MCSD: Windows Architecture I
Study Guide

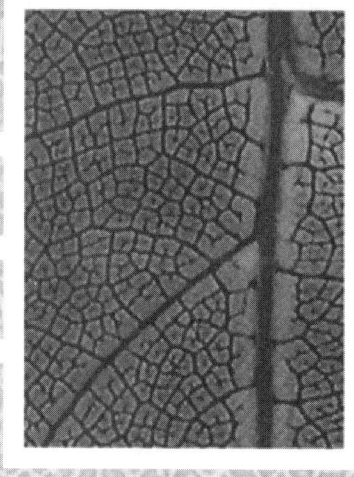

MCSD Windows Architecture I Study Guide Companion CD-ROM

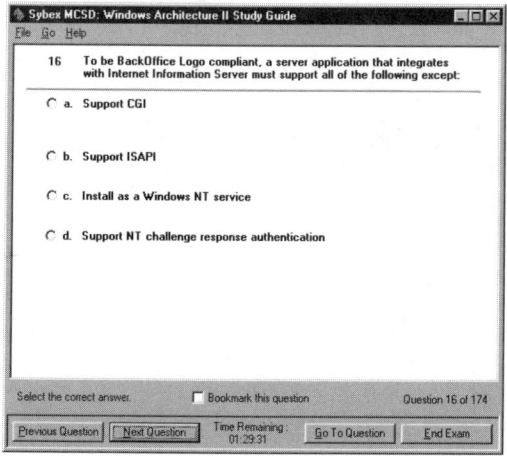

For Windows 95, 98, and NT4 users, this *autoplay* CD-ROM automatically displays the Sybex Test Engine Interface for access to the different products on the CD. Just pop it in the CD-ROM drive and let the autoplay CD boot the Sybex interface. You'll find the following software products on the CD:

The Exclusive Sybex MCSD ExamReady Test Engine. All the questions and answers in this book are included on the Sybex MCSD Exam-Ready Test Engine, an easy-to-use program for test preparation.

MCSD Offline Update. The latest Microsoft information on the MCSD certification program. Internet Explorer 4 is required to run this HTML-based document.

Internet Explorer 4.02. Just in case you don't have it or feel like downloading it, we've included this powerful browser.

MCSD on the Web. Popular MCSD Web sites listed in order of importance to MCSD students.

Using the Sybex MCSD ExamReady Test Engine

The Sybex test engine is an autorun test engine created exclusively for the Sybex MCSD Study Guides. To prepare for the real exam:

1. Put the CD in the CD drive and wait a few seconds until the MCSD test engine interface appears.
2. Click Name and enter your name, then press Enter.
3. Click Exam, then Timed Exam to begin the timed, mock MCSD exam.
4. You're ready to go! Start the timer, then answer the questions one by one. Click Next Question at the bottom of the screen to proceed.

To access other elements of the CD, use Windows Explorer or File Manager.

MCSD: Windows®
Architecture I Study Guide

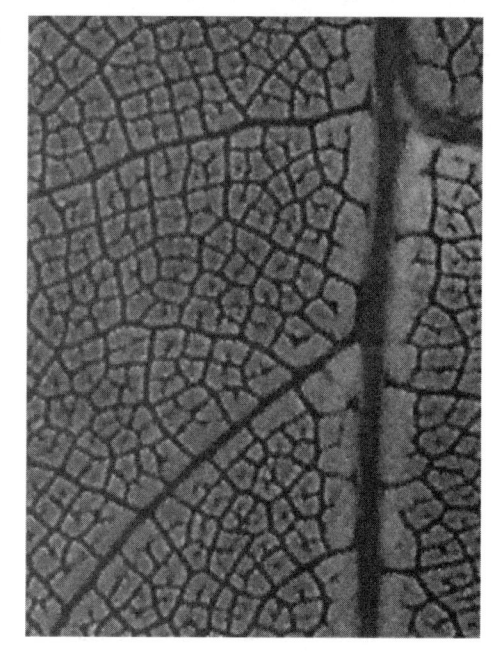

Ben Ezzell with
Michael Lee

San Francisco • Paris • Düsseldorf • Soest

Associate Publisher: Gary Masters
Contracts and Licensing Manager: Kristine Plachy
Acquisitions & Developmental Editor: Peter Kuhns
Editor: Davina Baum
Technical Editor: Richard Waymire
Book Designer: Patrick Dintino
Graphic Illustrators: Michael Gushard, Tony Jonick
Electronic Publishing Specialist: Bill Gibson
Production Coordinator: Rebecca Rider
Indexer: Ted Laux
Companion CD: Molly Sharp and Ginger Warner
Cover Designer: Design Site
Cover Illustrator/Photographer: Design Site

Screen reproductions produced with Collage Complete.

Collage Complete is a trademark of Inner Media Inc.

SYBEX, Network Press, and the Network Press logo are registered trademarks of SYBEX Inc.

TRADEMARKS: SYBEX has attempted throughout this book to distinguish proprietary trademarks from descriptive terms by following the capitalization style used by the manufacturer.

Microsoft® Internet Explorer ©1996 Microsoft Corporation. All rights reserved. Microsoft, the Microsoft Internet Explorer logo, Windows, Windows NT, and the Windows logo are either registered trademarks or trademarks of Microsoft Corporation in the United States and/or other countries.

The CD Interface music is from GIRA Sound AURIA Music Library © GIRA Sound 1996.

The author and publisher have made their best efforts to prepare this book, and the content is based upon final release software whenever possible. Portions of the manuscript may be based upon pre-release versions supplied by software manufacturer(s). The author and the publisher make no representation or warranties of any kind with regard to the completeness or accuracy of the contents herein and accept no liability of any kind including but not limited to performance, merchantability, fitness for any particular purpose, or any losses or damages of any kind caused or alleged to be caused directly or indirectly from this book.

Photographs and illustrations used in this book have been downloaded from publicly accessible file archives and are used in this book for news reportage purposes only to demonstrate the variety of graphics resources available via electronic access. Text and images available over the Internet may be subject to copyright and other rights owned by third parties. Online availability of text and images does not imply that they may be reused without the permission of rights holders, although the Copyright Act does permit certain unauthorized reuse as fair use under 17 U.S.C. Section 107.

SYBEX is an independent entity from Microsoft Corporation, and not affiliated with Microsoft Corporation in any manner. This publication may be used in assisting students to prepare for a Microsoft Certified Professional Exam. Neither Microsoft Corporation, its designated review company, nor SYBEX warrants that use of this publication will ensure passing the relevant exam. Microsoft is either a registered trademark or trademark of Microsoft Corporation in the United States and/or other countries.

Library of Congress Card Number: 98-85473
ISBN: 0-7821-2271-X

Manufactured in the United States of America

10 9 8 7 6 5 4 3 2 1

November 1, 1997

Dear SYBEX Customer:

Microsoft is pleased to inform you that SYBEX is a participant in the Microsoft® Independent Courseware Vendor (ICV) program. Microsoft ICVs design, develop, and market self-paced courseware, books, and other products that support Microsoft software and the Microsoft Certified Professional (MCP) program.

To be accepted into the Microsoft ICV program, an ICV must meet set criteria. In addition, Microsoft reviews and approves each ICV training product before permission is granted to use the Microsoft Certified Professional Approved Study Guide logo on that product. This logo assures the consumer that the product has passed the following Microsoft standards:

- The course contains accurate product information.
- The course includes labs and activities during which the student can apply knowledge and skills learned from the course.
- The course teaches skills that help prepare the student to take corresponding MCP exams.

Microsoft ICVs continually develop and release new MCP Approved Study Guides. To prepare for a particular Microsoft certification exam, a student may choose one or more single, self-paced training courses or a series of training courses.

You will be pleased with the quality and effectiveness of the MCP Approved Study Guides available from SYBEX.

Sincerely,

Holly Heath
ICV Account Manager
Microsoft Training & Certification

MICROSOFT INDEPENDENT COURSEWARE VENDOR PROGRAM

To all of those who try ... and, I hope, succeed ...

Acknowledgments

Every time I set out to write a new book, it is a venture undertaken with a mixture of joy and trepidation. The joy is easy; I enjoy writing, I enjoy sharing information (which is one commodity that is enhanced rather than diminished by distribution) and, not least, I enjoy being paid for my efforts.

The trepidation portion is another matter; an inborn fear of making a mistake, of saying (writing) the wrong thing, a hesitation over misleading the reader in some fashion. Or simply of overlooking some important factor.

The process of writing a book is never simple: there is a great deal to cover in any book, and a book of this type is not only far from being an exception but, in actual fact, covers far more than most titles are expected to.

Happily, the staff at Sybex—from my editors (Peter Kuhns and Davina Baum) and technical reviewer (Richard Waymire), to the artists (Michael Gushard and Tony Jonick) who rendered the illustrations, the electronic publishing specialist who turned the text into print (Bill Gibson), the production coordinator (Rebecca Rider), and all the rest of the people involved in this volume—are true professionals who put in untold hours and Herculean efforts toward ensuring that this book becomes what it is intended to be: a useful resource presented in a coherent and proper fashion.

Finally, a big thanks goes to Michael Lee for all of his help.

To everyone involved, my very sincere thanks ….

Ben Ezzell

Contents at a Glance

Table of Contents

Introduction

The Microsoft Certified Solutions Developer exams combine to form an extremely comprehensive certification covering all aspects of the Microsoft operating systems, Microsoft Office products, and Microsoft Development tools. Because of the sweeping scope of the examination, this study guide also must cover a broad and varied assortment of topics.

One approach to preparing the reader would have been simply to provide a series of questions mirroring the exams, together with a discussion of each and an explanation of why specific answers were appropriate or inappropriate. However, while a study guide of that type might assist the reader in passing an exam, it is an approach which would do very little to prove that the reader could meet the standards the examinations are intended to ensure.

A second approach would simply be a massive document covering all aspects of all Microsoft products, but meeting this objective would require a multi-volume set, tremendous preparation time, and would do more to produce information overload than to help the reader prepare for the examination.

The third approach—and the one followed here—is to provide the reader with comprehensive coverage of the material which appears on the exams, discussing each of the relevant topics in sufficient breadth to provide the background necessary to understand the exam questions, and of course, to be able to answer the questions correctly.

Again, however, because of the nature of the Windows Architecture exams, you may also find it useful to refer to other documentation, including the wide variety of documentation available online. Additional suggestions and recommendations for preparing for the examinations are offered here.

Your Key to Passing Exam 70-160

This book provides you with the key to passing Exam 70-160, Windows Architecture I. Inside, you'll find information relevant to this exam and practice questions, all designed to make sure that when you take the exam, you are ready.

To help you prepare for certification exams, Microsoft provides a list of exam objectives for each test. This book is structured according to the objectives for Exam 70-160, designed to measure your understanding of Windows Architecture and development.

Is This Book for You?

If you are interested in preparing for the Windows Architecture I exam, this book is for you. If you are trying to complement your general understanding of Microsoft technologies, this book is also for you. The exams are written at a survey level, discussing many different topics in general terms, and a few topics in specific terms. This book is designed to give you the information you need to pass the exam and supplement your understanding without overburdening you with unnecessary detail.

There is a significant amount of crossover in the two Windows Architecture exams. Although every effort has been made to address the exam objectives in appropriate detail, you may still draw a few questions on this exam that fit more logically with the objectives for the Windows Architecture II exam. Reviewing the companion volume to this book, *MCSD: Windows Architecture II Study Guide*, by Michael Lee, before taking this exam would be extremely beneficial.

Understanding Microsoft Certification

Microsoft offers several levels of certification for anyone who has or is pursuing a career as a network professional working with Microsoft products:

- Microsoft Certified Professional (MCP)
- Microsoft Certified Solution Developer (MCSD)
- Microsoft Certified Systems Engineer (MCSE)
- Microsoft Certified Professional + Internet
- Microsoft Certified Systems Engineer + Internet
- Microsoft Certified Trainer (MCT)

The one you choose depends on your area of expertise and your career goals.

Microsoft Certified Professional (MCP)

This certification is for individuals with expertise in one specific area. MCP certification is often a stepping stone to MCSE certification and allows you some benefits of Microsoft certification after just one exam.

By passing one core exam (meaning an operating system exam), you become an MCP.

Microsoft Certified Solution Developer (MCSD)

The MCSD certification identifies developers with experience working with Microsoft operating systems, development tools, and technologies. To achieve the MCSD certification, you must pass four exams:

1. Windows Architecture I

2. Windows Architecture II

3. Elective

4. Elective

Some of the electives include:

- Microsoft Visual Basic 5.0

- Microsoft Access for Windows 95

- Implementing a Database Design on Microsoft SQL Server 6.5

- Developing Applications with C++ and MFC

- Microsoft FoxPro 3.0

Microsoft Certified Systems Engineer (MCSE)

For network professionals, the MCSE certification requires commitment. You need to complete all of the steps required for certification. Passing the exams shows that you meet the high standards that Microsoft has set for MCSEs.

The following list applies to the NT 4.0 track. Microsoft still supports a track for 3.51, but 4.0 certification is more desirable because it is the current operating system.

To become an MCSE, you must pass a series of six exams:

1. Networking Essentials (waived for Novell CNEs)

2. Implementing and Supporting Microsoft Windows NT Workstation 4.0 (or Windows 95)

3. Implementing and Supporting Microsoft Windows NT Server 4.0

4. Implementing and Supporting Microsoft Windows NT Server 4.0 in the Enterprise

5. Elective

6. Elective

Some of the electives include:

- Internetworking with Microsoft TCP/IP on Microsoft Windows NT 4.0
- Implementing and Supporting Microsoft Internet Information Server 4.0
- Implementing and Supporting Microsoft Exchange Server 5.5
- Implementing and Supporting Microsoft SNA Server 4.0
- Implementing and Supporting Microsoft Systems Management Server 1.2
- Implementing a Database Design on Microsoft SQL Server 6.5
- System Administration for Microsoft SQL Server 6.5

Microsoft Certified Trainer (MCT)

As an MCT, you can deliver Microsoft-certified courseware through official Microsoft channels. The number of exams you are required to pass depends on the number of courses you want to deliver. Certification is granted on a course-by-course basis.

In addition to passing exams for the courses that you want to deliver, you must also attend a trainer skills course that is approved by Microsoft. You must also demonstrate that you have prepared adequately for each new class. This can be done by either attending the class or completing a self-study checklist and sending it to Microsoft.

For the most up-to-date certification information, visit Microsoft's Web site at www.microsoft.com/train_cert.

Preparing for the MCSD Exams

To prepare for the MCSD certification exams, you should try to work with the products as much as possible. In addition, a variety of resources from which you can learn about the products and exams are available:

- Instructor-led courses can be a valuable resource.

- As an alternative to instructor-led courses, online training is available. This is a useful option for people who cannot find any courses in their area or who do not have the time to attend classes.

- If you prefer to use a book to help you prepare for the MCSD tests, you can choose from a wide variety of publications. These include study guides, such as the Network Press *MCSD Study Guide* series, which cover the core MCSD exams and key electives.

For more MCSD information, point your browser to the Sybex Web site, where you'll find information about the MCP program, job links, and descriptions of other quality titles in the Network Press line of MCSD-related books. Go to http://www.sybex.com.

Scheduling and Taking an Exam

Once you think you are ready to take an exam, call Prometric Testing Centers at (800) 755-EXAM (755-3926). They'll tell you where to find the closest testing center. Before you call, get out your credit card: Each exam costs $100. (If you've used this book to prepare yourself thoroughly, chances are you'll only have to shell out that $100 once!)

You can schedule the exam for a time that is convenient for you. The exams are downloaded from Prometric to the testing center, and you show up at your scheduled time and take the exam on a computer.

Once you complete the exam, you will know right away whether you have passed or not. At the end of the exam, you will receive a score report. It will list the six areas that you were tested on and how you performed. If you pass the exam, you don't need to do anything else—Prometric uploads the test results to Microsoft. If you don't pass, it's another $100 to schedule the exam again. But at least you will know from the score report where you did poorly, so you can study that particular information more carefully.

Test-Taking Hints

If you know what to expect, your chances of passing the exam will be much greater. The following are some tips that can help you achieve success.

Get There Early and Be Prepared   This is your last chance to review. Bring your book and review any areas about which you feel unsure. If you need a quick drink of water or a visit to the restroom, take the time to do so before the exam. Once your exam starts, it will not be paused for these needs.

When you arrive for your exam, you will be asked to present two forms of ID. You will also be asked to sign a piece of paper verifying that you understand the testing rules and that you will not disclose the content of the exam to others.

Before you start the exam, you will have an opportunity to take a practice exam. It is not related to Windows NT and is simply offered so that you will have a feel for the exam-taking process.

What You Can and Can't Take In with You   These are closed-book exams. The only thing you can take in is scratch paper provided by the testing center. Use this paper as much as possible to diagram the questions. Many times diagramming questions will help make the answer clear. You will have to give this paper back to the test administrator at the end of the exam.

Many testing centers are very strict about what you can take into the testing room. Some centers will not even allow you to bring in items like a zipped purse. If you feel tempted to take in any outside material, beware that many testing centers use monitoring devices such as video and audio equipment (so don't swear, even if you are alone in the room!).

Prometric Testing Centers take the test-taking process and the test validation very seriously.

Test Approach   As you take the test, if you know the answer to a question, fill it in and move on. If you're not sure of the answer, mark your best guess, then "mark" the question.

At the end of the exam, you can review the questions. Depending on the amount of time remaining, you can then view all of the questions again, or you can view only the questions about which you were unsure. Double-check your answers, just in case you misread any of the questions on the first pass. (Sometimes half of the battle is in trying to figure out exactly what the question is asking you.) You may find that a related question provides a clue for a troublesome question.

Be sure to answer all questions. Unanswered questions are scored as incorrect and will count against you. There is no penalty for guessing. Also, make sure you keep an eye on the remaining time so that you can pace yourself accordingly.

If you do not pass the exam, note everything that you can remember while the exam is still fresh in your mind. This will help you prepare for your next try. Although the next exam will not be exactly the same, the questions will be similar, and you don't want to make the same mistakes.

After You Become Certified

Once you become an MCSD, Microsoft kicks in some goodies, including:

- A one-year subscription to the Microsoft Beta Evaluation program, which is a great way to get your hands on new software. Be the first kid on the block to play with new and upcoming software.

- Access to a secured area of the Microsoft Web site that provides technical support and product information. This certification benefit is also available for MCP certification.

- Permission to use the Microsoft Certified Professional logos (each certification has its own logo), which look great on letterhead and business cards.

- An MCP certificate (you will get a certificate for each level of certification you reach), suitable for framing or sending copies to Mom.

- A one-year subscription to *Microsoft Certified Professional Magazine*, which provides information on professional and career development.

How to Use This Book

The Windows Architecture exams are mostly conceptual, rather than applied. Or theory as opposed to practice. And this is particularly true for the Windows Architecture I exam where the topics covered admit to very few hands-on exercises. Still, a few exercises are included here and even more will be found in the Windows Architecture II study guide. For both titles, the exercises provided are designed to reinforce some of the important topics on this exam, especially those topics where implementation detail will be tested. To address the wide range of topics on this exam, many Microsoft Applications and development tools have been referenced in this book. To do all of the exercises in these books, you must have the following software installed:

- Windows Operating Systems selected from the following configurations:

  - Windows 95 with Personal Web Server

- Windows NT Workstation with Peer Web Services

- Windows NT Server with Internet Information Server (required for any BackOffice products)

- Microsoft Visual InterDev 1.0 with Active Server Pages installed on Web server

- Microsoft Access 97 (version 8.0) with the Northwind sample database installed

- Microsoft Visual Basic 5.0 at a default installation

- Microsoft Internet Explorer 4.0 (included on accompanying CD) Note that all exercises and screen shots in this book assume that the Active Desktop is not installed with IE 4.0.

All of the exercises in the book assume that products have been installed according to the defaults and no consideration is given for additional customizations that you have made on the installation.

As you work through this book, you may want to follow these general procedures:

1. Review the exam objectives as you work through the chapter. (You may want to check the Microsoft Train_Cert Web site to make sure the objectives haven't changed.)

Exam objectives are subject to change at any time without prior notice and at Microsoft's sole discretion. Please visit Microsoft's Training & Certification Web site (www.microsoft.com/Train_Cert) for the most current exam objectives listing.

2. Study a chapter carefully, making sure you fully understand the information.

3. Complete all hand-on exercises in the chapter, referring to the text so that you understand every step you take.

4. Answer the practice questions at the end of the chapter. (You will find the answers to these questions in Appendix A.)

5. Note which questions you did not understand, and study those sections of the book again.

To learn all of the material covered in this book, you will need to study regularly and with discipline. Try to set aside the same time every day to study, and select a comfortable and quiet place in which to do it. Good Luck!

What's on the CD?

The Exclusive Sybex MCSD ExamReady Test Engine All the questions and answers in this book are included on the Sybex MCSD ExamReady Test Engine, an easy-to-use program for test preparation.

MCSD Offline Update The latest Microsoft information on the MCSD certification program. Internet Explorer 4 is required to run this HTML-based document.

Internet Explorer 4.02 Just in case you don't have it or feel like downloading it, we've included this powerful browser.

MCSD on the Web Popular MCSD Web sites listed in order of importance to MCSD students.

About the Author

Ben Ezzell is a consulting software engineer and the author of more than twenty books dealing with application programming and development including both *NT 4/Windows 95 Developer's Handbook* and *Windows 98 Developer's Handbook,* also from Sybex, and *Developing Windows Error Messages* from O'Riley and Associates.

You can e-mail Ben at the following address:

ben@ezzell.org

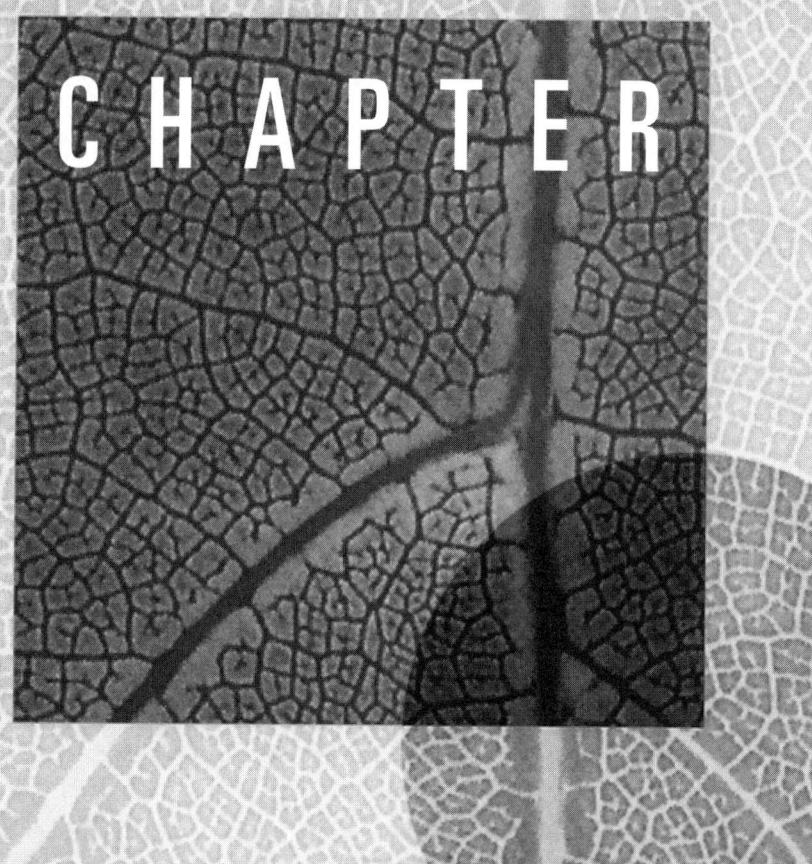

CHAPTER

1

Operating System Awareness

F our topics are relevant to operating system awareness. This chapter begins with the Windows registry and the storage of persisted data, and then moves on to discuss the Windows Open Services Architecture (WOSA) and the component services provided by WOSA, including Dynamic Link Libraries and memory management. Finally, the chapter concludes with a few notes on common issues related to Dynamic Link Libraries under both Windows 95/98 and Windows NT.

For discussion of a final topic relevant to operating system awareness—threads, processes, and scheduling—see Chapter 12.

The Windows Registry

T he Windows registry is a database where system and application configuration information is registered. Previously—i.e., Windows 3.*x* and earlier—the AUTOEXEC.BAT and CONFIG.SYS files together with the WIN.INI, SYSTEM.INI, and PROTOCOL.INI files contained system setup information. Application configuration data was stored both in application-specific .INI files and as entries in the SYSTEM.INI and WIN.INI files, at the same time.

Today, the Windows registry takes the place of most configuration and initialization files for Windows and new Windows-based applications. This does not mean, however, that the previously cited .INI files (nor the AUTOEXEC.BAT and CONFIG.SYS files) are completely superseded, since these will still be found on most systems. These files have been relegated to the secondary role of providing compatibility with older applications.

Initialization (.INI) files were used to store the following:

- information used to initialize software and hardware configurations

- information about user preferences which would otherwise be lost at system shutdown

- status information about applications and programs, including directory information and file usage

The shortcomings of the AUTOEXEC.BAT, CONFIG.SYS, and various .INI files were numerous:

- Damaged .INI files were not recoverable.

- Information in .INI files was available only to the application creating the file.

- Security was lacking against deliberate corruption as well as casual manipulation, accidental corruption, and deletion by users.

- There were no consistent remote-access or remote-administration facilities.

- There was no support for multiple users, i.e., profiles could not be customized for individual users.

- There was a proliferation of .INI files and orphaned .INI files.

Windows 3.1 introduced a new feature: the registry, or registration database, which contained information to support shell applications. In this early format, support was provided for utilities such as the File Manager and, of course, for OLE applications.

In its earliest inception, the registry's database consisted of entries identified by a key and a single data value. At this time, the registry was not designed for use by applications for user-specific configuration data. Therefore applications continued to use individual .INI files, or they simply inserted settings and parameters in the SYSTEM.INI and WIN.INI files as well as, less frequently, the CONFIG.SYS and AUTOEXEC.BAT files.

The Win32 API (application programming interface) revised the structure and use of the registry in two important fashions: It expanded the number of keys and allowed each key to contain multiple values.

While the API functions providing registry access under Windows 3.1 are still functional, the original functions were limited in how they operated: They could only access the single "default" value for a registry key. Today, these have been superseded by new, extended API functions just as the registry itself has been redesigned to satisfy broader goals.

The registry is used to store and retrieve information on a per-user, per-application, and per-system basis. All data is stored in a binary format requiring applications to use the API registry functions to access the data. The information contained in the registry is stored in a hierarchical tree structure. Each node in the tree—each key—may contain both further subkeys and data entries (values).

The present functional scope supported by the registry includes the following:

- Providing a single source for configuration information superseding the original configuration and initialization files

- Eenumerating and tracking the hardware configuration for a system

- Separating user-, application-, and hardware-related information and maintaining separate configurations for multiple users

- Providing keys to enumerate, track, and configure applications, device drivers, and operating-system control parameters

- Providing configuration storage that is recoverable after a system crash

- Maintaining security for configuration data by preventing casual or unauthorized access to critical information while still permitting full access to user-specific configuration settings

- Providing network-independent functions to permit querying and setting system configuration information across a network

- Using the Windows Control Panel to standardize the user interface for configuration information

- Eliminating the probability of syntax errors in configuration information

Registry Structure

The Windows NT/95/98 registry is stored as a binary database in two files in the Windows directory: SYSTEM.DAT and USER.DAT. Internally, the registry is divided into a number of root or primary keys (also called *hives*) which separate the registry contents into collections of related data.

For more information on how the registry functions specifically within Windows NT, see *MCSD: Windows Architecture II Study Guide* (Sybex, 1998).

The size of the registry is user-configurable, limited only by the system resources. By default, the registry limit is one-fourth of the size of the system's paged pool size.

Figure 1.1 shows the registry opened using the registry Editor (RegEdit).

FIGURE 1.1

A view of the system registry

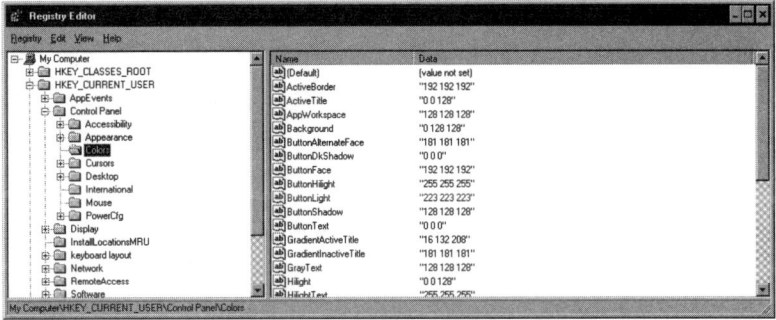

Here, the registry shows two root keys identified by HKEY_*xxxx* mnemonics. In the left pane, under HKEY_CURRENT_USER, the subkey *Control Panel* is opened to the further subkey *Colors* while the right pane shows the values stored in this key.

Applications accessing the registry locate information in much the same format as they would access a file in a directory/subdirectory structure. Functionally, the registry is used much like previous initialization files; the registry is simply a location where information is stored and retrieved.

In some cases, the presence of a key may be the only information an application requires, and the key alone may appear with no value entries. In this case, the *(Default)* value will appear but will be identified as *(value not set)*.

More commonly, an application or process will open a key and request a specific value from the key.

Under Windows 3.x, a registry key contained only one value, *Default*, which was always an ASCII string and there were no provisions to identify individual values.

For the 32-bit version of the registry, any key can hold any number of data entries—called values—and the individual entries may take many different forms. Table 1.1 lists the possible components of keys, and Table 1.2 lists the components of the values.

T A B L E 1.1 Key Components	**Key Component**	**Description**	**Status**
	Name	A string used to identify the key. Each name—within a specific sub-level key—must be unique. The key name cannot contain a backslash (\) or any null characters, but may contain spaces or punctuation.	Required
	Class	Object class name, intended for use in associating a class method with class instances stored in the registry.	Optional
	Security Descriptor	Used by Windows NT security descriptors for auditing and access control. Normal security inheritance rules apply.	Optional; Windows NT only
	Last write time	Time stamp indicating the date/time a key was last modified. Any change to a value is regarded as a change to the parent key.	Windows NT only
	Value(s)	None, one, or multiple items of data stored under a key.	Optional

T A B L E   1.2:   Value Components

Value Component	Description
Name	Identifier for the value. Names may be up to 64K in size (32,767 Unicode characters). The backslash character (\) is permitted in a value name. Also, to provide compatibility with Windows 3.x, a null name ("") is also permitted.
Type	Defines the data type stored in the value. For Windows 3.x, the value type was always REG_SZ, identifying a null-terminated string. In the Win32 API, REG_xxxx type identifiers are provided for most common data types. While the system itself does not use this type of information, applications should use the identifiers to allow registry tools to find and manipulate the value data. Type identifier values below 0x7FFFFFFF are reserved for system use, that is, custom type identifier values must have the high-bit of the high-word set.
Data	Application-specified data. The data length and format are arbitrary, but Windows NT 3.1 did impose a 1MB limit on size.

While all name strings in the registry are stored in Unicode format and the registry does preserve string case, case is ignored in all search operations. Value names are not case sensitive.

While the data stored in a value is arbitrary, storing string values in Unicode format is recommended.

Consistency and Integrity

The registry enforces a strict granularity (atomicity). This insures that, for any value entry, a given change is not committed until it is complete, at which time it is committed entirely and as a whole. This ensures that the name, type, size, and data will always match and that the data in a value entry will be complete and consistent. This protective atomicity is enforced even if—as an extreme example—the system crashes during a change.

Consistency across values, however, is not enforced, even within multiple values belonging to a single key. Consistency on this level is the responsibility of the application providing these values. (Rather obviously, given the unconfined nature of the registry, only the applications entering values can determine what is consistent or inconsistent.)

Opening Registry Keys

Before an application can locate or open a registry key, the application must begin with the handle of an existing key. Depending on your version of Windows, the system defines four or six standard handles that are always open. An application uses one of the predefined handles as an entry point to access the registry. Refer to Table 1.3 for an explanation of the usage of those handles.

T A B L E 1.3: Predefined Keys and Their Usage

Predefined Key	Usage
HKEY_CLASSES_ROOT	Contains entries defining types or classes of documents and properties associated with these classes. This was the original entry point used in Windows 3.1.
	Entries under HKEY_CLASSES_ROOT are used by the Windows shell and OLE applications. This includes file extensions associated with applications to open files of that type. OLE information includes the server command line, the appropriate data types and actions taken by activated OLE objects.
	HKEY_CLASSES_ROOT is an alias for HKEY_LOCAL_MACHINE\SOFTWARE\Classes.
HKEY_CURRENT_USER	Contains entries defining the preferences of the current user, including application preferences, color settings, environmental variables, network connections, printer types, and program groups. HKEY_CURRENT_USER is an alias for HKEY_USERS*user_name* (or HKEY_USERS\sid on NT) or, if there is only one user on the system, HKEY_USERS\DEFAULT.
HKEY_LOCAL_MACHINE	Contains entries defining the configuration state of the system, including the bus type, system memory, and installed software and hardware.
HKEY_USERS	Contains a default user configuration and individual user configuration (if more than one user configuration is installed). In Windows 98, the HKEY_USERS key contains some software configuration information.
HKEY_CURRENT CONFIG	Defined for WINVER 4.0 or later; contains system hardware configuration settings.
HKEY_DYN_DATA	Defined for WINVER 4.0 or later; contains system plug-and-play information. It may be empty on Windows NT.

The HKEY_CURRENT_CONFIG and HKEY_DYN_DATA would not normally be used by applications.

While the HKEY_CURRENT_USER key contains data similar to HKEY_LOCAL_MACHINE, these are per-user preferences that would normally override per-machine defaults. This is not a system-enforced convention, however, and observing these preferences is the responsibility of the application.

Registry Access

The registry Editor (REGEDIT.EXE in Win95/98/NT systems or REGEDT32.EXE in the Windows NT system only) can be used to open, examine, and edit the system registry. The registry Editor is not intended to be used for generic access to the registry—it is possible to do a lot of damage to your system using this tool—but it does provide a convenient method of examining the registry entries. And, occasionally, it also provides an essential access for changing values.

Registry information is not necessarily cross-compatible between system versions; registry information saved from Windows NT 4.0 cannot be restored on a Windows NT 3.1 system because the formats are different. Backwards compatibility, however, is maintained and later versions can usually import registry data from earlier versions. Of course, problems may occur if an attempt is made to copy registry information from NT to 95/98 or vice versa.

Initialization Files and the Registry

Originally, 16-bit Windows-based applications used the GetPrivateProfile-String and PutPrivateProfileString functions to retrieve and write application profile values, as strings, from and to specific sections of an initialization (.INI) file. Under 32-bit Windows applications, these functions continue to be supported. Under Windows NT—but not under Windows 95/98—rather than relying strictly on the presence of .INI files, these functions now begin by looking in the registry, under IniFileMapping, for the name of the .INI file. More precisely, the location searched first would be:

```
HKEY_LOCAL_MACHINE\Software\Microsoft\Windows NT\
CurrentVersion\IniFileMapping\filename.INI
```

If there is no key or subkey corresponding to the .INI file in the Windows NT registry, then the operation will look for an actual .INI file.

Storing Application-Specific Information

Any application that relies on initialization information, as most applications do to one degree or another, should use the registry to store and to retrieve this information.

Microsoft *Exam* *Objective*	**Identify situations in which it is appropriate to store persisted data in the registry.**

One of the first points where an application should look for persisted data is during installation. Simply by checking the registry during setup, an application can determine if there has been a previous installation of a product—or if an earlier version is or has been installed—and can respond accordingly. If the present installation is an upgrade, it may be appropriate to retrieve (and preserve) existing user preferences or to take other actions.

Setup aside, any kind of persisted configuration data used by an application should be stored in the registry.

If the information is user-specific, then the entries would appropriately be registered under:

```
HKEY_CURRENT_USER\Software\VENDOR\ApplicationName\VERSION\
```

This would be the same type of information, which, under earlier versions of Windows, would have been stored in the WIN.INI file.

Alternately, if the information simply applies to the installation as a whole, i.e., the same data will be applied irrespective of the user, the entries would be registered under:

```
HKEY_LOCAL_MACHINE\Software\VENDOR\ApplicationName\VERSION\
```

Other items that applications should store in the registry include application-specific path information. Under DOS, applications commonly tried to insert their installation path information in the PATH= statement in the AUTOEXEC.BAT file. This approach was problematic in that the PATH statement was limited in length and there was little point in having all applications searching each other's paths.

Once an application has registered a path, Windows will automatically set the PATH environment to the registered directory (or directories) when the application is started. Environmental PATH information is registered under the HKEY_LOCAL_MACHINE root as \Software\Microsoft\ Windows\CurrentVersion\AppPaths\.

The subkey must have the same name as the executable application. Also, if your application consists of more than one executable, each executable should have its own PATH environment registered.

For example, under the subkey EXCEL.EXE, two entries are found as:

```
[HKEY_LOCAL_MACHINE\Software\Microsoft\Windows\CurrentVersion\
App Paths\EXCEL.EXE]
    @="E:\program files\microsoft office\Office\EXCEL.EXE"
    "Path"="E:\program files\microsoft office\Office"
```

The @ symbol designates the default entry for the key and supplies the path where the application is installed. The "Path" value designates the default directory used during execution.

Use the REGSTR_PATH_APPPATHS macro to register application path entries.

Tracking Shared DLLs

Application programs should also keep track of shared DLLs. When an application is installed that uses a shared DLL—system-supplied DLLs excepted—the usage counter in the registry for the DLL should be incremented. Or, when the application is removed, the usage counter should be decremented.

In this fashion, if the usage counter reaches zero, the presumption would be that the DLL could be safely removed from the system. The following example shows the general format for a registry usage counter.

```
\HKEY_LOCAL_MACHINE\Software\Microsoft\Windows\CurrentVersion
\SharedDLLs
    C:\Program Files\Common Files\System\vbrun400.DLL=3
```

While incrementing and decrementing a usage counter for Dynamic Link Libraries is a laudable thought, this practice appears to be much more honored in the breach than the observance. Thus, those usage counts actually found in the registry cannot be considered reliable.

Initializing Registry Information

While normal registry operations are carried out through API function calls, it is also possible to use a .REG file—normally during application installation—to preset registry entries. Following is a brief example of a .REG file excerpted from an example in the *Windows 98 Developer's Handbook*, published by Sybex, 1998.

In this sample, the terms in brackets denote registry keys to be created and the value for each key follows the key entry.

```
REGEDIT4

[HKEY_LOCAL_MACHINE\SOFTWARE\registry Demo]
[HKEY_LOCAL_MACHINE\SOFTWARE\registry Demo\Charlie Brown]
    "Password"="@ABCDGCGJ"
    "Status"=dword:000003e9
[HKEY_LOCAL_MACHINE\SOFTWARE\registry Demo\Henry Ford]
    "Password"="B@@EC"
    "Status"=dword:000003ea
[HKEY_LOCAL_MACHINE\SOFTWARE\registry Demo\Billy Sol Estes]
    "Password"="ABDABBCGE"
    "Status"=dword:000003eb
[HKEY_LOCAL_MACHINE\SOFTWARE\registry Demo\Thomas Alva
Edison]
    "Password"="AA@@F"
    "Status"=dword:000003ec
[HKEY_LOCAL_MACHINE\SOFTWARE\registry Demo\Blaise Pascal]
    "Password"="ACBBDEGE"
    "Status"=dword:000003ed
[HKEY_LOCAL_MACHINE\SOFTWARE\Not Very Secret]
    "Secret Key"="Rumplestiltskin"
```

This approach is especially useful when you need to establish a large number of keys and/or values as, for example, to register a series of default values or configuration parameters, which an application will use to present selections for configuring a system.

One example may involve an application where any individual computer with the application installed might be configured to drive a variety of different external systems. To provide options without requiring these to be 'hardwired' in the application code, a .REG registry file would be supplied with the installation to create registry entries with default parameters for each system type and each configuration.

Subsequent to installation, a configuration utility would use the pre-established registry information to offer choices to set up each individual machine according to the external equipment configuration. Of course, the default settings would be available later if the configuration required alteration, repair, or a change in the external system.

Windows Open Services Architecture

Microsoft *Exam* *Objective*	Describe the architecture of Windows Open Services Architecture (WOSA) technologies, including Dynamic Link Libraries (DLLs), memory management, and scheduling.

The Windows Open Services Architecture (WOSA) is Microsoft's standard to provide an open environment for Windows-based applications. WOSA takes a far broader stance than an API by proposing an architecture for integration between the Windows operating system and Windows-based applications under the cloak of a heterogeneous enterprise-wide computing environment.

To this end, WOSA offers standards for seamless access in three categories of information resource services: common application services, communication services, and vertical market services.

The standards for WOSA's component services are being defined through the Open Process program with the cooperation of hardware manufacturers, corporate developers, and independent software vendors. While the WOSA development effort enjoys wide backing by hundreds of industry members, Microsoft has also adopted *de jure* specifications where gaps exist.

Like the Microsoft Foundation Classes (MFC), the WOSA APIs function as a very thin layer over the Windows API, wrapping the functionality of Windows without adding unnecessary overhead.

Common Application Services

The use of a consistent and open architecture is intended to allow Windows-based applications to transparently access key services across multiple software vendors' implementations, including services which span different hardware and operating system environments. Among these services are ODBC, MAPI, TAPI, and LSAPI.

Open Database Connectivity (ODBC)

Open Database Connectivity will be covered in more detail in Chapters 9 and 10. In brief, ODBC offers a common method of data access from a variety of heterogeneous environments. ODBC is an open standard defined by a number of industry groups including ANSI, the SQL Access Group, X/Open, and others. The objective behind ODBC was to develop an open and vendor-neutral standard. As a portable API, ODBC offers cross-platform support for data access from both the Windows and Macintosh environments.

Messaging API (MAPI)

The Messaging API, like ODBC, is an open standard developed in cooperation with a broad base of independent software vendors to offer a common method for Windows-based applications to gain access to a wide variety of electronic messaging services in enterprise environments.

MAPI standards allow a single application—for example, a workgroup scheduling application—to gain access to all aspects of a company's messaging systems, including e-mail systems, voice mail, and fax.

MAPI has been refined in consultation with XAPIA, the standard-setting body for X.400 communications.

Windows Telephony (TAPI)

The Windows Telephony API (TAPI) offers easy access for applications to interact with the telephone network. It facilitates visual call control, and allows for the integration of electronic mail, voice mail, and fax, as well as the support of desktop audio and video conferencing.

The TAPI specification has been developed in cooperation with major companies in the telecommunications and PC industries, including chip manufacturers, network operators, PC vendors, software developers, telephone system companies, and voice-mail providers. In response, every major PBX manufacturer has announced support for TAPI and has agreed to offer access to their previously closed and proprietary PBX systems.

License Service API (LSAPI)

The License Service API is designed to automate software licensing and to reduce the overhead involved in implementing custom licensing systems. The LSAPI has been developed in cooperation with industry participants including the Software Publishers Association and the Microcomputer Managers Association.

Network Communication Services

The existing multiplicity of network standards has been a major stumbling block to application development and is one of the areas addressed by the Windows Open Services Architecture. Services include SNA API, Sockets API, and the RPC API.

Windows SNA API

The SNA API offers a standard for corporate-host connectivity by providing open access to the existing IBM SNA API categories.

Windows Sockets API

The Windows Sockets API is used to integrate both Windows- and Unix-based applications across a network. The Sockets API provides a single Windows-based application interface supporting communications with Sockets-based applications through a variety of transport protocols including TCP/IP, AppleTalk, and IPX/SPX.

Microsoft Remote Procedure Call (RPC)

The Microsoft RPC API supports the Open Software Foundation's Distributed Computing Environment (DCE) RPC. The RPC API is discussed in Chapter 7.

Vertical Market Extensions

WOSA has announced a number of vertical market extensions which provide specialized services to support or extend tasks required by particular market segments. These include:

- **Financial Services** Working in cooperation with the Banking Systems Vendor Council, WOSA defines a standard API extension for branch banking applications. This API includes functions for varying services, such as receipt printers and magnetic PIN-pads.

- **Real-Time Market Data** The Open Market Data Council for Windows—a group of market data vendors, trading, and brokerage systems suppliers—initiated the development of WOSA extensions to permit Windows-based applications to receive live market data, including stock quotes and news. The WOSA extensions provide a standard format independent of the data source.

- **Controls, Engineering, and Manufacturing** Other WOSA extensions are under development for such diverse areas as control systems, engineering, and manufacturing.

Dynamic Link Libraries

Because neither Windows 95/98 nor Windows NT use the MFC30 (Microsoft Foundation Classes version 3.0) Dynamic Link Libraries (DLLs) as part of their core functionality, neither installs the MFC30 DLLs as part of a minimum installation.

Many applications used with Windows 95/98, however, are MFC30-dependent and these will install the MFC30 DLLs as part of their own installations. Because many—or most—Windows 95/98 users accept the default setup (which does include WordPad) they will find MFC30 DLLs present on their systems.

Conversely, the Windows NT version of WordPad doesn't use the MFC30 DLLs nor do any of the other applications shipped with Windows NT. Unless the user installs another application or package, such as Office 95, which uses and installs the MFC30 DLLs, these DLLs are not commonly found on NT installations.

The problem occurs when other Windows 95 applications depend on the MFC30 DLLs but fail to install these libraries as part of their own installation. In many cases, the developers may simply be unaware of the dependency because of the presence, coincidentally, of the MFC30 DLLs as a result of other installations. The result is that these applications will fail to install or fail to function correctly on Windows NT systems.

To prevent such failures, applications should verify the presence of all required DLLs and should be prepared to install these if necessary.

Also, applications should warn the user—clearly and explicitly—any time that they find what appears to be an older version of a required DLL and should offer the user the option of replacing the original or of leaving it in place.

Further, applications should refcount DLLs which they use and which are already installed on the system (see the "Storing Application-Specific Information" and "Tracking Shared DLLs" sections, above). When an application is uninstalled the refcount should be decremented for all DLLs used by the application.

MFC and system DLLs should never be removed from the system, even when the refcount falls to zero.

Replacing System DLLs

In some cases, during installation, applications may attempt to replace a system DLL—such as the URL.DLL—with newer versions. When applications fail to verify the operating system version and platform information correctly, they may install the wrong DLL for the system or version. For example, many applications that replace the URL.DLL on Windows NT systems install a Windows 95–specific version. When encountering the wrong version, applications initializing the URL.DLL display an error dialog box. This occurs because the Windows NT KERNEL32.DLL does not contain the entry point `ReinitialeCriticalSection`, which the Windows 95–specific URL.DLL employs.

If, during installation, an application intends to replace any system DLL, the user should be clearly advised. In addition, applications should also provide platform-specific DLLs if any calls are made from the DLL to any platform-specific functions.

Advantages of DLLs

Under Windows, DLLs are loaded once and shared by two or more processes. The DLL is loaded into physical memory with LoadLibrary called by an application. Subsequent calls to LoadLibrary for the same DLL cause the physical memory to be mapped—through the Virtual Memory Manager's file mapping facility—to the virtual address space of the new process.

Each process sharing a DLL maintains its own set of global and static variables. DLLs receive their own local heap only under 16-bit versions of Windows.

Summary

The Windows registry is a database containing system and application information and replaces the AUTOEXEC.BAT, CONFIG.SYS, and a multitude of .INI files used under DOS and earlier DOS-based versions of Windows. The registry is used both by the system and by applications directly to store configuration and startup information, user preferences, settings required by applications for peripheral devices, file usage, and directory information, among other things. In addition, the registry offers a number of advantages over flat-ASCII .INI files, including security, multiple-user support, remote-access capabilities, and crash-recovery capabilities.

Originally, in Windows 3.1, the registry was limited to single value entries under each key. Subsequently, the original specification has been expanded to permit multiple entries under each registry key while the registry API functions have also been enhanced to satisfy a more flexible access.

Because an application must have a handle to an existing registry key before it can locate or open a registry key, the system supplies a series of predefined handles as entry points. The keys provided offer entry points to areas of the registry devoted to such elements as user preferences, hardware configuration, and software settings.

With the expansion of the registry, a great deal of emphasis is placed on moving application-specific settings from separate .INI files to the registry along with user preferences, application path information and even usage (application dependency) information for Dynamic Link Libraries.

The Windows Open Services Architecture, or WOSA, offers standards for component services include memory management, common application services, network communication services, and vertical market extensions. These standards seek to integrate the computing environment.

Conflicts may occur when applications fail to install required DLLs or if they replace existing DLLs with incorrect versions. Careful planning can forestall these problems. To avoid such problems, developers should take care when installing libraries to ensure that all necessary DLLs are supplied—including Microsoft redistributable DLLs—and that later DLL versions are not being overwritten by earlier copies.

 For more information on the registry, refer to the Windows 95 Resource Kit.

Review Questions

1. Registry entries contained in the HKEY_LOCAL_MACHINE hive will be overridden by data contained in which of the following?

   A. The CONFIG.SYS file

   B. The HKEY_CURRENT_CONFIG hive

   C. The HKEY_CURRENT_USER hive

   D. The WIN.INI file

2. The functional scope supported by the registry services includes which of the following? (Select all that apply.)

   A. Enumerating and tracking a system's hardware configuration

   B. Providing keys to enumerate, track, and configure applications, device drivers, and operating system control parameters

   C. Providing multi-user configuration support

   D. Providing system global storage for information exchanged between applications

3. In which two disk files is the Windows NT/95/98 registry stored?

    A. SYSTEM.DAT and USER.DAT

    B. SYSTEM.DAT and WIN.DAT

    C. SYSTEM.INI and USER.INI

    D. SYSTEM.INI and WIN.INI

4. The registry is organized into sections called:

    A. Hives

    B. Keys

    C. Nests

    D. Swarms

5. Information in the registry is accessed through keys and subkeys that serve which of the following functions?

    A. They are required to unlock successive layers of security for access.

    B. They are used like directories and subdirectories to identify where the information is stored.

    C. They are used to decode the encrypted information.

    D. Both A and C

6. A registry key under Windows 95/98 or Windows NT may contain how many individual values?

    A. One

    B. Two

    C. Four

    D. Eight

    E. Any number

7. Individual key data entries may take which of the following forms? (Select all that apply.)

    A. Names and object class names

    B. Pointers to memory

    C. Security descriptors and time stamps

    D. Values

8. All registry data entries:

    A. May be of any data type, including custom and binary data

    B. Must be ASCIIZ string values

    C. Must conform to either a predefined or a registered custom data format

    D. Must match a predefined data format

9. What does the registry enforce?

    A. Consistency across registry data values

    B. Security for read and read/write access

    C. Strict granularity (atomicity) to ensure that changes are committed entirely

    D. Unicode string formats for string entries

10. Before an application can open a registry key, the application must first do which of the following?

    A. Create a new registry entry

    B. Have security rights for access

    C. Use any existing handle to find a registry entry point

    D. Use one of the predefined handles as an entry point

11. A registry key value consists of which of the following segments? (Select three.)

   A. Data

   B. Name

   C. Security access

   D. Type

12. A key entry for an OLE class would be found under which root key?

   A. HKEY_CLASSES_ROOT

   B. HKEY_CURRENT_CONFIG

   C. HKEY_DYN_DATA

   D. HKEY_LOCAL_MACHINE

13. HKEY_CLASSES_ROOT is an alias to a subkey under which of the following?

   A. HKEY_CURRENT_CONFIG\Software\Classes

   B. HKEY_CURRENT_USER\Software\Classes

   C. HKEY_DYN_DATA\Software\Classes

   D. HKEY_LOCAL_MACHINE\Software\Classes

14. User preferences, including color settings, environment variables, program groups, and network connections would be found under which key?

   A. HKEY_CURRENT_CONFIG

   B. HKEY_CURRENT_USER

   C. HKEY_DYN_DATA

   D. HKEY_LOCAL_MACHINE

15. System configuration identifying the bus type, system memory, and installed software and hardware would be found under which key?

    A. HKEY_CLASSES_ROOT

    B. HKEY_CURRENT_CONFIG

    C. HKEY_DYN_DATA

    D. HKEY_LOCAL_MACHINE

16. Where should application-specific information be stored?

    A. In .INI files outside the registry

    B. Under HKEY_CURRENT_CONFIG\Software\Vendor\ AppName\Version key entries for all application data

    C. Under HKEY_CURRENT_USER\Software\Vendor\AppName\ Version key entries for user-specific preferences

    D. Under HKEY_LOCAL_MACHINE\Software\Vendor\AppName\ Version key entries for initialization and run-time data which applies to all users

17. Windows Open Services Architecture (WOSA) proposes:

    A. A cooperative development effort toward a single unified operating system

    B. A single integrated API providing functional database access across multiple types of operating systems

    C. Standards for seamless access in information resource services

    D. Standards for transporting the Windows operating system to Macintosh, Unix, and Sun workstation platforms

18. In a 32-bit Windows environment, when two processes use the same DLL:

   A. The DLL is loaded once and mapped to the virtual address space of the first process calling the DLL.

   B. The DLL is loaded only once but mapped to the virtual address space of both processes.

   C. The DLL is loaded twice but each process shares one set of global and static variables.

   D. The DLL is loaded twice, giving each process its own copy.

19. The WOSA Common Application Services include which of the following? (Select three.)

   A. Financial Services API (FSAPI)

   B. Messaging API (MAPI)

   C. Open Database Connectivity (ODBC)

   D. Windows Telephony API (TAPI)

20. The Windows Telephony API offers applications access to interact with which of the following?

   A. Broadcast video transmissions

   B. Desktop audio and video conferencing

   C. Electronic mail

   D. The telephone network

21. What is the advantage of dynamic linking over static linking?

   A. It allows global and static variables to be shared between processes for Dynamic Link Libraries.

   B. It gives 32-bit DLLs their own local heaps.

   C. It allows multiple copies of a DLL to be created in memory.

   D. It requires that only one copy of a DLL be created in memory.

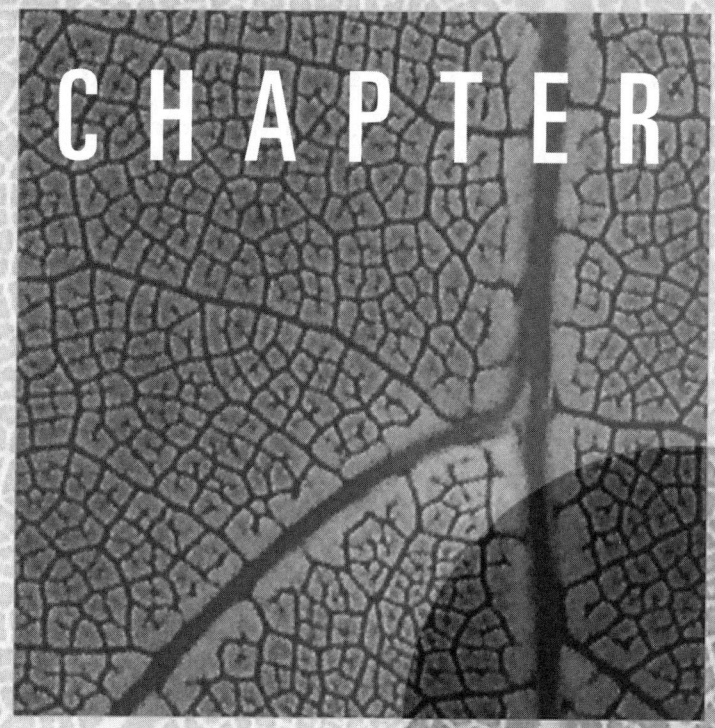

CHAPTER

2

Architectural Differences between
Windows 95/98 and Windows NT

The Windows 95/98 and Windows NT operating systems are aimed at different market requirements and different platform capabilities. This chapter will look at those differences from an architectural standpoint, and at why one OS would be selected over the other in various deployment scenarios.

Understanding the Differences

While Windows 95/98 and Windows NT support the same "look and feel" in their interfaces and both systems offer support for both 16-bit and 32-bit applications, there are differences between the 95/98 and NT systems. The major differences are the ways in which each operating system deals with multitasking, services, protected memory, file system security, multiple CPU support, and drivers and peripheral support.

Multitasking

Both Windows 95/98 and Windows NT support multitasking and multi-threaded applications, but there are significant differences in how the different operating systems handle multitasking.

Very briefly, multitasking is a system which suspends one application—while preserving its registers, memory, and execution status—to permit another application an opportunity to execute. Multithreading is similar to multitasking, except, instead of multiple applications, a single application is executing two or more tasks as independent or semi-independent threads. In this case, one thread must be suspended before a second thread can execute. (See the "Multiple CPU Support" section later in this chapter.)

Under Windows 3.x, multitasking is handled on a cooperative basis. This means that applications and threads must relinquish control of the CPU so that the operating system can manage the rotation of tasks to allow other applications or threads an opportunity to perform their tasks. The weakness of cooperative multitasking is simply that badly-behaved applications—and there are many—may not readily relinquish control and permit other tasks to function.

In contrast, under Windows NT and Windows 95/98, multitasking is handled on a preemptive basis. (Unfortunately, 16-bit applications under Windows 95/98 continue to be handled on a cooperative multitasking basis.) Under preemptive multitasking, the operating system itself is able to suspend an application or thread without waiting for the executing process to relinquish control. The strength of preemptive multitasking is that badly-behaved applications are not able to hold control and cannot monopolize the CPU and system resources.

When an application is launched, the operating system begins by creating an initial thread for the process. The initial thread may create other threads which may then create subsequent threads. A process (application) remains active as long as any one of these threads remains active.

Protected Memory

Both Windows 95/98 and Windows NT provide a memory address space for executing applications, using a virtual memory table to translate application memory addresses to physical memory addresses. Virtual memory is simply a set of logical addresses which may correspond either to RAM or to data in a *page file* (the page file is a physical extension of memory written to the hard drive). The use of virtual memory allows a process access to memory addresses beyond the limits of physical RAM.

Virtual memory is allocated by pages: 4096-byte (4KB) blocks in virtual address space. In contrast, RAM refers only to physical memory, which is unrelated to virtual memory space.

The difference between the two systems, however, is that Windows NT provides protected memory spaces and actively prevents applications from attempting to read from or write to physical memory outside of the allocated memory space. Under NT, applications that attempt to violate memory address spaces are simply terminated, and a badly-behaved application cannot cause a system crash nor interfere with the execution of other applications.

Under Windows 95/98, where protected memory is not enforced, it is possible for applications to access memory outside of their allocated space, and the results can crash other applications or the system itself. In all of the 32-bit Windows systems, the Virtual Memory Manager allocates 4GB of memory (virtual address space) to each process. Within this virtual address space, the lower 2GB is allocated to the process or application, while the upper 2GB is reserved for system use. 16-bit applications commonly rely on 16-bit global segments located below 1MB with remaining segments located at virtual addresses in the 2GB to 3GB range, which is also where 32-bit system DLLs are located.

File System Security

DOS, Windows 95, Windows 98, and Windows NT all recognize the standard 16-bit FAT (File Allocation Table, a.k.a. FAT16) system. The shortcomings of the FAT16 system—aside from poor usage and inadequate support for larger drives—are that all drives, directories, and files are freely available to all users.

Windows NT also supports the NTFS (NT File System) file format. As a 32-bit file system, NTFS has a number of strengths over FAT16, including better support for larger drives and better usage by supporting smaller cluster sizes, thus making more efficient use of storage space. Windows 95 OSR2 (Operating System Release 2) has also introduced a 32-bit file system—FAT32—which shares NTFS's improved support for larger drives and more efficient usage. Windows NT 5.0 and Windows 98 will also support FAT32 drives.

The important advantages of NTFS over both the FAT and FAT32 systems are the file security features which permit the assignment of security rights to govern access both to drives and directories, and to individual files. File security allows access to be offered and restricted to individuals or groups, and can grant access to read files while not offering access to write or alter files. File security also records when a file was last accessed or changed and conforms to C2-level certification requirements.

Multiple CPU Support

Windows NT supports symmetric multiprocessors. Using multiple CPUs allows multitasking operations—including multithreading—to be shared across two or more CPUs, greatly enhancing performance.

Multiple CPUs are advantageous even for single-threaded applications because Windows NT itself is multithreaded and constitutes a part of the workload.

Drivers and Peripheral Support

The one area where Windows 95/98 has an advantage over Windows NT is in the drivers and support for peripheral devices. Because drivers for Windows 95/98 are not always compatible with Windows NT, and because developers and OEMs are not as quick to develop NT-version drivers, Windows 95/98 does have better support for modems, video cards, and other peripherals than Windows NT.

Of course, unlike Windows NT, Windows 95/98 is not portable to non-Intel platforms.

Selecting an Operating System

While the future of Windows—according to Microsoft's announced intentions—is to drop all Windows versions except for the Windows NT client and server platforms, Windows presently exists in three principal forms: the 16-bit Windows 3.*x* versions, the 32-bit Windows 95/98, and the 32-bit Windows NT client/server platforms. Each of these offer different potentials for satisfying user requirements.

Microsoft ✓ *Exam Objective*

Choose from 16-bit Windows operating systems, Windows 95/98, Windows NT Workstation, and Windows NT Server for satisfying a set of requirements.

Window 3.*x* (16-Bit Windows Systems)

The Windows 16-bit operating systems, all of which are DOS-based, include Windows 3.0, Windows 3.1, and Windows 3.11 (Windows for Workgroups).

Windows 3.0 was the first version to introduce a completely graphical user interface. However, version 3.0 also had some serious problems, such as the infamous Unrecoverable Application Error message (commonly referred to as "that damned UAE"), and never did become popular. The passing of Windows 3.0 was lamented by very few... if, indeed, any at all.

Windows 3.1 was a major improvement over 3.0; it was more stable, more powerful and, even though it was still essentially a DOS shell, proved to be a very popular system and was widely adopted by users who were tired of purely text-based applications and command line prompts. Windows 3.1 was also popular with developers, who flocked to convert existing applications and to create new applications for the system.

Windows 3.11, a.k.a. Windows for Workgroups, added networking support, thereby allowing Windows systems to interact with each other and with network server systems.

Except for circumstances where older, legacy machines require support, there are few reasons for selecting any 16-bit operating system as a solution. Further, given the considerations of support and of compatibility with current and future application development, long-term economics strongly suggest that the appropriate hardware upgrades (to 32-bit systems) would produce the less expensive solution.

Windows NT 3.1 / 3.5 / 3.51

The first version of Windows NT—version 3.1—appeared a few years after the split between Microsoft and IBM, around 1993, over disagreements about the future and development of OS/2, the operating system which, originally, had been billed as the universal replacement for DOS.

This first version of Windows NT was a significant departure from previous OSs—excepting, of course, its similarities to OS/2. Windows NT did not run on top of DOS, but was a true operating system, offered 32-bit functionality, took full advantage of the current generation of CPUs, could run both as a server and as a workstation, supported larger hard drives... well, the complete list of advantages are simply too many to list. But the big disadvantage of Windows NT was inherent in its capabilities. This was a time when memory was still expensive and, in order to do everything it was capable of, Windows NT simply needed more memory and more sophisticated equipment than any other operating system.

To developers, Windows NT was the answer to a dream. To the average user, unfortunately, Windows NT was simply too expensive to support. And, given the lack of general popularity, there was also a lack of development support and relatively few applications were moved to the new platform. Partially as a result, Windows NT systems were more widely deployed as servers than as desktops.

Windows 95/98

Windows 95 was the product that made the break from DOS irreversible, partly because of its improved interface, which strongly resembled the original OS/2 design. This break, however, occurred less because of its technical superiority than because falling prices for memory, hard drives, and other equipment made it more practical for the average user to take advantage of the improvements.

Windows 98—marketing hype aside—is less of a major change from Windows 95 than it is a step-upgrade to fix some problems in Windows 95. For most purposes, Windows 98 can, and will, be discussed as indistinguishable from Windows 95.

This is not to denigrate the changes between the two systems but simply because, for purposes of selecting an OS, the differences between Windows 95 and Windows 98 are not important.

Windows NT Workstation and Windows NT Server

The successors to Windows NT 3.1 and 3.5, the Windows NT Workstation 4.0 (for client workstations) and Server 4.0 are the two preeminent operating systems available today. Since the differences between the two are simply the purpose to which each is directed—both versions are compiled from the same source and, functionally, they differ only in the settings of a few switches—both the Workstation and Server versions of NT are discussed simply as Windows NT.

Comparing Operating Systems

Since it isn't possible to have a single operating system that can fully exploit the broad range of hardware systems available, Windows has taken a two-tiered approach, with the Microsoft family of operating systems focusing on two distinct design points. The first is aimed at the mainstream—the average home/office user and portable systems—and the second is aimed at the high end, leading-edge power users—developers, server systems, and high-performance workstations.

The Windows 95/98 operating system is aimed at the mainstream market, including everything from sub-notebook and entry-level desktop machines to average and advanced home/office users. Windows 95/98 is designed to deliver responsive performance for a broad range of applications while still conserving system resources. At the same time, the Windows NT system is designed to support the leading-edge power users, providing support for high-end systems including dual-processor workstations and multi-processor RISC servers. Windows NT is designed to exploit the full capabilities of top-end hardware systems and to provide the most advanced services for the most demanding applications.

Currently, all major operating system developers are moving to a micro-kernel architecture for their leading-edge operating systems. This includes Microsoft, IBM, Sun (together with most UNIX vendors), and Novell. Micro-kernel architecture offers vendors the ability to enhance systems in response to rapid changes in the requirements for business solutions under development, as well as maintain the flexibility to exploit new hardware and peripherals.

Since Microsoft is maintaining two separate but parallel operating systems—Windows 95/98 and Windows NT—they have committed to maintaining parity in basic functionality (including the user interface) between the two platforms. The differences that do exist between these two platforms are simply the result of different design goals.

Following these standards, Windows 95/98 is focused on ease of computing and on making a wide range of personal and business applications available to everyone across a wide range of desktop and portable computers. One element behind this broad support is a wide range of drivers providing peripheral support as well as a high level of compatibility with contemporary applications.

Windows NT, or, more explicitly, the Windows NT Workstation, is focused on providing a powerful desktop operating system for solving complex business requirements. Also aimed at developers, technical, engineering, and financial users, and business operations application users, Windows NT delivers high performance to support demanding business applications. Further, Windows NT also delivers reliability, protection, and security for applications in circumstances where operation failure is of major importance. Support includes exploiting the latest hardware innovations, such as RISC processors and multi-processor configurations, as well as keeping an emphasis on maintenance and regular system updates.

In the future, as the mainstream systems become increasingly sophisticated, market demands will ensure that the technologies first implemented on the leading-edge Windows operating system product will migrate to the mainstream product. For example, generalized support for high-resolution direct video might be introduced first on leading-edge systems where machine vision system—demanding extensive processing capabilities—would be used in manufacturing and industrial control processes.

In other circumstances, technical innovations may first appear on the mainstream operating system, either because of the timing of release versions or because certain features are focused on ease of use for less technical users. For example, a generalized voice recognition engine might prove more popular with casual users than in technical environments. In general, however, the intention behind product planning is for the leading-edge operating system to provide a superset of the functionality found in the mainstream operating system.

To provide commonality for application developers, the Windows programming platform is defined by Win32 (the 32-bit Windows application programming interface) and COM (the Common Object Model, including OLE). Given these standards and by following a few simple guidelines, developers can write a single application version which will execute across the entire Windows operating system family. This does not, of course, exclude developers from targeting specific operating systems to make use of functional elements which are important to particular objectives or tasks.

Deployment Scenarios

Deciding which platform to deploy should ideally be based on the tasks individuals expect to accomplish. Between the 95/98 and NT platforms, a very complementary set of services and capabilities offer a broad range of usage scenarios. For example, most office environments require general tasks such as word processing, database queries, or spreadsheets. In many cases, the office environment may be centered around productivity products such as

Lotus Suite or Microsoft Office together with more specialized, industry-specific applications. Further, because most offices will have an installed base of desktop computers, peripheral devices, and legacy applications, they will also want to maximize their existing investment and may well choose to rely on the Windows 95/98 operating system.

Many business have a number of remote employees—employees who spend a good part of their time away from the office, either as support personnel at customer sites, on sales calls, or performing other types of field work. In such circumstances, workers commonly rely on portable computers to perform a multitude of tasks. While their computing requirements are similar to office workers in terms of application and device compatibility, the limitations of portable systems also place an emphasis on minimizing hardware demands, including memory, drive space, and battery power. Again, the Windows 95/98 operating system is the optimum choice.

Engineers, researchers, statisticians, and other technical users commonly require the capacity for processing-intensive applications, whether for data analysis or complex design activities. Windows NT Workstation—supporting symmetric multiprocessing and offering portability to multiple high-performance platforms such as those using Pentium, DEC Alpha, or MIPS CPUs—can provide performance equal to leading-edge workstations or minicomputers, but can do so at a fraction of the cost. As an added advantage, a Windows NT Workstation still accommodates the same productivity software as a Windows 95/98 system.

In other circumstances, the primary consideration is the need to protect sensitive data or even application files, such as in the banking industry or in the military. For this purpose, the Windows NT Workstation offers platform security. The NTFS file system, combined with the appropriate security procedures, can prevent unauthorized access to both systems and data. Because the security model in Windows NT Workstation is designed for C2-level security certification, an NT system can be shared by multiple users while still maintaining full security for all files on the system.

In some settings, the primary requirement is for high levels of availability and performance with a minimum of downtime irrespective of the applications being run. Quite often, mini and mainframe systems are being "right-sized" to provide platforms for this type of system. For example, many manufacturing systems use 16-bit applications to manage company production lines. Under Windows NT, Win16 applications are executed in separate address spaces—a.k.a. virtual machines—while Windows NT provides strongly protected memory spaces. The end result is that, if one or more applications fail to execute correctly, all other applications on the system continue to function without effect or interruption.

Finally, Windows NT Workstation also offers complete protection for 32-bit applications, as well as the ability to automatically recover (with a complete reboot if necessary) in the event that the system crashes.

Similarities and Differences between Windows 95/98 and Windows NT

Table 2.1 shows similarities between the Windows 95/98 and Windows NT (4.0) operating systems.

T A B L E 2.1 Comparing Windows 95/98 and Windows NT 4: Similarities	Benefit/Feature	Windows 95/98	Windows NT Workstation
	Ease of use		
	Hardware auto-detection during installation and configuration	Yes	Yes
	Next-generation Windows user interface	Yes	Yes
	Power		
	32-bit, preemptive multitasking design	Yes	Yes
	Win32 API for application development, OLE 2.0 for linking data across applications	Yes	Yes
	Connectivity		
	LAN connectivity and peer-to-peer networking, with all popular protocols including TCP/IP, IPX/SPX, and NetBEUI	Yes	Yes
	Open networking architecture providing choice of clients, transports and drivers and extensibility for support of third-party networking applications	Yes	Yes
	Remote built-in access services	Yes	Yes

T A B L E 2.1 *(cont.)* Comparing Windows 95/98 and Windows NT 4: Similarities	Benefit/Feature	Windows 95/98	Windows NT Workstation
	Manageability		
	Open system management architecture providing infrastructure for third-party system management solutions	Yes	Yes
	Support for existing and emerging system management standards (SNMP, DMI)	Yes	Yes
	Desktop user profiles (can be modified by anyone on the system) and monitoring tools	Yes	Yes
	Application support		
	Runs Win16 applications	Yes	Yes
	System and peripheral support		
	Runs Win32 and OLE 2.0 applications	Yes	Yes
	Fully exploits 386DX, 486, and Pentium platforms	Yes	Yes

Table 2.2 shows differences between the Windows 95/98 and Windows NT (4.0) operating systems.

T A B L E 2.2 Comparing Windows 95/98 and Windows NT 4: Differences	Benefit/Feature	Windows 95/98	Windows NT Workstation
	Protection and security		
	Complete crash-protection between Win16 applications by running Win16 applications in separate address spaces	No	Yes

TABLE 2.2 (cont.) Comparing Windows 95/98 and Windows NT 4: Differences	Benefit/Feature	Windows 95/98	Windows NT Workstation
	Protection and security (cont.)		
	Offers C-2 certifiable user-level security over access to a standalone workstation. Files, folders, and applications on both desktop and server can be made "invisible" to specific users	No	Yes
	Secure user profiles to control access to desktop, applications, and system configuration files	No	Yes
	Data protection through transacted file system	No	Yes
	Has automatic recovery from a system failure	No	Yes
	Application support		
	Runs MS-DOS applications	Yes	Most
	Supports multiple file systems beyond the MS-DOS FAT file system (NTFS)	No	Yes
	Support for FAT32 file system	Windows 98	version 5.0
	Uses OpenGL graphics library to enable advanced 3-D graphics	Windows 98	Yes
	Runs IBM Presentation Manager (through 1.3) and POSIX 1003.2 applications	No	Yes

T A B L E 2.2 *(cont.)* Comparing Windows 95/98 and Windows NT 4: Differences	Benefit/Feature	Windows 95/98	Windows NT Workstation
	System and peripheral support		
	Runs MS-DOS device drivers	Yes	No
	Runs Win16 device drivers	Yes	No
	Supports disk compression	Yes	Yes
	Runs on PowerPC, MIPS, and DEC Alpha based RISC systems	No	Yes*
	Supports multi-processor configurations for scaleable performance without changing operating system or applications	No	Yes
	Plug-and-Play technology	Yes	Limited**
	Support and service		
	Quick-fix engineering teams to solve problems in critical sites (issues that block business systems usage or deployment)	No	Yes
	Periodic maintenance releases posted to electronic services (e.g., Compuserve, Internet)	No	Yes
	Quarterly service pack releases		
	Distribution vehicle (CD-ROM and floppy) for maintenance releases	No	Yes

* Support for some platforms was phased out after Windows NT 4.0 service pack 1.

** Plug-and-play support under Windows NT is limited for versions 4.0 and earlier.

Summary

In discussing the architectural differences between Windows NT and Windows 95/98, the biggest (and most critical) difference is the support for protected memory. A second important consideration is found in file systems: Windows NT supports the NTFS file system, which is not recognized by Windows 95/98; while Windows 98 introduces the FAT32 file system, which is not recognized by Windows NT 4. Other important differences between the Windows 95/98 systems and the Windows NT system lie in NT's support for multiprocessor systems and in Windows 95/98's superior support for peripherals.

In selecting an operating system for deployment, the primary consideration should be security: Windows NT should be used in circumstances where intensive computation, file security, or failure recovery are primary considerations. Both file and general security are major considerations in the selection of Windows NT as an operating system. The Windows 95/98 operating system is more suitable for general office use, with laptops, and in circumstances where less powerful desktop systems are in use.

Review Questions

1. Both Windows 95 and Windows NT fully support which of the following? (Select all that apply.)

   A. MAPI

   B. ODBC

   C. Unicode

   D. User-level security functions

2. Which of the following is true?

   A. Both Windows NT and Windows 95/98 enforce protected memory for all applications.

   B. Protected memory is enforced by application design only.

   C. Windows NT and Windows 98 enforce protected memory but Windows 95 does not.

   D. Windows NT enforces protected memory but Windows 95/98 does not.

3. The virtual address space shared by 16-bit applications and 32-bit DLLs in Windows 95 is:

   A. 1GB to 2GB

   B. 1MB to 4MB

   C. 2GB to 3GB

   D. 3GB to 4GB

4. The only file system recognized by DOS, Windows 95, Windows 98, and Windows NT is:

   A. FAT16

   B. FAT32

   C. HPFS

   D. NTFS

5. Virtual memory address space in the 32-bit Windows environment is arranged with:

   A. The lower 2GB allocated to the application and the upper 2GB allocated to the system.

   B. The lower 2GB allocated to the system and the upper 2GB allocated to the application.

    C. The lower 2MB allocated to the application and the upper 2MB allocated to the system.

    D. The lower 2MB allocated to the system and the upper 2MB allocated to the application.

6. Which of the following are true? (Select all that apply.)

    A. FAT file systems provide efficient support for larger hard drives.

    B. FAT32 file systems provide efficient support for larger hard drives.

    C. FAT32 file systems support file access security.

    D. NTFS file systems provide efficient support for larger hard drives.

7. In a 32-bit Windows process, the termination of which thread causes the process to terminate?

    A. The initial thread

    B. The last thread executing

    C. The primary thread

    D. The semaphore thread

8. Multiple processors are supported by which of the following?

    A. Both Windows 95/98 and Windows NT

    B. Windows 95/98 only

    C. Windows NT only

    D. None of the above

9. Which of the following elements are features of Windows 95? (Select all that apply.)

    A. Portability to non-Intel platforms

    B. Preemptive multitasking

    C. Support for symmetric multi-processors

    D. Virtual memory management

10. Which of the following are true? (Select all that apply.)

    A. 16-bit Windows operating systems offer a method of leveraging older, legacy systems.

    B. Windows 3.1 supports 32-bit addressing.

    C. Windows 95 operates independently of the DOS operating system.

    D. Windows for Workgroups adds networking support to Windows 3.1.

11. In a 32-bit Windows environment, what is the maximum amount of virtual address space each process can use?

    A. 4MB

    B. 2GB

    C. 4GB

    D. 8GB

12. Which of the following are true of the Windows 95/98 operating system? (Select all that apply.)

    A. It's aimed at top-end, leading-edge power users with high performance workstations.

    B. It's an independent 32-bit operating system.

    C. It's designed to deliver responsive performance for a broad range of applications while still conserving system resources.

    D. It's designed to support multiple-processor RISC systems.

13. Which of the following is true of the Windows NT operating system? (Select all that apply.)

    A. It's aimed at the mainstream market.

    B. It's designed to exploit the full capabilities of top-end hardware systems.

    C. It's designed to provide the most advanced services for the most demanding applications.

    D. It's optimized for 16-bit applications.

14. C2-level file security is supplied by which of the following?

    A. Windows 3.11

    B. Windows 95/98

    C. Windows NT

    D. All of the above

15. What are units of virtual memory called?

    A. Allocation units

    B. Extents

    C. Pages

    D. RAM

16. For which of the following situations is the Windows 95/98 operating system a valid selection? (Select all that apply.)

    A. Engineering and scientific applications requiring intensive data analysis

    B. General office environments

    C. Manufacturing systems using multiple 16-bit applications to manage production lines

    D. Sales and field representatives who use portable computers

17. How is multitasking handled?

    A. On a cooperative basis by Windows NT, but on a preemptive basis by Windows 3.x and Windows 95/98

    B. On a preemptive basis by all versions of Windows, including Windows 3.x, Windows NT, and Windows 95/98

    C. On a preemptive basis by Windows NT, both a preemptive and cooperative basis by Windows 95/98, and on a cooperative basis by Windows 3.x

    D. On a preemptive basis by Windows NT, but on a cooperative basis by Windows 3.x and Windows 95/98

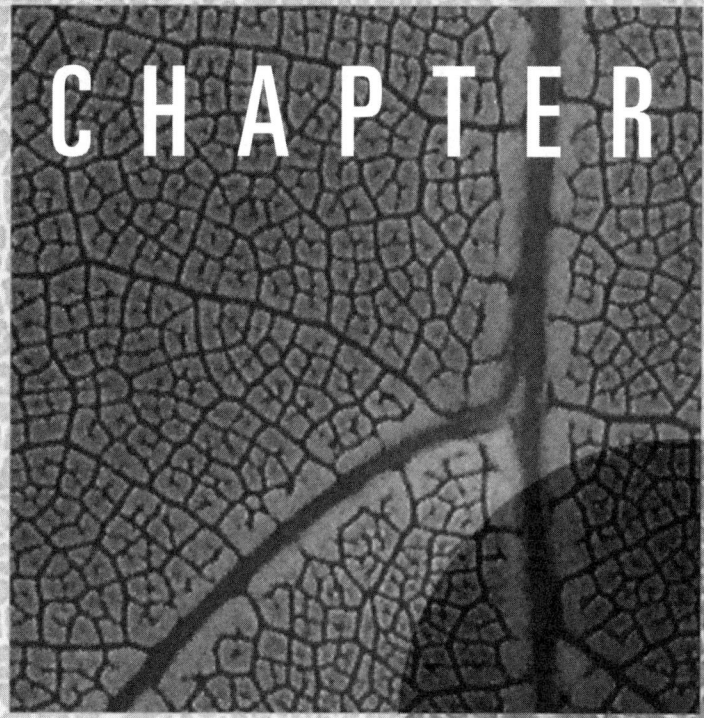

CHAPTER

3

Choosing Development Tools

Together, Microsoft Office, Microsoft BackOffice and Microsoft Visual Studio are designed to function as three complementary and interrelated suites, providing components for creating application solutions.

The Microsoft BackOffice suite, together with Windows NT, provides a group of server-side components for Internet and intranet support. The Microsoft Office suite offers applications to satisfy a variety of the most common office requirements, including document processing (Microsoft Word), spreadsheets and financial tools (Microsoft Excel), and database creation (Microsoft Access). The Microsoft Visual Studio suite completes the triad by supplying application development tools—including Visual Basic, Visual C++, and Visual FoxPro—for creating complete, custom applications.

Microsoft BackOffice Integrated Server Suite

Microsoft's BackOffice is an integrated server suite designed for both the Internet and intranets. In this section, we will look at the key capabilities of BackOffice, at methodologies for evaluating BackOffice, and at the circumstances and situations where BackOffice is employed.

Information Technology Infrastructures

Traditionally, the server side of a client/server system has been a conglomeration of tools, systems, and utilities, with the server's information technology (IT) infrastructure being restructured and evolving as new business applications are added, new network services incorporated, or existing components upgraded or updated. Overall, this process has commonly resulted in an ad-hoc system—one which functioned but was rarely, if ever, optimal.

A typical, mixed client/server architecture is illustrated in Figure 3.1, with six separate operating systems supported by a variety of network services.

FIGURE 3.1

A traditional (mix and match) client/server architecture

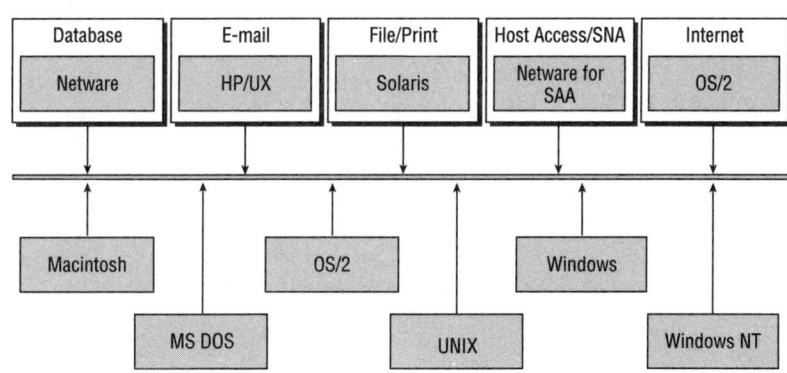

The problems with relying on a mix-and-match IT infrastructure are numerous. They include high support and training costs as well as software/hardware expenses. Further, since mixed applications rarely function cooperatively, mixed systems commonly require special programming before information from different and disparate sources can be integrated.

The requirement for custom solutions, of course, adds another layer of expense in the IT overhead required to manage both individual applications and the linking infrastructure itself. Historically, these inconveniences were simply a fact of life, tolerated as a necessity but appreciated by few people.

Currently, with the rapid growth of the Internet and World Wide Web as well as the growing use of intranet services, a further layer of infrastructure is imposing its own demands for seamless access to information across files, documents on distributed systems, messages, local and remote databases, and, of course, Web pages themselves.

The problems inherent in the mix-and-match approach to a server architecture can be categorized from three perspectives: that of the system administrator, the user, and the solution developer.

From a system administrator's perspective, the major problems with mix-and-match server systems include:

- Both in terms of financial and man-hour requirements, costs for maintaining multiple directories of user accounts and permissions for each separate network service and application can be high.

- Different setup and administration tools are required to perform similar tasks across different applications. Differences require additional training and make administration tasks increasingly time-consuming.

- Application licensing from multiple vendors with different requirements and standards results in complex purchasing and increased expenses.

- Requiring support from multiple sources for multiple applications results in higher costs. The quality of support is often poor in terms of resolution and is too frequently complicated by conflicts between applications where neither vendor is willing to accept responsibility.

From a user's perspective, problems include:

- Multiple accounts and passwords are required to access printers, files and applications.

- Multiple information sources are stored on different systems and it is necessary to learn multiple applications to access the information.

- It is difficult to integrate and analyze information derived from multiple sources in multiple formats.

From a solution developer's perspective, the downside is found in:

- Time and expense are required to ensure that applications can work together and will not cause fatal system crashes.

- The developer must be familiar with multiple, proprietary development tools and APIs in order to function across different applications and across network services.

All of these problems—and others—are behind the growing demand for solutions in the form of integrated server suites.

Server Suites

Integrated server suites must supply a variety of system services including:

- complete management solutions for networked systems

- fast access to files, printers, and peripherals through a network foundation

- reliable messaging services to support communications, collaboration, and the free and ready exchange of information

- robust and scaleable database services for information management

- tools for both Internet and intranet publishing support

- tools for secure access to host (AS/400 or Mainframe) applications and data

The Microsoft BackOffice Strategy

In the past, problems similar to those described for server systems were also notable in desktop systems where word processors, spreadsheets, graphics programs, and others all existed as disparate applications, lacking both common interfaces and the ability to exchange and share information. In response, many application developers set about creating integrated office systems such as Microsoft Office and Lotus Office Suite.

On the server side, Microsoft has adopted a similar strategy by developing and offering an integrated Server Suite to address the problems inherent in mix-and-match server systems while, at the same time, offering choice.

Advantages promised by BackOffice include:

- better pricing than individually marketed applications

- a common user environment

- common system management tools

- common development tools

In addition, by integrating Microsoft's BackOffice with their desktop applications—including Microsoft Office—the following user benefits are promised:

- a fully integrated and optimized client/server environment

- applications which can be:

  - shared and divided between client and server components

  - developed and managed through a common set of tools

The most important long-term advantage is that solution developers will be free to employ their resources to address business solutions instead of spending time and effort duplicating integration efforts which are more efficiently handled by application vendors.

Traditional Solutions

Traditionally, Unix was the platform of choice for the server side of client/server systems. The disadvantage of Unix, however, was that Unix comes in many different flavors, and each Unix application is tied to a specific hardware platform and/or to a specific version of Unix. The result was that customers were faced with proprietary solutions which were difficult or even impossible to integrate with other Unix platforms or solutions.

Alternately, the AS/400 platform has traditionally offered the built-in integration that customers have preferred. However, the AS/400 is expensive, only executes on IBM hardware platforms, and makes it difficult to add third-party applications.

In contrast, Microsoft BackOffice provides the integration of the AS/400 platform while being less expensive—both in terms of hardware and software—and provides easier third-party integration.

Microsoft BackOffice as a Server Solution

BackOffice offers a complete server solution including:

- a single management model using Windows-based administration tools across the network suite, as well as integration with the Windows NT Server directory services and management tools

- a single, Windows-based development environment with standard APIs (ODBC, OLE, MAPI, and Win32) as well as common, integrated networking (TCP/IP and IPX/SPX) for both the client and server sides

- acceptance for a broad variety of third-party, off-the-shelf applications without extensive integration efforts

- fast file and printer sharing, communications, messaging, database, host connectivity, systems management, and Internet and intranet publishing

- twenty-four hour, seven-days-a-week mission-critical support as well as on-site, multi-vendor systems integration

Microsoft BackOffice as a Solution Development Platform

Microsoft BackOffice provides a complete and extensible development platform for both intranet and Internet business solutions, providing support for the full spectrum of data storage, including a secure file system for files and Web pages, a messaging store, and a relational database for structured data. BackOffice includes common administrative tools, host integration, intranet information query, replication, systems management, and a unified security model.

BackOffice Application Integration

Microsoft BackOffice applications are designed to work on an integrated basis. They offer the following benefits:

- fully designed for both the Windows NT Server and cross-application compatibility

- a high-performance, reliable, and secure platform supporting centralized, consistent, and convenient administration

- compatible with existing customer systems and the Internet

- integrated with the desktop, providing users with a single logon for access to desktop, network, and business applications as well as seamless access across servers, legacy systems, and the Internet

This design for integrated operation provides a variety of benefits for solution developers, end users, and IT administrators.

Solution developers, including ISVs, VARs, and corporate developers, are able to take advantage of the integrated design to concentrate efforts on creating customized solutions and adding value to customers' technology investments. By removing the need for creating interoperation solutions, developers are able to develop applications faster and at lower development costs, and to concentrate on value-added services rather than spending time on network integration.

End users will find familiar, Windows-based desktops where a single network logon provides seamless, consistent, and convenient access to a variety of information from an assortment of sources including intranets and the Internet.

For IT administrators, Microsoft BackOffice is easily installed and administered as well as convenient to use. A single integrated installation with online help, consistent licensing, and graphic administration tools make both local and remote management for BackOffice applications convenient. Using the integrated BackOffice suite, managers are offered single-seat administration—both local and remote—for intranets through consistent, Windows-based utilities. With a single directory service, administrators are able to deploy and administer both desktops and servers using a single set of tools.

In addition, BackOffice is also scaleable from small/branch office installations to enterprise-wide deployment. Because BackOffice (and the Windows NT Server) run on a variety of Intel and RISC single and multiprocessing systems, systems are scaleable supporting growing business needs without making existing IT investments obsolete.

Because Microsoft BackOffice is designed for Windows NT Server, Back-Office applications are able to take full advantage of the Windows NT services, including:

- Micro-kernel–based architecture which is extensible, offers multi-threading and dynamic load balancing across processors, and provides asynchronous I/O. At the same time, the protected virtual memory space offers great scaleability. Because Windows NT is a portable architecture, systems can execute on a variety of hardware platforms ranging from single processor Intel-based systems to SMP RISC-based systems, allowing organizations to take full advantage of the optimum price/performance choices available.

- Windows NT's memory protection permits secure execution for multiple applications on a single computer.

- Structured exception handling and built-in support for such fault-tolerant features as disk-striping, mirroring, duplexing, and UPS-support offer a reliable foundation.

- C-2 level security provides protection against unauthorized access to data, both locally and across the Internet. Protected access covers files, documents, Web pages, e-mail, databases, and host data.

- Windows NT's built-in networking API provides support for Windows Sockets (WinSock API), remote procedure calls (RPCs), and named pipes while OLE/COM offers network transport independence.

All of these elements together offer a reliable and secure platform for mission-critical applications. Further, reliability is enhanced using Microsoft SQL Server and Microsoft Exchange Server to provide data replication between servers and SNA Server's support for hot backup and fault-tolerant host connections.

BackOffice Standards

While server suites can be designed to operate across multiple platforms, they necessarily suffer from three principal shortcomings:

- Applications must be designed to incorporate functionality duplicated for multiple platforms.

- Multiple platform applications must be written to only take advantage of the lowest common denominator services common to all server platforms.

- The performance benefits of being integrated with the operating system architecture are compromised.

Because BackOffice is designed specifically for the Windows NT Server platform, BackOffice applications avoid the shortcomings of cross-platform designs while providing powerful client/server and enterprise-class functionality.

Together with other Microsoft products and third-party applications, Back-Office offers a single, integrated development infrastructure supporting the standard APIs together with common built-in networking on both the server and desktop sides. As a development platform, BackOffice consists not only of the operating system and applications but also the development and testing tools necessary to build applications for intranet and Internet use.

For solution developers, Microsoft offers a variety of programs which include developer conferences, the Microsoft Developer Network (MSDN), porting labs, and software development kits (SDKs).

The "Designed for Microsoft BackOffice" logo is intended to allow customers to select off-the-shelf applications that are not only compatible with BackOffice but that also take advantage of the integration and functionality of BackOffice. To qualify for the BackOffice logo, products must comply with the technical criteria listed in Table 3.1.

TABLE 3.1

Requirements for the BackOffice Logo

For Server Applications	For Client Applications
must run as a Windows NT service	must be developed on the Microsoft Windows platform
must support the Windows NT unified logon	must use APIs appropriate to the server application (i.e., MAPI, TAPI, ODBC)
must be deployable using the Microsoft Systems Management Server	must be deployable using the Microsoft Systems Management Server

T A B L E 3.1 *(cont.)*	**For Server Applications**	**For Client Applications**
Requirements for the BackOffice Logo	must be network independent by supporting both the TCP/IP and IPX/SPX protocols	
	must support ISAPI (Internet applications only)	

The Open Systems Environment

The Open Systems Environment is a standard intended to increase the number and variety of products for business solutions available to users—assuming functionality and price—by encouraging third-party add-on product developers. Products are deemed to be open on the basis of the following:

- The application's use of published interfaces and protocols which are publicly accessible for use by any party for any purpose. This includes purposes of interoperability and integration with other applications or systems.

- The application is available from multiple vendors.

Microsoft BackOffice itself supports a broad variety of both *de jure* and *de facto* standards, including:

- database standards: DB-Lib, ODBC, OLE DB, and ODS

- industry standard APIs: MAPI, ODBC, OLE, RPC, SNA API, Win32, WinSock, and WOSA APIs

- Internet standards: CGI, HTTP, ISAPI, Java, ODBC, and Perl

- management standards: DMTF and SNMP

- messaging standards: CMC, MAPI, SMTP/MIME, UUDECODE, UUENCODE, X.400, and X.500

- most major network protocols: AppleTalk, DECnet, IPX/SPX, NET-BEUI, OSI, SMB, and TCP/IP

In addition to adopting customer standards, the portability of BackOffice across multiple hardware platforms and open systems environment gives customers an open choice of hardware, vendors, and applications.

- **Hardware choices** BackOffice (via Windows NT) runs on a wide variety of Intel (and Intel-compatible) and RISC CPUs on unmodified single and multiprocessor systems. Furthermore, BackOffice functions with a wide variety of peripherals including CD-ROMs, fax/modems, and various input devices.

- **Vendor choices** Because neither Windows NT nor BackOffice are hardware dependent, hardware platforms and vendors can be changed without changing applications.

- **Applications choices** Under the Open Systems standard, a wide variety of off-the-shelf server and desktop applications are available to run on the BackOffice platform.

Integration within BackOffice

Microsoft BackOffice is designed to run exclusively on Windows NT Server. BackOffice consists of five principal components:

- Microsoft Exchange Server

- Microsoft Internet Information Server

- Microsoft SNA Server

- Microsoft SQL Server

- Microsoft Systems Management Server

Each of these components is designed to take full advantage of Windows NT's micro-kernel architecture, making BackOffice extensible and scaleable.

The Windows NT operating system provides file and print services as well as client/server and Internet application services. NT's portable SMP (Symmetric Multiprocessing) architecture permits applications to execute unmodified on everything from small single processor systems to SMP RISC-based systems. This range of choice permits taking advantage of the optimum price-performance hardware and allows hardware to be upgraded as system needs grow, while ensuring that the installed applications will automatically take advantage of hardware upgrades and increased performance.

Memory protection for both applications and subsystems, structured exception handling, and built-in support for disk striping, mirroring, duplexing, and UPS (Uninterruptable Power Supply) services offer a highly reliable environment for the entire BackOffice application family.

Supporting C-2 level security as specified by the U.S. Department of Defense's National Computer Security Center (NCSC), Windows NT Server prevents unauthorized access to corporate data and provides full auditing capabilities.

Integrated Directory and Security Model   Supporting a single user login to the network, to the BackOffice server applications, and to third party applications eliminates the requirement for users to remember multiple account names and passwords and obviates the need for administrators to maintain separate user account databases. Third-party applications—under the BackOffice label standards—also leverage this integrated directory and security model.

Because of the centralized management scheme for user accounts and passwords, management is convenient from any administrative console, whether over a private network, an intranet, or through dial-in access. This also reduces administrative overhead.

Setup, Installation, and Configuration   BackOffice server and client applications support unified server/client installation programs providing an automated, point-and-click setup process.

Setup is simplified and manual configurations eliminated by using auto-detection for network protocols and hardware, including CD-ROM drives, network cards, and SCSI adapters. All BackOffice components automatically use the same single hardware configuration, and online help is available from all BackOffice applications.

Windows NT Server's network client utilities and automated setup for Windows clients over the network reduces the time required for manually setting up each client.

Systems Management and Administration   BackOffice's Windows-based administration simplifies complex administration tasks, while a knowledge of Windows NT Server simplifies learning other BackOffice applications.

BackOffice leverages the Windows NT Server administration tools, allowing administrators to use a common tool set for such tasks as performance monitoring, event viewing and logging, application license management, and alert monitoring.

By centralizing the administration of shared resources—i.e., files, printers, and peripherals—the complete network solution can be managed from any administrative console, reducing travel costs, system downtime, and the need for system expertise at remote locations.

Desktop Integration Microsoft BackOffice shares the same graphical user interface, Win32 API, development environment, and management model as the Windows NT desktop. This integration permits solution developers to take advantage of existing skills, such as knowledge of Win32, OLE, and other standards, as well as common visual tools to develop and extend client/server applications for intranets and the Internet.

Because both the desktop and the server incorporate the same technology, third-party and custom business solutions are more reliable. Administrators are able to manage both desktops and servers in a similar fashion.

Industry Standard Support BackOffice provides support for such industry standards as ODBC, MAPI, and OLE on both the desktop and server sides. This provides flexibility for desktop applications both in taking advantage of BackOffice capabilities and in a choice of applications.

ODBC supports applications such as Microsoft Excel and Microsoft Access by providing convenient access to information on SQL Server or on hosts via Microsoft SNA Server. OLE supports information exchange between applications through drag-and-drop, visual editing, and custom document properties. Using OLE, documents can be dragged and dropped into e-mail messages, and e-mail messages can be dragged and dropped into files. Custom OLE properties can be incorporated in Microsoft Office documents, which can then be sorted in Microsoft Exchange views.

OLE Automation supports the standard visual development tools to permit building custom applications that integrate Microsoft Office and Microsoft BackOffice applications. The visual development tools include Visual Basic or Visual Basic for Applications with desktop productivity tools (i.e., Microsoft Excel or Microsoft Access).

MAPI support permits e-mail systems to interact with both desktop and server applications. Using MAPI, the Microsoft Exchange client can query the Microsoft SQL Server database and deliver a response to the e-mail inbox or administrators can have SQL Server alerts sent to their e-mail inbox or to their pager. MAPI support allows automatic mailing, the addition of routing slips to documents, or the posting of documents to public folders in Microsoft Exchange.

Other Features Long filename and fast query support provides easy document access from Windows 95/98 and Office 97 to the Windows NT Server file system.

The Dynamic Host Configuration Protocol (DHCP), Domain Name System (DNS), and Windows Internet Naming Service (WINS) services provide automatic IP address configuration for Windows clients as well as automatic resolution of a client's "friendly name." This conserves IP addresses and eliminates the requirement for manual updates of host files and broadcast names, as well as allowing end users to log on to the network automatically using TCP/IP.

Software deployment and system management costs and administration overhead are reduced by using automated scripts for Windows 95/98 and Office 97 installation.

Integration with Existing Systems

Integrating BackOffice into existing network architecture is simplified by the built-in networking support (for TCP/IP, IPX/SPX, NetBEUI, SNA DLC, AppleTalk, RAS, etc.) in Windows NT Server. This also reduces deployment costs and protects existing IT investments.

Non-Windows Operating Systems   Seamless integration between the Windows NT Server, BackOffice, and the NetWare environments is provided by Client Services for NetWare, Directory Services Manager for NetWare, File and Print Service for NetWare, Migration for NetWare, and NWLink (IPX/SPX) utilities. These utilities provide the means for a smooth transition between Novell NetWare networks and the Windows NT Server network.

Integration between the Windows NT Server, BackOffice, and Unix environments is provided by support for TCP/IP and DNS, by FTP (File Transfer Protocol), by Telnet and NFS (from third party developers), by X Windows, (from third party developers), and by LPR/LPD.

The Windows NT Server and services for the Macintosh provide an integrating platform for mixed PC/Macintosh networks.

E-Mail Systems   Gateways and migration tools provide connections and conversions between e-mail systems. Internet Mail Connector (SMTP/MIME), Microsoft Mail Connector, X.400 Connector, X.500 support, and gateways from vendors, including Attachmate, IMI, and Fennestrae, provide communications to and from Fax Server, the Internet, PROFS, and SNADS environments, as well as SMTP-based and X.400-based e-mail environments.

For LAN-based and host-based e-mail systems, migration tools include DEC ALL-IN-1, IBM PROFS/Office Vision, Lotus cc:Mail, Microsoft Mail for AppleTalk, and Microsoft Mail for PC Networks. These migration tools can be used to automate and to simplify the task of migrating users to Microsoft Exchange.

Non-Microsoft Databases   Microsoft SQL Server is able to interoperate with other databases in a heterogeneous environment using data replication and Open Data Services (ODS)–based gateways. Heterogenous gateways are provided by such partners as Information Builders, Showcase, and Micro Decisionware (MDI/Sybase).

Microsoft SQL Server databases can be replicated to ODBC subscribers such as Microsoft Access, Oracle, Sybase, and DB2. Replication with an AS/400 database is provided by third-party applications such as Symbiator from Execusoft.

SNA Networks and Hosts   Microsoft SNA Server provides support for all SNA APIs, communication adapters (via the SNADIS interface), protocols (LU, PU and data link), and standards (3270 and 5250 emulators, TN3270 service, and AFTP), as well as all major LAN protocols. This enables the SNA Server to provide secure and reliable connections between desktops and hosts along with support for Internet connectivity, systems management, remote access, and messaging over SNA networks.

ODBC/DRDA drivers supplied with the Microsoft SNA Server allow Microsoft Access and Microsoft Excel access to mission-critical data on host-based databases. These include DB2 for MVS, SQL/DS on VM, and DB2/400 on OS/400.

Client Management Services   In a heterogeneous environment, client management can be managed via popular LAN and WAN protocols using the Microsoft Systems Management Server. The Microsoft Systems Management Server can manage Macintosh, MS-DOS, OS/2, Windows 3.*x*, Windows 95/98, Windows for Workgroups, and Windows NT, client-connected network operating systems including IBM LAN Server 3.0 and 4.0, Microsoft LAN Manager (versions 2.1 and later), Microsoft Windows NT Server (versions 3.5 and later), NetWare 3.1*x* and 4.*x*, PathWorks, Unix, and VMS.

BackOffice Components

In addition to Microsoft Windows NT, the Microsoft BackOffice suite consists of five principal components. These components are illustrated in Figure 3.2.

F I G U R E 3.2

Using Microsoft Back-
Office for a unified cli-
ent/server architecture

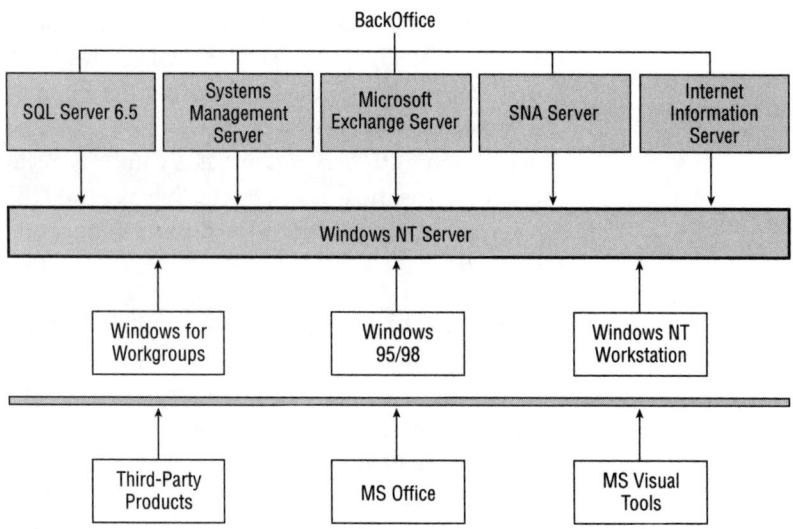

Microsoft Windows NT Server 4

Windows NT Server 4 is a fully functional network server supporting a variety of client systems, including MAC, MS-DOS, OS/2 (requires OS/2 Warp Connect), Unix (requires third party NFS server or LM/X), Windows 3.1, Windows 95/98, Windows for Workgroups, and, of course, Windows NT Workstation or other versions of Windows NT Server.

Windows NT Server also supports connectivity to other servers, including Banyan, DEC Pathworks, Internet, LAN Manager, NetWare, Unix, and others.

BackOffice/NT Server integrates with NetWare servers providing:

- Client Services for NetWare

- Directory Services Manager for NetWare (DSMN)

- File and Print Services for NetWare (FPNW)

- Gateway Service for NetWare (GSNW)

- IPX and SPX support

- NetWare migration tool

- PPP for IPX support

BackOffice/NT Server integrates with Unix servers, providing:

- TCP/IP and DNS support

- FTP and Telnet support (with third party NFS Server)
- built-in LPR/LPD (printing) support
- NFS servers (Beame & Whiteside, FTP Software, Intergraph, Net-Manage, and SunSelect)
- X Windows servers (AGE Logic, Congruent Corporation, Digital, Hummingbird, JSB, and Network Computing Devices)

Connectivity for IBM Mainframes and AS/400 servers require the Microsoft SNA Server. Macintosh requires Services for Macintosh. Finally, Internet connectivity is supplied through the Microsoft Internet Information Server and Windows NT Server, providing CGI, HTTP, ISAPI, ODBC, and Perl support.

Supported application protocols include NetBIOS, OLE, RPC, Streams, TAPI, Win32, and WinSock while Windows NT has built-in support for AppleTalk, DLC, IPX/SPX, NetBEUI, RAS (Remote Access Service), and TCP/IP.

Microsoft Exchange Server

Microsoft Exchange Server is a replacement for Microsoft Mail Server and consists of a series of services and agents providing e-mail and groupware services. One of these—the *System Attendant*—is a maintenance service which must be executed to support the Microsoft Exchange Server services.

Exchange Server provides a directory, based on the X.500 specification, to hold information for mailboxes, public folders, distribution lists, and servers. An *information store* is also supported, which holds users' mailboxes as a private information store and public folders as a public information store while enforcing security access for both.

The Exchange Server *directory synchronization component* exchanges directory information between systems using the Microsoft Mail 3.*x* directory synchronization protocol.

Within an Exchange Server organization, the *key management component* provides security information used to digitally sign and encrypt messages exchanged between users.

The Exchange Server *message transfer agent* (MTA) provides an engine for submitting, routing, and delivering messages to other Microsoft Exchange Server MTAs, connectors, information stores, and third-party gateways. Routing and data transfers are performed using the site, RAS (Remote Access Service), and X.400 connectors.

Within the Exchange Server, connectors provide connectivity to various messaging systems. Supplied connectors include:

- **X.400 connector** Provides complete, native support for the 1984 and 1988 X.400 messaging protocol, and can either plug in to an existing X.400 backbone or serve as an X.400 backbone itself.

- **Microsoft Mail connector** Provides connectivity to both the PC and AppleTalk versions of Microsoft Mail and to Microsoft Mail gateways including AT&T Mail, Fax, MCI Mail, MHS, PROFS/Office, SNADS, and Vision. These gateways, however, must be purchased separately.

- **Internet Mail connector** Offers native, built-in support for both Internet and SMTP/MIME mail.

Microsoft Exchange Client The Microsoft Exchange Client is supported by MS-DOS and all versions of Windows. Each client contains an Address Book, Personal folders, Public folders, and a user's mailbox. The Exchange Client is used to access, organize, and exchange information of varying types, including documents, e-mail, expense reports, faxes, graphs, meeting requests, sales orders, spreadsheets, and voice mail.

Microsoft Schedule+ Microsoft Schedule+ is used for time management (tracking appointments and schedules), for organizing tasks (grouping by project and sorting by start date, end data, priority, billing codes), and to communicate schedules with other users (for example, meeting requests and notifications, and managing resource bookings, such as conference rooms and equipment).

The Exchange Server's Schedule+ Free/Busy connector exchanges free and busy information via Microsoft Mail, thereby allowing Schedule+ users to check other users' schedules for free periods.

Microsoft Outlook is the replacement client for Schedule+.

Microsoft Exchange Forms Designer The Exchange Forms Designer is used to design custom forms, such as purchase requisition, expense reports, or forms for posting information to a folder, which are built in to groupware applications.

Microsoft Exchange Server Clients Microsoft Exchange Server clients include MS-DOS, all versions of Windows, OS/2 Warp, Macintosh, and Unix.

Microsoft Exchange Server Messaging Standards   The Microsoft
Exchange Server supports a variety of messaging standards including:

- CMC (Common Mail Calls) support for cross-platform APIs

- MAPI (Messaging Application Programming Interface)

- MIME (Multipurpose Internet Mail Extensions) for full-fidelity
  exchange of file attachments and multimedia objects

- SMTP (Simple Mail Transfer Protocol) support to communicate with
  the Internet and with SMTP-based mail systems

- UUENCODE and UUDECODE support to encode and decode non-
  text attachments accompanying messages

- X.400 support to communicate with other X.400 mail systems
  including Control Data, DEC Mailworks, DEC MRX, HP Open Mail,
  INFONET, Lotus Message Switch, Retix Open Server, X.400 Mail
  System, and others

- X.500 Addressing

Other support includes standards-based remote access support for RAS
(Remote Access Service), SLIP (Serial Line Internet Protocol), and PPP
(Point-to-Point Protocol), while third-party gateways are available for
PROFS (Attachmate ZIP!) and SNADS (IMI Connect-ME).

Microsoft Internet Information Server

The Microsoft Internet Information Server (IIS) is provided with Windows NT
Server 4 and provides both HTTP and FTP services as well as software for
Internet security and database access. Supported services include:

- FTP (File Transfer Protocol) service for both binary and ASCII file
  transfers

- Internet Database Connector gateway (ODBC database gateway for the
  WWW service) supporting publication of database information on the
  Internet

- Internet Service Manager used for remote, secure administration of
  all Internet Information Servers and services

- Secure Sockets Layer (SSL) supporting encrypted communications
  between client and server

- WWW (World Wide Web) service

- Web Browsers (hypertext clients for all Windows versions)

Gopher service is obsolete, and has been eliminated from IIS 4.0.

Using the ODBC/DRDA drivers supplied with Microsoft SNA Server with the Internet Database Connector (supplied by Microsoft Internet Information Server) Web browser clients are able to access host-based mainframe and AS/400 data sources.

Internet Information Server Clients   The Microsoft Internet Information Server supports MS-DOS, all versions of Windows, Macintosh, OS/2, and Unix.

Internet Information Server Standards   The Microsoft Internet Information Server supports a variety of standards including:

- CGI (Common Gateway Interface)

- HTML (HyperText Markup Language)

- HTTP (HyperText Transport Protocol)

- ISAPI (Internet Server API)

- ODBC (Open Database Connectivity through the Internet Database Connector for publishing database information on the Internet)

- Perl (the most common language for developing simple Web applications)

Internet Database Connector   The Internet Database Connector is an ISAPI application provided with Microsoft Internet Information Server which allows Microsoft SQL Server database information to be dynamically published on the Web, and allows Web users to query information from the database and to send information to the database.

Internet Information Server can log its activities to an SQL Server database allowing Microsoft Excel, Microsoft Access, or other data analysis tool to be used to analyze Web site traffic.

Microsoft SNA Server

The Microsoft SNA (Systems Network Architecture) Server is used to communicate with remote computers, such as IBM mainframes, AS/400s, or other PCs on an SNA network.

SNA Server Clients   The Microsoft SNA Server supports MS-DOS, all versions of Windows, Macintosh, OS/2, and Unix.

SNA Server Supported APIs   APIs support by the SNA include:

- APPC (Advanced Program to Program Communications)
- CPI-C
- CSV (Common Service Verb)
- EHNAPPC
- LUA (Logical Unit Application)

SNA Server Supported Protocols   The SNA Server supports a wide variety of protocols, including:

- APPC File Transfer Protocol (AFTP), which performs high-speed file transfers between IBM hosts and Windows NT-based systems
- Data Link protocols (802.2/LLC, Channel Attachment, DFT, SDLC, Twinax, and X.25/QLLC)
- LU protocols (LU 0, 1, 2, 3 and 6.2)
- Network protocols [AppleTalk, Banyan VINES/IP, DLC 802.2 (for DSPU connections), IPX/SPX, NetBEUI, RAS (Remote Access Service), and TCP/IP]
- PU protocols [APPN LEN Node, DSPU (downstream PU), and PU 2.0 and 2.1]

Other SNA Server Standards   Other SNA Server standards include:

- 3270 and 5250 emulators
- Open Database Connectivity / Distributed Relational Database Architecture (ODBC/DRDA) drivers providing desktop connectivity to DB2 for MVS, SQL/DS for VM, and DB2/400 for OS/400
- Support for a variety of SNA communications adapters through open SNADIS interface
- TN3270 service permitting any TN3270/E client, such as a Unix workstation, to connect to an IBM host via an SNA Server through a TCP/IP internetwork

In addition, NetView Services allow host administrators to execute Windows NT commands from IBM NetView consoles using NVRunCMD. Alerts generated by Windows NT, BackOffice, or other Windows NT applications can be forwarded to NetView using NVAlert. Finally, NetView Services permit LAN administrators to view NetView performance data on any Windows NT performance monitor.

Microsoft SQL Server

Microsoft SQL (Structured Query Language) Server is used to access data in SQL databases and includes support for Heterogeneous Data Replication to ODBC subscribers, including Microsoft Access, Sybase, Oracle, and IBM DB2.

The SQL Server Distribution Transaction Coordinator (DTC) provides transaction management spanning two or more SQL Server systems to guarantee transaction integrity and recovery. Two-phase commit support is provided for server-to-server procedures, removing the burden from the client application. Support is included for multiple programming interfaces including DB-Library, ODBC, OLE DB, OLE Transactions, Transact-SQL, and XA.

SQL Server uses Dynamic Locking to select the appropriate level of lock (i.e., row, page, table, or database) to maximize both concurrency and speed to fit the application needs. Page locks provide increased speed while row locks offer improved concurrency for data access.

SQL Server's data warehousing enhancements offer new online analytical query processing (OLAP) capabilities including the CUBE and ROLLUP operators, which allow a single query to return detailed data and aggregates across multiple dimensions, thus simplifying information retrieval for analytical purposes. Other SQL Language enhancements include DDL statements within transactions, improved cursor processing with relaxed update requirements, distributed transactions, and improved syntax for outer joins.

SQL Server database information can be staged in an Exchange Public Folder, allowing groupware applications to share the information and allowing users to view key database information from their e-mail inboxes.

SQL Server industry standard support includes:

- ANSI SQL-92 and FIPS 127-2 compliance using the NIST 5.1 certification suite

- SNMP MIB and SNMP traps for managing SQL Server with SNMP-based management tools

- XA support for managing SQL Server as a resource with XA-compliant transaction monitors

Performance and scaleability have been enhanced by providing:

- additional counters and high-water marks for performance monitoring and tuning

- faster sort and index performance for better throughput and response times

- reduced checkpoint serialization

Microsoft SQL Server provides support for Intel and Alpha-based systems. A 32-bit OCX implementation of the DB-Library is supplied for Visual Basic developers.

For very large databases (VLDB), Microsoft SQL Server has enhanced support including dumping and loading for individual tables, and index rebuild capabilities without requiring a drop and recreate.

SQL Enterprise Manager   The SQL Enterprise Manager is equipped with enhanced administration capabilities, including:

- built-in SNMP monitoring and traps

- built-in Transfer Manager for moving schemas and data

- DBA Assistant

- domain-wide shared server groups

- extensible toolbars and menus for both Microsoft and third-party add-ins

SQL Distributed Management Objects   SQL Distributed Management Objects (SQL-DMO) have been enhanced with new objects for data transfer and bulk copy, server groups and registered servers, as well as a multi-threaded call-back for task progress notification.

SQL Server Web Assistant   The Microsoft SQL Server Web Assistant—shipped with SQL Server 6.5—is an HTML generation tool. As such, Web Assistant can be used to automatically generate HTML pages using data from the SQL Server, and these pages can be updated automatically as data changes or in response to scheduled tasks.

The SQL Server Web Assistant can only generate Web pages based on queries which are defined by a pointer to an entire table, a view, or a stored procedure. This could include, for example, database-driven Web sites with automated information content to deliver stock prices or product availability. The viewer of the Web page, however, has no control over what is displayed or when the Web page is refreshed.

The SQL Server Web Assistant cannot be used to update, insert, or delete rows in any database table. Almost any SQL SELECT statement, however, can be specified and the output will be generated by a task created by the SQL Server Web Assistant.

Microsoft SQL Server Clients   Microsoft SQL Server Clients include MS-DOS, all versions of Windows, Macintosh (ODBC), OS/2 (Visigenic ODBC), and Unix (Visigenic ODBC).

Microsoft SQL Server Support for Other Databases   SQL Server provides support for other databases, including:

- ODS-based gateways from Information Builders, Micro Decisionware (MDI/Sybase), and Showcase for interoperation with DB2, Oracle, and Sybase, among others

- ODBC replication to Access, Oracle, Sybase, and DB2

- ODBC/DRDA drivers in the SNA Server or from third-party suppliers provide access to DB2 in MVS, SQL/DS in VM, and DB2/400 in OS/400

Microsoft Systems Management Server

From a management standpoint—or a system administrator's viewpoint—perhaps the biggest headache in maintaining a distributed system, or even a local network, is the job of installing applications and keeping track of diverse systems.

In the days of mainframes and dumb terminals, maintenance was relatively simple since the real system was all in one place. And a certain element of nostalgia may be part of the current interest, however unrealistic, in 'thin client' systems.

In the real world, however, because individual computers are not gathered in a single location and—especially when portables are involved—may not even be in an established location, maintenance often involves running from one place to another, carrying a case full of diskettes or CDs and then waiting while a manual installation concludes. On a network system, even when the installation source is centrally located—as on a network hard drive or shared CD-ROM drive—many applications require manual intervention during installation. This may be nothing more than hitting the Enter key at requested intervals, or may involve answering certain questions or confirming some details of configuration but, regardless of the reasons or responses, this interactive demand during installation makes the applications poorly suited for centralized distribution.

The Microsoft Systems Management Server Installer is designed to eliminate the need for a personal presence during installation by providing advanced installation scripting and *snapshot* installation techniques. By freeing administrators from such routine tasks, automated deployment for software applications—to any Windows-based system—minimizes ownership and overhead costs.

Simple installation labor costs aside, the Systems Management Server Installer offers much more extensive benefits. In addition to allowing administrators to install new and updated applications in a convenient and controlled fashion, the Systems Management Server Installer also makes it possible to roll back changes quickly and efficiently.

Further, by building on the functions found in the Systems Management Server, administrators are vested with the ability to manage software distribution without the need to learn sophisticated procedures or to learn to develop code or scripts. In addition, the Systems Management Server Installer extends the distribution capabilities of Systems Management Server by providing an installation engine allowing administrators to automate installation, customize installation processes, and monitor the distribution of applications to multiple desktop systems.

Using the Systems Management Server, hardware and software inventory data is stored in an SQL Server database where the information is available, through Excel or Word, for custom inventory reports. Database information can also be employed in building custom applications for help-desk support.

Systems Management Server Clients   Systems Management Server clients include:

- Apple Macintosh System 7, IBM OS/2 (2.*x*) and OS/2 WARP, MS-DOS 5.0 and later, and all versions of Windows

- Unix (versions AIX, HP-UX, OSF/1, Solaris, Sun OS, and Ultrix) and VMS clients with third-party add-on applications

Systems Management Server Servers   Native servers for System Management Server include:

- LAN Server (3.0 and 4.0)

- Microsoft LAN Manager (2.1 and later)

- Novell NetWare (3.1*x* and 4.*x*)

- Windows NT (3.5 and later)

- DEC PATHWORKS from Digital

Systems Management Server Management Standards   Management standards supported by the Systems Management Server include:

- DMTF Desktop Management Interface (DMI)
- Simple Network Management Protocol (SNMP)
- IBM NetView

Systems Management Server Network Management Tools   Network management tools supported by the Systems Management Server include:

- CA UniCenter
- IBM NetView/6000
- Network Managers NMC Vision 4000
- Openview (Hewlett-Packard)
- PolyCenter Manager on NetView (Digital)

Systems Management Server WAN Protocols   Wide Area Network (WAN) protocols supported by the Systems Management Server include:

- Asynchronous Public Switched Telephone Network (PSTN) dial-up circuits
- Internet
- ISDN services
- Private leased lines
- Private or public X.25 services
- SNA Networks (using MS SNA Server)
- TCP/IP and IPX/SPX routed networks

Microsoft Office

The Microsoft Office suite consists of ten principal components. Depending on the user's requirements and tasks, individual installations may consist of only one, two, or several of these components. The entire list is detailed in Table 3.2.

	Component	Purpose
T A B L E 3.2 Components of the Microsoft Office Suite of Products	Word	Word-processing program with capabilities for efficient online communication and collaboration
	Excel	Supports spreadsheets and Shared Workbooks, enables groups to work together more effectively
	Outlook	E-mail, scheduling, and desktop information-management
	Access	Relational database-management, local, LAN, and Internet
	PowerPoint	Tool suite for presentations both in person and via the Web
	Publisher	Tools for creating both hard-copy publications and Web pages
	FrontPage	Tools for creating and managing Web sites, with no programming required (see also Microsoft InterDev)
	Project	Project management tool for tracking schedules and budgets
	Team Manager	Consolidates, coordinates, and tracks team activities

Microsoft Office Container Collections

Each of the Microsoft Office applications has an application object model with a Container collection which is used to store objects. For Microsoft Excel, Workbooks contain Worksheets; for Microsoft Access, containers store documents such as forms, tables, and macros; and for Outlook, the Items collection is used to store messages, contacts, and appointments.

These collection objects are discussed below for individual applications.

Microsoft Word

For a writer, trying to describe Microsoft Word is a little like a fish describing water: After using it so long and for so many hundreds of thousands of words, it's just too close and too familiar to describe.

Principally, Microsoft Word is a text editor. What distinguishes Word from applications such as NotePad and WordPad is that it is much more than simply an editor. Word is, rather, a document production tool or, if you prefer, a communications tool.

Because Word offers far more than simply editing words—by providing spellchecking, typesetting, and elaborate formatting—Word makes it easier than ever to present ideas in a coherent format. Further, Word makes it possible to share information through online technologies, to share document creation with others while tracking changes and revisions, and, of course, to author HTML documents for Internet publication.

Features supplied by Microsoft Word include:

- **Address Book integration**   Maintains contact information in a single location accessible by Microsoft Word, Microsoft Exchange, and Microsoft Schedule+

- **Annotations**   Allows insertion of comments into documents, with a separate window for reviewing annotations. Annotations may include text, graphics, and voice notations.

- **Answer Wizard**   Offers help in response to user questions

- **AutoFormat**   Allows the user to add style and formatting to a document during composition

- **Document Templates**   Offer forms for the creation of letters, memos, and faxes. Custom template designs can be created.

- **Enhanced AutoCorrect**   Auto-correction for pre-defined as well as user-defined typos

- **Find Fast technology**   Provides high-performance indexing tools to manage and organized files

- **Internet Assistant**   (add on extension) Supports HTML authoring and browsing in Microsoft Word

- **Mail Merge**   Supports importing data from Microsoft Excel, Microsoft Access, and Microsoft Schedule+

- **Office interactivity**   Shares a consistent interface with other Office applications, reducing training and support costs

- **OLE support**   Supports drag-and-drop operations to integrate and share information between Office applications

- **Revision marking**   Allows editing and tracking of changes in documents more efficiently

- **Spell It**   Checks spelling during typing, underlining misspelled words and displaying alternative spellings

- **TipWizard**   Offers interactive assistance to teach users how to accomplish tasks.

- **WordMail**   Provides access to e-mail and allows Word to compose messages

Microsoft Word also provides features and utilities that offer convenient conversion and upgrade, making transitions from other word processors or office suites convenient. Conversion and upgrade features include:

- **Built-in file conversion**   Allows document files to be transferred to and from other popular word-processing programs, including all versions of WordPerfect as well as earlier versions of Microsoft Word

- **Online help for WordPerfect users**   Supports the familiar Word-Perfect commands while learning to use Microsoft Word

- **High-performance 32-bit platform**   Allows full support for long filenames, complete Windows 95 compatibility, intuitive control buttons, and easy desktop shortcuts

Word 97 can also be used to send documents directly through a network connection by using the File/Send To option.

Microsoft Excel

Microsoft Excel 97 extends the tradition spreadsheet concepts, offering features which make it easier to analyze, report, and share data while also offering support for both novice and expert users.

Access to Excel Elements

Excel uses an object model hierarchy which begins at the top with the Excel Application. The Application can create Workbook objects which, in turn, create Worksheet objects. Each Worksheet object contains Range objects and can call the Cell method.

For example, to refer to a single cell in the spreadsheet, an application would point to a Range object using the column letter and row number. To call the Cell method, the application would again use the row and column numbers separated by a comma. An example would be: "`Application .Cells(row:column)`".

Support Features

Excel formula creation makes it easier to create spreadsheets and reduces the time required for building formulas by using natural language terminology in place of cell coordinates (see the "Access to Excel Elements" section, below). The Formula AutoCorrect feature provides on-the-fly correction for common errors.

Charting and spreadsheet formatting options help to present information in useful and meaningful forms while the ChartWizard assists in chart-building. Custom Cells allow cell information to be presented in new formats.

Connectivity in Excel makes it convenient to share data and spreadsheets, allowing multiple users to collaborate on budgets or lists by simultaneously working through single shared workbooks. Changes to spreadsheets are tracked by time and by the person making the change. Spreadsheet documents can be shared over an intranet or the Internet, or published as HTML documents without requiring coding.

Because Excel is part of the Microsoft Office suite, it shares a common interface, look, and feel with other components, reducing training time and expenses. The interactive Office Assistant offers easy access to answers, tips, and suggestions during work, making it easier to train novices or to convert experts familiar with other systems. Table 3.3 lists the principal features of Excel together with brief explanations of their use and purposes.

T A B L E 3.3 Excel Features	Feature	Purpose
	Calculated Fields and Items	Perform additional analysis and modeling. Add custom formulas to existing PivotTable reports.
	Charts	Chart types such as bubble, conical, and pie-of-pie illustrate reports and offer graphical impact
	ChartWizard	Build chart data easily and consolidate all chart options for convenience in formatting, building, and modify charts
	Conditional Formatting	Highlight key data points according to specified parameters and show critical variables at a glance
	Custom Cells	Permit cells to be rotated, indented, and merged, supports automatic resizing for text

TABLE 3.3 (cont.) Excel Features	Feature	Purpose
	Enhanced PivotTables	Supports multidimensional data analysis. The Excel PivotTable is a reporting tool which can be used to automatically create configurable drag-and-drop crosstab reports while requiring little or no programming, and can be created with or without Visual Basic for Applications programming.
	Formula AutoCorrect	Auto-correction for common equation errors, quickly correcting formulas
	Microsoft Excel Viewer	Attaches to spreadsheets, allowing sheets to be viewed without Microsoft Excel
	Multiple Level Undo	Used to roll back changes in equations or formatting
	Natural language formulas	Custom row and column names can be used in formulas in place of cell coordinates
	Page Break Preview	Shows where page breaks occur for printed pages, allows page breaks to be dragged and dropped with automatic resizing to fit for data
	Persistent formatting	Retains custom formatting through changes in data display
	Range Finder	Uses color-coded frames to highlight cells used in equations. Supports drag-and-drop frames to change formulas and charts.

Sharing Spreadsheets

The Shared Workbooks feature allows multiple users to edit the same spreadsheet without restrictions. Two or more users can change formatting, enter and edit data, edit formulas, and add and delete cells.

For remote, offline users, the MergeWorkbooks feature permits changes to spreadsheets which are made away from the shared spreadsheet to be consolidated to the original workbook.

The Track Changes feature provides color-code frames and popup cell tips to report which elements have been changed while a change log keeps a record of when changes were made and by whom.

While Microsoft Excel can be used as a database and does provide an excellent solution for business price modeling, complex calculations, and cost of accounting applications, Excel is not a practical database tool where a large number of records are involved.

Using Spreadsheets on the Internet

Excel supports using spreadsheets on the Internet and using the Internet in spreadsheets. URLs can be incorporated in formulas to offer access to current data from remote locations. The indicated data is imported automatically from local or remote Web locations.

Web Queries support the import of dynamic, real-time data such as currency exchange rates, stock quotes, or sport scores. Data can be entered directly into formulas or charts and updated automatically.

Excel spreadsheets can be saved directly to URLs, allowing the spreadsheets to be viewed through the Internet or via corporate intranets. Spreadsheets can also be automatically converted into HTML format for Internet publication with no coding required.

Hyperlinks can be used in spreadsheets to provide connections directly from the spreadsheet to supporting information in documents on the local system, intranet, or Internet.

Microsoft Access

The Microsoft Access relational database management system provides the means to structure data to make it easy to find answers, to make it possible to share information over intranets and the Internet, and to build fast solutions to help make appropriate business decisions. Using an .MDB database with either Microsoft Access or Visual Basic is a fast and convenient technique for prototyping a client/server database system. Access provides the means to generate, analyze, and create reports with minimal development time and integrates ease of use from the data entry point through printing in HTML format.

Access provides the means to share information across a network, through an intranet, or through Internet features, allowing reports to be published on paper, in an online format, or in an HTML format.

Because Access is a scaleable relational database, it can be employed from home businesses through corporations and can provide support from startup operations, growing as business demands expand.

Microsoft Access Objects

Microsoft Access employs a variety of object types including Documents, Forms, Macros, Modules, Queries, Reports, and Tables as well as object Containers.

A Container object, for example, might be used to group similar Document objects. To programmatically check to determine if an object named MyForm exists, the application could loop through the Documents collection of the Forms Container object looking for a Document object with the Name property of "MyForm."

The Access Container object is not the same as a Data Access Object Container object. The DAO container contains Tables, Queries, or Relations.

Getting Started with Access

Access 97 provides tools for both expert and novice users, helping first-time users to get up and running quickly. Startup tools include:

- **Access Database Wizard**   Offers 20 custom database structures as starting points for database projects

- **Access Table Analyzer Wizard**   Identifies underlying structures in flat-file lists, transforming them to related tables, allowing novices to harness the capabilities of relational databases without requiring a deep understanding of relational database systems

Sharing Information   Access 97 provides tools that make it convenient to share up-to-date information with others both over enterprise intranets and over the Internet.

The Publish to the Web Wizard makes it possible to share dynamic or static database information—without writing code—across a company's intranet or via the Internet. Using the Publish to the Web Wizard, data can be incorporated in a Web site, allowing others access to the data both across a workgroup or across the world in an HTML format. The Publish to the Web Wizard can also set up live, interactive database pages allowing Web users to query, update, and add information.

Hyperlinks can be incorporated to provide links to other Access forms, reports, and tables; to other Office documents; and to internal and external Web sites. Hyperlinks can be made to Office documents or to specific locations in documents, such as to a specific paragraph in a Word document or to a cell in an Excel spreadsheet. Through FTP or HTTP servers, links can also import or attach (in a read-only format) to tables.

Building Solutions   Strengths found in Access 97 include enhanced 32-bit performance, smaller forms, efficient compilation, improved data-manipulation technology, and assistants to substantially reduce the technical expertise required to build fast and flexible business solutions.

The Performance Analyzer Wizard provides automatic recommendations for the creation of a responsive and well-organized database. By examining the database and seeking ways to speed access, the Performance Analyzer Wizard offers suggestion to improve performance and, with user approval, can automatically incorporate the suggested changes.

Visual Basic for Applications, using an intuitive and integrated development environment and including ActiveX support, is available to develop powerful databases and to integrate them with other Microsoft Office components to create comprehensive business solutions.

Features provided by Microsoft Access include:

- **Database Wizard**   Uses more than 20 types of fully featured templates to automatically build tables, queries, forms, and reports. Results can be further customized to suit application needs. New elements are easily incorporated using other wizards.

- **Simple Query Wizard**   Sorts through database information, gathering data from multiple tables and combining results to respond to queries. Together with the Form and Report Wizards, a common background intelligence engine allows users to focus on asking questions without needing to consider how data is stored.

- **Filter By Selection**   Filters data according to highlighted selections, presenting information corresponding to selections.

- **Filter By Form**   Permits search criteria to be entered in familiar forms with data-matching request criteria and supports selections using complex Boolean queries.

- **Calendar Control**   32-bit OLE calendar control can be incorporated in forms, providing a convenient date selection method. Changes made to data using the calendar control are stored in the underlying tables.

- **Multi-Select List Boxes**   Permit either single or multiple selections.

- **Image Controls**   Provide a simple means to incorporate graphical information in forms or reports while improving the image display performance. Previously, displaying images required OLE and included a number of steps.

- **Import/Export Wizard**   Offers a convenient means of translating and moving data from one format to another. By selecting from a list of supported formats, the Wizard provides a step-by-step guide through the conversion process and also shows how selected choices will affect the appearance of the finished database.

Web and Hyperlink Support

Access provides sophisticated mechanisms, utilities, and links to manage hyperlink, network, and Internet operations, including:

- **Hyperlink Datatype**   Access provides a native datatype for storing hyperlinks. For example, an applicant's name stored in a job candidate database can become a permanent hyperlink to the candidate's resume. In addition, hyperlinks can go to URLs as well as locations in Office 97 documents and entire databases can be built using hyperlinks as the mechanisms to connect objects.

- **Save to HTML**   Access's Save As HTML/Web Formats command allows static views of data to be shared on the Web by outputting table, query, and form datasheets as well as formatted reports directly to HTML format.

- **Output to IDC/HTX**   Access 97 leverages the Internet Database Connector functionality native to the Microsoft Internet Information Server and Personal Web Server, offering an easy way for users to share structured data for a workgroup or over the Internet.

- **Parameterized Queries**   Parameterized queries can be used through the Web to create a data source which is both dynamic and interactive. Using parameterized queries, queries can be made requesting only information which is relevant to the queriant and returning responses using the most current data.

- **Publish to the Web Wizard**   Allows users to publish database objects either statically or dynamically and includes custom HTML formatting using templates. Users may also save settings to output the objects.

- **HTML Importing and Linking**   The Import/Export Wizard can read HTML documents containing data tables, either importing the data directly into a new table or appending the records to an existing table.

An .ASP file is an Active Server Pages (ASP) page containing the instructions for generating an HTML Web page. The .ASP file uses server-side scripts to create and present a visual interface in a Web browser with the Web page displaying controls allowing access to a database in a fashion similar to a Microsoft Access form.

Performance and Results

Access 97 offers facilities for improving performance, organizing data, and creating reports and forms:

- **Performance Analyzer Wizard**   Analyzes database structures to identify means of optimizing access speed and performance and, if requested, to automatically perform changes when requested.

- **Table Analyzer Wizard**   Identifies relationships in unstructured data (such as a flat-file database) and reorganizes the information into a relational structure.

- **Form Wizard**   Provides intelligent assistance in deciphering how to bring together the desired date and in creating a custom view of the data. The Tab control is used to create tabbed dialog boxes and forms.

- **Report Wizard**   Offers a series of suggested layouts for creating professional-quality forms or reports. For example, to provide clients with order information, the wizards can be used to build a report showing customer information and related orders.

- **Database Replication**   Allows data from remote locations to be synchronized using the enterprise intranet or Internet. For example, Database Replication permits sales or service people in the field to update customer data providing everyone in the company with current information. (See Chapter 10, *Database Access Technologies*, for more on Database Replication.)

The terms *replica* and *design master* are used with Microsoft Access Jet Database Engine Replication. Under Jet Replication, one copy of an .MDB file is designated as a design master. Additional copies, called replicas, are generated from the design master. Design masters and replicas can be synchronized at any time while intelligent algorithms are used to resolve any differences between the object definitions and the data.

- **The Relationships window**   Allows users to view database schema and to draw or edit relationships between tables.

Overall, 32-bit performance makes Access 97 faster and more responsive while providing smaller forms, improved compilation, and faster 32-bit data manipulation.

Development Features

Access 97 offers a wide variety of development features, supporting convenient development and debugging. These features include:

- **Programmable Command Bars**   Permit the Access 97 interface to be conveniently customized by providing full control for toolbars and menus. Toolbars, menu bars, and shortcut menus can be created and existing ones customized by dragging and dropping menus, commands, and buttons and by setting properties. Menus can also be added to toolbars and toolbar button icons can be added to associated menu commands.

- **Hierarchical Object Browser**   Allows developers to explore an object hierarchy to locate development information by differentiating between built-in properties, custom properties, methods, event handlers, and user-defined procedures.

- **Class Modules**   Contain the definitions for new objects. When a new instance of a class is created, a new object is created and any procedures defined in the module become the properties and methods for the object.

- **Multi-Instance Forms**   By programmatically creating multiple instances of a form within an application, developers can provide branching within the application. Each form maintains its own underlying record set and can update the form's data independent of other data.

- **Conditional Compilation**   Compilation flags within the code allow developers to control application behavior, making it easy to create both debug and release compilations simply by setting or clearing flags.

- **Auto Conversion**   Allows users to migrate earlier Access databases to the latest version. When databases created under earlier versions of Access are opened, users are prompted to convert the database to the current format.

- **Partial Table Replication**   Database replication is used to replicate database objects across corporate networks. Users can specify subsets of data for replication. Access provides extensions for partial table replication using DAO (Data Access Objects).

- **Removable Source Code**   Permits developers to remove the source code from their Access applications. This reduces size, makes applications run faster, and offers protection for intellectual property.

- **Automation Object and Controller** Access drivers can be driven by an application supporting Automation. This gives developers programmatic control of product functionality—such as the reporting engine—from outside of Access.

- **Databound ActiveX Controls** The Access container is updated to support the latest ActiveX controls produced through the Visual C++ development system Control Development Kit.

- **Source Code Control** Access supports integration with various source code control providers including Visual SourceSafe. Visual SourceSafe is available as an add-in in the Office 97 Developer's Edition.

Visual Basic for Applications/ActiveX Support for Access Microsoft Visual Basic for Applications provides an integrated development platform and support for ActiveX components within Access. The intuitive IDE features drag-and-drop code, color-coded syntax, an improved debug window, and in-place object browsing. VB for Applications provides sophisticated programming, interface, and debugging tools.

Using ActiveX makes it possible to automate database functions, to create links to other applications and objects, and to deploy custom solutions using rapid, automated controls.

Microsoft Outlook

Microsoft Outlook combines e-mail management, contact management, and schedule management in a single package and can be employed together with a variety of e-mail servers and services. Services include the standard Internet SMTP/POP3 or IMAP4 mail servers and integration with Microsoft Exchange Server.

Outlook can also be used without an e-mail server for standalone contact and task and schedule management. Since the capabilities supported by e-mail servers vary, differences will be found in the features available in Outlook according to the e-mail server employed.

In general, Outlook works with all SMTP/POP3, IMAP, or MAPI servers. This includes a broad range for messaging services from Internet Service Providers (SMTP/POP3 or IMAP) to LAN-systems such as the Exchange Server (MAPI). Because Outlook uses the MAPI extensibility interface, other supported information and messaging sources include Compuserve, Digital's ALL-IN-1, Hewlett-Packard OpenMail, Lotus cc:Mail, Lotus Notes, Microsoft Fax, Microsoft Mail, and Novell GroupWise.

The Microsoft Outlook Hierarchy and Methods

Microsoft Outlook operates on a hierarchy beginning with the Application object at the top with Folder objects as the second level. Folder objects may contain Item objects that consist of `AppointmentItems`, `ContactItems`, `JournalItems`, `MailItems`, and `TaskItems`.

The `CreateItem` method is used to add items to a Folder by including the folder name as an argument.

The Folder object can be used to search for items in Outlook folders— a procedure identical to the `NewSearch` method used in Microsoft Office to search for files on a hard drive.

Because Microsoft Outlook is based on a folder paradigm, Outlook can easily be integrated with Microsoft Exchange Server public folders. This allows Outlook users to read and write to items in a local folder that is synchronized with Microsoft Exchange Server public folders stored on a shared network drive. (This is known as Microsoft Exchange Server Folder Replication.)

Optimized Outlook Installations

Because there are a variety of ways to send and receive e-mail, the Outlook Setup Wizard offers three optimized installations according to how Outlook will be used.

When no e-mail support is present but Outlook's contact, task, and schedule management features will be used, the No E-mail configuration is selected at setup. When either an Internet Service Provider (ISP) or an Internet-standard (i.e., POP3/SMTP or IMAP) server is used at the enterprise level, the Internet Only configuration is selected at setup. For corporate or workgroup users who primarily work with a LAN-based mail system, such as the Exchange Server or MS Mail, but who may also use Internet mail, the Corporate or Workgroup configuration is selected at startup.

Commonly, Outlook will select the configuration automatically during setup on the basis of the e-mail client presently in use. In some situations, when ambiguity occurs, Outlook may request a specific choice be made from the three configurations.

The optimized configuration can be changed when user requirements change. For example, a No E-mail configuration can be changed to Internet Only simply by adding an e-mail account. Alternately, an Internet Only configuration can be changed to Corporate or Workgroup using the Outlook 98 Add Components Web page.

While Outlook does make full use of whatever e-mail, scheduling, and collaboration features are supported by whichever server the product is used with—if any—different mail servers or services support quite different feature sets.

For example, the most common type of mail service, POP3/SMTP, does not support managing and storing e-mail messages on multiple folders on the server. Conversely, both IMAP4 and the Microsoft Exchange Server support this feature. Of course, some features—such as contact, task, and calendar management—are supported independently of mail servers of any kind. The three support configurations and servers providing support are discussed in further detail following.

No E-Mail: Information Management Only   Even without an e-mail server or Internet Service Provider, Outlook is still a complete PIM (personal information manager). While Outlook cannot send or receive e-mail or schedule meetings, the personal contact lists, calendars, task lists, and documents are still handled using Outlook's information management tools.

Internet Only: E-Mail, Limited Group Scheduling, and PIM   Used with an Internet Service Provider or some other SMTP/POP3 or IMAP4 mail server, Outlook adds a rich set of e-mail features to the personal contact, schedule, and task management facilities. While there are some differences in the features supported by STMP/POP3 and IMAP4 servers, both enable secure messaging together with a host of inbox management tools. Meeting requests can be exchanged via e-mail using the vCalendar protocol and Internet free/busy information can be shared using the iCalendar format. All e-mail addresses are stored as contacts in the user's personal contacts folder though the Internet Explorer Address Book user interface.

Corporate/Workgroup: Full E-Mail, Scheduling, and Collaboration
When Outlook is used with the Microsoft Exchange Server, another set of messaging, scheduling, and collaboration features are enabled, more powerful than those provided by the No E-mail and Internet Only configurations. Through the Exchange Server, special messaging features such as message recall and voting buttons are enabled. Also, Outlook and Exchange Server offer complete group scheduling integrated with Schedule+. Further, using the Exchange Server permits a wide range of collaboration, including sharing contact information across workgroups, and managing enterprise-wide workflow and tracking applications.

A driver connecting Outlook to the Microsoft Exchange Server is included with the product but the Exchange Server client access license must be purchased separately.

Those using MS Mail or third-party systems such as Lotus cc:Mail in the Corporate/Workgroup configuration also gain messaging and scheduling capabilities. Supported services include Compuserve, Digital's ALL-IN-1, Hewlett-Packard OpenMail, IBM PROFS, Lotus Notes, and Novell Group-Wise XTD.

Outlook 98 Configurations: Feature Details   Information Management Features are supported by all configurations. Information Management Features include:

- activity journal with scrolling time-line views
- Advanced Outlook Searching
- AutoArchiving
- AutoCreate (create new contact from e-mail message)
- categories on all Outlook items
- contact manager
- create customized versions of Outlook forms
- integrated document explorer
- multiple views on folders and creation of new views
- Outlook free-form notes
- personal calendar
- task list
- Web-style Find Tool and Organize Tool

E-Mail–Based Features in Outlook   Outlook's e-mail–based features are dependent in part on the mail server in use. Table 3.4 shows features supported by e-mail types.

None of these features are available in the No E-Mail configuration.

Feature	Internet Only	Corporate/ Workgroup
Access to SMTP/POP3 Servers and ISPs	Yes	Yes
Access to IMAP4 Mail Servers	Yes	No
Access to LDAP Directories	Yes	Yes[1]
Access to Exchange Mail Servers	Yes[2]	Yes
Access to MS Mail and third-party systems	No	Yes
S/MIME Digital Signatures and encryption	Yes	Yes
Store e-mail on the server	Yes	Yes
Offline access to messages	Yes	Yes[3]
Preview Pane	Yes	Yes
Use Outlook contacts for addressing	Yes	Yes
Personal distribution lists	Yes	Yes
Stationary	Yes	Yes
HTML Mail and M/HTML Mail	Yes	Yes
File attachments	Yes	Yes
Reply and forward options	Yes	Yes

Note 1 Third-party drivers are required for direct access to LDAP directories in this configuration.

Note 2 Exchange Server 5.0 supports POP3/SMTP, and Exchange Server 5.5 supports IMAP4 as well, enabling Outlook 98 to be used with Exchange Server in this configuration.

Note 3 Exchange Server is required for synchronization to Outlook offline store. Access to offline messages in a personal data store is available to all Outlook e-mail users.

T A B L E 3.4 *(cont.)*

E-Mail, Directory, and
Security Features

Feature	Internet Only	Corporate/ Workgroup
AutoNameCheck when addressing	Yes	Yes
Automatic dial-up of mail accounts	Yes	No
AutoSignature with multiple signatures	Yes	Yes

Feature	SMTP/ POP3	IMAP4	Ex- change	MS Mail and others
Inbox rules (mail filters)	Yes	No	Yes	Yes
Store messages in multiple server folders	No	Yes	Yes	Yes
Client/Server replication of messages	No	No	Yes	No
Server-based inbox rules (mail filters)	No	No	Yes	No
Exchange Server Global Address List	No	No	Yes	No
Voting, Message Flags and Message Recall	No	No	Yes	No
Deferred delivery and message expiration	No	No	Yes	No
Read and Delivery receipts	No	No	Yes	No
Remote (dial-up) Mail	Yes	Yes	Yes	No

Group Scheduling and Collaboration in Outlook   Group scheduling and collaboration features in Outlook are also dependent on the server used. Table 3.5 shows a breakdown for features supported without e-mail, using the Internet and, for the Corporate/Workgroup configuration, showing features available only using Microsoft Exchange.

T A B L E 3.5:   Group Scheduling and Collaboration Features

Feature	No E-mail	Internet Only	Corporate /Workgroup Exchange	MS Mail, others
Access other user's schedule free/busy information	Yes	Yes	Yes	No
Access to Exchange Server Public Folders for collaboration	No	No	Yes	No
Collaboration, workflow, and tracking applications	No	No	Yes	No
Create private discussion groups	No	Yes	Yes	No
Delegate Access for scheduling	No	No	Yes	No
Interoperability with Microsoft Schedule+ for group scheduling	No	No	Yes	No
Open other's calendars	No	No	Yes	No
Participate in Internet (NNTP) newsgroups	No	Yes	Yes	No
See details of free/busy information	No	No	Yes	No
Send and receive meeting requests for group scheduling	No	Yes	Yes	Yes
Share Outlook 98 contacts or personal schedule with others	No	Yes	Yes	Yes
Task delegation	Yes	No	Yes	No
vCard and vCalendar Support	Yes	Yes	Yes	Yes

Microsoft PowerPoint

Microsoft PowerPoint is a graphics presentation package used to organize, illustrate, and present ideas either in informal meetings, for audience presentations, or via the Internet. PowerPoint provides professionally designed templates with a design wizard for generating content and links. PowerPoint Central provides links to additional tips, content, and multimedia effects.

Features provided by PowerPoint include:

- **AutoContent Wizard**   Offers professionally designed content templates as a basis for presentations, flyers, or Web-page designs.

- **Comments**   Allow others to provide feedback by annotating slides.

- **Custom Shows**   Allow a single presentation to be tailored to multiple audiences by creating different versions within one file.

- **Expand Slide**   Automatically expands bulleted points from one slide to multiple slides, offering a cleaner, more organized presentation.

- **Outline Mode**   Offers miniature views of slides for organization and allows users to write speaker's notes.

- **PowerPoint Central**   Offers links to resources such as learning aids, clip art, textures, sounds, and animations both on CD-ROM and through the PowerPoint Internet site.

- **Slide Finder**   Organizes presentations by locating and previewing slides.

- **Spell It**   Highlights misspellings and suggests corrections.

- **Summary Slide**   Creates a single summary slide using titles from existing slides.

PowerPoint also offers powerful illustration tools, including 3-D Action Buttons, AutoClipArt, and Multimedia Clip Gallery, among others.

PowerPoint Portability

PowerPoint offers the following portability features:

- **Action Buttons**   Allow others to navigate through presentations with 3-D buttons for hyperlinks to slides, documents, or Internet sites using universally recognizable icons for forward, reverse, home, and information.

- **Action Items**   Record due dates and assigned owners in the Meeting Minder. Using Microsoft Outlook, Action Items can be sent, tracked, and scheduled with the task manager.

- **Animation Player for ActiveX**   Permits publishing work on the Internet as Web pages with animation and narration. The Animation Player Internet browser extension can be freely distributed to allow others to view animated Web pages.

- **Home Page Template**   Used to create personalized Internet or intranet home pages using the AutoContent Wizard, complete with links to desired Web sites.

- **Pack and Go Wizard**   Compresses presentations for portability on laptop systems and provides a Viewer allowing presentations to be run from systems which do not have PowerPoint.

- **Save as HTML Wizard**   Converts a presentation to a standard HTML format for Internet publication, with no technical knowledge of HTML required. Images are converted to GIF or JPEG format. Hyperlinks provide links to other files or Web sites and image maps can be created for graphical navigation on the Internet.

- **View on Two Screens**   Using a direct cable connection, the presenter can see notes, slide navigator, and time on one screen, while the audience sees only the presentation on a second screen.

- **Voice Narration**   Allows recording and saving voice-overs for presentations. PowerPoint automatically links slides to the corresponding narrative to create a self-executing slideshow which can be distributed online or on disk to reach remote audiences.

PowerPoint Document Distribution

A PowerPoint document viewer is available on the Internet and can be downloaded free of charge from www.microsoft.com/office/. The PowerPoint document viewer allows anyone to view a .PPT file in its native format.

While Internet Explorer also has provisions to allow users to view Microsoft Office documents—using the ActiveX document technology—the corresponding Office application (i.e., PowerPoint, Word) must be installed on the user's computer.

Microsoft Publisher

Microsoft Publisher is a business desktop-publishing program offering wizards, templates, and tools to produce quality publications either in print or online.

Microsoft Publisher is not shipped as a part of Microsoft Office, but must be purchased separately.

Where typesetting and design have traditionally been the parvenu of professional publishing companies, computers and advanced software have made possible in-house production of professional publications. Microsoft Publisher, in particular, has focused on the smaller publishing client, including, but not limited to, the small office/home office (SOHO) market seeking to design professional-quality publications ranging from newsletters, brochures, and flyers, to letterheads and invitations.

All in all, Microsoft Publisher has been designed to satisfy three principal markets: the publisher user, the small business user, and the home or in-house user. For the publisher user, Microsoft Publisher is a business desktop publishing program providing professional-quality materials without demanding professional level expertise. As a business desktop publisher, Microsoft Publisher appeals to a diverse group, ranging from business people to organization volunteers.

For the small business user, working in small offices/home offices with fewer than 10 employees, principal uses for Microsoft Publisher are to create brochures, flyers, and newsletters for colleagues and customers; to land new customers; to project a big-company image; and to prepare proposals and bids, etc. Small office/home office users form the principal market for Microsoft Publisher.

Home and in-house users in large organizations form the third market segment for Microsoft Publisher. Home users include people working in volunteer groups, though schools and community groups, as well as people using Publisher for personal uses. In-house users in large organizations may use Publisher for internal communications such as departmental newsletters.

Microsoft Publisher Features

Automated design makes it possible for non-professional users to create publications with a professional image while minimizing the time requirements.

PageWizard assistants offer task-based, step-by-step guidance to creating common publications such as newsletters, brochures, flyers, or Web sites. To finish publications, all users are required to do is to add text and, if desired, illustrations. Publisher includes a wide variety of publication types and more than 20 PageWizard assistants.

Tippages provide hints about more efficient ways to work.

The Web Site Wizard provides design assistance for creating multi-page Web sites complete with navigational links. Web pages are saved in HTML format, which can be transferred directly to a Web Server or published to an Internet Service Provider. Pages can be previewed in Internet Explorer or other compatible Web browsers.

Other tools and support elements include:

- 150 predesigned borders; custom borders can be created from any clipart

- 200 professional designed styles or prefabricated publications

- coordinated design elements such as mastheads and pull quotes

- the Design Checker, which reviews publications for design problems including excessive colors or too many fonts

- four AreaWizards aid in designing ads, logos, calendars, and coupons

- integrated help and First-time Help support as well as online demonstrations

- World Wide Web special content includes backgrounds, photo images, and Design Gallery elements optimized for browser viewing

Integrated Design in Microsoft Publisher

Microsoft Publisher is designed to work with other Microsoft Office components. To this end, it includes such features as:

- **Clip Gallery Live** An integrated extension of the Internet-based Clip Gallery offering video and sound clips for use in publications

- **Integration Publisher** Imports text directly from the most popular word processors including Microsoft Word, Microsoft Works, and WordPerfect

- **Mail Merge**   Allows users to create address lists in Publisher, or allows Publisher to read lists created by Word, Works, Access, dBASE, FoxPro, or other databases
- **Word Story Editor**   Allows users to write and edit in Microsoft Word, then to return to Publisher to edit the layout and text flow

Publisher is also consistent with other Microsoft Office components, sharing the same menus, shortcuts, and toolbars for common actions such as cut and paste. The tab and indent rulers, tables, bullets, and numbered lists are similar to Microsoft Word. And, of course, Publisher is an OLE application allowing documents and spreadsheets to be edited using drag-and-drop and in-place editing.

Microsoft FrontPage

While both Microsoft Word, Publisher, and Internet Explorer can be used to create Web sites, FrontPage—together with the Bonus Pack—not only makes creating Web sites easy but also offers powerful functionality, support for the latest Web technologies, and seamless integration with Microsoft Office.

Microsoft FrontPage is not shipped as a part of Microsoft Office, but must be purchased separately.

WYSIWYG editing eliminates the need to know HTML to develop Web pages. The FrontPage Editor allows editing and refining previously created or new Web pages, and creates custom looks by adding text and images to blank Web pages.

Microsoft FrontPage is paralleled by the Microsoft Visual InterDev Web development system. The principal difference is that Visual InterDev is designed for programmers and for Active Server Page development, while FrontPage does not demand programming skills.

Tools supplied include:

- **Import Wizard** Used to import existing files or entire folders of information into FrontPage Web sites

- **Wizards and templates** Used to generate Web sites or pages from predefined formats before replacing the structured content with suitable words, images, and ideas

- **Hyperlink View** Provides a hierarchical and link display of all paths to and from Web pages. The Hyperlink View graphically displays all hyperlinks between pages, with arrows indicating the direction of each link. Positioning the pointer over a page icon calls up the page's address.

- **Folder View** Displays the entire Web site directory structure. The Folder View provides a directory of the Web site displaying a sortable list of the properties for each file, making it easy to manage Web site content more effectively.

- **Link verification** Automatically verifies that all hyperlinks, including those pointing to files outside the immediate Web site, are valid. When a broken hyperlink is corrected in one location, FrontPage automatically corrects all occurrences throughout the site.

- **Enhanced drag-and-drop** Allows dragging Microsoft Office files into FrontPage or moving hyperlinks, tables, and images into the editor

Connectivity support is provided by technologies such as JavaScript and ActiveX controls. Connectivity features include:

- Database connectivity to dynamically link to ODBC-compliant databases allows Web pages to be created from database queries and provides easy access to information.

- ActiveX control and Java applet support gives users the ability to develop powerful Web applications in an intuitive WYSIWYG environment.

- VBScript and JavaScript authoring support allow custom scripts to be added to Web pages.

- WebBot components provide sophisticated interactive functionality such as full-text searching and forms while eliminating the need to write custom programs.

- Support for both Microsoft and Netscape plug-ins make it possible to author dynamic Web pages easily.

- Tables and Frames can be created handily using the Frames Wizard and templates to create custom frame pages.

- Discussion Web Wizard is used to build a threaded discussion bulletin board using frames.

Other features supporting Web development and operation include:

- Remote and collaborative authoring and editing allows multiple authors to develop and manage Web sites on local or remote Web servers and update different pages on the same server simultaneously.

- HTML code can be edited directly in FrontPage and previewed in any installed browser without leaving FrontPage.

- Microsoft Image Composer is used to create graphics for Web pages and includes thousands of image samples.

- Microsoft Personal Web Server (included in the Bonus Pack) permits hosting Web sites directly from any PC.

- Internet Mail and News permits sending and receiving electronic mail as well as participation in Internet newsgroups.

- Microsoft Visual SourceSafe integration allows Web site managers using Microsoft Visual SourceSafe (not included) to provide Web site version control.

Additional support is provided through integration with the Microsoft Office and includes the following features:

- FrontPage Explorer can be used to display, verify, and correct Office 97 hyperlinks.

- Microsoft Thesaurus can be used while composing text.

- Global spelling checker can check the spelling of all HTML documents in a Web site in one single step.

- Global Find and Replace searches for and replaces text across all HTML documents in the Web site.

- Text Import Converters import a variety of file formats directly into Web pages.

Microsoft Project

Microsoft Project is a project management application designed to plan and track projects to maintain schedules and budgets. Microsoft incorporates planning, analysis, and management tools for building enterprise-wide, mission-critical project management solutions.

Microsoft Project is not shipped as a part of Microsoft Office but must be purchased separately.

Using Microsoft Project, complex project plans can be broken down into manageable steps to show how various tasks are related, identify which tasks are most critical to the overall schedule, locate bottlenecks, and estimate project development costs.

Likewise, separate projects can be consolidated to assess the demand for shared resources, evaluate team workloads, and ensure that concurrent projects can accomplished within the available resources and budget.

Built-in links to Microsoft Exchange make it easy to keep others abreast of progress by reporting project status elements—for example, due dates for deliverables—without requiring everyone to be involved in all details. Links can also be made through Microsoft Mail, Schedule+, BackOffice, or a wide variety of other add-on programs designed for use with Microsoft Project.

A variety of elements and tools are supported by Microsoft Project, including:

- Planning Wizards and templates can be used to setup projects. Wizards also can monitor actions and offer suggestions which may be incorporated into the project plan.

- Critical Path tasks are used to identify elements that are critical to the success of the project and that will result in major problems if due dates are missed.

- Resource Tools are used to track resource demands and usage, to identify bottlenecks and shortages in advance, and to balance workloads across tasks or projects.

- Baseline Chart allows the current schedule to be compared to the original project plan.

- Filters permit viewing task subsets within a plan. Filters might be used to view project milestones or to examine tasks assigned to a specific person.

- OfficeLinks allow data to be exchanged among spreadsheets, slides, reports, and other documents created by Microsoft Office components.

- Save to Database allows direct data exchange with Microsoft Access databases, Microsoft BackOffice, and other ODBC-compliant databases.

Teamwork Facilities and Workgroup Tools

Microsoft Project communicates through MAPI- or VIM-compliant e-mail (such as Microsoft Mail), allowing projects to be routed to reviewers. E-mail can also be used with TeamAssign to communicate assignments and with TeamStatus to collect status information and keep schedules current.

Microsoft Project can also set task reminders and add tasks to the To Do list in Microsoft Schedule+. Project's Copy Picture utility creates a snapshot of project plans which can be distributed to others without requiring them to use Microsoft Project to view the project. Report Gallery offers preformatted reports for current activities, assignments, costs, and workloads. Custom reports can also be designed.

Exchange Support allows documents to be posted and displays custom OLE properties for projects for viewing by group members and others outside of teams.

Building Custom Solutions

Microsoft Project can be customized internally and can be extended to create custom solutions. Customizing options include:

- Customization can be applied to buttons, menus, and toolbars and to the format used for messages between team members.

- Filters, tables, and views provide access to the information most important at any time.

- Macro Recorder is used to create powerful macros and to automate routine tasks. Most importantly, Macro Recorder does not depend on programming skills.

- Multiproject Consolidation permits combining multiple projects to ensure efficient resource usage.

An example of a custom solution using Microsoft Project would be creating a Gantt chart. While other Office components such as Outlook, Excel, or Word could also be used for this purpose, Project has the advantage—in addition to using Visual Basic for Applications as its macro language—of storing its files in ODBC database format.

Microsoft Project can also be used with a variety of tools including MAPI (messaging application programming interface) and VIM (vendor independent messaging) support, Object Libraries, ODBC, OLE Automation, and Visual Basic for Applications, as well as Microsoft Exchange to create enterprise-level mission-critical applications. Also, more than a hundred add-on products are available for charting, client/server computing, costing, estimating, resource management solutions, risk analysis, timesheeting and other specialized tasks.

Microsoft Team Manager

The Microsoft Team Manager is used to consolidate, coordinate, and track team activities, to enhance team members' communications and cooperation, and to build a more collaborative and productive team. Team Manager is designed to enhance the task management capabilities of Microsoft Outlook (see the "Microsoft Outlook" section, above). Team Manager provides a single source/single tool manager to track team information with team members' workloads, tasks, and progress status consolidated into one team file, making current information available at all times. For example, the Task Organizer and Workload Planner views offer summaries of individuals' current projects, schedules, and assignments.

Using Team Manager, team members can also become a part of the planning process using a consolidated team file to view team activities and adjust their own priorities accordingly. Red Alerts permit everyone to communicate urgent details, such as impending or missed deadlines, while Team Manager makes it easy for members to track and manage their own tasks using task tracking and automated Status Reports.

Team Manager provides tools to group, sort, and filter project details. For example, Best-Fit Scheduling assists managers in determining whether team members can finish tasks on time based on current priorities and deadlines, while goal and performance tracking automatically consolidates notes and personal information on employees for later use in judging performance. Since all confidential information is password protected, private details stay private.

Team Manager organizes, coordinates, and tracks details, allowing the user to focus on the big picture. Activities are supported by a series of Team Manager modules.

Initially, Team Manager tabs offer several views to access information:

- The Tasks tab holds task information such as priorities and task status.

- The People tab stores individual team member information ranging from performance goals to personnel information.

- The Notebook tab provides a confidential location for managers to enter notes on group tasks, employee performance, and team activities.

- The Vital Signs tab helps to identify loose ends before they become problems.

Other Team Manager features include:

- Status Reports submitted by team members, including individual achievements, objectives, issues, or other specified topics. Individual Status Reports can be consolidated into a single, comprehensive team Status Report.

- Task Organizer is used to review a team's tasks, deadlines, who's working on what, and task status.

- Workload Planner provides an overview and an automatic summary of team members' workloads to help scheduling deadlines and assignments.

- Completed tasks can be automatically archived, saving all associated information including custom views, assignments, notes, and goals.

- Profile Information stores vital statistics for team members, including names, titles, phone numbers, and addresses. Private performance notes can also be stored in Profile Information.

Team Manager creates a variety of views and reports to make information readily available and visible. Elements include:

- Red Alerts can be used to notify team members about urgent issues, missed deadlines, or tasks needing attention.

- Multiple views provide subsets of details from the Task Organizer. Views can be used to show all team projects and details at once, or narrowed to show project specifics.

  - Sorting shows information by task name, deadline, finish date, or by custom sort parameters.

  - Filtering displays team tasks by priority, incomplete tasks, overloaded tasks, Red Alerts, unassigned work, completed tasks, tasks in progress, tasks not started, and tasks with deadlines.

- Grouping arranges information in windows by people assigned, priority, project, status, or by custom groupings.

- Quick Filter is used to customize the view to display only the tasks and details desired.

- Work Calendar shows team tasks by day, week, or month, offering both the big picture or a view of day-to-day activities.

- Working Times tracks team members' work schedules and vacation time in a single calendar showing non-working days for each team member.

- Goal Reviews can be created by compiling employee goals, supporting tasks, and the manager's notes and ratings into a single document.

- Performance reviews can be compiled by consolidating Goal Reviews with performance notes. The Team Manager review scale can be customized to suit your team and industry.

Because Team Manager can track hours spend on individual tasks, time sheets are built automatically. For remote operations, Team Manager can be used while traveling and while working off-site.

Finally, Team Manager is an integrated part of Microsoft Office and functions together with Microsoft Exchange, Microsoft Outlook, Microsoft Schedule+, Microsoft Project, Lotus cc:Mail, or Lotus Notes Mail.

Microsoft Visual Studio

The Microsoft Visual Studio development system is a comprehensive suite of Visual Tools for creating multi-tiered applications and Web applications, and integrating client/server solutions and Internet technologies. Providing support for open standards as well as tools for building scaleable solutions, Visual Studio supports both traditional client/server development and the newest Internet technologies including HTML and Java.

Visual Studio is available in two versions: the Professional Edition and the Enterprise Edition.

Professional Edition

The Professional Edition includes:

- Visual C++ (Professional Edition)
- Visual Basic (Professional Edition)
- Visual InterDev Web development system
- Visual J++ (Professional Edition)
- Visual FoxPro database (Professional Edition)

Visual Studio also includes a special edition of the MSDN Library on CD with comprehensive of development information and documentation.

Visual Basic

Visual Basic is probably the most popular development tool for the Windows environment. Because Visual Basic handles so many of the details behind application development, Visual Basic is the preferred tool for many novices and inexperienced programmers, as well as experienced developers.

Visual Basic for Applications, while not strictly speaking part of the Visual Studio, nor as powerful and flexible as Visual Basic proper, is used extensively in Microsoft Office and Microsoft Project. Also, Visual Basic for Applications is expected to be used in conjunction with third-party applications in the future.

Visual Basic features a variety of significant performance and productivity enhancements which increase developer efficiency as well as making the end-user solutions perform faster and more flexibly.

Visual Basic incorporates such advanced features as native code compilation, high-speed database access, and an improved development environment. Because Visual Basic supports the component creation capabilities of the ActiveX technologies, Visual Basic is also popular with developers targeting client/server environments, intranets, and the Internet.

Visual C++

In addition to full support for the Windows APIs and the Microsoft Foundation Classes, current versions of Microsoft Visual C++ include support for creating ActiveX component-based applications for use in integrating client/server and Internet technologies. Enhanced features in Visual C++ include support for the Component Object Model (COM) and a number of new class libraries. Improvements in the compiler generate smaller—and presumably faster—code.

Visual FoxPro

Visual FoxPro provides an object-oriented database development system with support for ActiveX extensibility. Visual FoxPro can be used to develop desktop and client/server database applications.

A wide variety of ActiveX controls are supported and can be subclassed to create customized reusable objects. This includes support for ActiveX controls developed using other tools from the Visual Studio suite. Automation servers created using Visual FoxPro can be employed in any environment supporting automation.

FoxPro's debugging capabilities have been enhanced to include color-coded syntax as well as a tree view with the capabilities of modifying objects, properties, and events.

Visual J++

Java is an object-oriented cross-platform programming language for building Web applets and components that can run on either the Web client (inside the browser) or on the Web server.

The Microsoft Visual J++ Professional Edition provides all of the tools and information necessary to design applications using Java and ActiveX technologies. Visual J++ includes sample code, development wizards, a graphical debugger, and ActiveX integration as well as the full set of Java language documentation.

Java applets and applications can be built with or extended with ActiveX integration, permitting them to work with other applets and ActiveX controls. Also, functionality can be added to Java applets using prebuilt ActiveX controls and COM objects such as Data Access Objects (DAO) and Remote Data Objects (RDO). In addition, wizards supplied by Visual J++ can be used to create fully functional applications in minutes.

Enterprise Edition

The Visual Studio Enterprise Edition includes the tools found in the Professional Edition but extends their functionality by providing support for multi-tiered development with transaction, data management, and performance enhancements. Support is included for development teams, tools for creating large-scale solutions, and integration tools for large data stores.

Although 16-bit versions of Visual Basic, Visual C++, and Visual FoxPro are available, the current shipping versions of all products are 32-bit.

In addition to the tools supplied in the Professional Edition, the Enterprise Edition also provides:

- Microsoft Repository
- Microsoft SQL Server, Developer Edition
- Microsoft Transaction Server, Developer Edition
- Microsoft Visual Database Tools
- Microsoft Visual SourceSafe

Visual SourceSafe

Visual SourceSafe provides project-version control management compatible with any file types and any development language or authoring tools. Visual SourceSafe allows users to work at both file and project levels and can be used by any size team for any size project.

Visual SourceSafe, using project-oriented features, enables team development with the aim of efficiently managing the day-to-day tasks found in team-based development environments.

While most commonly used for software development, Visual SourceSafe is also useful for managing Web content. (Visual SourceSafe is discussed in more detail in Chapter 6, *Source Control as a Development Methodology*.)

Microsoft SQL Server

Visual Studio, Enterprise Edition includes a develop-and-test edition of the Microsoft SQL Server, providing a database engine for powering Web sites and client/server applications.

For a detailed discussion on SQL Server, see the "BackOffice Components" section, above.

Microsoft Transaction Server

Microsoft Transaction Server allows developers to create server applications as "single user" ActiveX components using any of the Visual Tools, and then to deploy the components in Transaction Server as reliable, multi-user applications.

Transaction Server saves the component developer from worrying with the complexities of server programming by providing automatic support for distribution, transactions, security, and scaleability both across client/server networks and across the Internet.

In brief, Transaction Server offers a convenient means to develop and deploy scaleable, multi-tiered applications for Windows NT Server.

Microsoft Visual Database Tools

The Visual Studio, Enterprise Edition data environment allows developers to visualize and edit key database objects used in applications. The data environment includes a data dictionary for all relevant database objects, including tables, views, and stored procedures, as well as editors for query design, creating stored procedures, and debugging.

This tool set makes it possible for developers to completely integrate database development into a Rapid Application Development (RAD) environment. The visual database tools are seamlessly integrated with Visual InterDev, Visual C++ (Enterprise Edition), and Visual Basic (Enterprise Edition).

Microsoft Repository

At present, the Microsoft Repository functions only with Visual Basic. It is a database used to store and share components, models, objects, and relationships together with descriptive information. The Repository provides important capabilities in five key areas for client/server environments: reuse, tool interoperability, team development, data resource management, and dependency tracking.

The Repository sits on top of the Microsoft Jet and Microsoft SQL Server.

Summary

Necessarily, this chapter has had to cover quite a lot of ground and to talk about the large number of products that encompass Microsoft Office, Microsoft BackOffice, and Microsoft Visual Studio. The two stated objectives at the opening of this chapter call on users to identify how elements and objects from these three suites could be used as solution components.

Beginning with the BackOffice suite and the Microsoft NT Server, we discussed a variety of server-side components providing Internet and intranet support.

The Microsoft Office suite provides applications to satisfy most common office requirements, including document processing, spreadsheets, financial tools, and database creation, as well as Web page design.

The Microsoft Visual Studio tools completes the discussion, with application development tools including Visual Basic, Visual C++, and Visual FoxPro, providing the means for creating complete, custom applications. Visual Studio, however, appears in two forms: the Professional and Enterprise Editions, with the latter offering a number of extended tools and features for team development and larger projects.

Review Questions

1. The sales department is interested in creating a slide presentation that will include audio/visual clips and that will be used for live presentations as well as being distributed both on CD and over the Internet. What would your recommendation for this project be?

    A. Microsoft FrontPage

    B. Microsoft Outlook

    C. Microsoft PowerPoint

    D. Microsoft Publisher

2. Your office manager asks for a recommendation for a package which can be used to create the company newsletter and prepare brochures and documents for internal distribution. What would your recommendation(s) be?

   A. Microsoft FrontPage

   B. Microsoft InterDev

   C. Microsoft Publisher

   D. Microsoft Word

3. Microsoft Outlook supplies support for which of the following? (Select all that apply.)

   A. Creating and printing formatted text

   B. Performing calculations on data

   C. Sending e-mail

   D. Tracking schedules

4. The Microsoft Internet Information Server supports Internet publishing, providing all of the basic services required including:

   A. Dynamic Host Configuration Protocol (DHCP) services

   B. Internet Database Connector gateway supporting publication of database information on the Internet

   C. Internet Service Manager supporting encrypted communications between client and server

   D. Windows Internet Naming Services (WINS) for automatic IP address configuration

5. Microsoft Project supplies support for which of the following? (Select all that apply.)

   A. Creating and printing formatted text

   B. Performing calculations on data

   C. Sending e-mail

   D. Tracking schedules and budgets

6. The corporate sales force needs e-mail, contact, task and schedule management both in the office and in the field. Select the optimum package(s) for in-house support for these functions.

   A. Internet Explorer with Microsoft Team Manager

   B. Lotus cc:Mail, Lotus Notes, and Novell Groupwise XTD

   C. Microsoft Outlook and Exchange Server

   D. Microsoft Word and MS Mail

7. Microsoft FrontPage supplies support for which of the following? (Select all that apply.)

   A. Creating formatted text

   B. Managing Web sites

   C. Sending e-mail

   D. Tracking schedules and budgets

8. Internet Information Server supports a number of standards, including:

   A. APPC

   B. HTML and HTTP

   C. ISDN services

   D. SNMP and SNMP MIB

9. To setup an Excel spreadsheet for calculating point spreads for NFL teams without needing to enter the data manually, the optimum solution would be to:

   A. Ask the receptionist to maintain the spreadsheet as a shared intranet link.

   B. Link the spreadsheet to an Access database containing updated scores.

   C. Subscribe to a data service to have scores sent by e-mail in an import-compatible format.

   D. Use Web Queries to directly import dynamic, real-time data.

10. To share an Excel spreadsheet across a workgroup or enterprise, what would be the optimum solution?

   A. Distribute printed copies via company mail.

   B. E-mail exported copies of the spreadsheet to all interested parties.

   C. Import the spreadsheet into PowerPoint and use the viewer to create a distributable package.

   D. Save the spreadsheet directly to a URL, allowing the spreadsheet to be viewed via the corporate intranet.

11. The Microsoft SNA Server supports a number of APIs including:

   A. APPC

   B. HTML and HTTP

   C. ISDN services

   D. SNMP and SNMP MIB

12. Microsoft Word supplies support for which of the following? (Select all that apply.)

   A. Creating and printing formatted text

   B. Performing calculations on data

   C. Sending e-mail

   D. Tracking schedules and budgets

13. Using Microsoft SQL Server Web Assistant, which of the following database operations can be accomplished? (Select all that apply.)

   A. A GROUP BY operation within a SELECT statement

   B. A sub-query operation within a DELETE statement

   C. A sub-query operation within an INSERT statement

   D. An ORDER BY operation within a SELECT statement

14. The sales and engineering departments are collaborating on the creation of a company Web site. To maintain compatibility between the departments while offering both the optimum development package for the joint project, you select:

A. Microsoft Explorer

B. Microsoft FrontPage

C. Microsoft InterDev

D. Microsoft Word

15. PowerPoint presentations can be which of the following? (Select all that apply.)

A. Converted to HTML Web pages

B. Printed in book or brochure format

C. Run without having PowerPoint installed

D. Sent as e-mail messages

16. In a company with an increasing number of computers, the need is for software which will make it possible to troubleshoot problems remotely. Objectives include being able to examine the registry on a remote computer and being able to consult an inventory database to determine what software is installed on a specific computer. Select the BackOffice component which would provide these features from a server computer.

A. Microsoft Internet Information Server

B. Microsoft SNA Server

C. Microsoft SQL Server

D. Microsoft Systems Management Server

17. HTML pages can be automatically created and updated:

A. From the SQL Server using SQL Server Web Assistant

B. Through Excel pages and Shared Workbooks

C. Using ActiveX components to search for changed data

D. Using Stored Procedures on UNIX database servers

18. Which of the following is true of BackOffice applications? (Select all that apply.)

   A. They are hardware dependent.

   B. They operate only on RISC systems.

   C. They operate only on multiple-CPU systems.

   D. They support the Open Systems standard.

19. A company desires to create an Internet server with support for interactive Web pages allowing clients to access company database records for product pricing and availability and to place orders. This application design would be best satisfied by:

   A. Using a UNIX/XENIX Server with a FoxPro database using the Publish To The Web Wizard

   B. Using a UNIX/XENIX Server with an Access database for calculations and ActiveX objects to render data in HTML format

   C. Using a Windows NT Server with an Access database using the Publish To The Web Wizard

   D. Using a Windows NT Server with an Excel spreadsheet for calculations and ActiveX objects to render data in HTML format

20. How is it that BackOffice applications work on an integrated basis?

   A. They are fully designed for the Windows NT Server and cross-application compatibility.

   B. They rely on SQL transaction commands and the Windows SQL Server.

   C. They use ActiveX components to promote transaction compatibility between applications.

   D. They use the Performance Analyzer Wizard to recommend changes to improve performance.

21. Which standards does BackOffice support? (Select all that apply.)

   A. AppleTalk, DECnet, IPX/SPX, NETBEUI, OSI, SMB, and TPC/IP network protocols

   B. ASCII and FTP file transfer protocols

   C. DMFT and SNMP management standards

   D. SSL and WWW encrypted communications

22. What does Outlook use to add a new Appointment object to the Appointments folder?

   A. The `AddAppointment` method

   B. The `AddFolder` method

   C. The `CreateFolder` method

   D. The `CreateItem` method

23. IT managers and administrators using Microsoft BackOffice:

   A. Are able to deploy and administer desktop and server system using a single tool set

   B. Are able to deploy and administer server systems using Back-Office tools while desktop systems require the Windows NT or Windows 95/98 tool sets

   C. Are expected to choose from third-party tools for deploying and administering desktop and server systems

   D. Are provided with separate tools for deploying and administering desktop and server systems but each with a common look and feel

24. Select the product(s) included with Windows NT Server 4.0:

   A. FrontPage

   B. Internet Information Server (IIS)

   C. SQL Server

   D. Systems Management Server (SMS)

25. BackOffice is designed to run on which of the following? (Select all that apply.)

  A. Windows 95/98

  B. Windows for Workgroups

  C. Windows NT Server

  D. All of the above

26. Select the items that are designed to operate as integrated components under Outlook.

  A. Excel PivotTables

  B. Exchange Server Public Folders

  C. Team Manager

  D. Word spell checker

27. Windows NT supplies which of the following? (Select all that apply.)

  A. Built-in support for Internet standards: CGI, HTTP, ISAPI, ODBC, and Perl

  B. Built-in support for fault-tolerant features including disk-striping, mirroring, duplexing, and UPS-support

  C. C-2 level security for protection against unauthorized access to data

  D. Memory protection permitting securing execution for multiple applications on a single computer

28. While using the Microsoft SQL Server 6.5 Web Assistant to develop a Web page, the results set to be displayed can be specified by:

  A. Selecting a rule

  B. Selecting a stored procedure

  C. Selecting a view

  D. Writing a SELECT statement

29. Microsoft BackOffice offers which of the following advantages? (Select three.)

   A. A common user environment

   B. A single, integrated server supplying complete server-side functionality

   C. Common development tools

   D. Common system management tools

30. The Microsoft BackOffice suite includes which of the following?

   A. Microsoft Exchange Server

   B. Microsoft SQL Server

   C. Microsoft Systems Management Server

   D. Microsoft Transaction Server

   E. All of the above

31. To send a document to several developers for review, while working in Microsoft Word 97, which of the following should you select?

   A. The Exchange item from the Tools menu

   B. The Exchange item from the Windows menu

   C. The Send To item from the File menu

   D. The Send To item from the Windows menu

32. BackOffice offers a complete server solution, including:

   A. A single management model using the Window for Workgroups administration tools

   B. A single management model using Windows-based administration tools

   C. Two management models for Professional and Enterprise platforms

   D. Two management models for the client and server sides of the database enterprise

33. Your objective is to design a Web site where customers can (a) query the company database for price and availability information, (b) place order requests, and (c) provide contact information. To handle pricing and stock availability, you would choose:

   A. Microsoft Access

   B. Microsoft FrontPage

   C. Microsoft Visual Basic

   D. Microsoft Visual J++

34. Microsoft Access offers developers a variety of tools used in form design, including which of the following? (Select all that apply.)

   A. Auto-conversion tools to convert ODBC and SQL data sources

   B. Edit boxes with built-in spell checking

   C. Image Controls providing a means of displaying graphical information in forms or reports

   D. Multi-select list boxes permitting either single or multiple selections

35. Static database information can be presented on a Web site by saving the output from a Microsoft Access query, table, or report as an HTML file. To present dynamic data on the Web, Access objects would be created by saving:

   A. Access forms as .ASP files

   B. Access forms as .HTML files

   C. Access macros as .ASP files

   D. Access macros as .HTML files

36. A development application requires maintaining an index to a large number of Web sites as hyperlinks. To satisfy this requirement, what is the optimum development tool?

A. Microsoft Access

B. Microsoft InterDev

C. Microsoft Visual C++

D. Microsoft Visual J++

37. Using Visual Basic for Applications in Microsoft Excel, what should the instruction to reference the value in cell A1 be?

A. `Excel("Book1").Range("A1:A1")`

B. `Excel("Sheet1").Cell "A1"`

C. `Worksheet("Book1").Cells("A1:A1")`

D. `Worksheet("Sheet1").Range("A1")`

38. In order to use Visual Basic for Applications (VBA) to create e-mail macros within Word, what is the first requirement?

A. Add the OLE Messaging control to the Word document

B. Register the MAPI control in a Word macro

C. Set a reference to the OLE Messaging library

D. Set a reference to the TAPI custom controls

39. A replica and a design master would be used to synchronize a local database with a Web-based database by:

A. Access

B. Internet Explorer

C. Internet Information Server

D. SQL Server

40. Microsoft Access supports which of the following? (Select all that apply.)

A. Distributed n-tier applications including middle-tier business rule servers

B. Parameterized Queries allowing Internet users to create a data source which is both dynamic and interactive

C. Partial Table Replication to replicate database objects across corporate networks

D. Reverse engineering using the Microsoft Visual Modeler

41. What is the appropriate tool to visually display an Entity-Relationship diagram for a database?

A. Access

B. SQL Server

C. Visual Basic

D. Visual C++

42. Using Visual Basic for Applications (VBA), a generic object named xl has been dimensioned (declared). Before methods can be invoked and properties set using xl as a Microsoft Excel object, xl must be assigned as an Excel object as:

A. `Set xl = CreateObject("Excel.Application")`

B. `Set xl = GetObject("Excel.Application")`

C. `Set xl As Excel.Application`

D. `Set xl As New Excel.Application`

43. An existing mainframe database application is designed to track interest rates and calculate closing costs, payments, and total interest paid for loans, presenting the information on screen. The existing mainframe application is to be replaced with Microsoft Windows applications. To convert the load amortization program to a Microsoft Office application, what would be the optimum tool?

A. Access

B. Excel

C. Outlook

D. Project

44. Microsoft Access objects include forms, macros, modules, reports, and tables, each of which constitute a document. Which Access object is used to group these documents into collections?

A. Container

B. Database

C. DBEngine

D. Workspace

45. A decision-support application is designed to show cross-tab reports by customer, product, sales, and salesperson. Reports should cover all combinations of sales according to customer, customer region, product, and salesperson as well as sales by date by week, month, and year. Having developed a stored procedure within the database to extract the raw data, the next step is to create a configurable drag-and-drop crosstab report with a minimum of programming. What is the ideal tool for this purpose?

A. A Visual Basic ActiveX control

B. An Access AutoTable

C. An Access dynaset

D. An Excel PivotTable

46. The objective is to create a Gantt chart showing task start and end times together with critical paths. The chart data will be stored in ODBC database and the application created using Visual Basic for Applications. Which VBA and ODBC-enabled application is best suited for this task?

A. Microsoft Excel

B. Microsoft Outlook

C. Microsoft Project

D. Microsoft Word

47. After creating a slideshow in PowerPoint, the finished .PPT file will be distributed over the Internet. In order for people who do not have PowerPoint installed to be able to view the presentation, which tool is available on the Internet to show the presentation in the original format and backgrounds?

A. Microsoft FrontPage

B. Microsoft Internet Explorer

C. Microsoft Office document viewer

D. PowerPoint document viewer

CHAPTER

4

Application
Development Languages

Microsoft Exam Objectives Covered in This Chapter:

- Choose a development system to use as a tool to provide a solution for a given business problem.
    - Microsoft Visual Basic®
    - Microsoft J++™
    - Microsoft Access
    - Microsoft Visual C++®
    - Microsoft Visual FoxPro™

Microsoft Visual Studio 97 gives developers a comprehensive suite of tools for integrated client/server computing, including support for Internet technologies. Visual Studio provides the tools to build open, distributed Web applications; to scale traditional client/server applications for multi-tiered, server-based solutions; and to access the flexibility of component-based development. Visual Studio includes the MSDN library, which offers a comprehensive source of technical information on Microsoft tools, platforms, and technologies.

Visual Studio is available in two versions: the Professional Edition and the Enterprise Edition. The Professional Edition offers the following set of development tools:

- Microsoft Visual Basic, Professional Edition, version 5.0

- Microsoft Visual C++, Professional Edition, version 5.0

- Microsoft Visual FoxPro, Professional Edition, version 5.0

- Microsoft Visual J++, Professional Edition, version 1.1

- Microsoft Visual InterDev

Visual Studio 97, Enterprise Edition includes all of the tools offered in the Professional Edition but adds support for multi-tier development with new transaction, data management, and performance enhancements. The Enterprise Edition is designed to provide support for development teams, tools for designing large-scale solutions, and integration with large data stores. The

Visual Studio Enterprise Edition contains the Enterprise Editions for Visual Basic, Visual C++, Visual FoxPro, and Visual J++, and adds the following components:

- Microsoft Visual SourceSafe, version 5.0
- Microsoft SQL Server, Developer Edition, version 6.5
- Microsoft Transaction Server, Developer Edition, version 1.0
- Microsoft Visual Database Tools
- Microsoft Repository, version 1.0

Microsoft ✓ ***Exam*** ***Objective***	**Choose a development system to use as a tool to provide a solution for a given business problem. Development systems include:** - Microsoft Visual Basic® - Microsoft J++™ - Microsoft Access - Microsoft Visual C++® - Microsoft Visual FoxPro™

Visual FoxPro

Visual FoxPro (5.0) is an object-oriented database development system featuring ActiveX extensibility, improved performance (over 3.0), improved connectivity features, and an enhanced development environment. Visual FoxPro can be used to develop desktop and client/server database applications.

Visual FoxPro supports a variety of ActiveX controls and can be subclassed to create customized reusable objects. This includes support for ActiveX controls developed using other tools from the Visual Studio suite. Automation servers created using Visual FoxPro can be employed in any environment supporting automation.

Visual FoxPro version 5.0 gives a developer the tools necessary to manage data—whether for organizing tables of information and running queries, creating an integrated relational database management system (DBMS), or programming a fully developed data-management application for end users.

Debugging capabilities in Visual FoxPro are enhanced and include color-coded syntax and a tree-view with capabilities for modifying objects, properties, and events. FoxPro can be used to build database applications using object-oriented programming (OOP) techniques. ActiveX controls and Visual FoxPro class libraries can be used to assemble applications from pretested components for rapid development.

Visual FoxPro's improved editor, new debugger, and Visual SourceSafe integration assist developers, either alone or in teams, to increase productivity.

Improvements in the current Visual FoxPro database engine and user interface offer execution improvement up to 40 percent faster than earlier versions. Speed improvements ensure that forms load and refresh faster and both local and client/server data are retrieved faster.

Features and capabilities supported by Visual FoxPro include the following:

- **ActiveX automation servers** FoxPro applications can be deployed as ActiveX automation servers which can be called by a variety of front-ends, locally, over a LAN or intranet, or over the Internet.

- **Distributed, n-tier applications** Multi-tier applications can be used to centralize business rules while maximizing network resources. Visual FoxPro can be used to create middle-tier business rule servers and to build front-ends for middle-tier servers created using other tools or development platforms.

A multi-tiered application, using a three-tiered client/server application as an example, would be one employing an architecture where the user interface (front end) for the application is contained in one component, i.e., an .EXE. The second tier would be a separate .EXE or .DLL (code component) supplying all of the business rules and data access routines, while the third tier would be a database engine.

- **Web server integrated applications**   Visual FoxPro includes tools to integrate FoxPro applications with the Microsoft Internet Information Server. Web-based applications allow users to find and update information in Visual FoxPro databases and to share data with LAN-based users.

- **Internet Search Wizard**   Web searches for Visual FoxPro databases are created using the Internet Search Wizard to create search pages where users can formulate queries which are passed to a Visual FoxPro database. Results returned by the database are automatically converted to HTML pages for presentation.

Visual FoxPro's Offline View offers support for mobile and remote users, permitting users who do not have immediate access to the FoxPro database to share data, partition, and then resynchronize multiple changes to the database.

Using the optional Visual SourceSafe, Visual FoxPro developers can save versions of each component and the application as a whole and can then roll back to a previous version at any time. Multiple developers working on a common project can use Visual SourceSafe to coordinate team development using the advanced check-in, check-out, merging, branching, and differencing features.

Visual FoxPro's new debugger provides such advanced features as the ability to save and reload debugging sessions, provide a tree-view to inspect application objects, and complex breakpoint support. All debugging surfaces are fully drag-and-drop enabled.

Field mappings defined at the database level permit developers to customize elements ranging from fields' labels to custom classes representing fields across every form in an application. Field mapping speeds the creation and maintenance of forms and screens.

Visual FoxPro supports outer joins using native ANSI-standard SQL, saving coding over using multiple SQL statements for outer joins. Visual FoxPro's Query Designer uses this syntax automatically.

Visual FoxPro's editor provides color-coding for keywords with customizable color schemes. Drag-and-drop support is provided for arranging code segments and subprocedures can be located instantly using improved editor navigation.

> ### Visual FoxPro versus Microsoft Access
>
> While Microsoft Access—in general—is superior to Visual FoxPro for database development (if only because Access is more easily integrated with other Microsoft products), there are situations where Visual FoxPro holds the advantage.
>
> - Where a team has existing experience using the xBase language—the basis for Visual FoxPro—then FoxPro becomes the obvious choice.
>
> - Visual FoxPro, unlike Microsoft Access' Visual Basic, offers support for object-oriented inheritance.
>
> - Visual FoxPro is the only (Microsoft) development language that is supported on the Macintosh platform.

Performance Improvements

Visual FoxPro reduces the memory overhead on commonly used form controls, allowing forms to run 40 percent faster than earlier versions of FoxPro. By supporting delayed data binding, Visual FoxPro forms render and refresh faster—particularly multi-page forms—because less data is being accessed as users navigate to the desired record. Visual FoxPro (5.0) offers faster data retrieval for local data and improved access to server-based data (such as Microsoft SQL Server).

ActiveX Controls

Visual FoxPro provides 26 ActiveX controls with support for third-party ActiveX controls including controls created using tools in Visual Studio. While Visual FoxPro cannot be used to create ActiveX controls, controls created using Visual Basic, Visual C++, or Visual J++ can be used in a Visual FoxPro form.

Visual Basic

Since the Visual Basic program system was introduced roughly six years ago, Visual Basic has become an extremely popular development tool for Windows. Using Visual Basic, even novice programmers are able to rapidly develop working Windows-based applications while needing only a minimal knowledge of the Windows APIs, messaging protocols, and information structures.

Visual Basic for Applications, while not strictly speaking part of the Visual Studio, nor as powerful and flexible as Visual Basic proper, is used extensively in Microsoft Office and Microsoft Project. Also, Visual Basic for Applications is expected to be used in conjunction with third-party applications in the future.

Benefits found in Visual Basic include such advanced features as optimizing native code compilation, accelerated form rendering and enhanced database access—all allowing developers to create functional applications and components.

On the down side, even though Visual Basic is optimized for speed, for computation-intensive operations Visual Basic applications continue to be slower than parallel applications created using more sophisticated development tools, such as Visual C++.

Because Visual Basic can work with DLLs created using Visual C/C++, one method of leveraging Visual C++'s speed and efficiency is to create libraries to support computation-intensive operations using Visual C++ and to then call library-supplied functions from Visual Basic.

Because Visual Basic supports the component creation capabilities of the ActiveX technologies, Visual Basic is also popular with developers targeting client/server environments, intranets, and the Internet.

Visual Basic is available in two forms: the Professional Edition and the Enterprise Edition. The latter offers tools for team development and scaleability, including the following:

- **Microsoft Visual Modeler** A tool for reverse engineering existing Visual Basic applications and creating models of applications prior to development

- **Visual Database Tools** Tool suite used to create and manage data-driven applications relying on live connections to databases

- **Visual SourceSafe** (Discussed in Chapter 3) Provides version control for team development projects

- **SQL Server, Developer Edition** (Discussed in Chapter 10) Provides a variety of graphical and command-line utilities enabling data access

- **Transaction Server** A component-based transaction processing system for developing, deploying, and managing high performance, scaleable, and robust enterprise, Internet, and intranet server applications

Other features found in Microsoft Visual Basic 5.0 Enterprise Edition include the following:

- **Native code compiler** The built-in optimizing native code compiler produces applications which can run up to 20 times faster than parallel applications created using Visual Basic 4.0.

- **Microsoft ActiveX Controls** Visual Basic can be used to create ActiveX Controls which can be reused by other development tools including Visual Basic, Visual C++, Visual FoxPro, Microsoft Office, and Microsoft Internet Explorer.

- **Microsoft IntelliSense features** The IntelliSense features, including DataTips for popup information, Quick Info, and List Properties/Methods, eliminate the need for VB programmers to memorize complex syntax, optional arguments, and component properties.

- **Application Wizards** Visual Basic includes 13 wizards for fast creation, including MDI (multi-document interface), SDI (single document interface), database-centric, and Microsoft Explorer-based applications.

- **Enterprise scaleability** Scaleability allows Visual Basic to be used to build multi-tiered applications using an distributed component environment.

- **RDO/RDC Enhancements**   The Remote Data Objects library and the Remote Data Control (version 2.0) feature enhances local cursor support and optimistic batch updates as well as stand-alone connection and query objects.

- **MDI/SDI/Explorer-Style Interface Options**   These options offer the ability to create single, multiple, or Microsoft Explorer-style document interface applications.

In addition, the Enterprise Edition of Visual Basic supports operations with the Microsoft Visual Modeler, Visual Database Tools, Visual Source Safe, SQL Server, Developer Edition, TSQL debugging, and Transaction Server.

Visual Basic and Messaging

Visual Basic programs can be written into a Microsoft Word 97 macro to send and receive mail using the OLE Messaging library. This requires using the Visual Basic Editor and setting a reference—in the References dialog box from the Tools menu.

The OLE Messaging Library must also be installed on your computer. To use an ActiveX control, such as the MAPI control, you must place it on a form or visible document. While MAPI (Messaging API) controls simplify the implementation of messaging functionality on Visual Basic forms, these do require programming.

VB UserControl Module

A UserControl module is a container holding the source code for an ActiveX control. UserControl modules can be incorporated in any Visual Basic project but, unless the project itself is an ActiveX Control project, the control defined in the UserControl module will only be available within the project application.

The advantage of limiting the scope of a control in this fashion is that it permits developers to create proprietary controls which can not be used by other developers or other applications.

Callback Functions

A variety of Windows API functions accept pointers to a user-defined function as one of their arguments. These user-defined functions are referred to as "callback functions."

In Visual C++, callback functions are quite common, but the equivalent in Visual Basic can be created using the AddressOf operator.

Visual C++

Visual C++ is presently the preeminent object-oriented development tool for Windows-based applications, offering fast, efficient execution while still offering developers direct access to full system functionality and flexibility in application design. Visual C++ provides the means for building small, fast applications and components.

In addition to offering full support for the Windows APIs and the Microsoft Foundation Classes, Visual C++ supports the Component Object Model (COM), the creation of ActiveX component-based applications, and provides integrated support for distributed computing and for the deployment of applications on the Internet.

For component-based development, Visual C++ offers extensive native COM support for creating fast, lightweight COM objects for desktop, Internet, and server use. Also, the Visual C++ development system is designed not just for C/C++ applications but also for mixed-language systems, and for Internet and intranet applications.

Like Visual Basic, Visual C++ is marketed in both Professional and Enterprise Editions with both editions offering a variety of support and development features, including:

- **Developer Studio IDE**   The Developer Studio Integrated Development Environment supports using the Visual Basic Scripting Edition to automate repetitive tasks and makes debugging convenient with the Variables and Watch windows. Editing HTML and C++ code is supported with syntax coloring.

- **MFC and Templates**   Improved MFC and template wizards make application and component creation more efficient while the Active Template Library supports creating small, fast COM objects for both the Internet and Microsoft Transaction Server. Improved ODBC classes boost performance and data integrity.

- **Optimizing compiler**   The compiler generates smaller, faster applications and components. Existing code, using previous versions of C/C++, can be recompiled to decrease size and increase speed by 10 percent (depending on applications).

- **Native COM support**   Compiler support for COM makes it easy to develop C++ clients using COM objects. Support includes Visual COM editing, location- and language-independent COM browsing, and MFC templates, as well as wizards supporting component-based development.

- **Active Document server support**   Wizard and programmatic support are supplied for the creation of Active Document servers, which can be invoked by any Active Document container (i.e. Microsoft Office 95/97, Internet Explorer 3.0, or Microsoft Visual Studio 97).

- **ANSI/ISO C++ Conformance**   Visual C++'s Standard C++ Library conforms to the ANSI/ISO (X3J16) Working Paper including standard support for the bool, mutable, and explicit data types.

- **MSDN Library CDs**   This resource provides a wealth of development information including sample code, Microsoft Knowledge Base articles, technology specifications, product documentation, books, and conference papers.

The Visual Basic Enterprise Edition offers tools for team development and scaleability, including:

- **Visual Database Tools**   For fast database development with support for remotely debugging stored procedures in Microsoft SQL Server databases and the ability to remotely review tables, queries, and stored procedures in any ODBC-compliant database

- **Visual Schema designer**   Provides the means to remotely analyze the schema for a Microsoft SQL Server database and to enhance database application development

- **Transaction Server, Developer Edition**   Provides tools for building high-performance, transaction-based applications

Visual J++

Java is a cross-platform programming language for building Web applets and components that can run on either the Web client (inside the browser) or on the Web server. Further, Visual J++ is also an object-oriented language and, like Visual C++ or Visual Basic, can also be used to create stand-alone applications.

Microsoft Visual J++ Professional Edition offers a complete development environment with all of the tools and information necessary to design 100 percent Java-compatible applications and applets using the Java and

ActiveX technologies. Visual J++ provides an Integrated Development Environment (IDE) together with a collection of interrelated components for creating, testing, tuning, and deploying Java code for multiple platforms.

Visual J++ includes sample code, development wizards, a graphical debugger, and ActiveX integration as well as the full set of Java language documentation.

Visual J++ does not have pointers.

Java applets and applications can be built or extended with ActiveX integration, permitting them to work with other applets and ActiveX controls. With ActiveX integration, Java applications can access databases and other existing applications, making it easy to create reusable components in Java. Also, functionality can be added to Java applets using prebuilt ActiveX controls and COM objects such as Data Access Objects (DAO) and Remote Data Objects (RDO).

Java is a full-featured development language, and its applications can run on any computer that has the Java virtual machine software installed. The Win32 virtual machine is the Microsoft Windows version of the Java virtual machine.

In addition, wizards supplied by Visual J++ can be used to create fully functional applications in minutes.

Visual J++ offers the means to maximize Java development and performance, to create portable applications, and to take advantage of current and emerging standards, all within a proven development framework. Visual J++ offers a variety of tools and support including:

- **ActiveX Wizard**   Provides support for creating ActiveX components in Java, allowing Java programs to be used in applications such as Visual Basic, Delphi, and Excel, as well as in Web pages

Visual J++ applications can act both as ActiveX components and as consumers for ActiveX component services.

- **Database Wizard**   Provides connections from Java applications to popular ODBC and SQL databases through DAO and RDO interfaces

- **Java Type Library Wizard**   Provides the means to integrate COM-based applications, written in other programming languages, into Java applications without needing to rewrite the applications from scratch

- **Post-Build Step**   Permits developers to have applets automatically compressed, signed, or posted to a Web server

In addition, Visual Basic Script can be used with Visual J++ to create macro scripts to automate development tasks and increase productivity with Visual J++. Also, because the Visual J++ IDE is shared with Visual C++, Visual InterDev, and MSDN, users familiar with any of these tools will be able to come up to speed in Visual J++ without having to learn a new operating environment.

Just-In-Time Compiler and Byte Codes

By not compiling Java executables until run time, Java applications become essentially platform independent.

Each platform (or Web browser) supporting Java applications must also provide a Java virtual machine (JV Machine). The JV Machine turns the Just-In-Time byte codes into machine code at run time.

NOTE   The Microsoft Internet Explorer includes a JV Machine called the Win32 virtual machine.

A Just-In-Time compiler can be built for any platform. Once a Visual J++ executable file has been created on any platform, it can be compiled by the JIT compiler on any other platform. This transportability makes Visual J++ extremely platform independent. Since ActiveX controls can be created using Visual J++, it can be used to generate platform-independent ActiveX controls.

Visual J++ and COM

Unlike most ActiveX or COM (Component Object Model) components, Java COM components are not required to provide an explicit iUnknown interface. Visual J++ programmers are not required to use COM to create package objects or class libraries to expose Java objects. All that Visual J++ requires is for programmers to make Java objects public and to create a type library for the Java objects.

Visual InterDev

Microsoft Visual InterDev provides an integrated Web application development system offering tools to develop, publish, and manage database-driven Web applications, creating applications which are accessible from any Web browser. Database tools supplied in Visual InterDev offer the means for connecting a Web site to any database supporting Open Database Connectivity (ODBC). Together with a variety of database wizards and programmable data access components, Visual InterDev offers visual database tools including an integrated Data View, Query Designer, and Database Designer.

With these facilities, Visual InterDev makes creating sophisticated database-driven Web applications easy and convenient and can also be used to integrate both client-side and server-side Java components for a Web site.

Microsoft FrontPage versus Visual InterDev

While Microsoft FrontPage is also a Web authoring tool, FrontPage is designed for non-programmers and is a member of Microsoft Office with the same look and feel as other Microsoft Office components. In contrast, Visual InterDev is a member of the Visual Tools family and shares the look and feel of Microsoft development tools such as Visual C++.

Because Web sites may be—and often are—created by teams composed of both programmers and non-programmers, Visual InterDev and FrontPage are designed to be interoperable, allowing people with different skill sets to work together on the same Web site. For more on Microsoft FrontPage, see Chapter 3.

Visual SourceSafe

Microsoft Visual SourceSafe provides a project-oriented version control repository and a means for managing software source control for team development projects and for Web content. Visual SourceSafe manages any type of source file created by any development language or authoring tool and allows users to work at both project and file levels while promoting component reuse.

With project-oriented features, Visual SourceSafe makes managing team development projects simple, offering the means to handle most of the day-to-day tasks required for multi-developer coordination. Visual SourceSafe also supports roll-back operations to recover earlier versions of project components or of entire projects. Visual SourceSafe is discussed further in Chapter 3.

SQL Server, Developer Edition

Microsoft SQL Server, Developer Edition offers a develop-and-test version of the Microsoft SQL Server. SQL Server is tightly integrated with the Microsoft BackOffice family of server products and provides a database engine for powering Web sites and for client/server applications that scale up to the enterprise. With built-in data replication, powerful management tools, Internet/intranet integration and open-system architecture, SQL Server provides cost-effective information solutions.

Further, SQL Server allows extended stored procedures using C/C++ for enhanced system configuration. Distributed transactions are supported by DB-Library, ODBC, Transact-SQL, XA, and OLE Transaction interfaces.

Using the Transact SQL debugger, developers can interactively debug and view SQL stored procedures in SQL Server from within Visual Basic and Visual C++.

SQL Server is discussed in further detail in Chapter 10.

Transaction Server, Developer Edition

The Transaction Server, Developer Edition provides support for developing and deploying scaleable, multi-tier applications for the Windows NT Server. Developers can build server applications as "single user" ActiveX Components using Visual Tools, then deploy the components through the Transaction Server as reliable, multi-user applications. Using Transaction Server masks the complexity of server programming from the component developer by providing automatic support for distribution, transactions, security, and scaleability both across the Internet and client/server networks.

Microsoft Transaction Server is also discussed in Chapter 3.

Visual Database Tools

The Visual Database Tools included with Visual Studio Enterprise Edition provide developers with the means to visualize and edit the database objects used in an application. The Database Tools include a data dictionary for all relevant database objects, including tables, views, and stored procedures, as well as editors for query design, stored procedures, and debugging. The Visual Database Tools allow developers to completely integrate database development into a RAD (Rapid Application Development) environment and work seamlessly with Visual InterDev, Visual C++ Enterprise Edition, and Visual Basic Enterprise Edition.

Microsoft Repository

Microsoft Repository is a database that stores and shares components, models, objects, and relationships together with their descriptive information. The Repository provides important capabilities in five key areas for client/server environments: reuse, tool interoperability, team development, data resource management, and dependency tracking.

Repository sits on top of Microsoft Jet and Microsoft SQL Server but is presently exclusive to Visual Basic.

Microsoft Developer Network Library

The Microsoft Developer Network (MSDN) Library CD-ROM, included with Visual Studio, offers a comprehensive source for technical information about Microsoft tools, platforms, and technologies. The MSDN Library contains thousands of articles and code samples from Product Support Specialists addressing specific technical challenges faced by developers. All product documentation from the individual tools in Visual Studio is indexed and cross-reference on the CD.

Summary

Microsoft supplies a series of development tools including Access and Visual FoxPro for database applications, Visual Basic and Visual C++ for general application development, and Visual J++ for Web and network applications.

FoxPro, like Access, is a relational database management system but, unlike Access, is fully object-oriented and includes support for ActiveX controls developed using other tools from the Visual Studio suite. FoxPro is designed to create and support distributed, multi-tier database applications used to centralize business rules; to create middle-tier business rule servers and to build front-ends for middle-tier servers created by other development platforms.

Visual Basic provides an application development platform which places minimal demands on the developer's knowledge of Windows APIs by hiding most of the details involved in procedure calls, and by providing extensive wizard support to assist developers in programming details, including prompts for supplying the required arguments, testing parameter types, and imposing a relatively heavily structured development environment. The result is a system allowing even novice programmers to create functional applications while still permitting experienced programmers a high degree of flexibility in application design.

The Enterprise Edition of Visual Basic is designed for team development circumstances by adding additional tools for scaleability, database access and version control.

In both the Professional and Enterprise Editions, Visual Basic is also a popular tool for the development of ActiveX Controls, while the Visual Modeler can be used with Visual Basic to reverse engineer existing applications and to create application models prior to developing the actual application.

For computation-intensive processes or for time-critical circumstances requiring faster responses than Visual Basic supplies, Visual C++ can be used to create dynamic link libraries supplying maximum performance when called from Visual Basic applications.

Visual C++, in contrast to Visual Basic, is strictly a professional development environment demanding a more sophisticated knowledge of programming than Visual Basic. In return for these demands, however, Visual C++ produces a faster product while placing virtually no restrictions on how applications are developed, giving developers full and complete access to all aspects of the Windows system.

Among the strengths of Visual C++ are native COM support for creating fast, lightweight COM objects, distributed computing support, creation of ActiveX components, and strong Internet and intranet application support.

Again, like Visual Basic, Visual C++ is available in both a Professional and Enterprise Edition, with the latter offering support for larger projects, team development, and high-performance database access.

Visual J++ is a cross-platform development language intended primarily for building Web applets and components which can run both on Web clients (i.e., browsers) and on Web servers. Java applets and applications support ActiveX integration and work with COM objects such as Data Access Objects and Remote Data Objects.

Review Questions

1. An ActiveX control created with Visual Basic can be embedded in an Active Server Page (ASP) or in:

   A. A macro for an Access .MDB file

   B. A Visual Basic .CLS file

   C. A Visual Basic .FRM file

   D. The code for a Visual FoxPro .PRG file

2. Visual FoxPro uses the Internet Search Wizard to:

   A. Access data tables through the Microsoft Internet Server

   B. Create search pages where users can formulate queries which are passed to a Visual FoxPro database.

   C. Execute topic searches across the Internet to locate requested Web pages

   D. Locate Internet URLs where data tables are stored

3. In creating a Visual Basic ActiveX controller application to send e-mail messages, which Outlook collection would be used to add a new message to the Outbox?

   A. Items

   B. Messages

    C. Outbox

    D. Profiles

4. Visual FoxPro supports which of the following? (Select all that apply.)

    A. Distributed n-tier applications including middle-tier business rule servers

    B. Removable source code to reduce size, make applications run faster, and provide protection for intellectual property

    C. Auto-conversion to migrate Access databases to FoxPro databases

    D. Reverse engineering using the Microsoft Visual Modeler

5. For database development, why would Visual FoxPro be selected over Access 97?

    A. FoxPro can be used to create ActiveX controls.

    B. FoxPro is more compatible with other Microsoft tools than Access Visual Basic for Applications.

    C. FoxPro is more efficient than the Jet Database Engine.

    D. FoxPro provides more object-oriented programming capabilities.

6. Byte codes—Java executables which are not compiled into machine code until run time—offer which of the following advantages? (Select all that apply.)

    A. Direct hardware access at run time

    B. DirectX technology

    C. Faster performance at run time

    D. Platform independence

7. Visual FoxPro provides support for outer joins using:

    A. ActiveX controls

    B. Custom classes representing fields

    C. Multiple SQL statements

    D. Native ANSI-standard SQL

8. The Microsoft Visual Modeler is provided in which of the following tools:

A. Microsoft Visual Basic Enterprise Edition

B. Microsoft Visual Basic Professional Edition

C. Microsoft Visual C++ Enterprise Edition

D. Microsoft Visual J++ Professional Edition

9. To what kind of user-defined function do a number of Windows API functions accept a pointer, as an argument?

A. Aggregate

B. Allocation

C. Callback

D. Thunking

10. The results of queries submitted to a Visual FoxPro database through the Internet Search Wizard are:

A. Automatically converted to HTML pages for presentation

B. Passed to an ActiveX control for presentation

C. Returned in raw format to be displayed by the client's own FoxPro forms

D. Viewed using a Visual Basic supplied display control

11. The Visual Basic Enterprise Edition includes which of the following? (Select all that apply.)

A. Internet Search Wizard

B. SQL Server, Developer Edition

C. Visual Database Tools

D. Visual SourceSafe

12. Which Microsoft Visual Basic module is used to create an ActiveX control?

   A. A Control (.CTX file) module

   B. A Custom Control (.OCX file) module

   C. A UserControl (.CTL file) module

   D. A UserDocument (.OCA file) module

13. Visual Basic supports creating documents with which of the following? (Select all that apply.)

   A. Explorer-style document interface applications

   B. HTML document interface applications

   C. Multiple-document interface applications

   D. Single-document interface applications

   E. All of the above

14. The Microsoft Visual Modeler is a tool for which of the following? (Select all that apply.)

   A. Creating graphic models of database structures

   B. Creating models of application prior to development

   C. Reverse engineering Visual Basic applications

   D. Reverse engineering Visual C++ applications

15. Using Microsoft Visual J++ as a Java development tool, how do Visual J++ components interact with ActiveX components?

   A. Visual J++ applications may act as ActiveX components.

   B. Visual J++ applications may use ActiveX components.

   C. Both A and B

   D. Neither A nor B

16. As the IS manager for a company with mainframe, Macintosh, and PC systems running Windows, you are considering using Visual J++ as one of the development tools because applications written in Visual J++:

A. Are easily integrated with other Microsoft applications

B. Are specifically designed for the Internet

C. Offer a single compiled application which can execute on any platform including Windows, Macintosh, and UNIX

D. Operate faster than applications developed in Visual C++ or Visual Basic

17. For an application requiring computation-intensive data processing, what is the optimum development tool?

A. Visual Basic

B. Visual C++

C. Visual FoxPro

D. Visual J++

18. A series of applications are needed for in-house use to perform specialized calculations. These applications will require a user interface for data entry and responses but are not computation-intensive. Because the coding staff is heavily invested in other critical development tasks, you decide that these modules can best be developed by:

A. Assigning a relatively inexperienced programmer to create the modules using Visual Basic

B. Creating ActiveX components using Visual J++

C. Reassigning your top Visual C++ engineer to the development project

D. Hiring additional engineering staff on a contract basis for the development

19. After developing a Visual Basic application, you discover that the application as a whole is running too slow. After further profile testing, three computation-intensive functions in the application account for better than 90 percent of the execution time. In order to speed up the application to suitable performance standards, the optimum choice is to:

A. Create a dynamic link library, using Visual C++, to support the three computation-intensive operations.

B. Create ActiveX components, using Visual J++, to handle the three computation-intensive operations.

C. Rewrite the entire application in Visual C++ to speed up all operations in the application.

D. Rewrite the Visual Basic application to speed up the three computation-intensive operations.

20. Microsoft Visual J++ offers which of the following? (Select all that apply.)

A. A Just-In-Time (JIT) compiler

B. ActiveX technology

C. Pointer addressing

D. The Component Object Model (COM)

21. Functionality can be added to Java applets using which of the following? (Select all that apply.)

A. COM objects such as Data Access Objects and Remote Data Objects

B. Dynamic link libraries

C. Prebuilt ActiveX controls

D. Visual InterDev

22. What is required in order to run a Visual J++ application in the Windows environment?

A. Web browser

B. Web server

C. Win32 virtual machine

D. Windows virtual machine

CHAPTER

5

Solutions Framework
as a Development Methodology

Microsoft Exam Objectives Covered in This Chapter:

- Given a scenario, discuss the use of the Microsoft Solutions Framework (MSF) to guide development, testing, and deployment of a business solution.

The image of software developers as 'otherworldly' geeks living on potato chips and Jolt cola, sleeping in their cubicles and sometimes not coming out for days on end is a popular myth which seems to be deliberately perpetrated by software developers (most of whom, of course, do not fit the image at all). And Dilbert cartoons aside, software development is every bit as serious a business as manufacturing cars... or, perhaps, even more serious given the current pace of change and the competitive nature of the business.

The result—after discarding these popular but invalid images—is that the software industry is just that, an industry. And, like other industries, developers are faced with making decisions about what to develop and when and how to develop it, about product cycles, about business alliances, about investment strategies... in short, decisions about how to conduct their business.

The Microsoft Solutions Framework (MSF) Models are a collection of practices gathered from customers, IT groups, partners, and product developers across the globe. These business practices have been analyzed for repeatable success rates, then integrated into reusable models which incorporate measurable milestones to guide technological decisions in a business context. Each of these models can be used independently or can be combined as required.

Microsoft ✓ ***Exam*** ***Objective***

Given a scenario, discuss the use of the Microsoft Solutions Framework (MSF) to guide development, testing, and deployment of a business solution.

Using the Solutions Framework models offers developers guidance and a framework for development methodologies. In effect, the Solutions Framework offers a "compass" for users of development methodologies to ensure that the tools deliver the desired results.

The Microsoft Solutions Framework is not a product and is less a development tool than it is a service marketed by Microsoft—by offering MSF experts for hire—to assist developers in planning development, testing, and deployment efforts.

The Solutions Framework is composed of seven models:

- The Team Model provides the means to build high-performance teams.
- The Process Model is used for judging development tradeoffs.
- The Development/Application Model offers guides for flexibility in design processes.
- The Solutions Design Model aids developers in anticipating user requirements.
- The Enterprise Architecture Model provides structures for business integration.
- The Infrastructure Model is used to guide systems deployment.
- The Total Cost of Ownership Model provides methods to identify and contain costs in technology investments.

The Team, Process, and the Development/Application models are the three major models in the Microsoft Solutions Framework.

Selecting Practices Appropriate to Needs

The Microsoft Solutions Framework offers a selection of models for business development practices together with the services of consultants to assist in applying Solutions Framework models to particular situations faced by project teams.

The models offered by the Solutions Framework are not necessarily intended to be applied individually, rather they are more appropriately used in combinations according to project requirements and the nature of the projects. Table 5.1 shows suggested model combinations for several common types of project.

T A B L E 5.1:   Projects and Model Recommendations

Objective	Team	Process	Application	Infrastructure	Solutions Design	Enterprise Architecture	Total Cost of Ownership
Planning a network architecture	✓	✓		✓		✓	✓
Designing an intranet	✓	✓		✓		✓	
Building a messaging infrastructure	✓	✓		✓		✓	
Building an intranet application	✓	✓	✓	✓	✓		
Building an electronic commerce site	✓	✓		✓	✓	✓	
Deploying a standard desktop	✓	✓		✓			✓

(Column grouping header: M O D E L S)

Team Model

The Team model is aimed at building teams who perform and deliver. Ideally, a team is not simply a collection of engineers assigned to a project. An effective team should:

- Possess the appropriate expertise for the project

- Be empowered to use their expertise

- Be accountable for results in the areas each own

Of these, accountability and empowerment are the two factors which must balance. Micro-management—accountability without empowerment—simply leads to disgruntled developers who feel blamed without having the freedom to do their best. And the converse—empowerment without accountability—simply leads to chaos.

But with both accountability and empowerment, competent developers will do their best to achieve everything possible. Without an effective team model, the problems which will occur are virtually predictable and include such familiar foul-ups as:

- No one is responsible for dealing with users or providing training materials.

- No one knows the status of the project.

- The choice becomes one of developing software or testing software but not both.

- Everyone claims responsibility for the same project elements.

  – and –

- There are project elements which no one will claim.

Peer-to-Peer Teamwork

The Solutions Framework team model is defined as a team of peers with interdependent and cooperative roles. When each member in the team has a well-defined role and a specific mission, the need for supervision becomes minimal. By giving team members objectives and responsibility, ownership is encouraged, and the result is a better product.

In a team composed of peers, team leaders take the responsibility for management, guidance, and coordination while team members are free to concentrate on their specific objectives.

The Team model is structured around six clearly defined roles:

- Development covers building or implementing a product or service which satisfies specifications and customer expectations as well as delivering a product which meets the stated functional specifications.

- Logistics provides for a smooth rollout, handling installation and migration of the product to operations and support groups.

- Product Management is responsible for providing objectives to be filled by the product or service, for defining and quantifying customer requirements, for developing and maintaining the business case, and for managing customer expectations.

The Product Manager is responsible for the vision statement and high-level project management and has the primary responsibility for ensuring that the software product offers the features required by the end users.

- Program Management is responsible for time-critical decisions, including when to release a product or service, as well as coordinating delivery in a fashion consistent with organizational standards and interoperability goals.

The Program Manager is responsible for the functional specification for a product.

- Testing is responsible for ensuring the functionality of the product or service, including complete testing of the user interface and all APIs, and ensuring software compatibility with existing systems.

- User education is responsible for ensuring that clients are able to deploy the product or service through performance solutions and training systems. User education also works to reduce support costs by ensuring that the product is designed in a fashion which is understandable and usable.

The Team model is **not** an organizational chart.

Unrestricted communications between the individuals or groups filling these roles is absolutely critical, as is communication between all team members, irrespective of their roles.

Product quality is not assigned to any group or individual but is jointly and severally owned by all team members. This shared and distributed ownership of product quality ensures that problems are noticed early rather than remaining hidden until the product or solution has been deployed.

When problems are addressed early—during development—costs across the board are reduced, including costs for rework, reduced help-desk costs, and minimized support costs during product transitions.

While the Team model has grown out of software development practices, this model has also been successfully applied to infrastructure deployment projects.

Who's in Charge Here?

While the Team model defines roles and responsibilities, it does not define the management structure for a team. Instead, a team may report to a business unit manager or may be drawn from several organizations for the project. While a table of organization determines who is in charge, the Team model defines how work is divided and who is responsible for ensuring that different aspects of the project are completed.

The Solutions Framework Team model offers the following tangible benefits:

- All roles are accountable for specific objectives.

- Each team member has an interest in the success of the product or service.

- Customer-focused products or services are produced.

- The team culture encourages clarity, efficiency, participation, commitment, and mutual cooperation.

The benefits of the Solutions Framework Team model are not theoretical: they have been proved by organizations—including Microsoft—using this model.

Process Model

The Process model is aimed at identifying and weighing development tradeoffs. Process management requires balance. Too little process management creates a chaotic environment where everything is always urgent, problems are chronic, and team members become exhausted from continually facing the same familiar but unresolved issues. Too much process management creates a straightjacket situation where there is a policy for everything but where nothing can change, no matter how critical the need.

The challenge in process management is to identify what is important, and to manage the important elements against known trade-offs. However, the lack of process management, in itself, can be expected to cause a variety of problems including:

- Project release is continually derailed by demands to add new and additional features.

- Projects assume a life of their own and no longer satisfy an objective.

- Projects change into creatures they were not designed to be.

- Projects run afoul of major issues and must be restarted.

- Projects take too long, absorb too many resources, and go over budget.

  – or, perhaps worst of all, –

- The project is completed, comes in within budget, everything works... but it is obsolete or unneeded when completed.

The Solutions Framework Process model is a milestone-based model providing guidelines for planning and controlling results-oriented projects on the basis of project scope, available resources, and scheduling. The Process model is an iterative and adaptable model which:

- Addresses explicit accountability for teams

- Addresses project risks early in the planning stages

- Defines critical but manageable milestones for tracking development

- Defines the variables and priorities affecting scheduling, features, and trade-off decisions

---

The Systems Development Life Cycle (Waterfall) model

The traditional Systems Development Life Cycle (SDLC)—a.k.a. the Waterfall model—used by many companies is activity- or task-driven. SDLC is not designed for RAD (Rapid Application Development) but rather assumes a single, large-scale development with a defined beginning and endpoint. In contrast, Windows applications are likely to be constantly changing with no marked endpoint in development.

The SLDC has been replaced by the Process model.

Characteristics of the Process Model

The Solutions Framework Process model departs from traditional development models in several fashions, including:

- Development is aimed at versioned releases, not at including every version the first time. Because technology rapidly changes the capabilities, versioned releases are necessary to leverage investments in PC-based computing environments.

- Milestones are customer-oriented, not development-oriented.

- Milestones are managed using known tradeoffs: resources, features, and schedules.

- Milestones are used as synchronization points to recalibrate efforts according to customer expectations.

- The emphasis is placed on the project Vision and the project Scope rather than on requirements.

The Process model is aimed at producing better design decisions, reducing rework, creating higher morale and, not least, creating a higher-quality product. By addressing support and performance issues as part of the development process, the Process model lowers the risk in rolling out new solutions and helps to lower the cost of ownership.

The Solutions Framework Process model consists of four phases: envisioning, planning, developing, and stabilization, with each phase terminating in a major milestone.

Envisioning

Envisioning before instituting a project saves investing major efforts on minor needs or wasting effort in trying to improve bad processes. This requires an open-minded approach to look not only at how a proposed solution addresses current visible objectives, but also at basic issues behind the immediate objective, at other similar issues both local and in other departments, and at potential issues which may arise in the future.

The milestone terminating the Envisioning phase is the VISION / SCOPE APPROVED milestone. Once this point has been reached—by a new product or service gaining approval—the next step will be for a project team to be assembled to define the product. The Vision statement provides the product or service goals and offers a clear direction for development.

The Scope element is the opposite of Vision and defines limits for a specific version of the product or service, while recognizing that further developments will be deferred for incorporation in future versions.

Planning

The Planning phase is devoted to defining customer expectations, team objectives and delivery standards, and how the product will be built or the service created. This is the opportunity for risk assessment, for establishing priorities, and for finalizing estimates for scheduling and resources.

The Planning phase terminates in the PROJECT PLAN APPROVED milestone where the project plan consists of functional specification and a schedule. The functional specifications are created from the combined plans of each team member—as defined in the Team model—and provide the project team with sufficient detail to determine resource requirements and to schedule commitments.

Developing

The Developing phase uses the functional specification and the associated project plan to provide a baseline for initiating development. The development team is responsible for establishing a series of interim milestones, each involving a full test/debug/fix cycle.

The Developing phase terminates in the SCOPE COMPLETE / FIRST USE milestone (a.k.a. CODE COMPLETE milestone). When this milestone is reached, customers and the team assess the product's functionality and verify that rollout and support plans are in place. At this time, the current development is completed and any deferred functionality is documented for a future release.

Stabilization

The Stabilization phase is different from the previous phases and requires a change in focus. Previously, the objective was to find elegant development solutions. Now the objective becomes the rigid operational requirements of a thorough and complete testing.

During the Stabilization phase, the product or service is being tested concurrently with code development to correct bugs and performance problems. During the Stabilization phase, bug finding and bug fixing become the primary focus of activity.

The Stabilization phase culminates in the RELEASE milestone (a.k.a. RELEASE OF PRODUCT milestone). When this milestone is reached, the product is formally released to the operations and support groups and, typically, the project team either returns to the Envisioning phase to begin work on the next version of the product or is dispersed to other development projects.

MSF Process Milestones

The Process model is based on four major milestones:

- **Vision/Scope Approved**   Marks the end of the Envisioning phase.

- **Functional Specification Approved**   Marks the end of the Planning phase.

- **Code Complete**   Marks the end of the Developing phase. Only testing and bug fixes should occur after Code Complete.

- **Release of Product**   Marks the end of the Stabilization phase.

Any project requiring more than three months to complete, of course, should include frequent interim milestones.

Development/Application Model

The Development/Application model is aimed at designing for flexibility. Today's applications are commonly designed on the basis of a clear division between the user interface, business rules, and data—a logical partitioning of functionality which permits flexibility in design by allowing the user interface to be adapted over time or by applying new business rules to new data sources.

User services typically provide a user interface component; business services encapsulate business rules and application logic; data services provide the lowest common level of persistent storage functionality.

This separation of domains approach also encourages a vertical view of applications, eliminating the economies of scale which might be achieved by linking application design, infrastructure usage, and component reuse across functional departments.

This functional separation is also directly opposed to changes which are happening in today's business environments. As business practices become streamlined and hierarchies flattened, developers are expected to undertake a broader range of activities with new tasks spanning the traditional functional boundaries.

Information systems must also evolve to accommodate this trend. Business applications need to allow users more flexibility by allowing them to perform a broader range of activities and undertake more complex transactions without having to learn new software products. For example, ideally the interface elements used to view, locate, and modify information about a customer should be consistent to allow users to move from one application to another without having to relearn each. To achieve this type of consistency, however, requires fine-tuning the commonly accepted development approach.

Lacking a fine-tuned application model, problems which are likely to arise include:

- Applications function correctly in house but are unusable internationally.

- Projects grow until they are too large to understand.

- Projects use objects, but objects are never reused.

- Unexpected performance issues jeopardize deployment.

- User interface changes are impossible because they would throw development off schedule.

According to Microsoft's definition, applications are constructed from a logical network of consumers and suppliers of services where services can be distributed across both physical and functional boundaries to support the needs of many different applications.

The Solutions Framework Development/Application model describes the development process for multi-tiered applications constructed on user, business, and data services by establishing definitions, rules, and relationships to form an application structure. The Development/Application model also offers guidelines on separating an application into a network of services permitting features and functionality to be packaged for reuse across functional boundaries.

A service is defined as a unit of application logic implementing an operation, function, or a transformation applied to an object. Services may enforce business rules, expose features to enter, retrieve, view, or modify information, or perform calculations or manipulate data.

Service Categories

Viewing applications as networks of services, the Solutions Framework Development/Application model defines the following three categories of services which compose an application:

- **User services**   The user interface and supporting application logic. Because an application's user may be an individual or another application, the application interface may be either a graphical user interface or a programmatic interface.

- **Business Services**   The functions controlling the enforcement of business rules, sequencing, and the transactional integrity of the operations performed. Business services transform data into information through the application of business rules.

In the Solutions Framework, the business service component can be provided by ActiveX components on the Internet because no user interface or data services are required by the business services.

- **Data services**   The functions supporting the lowest visible layer of abstraction for manipulating data. Data services are responsible both for the maintenance of data in terms of availability and the integrity of both persistent and non-persistent data as corporate assets. Data services provide functionality such as Create, Read, Update, and Delete in such a fashion that business services (the consumers of the data services) are not required to know where data is located, how data structures are implemented, or how the data is accessed.

The Development/Applications model guidelines for multi-tier development are particularly applicable when business solutions are integrated with intranet and Internet technologies. Specifically, business solutions should:

- Establish and maintain a presence on the Internet

- Promote a consistent user-interface style and navigation model for all business applications

- Provide centralized maintenance of application logic to simplify the deployment of applications

- Provide cross-platform support for a heterogeneous workstation environment

Solutions Design Model

The Solutions Design model is designed to anticipate user needs. While research studies report that a key factor in designing a successful business solution is involving users throughout the design process and giving consideration to their views and desires, user involvement in the development and design process can also be a serious problem. Reasons given by developers for not involving users in the design process include the following:

- Users are reluctant to consider innovation, are not interested in new technologies, and are not interested in being involved in the design process.

- Users have divergent opinions about what new applications should and shouldn't include and have different preferences for screen designs, layouts, and color schemes.

- Users may be dissatisfied with their current systems but don't really know what they want beyond their familiar features.

- Users may request features but, when a feature is delivered, demand something different.

The downside of not involving the users is the lack of a clear perspective on how the application or system will be employed on a day-to-day basis and can result in predictable shortcomings, including:

- Application specifications have remained fixed while the business requirements have changed.

- Once completed, the project may create more workflow problems than it solves.

- The application is complete but will not be deployed because of high costs for training and help-desk support.

- The project solution solves infrastructure problems but nobody is willing to employ it.

- While the project is in development, users have created their own solutions to the problem.

The Solutions Design model offers a step-by-step strategy for the design of business-oriented solutions driven by specific business needs. This model ties together the Solutions Framework Team, Process, and Application models, making it possible for developers to apply resources efficiently.

Aligning the Solution with the Business

The Solutions Design model aligns solutions development with business goals in two key ways:

- **User involvement**   Solutions are driven from the business context, an essential consideration in developing workflow applications. Usability considerations are addressed by end users during design and development rather than waiting to become help-desk incidents. Information systems professionals become involved in creating the solution before end users arrive at their own solutions without addressing infrastructure requirements.

- **Iterative, sequential development**   Three perspectives—conceptual, logical, and physical—aid planners in identifying all business and technical requirements which the application should satisfy. By identifying these constraints and requirements up front, developers are better able to assign resources appropriately.

Three Perspectives

In complexity, software systems design can be related to the process of designing a business; the title Architect is often given to experts in software design. While the conceptual, logical, and physical perspectives work together to identify application requirements, individually, these perspectives can be related to architectural processes.

- Conceptual Design is similar to an architect's sketches for the design of a structure. The initial drawings offer clients views of a building and may contain a site plan, elevation drawings, floor plans, cut-away views, and other images to offer a perspective of what the finished product—the structure—is intended to look like. The Conceptual Design for a product serves the same purpose, by beginning with an understanding of what the users really need to do and creating a set of models which communicate this understanding.

- Logical Design is the equivalent of an architectural plan. The plan shows the structure in a form relevant to the architect and staff, providing detailed views combining the client's expectations with the architect's view and knowledge and communicating these to the various parties involved in the project. The architect's plans correspond to the MSF Logical Design, which lays out the requirements for structure and communications between the individual elements of a system.

- Physical Design is the equivalent of the architect's blueprints, which detail the designer's intentions with adjustments for the physical site environment and the technology and materials available for construction. The Physical Design view directs all construction activities and may provide detailed plans for individual subcontractors. This is the point where the constraints of real-world technology are applied to the model to arrive at realistic implementation and performance considerations and where real resources, costs, and schedules can be estimated.

These perspectives are not stages and do not imply cutoff points or rigid boundaries; it is not necessary for one perspective to be completed before work can begin on another.

Further, elements within each perspective can overlap. It may be that some portions of a system are being coded while other portions are still in the planning stage either conceptually or logically. When information is available before a particular design perspective would normally be expected to target the topic, there is no particular advantage in waiting to apply the information until some hypothetical trigger point is reached.

For flexibility, it might be appropriate to consider these three perspectives as points across a continuum, where designers apply a particular set of techniques and tools to address the needs of particular audiences. In effect, these are methods of describing the design process in a focused fashion.

Also, at any time, portions of the design can be revisited. Design is a continuing process of successive refinement, not a race from a starting point to a finish line.

Enterprise Architecture Model

The Enterprise Architecture model is aimed at integrating the business. In many ways, Enterprise Architecture resembles urban planning. Urban planning is concerned with developing infrastructures for the delivery of utilities and services which provide support for a wide variety of activities across a variety of communities. As populations and the economy grow—for both urban planners and enterprise architects—the infrastructure requires periodic improvements to accommodate growing numbers of users.

Enterprise architects plan for the necessary infrastructures, utilities, systems, and processes required for businesses to access and exchange critical information across the organization. Infrastructure development and management activities are the equivalent of civic public works required to support growth.

Without regular improvements to the infrastructure—or, at the very least, regular maintenance—predictable divisions occur between the business and old and new technologies. For example:

- Continuing support for legacy systems makes it impossible to define new technical guidelines.

- Keeping things running doesn't leave time to consider future improvements and upgrades.

- The need for new technology is obvious but departments are reluctant to agree.

- The technology changes faster than new corporate standards can be defined.

- Where managing was difficult when all assets were centralized, they're now distributed internationally.

Enterprise Architecture planning is not an occasional endeavor but, necessarily, is a continuing and continuous occurrence tracking the need for businesses to evolve. Enterprise Architecture planning relies on such Solutions Framework principles as a fixed release date mindset, activity-based planning, risk-driven scheduling, small teams, and visible milestones to parallel and sustain ongoing solution development projects.

In contrast to top-down methods, projects are not merely driven by an Enterprise Architecture model: They directly impact the evolution of the enterprise architecture. To support this, the Enterprise Architecture model provides a consistent set of guidelines for planning, building, and managing a technology infrastructure by encompassing four perspectives: Application, Business, Information, and Technology. Considering each business requirement from each of these perspectives supports developing better change-management strategies for the enterprise.

Application Architecture

The Application Architecture describes the standard interfaces, services, and application resources required by the business enterprise. For project teams, these interfaces, services, and resources translate into development resources (i.e., component and code libraries, standards documents, design guidelines).

The Application Architecture also describes the automated services supporting the business processes in the Business Architecture and the interactions and interdependencies in the organization's applications. It offers guidelines for developing new applications and for moving to new application models.

Key questions which should be prompted by the Application Architecture include:

- Are there core applications which inhibit customer service?
- Does the business enterprise demand stability or cutting-edge technology?
- What application models are used within the organization?
- What applications are unique to the business enterprise?
- What applications can be purchased from independent software vendors?
- What integration issues exist with current application systems?
- Where do application backlogs exist?

Business Architecture

The Business Architecture describes how the business enterprise operates by describing the functions and cross-functional activities performed by the organization. The process of describing business enterprise architecture reveals opportunities where technology can be employed to control expenses, enhance innovation, and increase revenues.

The Business Architecture also establishes boundaries for clear requirements and the development of Vision/Scope definitions for each project.

Key questions which should be prompted by the Business Architecture include:

- Do existing core processes meet customer's needs?
- How healthy are present margins?

- How will new systems affect cash flow, revenues, and expenses?

- Is the present market expanding or contracting?

- What are the business's core strengths and what trends affect the business enterprise?

- What industry is the business enterprise engaged in?

- What services and resources are required by the business enterprise?

- Where is the industry headed? Where will it be in five years?

Information Architecture

The Information Architecture describes what information is needed by an organization in order to run business processes and operations. This includes data models, data management policies, and descriptions of the patterns for information consumption and production throughout the organization. The Information Architecture also describes how data is bound to the workflow, documents, and personal files throughout the organization. Often, parts of the crucial information do not reside in database servers but are scattered across thousands of desktops in the enterprise.

Key questions which should be prompted by the Information Architecture include:

- What are the business process data and workflow requirements?

- What functional data requirements exist?

- What industry requirements and standards exist?

- What information does the business require?

- What statutory or legal constraints affect data and information needs?

- Where do the biggest data issues occur?

- Which information requirements are critical?

Technology Architecture

The Technology Architecture provides standards and guidelines for the acquisition and deployment of application building blocks, client/workstation tools, infrastructure services, network connectivity components, and platforms. The question of acquisition breaks down to build-or-buy decisions while deployment requires developing technology blueprints to guide the evolution of the technology infrastructure.

Key questions which should be prompted by the Technology Architecture include:

- Are the technical skills required today and tomorrow known?
- Do standards call for deploying approved, standard technologies or can ad hoc technologies be purchased?
- Does the technology infrastructure map to the enterprise business requirements?
- What are the key technology trends affecting IT operations?
- What level of technology risk is acceptable?
- What, where, and how is the technology deployed in the organization?

Used together, these four perspectives offer guides for organizations to plan during building, to use business-driven projects to evolve enterprise architecture, and to use new technologies to drive the business enterprise forward to competitive advantage.

Infrastructure Model

The Infrastructure model is used to guide systems deployment. The term *infrastructure* holds different meanings for different people. For a software engineer, an infrastructure may mean the software elements appropriate to a computing environment. For a hardware engineer, an infrastructure may be the physical elements forming the network. For someone from human resources, an infrastructure consists of personnel and services performed. In a more general sense, however, the computing infrastructure is a composite of all of these and much more.

The Solutions Framework defines an infrastructure as the total set of resources necessary to support the enterprise computing environment. Resources include the technologies and standards (defined by the Enterprise Architecture), the operational processes (policies, operating procedures, and services) and the people and organization skills (skill sets and management).

When an infrastructure is not well deployed, a number of predictable obstacles may be observed, including the following:

- Unresolved underlying technology issues keep important business projects on hold.

- No criteria exist for evaluating new technologies.

- User mobility increases the time spent administering security policies.

- As a project is being rolled out, the help desk discovers that a project cannot be supported.

- The deployment timeline is determined by whether or not the application functions as planned.

Projects which require more than a year to complete are likely to lose their value simply because of the rate of technological innovation. For larger projects, this means that the deployment of any single version may never be completed because, as one wave of deployment approaches completion, another wave will already be in the planning stages.

To manage overlapping developments, customers and project teams must collaborate to determine priorities and to decide how trade-offs will affect development and deployment. Such decisions are based on the three project management parameters: schedule, scope, and resources. These are, however, precisely the parameters driving the Solutions Framework Process model.

The Infrastructure model applies the roles, functions, and expectations of the Process and Team models to the requirements of rolling out a successful infrastructure, thus achieving dual goals.

- Established best practices are applied to complex operations, increasing the chances for success.

- Team members reuse familiar knowledge, allowing organizations to accomplish more in less time with fewer people.

By applying the Process model to infrastructure projects, some labels are changed to emphasize the characteristics specific to this project type. For one example, the Developing phase in the Process model becomes the Fulfillment phase in deployment to apply the core activities of envisioning, planning, developing, and stabilizing to an iterative deployment environment.

Here the core roles in the Team model remain valid, still own the same views of the project, and have the same interactions as before. However, to expand the Team model for an infrastructure deployment project, the previous six team roles are expanded to encompass wider responsibilities with three new areas added to the Logistics role:

- System Management assumes responsibility for the systems, technology, and the continued operation of the technology.

- Help desk provides ongoing user support.

- Communications is responsible for maintaining voice, video, and data communication capabilities.

The Infrastructure model provides a more flexible approach to deploying technology, making it possible to get new technology in place and delivering value in less time. Also, for teams who are already familiar with the Team and Process models, reusing this knowledge in the Infrastructure model benefits the organization.

Total Cost of Ownership Model

The Total Cost of Ownership model (TCO model) is aimed at improving the return on investment. While the concept behind the Total Cost of Ownership model is both simple and laudable, the issue itself is far from simple and must be evaluated on the basis of several considerations including:

- **The role of value** While it is possible to reduce the total cost of ownership to zero by the simple expedient of eliminating all computers from the organization, this would also eliminate the competitive advantage conferred by those same computers. Granted, the suggestion is extreme, but it also makes two key points: that value is an integral part of the equation and that the overall goal is not to minimize costs but to optimize costs against the values which are unique to each organization.

- **What constitutes a cost?** The industry is replete with TCO models which estimate annual costs to range from $3,200 to $31,000 per desktop PC. This discrepancy in costs is largely due to disagreements over what costs—software, hardware, training—should be included in a good TCO analysis. Microsoft's Solutions Framework Total Cost of Ownership model offers a comprehensive model to assist organizations in understanding the costs in owning and using each IT component.

- **Business enterprise requirements**   Some TCO models include large percentages under fully loaded costs which are ascribed to undefined end-user activities. This type of approach makes accurate costs difficult to measure, substantiate, or to apply in any meaningful fashion.

- **Seeing the entire picture**   Some TCO models treat costs as primarily acquisition costs, creating new classes of devices which transfer the acquisition cost to the network, to development, and to other cost areas.

In the absence of a measurable, customizable model for identifying and managing costs, predictable problems include:

- High costs are recognized but there are no plans for dealing with costs.

- High costs are suspected but there are no benchmarks for determining cost levels or making comparisons.

- A change to distributed computing has added flexibility but the resulting variety of platforms requiring support is hindering the ability to deliver cost-effective, flexible solutions.

- A move to less expensive equipment is matched by increasing costs of complexity.

- New technologies are being evaluated with total costs in mind but no firm knowledge of costs relative to the decision can be determined until after the technology has been deployed.

Collaboratively developed with Interpose—experts in TCO analysis—Microsoft's Solutions Framework Total Cost of Ownership model views costs as a continual process of ongoing improvement with three key stages: planning, building, and managing. The TCO model is useful in developing business cases and priorities for infrastructure projects in several areas, including:

- The planning phase uses the TCO model to calculate benchmarks, cost baselines, return on investment (ROI), and validation. The benchmark is a determination of total costs on the basis of industry average costs, while the baseline report accounts for the actual costs of acquiring, managing, and retiring network-based technology assets.

- The building phase calculates return on investment by simulating the impact of recommended improvement projects and cost savings over time on the basis of a specific migration/deployment strategy.

- The managing phase is used to validate the TCO optimization strategy by measuring actual results against the objectives and projections.

Using the lifecycle approach optimizes cost model elements including:

- Development covers code and content development.

- Downtime/Other categories account for planned and unplanned downtime as well as applications development and testing.

- End-user costs cover cooperative end-user training, peer support, and miscellaneous desktop support.

- Hardware and software includes desktop hardware and software, servers, routers, bridges, and upgrades.

- Management includes networks, systems, and data management.

- Support comprises maintenance, disaster recovery, help desk, administration, and user training.

- Telecommunications Fees include costs for leased lines and other communications expenses.

It is important to realize that the majority of costs are not covered in the acquisition of hardware and software but rather in the labor necessary to develop, support, and maintain IT infrastructures. Optimizing development, support, and maintenance costs requires a combination of good business practices, skilled IT resources, and the best use of technology.

Common shortcomings in today's technologies include organizations that fail to take advantage of system policies, logon scripts, and user profiles—problems which can only be overcome through education. Other useful best practices include well-defined asset management procedures, standard common operating environments, and training.

The Total Cost of Ownership model offers a comprehensive strategy built around improvements to the people, process, and technology elements of the business enterprise. The objective is to make all aspects of the enterprise's IT infrastructure processes—including network operations, network and data management, administration, help desk—as self-sufficient as possible with the goal of lowering user dependence on IT infrastructure processes.

Summary

The Microsoft Solutions Framework is a methodology for optimizing development processes. Based on a collection of practices derived from customers, IT groups, development partners, and product developers internationally, the Solutions Framework offers a selection of strategies to guide development and deployment of projects.

The Solutions Framework is composed of seven models: Team, Process, Development/Application, Solutions Design, Enterprise Architecture, Infrastructure, and Total Cost of Ownership. These models are intended to be used in varying combinations as required by different project types.

The Team model is directed at creating motivated, high-performance development teams with the appropriate expertise for the project and by empowering team members as well as making them accountable for results.

The Process model is directed toward judging and assessing development tradeoffs while balancing process management between the chaos produced by too little management and the stifling straightjacket of micro-management.

The Development/Application model provides guides for flexibility in the design process by viewing applications as services distributed across both physical and functional boundaries. The Development/Application model defines the three categories of applications services as User, Business, and Data services.

The Solutions Design model is used by developers to anticipate user requirements and needs by involving users in the design and development processes to create business-oriented solutions driven by specific business needs. The Solutions Design model relies on three perspectives: Conceptual, Logical, and Physical design.

The Enterprise Architecture model offers structures and guides for business integration, seeking to provide supporting infrastructures according to business growth and changing technological needs. The Enterprise Architecture model depends on four architectures: Application, Business, Information, and Technology.

The Infrastructure model is employed in guiding systems deployment in a computing infrastructure which is defined as the complete set of resources necessary to support the enterprise computing environment.

Finally, the Total Cost of Ownership (TCO) model offers methods to identify and contain costs in technology investments while balancing costs against values.

Strictly speaking, the Microsoft Solutions Framework is not a product: It would be better classified as both a service and a methodology. As a service, the Microsoft Solutions Framework offers MSF experts to assist developers in planning development, testing, and deployment efforts.

Review Questions

1. The Total Cost of Ownership model weighs costs based on which of the following? (Select all that apply.)

   A. Cost versus value

   B. Current interest rates

   C. International exchange rates

   D. Return on investment (ROI) rates

2. The Vericard Corporation provides credit card validation for Internet sales orders, employing Microsoft Transaction Server to provide credit card validation objects. The credit card validation object belongs to which component of the Microsoft Solutions Framework (MSF) Application Model?

   A. Active Servers

   B. Business Services

   C. Interface Services

   D. ODBC Services

3. Cost baselines in the TCO model account for which of the following? (Select all that apply.)

   A. Costs as reported in industry averages

   B. Costs of acquiring technological assets

   C. Costs of managing and maintaining technological assets

   D. Costs of retiring technological assets

4. The Team model aims to ensure that an effective team consists of members who:

    A. Are accountable for results in the areas each own

    B. Are empowered to use their expertise

    C. Are exam-certified professionals

    D. Possess the appropriate expertise for the project

5. The managing phase in the TCO model is used to:

    A. Control expenses during implementation of the model processes

    B. Develop alternative strategies for maximizing return on investment (ROI)

    C. Treat costs as primary acquisition expenses

    D. Validate the optimization strategy by measuring actual results against projections

6. The Solutions Framework Infrastructure model is used to:

    A. Anticipate user requirements

    B. Assess development tradeoffs

    C. Guide systems deployment

    D. Support infrastructures according to business growth requirements

7. Major milestones defined by the Microsoft Solutions Framework (MSF) include which of the following? (Select all that apply.)

    A. Application Design

    B. Code Complete

    C. Project Analysis

    D. Project Definition

8. The Solutions Framework defines an infrastructure as:

A. Personnel and services performed.

B. The physical elements forming a network.

C. The software elements appropriate to a computing environment

D. The total set of resources necessary to support the enterprise computing environment

9. The Infrastructure model applies the roles, functions, and expectations of which model or models to the requirements of rolling out a successful infrastructure?

A. The Enterprise Architecture model

B. The Process and Development/Application models

C. The Process and Team models

D. The Solution Design and Development/Application models

10. The Microsoft Solutions Framework (MSF) consists of which three major models?

A. The Process model, System Development Life Cycle (SDLC) model, and Team model

B. The Team model, Client/Server model, and Application model

C. The Team model, Process model, and Development/Application model

D. The Team model, System Development Life Cycle (SDLC) model, and Application model

11. The Microsoft Solutions Framework assigns responsibility for ensuring that the functional specifications for a project fit the requirements of the business to the:

A. Development Manager

B. Product Manager

C. Program Manager

D. Project Manager

12. The Enterprise Architecture model is based on managing a technology infrastructure by encompassing which four perspectives?

  A. Application and Business

  B. Component and Services

  C. Information and Technology

  D. Infrastructure and Networking

13. The planning phase in the TCO model is used to calculate which of the following? (Select all that apply.)

  A. Cost baselines

  B. Cost benchmarks

  C. Return on investment (ROI) estimates

  D. The impact of improvement costs on return on investment (ROI)

14. What are the major milestones in the software development process (according to the Microsoft Solutions Framework)? (Select all that apply.)

  A. Code Complete

  B. Envisioning

  C. Planning

  D. Release of Product

15. Problems that occur between businesses and old and new technologies in the absence of regular improvements to the infrastructure include which of the following? (Select all that apply.)

  A. Companies are unable to compete against rivals who are investing in newer systems and applications.

  B. Continuing support for legacy systems makes it impossible to define new technical guidelines.

  C. IT professionals loose touch with industry vendors and lack familiarity with state-of-the-art developments.

  D. Technology changes faster than new corporate standards can be defined.

16. What are the perspectives used by the Solutions Design model? (Select all that apply.)

   A. Conceptual Design

   B. Industrial Design

   C. Logical Design

   D. Physical Design

17. The Solutions Design model involves users:

   A. In both the initial planning and final testing stages

   B. In study groups to determine user needs and expectations

   C. Only in the initial planning stages

   D. Throughout the design process

18. The Solutions Framework Process model is aimed at:

   A. Anticipating user needs

   B. Designing for flexibility

   C. Identifying and weighing development tradeoffs

   D. Producing customer-focused products or services

19. Information Architecture (in the Enterprise Architecture model) is concerned with which key questions? (Select all that apply.)

   A. Is the present market expanding or contracting?

   B. What functional data requirements exist?

   C. What industry requirements and standards exist?

   D. What integration issues exist with current application systems?

20. What are the reasons cited by development professionals for keeping users from being involved in the design process? (Select all that apply.)

   A. Users are frivolous and tend to make impractical suggestions.

   B. Users are reluctant to consider innovation and are not interested in being involved in the design process.

   C. Users become overly demanding and expect all requests to be immediately implemented.

   D. Users have divergent opinions about what features new applications should and shouldn't include.

21. Benefits offered by the Solutions Framework Team model include which of the following? (Select all that apply.)

   A. A team culture encouraging clarity, efficiency, participation, commitment, and mutual cooperation

   B. Centralized maintenance of application logic

   C. Producing customer-focused products or services

   D. Tight, compact application code with well developed features

22. What are the three categories of services which compose an application, as defined by the Solutions Framework Development/ Application model?

   A. Business services, including business rules, sequencing, and transaction integrity

   B. Data services, including data manipulation abstractions

   C. Internet services, including posting and HTML support

   D. User services, including the user interface and supporting logic

23. The Solutions Framework Process model is aimed at:

   A. Creating a higher quality product

   B. Directing development along profitable lines

   C. Improving developer morale

   D. Producing better design decisions

24. The Solutions Framework Process model departs from traditional development models in several fashions, including which of the following? (Select all that apply.)

    A. Directing development toward versioned releases

    B. Placing the emphasis on product Vision and Scope rather than requirements

    C. Placing the emphasis on realizable milestones

    D. Using customer-oriented rather than development-oriented milestones

25. The Team model is structured around clearly defined roles which include which of the following? (Select all that apply.)

    A. Design and Cost Containment

    B. Development and Logistics

    C. Product Management and Testing

    D. Program Management and User Education

26. Select the Microsoft Solutions Framework (MSF) Application Model component which resides between User Services and Data Services.

    A. Active Servers

    B. Business Services

    C. Interface Services

    D. ODBC Services

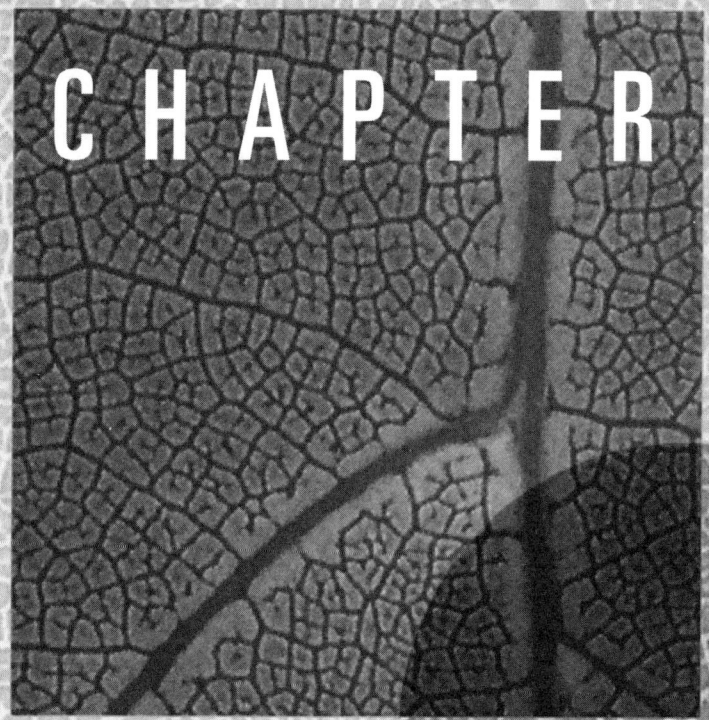

CHAPTER

6

Source Control as a
Development Methodology

Microsoft Exam Objectives Covered in This Chapter:

- Identify strategies for using source-code control to help manage the development process in a given development environment.

A century or more ago, back when Ford, Olds, and others were inventing automobiles in their barns or workshops, a development project involving one or two workers was perfectly normal. Today, of course, a new automotive design involves hundreds—if not thousands—of engineers.

Computer programming has followed this same pattern. A decade or two ago, quite sophisticated applications were put together by single individuals or, at most, by small groups of two or three people. Today, applications are designed and developed by teams consisting of anywhere from a half-dozen to hundreds of people.

However, as the size of development teams increases, the problems involved in tracking and coordinating development increase in direct proportion—or, perhaps, logarithmically.

One of the biggest problems is simply ensuring that everyone has the current version of all relevant source files and libraries, and, of course, that changes made in the course of a day's work do become part of the combined effort and are not lost by being accidentally overwritten. Rather obviously, one of the most important tools in contemporary team development is some form of source-code control. But simply having facilities for source-code control is only one part of the problem, because knowing how to use source-code control is every bit as important as having the facilities.

Microsoft ✓ ***Exam*** ***Objective***

Identify strategies for using source-code control to help manage the development process in a given development environment.

One strategy for managing source control for complex development projects is to use some form of source control software, such as Microsoft Visual SourceSafe.

Source Control Operations

Source control is a generic term for tools used to manage files in a multi-developer environment. In general, source control tools are analogous to a library, with the source control tool functioning as a central repository of files (which may be images, source code, documents, etc.) that is accessible to all developers. The library analogy only goes so far, however, because where library patrons are able to check out books, source control tools allow users two quite different types of access to stored files.

In one type of operation, individual developers may request copies of whichever project files they need at any time for development. These files are delivered to the working directories on the developer's system (or to other locations if specified) but cannot be returned to the source safe. In Visual SourceSafe, this would be a *Get* operation and the delivered files would automatically be marked *Read Only*.

The second type of operation delivers one or more files to the developer in a *Check Out* operation. This means that the developer is assuming ownership of the files so that they can be modified, edited, revised, or extended.

When the modified files are checked back in—returned to the source control repository—the revisions then become available to all developers. As a general rule, developers will ask for copies of all files belonging to a project, or all files affecting the portion of the project they are working on, using a Get operation. They will then Check Out only those files they actually need to work on. Also unlike the library analogy, a good source control repository maintains an incremental record of changes made to individual files, allowing developers to view changes and, if necessary, to revert to earlier versions.

Typical Features

Given the basic features—access to files, control over changes, and a record of changes—source control repositories become a powerful tool in project management. In virtually all cases, however, source control tools provide much more than these simple basics. Typical features found in source control tools are discussed below.

Check In/Check Out

Working files are checked in to the source control repository and then checked out by developers to their local computers for work and modification. In general, once a source file has been checked out by one party, others can get copies of the file but can not check out the file (i.e., can not assume ownership nor modify the stored copy).

Once the file owner is finished modifying a file, changes are preserved by uploading or checking in the file to the central repository. Commonly, as a part of the Check In process, developers are prompted to enter comments about changes made to the file.

Updates can also be made without checking in a file (or files) in order to allow others to synchronize their file copies while the developer continues working with the file (or files). Functionally, this is the same as a Check In operation except that the ownership of the checked-out file does not change.

Shadow Folders

A shadow folder is a directory where a separate copy of all up-to-date project files are stored outside of the SourceSafe repository. The project files in the shadow folder can be used when access is required to the most recent versions of the project files without accessing the master copy.

Obviously, of course, files from the shadow folder can not be used for development but do provide a ready reference. Files in the shadow folder should be maintained as read-only.

Branching

Branching is used when a new project version (a version branch) is initiated while the original project is left intact. Branching produces two separate projects; the original, and a new project, which begins with the source files of the original.

Once a project has branched, both project versions can be developed simultaneously. For example, the original project could be undergoing a debug revision to produce minor bug fixes at the same time the branched project is undergoing development as a new product version.

Merging

In order for multiple developers to work concurrently on the same file, source control systems may allow multiple developers to check out the file at the same time. Commonly, this is only permitted for text source files (i.e., ASCII text files).

Normally, merging is only supported for ASCII text files, since merging changes in binary (non-ASCII, non-text) files would require a custom engine for each file type.

After another developer has made changes to a file and checked their copy of the file back in, on request, the source control system can integrate the changes into other copies which are already checked out by other developers.

Before a source control system can check out a file concurrently to separate developers, options for simultaneous usage must be enabled. For details, refer to the documentation for the specific source control software.

Merging, like branching, can also be used to reconcile changes made for bug fixes with the new version source files. Where merely overwriting the original files on the new version with the fixed files from the original would also overwrite changes made since the versions branched, merging can incorporate the bug fix changes without disturbing the code revisions for the later version.

Project Control

Developers use project control features to organize repository files into projects and subprojects (or other work-specific categories). Commonly, files can also be shared between projects.

A file shared between projects maintains only one copy of the file, and changes made to the file affect all projects using the file.

Change Tracking

Change tracking is a feature supported by most source control systems to preserve a record of incremental changes made to individual files each time the file is checked in to the repository. With change tracking, developers can reconstruct earlier file versions. This is an important service, as it makes it possible to recover earlier work or, occasionally, to discard undesirable changes which have been made.

Difference Checking

Difference checking goes hand-in-glove with change tracking, and is a feature supported by most source control software to allow developers to compare file versions and to review differences between two files.

Files saved in proprietary formats—such as Microsoft Word documents or Microsoft Excel spreadsheets—are treated as binary files. SourceSafe will report when these files are different, but will not show the differences in detail.

History

File history is also a common feature, allowing developers to examine the check-in history for each file, showing when each version was checked in, by whom, and the comments recorded by the developers.

File version comments—which most source control software supports— are a valuable resource and their use should be mandatory in any well-organized development environment. Even brief comments concerning changes made to source files can be invaluable in tracking changes and in providing a history of the development process.

All of the features listed here, of course, are supported by Microsoft's Visual SourceSafe.

Team Development Processes/Advantages

Team development offers a number of advantages over the individual developer. Using teams, more complex applications can be created in less time and the skills of different developers can be combined to create applications, which would be difficult or impossible for single developers.

The down side of team development, however, is that it does require some additional effort in assigning and coordinating tasks. A successful team development is dependent on:

- Multiple developers being able to access project, database, and source files

- Coordinating and synchronizing changes to project source files such that all developers have access to work on project files done by others and, at the same time, ensuring that changes made by one developer do not overwrite work done by another

- Developers being able to enhance existing application elements (i.e., resources, programs, class libraries) without interfering with efforts by other developers who are using the same elements

For an example, imagine a project which will involve developing five principal elements:

- Data entry forms

- Business rules

- Reports

- Graphs and charts

- Database and records

For our hypothetical project, either Visual FoxPro or Access would be an appropriate development platform. Certainly either program offers a full set of development tools appropriate to the task. However, since this particular project needs to be created in a relatively short time, the reasonable approach is to assign each of these project elements to a different developer, maximizing the division of labor and team effort.

Of course, doing so will involve giving multiple developers access to different components, but will also involve all developers sharing access to many of the program elements. At the same time, means are necessary to ensure that only one engineer at a time is working on any individual element and that changes made by one developer do not overwrite the work done by another.

In addition, developers need to be able to code, test, and debug the forms or processes they are working on without interfering with other developers who are working on other elements. Once a particular form, process, or element is completed or when any significant enhancement is completed, however, the element needs to be integrated in the full application and made available to the other developers.

This, of course, is precisely where a source control system—a source code repository—becomes the essential tool for coordinating development tasks.

Introduction to Visual SourceSafe

SourceSafe is a file repository which stores project source files, tracks differences between file versions, and allows developers access to either current or previous version of the source files. In effect, SourceSafe provides a historical archive for files during development, as well as a central repository making it possible for multiple developers to remain synchronized on large projects. In this chapter, we will discuss strategies for successful team development using Visual SourceSafe together with Visual FoxPro and Visual C++ as language examples.

Note, however, that Visual SourceSafe is not limited to just these languages, but can be used with all types of files, development languages, and document types. As an example, the working files used in preparing this book have been saved in SourceSafe and include a wide variety of file types ranging from Microsoft Word document files, to .TIF image files, to FlowCharter diagram files. Figure 6.1 shows Visual SourceSafe with the files contained in the MCSD project.

FIGURE 6.1

Visual SourceSafe with mixed files

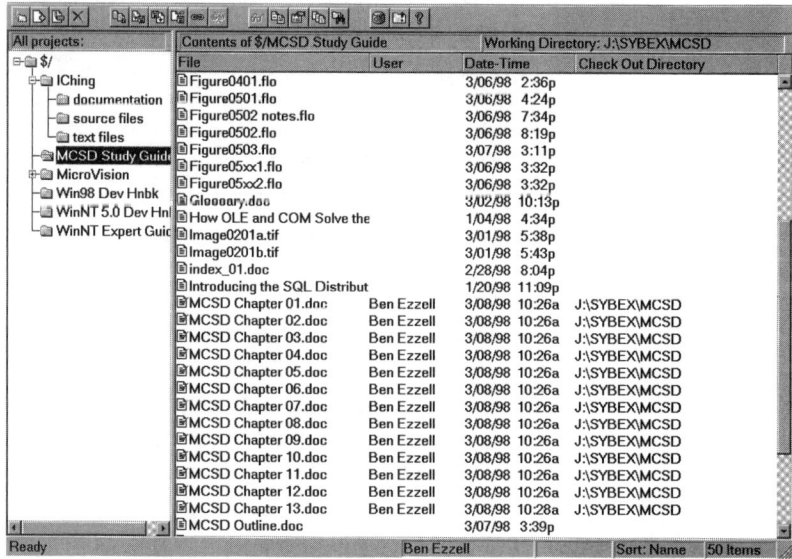

Notice particularly that in the example, Visual SourceSafe contains several projects (left pane) and that these are arranged as directories and subdirectories shown in the familiar tree format.

In the right pane, the contents of the selected project (or subproject) are shown in a columnar format as follows:

- **Filename**   Gives the name and file type extension while the icons to the left of each filename offer graphic cues to the file status. Typical status icons are shown below (exact icons and status flags may vary with different versions of SourceSafe):

   File exists in current project only.

   File exists in (is shared by) two or more projects (only one copy of the file is kept but the single copy is used by multiple projects).

   File is checked out.

   File is checked out by two or more persons.

   File is pinned to a specific version.

The single and multiple checked-out status marks may be combined with any of the other status symbols.

- **User**   If a file has been checked out, identifies the person who has control of the file.

- **Date/Time**   Time and date when the file was last modified – *or* – the time and date the file was checked out from SourceSafe.

- **Check Out Directory**   Directory where checked-out files are located. On a network system, the drive/directory will be prefaced with the workstation name.

Above the Files pane, the selected project is shown to the left with the working directory for the project shown to the right.

Installing Visual SourceSafe

When Visual SourceSafe is installed—either on a network or on a local system—the installation consists of two components: the Visual SourceSafe Explorer interface and the Visual SourceSafe database, which holds the project files, version information, and notes.

Visual SourceSafe can be installed in any of three configurations:

- **Local**   SourceSafe is installed on a local computer with both the interface and database on the same system. This is essentially a single-user configuration and makes limited use of SourceSafe's version control features.

- **Network**   SourceSafe is installed on a network server with the Visual SourceSafe Explorer executed remotely, from the server. This configuration may, however, limit performance since all users must rely on a single copy of the SourceSafe Explorer executing across the net.

- **Distributed**   SourceSafe is installed on a network server supporting the database and an administrative installation of the Visual SourceSafe Explorer while Visual SourceSafe executables (interface components) are installed on all workstations. Because each user has their own copy of the Visual SourceSafe Explorer, performance is not limited, but all users are sharing a single SourceSafe database, maximizing SourceSafe's version control facilities.

Commonly, the administrator will setup Visual SourceSafe in the Network configuration. If, however, network performance becomes a problem, the Client Visual SourceSafe setup will copy the SourceSafe executables from the network server to local computer, requiring 2 megabytes of storage space on each system.

The Client Visual SourceSafe setup is a button option appearing when the SETUP.EXE program is executed. However, this option appears only when installation is performed on a network, but not on a local installation.

Using Visual SourceSafe

On one level, using Visual SourceSafe is very simple; on a second level, using SourceSafe can be as complex and complicated as your project requirements dictate. While detailed instructions for operating Visual SourceSafe—including coverage for many of the advanced features—are included in SourceSafe's online documentation, an overview of the process will be relevant to later discussions. Therefore, we will begin with the simple uses if only because the basics are relevant to any project. Figure 6.2 illustrates the six principal steps using Visual SourceSafe while developing a project.

FIGURE 6.2

Using Visual Source-Safe during project development

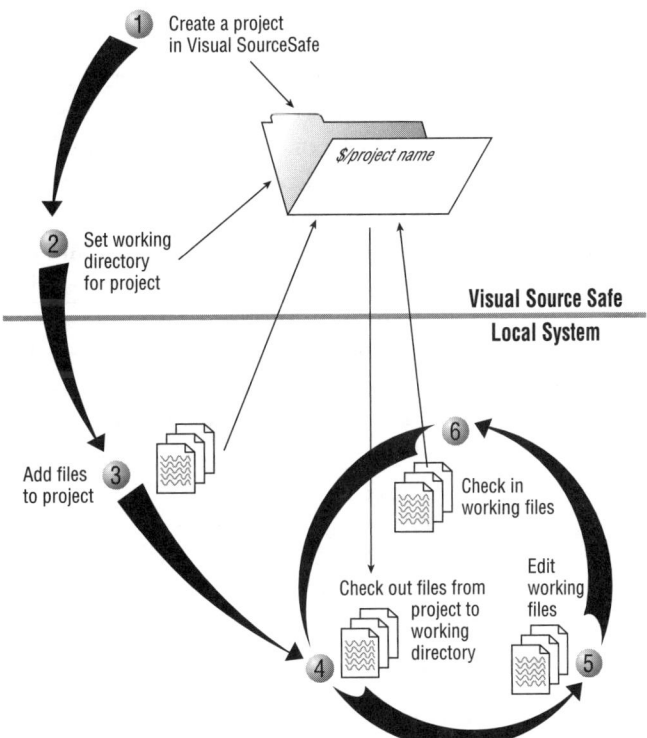

First Step

The first step in any development process using SourceSafe—assuming, of course, that you have already installed the software—is to create a project in Visual SourceSafe. SourceSafe is arrange very much like a disk drive with a root directory ($\) where projects can be created as subdirectories. Of course, within a project directory, further subdirectories can also be created just as on a file system.

For example, for a project we'll call MicroMech, we might want to start by creating subprojects (subdirectories) with these titles: Source Files, Libraries, Documentation, and Project Design, using each of these to store different files associated with this project.

Second Step

After creating a project directory, a working directory for the project needs to be assigned. For example, as shown in Figure 6.1, the MCSD Study Guide project has a default working directory specified as J:\Sybex\MCSD.

The restriction here—on a network system—is that everyone has to have the same working directory on their local systems. Since different physical systems may have different drive and partition setups, one way of assuring a uniform drive on all workstations is to create an alias drive.

For example, on one recent project where some developers were local and on the office LAN and others used remote access (dial-in), no two physical systems were the same. Some had only one or two drives/partitions and others had multiple drives/partitions. The solution was to create a directory on each machine—on whichever logical drive was desired or had free space—and then to alias the directory as drive P:.

In SourceSafe, the working directories for projects and subprojects became P:\MicroMech\Source Files, P:\MicroMech\Libraries, etc. And, on the individual workstations, the \MicroMech\... directories became subdirectories under the phantom P:\ drive—i.e., subdirectories under the directory assigned to the project.

As far as SourceSafe was concerned, each machine connecting to retrieve files had a physical (virtual) drive identified as P:\ , and it did not need to know further.

Third Step

Before files can be checked out from SourceSafe, some files need to be checked in. These may be skeletal project files or design documents, but the point is that SourceSafe can not originate document files. These files must always be created outside of SourceSafe and checked in for the first time.

Obviously, step 3 will be repeated many, many times in the course of a project as new files are created and added to the project archives.

Fourth Step

Files must be checked out of SourceSafe to the working directory on a workstation before they can be modified, edited, expanded, or otherwise developed.

In general, we will use the Get function to get copies (without checking them out) for all project files or, at least, for all files we will need during our current development efforts.

WARNING Files that are retrieved from the archive but not checked out will be flagged with read-only status. While the file status flag can be changed, modifications to files that have not been checked out cannot be written back to the SourceSafe archive.

After selecting a project (from the All Projects pane), we can select the Tools ➢ Show Differences option to find out which files in the project no longer correspond to our local copies. Once we've identified changed files (see Figure 6.3) we can select only those files which need to be updated rather than wasting time—especially if we're using dial-up access—copying all project files.

FIGURE 6.3

Identifying differences between project and local files

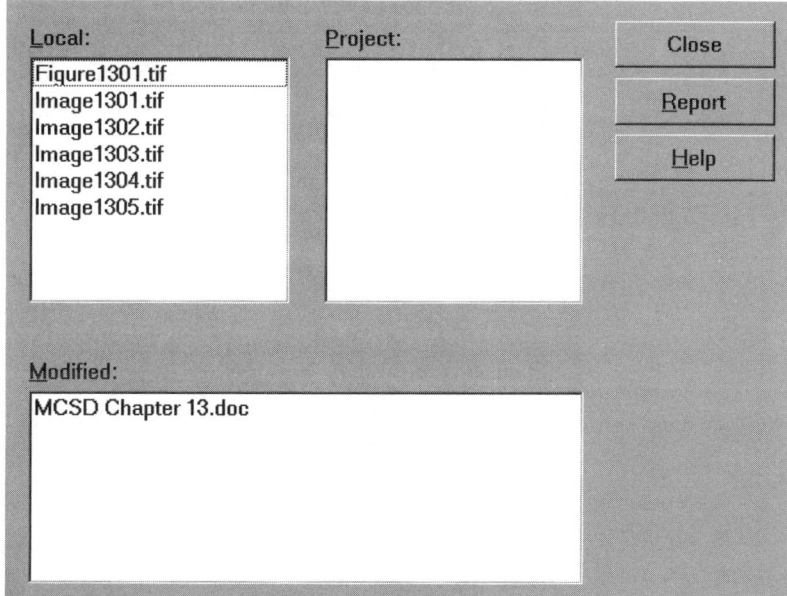

In Figure 6.3, the only differences identified are six files in the Local list (upper left), which have not been added to the project's archive, and one file in the Modified list (bottom), which is different from the version found in SourceSafe. Any files that had been added to the project archive but that were not on the local drive would have appeared in the Project list (upper right).

Once we've updated our local project, any files that we need to modify—assuming, of course, that we intend to save the modifications—need to be checked out at this point.

Fifth Step

Now that our local project copy has been updated, the next step is to compile and test, modify, edit, or in some fashion work on one or more of the files from the project. Of course, we could simply be retrieving documents for printing or something similar but, as a programmer/engineer, my usual purpose in retrieving project files involves either testing or programming.

Sixth Step

Once project files have been modified, the files need to be checked in again so that the revisions can be shared with other developers. As the updates are added to the SourceSafe repository, comments should also be included, however brief, to provide a record of project modifications. For convenience, several files can be updated at the same time, applying a single comment to all.

Once the files have been checked in, if you wish to continue work on the same files, they should be checked out again (Fourth Step). Alternately, you can simply check the Keep checked out option during the update. This will update the archive but the files will remain checked out and the local files will not be marked read-only.

Development Cycles

Typically, developers will check in or update working files once per day or, sometimes, twice daily to allow other team members access to changes and modifications. Most often, the practice is to update or check in working files as the last task before leaving work. By checking in working files—and then checking files out as necessary the next day—not only are all team members able to access the latest files at regular intervals, but also unexpected illnesses or accidents will not prevent others from being able to take over and fill in during absences.

Because workstations are normally password protected, the checked out versions of project files are essentially inaccessible if not checked in at regular intervals. While files can be unchecked out, if necessary, by someone with administrative privileges, this action only frees the versions currently in the archive but does not recover modifications from the workstation files.

Accountability

One further advantage of using source-file archiving such as Visual Source-Safe is that it is very easy to find out who is working on which file(s) at any time since the User list shows immediately who has ownership of each file, while the Check Out Directory list—on a network installation—shows which workstation the file is located on.

This makes the task of finding out who and where convenient; without these aides, this would be virtually impossible to accomplish.

Visual SourceSafe Operations

Visual SourceSafe is not merely a repository for information but provides a variety of services for managing version control. The simplest and most obvious services are being able to add files, to get files, and to remove files from the repository. Other—less obvious but useful—services include viewing file (version) histories, retrieving specific file versions from SourceSafe, and viewing differences between file versions.

Adding Files to SourceSafe

To add files to the Visual SourceSafe repository, it is necessary to specify a drive, directory, and filename. The file is then copied to the selected Visual SourceSafe project. Exercise 6.1 details the steps involved.

EXERCISE 6.1

To Add a File to Visual SourceSafe

1. From the File menu, select Add Files to display the Add Files dialog box.

2. Use the Drives list box to select the drive where the file is located.

3. Use the Directories list box to select the desired directory.

4. Optionally, use the List Files of Type list box to select a file type and to filter the list of files to a more manageable list.

5. Files which are already in the repository will not be displayed in the File Name list box.

6. Select a file (or files) from the File Name list box.

Multiple files are selected by holding the Ctrl key while clicking the filenames desired. Blocks of files can be selected by selecting the first file, then holding the Shift key while selecting the last file in the block.

7. Click Add Files to incorporate these files in the Visual SourceSafe repository.

8. When files are added, Visual SourceSafe displays a dialog box where a comment can be entered. To have the comment applied to all selected files, check the Use For All check box. Otherwise, the comment dialog box will be repeated for each file selected.

9. Click the OK button to add the files with a comment or click Cancel to exit the Add Files operation. When Visual SourceSafe returns to the Add File dialog box, select Close.

Exercise 6.2 outlines the steps for adding a directory.

To Add a Directory to Visual SourceSafe

1. Select a project in Visual SourceSafe where the directory will be added as a subproject.

To create a new project in Visual SourceSafe, select the $\ (root) project.

2. Select a directory from the Directory list box in the Add Files dialog box.

3. Click the Add button, the Comment dialog box will appear.

4. Enter a comment and proceed as before.

Subdirectories and the files included in the subdirectories can be added recursively by selecting the Recursive checkbox.

Exercise 6.3 will take you through using drag-and-drop operations in SourceSafe.

To Add Files Using Drag and Drop

1. Open and display both Visual SourceSafe Explorer and Windows Explorer (or any other file/directory utility supporting drag and drop).

2. Select a target project in Visual SourceSafe.

3. Select one or more files or folders from Windows Explorer and drag and drop the selection in the Visual SourceSafe Explorer window.

Files are added to the current Visual SourceSafe project while directories are added as subprojects of the current project.

Checking In Files to SourceSafe

Adding files to Visual SourceSafe and checking in files to Visual SourceSafe are not precisely the same, since checking in implies that files have been checked out from the repository, a topic which is discussed below.

Checking in a file to the repository means updating an existing file by creating a new version of the file.

After editing a file (or files) in your working directory, the Check-In operation is used to return the revised file(s) to the Visual SourceSafe project. Figure 6.4 shows the process of checking in several files, and Exercise 6.4 details the steps.

FIGURE 6.4

Checking in files in Visual SourceSafe

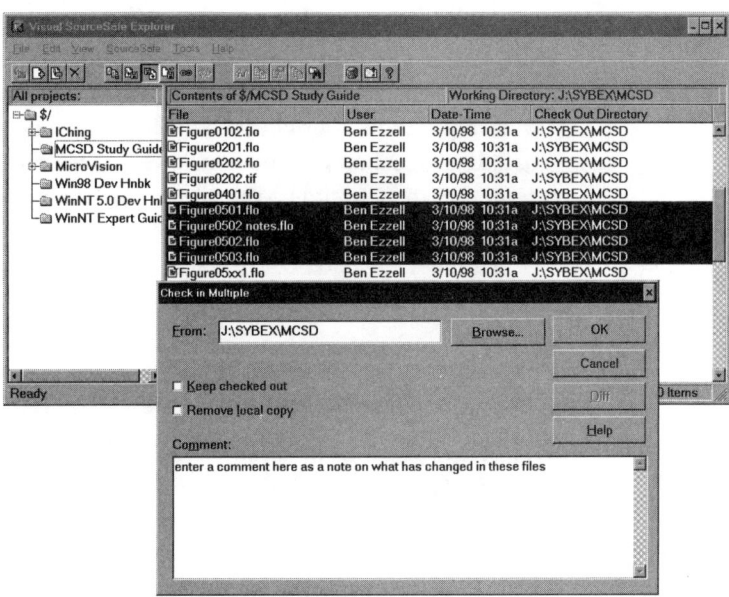

EXERCISE 6.4

To Check In Files to Visual SourceSafe

1. Select the file(s) from the Files pane in Visual SourceSafe Explorer.

2. Select Check In from the SourceSave menu.

3. The Check In dialog box shown in Figure 6.4 appears containing a number of options.

   - **Keep checked out**   The file(s) are checked in (updated) but kept checked out as well so that the user can continue working after saving the changes.

   - **Remove local copy**   The local copy (or copies) is removed from the working directory after the check in is complete. By default, Visual SourceSafe leaves a read-only copy of the file(s) in the working directory after the file(s) is checked in.

   - **Diff**   Displays the differences between the file presently being checked in and the file version which was checked out. This option is disabled if more than one file is selected. (Refer to the "Differencing Files in SourceSafe" section.)

   - **Browse**   Browses directories in search of other checked out files.

4. Enter a comment to record the type of changes made to the file(s).

5. Click OK to complete the operation.

In Figure 6.4, four checked out files have been selected in Visual SourceSafe Explorer before choosing Check In from the SourceSafe menu. In response, the Check in Multiple dialog box appears as shown and the Diff button is disabled.

If a single file had been selected, the dialog box would appear as Check In, followed by the name of the selected file and the Diff button would be enabled.

Getting and Checking Out Files from SourceSafe

To retrieve files from Visual SourceSafe, two different operations are supported: Get and Check Out.

To get a source file simply creates or updates a local copy of the file in the designated working directory, marking the file as read-only.

To check out a file also creates or updates a local copy but, in addition, marks the local file copy as read/write, marks the SourceSafe copy as checked out, and shows who has taken ownership of the file and when.

Files that are already checked out can not be checked out a second time nor to a second user.

To get or check out a file or files:

1. Select the file(s) in the Files pane.

2. Select the SourceSafe menu.

3. Select either Get or Check Out.

The selected file(s) are copied to the working directory on the local machine and marked appropriately.

If a file (or files) is *pinned* to a specific version, the file(s) cannot be checked out for revision. Pinned files, however, can be shared with another project, and the shared version will not be pinned, nor will changes made to the shared file in the other (shared) project affect the current project's file.

Getting or Checking Out Projects   An entire project can be retrieved from SourceSafe by selecting the project or subproject in the Project pane. To 'get' or 'check out' a project or subproject:

1. Select the project or subproject(s) in the Project pane.

2. Select the SourceSafe menu.

3. Select either Get or Check Out.

The selected project(s) are copied to the working directory on the local machine, creating subdirectories as required and marking the files appropriately.

Use the Uncheck Out option to cancel checked out files without updating the repository.

Removing Files from SourceSafe

Files or projects can be removed from Visual SourceSafe. When a file or project is removed, the file or project may be recoverable or may be permanently removed.

The Add Access right is required before this command can be used.

To remove a file or project:

1. Select the file(s) in the Files pane or the project in the Projects pane.

2. Select the File menu.

3. Select the Delete option.

The Delete dialog box appears in Figure 6.5.

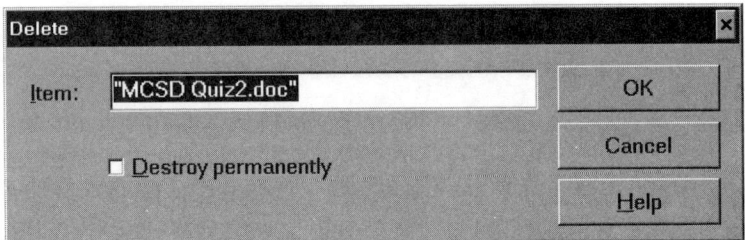

The Destroy Permanently checkbox in the Delete dialog box removes the selected file(s) or project permanently and unrecoverably. If the Destroy Permanently checkbox is not selected, the deleted file(s) or project remain in the repository and can be recovered later using the Recover command.

Destroy access rights are required before the Destroy Permanently checkbox can be selected.

A deleted subproject or file(s) that has not been permanently removed can later be permanently destroyed using the Purge command.

To recover the file, use the Recover command. Another way to retrieve the file (if it hasn't been purged or destroyed) is to return to an earlier version of the project that contains the file.

The Destroy Permanently option should be used with caution.

Viewing and Retrieving File Versions (Using Histories)

Visual SourceSafe tracks all changes made to files and projects. This includes file-level changes to lines added, deleted, or revised in specific files and project-level changes covering files and subprojects which are added, deleted, or renamed. Because of this tracking, Visual SourceSafe offers the ability to retrieve any version of a file or project.

To retrieve a specific version of a file or project:

1. Select the file or project in Visual SourceSafe Explorer.

2. From the Tools menu, select Show History.

3. Select the version desired from the History of File or History of Project dialog box (Figure 6.6).

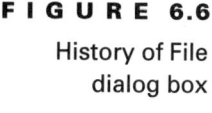

FIGURE 6.6

History of File dialog box

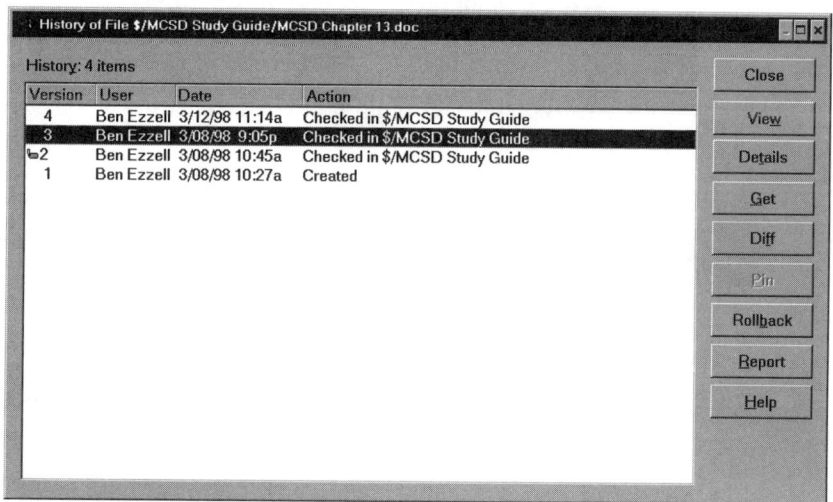

4. Select the option button for the operation desired: View or Get.

- The View option will open the selected file version for viewing, launching an application to display the file as necessary.

- The Get option will copy the selected file version to the working directory.

5. Click Close to finish.

The History dialog box offers several other options, including:

- Details displays comments associated with an event, along with more detailed event information, such as label information, version information, and check-out comments.

- Diff performs the Show Differences command on the selected file (see "Differencing Files in SourceSafe").

- Pin/Unpin performs the Pin or Unpin command on the selected file, toggling between Pin and Unpin depending on the state of the selected file.

- Rollback performs the Rollback command on the selected file or subproject, discarding all versions of a file subsequent to the selected version, returning the current version of the file to the selected version.

- Report sends a report to the Clipboard, a file, or a printer.

Versions   Visual SourceSafe offers two different types of version identification, both useful in different situations.

First, the internal version number is maintained automatically by SourceSafe. A version number is assigned to each version of each file and project. This version number is displayed in the History of File or History of Project dialog boxes.

The internal version number may skip a number occasionally, but is always an integer value.

Second and more useful are the user-defined labels. A label can be applied to any version of any file or project as a string up to 31 characters. Examples of user-defined labels might be: "version 1.2," "3.02b," "Beta Release 2," or "QA 2.03."

Users experienced in employing Visual SourceSafe often prefer user-defined labels applied at a project level over the internal version numbers. At the same time, it is unusual to label individual files.

Unlike many other source control applications, Visual SourceSafe uses labels to identify both projects and files versions within projects and also allows multiple labels to be applied even if the files have not changed.

In this fashion, the file MYSOURCE.CPP can be labeled Release 2.0 and then later, without the file having changed, also be labeled Release 2.5, indicating that the same version of the file belongs to both release versions of the project. In effect, each label creates a new version in Visual SourceSafe even though the two versions are identical.

In like fashion, entire projects can be assigned multiple labels even when the project contents remain unchanged. Exercise 6.5 goes over the steps involved.

EXERCISE 6.5

Labeling a Project or File Version

1. Select the project or files(s) in Visual SourceSafe Explorer.

2. Select Label from the File menu.

3. In the Label dialog box, enter a user-defined label in the Label field.

4. In the Comment field, an optional comment can also be included.

5. Click OK to close the dialog box.

Differencing Files in SourceSafe

The Show Differences feature in Visual SourceSafe provides a means to compare two file versions and to display the differences between them. Exercises 6.6 and 6.7 outline two means of comparison.

WARNING   The Diff command offers full comparisons only for ASCII-text files such as compiler source files. Other file types using proprietary formats, such as Word .DOC files, Excel .XLT files, or bitmap files, are all treated as binary files, and the Diff command will only report whether the files are identical or different.

EXERCISE 6.6

Comparing a SourceSafe File Version to the Working Version

1. Select the file to compare from the Visual SourceSafe Files pane.

2. Select History from the Tools menu.

EXERCISE 6.6 (CONTINUED)

3. Select the repository version for comparison from the History of dialog box list.
4. Select Diff to compare the selected version with the working version.

EXERCISE 6.7

Comparing Two SourceSafe File Versions

1. Select the file to compare from the Visual SourceSafe Files pane.
2. Select History from the Tools menu.
3. Select the first repository version for comparison from the History of File dialog box list.
4. Hold the Ctrl key while selecting the second repository file for comparison.
5. Select Diff to compare the two selected versions.

The two file versions will appear in a split window as shown in Figure 6.7.

FIGURE 6.7 Comparing two versions of a file

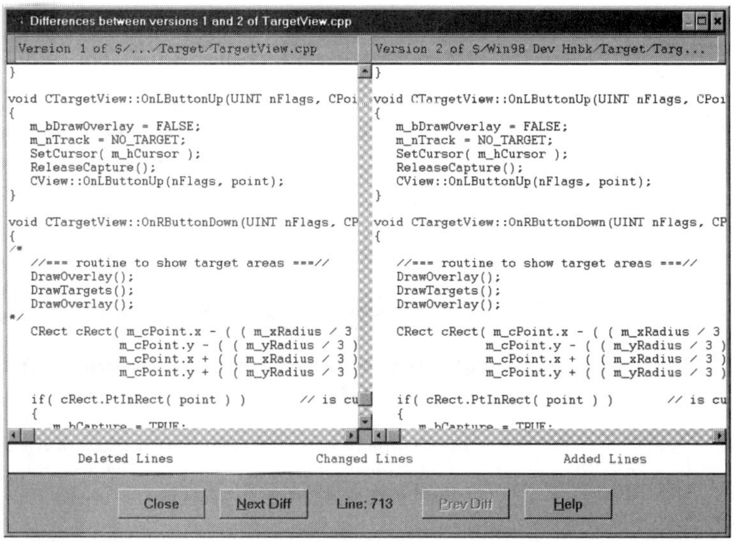

Figure 6.7 shows two versions of a .CPP source file being compared in which two lines in version 1 are different than version 2. Because the lines have been changed, in the version 1 pane these lines appear in red. Any lines of code in the version 1 pane which had been deleted—i.e., did not appear in version 2—would be displayed in green in version 1. Likewise, lines which had been added in version 2 would be displayed in blue in version 2.

The Next Diff and Prev Diff buttons can be used to step through the file differences or the scrollbar (between the two panes) can be used to scroll through both files simultaneously.

Integrating Visual SourceSafe

Visual SourceSafe is designed to work together with development tools using an integrated development environment (IDE) such as Visual Basic, Visual C++, or Visual FoxPro. For this purpose, however, the client setup must be run on the local computer to properly register Visual Source-Safe, and the client setup must be done after the administrative version of SourceSafe has been installed on the network server.

Alternately, a local installation can be performed—installing both the database and Explorer components—but setup must still be run a second time, using the Client button, to register the IDE correctly.

Once Visual SourceSafe is installed locally, it is also helpful to add Visual SourceSafe to the IDE for your development platform. While not absolutely essential, this step does make it convenient to call SourceSafe whenever there is a need to save or update source files to the repository or to get or check out files.

All developers on a project must use the same source code control software.

The following topics discuss methods for using Visual SourceSafe with several different development platforms: Visual C++, Visual FoxPro, Visual InterDev, and the Web. While some of this material is specific to particular development environments, the general principals discussed previously apply to all types of development platforms and projects.

Source Control for Visual C++

To add Visual SourceSafe to the Tools menu in the Visual C++ integrated development environment, follow these steps:

1. Open Visual C++.

2. Select the Tool/Customize option from the menu.

3. Select the Tools tab, shown in Figure 6.8, from the Customize dialog box.

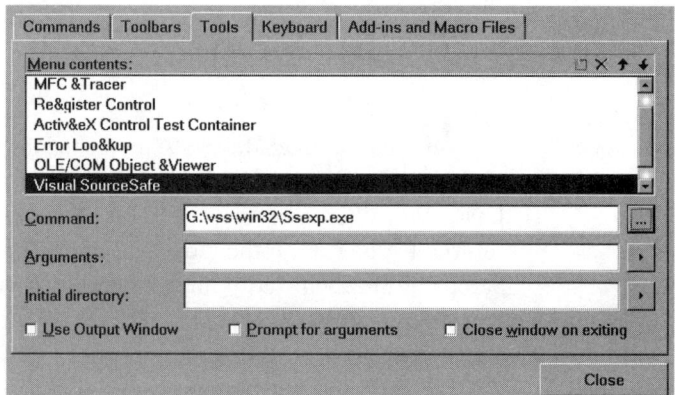

4. Scroll down the Menu contents list box to select the blank entry at the end. The Command, Arguments, and Initial directory edit boxes will be grayed and unavailable.

5. Double-click the blank entry, then enter the application name—Visual SourceSafe (or any other source control application)—and press Enter.

6. In the Command edit box, enter the full drive/path/filename for Visual SourceSafe, or click the browse button at the right and select the SSEXP.EXE (or other executable) from the directory browser.

7. Click Close when finished.

The Arguments field is not needed since Visual SourceSafe does not require any command line arguments when called.

The Initial directory edit field is also unnecessary since VSS has its own default directory information for each project and, in any case, will not recognize a working directory setting.

Likewise, the three check options—Use Output Window, Prompt for arguments, and Close window on exiting—do not apply when calling Visual SourceSafe.

Other commercially available source control packages or other tools such as PC-lint or Visual Intercept can be added to the Visual C++ Tools menu following this same procedure.

Once done, Visual SourceSafe will appear on the Visual C++ Tools menu as illustrated in Figure 6.9.

FIGURE 6.9

Visual SourceSafe appears on the Visual C++ Tools menu

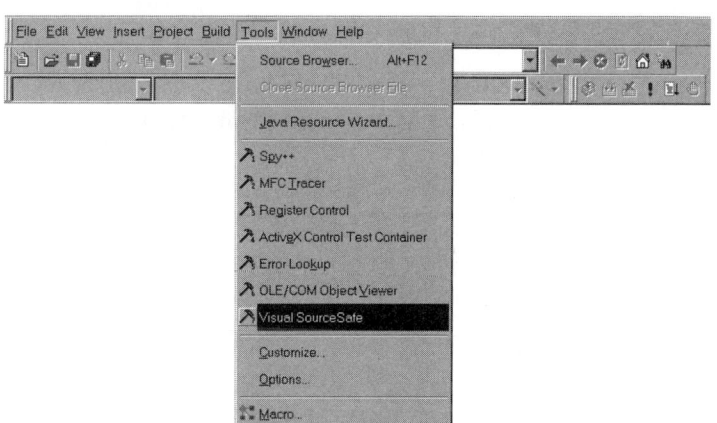

Even though Visual SourceSafe can be used with a variety of other development tools—including Microsoft Word—not all of these include convenient options for modifying their menus to add calls to external applications such as Visual SourceSafe.

Source Control for Visual Basic

To add Visual SourceSafe to the Visual Basic integrated development environment, use the following steps:

1. Open Visual Basic.

2. Select the Add-Ins menu, then select Add-In Manager from the menu.

3. Select Visual SourceSafe from the list in the Add-In Manager.

This installs Visual SourceSafe under the Tools menu in Visual Basic.

To run Visual SourceSafe together with Microsoft Visual Basic, you must perform the client setup to register Visual SourceSafe on your local computer.

Visual SourceSafe's check-in and check-out features can also be invoked by right-clicking a file in Visual Basic's Project box to manage files, forms, and .BAS modules.

Visual SourceSafe may also be called directly—as a standalone application—to manage Visual Basic files and projects.

Source Control for Visual FoxPro

Visual FoxPro offers source code control support by allowing commercially available source control software to be integrated directly into FoxPro projects.

Any of a variety of source control packages can be used, but do consult the vendors and ask if the software can be integrated with Microsoft development tools.

Source control in Visual FoxPro is managed through the Project Manager. When setting up a project in Visual FoxPro, an option is offered to create a corresponding source code control—a process which is referred to as "putting the project under source control."

Visual FoxPro manages source control in a much more integrated fashion than Visual C++ and, once the project is under source control, Visual FoxPro prompts the user to check out files for editing.

Visual FoxPro uses source control to manage files of all types, including .PRG, .SCX, .FRX, .LBX, .MNX, .VCX, and others. While individual files can be shared between different FoxPro projects, all source control operations are conducted on files within the context of a specific project.

Visual FoxPro does not prompt for data tables (.DBF or .DBC files) to be placed under source control when created. These can, however, be manually added to the source-controlled project.

When working in Visual FoxPro with a project under source control, the Project Manager displays icons similar to those discussed previously next to files under source control to identify their status.

Enabling Source Control for Visual FoxPro

Before source control can be enabled in Visual FoxPro, the source control program must be installed either locally or as a network installation with a client installation (see "Installing Visual SourceSafe," above).

Once the source control software is installed, options need to be set in Visual FoxPro so that the source control software will be recognized and so that defaults for projects will be specified.

1. To begin, select Options from the Tools menu in FoxPro.

2. From the Options dialog box, select the Projects tab.

3. Under Source control options, use the Active source control provider list to select the appropriate source control program.

4. Select Automatically add new projects to source control to have Visual FoxPro prompt to place new projects under source control.

When Visual FoxPro is opened, it will automatically check for a source control provider, allowing the user to manage projects under source control or to put projects under source control.

Managing FoxPro Projects under Source Control

Using source control software in Visual FoxPro requires:

- Putting projects under source control

- Adding files to source controlled projects

- Updating the project list for each project

Visual FoxPro maintains project information in a set of table and memo files with the .PJX and .PJT extensions. For example, on creating a project with the title "NewProj," all information about the project, including a list of files, file locations, and whether these are compiled to the application file (.APP or .EXE) is stored in the NEWPROJ.PJX and NEWPROJ.PJT files.

When working in a team environment, developers do not share common project files (.PJX and .PJT) but, instead, each have their own local copies of the project files.

To coordinate changes made by individual developers to source files in a project under source control, Visual FoxPro also maintains a project file list (.PJM, or project metafile). The project file list is contained in a text file that lists which files are currently included in the project. This is essentially the same information as that contained in the .PJX and .PJT files.

Synchronizing Development   The source control software also maintains a central project file list that is stored with the project files in the central repository, while each developer has a local (checked out) copy of the project file list that reflects their current version of the project.

For those accustomed to using source control on other development environments, the process described here is a divergence, but Visual FoxPro offers a much tighter integration of source code control than is typical of other environments.

These several copies of the project file list, however, will not remain identical and must be merged into the central project file list. For example, assume that one developer has added a new program file (.PRG) and has placed this file under source control. Visual FoxPro will update the local copy of the project and will show the new program file when the developer uses Project Manager. Other developers, however, will remain unaware of the addition and their local copies of the project will not show the added file.

Also, even though the project list has not been updated, the new program file can be checked in to the central repository for safekeeping and checked out again as needed.

Later, when the developer has finished with the program file, the project file list can be updated. When this is done, Visual FoxPro merges the information in the local project file list with the central project file list in the repository.

At the same time, Visual FoxPro updates the local project file list with changes made to the central project file list. Thus, assuming that other developers have added files to the project, the local project file list is updated and copies of the new files are written to the local computer before Visual FoxPro rebuilds the project (the .PJX and .PJT files).

The project file list only tracks those source files which have explicitly been placed under source control. If a project includes files which are not under source control, these files will not appear in the project file list and will not be updated to other developer's projects.

Managing FoxPro Multiple File Components

One of the benefits in Visual FoxPro's tight integration with source control utilities is found in project components which actually consist of multiple files, i.e., where a primary file and one or more implicit files are required for the component. For example, on creating a form, Visual FoxPro creates a primary .SCX file and an implicit .SCT file. Or, on creating a table, the primary file is a .DBF file accompanied by three implicit files identified by the extensions .FPT, .CDX, and .IDX.

Table 6.1 shows a list of Visual FoxPro components comprised of multiple files.

 **WARNING** When Visual FoxPro is used to generate or compile a menu, local .MPR and .MPX files are also created. These are not automatically placed under source control, but can be added to the project as files and then placed under source control just as would be done with any other file.

T A B L E 6.1
Visual FoxPro Components

Component	Primary file type	Implicit file type(s)
Class Library	.VCX	.VCT
Database	.DBC	.DCT, .DCX
Form	.SCX	.SCT
Label	.LBX	.LBT
Menu	.MNX	.MNT
Report	.FRX	.FRT
Table	.DBF	.FPT, .CDX, .IDX

Here, when a developer checks out a component file such as a form or a table, Visual FoxPro also checks out the implicit file or files. In like fashion, when a file is checked back in, or a new file is added to the repository, the implicit file(s) is also checked in or added automatically.

Other environments—Visual C++ for example—also have implicit files such as the .H headers accompanying .C/.CPP source files. These are not, however, managed automatically and must be explicitly added to the source repository.

Checking Out Files in Visual FoxPro

When Visual FoxPro is used with a source-controlled project and a file is opened for modification in the appropriate editor, FoxPro will prompt the user to check out the file(s). For example, by selecting a form and then selecting Modify to open the Form Designer, Visual FoxPro will issue a prompt for the file to be checked out. Alternately, if the file is not checked out, the form will be displayed in the Form Designer but will be read-only.

If exclusive access is required to a file or files—for example, to work off-site—files may also be checked out manually. Exercise 6.8 details the steps involved in checking out files.

EXERCISE 6.8

Checking Out Files in FoxPro

1. Select the file in the Project Manager.

2. From the Project menu, select Source Control and then select Check Out.

3. In the Check Out Files dialog box, select the file.

4. Click OK.

Checking In Files in Visual FoxPro

Since Visual FoxPro does not offer any provisions for automatically checking in files, files must always be checked in manually. See Exercise 6.9 for the steps involved.

Files should always be checked in when you have finished working with them. If files are kept checked out for lengthy periods, this can prevent other developers from having access, as well as preventing the latest version of the files from being backed up during normal network backup.

EXERCISE 6.9

Checking In Files in FoxPro

1. Select the file in the Project Manager.

2. From the Project menu, select Source Control and then select Check In.

3. Enter a comment describing the changes made.

4. In the Check In Files dialog box, select the file.

5. Click OK.

Checking In Text Files in FoxPro   In Visual FoxPro, when a text file such as a .PRG file is checked in and if multiple versions of the file are checked out, the source control software does not simply overwrite the version in the repository. Instead, the file is checked to determine if changes have been made to the central file since it was checked out. If changes are found, the source control software attempts to merge the file changes from the repository version with the local copy.

Visual FoxPro is more generous about permitting multiple check-outs than other developer platforms but also has provisions to attempt to resolve changes made by multiple developers.

Once this merger is complete, the user is given the opportunity to immediately check in the composite file. However, the application should be tested using the new version of the file, incorporating both the local revisions and the revisions of other developers.

Only after testing—and determining that the application continues to work correctly—should the file be checked in to the source repository. If, during this testing period, further changes have been made by other developers, another round of reconciliation and testing is necessary. If the source control software cannot resolve the differences, a merge conflict will be reported. This can occur, for example, when two developers have modified the same portion of a program.

When this occurs, the source control software creates a local file containing both sets of changes while marking the conflicts. The file then appears in the Project Manager with a merge conflict icon. To resolve the differences between files, the file must be edited again to satisfy the conflicts, the merge conflict markers removed, and the resulting product tested again. Once this is done, the file can be checked in again and, if no further merge conflicts are found, the revised file will become the current file version.

Microsoft InterDev and Team Development

The advantages of team development on projects are obvious: more complex applications can be created in less time, and the skills of different developers can be combined to create products which would be difficult or impossible for a single developer.

For this reason, Microsoft Visual InterDev offers the opportunity for multiple developers to simultaneously work with files in the same Web on a server. For this purpose, the first requirement is for the Web to exist on the server but, this provided, developers can then create local project files which point to the Web.

In this fashion, developers can maintain their own option settings and their own local copies of the master files. When a developer saves a file, the master copy on the server is automatically updated, allowing other developers to view the updated file.

The shortcoming in this shared access is that two developers may open the same file at the same time and, both making changes to the file, may well cancel each other's revisions.

To prevent such conflicts, Visual SourceSafe can be employed as an adjutant to Microsoft InterDev by providing source control service.

To enable source control for InterDev:

1. Ensure that Visual SourceSafe is installed on the server.

2. Open the Project menu.

3. Enable the Web Source Control option.

With source control enabled, only one developer will be able to check out any individual file for editing, and no conflict will occur from developer's changes.

Because Visual InterDev interacts with Visual SourceSafe, developers can continue to work with files on the Web just as they normally would. Visual InterDev will use Visual SourceSafe to check files in and out of the repository as they are requested.

Once source control has been enabled for the Web, using the Get Working Copy command creates a write-enabled copy in the developer's working directory. Likewise, the Release Working Copy command updates the repository, removing the working copy and making the file available to other users.

Setting Up Visual SourceSafe for a Web Server

To install Visual SourceSafe for a Web Server:

1. Run the Visual SourceSafe setup program on the Web server.

2. Select the Server setup to install all files.

   – or –

3. Select Custom setup but ensure that the installed components include:

   - Administrative Programs

   - Client Programs (Intel 32-bit)

   - Create SourceSafe Database

   - Enable SourceSafe Integration

For Windows 95/98 systems using the Microsoft Personal Web Server, the Distributed Component Object Model (DCOM) will also be required and can be downloaded from the Microsoft corporate Web site. Go to `http://www.microsoft.com/search/default.asp` and search for "DCOM."

There is no need to install Visual SourceSafe on the client systems.

Once Visual SourceSafe has been installed on a Web server, read/write permission must be granted for all users who will be authoring files using Visual InterDev or Microsoft FrontPage. See the "Setting Access Permissions for Visual SourceSafe" section below.

Setting Access Permissions for Visual SourceSafe

The Visual SourceSafe Admin utility is used to create users and to set access permissions for users. The Admin utility should appear in Start ➤ Programs ➤ Microsoft Visual SourceSafe as Visual SourceSafe 4.0 Admin – 32 bit. If not, check the installation to ensure that all of the necessary components have been installed.

If you are working from a client installation, the Admin utilities will not be present.

The Visual SourceSafe Admin utility appears in Figure 6.10 with the default Admin entry and three additional users.

FIGURE 6.10

The Visual SourceSafe Admin utility

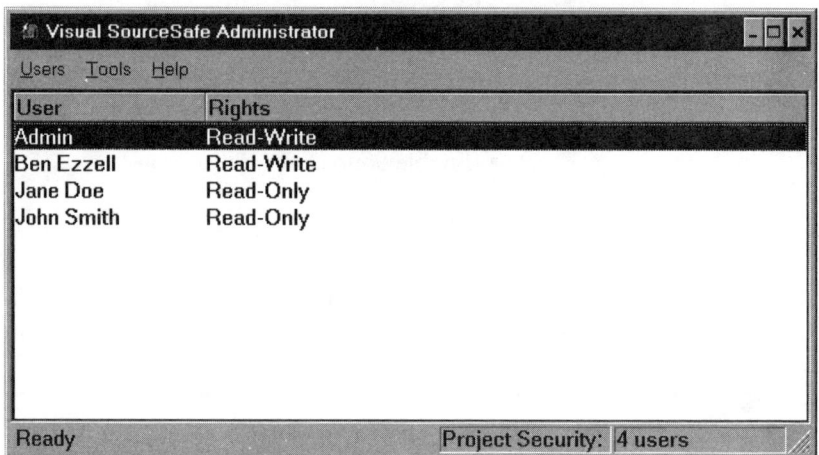

To Add a User

1. Select the Users menu from the Admin utility.

2. Select Add User. The Add User dialog box (Figure 6.11) will appear.

FIGURE 6.11

The VSS Admin Add User dialog box

3. Enter the user's name.

   - (optional) Enter a password for the user.

   - (optional) Check the Read-Only option to restrict access.

4. Click OK to conclude.

Window NT Server Installation Requirement   If Visual SourceSafe is installed on a Windows NT server, in addition to granting read/write permissions for individual users, permissions also need to be added to the Anonymous user account. To do this:

1. Run the Internet Service Manager application (on the Start menu under Programs ➤ Microsoft Internet Server).

2. Select the computer running the WWW (World Wide Web) service.

3. Select the Properties menu.

4. Select Service Properties.

5. Select the Service tab.

6. Copy the value from UserName property. (This property setting is always IUSR_*computer_name* where *computer_name* is the name of the server.)

7. In the Visual SourceSafe Admin utility, create a user account for the Anonymous user as described previously using the value copied from the UserName property.

8. Leave the Password blank and ensure that Read-Only is not selected.

For optimum results using source control, install Visual SourceSafe on a Windows NT server using an NTFS file system.

For Web servers installed on Windows 95/98 or Windows NT using the FAT16 file system, all files checked out through Visual SourceSafe are checked out to the same user account even though this account may or may not represent the user performing the operation.

- For a Windows NT FAT system, the anonymous user account performs all source control operations on the server.

- For a Windows 95/98 system, the user account specified at boot up performs all source control operations on the server.

Visual SourceSafe Limits

One potential problem in Visual SourceSafe that is worth being aware of is a limitation in the number of files which can be added to a project. Attempts to add more than 300 files to a project—perhaps using Developer Studio's Add To Source Control menu option—may produce an error message in the form:

```
Error accessing Source Code Control system. Check Installation.
```

This problem can be relieved by:

- Adding the files to the SourceSafe project directly from Visual Source-Safe Explorer

  – or –

- Using RegEdit to modify the HKEY_CURRENT_USER\SOFTWARE\ Microsoft\DevStudio\5.0\Source Control key and changing the Project-Threshold value by enter a number larger than the number of files in the project (including dependencies)

WARNING   Because increasing the ProjectThreshold value will impact the overall performance of Visual SourceSafe, this value should not be increased unnecessarily.

Summary

Application development, whether a small project with one or two developers or a large project with dozens or hundreds of programmers, has enough problems at the very best of times—enough problems that omitting proper source control isn't just foolish, it's down-right stupid!

Of course, source control—or version control—isn't limited just to application development, but can be applied equally well to versioning documents, Web pages, help files, or virtually any other type of on-going development project and, especially, any project where more than one person is sharing a group of files.

The principal features offered by source control software are:

- File check in/check out
- Document merging (does not apply to all file types)
- Project control
- Change tracking
- Version history

Microsoft's Visual SourceSafe is a source control/version control package that is designed to work with the Microsoft Visual Studio tools but which can also be used with virtually any other product that creates editable files of virtually any type. (Files which can not be edited or revised, of course, have no need of version control.)

Normally, source control applications permit multiple users to get copies but only permit one user at a time to check out a specific file. In this fashion, even though several people may be using an individual file, only one person is authorized to change the file's contents, preventing conflicts in which changes being made by one developer would overwrite changes being made by another.

An exception to this rule is found in Visual FoxPro, where multiple users are allowed to check out the same file concurrently. While FoxPro does provide mechanisms to resolve the potential conflicts from concurrent revisions, the proper resolution does still involve a developer's participation.

Regardless of whether the single developer access rule is applied or not, maintaining appropriate development cycles, i.e., seeing that files are checked in at regular intervals, optimally on a daily basis, are important to ensure that all team members are able to stay synchronized with the current revisions.

In addition to avoiding potential revision conflicts, other advantages conferred by proper version control include accountability in the form of a record of who has done what to each file.

Further, the differencing capability supplied by Visual SourceSafe (and others) provides a convenient method of identifying changes between versions. While not, perhaps, the only mechanism which can be used to try to identify problems, being able to see where changes have occurred is a definite aid at times in tracking down bugs and other idiosyncratic occurrences.

For many of the development tools in the Microsoft Visual Tool Suite, Visual SourceSafe can be integrated to one degree or another. For Visual C++ and Visual Basic, for example, Visual SourceSafe can be added to the Tools menu. Visual FoxPro offers an even tighter integration by actively prompting for and handling file check-out operations from SourceSafe as well as checking out implicit files to accompany the primary file.

All in all, Visual SourceSafe offers excellent version control. However, regardless of the source control package chosen, the one important factor is simply to install some form of version control and to use it to smooth the development process.

Review Questions

1. Source control applications commonly provide which of the following? (Select all that apply.)

A. A means of tracking successive versions of a file

B. A method of debugging source files

C. A repository for maintaining application source files

D. Facilities for viewing all types of file formats

2. Source control software organizes files using which of the following?

A. Directory trees

B. Linked lists

C. Projects

D. Virtual drives

3. A successful team development project depends on which of the following? (Select all that apply.)

A. Balancing the skill levels of the project developers

B. Coordinating and synchronizing changes to project files

C. Developers being able to enhance application elements without interfering with efforts by other developers

D. Multiple developers being able to access project, database, and source files

4. Version 1.0 of an application is presently being shipped while two new projects are under development. One is a service pack for version 1.0 while the second project is version 2.0 of the application. Using Visual SourceSafe, changes to the service pack code modules made to correct bugs can be incorporated in the version 2.0 project source code using which SourceSafe feature?

   A. Encapsulating

   B. Linking

   C. Merging

   D. Sharing

5. Services offered by source control applications include which of the following? (Select all that apply.)

   A. Automatic check-in of source files when the developer applications close

   B. Automatic check-out of source files when opened by developer applications

   C. Automatic tracking for different versions of each file

   D. Automatic version numbers to identify file versions

6. Files removed from Visual SourceSafe: (Select all that apply.)

   A. Are always permanently lost

   B. Are removed permanently if the Destroy Permanently option is selected

   C. Can be permanently removed later using the Purge option

   D. Can be recovered if not destroyed permanently or purged

7. Files under source control can:

   A. Be duplicated across projects

   B. Be shared between projects

   C. Belong to only one project

   D. Only be unique

8. Visual SourceSafe allows users to recover which of the following? (Select all that apply.)

   A. All file versions at once

   B. Any file version selected

   C. Any pinned file version

   D. Only the most recent file version

9. Version-control change tracking: (Select all that apply.)

   A. Can only be used with text-based files

   B. Compares separate copies of file versions to identify changes

   C. Preserves a record of incremental changes made to individual files each time a file is checked in

   D. Shows binary files in hexadecimal format

10. A shared file exists as which of the following? (Select all that apply.)

    A. A separate file for each project

    B. A single file belonging to more than one project

    C. A specific version copied to each project

    D. None of the above

11. In addition to using Visual SourceSafe to maintain archival and current copies of project files, SourceSafe can also be used maintain a central up-to-date copy of these files that is not in the archives but is accessible to users who do not have access to the archives (and who are not intended to change or revise the contents of these files). What is this central storage called?

    A. Mirror image

    B. Mirror project

    C. Project replica

    D. Shadow folder

12. Visual SourceSafe identifies file versions by which of the following? (Select all that apply.)

    A. Both decimal and letter increments

    B. Decimal increments only

    C. Integer version numbers only

    D. Letter increments only

13. Custom version labels in Visual SourceSafe are commonly applied to which of the following?

    A. Both project and file versions

    B. Individual files

    C. Project level versions

    D. None of the above

14. In Visual SourceSafe, which of the following is true? (Select all that apply.)

    A. Labels can be up to 128 characters in length.

    B. More than one user-defined label can be applied to a project version.

    C. Only one user-defined label can be applied to a project version.

    D. When applying multiple labels to a project, only the most recent label is retained.

15. Differencing files in Visual SourceSafe shows which of the following? (Select all that apply.)

    A. Added lines in the newer version

    B. Changed lines in each version

    C. Deleted lines in the older version

    D. Whether binary files are the same or different

16. Source control applications commonly support merging for which of the following file types? (Select all that apply.)

   A. Binary files

   B. Database files

   C. Text-based files

   D. Word-processing document files

17. Using Visual SourceSafe with a Web server requires which of the following? (Select all that apply.)

   A. Installing the client version of Visual SourceSafe on all workstations

   B. Installing the client version of Visual SourceSafe on the network server

   C. Installing Visual SourceSafe on the network server

   D. Installing Visual SourceSafe on the Web server

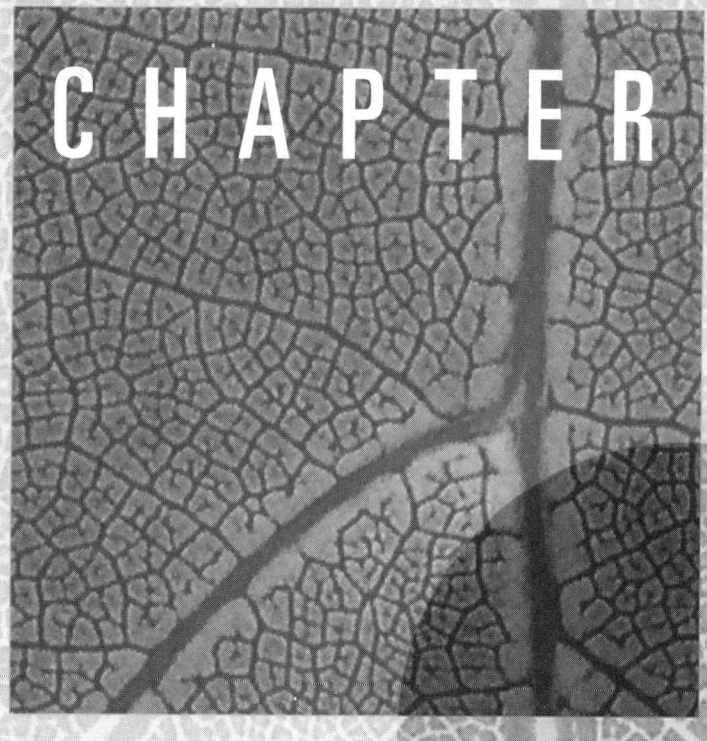

CHAPTER

7

The Component Object Model

Microsoft Exam Objectives Covered in This Chapter:

- Explain the benefits of the Component Object Model (COM) as a model for developing software.

- Compare component architectures on the basis of performance, maintainability, and extensibility.

As the name should suggest, the Component Object Model (COM) is based on the concept of reusable components. The concept of reusability in computer applications was first introduced by object-oriented programming languages where subroutines were encapsulated in classes (as methods), and classes became reusable, extendable, and inheritable in creating new custom classes.

The Component Object Model is an extension of the concept, applying reusability on a different scale by dealing with components as reusable objects. A component, in the COM sense, is a software service which can be 'plugged in' to work with other components—from the same or from different suppliers—with a minimum of adaptation and effort. In effect, the Component Object Model is intended to allow you to pull pieces of precompiled programming from different sources and make them work as services within another application.

In this fashion, COM provides the underlying architecture for higher-level services such as OLE, which includes compound documents, custom controls, inter-application scripting, data transfer, or other software interactions.

Explain the benefits of the Component Object Model (COM) as a model for developing software.

For example, you might want to include a spellchecker in your home planning package (see Figure 7.1). Using COM, rather than developing your own spellchecker, you would simply license an existing utility from another developer and include it. Or, equally possible, your end-users might select the spellchecker of their choice to work not only with your application but also with their word processor, their e-mail utility, their project planner, and their genealogy program. In this way, they could have one spellchecker which contains their custom dictionary and vocabulary and works exactly the same across all of their applications.

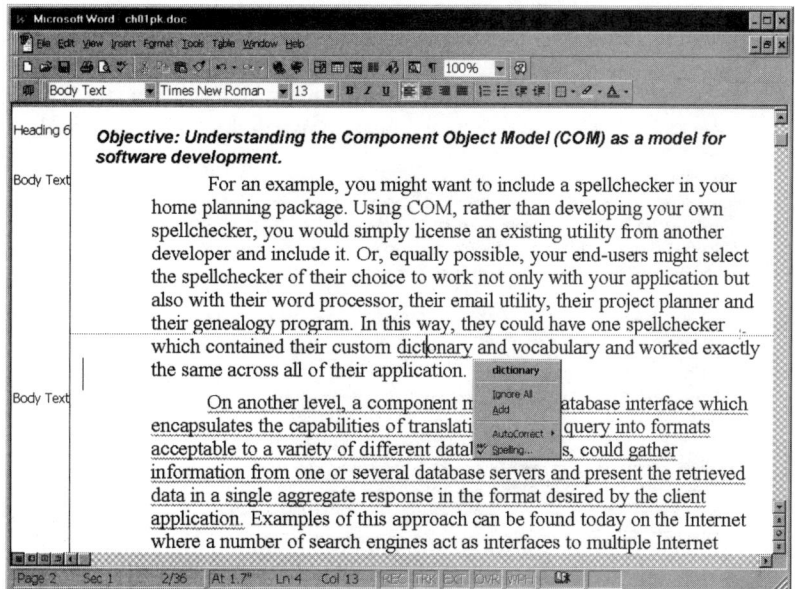

FIGURE 7.1

A typical spellchecker (but not a COM object yet)

On another level, a component might be a database interface which encapsulates the capabilities of translating a single query into formats acceptable to a variety of different database sources. The component could gather information from one or several database servers and present the retrieved data in a single aggregate response in the format desired by the client application. Examples of this approach can be found on the Internet, where a number of search engines act as interfaces to multiple Internet index services, allowing users to enter a single query, but receive responses provided by a host of sources.

The term *object* has developed a number of different interpretations since the introduction of object-oriented programming. In the Component Object Model, *object* simply means a body of compiled code which provide some service—or multiple services—to other system components. The terminologies *component object* or *component* are commonly employed to identify COM objects in an attempt to avoid confusion with OOP (object-oriented programming) objects such as those defined in C++ or Object Pascal.

Advantages in the Component Object Model

Even though component software technology is still in its infancy, there are a number of advantages in using the COM approach to development. Using COM objects, software development can be much more productive in designing components, marketing, and using and reusing software. The implications are significant for developers, vendors, users, and even corporations.

- For designers and developers, component software offers the opportunity to develop for niche applications, to offer custom programs suited to specific user needs, and to design specialty software components as add-ons or enhancements to existing packages.

- From a vendor's standpoint, component software provides the model for modularized applications where a distributed operating system can be tailored to users' requirements and populated by modularized components that provide the services desired for individual markets and even individual users.

- For end users, component software means a wide variety of choice: The user can select the component best suited to their needs rather than having to adapt their requirements to the services offered by generalized packages.

- From the corporate standpoint, component software can significantly reduce costs for in-house development. With component software, instead of having the corporate IS staff spending their time developing complete custom applications, staff programmers will be able to concentrate on business-specific solutions which can be implemented within a more generalized framework. Other advantages would include allowing existing legacy software components to be adapted by creating *object wrappers* to encapsulate legacy services while making the operations and data available as objects to other components, either across the network or locally.

Microsoft has defined a standard for component objects known as the Microsoft Component Object Model—an extended strategy encompassing both current and future technologies designed to facilitate component object development.

The Microsoft OLE (Object Linking and Embedding) standard was the first step in the creation of component software. Future implementations of OLE will continue to support the basic mechanisms of the Component Object Model but will incorporate new features including, for example, network operations.

The COM Component Software Architecture

All services provided to the user by the Component Object Model share a common requirement: the access to mechanisms to allow compiled software components from different software vendors to connect together and to share information in a well-behaved and well-defined fashion. These mechanisms are provided by COM in the form of the component software architecture, which defines binary standards for component interoperability. It is extensible, independent of programming languages, , and functional on multiple platforms, including Windows, Windows NT, Apple Macintosh, and UNIX.

Further, COM provides the supporting mechanisms for:

- The robust evolution of component-based applications and systems

- Communications between components, between processes, and across network boundaries

- Dynamic loading of components

- Error and status reporting

- Shared memory management between components

Even though the Component Object Model is used by Microsoft for specific purposes, including, among other things, automation, compound documents, controls, data transfer, storage, and naming, COM is still a general architecture for component software. More importantly, any developer is free to make use of the structure and the underlying foundation supplied by COM for whatever purposes they may find useful.

However, while the COM model is laudable in its overall intent, it's what's behind the intent that is important: the problems which COM addresses and the concepts which COM uses to solve these problems.

The Component Software Problem

Perhaps the most difficult fundamental problem inherent in component software is to provide a system which will allow binary executables, that is, programs, from disparate and diverse sources to cooperate smoothly. This does not merely include different programs written by a single company, but programs written by different companies, at different times, using different development tools.

To provide a single supporting mechanism, five specific areas must be supported:

- **Basic interoperability**   Developers must be free to create their own custom designs while still being able to determine that their applications will be interoperable with applications and components created by other developers.

- **Version compatibility**   Applications must be capable of upgrading without requiring all other components to be upgraded simultaneously.

- **Language independence**   Applications must be capable of interoperation regardless of the development tools and/or languages used in their creation.

- **Cross-process functionality**   The development model must provide the flexibility for developers to create components which will function not only in-process but also cross-process, and cross-network all within a single programming model as seen in DCOM (Distributed COM).

- **Performance**   Interoperability, compatibility, and independence cannot be achieved at the cost of performance. Specifically, the system overhead required to allow components to interact must not excessively impact performance.

Fundamental Concepts

Underlying the Component Object Model are a number of fundamental concepts addressing the requirements described in the previous section.

- A basic interface to provide the following:

  - Methods for components to discover—dynamically, at runtime—the interfaces supplied by other components

- Reference counting to permit components to track their own lifetimes and to automatically terminate themselves when they are no longer needed

- A loader to set up component interactions and, in cross-process and cross-network instances, to manage component interactions

- Binary standards for inter-process (inter-component) function addressing

- Mechanisms to uniquely identify components and component interfaces

- Provisions for strongly-typed grouping of functions into interfaces

Basic Interfaces

Using COM, applications interact—both with each other and with the system—through collections of functions called *interfaces*. An interface consists of a definition of expected behavior and responsibilities, together with a strongly-typed series of methods, or functions, providing related operations which can be used by other components for communication.

 All OLE services are simply COM interfaces.

For example, to provide OLE's drag-and-drop functionality, two COM interfaces are implemented: one for drag operations and a second target interface to receive dropped items:

- The IDragSource interface provides the functionality required for an object to be dragged—to be a drag source, whether for text, structured records, graphics, or other selections.

- The IDropTarget interface provides the functionality required for an object to be a drop target, allowing the application to receive an OLE object.

In the OLE drag-and-drop example, both the IDragSource and IDropTarget interfaces consist of multiple methods (functions), but only those functions belonging to a selected interface are available to other components. In other words, once a component has selected the IDragSource interface, methods belonging to the IDropTarget interface are not available unless the IDropTarget interface is also selected.

The OLE (Object Linking and Embedding) services offer a series of general purpose interfaces (commonly named using the format IOle*Xxxxx*).

By convention, all OLE interface names begin with "I," for Interface.

The existing interfaces, of course, do not prevent developers from defining their own custom interfaces when creating their own component-based applications. While there are no firm requirements, most developers continue to use the "I" preface to identify COM interface.

Interface Characteristics Despite the commonality of terminologies and the existing parallels between interfaces and classes, it's worth noting that some important differences exist.

The term *class* can mean several things, in part depending on which language you are working with. In C++, classes are understood as the basis for object instances, while in Visual Basic, the common terminology is simply to refer to objects without distinguishing between the class proper and the implementation instance. Also, most interfaces and components are implemented through C++ classes, but increasingly, may be implemented by Visual Basic objects. In brief, VC++ classes and VB objects may be considered equivalent, while either may provide the basis for implementing components.

The first difference is simply that an interface is not a class or an object. While a class can be instantiated to form an object, an interface, by itself, can not be instantiated. An interface does not contain its own implementation; instead, an interface is simply a collection of methods belonging to a component object and the object itself must be instantiated before the interface can be exposed. The interface is not the component object.

Instantiation is the process of creating an actual instance of an object class, i.e., creating the concrete instance (object) from an abstraction (class).

Second, different component object classes may implement an interface differently. The only real requirement is that the behavior conforms to the interface definition. For example, we could create two component objects which implement an interface called IDataSort where one version employs an array for data while the second employs a linked list.

Third, because component interfaces are simply groups of functions and exist only as binary operations, the component object supplying the interface can be implemented in any language, may use any internal operations desired, and may manipulate and store data in whatever fashion is appropriate. The single requirement is that the component can provide pointers to the interface member functions.

Interface Pointers (Addresses to Methods)   Because pointers to component objects are actually pointers to component object interfaces, the component object pointer can only be used to call a method and can not be used to modify data directly. Unlike classes, which can expose member data elements for public access, component objects can only expose interface methods and client objects can only access methods belonging to the selected interface.

When a client accesses a component object, the client application has a pointer giving it access to a particular interface and, through the interface, access to the methods defined for that interface. While this strong encapsulation may appear unnecessarily restrictive, the very stringency of the COM standard is what permits transparency and allows COM objects written in different languages and by different people to communicate successfully.

Multiple Interfaces for COM Objects   Typical component objects can—and do—implement multiple interfaces. In effect, rather than demanding that a COM object provide only one set of services, objects commonly provide multiple services and the services desired are selected by choosing the appropriate interface.

The OLE object was cited previously with the IDragSource and IDropTarget interfaces, each providing a different set of services while still belonging to the same object. Which services a client has access to depends on which interface is selected. Of course, if a client requires, more than one interface can be selected, but the services provided by each interface are only accessible through the pointer to the specific interface.

On another level, assume that the component supplying the IDataSort interface has methods—through the same interface—which allow the client to specify how the sort operations are handled, including what the object uses to sort records, and a provision to set the field order used for the sort. Now, perhaps the client application would like to store the settings, as persistent data, so that they could be reloaded the next time the object was used.

For this purpose, a provision might be made for a separate interface called IPersistSort which gives the object the ability to store its internal settings to a file (at the request of the client) and to reload these on request.

Figure 7.2 shows a hypothetical COM object with three interfaces: ISort-List, ISortArray, and IPersistSort. Both the ISortList and ISortArray interfaces include the SortBy function (for setting sort standards), but have different entry functions accepting different parameter types. The third interface, IPersistSort, has only one function in this example, a routine to save sorting standards to persistent storage, i.e., to a settings file or to registry entries.

FIGURE 7.2

A COM object with multiple interfaces

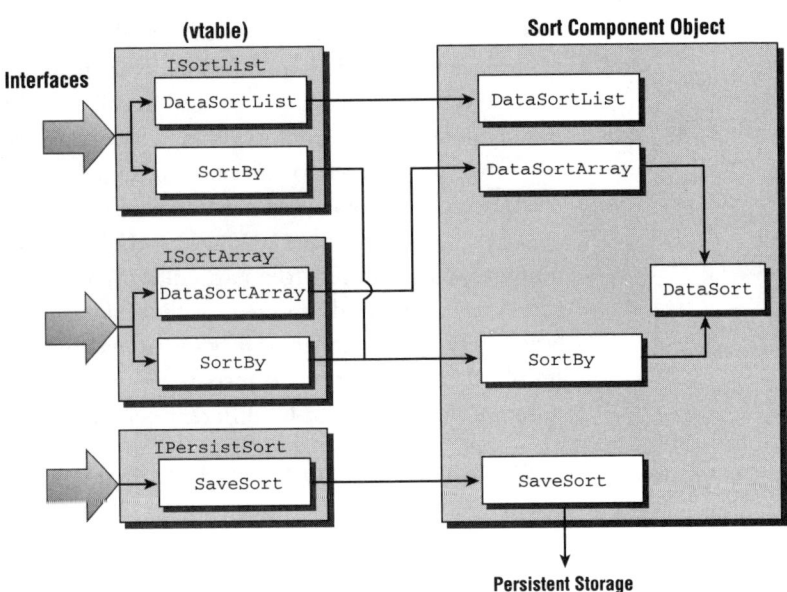

Strongly-Typed Interfaces   If you are familiar with OLE or have ever created an OLE server, you should be familiar with the *GUID* (Globally Unique ID) created for the server application. The GUID is a unique identifier generated to prevent any possibility (within reasonable limits) of a collision between names. Programmers, being human, tend to assign meaningful names to classes and to component objects but—because of limitations in human languages—this also means that there is a high probability of a collision occurring.

The use of a GUID, which is normally created by the development platform as a pseudo-random sequence, provides a unique non-human identifier which is used to request a pointer to an object interface and eliminates naming conflicts (and potential run-time failures). In effect, the GUID identifies not the component object, but the component interface providing access to the object.

GUIDs Identify Interfaces

Conventional DLLs, in order to support different interface functions—for example, to support conventional C/C++ apps, MFC-based apps, and Visual Basic—must define several separate entry points in the form of parallel exported methods, each with unique names.

Likewise, COM objects may define multiple interfaces. Rather than defining separate interfaces to support different languages, these interfaces are defined to expose specific groups of functions, even though these may provide similar functions with different calling parameters.

GUIDs are used to uniquely distinguish these interfaces not only from each other but also from other, similar interfaces supported by other COM objects.

Globally Unique Identifiers (GUIDs)   GUIDs are 128-bit integer values which are ostensibly guaranteed to be unique, both throughout the world and throughout time. They are used to identify each interface and each component object class.

 The GUID or UUID (Universally Unique IDs) values are defined by the Open Software Foundation's Distributed Computing Environment and—for all practical purposes—will not be duplicated accidentally.

Any human- (programmer-) defined names used while creating COM objects are strictly local in scope and have no referent validity outside of the COM object. (Or, more accurately, outside of the object's source code.) The use of GUIDs helps to ensure that COM components do not attempt to connect to incorrect components, component interfaces, or methods, even in situations (such as network operations) where thousands or even millions of component objects are present.

GUIDs (UUIDs) are referred to under a few different names according to their usage. For example, a CLSID (CLaSsID) is a GUID identifying a component object class while an IID (Interface ID) identifies a COM interface.

Microsoft supplies the uuidgen tool to automatically generate GUIDs while the CoCreateGuid function is provided by the COM API.

Commonly, regardless of how a GUID is created, developers rely on the use of defines to avoid handling the actual 128-bit GUID values.

For those who are not C/C++ programmers, a define statement—or the Visual Basic equivalent, a PUBLIC CONST statement—is a method of assigning a value such as a GUID to a mnemonic identifier for use in writing program code. After all, it is much easier type MY_CLSID than to type in a string like 53230327-172B-11D0-AD40-00A0C90DC8D9 every time a reference to the UUID is needed. Of course, errors are less likely to occur using the mnemonic.

If, however, you do want to get down to the nitty-gritty of GUID values, the following CLSID value was generated automatically for a simple OLE server application:

```
// This identifier was generated to be statistically unique
// for your app. You may change it if you prefer to choose a
// specific identifier.
// {C6A0FC60-3173-11D0-93D7-BA6083000000}
static const CLSID clsid =
    { 0xc6a0fc60, 0x3173, 0x11d0,
      { 0x93, 0xd7, 0xba, 0x60, 0x83, 0x0, 0x0, 0x0 } };
```

And, for an ActiveX control, a host of GUIDs were generated as:

```
const CLSID CLSID_LevelCtrl =
    { 0x59435B8E, 0x0B54, 0x11D1,
      { 0x85, 0xFB, 0x50, 0xA1, 0x4C, 0xC1, 0x00, 0x00 } };
const CLSID CLSID_LevelProp =
    { 0x59435B8F, 0x0B54, 0x11D1,
      { 0x85, 0xFB, 0x50, 0xA1, 0x4C, 0xC1, 0x00, 0x00 } };
```

```
const IID IID_ILevelCtrl =
  { 0x59435B8D, 0x0B54, 0x11D1,
    { 0x85, 0xFB, 0x50, 0xA1, 0x4C, 0xC1, 0x00, 0x00 } };
const IID LIBID_KnobCtrlLib =
  { 0x59435B80, 0x0B54, 0x11D1,
    { 0x85, 0xFB, 0x50, 0xA1, 0x4C, 0xC1, 0x00, 0x00 } };
const IID DIID__LevelEvents =
  { 0x59435B90, 0x0B54, 0x11D1,
    { 0x85, 0xFB, 0x50, 0xA1, 0x4C, 0xC1, 0x00, 0x00 } };
```

Here we have two class IDs (CLSIDs) and three interface IDs (IIDs), which should be sufficient to induce terminal ennui in even the most rabid numerologist.

For more examples of CLSID and IID values, refer to the Windows Registry (use RegEdit or RegEd32). Examples are plentiful but, if you have trouble finding one, use the search facility to hunt for the key string "CLSID."

After compiling, these GUIDs become embedded in the binary component object and are used dynamically by the COM system at bind time and during execution—to ensure that only the correct connections are made between components.

Dynamic binding, which is the only type of binding used with COM objects, occurs at run time, i.e., on execution. In contrast, static binding, used with conventional libraries, occurs at link time.

Immutability and Versioning   COM interfaces are never versioned, but remain immutable. When a COM interface is modified, the original COM interface remains unchanged and the revised interface becomes a new COM interface. This averts the possibility of version conflicts between old and new components. When a new version of an interface is created by adding, modifying, or removing functions or by changing the semantics of a method, the new version becomes an entirely new interface—with a new, unique identifier.

In this fashion, there are no conflicts between new and old interfaces even if the only differences are a single operation or a single change in the semantics of an existing method, and even if the two interfaces continue to share a common internal implementation.

As an example, assume that we want to add a new method to the IData-Sort interface but we also want to continue to support existing clients. For this purpose, we would add a new interface while, internally, keeping the old implementation and keeping the old interface as a subset of the new interface. Each of these interfaces, however, both the old and the new, would have different GUID values.

Benefits of COM Interfaces

The Component Object Model and the use of unique interfaces offer a variety of benefits, including:

- Increased process speed and minimal overhead

- Reusable interfaces and object evolution without losing existing application compatibility

- Local/remote transparency allowing objects to be local or networked

- Language independence allowing object sources to be transparent to calling applications

Process Speed   To begin, once a client application has established a connection to an object, all subsequent calls to the object's services—the object's interface functions—are simply indirect function calls through two memory pointers (see Figure 7.3). This immediate access minimizes the performance overhead for an in-process COM object—an object located in the same address space—because the calling code is minimal.

In-process calls, between COM components in the same process, require only a few more processor instructions than a conventional function call and are every bit as fast as a compile-time bound C++ object invocation. Further, the overhead for employing multiple interfaces is minimal because the processing requirements for negotiating interfaces (see the QueryInterface function in the section titled "The *IUnkown* Interface," below) is performed for groups of functions, not for each function individually. In other words, the entire negotiation overhead is contained in obtaining a pointer to the COM object interface, not in obtaining individual pointers to specific methods.

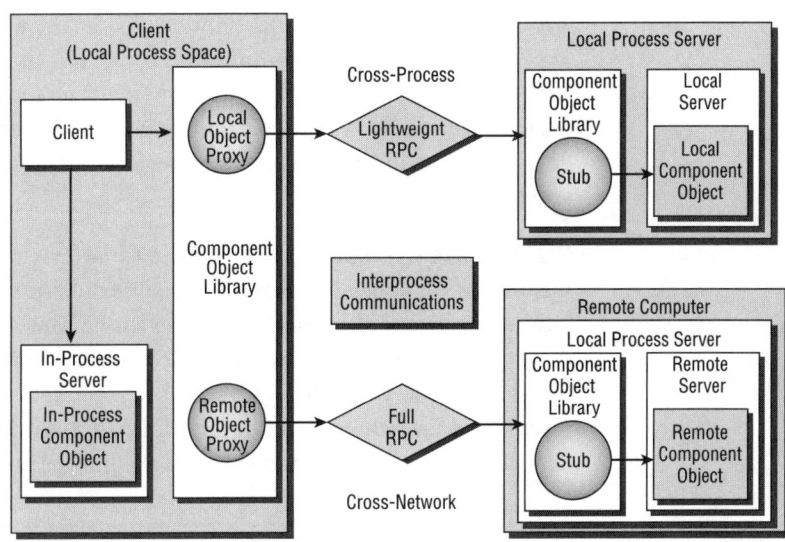

F I G U R E 7.3

COM Object
Connections

Here the client application makes three COM connections: the first directly to an in-process server in its own process space; the second as an out-of-process connection to a local process server in a separate process space through a lightweight RPC connection; and the third connection to a remote computer through a full RPC connection. In the latter two cases, the Component Object Library provides the object proxy and stub services.

From the component object server's view, all calls to the object's interface are made through a pointer to the interface. Because the pointer only has context in a single process, the caller must be some element of in-process code. As shown in Figure 7.3, when the component object is in-process, the caller is the client proper.

However, when the server object is cross-process or cross-network, the caller becomes a *stub* object provided by COM while the corresponding COM on the client side provides a *proxy* object in the client process. To complete the connection, the stub object receives the remote procedure call from the proxy object, turning it into an interface call to the server component object.

Therefore, from the viewpoint of both the client and server components, each is communicating directly with another in-process component object.

In sum, for both client and server objects the question of the location of another component becomes irrelevant and local and remote components are treated in identical fashion, like any in-process component object.

Reusable Interfaces   As most developers are aware, common sets of operations are normally functional and useful across a broad range of components. One such example would be a set of I/O functions to read and write streams of bytes. With COM, existing interfaces such as Istream, can be reused indefinitely. While reusing code is one benefit, another is that the developer is required to learn the interface only once, and can then apply it indefinitely.

COM Object Evolution   Because the isolation provided by encapsulation makes many changes in an object invisible outside of the object, internal evolution within a COM object—changes and improvements that do not affect the exposed interfaces—can be carried out without affecting the client processes using the COM object.

Evolutionary changes that are visible, that is, interface changes that are exposed, are also supported through the QueryInterface request.

WARNING

The QueryInterface request is absolutely required by all COM objects. If QueryInterface is not supported, the object is not a COM object. (The QueryInterface method belongs to the IUnknown interface discussed below; see "The *IUnknown* Interface.")

The QueryInterface method makes it possible for an object to create new interfaces, i.e., to support new groups of functions, and to make the interfaces available to new clients while still maintaining full compatibility with existing client applications. Because of the QueryInterface method, revising code to provide additional functionality does not require rewriting or recompiling existing client applications.

The QueryInterface method is COM's key to the versioning problem. Together with making established interfaces immutable to provide support for old interfaces and using GUID key values to make interfaces unique, the QueryInterface method provides robust versioning because the previously existing interfaces continue to be supported (or, if not, simply do not report the original interfaces) even when new interfaces and improved functionality are provided.

Local/Remote Transparency   One of the big advantages of the COM model is to make local and remote interface calls transparent. The client application does not necessarily know—nor does it need to know—whether it is calling a local procedure (a local COM object), calling a local server process, or calling a remote server process on another computer. Functionally, all of these appear the same to the client application and the connection proper is made through the COM processes which provide the necessary interprocess communication handling.

Granted, a remote process or a cross-network (remote) process call does impose some additional overhead, but this is still transparent and requires no special code in the client application to differentiate between in-process, out-of-process, and remote-process object calls.

As long as the client is written to handle RPC (remote procedure call) exceptions, all objects are available in the same uniform, transparent fashion.

A new, distributed version of COM, called DCOM, has been released, which requires no modifications to existing components to gain distributed capabilities. DCOM is designed to isolate programmers from networking issues, allowing existing component software to operate in a distributed environment.

Language Independence   Again, because of the isolation provided by encapsulation in the COM object model, any programming language which can provide structures of pointers (for interfaces) and, either implicitly or explicitly, call functions through pointers, is suitable both to create and to employ component objects. This means that component objects can be developed using a variety of tools (for example, in different languages) and that the resulting objects are completely independent of the languages used by the developers. This is illustrated in Figure 7.4.

The key point is that COM, unlike object-oriented languages which provide source code standards, provides a binary object standard with compatibility not merely across languages but independent of the languages used.

While DLLs (dynamic link libraries) are another approach to a binary-level compatibility, DLLs are not as fully cross-compatible, often requiring careful typecasting of variables to match the variable types used by the source compiler, and do not inherently provide the version independence designed in the COM model.

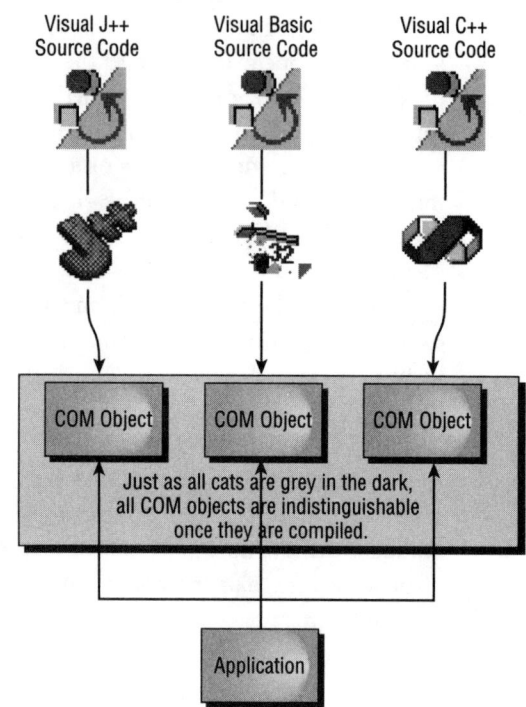

FIGURE 7.4

All COM objects are
gray in the dark.

Virtual Function Tables

Just as Windows requires a different implementation for different
hardware platforms (largely accomplished through the Hardware Abstraction Layer), the COM standard is also adapted to a variety of platforms
(both hardware and operating system). For COM, this adaptation consists of
defining standards for the *virtual function tables* (vtables) in memory, and
standards for how functions are called through the vtables.

In Figure 7.5, the client variable—a component object—is actually a
pointer to a component object while the component object itself owns
a pointer to the vtable and the vtable holds the point to the actual function.

With such standards, any language which supports function calls via
pointers, including Ada, Basic, C/C++, Pascal (Delphi), and Small Talk can
be used to write components. Any of these components can interoperate
with any other components that are written to the same binary standards.

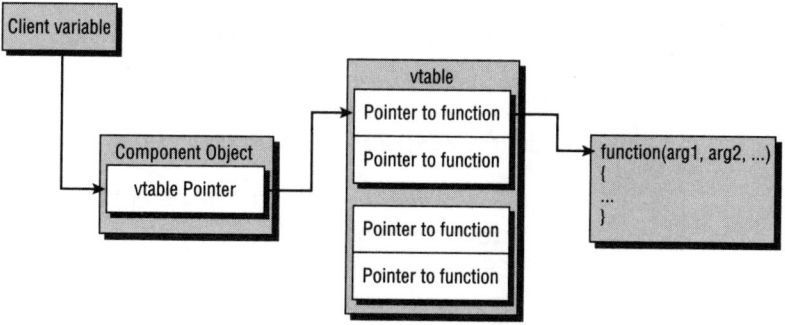

Because the vtable is accessed via a double indirection—the client has a pointer to a pointer to the vtable rather than a simple pointer to the vtable—the vtable can be shared among multiple instances of the same object class or among multiple object classes. For systems using hundreds or even thousands of object instances, being able to share vtables offers a significant reduction in memory requirements.

Component Object Interfaces

All component objects must support a base interface—IUnknown—along with any combination of other interfaces necessary to expose the functionality supplied by the component object.

While component objects may (and usually do) have associated data, unlike C++ or Pascal objects, the data elements belonging to a component object are never exposed. Instead, component objects always must access other component objects through the object's interfaces.

This feature is one of the primary architectural characteristics of the Component Object Model and is part and parcel of the structure (and strictures) which permit the COM model to enforce strict encapsulation of both data and processing. This architecture also permits transparent remote (cross-process or cross-network) access because all data must be passed through methods supported by proxy objects which forward the requests and vector the returning responses.

The *IUnknown* Interface

All COM objects define the IUnknown interface, which provides the implementation necessary for basic COM functionality. The IUnknown interface is also the base class used to derive all other COM and OLE interfaces. IUnknown provides three exposed methods: QueryInterface, AddRef, and Release.

In C++ syntax, IUnknown would appear as:

```
interface IUnknown
{
    virtual   HRESULT QueryInterface(IID& iid, void ppvObj) =
0;
    virtual   ULONG   AddRef() = 0;
    virtual   ULONG   Release() = 0;
}
```

If you are using MFC to develop your component applications, the definition of the IUnknown interface will not actually appear in your code since it is supplied, indirectly, through the Unknwn.H header.

The AddRef and Release methods are simple counting provisions. The AddRef method is called to increment the component's use count when another component object is using the interface; the Release method is called when the interface is no longer needed. The internal count is maintained to decide when the component is no longer needed and can be unloaded from memory.

The *QueryInterface* Method

The QueryInterface method is the provision which allows clients, at run time, to dynamically ask whether or not a specific interface is supported by the component object. In addition, this is also the means used by a client to retrieve an interface pointer.

Before an application can exercise any function supplied by a component object, the calling application must begin by querying the component's QueryInterface to request a pointer to the interface supporting (exposing) the desired function.

If the requested interface is supported, QueryInterface returns a pointer to the vtable pointer to the interface, together with a success code. However, if the component object does not support the requested interface, an error value is returned. On return, the calling application should examine the return code and, if it reports success, the application can use the interface pointer to access the desired method. Or, if the QueryInterface call returns failure, the application should choose some other course of action including, if necessary, informing the user that the request method is not available.

The following example implements a call to the IUnknown::Query-Interface method for the LevelCtrl component asking if the ILevelCtrl interface is supported. If the response reports success, then the pLookup pointer is a pointer to the ILevelCtrl interface which can be used to call methods belonging to the interface—in this instance, the ChangeLevel method.

```
LPLOOKUP   pLevelCtrl;
TCHAR      szNumber[64];
HRESULT    hResult;

// Call QueryInterface on the component object LevelCtrl,
asking for a pointer to the ILevelCtrl interface identified
by the unique interface ID: IID_ILevelCtrl.

hResult = pLevelCtrl->QueryInterface( IID_ILevelCtrl,
                                           &pLevelCtrl);
if( SUCCEEDED( hResult ) )
{
      // use ILevelCtrl interface pointer
    pLevelCtrl->ChangeLevel( 20 );
      // finished using the ILevelCtrl interface pointer
    pLevelCtrl->Release();
}
else
{
    // Failed to acquire ILevelCtrl interface pointer.
}
```

Of course, if hResult reports failure then we know that the requested interface is not supported.

There is no explicit call to the AddRef method since the QueryInterface method has already incremented the reference count before returning an interface pointer. Alternately, if QueryInterface had reported failure, the reference count would not have been incremented.

The Component Object Library

The Component Object Library is part of the Windows system providing the basic mechanisms supporting the COM model. The Component Object Library provides:

- Connections between components

- Mechanisms to make IUnknown calls across processes

- The underlying mechanisms for launching components

Commonly, for an application to create a component object, the application passes the CLSID of the component object class to the Component Object Library. In turn, the Component Object Library uses the CLSID to look up the component object in the registry.

If the component object is an executable server, COM launches the .EXE file, then waits for the component to register its class factory via a call to CoRegisterClassFactory. The class factory is a COM mechanism used to instantiate component objects.

Alternately if the component requested is a .DLL (dynamic-link library), COM loads the DLL, then calls DllGetClassFactory and uses the object's IClassFactory to create an instance of the component object.

In both cases, a pointer to the requested interface is returned to the calling application while the application does not know, nor care, where the server application is executing. All the calling application is concerned with is that the interface pointer is available and can be used to connect to the component object.

For Windows 3.1, the Component Object Library is part of COMPOBJ .DLL. For Windows NT/95/98, the OLE32.DLL provides the Component Object Library.

Component Object Servers

A component object *server* is a body of code implementing a component object's services (i.e., methods and functions). The Component Object Library uses the server code to create component object instances. In turn, the object instance provides the services to the component object client.

While component objects may be both servers or clients, server objects themselves may be implemented in three principal fashions: either as an in-process server, meaning that the object executes in the same process space as the client (as, for example, a DLL), as a local process, or as a remote process.

Both local and remote servers are out-of-process, meaning that they either run in a separate process space than the client (while still on the same machine) or that the server runs on a remote machine (networked).

While non-COM object models only permit objects to function as servers (while clients are never represented as objects), the Component Object Model allows components to expose separate interfaces such that they can act as both client and server component objects simultaneously. This is in keeping with the concept of peer-to-peer computing, and provides a flexibility which is lacking in other proposed object models.

When designing a component object server, the server type selected is based on consideration for how the object will be implemented and how it will be deployed. The COM standard accommodates a variety of circumstances, ranging from deploying numerous small in-process components such as OLE (ActiveX) controls, to very large components such as a database server object.

To the client objects, however, all server components are the same regardless of whether they are in-process, local, or remote servers.

Defining Component Interfaces   When creating a component object and a custom interface, the interface can be written using the interface definition language (IDL). The Microsoft IDL compiler (MIDL) will then create the appropriate header files for applications to use the interface, as well as the source code to create proxy and stub objects to handle remote procedure calls (RPCs).

Microsoft's IDL is based on extensions to the Open Software Foundation's Distributed Computing Environment (DCE) IDL.

The IDL itself is simply a tool provided for the convenience of programmers and is not defined by the Component Object Model standards. The IDL is not integral to COM's interoperability mechanisms. In effect, the IDL is simply a convenience which saves developers the need to manually create header files for each programming language (environment). The IDL and MIDL also save the effort of creating proxy and stubs.

While the Microsoft compilers provide the IDL file automatically when you create an ActiveX (COM) object project, this IDL file is only needed when defining a custom interface. The proxy and stub objects are already provided by the Component Object Library for COM and OLE interfaces.

The following IDL file defines the custom interface ILevelCtrl, which is implemented by the KnobCtrl object, an ActiveX component which presents a graphic rotary volume control knob with provisions to change the level using the mouse to manipulate the knob. This IDL file was created automatically for the KnobCtrl project by the Visual C++ compiler.

```
#include <olectl.h>
// KnobCtrl.idl : IDL source for KnobCtrl.dll
//

// This file will be processed by the MIDL tool to
// produce the type library (KnobCtrl.tlb) and marshalling code.

import "oaidl.idl";
import "ocidl.idl";

    [
        object,
        uuid(8B946F74-0A74-11D1-85FB-50914CC10000),
        dual,
        helpstring("ILevelCtrl Interface"),
        pointer_default(unique)
    ]
    interface ILevelCtrl : IDispatch
    {
```

```
            [ propput, id(DISPID_FILLCOLOR) ]
                HRESULT FillColor([in] OLE_COLOR clr);
            [ propget, id(DISPID_FILLCOLOR) ]
                HRESULT FillColor([out, retval] OLE_COLOR* pclr);
            [ propget, id(1), helpstring("property m_nLevel") ]
                HRESULT m_nLevel([out, retval] short *pVal);
            [propput, id(1), helpstring("property m_nLevel")]
                HRESULT m_nLevel([in] short newVal);
    };
[
    uuid(8B946F64-0A74-11D1-85FB-50914CC10000),
    version(1.0),
    helpstring("KnobCtrl 1.0 Type Library")
]

library KNOBCTRLLib
{
    importlib("stdole32.tlb");
    importlib("stdole2.tlb");

    [
        uuid(8B946F76-0A74-11D1-85FB-50914CC10000),
        helpstring("Event interface for LevelCtrl")
    ]
    dispinterface _LevelEvents
    {
        properties:
        methods:
            [id(1)] void ClickUp( [in] long x, [in] long y );
            [id(2)] void ClickDn( [in] long x, [in] long y );
    };

    [
        uuid(8B946F75-0A74-11D1-85FB-50914CC10000),
        helpstring("LevelCtrl Class")
    ]
```

```
coclass LevelCtrl
{
    [default] interface ILevelCtrl;
    [default, source] dispinterface _LevelEvents;
};

[
    uuid(8B946F79-0A74-11D1-85FB-50914CC10000),
    helpstring("LevelProp Class")
]
coclass LevelProp
{
    interface IUnknown;
};
};
```

COM and Component Structures   The Component Object Model specifies how component objects interoperate, but it is not concerned with how components are structured. The structure of a component object is strictly an internal matter and is determined by the programmer, the development language used, and the development environment.

In direct contrast, programming languages and environments do not set any standards relating to objects outside of their immediate environment: The strictures of a programming language apply only internally within an application during development.

In this fashion, COM, by defining language-independent interfaces, fills the gap between individual applications making it possible for separate components to function together, whether in-process, locally, or over network connections (remote). Further, by following the COM standard, applications can be relieved of the onus of supplying all services internally. This is accomplished by joining together with other component objects to share and acquire extended functions and capabilities, both locally and remotely, to create integrated applications.

Summary

The Component Object Model consists of the core handling specifications governing how components and clients function and intercommunicate. The COM standard defines interoperability mechanisms including:

- A binary standard permitting function calls between components

- Strongly typed groupings of functions making them accessible only through interfaces

- The base IUnknown interface, which provides:

  - Methods for components to dynamically query the interfaces provided by other components (the QueryInterface method)

  - Reference counting, which governs component lifetimes (through the AddRef and Release methods)

- The GUID identifier mechanisms to uniquely identify both components and interfaces

The Component Object Model, however, is more than simply a specification, but is also an implementation provided through the Component Object Library (in COMPOBJ.DLL for Win3.x or OLE32.DLL for WinNT/95/98). The Component Object Library supplies:

- The fundamental API functions providing services for the creation of both client and server COM objects. For client objects, COM provides the basic functions for creating component objects. For server objects, COM provides facilities to expose component object interfaces.

- Location services which use GUIDs (CLSIDs) to identify the server implementing a class and the location of the server object. This includes supporting a level of indirection—the system registry for Windows systems—which cross references from the component object class identity to the implementation packaging the component object class. In this fashion, client services are independent of the package, permitting the packaging to change over time.

- Provisions rendering remote procedure calls transparent so that a component object may be located on a local or a remote server.

Because the Component Object Model is not specific to Windows (even though Microsoft does implement COM for Windows, Windows NT, and the Apple Macintosh) COM can be implemented on other operating systems—including some versions of UNIX—by other vendors.

Further, COM does distinguish between the object model and the hardware-level protocols for distributed services and platform-specific O/S services, such as local security and network transport services. This differentiation assures that developers are not restricted to specific models when creating services for different operating systems, but may still design components which can interoperate with components on platforms using other operating systems.

By providing both binary and network standards, the Component Object Model provides for operations within a specific platform as well as a wire-level protocol for remote cross-system interactions, offering complete interoperability both between local components and across different machines on a networked system.

Review Questions

1. The Component Object Model depends on which of the following?

   A. The use of object-oriented programming languages such as C++, Smalltalk, or Delphi

   B. Developing ActiveX and OLE components as COM implementations

   C. Making use of the Windows common dialog boxes in application interfaces

   D. Employing third-party libraries in application development

2. Benefits of the Component Object Model include:

   A. Offering users a greater range of software choices

   B. Offering users a wider variety of specialized components

   C. Reducing the cost of redeveloping legacy applications

   D. All of the above

3. In COM objects, a GUID (Globally Unique IDentifier) is created for each:

   A. Object

   B. Interface

   C. Method

   D. All of the above

4. Local servers:

   A. Are commonly DLLs

   B. Are commonly EXEs

   C. Execute in a separate process space

   D. Execute in the same process space as the client

5. Three types of Component Object Model servers are:

   A. In-process

   B. Local

   C. Remote

   D. Internal

6. An individual COM object may act as:

   A. A server object

   B. A client object

   C. Both a client and a server object at the same time

   D. Either a client or a server object but not both at once.

7. The Component Object Model is supported by which of the following?

   A. Windows NT and Windows 98

   B. Windows NT, Windows 95, Windows 98, Windows 3.*x*

   C. Apple Macintosh

   D. Both B and C

   E. Any operating system providing COM services

8. Which of the following is applicable to the COM IUnknown interface? (Select two.)

   A. It must be supported by all COM objects.

   B. It provides a binary standard for function calls between components.

   C. It provides methods to query which interfaces an object supports.

   D. It reports the GUID identifier for a component object.

9. When a component calls an executable server object, what does COM do? (Select two.)

   A. It launches the .EXE file.

   B. It calls the CoRegisterClassFactory to instantiate the component object.

   C. It calls DllGetClassFactory to create an instance of the component object.

   D. It returns a pointer to the component object.

10. The Component Object Library supplies which of the following? (Select three.)

   A. Connections between components

   B. Mechanisms to make IUnknown calls across processes

   C. Mechanisms to launch components

   D. Mechanisms to create UUID values for component objects

11. Where is the CLSID value for a component stored for public reference?

    A. Only in the .DLL or .EXE binary file

    B. In the system registry

    C. In the SYSTEM.INI initialization file

    D. In the WIN.INI initialization file

12. After calling the `QueryInterface` method for a component, which of the following is true?

    A. If the result returned is failure, the `IUnknown` method should be called to report that the object is not valid.

    B. If the result returned is failure, the `Release` method should be called to close the component object.

    C. If the result returned is success, the `AddRef` method should be called to increment the reference count for the component object.

    D. If the result returned is success, the object's reference count is automatically incremented.

13. Developing component objects requires a language/development platform which supports which of the following?

    A. Passing pointers to data elements

    B. Passing pointers to functions

    C. Passing data elements by value

    D. Exposing internal data elements by address

14. How does the COM standard manage connections between components?

A. By using a vtable (virtual function table) to supply addresses for object functions

B. By using a vtable (virtual function table) to supply addresses for object interfaces

C. By querying an object's IUnknown function to retrieve the address of a function

D. By querying an object's IUnknown function to retrieve the address of an interface

15. Dynamic link libraries are:

A. Fully cross-compatible on a binary level and can be used on a cross-platform basis

B. Provide the same version independence as component objects

C. May be used for local component objects

D. May be used for remote component objects

16. The Component Object Model:

A. Provides compatibility between objects by translating parameter syntaxes between languages

B. Provides encapsulation to ensure language independence between objects

C. Requires compatible objects to be created using the same language

D. Requires compatible objects to be created using the same operating system

17. The Component Object Model relies on which of the following?

    A. ODBC handling for transparent communications between component objects

    B. RPC handling for transparent communications between component objects

    C. Static data structures for transparent communications between component objects

    D. Strict typecasting for transparent communications between component objects

18. Which of the following statements are valid? (Select two.)

    A. Existing COM interfaces always remain immutable.

    B. Existing COM interfaces may be modified to handle new provisions.

    C. New COM interfaces are identified by universally unique IDs.

    D. New COM interfaces are identified by version numbers.

19. Universally Unique ID values can be created by which of the following? (Select two.)

    A. The COM API `CoCreateGuid` function

    B. The Microsoft-supplied `uuidgen` tool

    C. The Universal ID Formula algorithm

    D. Tossing dice

20. Universally Unique ID values include which of the following? (Select two.)

    A. CLSIDs to identify component classes

    B. DIDs to identify component data elements

    C. FIDs to identify component files

    D. IIDs to identify component interfaces

21. Each component object interface:

    A. Receives a sequentially numbered GUID

    B. Receives a unique IID value

    C. Receives a GUID value supplied by the Open Software Foundation

    D. Shares the component object class's GUID

22. Component objects (COM objects) may contain:

    A. Both functions and data objects which are publicly exposed

    B. Neither publicly exposed functions nor data elements

    C. Publicly exposed functions and data elements that are never exposed

    D. Publicly exposed interfaces which provide access to functions and data elements that are never exposed

23. Which of the following are true about pointers to component objects? (Select two.)

    A. They are actually pointers to component object interfaces.

    B. They can be used to modify object data.

    C. They can only access object methods.

    D. They provide access to all methods belonging to an object.

24. Before a COM object can be used, which of the following must happen?

    A. The object interface must be instantiated.

    B. The object itself must be instantiated.

    C. The object methods must be instantiated.

CHAPTER

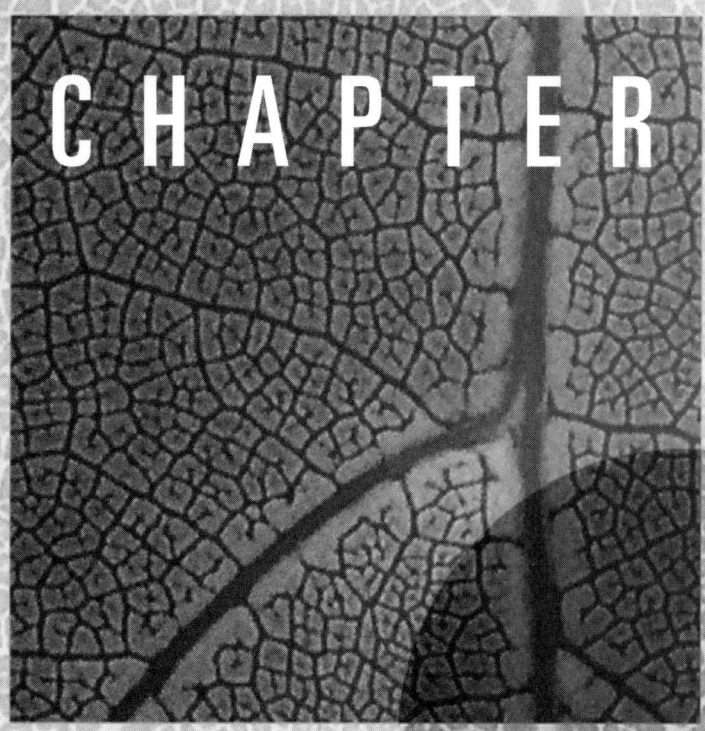

8

Object Linking and Embedding

Microsoft Exam Objectives Covered in This Chapter:

- Evaluate the use of one or more of the following in a given component solution: compound documents, OLE embedding and linking, and OLE drag and drop.

- Evaluate the use of Active Documents as a component of a solution for a given business problem.

Object Linking and Embedding (referred to as OLE) is a mechanism allowing users to create and edit compound documents. OLE documents (a.k.a. compound documents) are documents which contain objects created and maintained by multiple applications. OLE objects, whether linked or embedded, may include such diverse document elements as formatted text, spreadsheet excerpts, drawings and images, sound, or video clips.

Those parts of OLE which are not directly related to linking or embedding are now included in the ActiveX technology; see Chapter 10.

Applications supporting OLE permit users to create OLE documents without needing to switch between applications to access the various services. In effect, OLE itself manages the process of loading the various applications supporting the embedded items, making the compound document appear to be a single, integrated document belonging entirely to the parent application.

OLE applications consist of container and server applications. The container applications create compound documents and the server, i.e., component, applications provide the support for the items created within the container document. Individual applications may be either containers or servers, or, in many cases, may support both roles.

OLE is composed of a group of interrelated concepts which, working together, provide the mechanisms necessary to provide seamless interaction between otherwise independent applications. These concepts are explained below:

- *Linking and embedding* are two methods for storing items created by external server applications within an OLE document.

- *In-place activation* occurs when an embedded item is activated in the context of the container document. Activation of an embedded item changes the container application's interface to incorporate features of the OLE server application. In contrast, linked items can never be activated in-place because the linked item's data is not contained in the OLE document's context but, instead, is contained in a separate file.

Linking and embedding and in-place activation are the two main features behind OLE visual editing. Container applications retrieve commands from the system registry which apply to selected OLE objects. To locate the appropriate information, the container application uses the class identifier (CLSID) from the OLE object to locate the executable managing the embedded or linked object.

- *Automation* is the mechanism allowing one application to drive another. The driving application is referred to as the *automation client* or *automation controller*. The driven application is called the *automation server* or *automation component*.

Automation is used in both OLE and ActiveX contexts, and any object based on COM may be automated.

- *Compound files* provide a standard file format which provides for compound documents to be stored as structures, providing internal support for the formats required by different components. Within a compound file, structured storage contains many of the features found in file directories.

- *Uniform data transfer (UDT)* provides a set of interfaces allowing data to be exchanged between OLE client and server applications in a standard fashion, independent of the method used to effect the transfer. UDT provides the basis for drag-and-drop transfers, as well as Clipboard and dynamic data exchange (DDE) operations.

- *Drag-and-drop*, based on uniform data transfer, is the mechanism used to transfer data between applications, between windows within an application, or between locations within a single window.

- *Component Object Model (COM)*, introduced in Chapter 7, provides the infrastructure used by OLE objects for communication. The Component Object Model provides underlying support for both OLE and ActiveX.

OLE versus ActiveX

Currently, the name OLE is used to refer to the technologies and processes associated with linking and embedding. This includes OLE containers, OLE servers—a.k.a. ActiveX servers—OLE items, in-place activation, trackers, drag-and-drop, and menu merging.

The name ActiveX refers to the Component Object Model (COM) and to such COM-based objects as ActiveX controls.

OLE Automation is now simply referred to as Automation, and OLE Servers are now ActiveX servers.

OLE Structured Storage

OLE *structured storage* is an OLE-supported technology for storing and maintaining files composed of two or more OLE elements from different sources in a single document file. Accomplishing this task involves three principal elements: compound files, storage objects, and stream objects.

- A *compound file* is an OLE-supported structured storage implementation which incorporates the `IStorage`, `IStream`, and `ILockBytes` interfaces. The Stg*Xxx* helper functions are used to create and manipulate compound files.

- A *storage object* is a COM object implementing the `IStorage` interface. Storage objects contain nested storage objects or stream objects, resulting in the equivalent of a directory/file structure within a single file. A storage object is analogous to a directory and is the highest level object in the ActiveX storage system.

- A *stream object* is a COM object implementing the `IStream` interface and is analogous to a file in a directory/file system. For example, digitized audio or video files can be serialized to disk using a stream object.

Also, the iPersist interface provides a common set of functions and properties for manipulating persistent data. (Examples include data saved by ActiveX servers or by embedded or linked objects inside OLE container documents.)

By combining inheritance with Structured Storage, two related objects can expose the same data using different property names.

Each of these elements, and other aspects of structured storage, are discussed below.

Compound Documents

A compound document is simply any document containing linked and/or embedded objects in addition to the document's native data. The advantages of compound documents are simple: different types of data, supported by different applications, can be combined in a single presentation or can be drawn on to create an integrated product. While compound documents are most often thought of as visual documents—letters, memos, spreadsheets, or other documents intended to be printed and read—compound documents may actually be worksheets or data sets where different elements are supplied by separate server utilities from different sources, with or without actually being visually presented. Figure 8.1 illustrates a compound document.

Microsoft ✔ *Exam* *Objective*	**Evaluate the use of one or more of the following in a given component solution: compound documents, OLE embedding and linking, and OLE drag and drop.**

Compound files are an integral part of OLE and are used to transfer data and for OLE document storage. Compound files are also an implementation of the ActiveX structure storage model. The advantage of compound files is the existence of consistent interfaces supporting serialization to storage, streams, or file objects.

Compound files, however, do not imply that the information originates from an OLE document or compound document: compound files are only one of the methods of storing compound files, OLE documents, or other data.

FIGURE 8.1

Inside a compound
document file

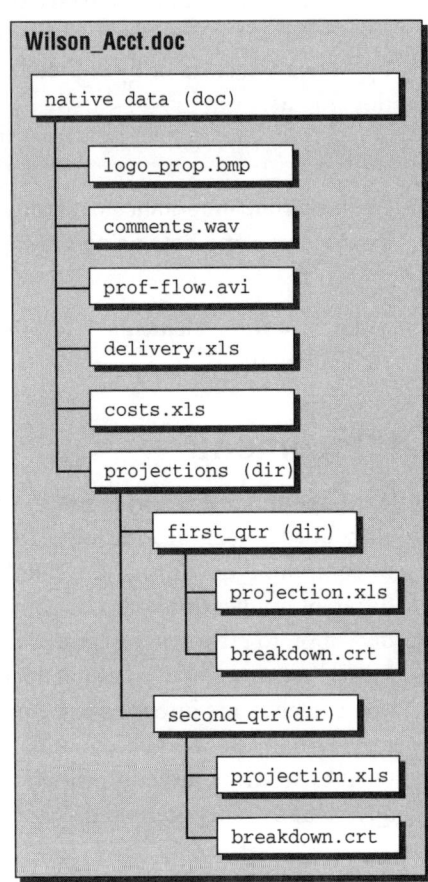

Advantages of Compound Files

The use of compound files offers benefits which were not available with earlier methods of file storage (i.e., storing each component as a separate file), including:

- Incremental file access

- File access modes

- Standardized file structures

Incremental File Access   Incremental file access is an automatic benefit of compound files. Since a compound file can be treated as a file system within a file, individual objects within the compound file, such as stream or storage objects, can be accessed without loading the entire file. This file-within-a-file format makes access to contained objects expeditious both for loading and for updating. When changes have been made to a stream or storage object, OLE does not need to rewrite the entire file but only the revised object.

File Access Modes   Compound files offer two access modes:

- **Transacted**   The transacted mode employs a two-phase commit operation, keeping both old and new copies of a document until instructed to either save the changes or to undo them.

- **Direct**   The direct mode makes immediate changes to a document without the ability to later undo the changes.

These access modes determine when changes to a file are committed.

Standardized File Structures   Because the structures of compound files are standardized, different OLE applications are able to use the compound files without requiring knowledge of the applications which originally created the files. This also supports the ability to update component objects within the file without rewriting the entire file.

Disadvantages of Compound Files

Compound files, however, also contain some potential disadvantages which include:

- Large file sizes

- Performance issues relevant to storing compound files on floppy disks

Size and Performance   The same standardization which provides advantages in compound files also incorporates a complexity of structure which makes files using the compound file format larger than other files using unstructured (flat-file) storage. Where frequent access for loading and saving data is a consideration, using compound files can also cause the file size to increase faster than conventional files. The resulting size can also affect access from floppy disks, resulting in slower access.

Fragmentation   The size of compound files—and the incremental updating of the file—can result in compound file fragmentation where compound files may contain areas of free space which are not actually used, i.e., do not contain data. These blank areas are created during the lifetime of a compound file when storage objects are inserted, updated, or deleted.

OLE Embedding and Linking

OLE linking and embedding operations allow documents, such as a word processor document, to contain images, graphs, formulas, charts, or other non-text objects, including non-graphic objects. Linking and embedding, of course, is not restricted to word processors but can be used with spreadsheets, drawing programs, typesetting applications, drafting programs, or with entirely non-graphic applications simply as a means of exchanging supporting data between applications.

An object is any set of data from one application treated as a unit. OLE applications create compound documents when they combine several objects in one file. The user sees all the objects from one document displayed together in a single window. To the client program, each object looks like a black box full of incomprehensible data. The program calls OLE functions to manipulate objects; it does not need to understand them.

An embedded component object is commonly created by employing the Paste command in a container application. The source data for an embedded item is stored as part of the OLE document (see "Compound Documents," above).

When importing an object, a client chooses between linking and embedding. *Embedding*, just like pasting, gives the client a complete and independent copy of the data. An embedded object, however, remembers its origin, and the user can edit an embedded document by double-clicking it. The double-click invokes the server application, and the editing happens there. When the user closes the server, the client receives the updated object.

The second way of storing objects is to *link* them. Linked component objects are also referred to simply as linked items or links but should not be confused—despite the common terminology—with hypertext links used to reference Internet or remote document locations.

Linking does not give the client its own independent copy of the data; instead, the client receives a live connection to a piece of the server's document—a kind of window opening into a view of the server's data. If the object is modified in the server, the modifications appear automatically in the client. If several clients link to the same object, an update in one place is visible in all the others (see Figure 8.2).

The process of creating a linked component object is similar to creating an embedded component object, except that the Paste Link command—rather than the Paste command—is used. The difference with a linked component, however, is that the link contains a path to the original data, which is generally located in a separate file.

FIGURE 8.2

A linked .WAV file
versus an embedded
.WAV file

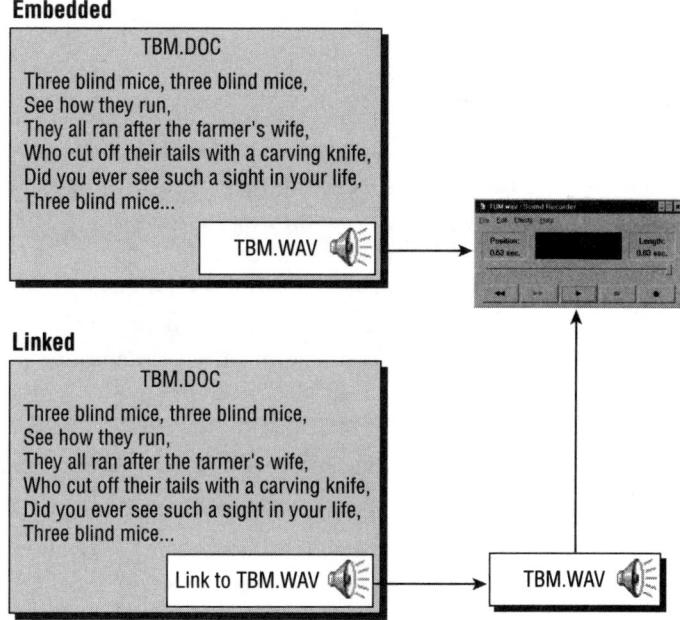

As an example, consider a word processor document which contains a link to cells belonging to a spreadsheet application, or, more accurately, to cells in a spreadsheet document. The word processor document contains only the link information, that is, the specification which indicates where the source document is found and which portion of the source document is linked.

OLE (ActiveX) objects know where their server application is located based on information in the registry. If a server application is moved without updating the registry, then the objects will be unable to execute.

The OLE (ActiveX) Adaptable Links feature applies only to linked OLE document objects.

When the word processor document is opened and the link is clicked, the original spreadsheet document is launched and updates the information shown in the word processor document.

When a link is broken, the pointer to the linked information remains in the document but the source file for the link is no longer reachable. Instead, only the image of the original link source is available.

The difference is that the embedded data is static—the content of the embedded information does not change outside of the container—while the linked data is updated and changed by an external application and source.

Linked objects have the advantage of taking less space in the document file. Embedded objects have the advantage of being very portable; documents that contain only embedded objects can move from system to system. Because they carry all their data with them, they do not require the OLE server to reside on the destination system. The user can change linked objects into embedded objects at will.

OLE embedding maintains data within the application, making the application file size larger and less efficient. Also, because OLE-embedded source data is local to the application, it can not be edited by other users.

NOTE OLE embedding has no effect on data security.

In summary, when a document file contains all the data for an object, the object is *embedded*. When a document contains only a reference pointing to data in another document, the object is *linked*. Both methods produce the same result on the screen, but only linked objects receive updates. Embedded objects are transferred through the equivalent of a DDE cold link; when you copy them into your document, they become independent of their source. By contrast, if you link an object into several documents, changing the object in one place causes it to change in all the others.

Every OLE component item, however, whether it has been embedded or linked, has an identifier associated not only with the application creating the component but with the item type. For example, Excel is one type of component item, while Quattro Pro is another, even though both are spreadsheet applications supporting OLE. At the same time, Excel can create three different types of OLE components: worksheets, charts, and macrosheets, each of which is identified by a unique CLSID.

OLE Drag and Drop

Using OLE, when performing data transfers either with the Clipboard or with drag and drop, the data always has both a source and a destination. One application—the source—is providing the data for the copy, while another application—the destination—accepts the data for pasting. To accomplish this, each side of the transfer operation has to execute different operations on the same data for the exchange to take place successfully.

The Microsoft Foundation Classes (MFC) provide two classes supporting OLE transfers.

- **Data source objects**   These classes are implemented through the `COleDataSource` class and support the source side of the data exchange. Data source objects are created by the source application whenever data is to be copied to the Clipboard or transferred though a drag-and-drop operation.

- **Data objects**   These classes are implemented by the `COleDataObject` class. They provide the destination side of the data transfer and are created when a drag-and-drop operation supplies data to the application or when the application is asked to paste information from the Clipboard.

Because they retain full-featured editing and operating capabilites, ActiveX-embedded objects are well suited for drag-and-drop operations when copied between containers. When memory space is limited or when a large number of memory-intensive objects are used in a single form, however, OLE linked objects are more efficient than ActiveX-embedded objects.

Creating Data Sources   Data transfer source applications, which may be on either the client or server side of an OLE relationship, use data objects as containers to transfer the information. The data source is created when the application needs to copy data for transfer.

Typically, a data copy operation would follow this format:

1. A block of data is selected (either by the user or by a scripted operation).

2. The Copy or Cut operation is selected from the Edit menu or a drag-and-drop operation is started.

3. The application creates a `COleDataSource` or a `COleDataSource`-derived data object.

4. A function from either the `CacheData` or `DelayRenderData` group inserts the selection into the data object.

5. Either the `SetClipboard` member of the data object is called to copy the object to the clipboard or the `DoDragDrop` member is called for a drag-and-drop operation.

6. If the operation is a Cut operation or if `DoDragDrop` returns `DROPEFFECT_MOVE`, the data selected is deleted from the original (source) document.

For examples of the scenario described preceding, refer to the MFC OLE samples OClient and HierSvr distributed with Visual C++.

Destroying Data Sources Data sources must always be destroyed by the application that is the current owner of the data source. When the source data object is handed to OLE as through the COleDataSource::SetClipboard member, OLE becomes the owner of the data object and is then responsible for destroying the object.

On the other hand, if the application retains ownership of the data object, the application retains the responsibility as well. This is exactly the same treatment as would be accorded to any C++ object instance.

Creating Data Objects On the receiving end of the process, data objects are commonly needed either when data is dropped into an application using drag-and-drop or when a Paste or Paste Special operation is selected from the Edit menu.

In the first circumstance—drag and drop—there is no need to create a new data object because a pointer to the existing data object is passed to the application's OnDrop function. This data object was created by the framework as part of the drag and drop operation and will be destroyed by it (see "Destroying Data Objects," below).

When the receiving end of the process is performing a Paste or a Paste Special operation, however, the application should first create a COleDataObject object and then call the object's AttachClipboard member function. This action associates the data object with the data contained in the Clipboard. Finally, the data object can be used in the actual paste function.

For an example, refer to the OClient demo program distributed with Visual C++ and note the OnDrop, OnPaste, and OnPasteLink functions.

Destroying Data Objects Assuming that object-oriented programming or MFC are employed, a data object created for a paste function will be destroyed automatically when the object goes out of scope as the function ends.

If any other type of handling is employed, however, the application must be explicitly destroyed after completing the paste operation. Until the data object has been destroyed, no other application will be able to copy data to the Clipboard.

Using Active Documents

Active Documents are also called *Doc Objects* or *Document Objects* and—in contrast to OLE embedded objects displayed within another document—are full-scale documents which are embedded in a container application. Thus an active document may be presented in a Web browser or in an ActiveX container, such as the Microsoft Office Binder, Microsoft Excel, or Microsoft Word, which provides support for ActiveX documents.

Microsoft ✓ *Exam* *Objective*	**Evaluate the use of Active Documents as a component of a solution for a given business problem.**

While objects embedded in documents are at least partially at the mercy of the container document, Active Documents have the advantage of owning their pages and exercising complete control over their presentations. Active documents also have the freedom to exploit the full native functionally of their servers (the server application creating the document).

Further, because Active Documents exploit the complete functionality of the server application, document creators can use all of the features of their favorite applications while treating the end product as a single entity. Of course, many—if not most—Active Document servers may also support embedded objects. This means that the resulting active document may include other objects supported by multiple servers but the advantage—treating the result as a single project—remains.

For an example of Active Document technology, use Internet Explorer to open a Microsoft Word document (see Figure 8.3).

You will find the document displayed just as if it were being edited in Word, even though it is contained by Internet Explorer. Internet Explorer is supplying the basic menus, toolbars, and status bars. At the same time, Word adds its own menus, toolbars, and status bars, providing an interface which, presumably, will be familiar to the user.

FIGURE 8.3

Editing a Word document in Internet Explorer

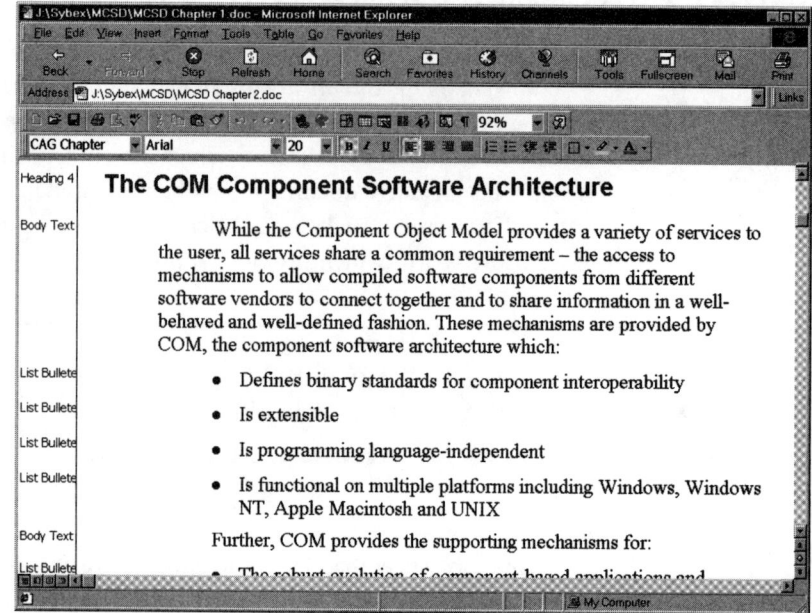

In Visual C++, Active Documents are supported by two classes:

- CDocObjectServer class maps the ActiveX document interfaces as well as initializing and activating ActiveX document objects.

- CDocObjectServerItem class specifically implements OLE server verbs for ActiveX document servers.

While both Visual Basic and Visual C++ support creating Active Document servers and containers, the following description uses Visual C++ but does not depend on MFC.

The DocObj.h header contains the Active Document-specific definitions while no special libraries are required.

Creating an Active Document Server

An Active Document server functions as an OLE local server and is very similar to an OLE in-place server. An Active Doc server provides the full functionality of the document application while being contained within an Active Document container. Within the container, the Active Doc is allowed to combine the document's menus (the server application's menus) with the container's menus (see Figure 8.3).

An Active Document assumes full control of the container application's client window (the view area) and can display its own toolbars, status bars, and scrollbars within this area. In this fashion, the Active Document can be hosted by any of a variety of containers while still presenting and using the original application's interface.

Step 1: Create an OLE Server   The first step in creating an Active Document server is to create a file-based OLE local server which implements the interfaces shown in Table 8.1. While not all of these interfaces are necessary for all servers, many of these—as noted—are required for the minimal implementation of any server.

Interface	Required	Description
T A B L E 8.1 Active Document interfaces		
IOleDocument	Yes	Used to create views of an Active Document, to enumerate the views the object supports, and to provide miscellaneous information about the object's capabilities
IOleDocumentView	Yes	Used to activate, deactivate, close, and communicate with a document's view object.
IPersistStorage	Yes	Used to initialize the document object and place it in the loaded or running state. Also used to instruct an object to perform various save operations or to release its storage
IOleObject	Yes	Used to execute verbs, communicate site information, and close the view
IDataObject	Yes	Used to get and set data in the object
IOleInPlaceObject	Yes	Used to activate and deactivate the view object
IOleInPlace-ActiveObject	Yes	Used to control the view object while active

TABLE 8.1 *(cont.)*	Interface	Required	Description
Active Document interfaces	IEnumFORMATETC	No	Used to determine the data formats supported by the object
	IEnumOleDocument-Views	No	Used to determine the views supported by the object
	IOleCommandTarget	No	Used to dispatch commands and receive command status information from an objec
	IPrint	No	Used to print an Active Document

Step 2: Register the Active Document Server Before an Active Document can be contained by a server application, the Active Document class must be registered. The following represents the minimum registry information needed to register an Active Document server (the information shown in <> brackets is implementation-specific):

```
HKEY_CLASSES_ROOT\<file extension> = <prog ID>
HKEY_CLASSES_ROOT\<prog ID> = <document name>
HKEY_CLASSES_ROOT\<prog ID>\CLSID = <clsid>
HKEY_CLASSES_ROOT\CLSID\<clsid>\LocalServer32 =
     <server path and file>
HKEY_CLASSES_ROOT\CLSID\<clsid>\InprocHandler32 = "ole32.dll"
HKEY_CLASSES_ROOT\CLSID\<clsid>\Insertable = ""
HKEY_CLASSES_ROOT\CLSID\<clsid>\DocObject = ""
```

The \Insertable and \DocObject registry keys shown are not necessary if the CATID_Insertable and CATID_DocObject component categories have already been registered for the server. Registering these component categories automatically causes these keys to be added. (Refer to the ICat-Register::RegisterClassImplCategories method.)

One additional registry entry may be provided (optionally) to have an icon displayed for the file type in Explorer.

```
HKEY_CLASSES_ROOT\CLSID\<clsid>\DefaultIcon = <server path
and file>,<icon index>
```

The *IDataObject* Interface

While an IDataObject interface is not specific to an Active Document, some Active Document containers store document information using container-specific formats rather than server-specific formats. When this is done, the container makes a copy of the data before activating the document by requesting the data via the IDataObject::GetDataHere method using the "Embed Source" registered DVASPECT_CONTENT and TYMED_ISTORAGE clipboard format.

To respond to the IDataObject request, the server stores the document's data in the IStorage interface provided through the STGMEDIUM structure. For implementation, refer to the OleSave API function.

The *IOleDocument* Interface

The IOleDocument interface forms the basis for the Active Document server and is used by the container to create views, to request a view enumerator (IEnumOleDocumentViews), and to retrieve document status information.

Step 3: Create the Document View   When opening an Active Document, the container sends a request to the server asking for a document view to be displayed. The process that unfolds involves three steps:

1. The container calls the server's IOleObject::DoVerb method with the iVerb parameter set as OLEIVERB_SHOW, OLEIVERB_PRIMARY, or OLEIVERB_UIACTIVATE.

2. The server calls the IOleClientSite pointer—by calling QueryInterface—to obtain the container's IOleDocumentSite pointer.

3. The server calls the container's IOleDocumentSite::ActivateMe method, passing either a valid IOleDocumentView pointer or NULL. If a valid pointer is supplied, the document view will be activated but, if the argument is NULL, the container calls the server's IOleDocument::CreateView method to create the view.

A simple example of an `IOleObject::DoVerb` implementation is shown below:

```
STDMETHODIMP COleObject::DoVerb( LONG iVerb,
                                 LPMSG lpmsg,
                                 LPOLECLIENTSITE pActiveSite,
                                 LONG lindex,
                                 HWND hwndParent,
                                 LPCRECT lprcPosRect )
{
    HRESULT  hr = E_FAIL;

    switch (iVerb)
    {
        case OLEIVERB_SHOW:
        case OLEIVERB_PRIMARY:
        case OLEIVERB_UIACTIVATE:
        {
            //try to get the IOleDocumentSite pointer
            LPOLEDOCUMENTSITE pOleDocSite;
            hr = pActiveSite->QueryInterface(
                            IID_IOleDocumentSite,
                            (LPVOID*)&pOleDocSite );
            if( SUCCEEDED(hr) )
                // passing NULL will cause the site to call
                // the CreateView method
                hr = pOleDocSite->ActivateMe( NULL );
        }
        break;

        default:        break;
    }
    return hr;
}
```

A simple example of an `IOleDocument::CreateView` implementation follows:

```
STDMETHODIMP COleDocument::CreateView(
        IOleInPlaceSite    *pInPlaceSite,
```

```
            IStream            *pStream,
            DWORD              dwReserved,
            IOleDocumentView **ppOleDocumentView )
    {
        HRESULT  hr = E_FAIL;

        *ppOleDocumentView = NULL;  // the view pointer is NULL
            // since only one view is supported,
            // fail if the view already exists
        if( ! m_pOleDocView )
        {
            m_pOleDocView = new COleDocumentView();
            if( m_pOleDocView )
            {
                // since the pointer is being given away, do AddRef
                m_pOleDocView->AddRef();

                if( pInPlaceSite )
                        // if given pInPlaceSite, use as site
                        // for view just created
                    m_pOleDocView->SetInPlaceSite( pInPlaceSite );

                if( pStream )
                        // if given pStream, initialize view state
                    m_pOleDocView->ApplyViewState( pStream );

                *ppOleDocumentView = m_pOleDocView;
                hr = S_OK;
            }
        }
        return hr;
    }
```

The Active Document container uses the IOleDocumentView interface to manage the display by setting the view's site, or by activating and deactivating the view.

Step 4: Retrieve the Active Document's View Site When the server's
IOleDocumentView::SetInPlaceSite method is called, if the server is maintaining an existing IOleInPlaceSite pointer, the server is responsible for
releasing the pointer, then calling AddRef (to increment the object's access
count) and, finally, storing the new IOleInPlaceSite pointer.

The IOleInPlaceSite pointer is used to inform the site of in-place activa-
tion and deactivation and to retrieve a handle to the view's parent window.
The parent window handle is retrieved by calling the interface's IOleWindow::
GetWindow function as shown in the following example:

```
STDMETHODIMP COleDocumentView::SetInPlaceSite(
                               IOleInPlaceSite *pNewSite )
{
    // if prior site exists, clean it up
  if( m_pInPlaceSite )
  {
    if( m_fUIActive )     // call view's private method
       DeactivateUI();    // to handle UI deactivation
    m_pInPlaceSite->Release();
    m_pInPlaceSite = NULL;
  }
  m_pInPlaceSite = pNewSite;
  if( m_pInPlaceSite )
     m_pInPlaceSite->AddRef();
  return S_OK;
}
```

Step 5: Activate the Document View A document is activated by the
following:

1. The server's IOleDocumentView::UIActivate method is called with a
   non-zero (TRUE) fActivate parameter.

2. The server ensures that the object becomes in-place active by calling
   the site's IOleInPlaceSite::OnInPlaceActivate method and then
   showing the view window.

3. The server performs the necessary tasks to become UI-active, including
   adding toolbars, merging menu items, and supporting any other UI
   objects desired by the Active Document.

4. The server notifies the site that the view is being UI-activated by
   calling the site's IOleInPlaceSite::OnUIActivate method.

Deactivating the Document View

A document is deactivated whenever the user is finished editing the embedded document, returns to the container application for some other operation, or begins operations on another embedded document. Or, of course, automatically on closure. The Active Document's view deactivation is similar to activation:

1. The document server's `IOleDocumentView::UIActivate` method is called with a zero (FALSE) `fActivate` parameter.

2. The document server removes its toolbars, status bars, or other UI objects.

3. The document server calls the site's `IOleInPlaceSite::OnUI-Deactivate` method to notify the site that the view is being UI-deactivated.

Multiple Document Containers

Since some container objects may hold more than one Active Document, the containers notify the object that the Active Document window is being activated by calling the document's `IOleInPlaceActivateObject::OnDocWindowActivate` method with a non-zero (TRUE) argument. Normally, this would occur after the object was already UI-active. When this notification is received, the object must display its UI objects, i.e., menus, toolbars, status bars.

Likewise, when an Active Document is being deactivated, the object's `IOleInPlaceActiveObject::OnDocWindowActivate` method is called with a zero (FALSE) argument. The deactivated document object is responsible for hiding its UI objects, such as toolbars and status bars, but the object is not responsible for removing its menus: The container object is responsible for this part of the task.

However, when an Active Document is being deactivated, it is not necessary to completely UI-deactivate the object.

Active Document Server Palette Management

Active Documents, in general, use the same palette management scheme as ActiveX controls with the exception that Active Documents do not receive ambient properties from their clients. In managing palettes, the Active Document server is responsible for:

- Notifying the container of which palette the Active Document requires by implementing the `IViewObject::GetColorSet` method (the same method OLE controls use to manage palettes)

- Realizing its own palette in the background—except in response to the WM_QUERYNEWPALETTE message, which is forwarded by the container (again, the same method OLE controls use)

The only real difference between Active Documents and OLE Controls is that Active Documents are not required to handle the DISPID_AMBIENT_ PALETTE property.

Active Document Requirements

Before Active Document servers can open in-place in Active Doc containers, the ACTXPRXY.DLL must be installed on a system. ACTXPRXY.DLL is installed when Office 97 or Internet Explorer (3.0 or later) are installed but, if neither of these products is present on a system, it will be necessary to redistribute the dynamic link library with the container application.

The ACTXPRXY library provides support for out-of-process marshalling for the Active Document interfaces. If the library is not present or if it is not registered, out-of-process containers will fail when attempting to negotiate with an Active Document server.

The ActXPrxy.DLL library is available as a self-extracting executable, AxRedist.exe, which contains the complete ActiveX redistributables for the ActiveX SDK with a single version supporting Windows 95, Windows 98, and Windows NT 4.0.

Summary

OLE provides a means for creating compound documents and is supported by a number of services including structured storage, drag-and-drop data transfers, and UDT (Uniform Data Transfer). UDT provides the model for clipboard data transfer, drag-and-drop operations and automation through the IDataObject interface. The IDataObject interface provides methods to enumerate available formats and, in some cases, to manage connections which include advisory sinks for notifications of changes in data.

Structured storage is a hierarchical organization permitting both native and linked or embedded document data to be stored in a single file while still maintaining the internal organization and separation of data elements.

Compound documents are documents containing linked or embedded data as well as the document's native data. They permit the creation of documents with resources—both data and services—drawn from a variety of different server applications.

Object Linking and Embedding is one form of operation supporting compound documents, but compound documents are not limited to OLE.

Active Documents, a.k.a. Doc Objects or Document Objects, are full-scale documents which are embedded (displayed by) a container application. Active Documents have the advantage over OLE objects in being able to exploit the full functionality of the server application.

In Visual C++, Active Documents are supported by the `CDocObjectServer` class, which maps the ActiveX document interfaces, as well as initializing and activating ActiveX document objects, and the `CDocObjectServerItem` class which implements OLE server verbs for ActiveX document servers.

Active Documents are responsible— on activation and deactivation—for their own toolbars, status bars, and scrollbars, while the container applications are responsible for presenting the server's menus. Some document containers may support multiple Active Documents.

Review Questions

1. The ACTXPRXY.DLL library supporting out-of-process marshalling for Active Document interfaces requires which of the following?

    A. A single version for Windows 95, Windows 98, and Windows NT 4.0

    B. Either Office 97 or Internet Explorer (3.0 or later) to be installed

    C. One version for Windows 95 and Windows 98 and a separate version for Windows 4.0

    D. Separate versions for Windows 95, Windows 98, and Windows NT 4.0

2. What is the advantage of OLE embedding over OLE linking?

    A. OLE embedding allows concurrent data access to multiple users.

    B. OLE embedding offers improved data security.

    C. OLE embedding prevents file sizes from expanding.

    D. OLE embedding supports in-place editing.

3. When an Active Document is being deactivated, what is the Active Document server responsible for?

 A. Adding its menus to the container object's menu bar

 B. Displaying all UI objects such as toolbars and status bars

 C. Hiding all UI objects such as toolbars and status bars

 D. Removing its menus from the container object's menu bar

4. When memory resources are limited, what is the best type of OLE object for drag-and-drop operations?

 A. An Internet object

 B. An OLE Java object

 C. An OLE-embedded object

 D. An OLE-linked object

5. When an Active Document is being activated, what is the Active Document server responsible for? (Select two.)

 A. Calling the server's `IOleDocumentView::SetInPlaceSite` method

 B. Calling the server's `IOleDocumentView::UIActivate` method with a non-zero (TRUE) `fActivate` parameter

 C. Displaying all UI objects such as toolbars and status bars

 D. Merging the server's menus to the container object's menu bar

6. To respond to an `IDataObject` request, how does the server store the document's data in the `IStorage` interface?

 A. Through the `IDataObject::GetDataHere` method

 B. Through the `IOleDocument` interface

 C. Through the `OleSave` API function

 D. Through the `STGMEDIUM` structure

7. Assume a Word document contains a linked Exel spreadsheet. If the Word document is opened after all references to Microsoft Excel are deleted from the registry:

    A. The linked spreadsheet will be visible but cannot be edited until Excel is reinstalled.

    B. The linked spreadsheet will be visible but must be relinked before it can be edited.

    C. The linked spreadsheet will be visible but the Excel type library must be reinstalled before editing.

    D. The linked spreadsheet will not be visible.

8. What is the advantage of OLE linking over OLE embedding?

    A. Linking does not inflate file sizes.

    B. Linking ensures that data is encapsulated within an application.

    C. Linking supports frame adornment.

    D. Linking supports in-place editing.

9. When registering an Active Document server, the \Insertable and \DocObject registry keys:

    A. Are always required

    B. Are required only if the CATID_Insertable and CATID_DocObject component categories have already been registered

    C. Are not required if the CATID_Insertable and CATID_DocObject component categories have already been registered

    D. Are never required

10. The Active Document IOleDocument interface is *not* used to:

    A. Activate and deactivate a document's view object

    B. Create views of an Active Document

    C. Enumerate the views the object supports

    D. Provide miscellaneous information about the object's capabilities

11. An `iAdviseSink` interface would offer the greatest benefit to:

   A. A budget application using linked Excel spreadsheets

   B. A DCOM application relying on synchronous event notification

   C. A document control application managing large print jobs

   D. A remote automation application using standard marshalling

12. The Active Document `IDataObject` interface is used to:

   A. Activate and deactivate the view object

   B. Get and set data in the object

   C. Initialize the document object and place it in the loaded or running state

   D. Perform various save operations or to release storage

13. Assume that a new hard drive has been added to a desktop system and that Microsoft Excel has been moved to the new drive without re-installation. After this is done, a Word document is opened which contains an embedded Excel spreadsheet. What is the effect of moving the EXCEL.EXE application on the document?

   A. The Adaptable Links feature of ActiveX will allow the embedded spreadsheet to be edited.

   B. The embedded spreadsheet can only be updated from within Excel.

   C. The embedded spreadsheet will appear but the system registry must be updated before the spreadsheet can be edited.

   D. The embedded spreadsheet will not appear but will be replaced by an icon.

14. An Active Document:

   A. Assumes full control of the container application's client window

   B. Assumes full control of the container application's frame window

   C. Acts as an embedded object

   D. Acts as a linked object

15. When an OLE-embedded or linked object is selected in an OLE document, the container application may perform object-specific operations which are identified by data entries stored in:

  A. An .INI file

  B. The container

  C. The OLE object

  D. The registry

16. When an Active Document is displayed by a container:

  A. The Active Document's menu replaces the container application's menu.

  B. The Active Document's menu is merged with the container application's menu.

  C. The Active Document's menu appears below the container application's menu.

  D. The Active Document supplies a composite menu for both the server and client applications.

17. Assume that a Word document has a link to a Paintbrush bitmap image file which is stored on the same drive as the document file. When the document file is copied to a floppy disk, without copying the bitmap file, and then opened from the floppy disk on another computer, what will occur:

  A. An icon will appear in place of the bitmap image.

  B. The bitmap image will appear but an error will occur if the image is deleted.

  C. The bitmap image will appear in the document but the original image file can not be updated.

  D. The bitmap image will not appear in the document.

18. In Visual C++, Active Documents are supported by what two classes? (Select two.)

    A. CDocObject class

    B. CDocObjectServer class

    C. CDocObjectServerItem class

    D. CDocObjectClientItem class

19. The COM Structured Storage System provides two types of objects:

    A. A binary object and a file object

    B. A binary object and a stream object

    C. A storage object and a file object

    D. A stream object and a storage object

20. Which statement is false?

    A. Active Documents have the advantage of owning their pages and exercise complete control over their presentation.

    B. Active Documents have the freedom to exploit the full native functionality of their servers.

    C. Objects embedded in documents are at least partially at the mercy of the container document.

    D. Objects embedded in documents have the freedom to exploit the full native functionality of their servers.

21. Interfaces provided by the COM Structured Storage SDK can be implemented using inheritance in Visual C++. Select the interface(s) which allow separate applications to share data in a storage object without relying on global memory.

    A. iCreateFileMoniker

    B. iMemAlloc

    C. iPersist

    D. iVirtualAlloc

22. What can Active Documents be presented by?

   A. ActiveX containers

   B. OLE client applications

   C. OLE servers applications

   D. Web browsers

23. Which of the following do compound files offer?

   A. Direct access mode which makes differed changes to a document

   B. Direct access mode which makes immediate changes to a document

   C. Transacted access mode which makes differed changes to a document

   D. Transacted access mode which makes immediate changes to a document

24. Which of the following are structured storage features? (Select all that apply.)

   A. Compound files

   B. Directory objects

   C. Folder objects

   D. Two-phase commits

25. In comparing embedded and linked data using OLE, which of the following is correct? (Select two.)

   A. Embedded data is static.

   B. Embedded data occupies less space in a document file.

   C. Linked data is static.

   D. Linked data occupies less space in a document file.

26. Which of the following are true of the Component Object Model (COM) Structured Storage System?

A. Storage objects are analogous to files within directories.

B. Storage objects can contain both streams and other storage objects.

C. Storage objects can contain streams but cannot contain other storage objects.

D. Storage objects form the highest level object in the ActiveX storage system.

27. The Component Object Model (COM) reduces the use of global system resource through dependence on:

A. ActiveX components

B. ActiveX controls

C. ActiveX documents

D. Uniform Data Transfer

28. An ActiveX object created using Visual Basic has control of a Microsoft Excel object. When a new hard drive is installed on a system and the user moves Microsoft Excel to the new drive (including all associated files) without reinstalling Excel, what is required for the ActiveX object to retain control of the Excel object?

A. The ActiveX object must be rewritten.

B. The adaptable links in ActiveX will allow everything to function unchanged.

C. The registry entries for Excel must be updated.

D. The user must reinstall the VBRun Dynamic Link Library.

CHAPTER

9

ActiveX (OLE Controls)
as COM Implementations

- Identify the appropriate use of ActiveX controls within component solutions.

- Discuss the use of the ActiveX™ and the OLE technologies as implementations of the COM.

- Identify which ActiveX technologies are appropriate for use in implementing a given business solution.

- Explain the implementation of Automation in the Microsoft Windows operating systems.

- Identify situations in which Remote Automation is an appropriate technology to use in order to provide a desirable solution.

- Discuss the use of Uniform Data Transfer (UDT) as part of a component solution.

- Assess structured storage as a component of a given solution.

The ActiveX Technology family—which includes ActiveX controls—comprises a group of technologies with one primary function: to allow the developer to create Internet applications using familiar tools and technologies. Table 9.1 details the components of the ActiveX technology family.

T A B L E 9.1: ActiveX Family

Component Group	Function	Formerly Called
Active Scripts	Scripting languages used to connect controls and to add interactive functionality to Web pages, includes VBScript and others	n/a
ActiveX controls	ActiveX objects can be incorporated into Web pages and other ActiveX containers, including applications developed using Access, FoxPro, Visual Basic, and Visual C++	OLE controls

T A B L E 9.1: ActiveX Family *(continued)*

Component Group	Function	Formerly Called
ActiveX documents	Can be displayed by Web browsers using Active Document servers	n/a
ActiveX server framework	Supports customized Web pages using data-base content and other customizations	ISAPI (Internet Server API), other server-side extensions
Code Download and Verification	Support for automatic downloading, verification, and installation	n/a
HTML extensions	Support for controls and scripting	n/a
Internet ActiveX controls	ActiveX controls for including browser and Internet communications capabilities in applications	n/a
Internet Data Download Services	APIs providing Internet access to data	n/a

---

Microsoft **Identify the appropriate use of ActiveX controls within**
✓ Exam **component solutions.**
Objective

ActiveX control objects—and to some degree ActiveX documents—are the component members of the ActiveX technology family and allow the application designer to create custom components. The reason for creating custom components is simple: components allow developers to create tools for specific tasks without having to create entirely new application suites to support these tools. Instead, using the COM model and ActiveX technology, applications can be created as an aggregate of existing components, customized by using only the components appropriate to the task or to the user's needs and adapted to new requirements by creating new components—instead of by creating new applications.

With the pervasive marketing of application suites such as Microsoft Office 97, development times are slow, requiring years to design, develop, and market a new application suite.

Using the COM model and component technology, the emphasis changes from monolithic application suites that supply everything as part of one single integrated package to slimmer root applications that are expanded by introducing COM and ActiveX components to serve specific needs and to fill specific requirements. This is, of course, an approach which will not be popular with marketing if only because components are not marketable in the same fashion as application suites. This will be unpopular for other reasons as well since COM certainly infers the capability of many developers to contribute components to a solution rather than a single company supplying a solution package.

The end result, however, of this evolutionary path in application development will be that every user will be able to design his/her own applications to suit their personal requirements instead of simply settling for whichever package comes closest to filling their needs.

Microsoft ✓ *Exam* *Objective* | **Discuss the use of the ActiveX™ and the OLE technologies as implementations of the COM.**

The Basics of ActiveX Controls

The foundation supporting ActiveX controls (previously called OLE controls) consists of eight principal elements:

- **COM (Component Object Model)**   Every ActiveX control is essentially a COM object which exposes the IUnknown interface to allow clients to obtain pointers to other interfaces supported by the object. Using the IClassFactory2 interface, ActiveX controls can support licensing and can also support self-registration.

- **Compound documents**   A compound document is any document that includes any linked or embedded objects, as well as its own native data. An ActiveX control is often an in-place active object embedded in a client container such as a compound document. In use, the control is activated to initiate an action in the container application. These were examined in Chapter 8.

- **Connectable objects**   ActiveX controls may support both incoming and outgoing interfaces, using outgoing interfaces—through connectable objects—to allow the control to communicate with the client object. Such bi-directional connectivity means that a control can initiate an action in the client, can notify a client that a change has occurred in the control object, or can query the client before taking action.

- **OLE automation**   OLE automation can be used in ActiveX controls to permit clients access to the control's features through a client-supplied programming language. ActiveX automation controls (or other server objects) are objects which expose programmable objects to client applications (automation clients). By exposing programmable objects, the client applications are able to automate certain procedures through direct access to the objects and through functionality made available by the server.

- **Persistence storage**   An ActiveX control can implement one (or more) of several persistence interfaces to support a means of saving a control's state. Optimally, control objects should implement multiple interfaces to offer the container object the widest choice of means. It is the control object designer, however, who must determine which types of persistence are important and implement the appropriate interfaces; the client object selects which interface it prefers to use. At a minimum, control objects which have a persistent state—of any kind—must implement at least one IPersist interface.

- **Property pages**   The property pages of ActiveX controls allow an object to display its internal properties in a tabbed dialog box. This display permits the users to view and change the control's properties. A component object can display its property pages independently from the client or the client may display the property pages from multiple contained objects in a single property sheet. The property pages also provide a means for the object to notify the client of changes in an object's properties.

A property page is a COM object with its own CLSID which is part of a user interface, implemented by a control, and allows the control's properties to be viewed and altered. Property page objects implement the IPropertyPage interface. Alternately, a logically related group of properties associated with a persistently stored object comprise a property set and are implemented through the IPropertySetStorage interface.

- **Uniform data transfer**   Uniform data transfer is a model for exchanging data via the clipboard, through drag-and-drop or using Automation. Component objects conforming to the UDT model implement the IDataObject interface and the IAdviseSink interface for providing an event notification loop. The UDT model is a replacement for DDE (Dynamic Data Exchange).

  ActiveX controls can support drag-and-drop operations within a container object with support from the container using the IOleInPlace-ObjectWindowless interface's GetDropTarget method.

- **System-provided font and image objects**   ActiveX controls may use system-supported font and picture objects to provide visual representations of themselves with the client container. Both the font and picture objects implement several direct interfaces, and both font and picture objects can be created indirectly using functions such as OleCreateFontIndirect, OleCreatePictureIndirect or, to load an image from a stream, OleLoadPicture. The important fact to understand is that these features are usable in any OLE object and there is no requirement to implement a control first.

Supporting DLLs

For Windows NT (4.0 and later), Windows 95, and Windows 98, the system library OLEAUT32.DLL provides the implementation for all standard font and picture API functions including OleCreateFont-Indirect, OleCreatePictureIndirect, OleCreatePropertyFrame, OleCreatePropertyFrameIndirect, OleIconToPicture, OleLoad-Picture, and OleTranslateColor.

For older systems, the corresponding APIs are found in the OLEPRO32.DLL.

ActiveX Controls

An *ActiveX control* is a reusable component supporting a variety of OLE functionality. Equally important, an ActiveX control can be customized to satisfy a variety of design objectives and software requirements. ActiveX controls can be used both in desktop applications in ActiveX control containers and, on the Internet, in Web pages. ActiveX controls can be created using the Microsoft Foundation Classes (MFC) or using the Active Template Library (ATL), as well as Visual Basic 5.

Microsoft ✓ *Exam Objective*	Identify which ActiveX technologies are appropriate for use in implementing a given business solution.

A typical ActiveX control is a small object implemented as an in-process server (see Chapter 6 for more information on dynamic link libraries) which can be used in any OLE container. However, there is one consideration to be aware of when using ActiveX controls: the full and complete functionality of an ActiveX control is available only when the control is used within an OLE container which is designed to be ActiveX-aware.

ActiveX controls (component objects) are fully supported by OLE containers created using Visual C++ with MFC and by Access, Visual Basic, and FoxPro applications. Generically, these containers are called *control containers* and operate ActiveX controls by using the exposed component interfaces to access the control's properties and to receive notifications from the controls as event messages.

ActiveX controls are commonly in-process servers which run in the same process space as the container and do not load the CLASS identifier for a local server. ActiveX controls are built for speed and efficiency.

ActiveX components communicate with each other using the Component Object Model library.

The ideal candidates for ActiveX controls are components providing user interface functionality. For example, an ActiveX component might receive and parse a plain language query from a user to be submitted to a database engine.

In contrast, components providing features such as Remote Automation, business-rule processing, or database access which do not support user interactions are not commonly developed as ActiveX controls.

 Because a type library is an ActiveX component mechanism, it can be used for object access, Object Browser display, and properties and methods type checking. A type library can provide pointers to Help (.HLP) files, but not to .CAB files. The easiest method to view object libraries in server applications is to use the VBA Object Browser.

ActiveX Elements

In order for an ActiveX control to interact efficiently with control containers and with the user, several programmatic elements are employed:

- The class COleControl

- A dispatch map

- A series of event-firing functions

The *COleControl* Class

Because the COleControl class is used as the base class for ActiveX controls developed using MFC, the ActiveX control inherits features including in-place activation and Automation.

The COleControl base-class also provides the ActiveX control object with the functionality of an MFC window object as well as the ability to fire events. Further, for windowless controls, which depend on their container for window support features such as mouse capture, keyboard focus, and scrolling, the COleControl parent provides the same functionality but also offers faster display.

When the ActiveX control is derived from COleControl, the control also inherits the ability to generate event messages which are sent to the control container.

ActiveX Control Events

ActiveX controls use event messages to report to the container when important events have occurred. Typical events include mouse clicks on the control, keyboard data entry, and other changes in the control's state, but may also include results of operations taken by the control. The event messages may be accompanied by parameters to provide additional information.

Using MFC, two types of event are supported: stock events and custom events.

Stock Events   COleControl contains predefined member functions which handle common actions by generating event messages automatically. These include mouse single- and double-clicks on the control, common keyboard events, and changes in the state of the mouse buttons.

Event map identifiers for stock events are always prefixed by EVENT_STOCK_.

The COleControl class supports the nine stock events listed in Table 9.2.

T A B L E   9.2:   COleControl Stock Events

Event	Trigger
Click	A mouse Click event is generated when the ActiveX control has the mouse capture and any mouse button (left, middle, or right) is released over the control, generating a BUTTONUP message from the system. A Click event will always be preceded by a stock MouseDown or MouseUp event.
DblClick	A mouse DblClick event is generated in the same fashion as the Click event but is triggered by a BUTTONDBLCLK message from the system.
Error	An Error event message is generated when an error occurs in an ActiveX control but the error is outside of the scope of a method call or a property access.
KeyDown	A KeyDown event message is generated when a system WM_SYSKEYDOWN or WM_KEYDOWN message is received.
KeyPress	A KeyPress event message is generated when a system WM_CHAR message is received.
KeyUp	A KeyUp event message is generated when a WM_SYSKEYUP or WM_KEYUP message is received.

T A B L E 9.2: COleControl Stock Events *(continued)*

Event	Trigger
MouseDown	A MouseDown event is generated when any BUTTONDOWN event (left, middle, or right mouse button) is received. Before the MouseDown event is generated, mouse capture is automatically initiated to ensure that the subsequent release event is received, regardless of where the event occurs.
MouseMove	A MouseMove event is generated when a system WM_MOUSEMOVE message is received.
MouseUp	A MouseUp event is generated when any BUTTONUP event (left, middle, or right) is received. Before the MouseUp event is generated, the mouse capture is released (see MouseDown).

Custom Events   Custom events are used by ActiveX controls to notify the container component when specific actions have occurred. Custom events can be anything from changes in the internal state of the control to a response to the receipt of a specific window message. In effect, a custom event is any event which is not already handled by the COleControl parent, or may be a supplement to the stock events.

Using Visual C++ to create an ActiveX control, use the ActiveX Events tab in ClassWizard to select both stock and custom events to be supported by the control.

ActiveX Dispatch Map

Once control events have been defined (and implemented), a dispatch map is required to expose a set of methods—an interface—to the control user.

An ActiveX dispatch map also allows control attributes (properties) to be exposed. This latter exposure, however, is in direct contradiction to the COM standard, which specifies that only methods should be exposed through an interface and that properties should only be accessible indirectly through interface methods.

Properties allow the control container—the client component—to manipulate the control in various fashions. Using interface controls, users are permitted to change the appearance of a control, to change specific values used (or displayed) by the control, or to issue requests of the control such as a request for an operation or for the return of some piece of data maintained by the control.

For an ActiveX control to generate event messages, the control class has to map each control event to a member function to be called when the related (internal) event occurs. The event map is the mechanism that provides the mapping between events and member functions providing the event response. During development, the event map allows Visual C++'s ClassWizard to access and manipulate the control's events.

An event map is declared by a macro, in the .H header file of the control class declaration as:

```
// Event maps
    //{{AFX_EVENT(CButtonCtrl)
    void FireClick()
        { FireEvent( DISPID_CLICK, EVENT_PARAM(VTS_NONE) );
}
    //}}AFX_EVENT
    DECLARE_EVENT_MAP()
```

This example declaration is taken from the Button control demo distributed with Visual C++ (in the Devstudio\Vc\Samples\Mfc\Controls\Button subdirectory).

Figure 9.1 shows the ActiveX Events tab in ClassWizard where provisions are offered to add both custom and stock events.

FIGURE 9.1

The ActiveX Events tab in ClassWizard

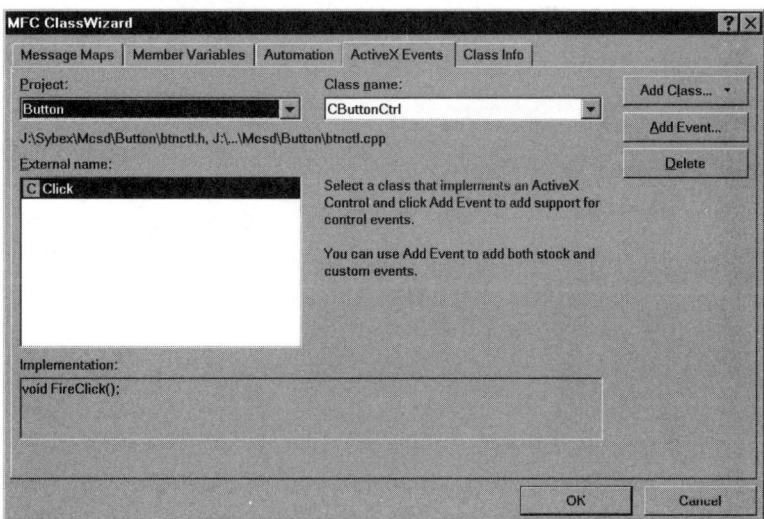

Once the event map has been declared, the implementation for the event map must be defined in the control's implementation file—in this case, in the BTNCRL.CPP file where a single custom event has been declared.

```
/////////////////////////////////////////////////////////
// Event map

BEGIN_EVENT_MAP(CButtonCtrl, COleControl)
//{{AFX_EVENT_MAP(CButtonCtrl)
EVENT_CUSTOM_ID( "Click", DISPID_CLICK, FireClick,
                        VTS_NONE )
//}}AFX_EVENT_MAP
END_EVENT_MAP()
```

The DISPID_CLICK UUID (Universally Unique ID) is a predefined identifier. Other custom events—when triggered by common occurrences—may rely on predefined UUIDs or have custom UUIDs declared in the project.

If you are using Visual C++ and MFC and you employ the ControlWizard to create the project, ControlWizard will add the event map declaration code automatically. If you are not using ControlWizard, the lines may be added manually.

Once the project has been created, using ClassWizard, both stock events supported by the COleControl and custom events can be added. With each event defined, ClassWizard will automatically add the appropriate code entry to the control's event map and to the control's .ODL file.

The .ODL file is created for OLE (OCX) projects and is processed by the Make Type Library (mktyplib) tool to produce the type library (.TLB) file used as a resource with the .OCX product. For ActiveX projects compiled as DLLs, the corresponding file is an .IDL source file which is processed by the MIDL tool to produce a .TLB type library and marshalling code.

> ### 16- and 32-bit ActiveX DLLs
>
> All ActiveX DLLs run in the process space of their controllers. For this reason, ActiveX DLLs must use the same memory model as their controllers and 16-bit ActiveX DLLs can not be used by 32-bit ActiveX controllers and vice versa.
>
> While Windows provides thunking and other mechanisms which allow 16-bit ActiveX EXEs to make calls to 32-bit ActiveX EXEs and 32-bit calls to 16-bit EXEs, DLLs running in the process space of their controllers are faster and better suited for low-level operations—such as memory block searching—than ActiveX EXEs.

Active and Inactive States of an ActiveX Control

ActiveX controls have two basic states: active and inactive. Originally, these states were determined by whether the control exhibited a window or whether it was not visible on the screen. If the control exhibited a window, it was an active control; if it did not have a window, it was an inactive control. However, since windowless activation was introduced, the distinction between active and inactive is not so clearly defined, although it may still apply.

Today, a windowless control may become active and, once active, may invoke mouse capture, acquire the keyboard focus, and acquire other window services from the control's container component. Also, mouse interactions can be provided to inactive controls or controls can be created which remain windowless until activated, at which time they create a window. Once a control with a window becomes active, the control is completely free to interact with the container (the client component object), the user, and with the Windows system.

Serialization

Object persistence—the ability to serialize data—permits a control to write property values to persistent storage. This allows a control to be re-created by retrieving the object's previous state from storage.

However, while object persistence is a property of a component object, the control itself is not responsible for handling I/O. Instead, the task falls to the container component (the client) for providing the control object with the appropriate access to storage both for initialization and to maintain changes. In this fashion, the settings for a specific control are stored (maintained) with the document where the control is used, rather than being stored globally for all instances of a control.

Interfaces

The properties and methods belonging to an ActiveX server are exposed though interfaces defined by an Interface ID (IID).

When adding methods to a server object, the existing interfaces should never be modified. Instead, to add methods, a new interface should be created to access the new features and provided as part of a new version of the ActiveX server. To improve performance for the new server version, the existing properties and methods should also be included in the new interface, thus reducing the number of vtable pointers required to access both the new and old features.

Licensing

License (.LIC) files for ActiveX components can be conveniently created using Visual Basic. These license files are used by ActiveX controls to ensure that developers are using licensed copies of a control. The .LIC file must be present when an application is running in design mode. If the license file is not found, an error will occur. License files are not checked in run mode. Instead, the expectation is that components are shipped freely with the application once the application has been developed.

ActiveX Automation

Automation is a mechanism which provides the means for one application to manipulate objects belonging to another application.

Microsoft ✓ *Exam Objective*	**Explain the implementation of Automation in the Microsoft Windows operating systems.**

Typically, Automation is used to:

- Create applications which expose objects, making them accessible to programming tools and macro languages

- Create and manipulate objects belonging to one application from within another application

- Create tools to access and manipulate objects

Any object that exposes an automation interface can be automated, offering methods and properties available for remote access, i.e., from another application. An automated object may be local (on the same machine as the automation client) or remote (on a separate machine accessed via a network connection). Further, Automation is a feature available for both OLE and ActiveX objects.

Quite commonly, commercial applications such as Microsoft Visual C++ or Word provide Automation interfaces. In Word, Word Basic can be used to write scripts (macros) while Visual C++ accepts both VBScript macros and Developer Studio add-ins which permit automating project builds, various code editing operations, or automated debugging.

An *automation client*, or automation controller, is any application which manipulates exposed objects belonging to another application. Conversely, an *automation server*, or automation component, is any application which exposes programmable objects to other interfaces. Automation comes in two categories: local automation or remote automation using DCOM (Distributed COM) over a network.

Because ActiveX Automation clients (controllers) require information about a server's properties and methods—particularly data types for properties and method parameters—a type library is the recommended method of providing this information.

Local Automation

An automation component object offers both properties and methods through their external interfaces. Properties are simply named attributes of the automation object, similar to the public data members of a C++ class. In like fashion, methods are functions which are available through the exposed interface, similar to the public member functions of a C++ class.

Commonly, even publicly exposed properties also have member functions which access them. Typically, a Get.../Set... function pair is provided for access to member properties. Since the COM standard requires object properties to not be exposed directly, interfaces should support Get.../Set... function pairs rather than direct exposure of object properties.

Using Parameters in Automation

A principal demand in designing automation methods is a means of providing a uniform and safe mechanism for exchanges between automation clients and servers.

The COleVariant class encapsulates the VARIANT data type for automation data exchange. The VARIANT data type is a tagged union which has one data member for the value—the raw data as an anonymous C++ union—and a second data member indicating the type of data contained in the union.

The VARIANT data type supports a variety of standard data types, including:

- Boolean values

- Both 2-byte and 4-byte integers

- Both 4-byte and 8-byte floating point values

- Strings

- HRESULT type (OLE error codes)

- CURRENCY type (fixed-point numeric, encapsulated in the COle-Currency class)

- DATE type (absolute date and time, encapsulated in the COle-DateTime class)

- Pointers to IUnknown and IDispatch interfaces

The complete VARIANT structure definition and the identifiers for each data type are show in the sidebar.

The VARIANT Type Structure

```
struct  tagVARIANT
{
   union
   {
      struct  __tagVARIANT
      {
         VARTYPE vt;
         WORD    wReserved1;
         WORD    wReserved2;
         WORD    wReserved3;
         union
         {
            LONG           lVal;          // VT_I4
            BYTE           bVal;          // VT_UI1
            SHORT          iVal;          // VT_I2
            FLOAT          fltVal;        // VT_R4
            DOUBLE         dblVal;        // VT_R8
            VARIANT_BOOL   boolVal;       // VT_BOOL
            _VARIANT_BOOL  bool;          // VT_BOOL
            SCODE          scode;         // VT_ERROR
            CY             cyVal;         // VT_CY
            DATE           date;          // VT_DATE
            BSTR           bstrVal;       // VT_BSTR
            IUnknown __RPC_FAR *punkVal;  // VT_UNKNOWN
            IDispatch __RPC_FAR *pdispVal; // VT_DISPATCH
            SAFEARRAY __RPC_FAR *parray;   // VT_ARRAY
            BYTE    __RPC_FAR *pbVal;     // VT_BYREF|VT_UI1
            SHORT   __RPC_FAR *piVal;     // VT_BYREF|VT_I2
            LONG    __RPC_FAR *plVal;     // VT_BYREF|VT_I4
            FLOAT   __RPC_FAR *pfltVal;   // VT_BYREF|VT_R4
            DOUBLE  __RPC_FAR *pdblVal;   // VT_BYREF|VT_R8
            VARIANT_BOOL   __RPC_FAR *pboolVal;
                                          // VT_BYREF|VT_BOOL
```

The VARIANT Type Structure (cont.)

```
        _VARIANT_BOOL __RPC_FAR *pbool;
                                          // VT_BYREF|VT_BOOL
            SCODE __RPC_FAR *pscode;    // VT_BYREF|VT_ERROR
            CY    __RPC_FAR *pcyVal;    // VT_BYREF|VT_CY
            DATE  __RPC_FAR *pdate;     // VT_BYREF|VT_DATE
            BSTR  __RPC_FAR *pbstrVal;  // VT_BYREF|VT_BSTR
            IUnknown  __RPC_FAR *__RPC_FAR *ppunkVal;
                                          // VT_BYREF|VT_UNKNOWN
    IDispatch __RPC_FAR *__RPC_FAR *ppdispVal;
                                          // VT_BYREF|VT_DISPATCH
            SAFEARRAY __RPC_FAR *__RPC_FAR *pparray;
                                          // VT_BYREF|VT_ARRAY
            VARIANT   __RPC_FAR *pvarVal;
                                          // VT_BYREF|VT_VARIANT
    PVOID  byref;       // (generic ByRef) VT_BYREF
            CHAR   cVal;                 // VT_I1
            USHORT uiVal;                // VT_UI2
            ULONG  ulVal;                // VT_UI4
            INT    intVal;               // VT_INT
            UINT   uintVal;              // VT_UINT
            DECIMAL __RPC_FAR *pdecVal;
                                          // VT_BYREF|VT_DECIMAL
            CHAR   __RPC_FAR *pcVal;     // VT_BYREF|VT_I1
            USHORT __RPC_FAR *puiVal;    // VT_BYREF|VT_UI2
            ULONG  __RPC_FAR *pulVal;    // VT_BYREF|VT_UI4
            INT    __RPC_FAR *pintVal;   // VT_BYREF|VT_INT
            UINT   __RPC_FAR *puintVal;  // VT_BYREF|VT_UINT
        } __VARIANT_NAME_3;
      } __VARIANT_NAME_2;
    DECIMAL decVal;
  } __VARIANT_NAME_1;
};
```

Using Remote Automation

OLE Automation can be used in ActiveX controls to permit clients access to the control's features through a client-supplied programming language. ActiveX automation controls (or other server objects) are objects which expose programmable objects to client applications (automation clients). By exposing programmable objects, the client applications are able to automate certain procedures through direct access to the objects and through functionality made available by the server.

Microsoft ✓ ***Exam Objective***   **Identify situations in which Remote Automation is an appropriate technology to use in order to provide a desirable solution.**

An ActiveX document is not a remoting mechanism.

One example of exposed object functionality would be for a word processor to expose its spell-checking or grammar-checking functionality such that other applications could make use of these features. Another example would be for a spreadsheet to provide in-place calculations within some other type of document whether a word processor or an engineering design package.

The principal advantage of Remote Automation is that a remote service can be supplied—from a single installation—to multiple clients and for multiple purposes.

Basics of Remote Automation

Remote Automation is simply a form of Automation which permits an interface client to execute an interface server which resides remotely, i.e., on a remote system via a network.

In effect, a Remote Automation component is an ActiveX component which can be controlled by a client application executing on a remote computer. Once an ActiveX component has been developed, it can be utilized from anywhere on a computer network.

Remote Automation is not language specific, but is wholly subsumed by DCOM and, in most cases, DCOM should be used instead of Remote Automation. While Remote Automation components may run from any computer on the network, they are designed principally for service from a central server.

 Since both Remote Automation and DCOM function over a network, adequate network bandwidth is a performance factor requiring consideration.

Still, there are a few circumstances where Remote Automation may be more appropriate than DCOM:

- 16-bit clients require support.

- A DCOM-enabled version of Windows NT or 95 is not available.

- An existing application suite—which uses Remote Automation—is being upgraded to use C++ components instead of Visual Basic components.

Aside from these exceptions, no particular differences exist between applications created using Remote Automation and applications created using Automation via DCOM. At the same time, configuration utilities conveniently permit switching operations between Remote Automation and DCOM, allowing a convenient upgrade once the initial infrastructure is installed.

Remote Automation Functionality and Limitations

Remote Automation permits applications to invoke the IDispatch implementation on a remote system over a network. Remote Automation also supports the IEnumVARIANT interface for collection support but, except for the IUnknown interface, does not provide the ability to distribute other COM interfaces. Both regular and Remote Automation contain marshalling support only for the data types recognized by Automation, i.e., those defined in the VARIANT data structure.

 *Marshalling* is the process of packaging and sending interface method calls across thread or process boundaries.

The Remote Automation facilities do allow programs access to the methods and properties exposed by remote objects. These include methods which return collections or return further automation objects as long as they are on an accessible network node.

Depending on the client machine's software, it may also be possible for the server application to call back to the client using Automation facilities. This call-back facility, however, is available only to 32-bit clients. While this process is similar to event messages, the mechanisms used are different.

Remote Automation is a multi-component remoting technology required for 16-bit client applications. While DCOM (Distributed COM) is a newer and more sophisticated technology, DCOM uses a 32-bit API, which is not compatible with 16-bit client applications.

For an application to function as a Remote Automation server, the application must be implemented as an executable (or out-of-process) rather than an in-process server.

Out-of-Process Communications under COM

When a client application uses an interface provided by an out-of-process object, a proxy object is created for each server in the client's process space and a stub is created in the server's process space. For out-of-process communications under COM, a proxy object receives calls made to server objects within the client's process space. In turn, the proxy creates a marshalling packet which is passed to a stub object in the server's process space.

Since marshalling is handled using remote procedure calls, there is no requirement for the client and server processes to reside on the same system.

Because inter-process communications do involve additional overhead, out-of-process communications are slower than in-process communications. Also, of course, in-process communications—as used with DLLs—do not require proxies or stubs.

Remote Automation Security

The Remote Automation design provides basic access security such that the server application administrator can determine how a specific object may be remotely accessed. Globally, on a given system, all automation objects may be set to disallow remote activation or to allow remote activation. Individually, specific automation objects may also be assigned the rights to allow or disallow remote activation.

Remote Automation depends on a key in the object's registry settings, `AllowRemoteActivation`, to determine whether a specific server permits Remote Activation. Where the system-wide (global) settings use this mode, each object in the registry is assigned an `AllowRemoteActivation` key with the individual status of each key set as "yes" to allow remote activation or "no" to disallow remote activation.

For Windows NT systems, a separate form of security is permitted using NT's ACL (Access Control List) to grant access to specific users or specific groups of users. Those users or groups who are given access can then remotely activate specific servers.

In both types of security, the permissions apply to the entire object: Permissions cannot be set only for specific interfaces nor for individual properties or methods belonging to an object.

The Remote Automation Connection Manager (RAC Manager) is used to set security options for server objects.

Uniform Data Transfer

Microsoft Exam Objective

Discuss the use of Uniform Data Transfer (UDT) as part of a component solution.

Uniform Data Transfer (UDT) is a model for transferring data either through the clipboard, through drag-and-drop operations, or through Automation. All objects conforming to the UDT model must implement the `IDataObject` interface.

The IDataObject interface replaces the older Dynamic Data Exchange (DDE) model.

The IDataObject interface provides methods for data transfer and for notifications of changes in data. The term *data object* refers to any object supporting an implementation of the IDataObject interface.

The data transfer methods specify both the data format and the medium used to transfer the data, along with options to render data for a specific target device. In addition to retrieval and storage methods, the IDataObject interface also offers methods to enumerate the available formats and to manage connections complete with advisory sinks to handle notifications for changes in data.

Depending on the requirements of the data object and how it will be used, implementations may vary. Some data objects do not support advisory sinks or change notifications, while others do not permit calling applications to transmit data to the objects and can only retrieve data. For methods which specific data objects do not support, the unsupported implementations may simply return E_NOTIMPL.

For objects which do not support change implementations, OLE offers the data advice holder object, available through the CreateDataAdvice-Holder helper function. Because a data object may have multiple connections, each with a separate set of attributes, the OLE data advice holder can simplify managing connections and sending appropriate notifications.

All COM technologies reduce the use of global memory and other global system resources. However, one of the primary design goals of Uniform Data Transfer (UDT) is the reduction of global memory usage. UDT makes it possible to represent and manipulate all data through a common object model and interface.

When to Implement the *IDataObject* Interface

The IDataObject interface should be implemented when developing any container or server application capable of transferring data. For example, the IDataObject interface would be implemented for an application which allows data to be pasted or dropped into another application.

OLE compound document servers which support objects that can be embedded or linked use the IDataObject implementation, while OLE provides implementations in the default object handler and cache.

While exchanging data between applications, using the clipboard, for instance, does not necessarily require the applications to support OLE, the Windows operating system and the clipboard itself are using the OLE mechanisms for the operation.

When to Use the *IDataObject* Interface

An application object designed to receive data uses the IDataObject interface methods. When the IDataObject interface data transfer methods are called, a format and medium are specified, and, optionally, a target device may also be specified for data rendering.

The IDataObject interface is also called by container objects which desire notification—through their advisory sinks—when values in the data object change. An advisory connection is created through which notifications can be sent.

Table 9.3 shows the methods supported by the IUnknown and IDataObject interfaces.

T A B L E 9.3: IUnknown and IDataObject Interfaces

IUnknown Methods	Description
QueryInterface	Returns pointers to supported interfaces
AddRef	Increments reference count
Release	Decrements reference count

IDataObject Methods	Description
GetData	Renders data described in a FORMATETC structure, transferring it via a STGMEDIUM structure
GetDataHere	Renders data described in a FORMATETC structure, transferring the data via the caller-allocated STGMEDIUM structure

T A B L E 9.3:   IUnknown and IDataObject Interfaces *(continued)*

IDataObject Methods	Description
QueryGetData	Determines if the data described in the FORMATETC structure can be rendered by the data object
GetCanonicalFormatEtc	Returns a FORMATETC structure that is logically equivalent but may be potentially different than the calling structure
SetData	Passes data described in a FORMATETC structure and contained in an STGMEDIUM structure to the source data object
EnumFormatEtc	Creates and returns a pointer to an object to enumerate the FORMATETC supported by the data object
DAdvise	Creates a connection between a data object and an advise sink so the advise sink can receive notifications of changes in the data object
DUnadvise	Closes a connection created with the DAdvise method
EnumDAdvise	Creates an object to enumerate the current advisory connections, returning a pointer to the object

Access to Structured Storage

Microsoft ✔ *Exam Objective*	**Assess structured storage as a component of a given solution.**

Structured storage is OLE's hierarchical organization of storage permitting both native data and linked or embedded document data to be combined in a single file without losing the internal organization and separation of data elements. In a structured storage environment, storage is organized into three object types:

- Stream objects
- Lock byte objects
- Storage objects

The stream and lock byte object types are both low-level objects which have direct access to data. Stream objects implement the IStream interface, which provides methods to read, write, position, and copy data. Lock byte objects implement the ILockBytes interface, providing data access as arrays of bytes, a method commonly used for custom access to underlying storage.

Storage objects may contain stream or lock byte objects, as well as other storage objects, and are layered overlying the stream or lock bytes objects. Storage objects implement the IStorage interface, which provides methods to access, create, and maintain nested objects.

Since the ILockBytes, IStream, and IStorage interfaces are OLE rather than MAPI, methods belonging to these interfaces return OLE error values rather than MAPI error values. Client and service providers should use the MapStorageSCode API to translate the OLE error values returned by these interfaces into MAPI error values.

Why Use Structured Storage?

Structured storage is used by both client and service providers to work with properties (data elements belonging to the client or server) that are too large to maintain using the IMAPIProp interface methods. Commonly, these are large string or binary data elements.

Typically, the IStream or IStorage interfaces would be calling in the IMAPIProp::OpenProperty method. For an example, to access a binary attachment in a message, a client object would call OpenProperty with the interface identifier IID_IStream and PR_ATTACH_DATA_BIN as the property tag.

Client and service providers may call API functions for access to MAPI or OLE implementations, or may implement their own stream and storage objects. However, custom implementations are rarely required because the supplied implementations are adequate for most purposes.

MAPI or Messaging API is a medium-independent messaging architecture enabling a variety of applications to interact with different systems on different hardware platforms. As a client-interface component, MAPI consists of the set of functions and object-oriented interfaces providing the foundation services for the MAPI subsystem's client and server interfaces.

There are a few aspects of the existing services which you should remain aware of, however. When a client calls a MAPI object's OpenProperty method for access through a storage object, the service provider may open the object storage in either direct or transacted mode. Even though the direct mode is typically used, this is not guaranteed behavior, and client objects should always assume that the transact mode has been used and that a call to IStorage::Commit is required. In addition, client objects should call IMAPIProp::SaveChanges after the final Commit to ensure that changes to storage objects are permanent.

While both MAPI and OLE offer a variety of API functions for defining and accessing stream and storage objects, the most common functions are as follows in Table 9.4:

T A B L E 9.4:   MAPI and OLE API Functions for Stream and Storage Objects

Function	Purpose
CreateDocfile	Commonly used by OLE and MAPI to create general purpose storage objects
HrIStorageFromStream	Creates a storage object to access a stream object or lock bytes object
OpenIMsgOnIStg	Creates a message object to access a storage object
OpenStreamOnFile	Creates a stream object to access a file
WrapCompressedRTFStream	Creates a stream object containing compressed or uncompressed versions of a stream holding the rich text of a message

Summary

ActiveX technology is designed to shield users from as much technical information as possible, allowing users to concentrate their attentions on higher-level tasks such as maintaining business information and data.

ActiveX controls are supported by eight core technologies:

- The Component Object Model
- Compound documents
- Connectable objects

- OLE automation

- Persistent storage

- Property pages

- System-provided font and image objects

- Uniform data transfer

An ActiveX control is an object implemented as an in-process server and can be used in any OLE/ActiveX-aware container including those created using Access, FoxPro, Visual Basic, and Visual C++. ActiveX controls fire event messages to communicate with the control container (the server component). In turn, the container uses exposed methods and properties to communicate with the ActiveX control.

ActiveX controls developed using MFC support two types of events: stock events and custom events. Stock events are supported by the `COleControl` class while custom events must be handled explicitly by the application. A dispatch map is used to expose a set of events, as an interface, to the control user.

ActiveX controls may be active or inactive but, while inactive originally referred to windowless controls, this distinction has blurred with windowless activation. An active control is able to invoke mouse capture, to acquire the keyboard focus and to obtain window services from the container. Object persistence permits a container to store and maintain an ActiveX component's settings.

ActiveX Automation permits:

- One application to manipulate objects belonging to another application

- The creation of tools to access and manipulate objects

- Objects to be accessible to programming tools and macro languages

To provide type-safe data exchange for automation, the `COleVariant` class encapsulates the VARIANT data type which supports a variety of standard data types.

Automation may be local or remote but Remote Automation is largely supplanted by DCOM (distributed COM) except for some special circumstances. Remote Automation also supports security access restrictions.

ActiveX controls permit the construction of custom components rather than custom applications, making it possible for users to create their own custom applications by combining components rather than depending on application suites.

Structured storage permits OLE clients to store compound files in native files systems and depends on five elements:

- **Compound document**   A document containing linked and/or embedded objects in addition to the document's native data

- **Root storage object**   The outermost storage object in a document; may contain other nested storage or stream objects. As an example, a compound document would be written to persistent storage (a disk) as a series of storage and stream objects within a root storage object.

- **Storage object**   Holds nested storage objects (or stream objects) to create the equivalent of a directory/file structure within a single file. A Storage object is also a COM object implementing the `IStorage` interface.

- **Stream object**   Analogous to a file in a directory/file system and refers to a COM object implementing the `IStream` interface.

Review Questions

1. How may a remote automation service be used?

   A. By many different client applications for different purposes

   B. By more than one instance of the same client application

   C. By multiple clients if they are using different interfaces

   D. By one client application at a time

2. Both Remote Automation and the Distributed Component Object Model (DCOM) enable remote communications between processes. On what do Remote Automation components execute?

   A. On a client system only

   B. On a server system only

   C. On either a client or server system with modifications to match the system

   D. On either a client or server system without modification

3. ActiveX controls are *not* based on:

    A. Local client objects and clipboard data transfers

    B. OLE automation and persistent storage

    C. Property pages and Uniform Data Transfer

    D. The COM model, compound documents, and connectable objects

4. Where are the proxies and stubs used for Remote Automation located?

    A. A proxy is located in the client's process space while the stub is located in the server's process space.

    B. A proxy is located in the client's process space while the stub may be located in either the client or server's process space.

    C. A stub is located in the client's process space while the proxy is located in the server's process space.

    D. A stub is located in the client's process space while the proxy may be located in either the client or server's process space.

5. In order to write an ActiveX control which will function in both the 16- and 32-bit environments, which of the following must be true?

    A. Only one version of the control is required, but it must be a 16-bit version with only one type library.

    B. Only one version of the control is required, but it must be a 32-bit version with only one type library.

    C. Two versions of the control (16- and 32-bit) are required but with only one type library.

    D. Two versions of the control (16- and 32-bit) are required, each with its own type library.

6. What is a compound document?

    A. A control activated to initiate an action in a container application

    B. Any ActiveX control containing data

    C. Any document containing an embedded Active Document

    D. Any document containing both its own native data and any linked or embedded object.

7. Given an application which uses object interfaces provided by two external ActiveX server applications—one local and one remote—how many proxy and stub objects are used?

    A. One stub and one proxy

    B. One stub and two proxies

    C. Two stubs and one proxy

    D. Two stubs and two proxies

8. ActiveX controls may support which of the following?

    A. Both incoming and outgoing interfaces

    B. Either incoming or outgoing interfaces

    C. Only incoming interfaces

    D. Only outgoing interfaces

9. Which of the following is the ActiveX-server remoting mechanism to use with a client application executing under a 16-bit operating system?

    A. ActiveX documents

    B. DCOM

    C. RCOM

    D. Remote Automation

10. An ActiveX control: (Select two.)

    A. Can implement one or more persistence interfaces

    B. Cannot implement more than one persistence interface

    C. Must implement at least one `IPersist` interface

    D. Must implement at least one `IPersist` interface if it has a persistent state

11. Select the appropriate (fastest) ActiveX component type for a processor-intensive application:

A. A Java server

B. An .EXE file

C. An ActiveX library

D. An in-process server

12. Which of the following is true about ActiveX controls property pages?

A. A component object can display its property page independent of the client.

B. Property pages from multiple contained objects may be displayed in a single property sheet.

C. The property sheet permits users to view and change a control's properties.

D. All of the above

13. In developing a multi-tier client-server application, which components would be good candidates for development as ActiveX controls?

A. Business-rule processing components

B. Custom remote automation objects

C. Database access components

D. Local user interface components

14. When do ActiveX controls check for license (.LIC) files?

A. In both design and run modes

B. In design mode

C. In run mode

D. When the control appears on a Web page

15. What is the greatest benefit to the user employing ActiveX technology?

A. The user knows how the registry works.

B. The user can manage and maintain information.

    C. The user can manage applications and versions.

    D. The user can use the events incorporated in ActiveX components.

16. For an ActiveX control to interact efficiently with a control container, which of the following programmatic elements are employed? (Select three.)

    A. A dispatch map

    B. A series of event-firing functions

    C. The `COleControl` class

    D. the `IPersist` interface

17. Given the objective of changing the interface to an existing ActiveX server in order to add additional features and to reduce memory overhead when multiple instances of the objects are created, what should be created?

    A. A new interface should be created to include both the new and existing features but without supporting the previously existing interfaces.

    B. A new interface should be created to include both the new and existing features while keeping the previously existing interfaces in the new server as well.

    C. A new interface should be created which supports only the new features while previously existing features would be accessible through the previously existing interfaces.

    D. The new features should be added to the existing interface.

18. Information about properties and methods can be provided to the controller of an ActiveX component by using which of the following?

    A. A .CAB file

    B. A type library

    C. An .INI file

    D. Dynamic Data Exchange (DDE)

19. Serialization is used to permit which of the following? (Select two.)

  A. An ActiveX control container to store state information for the control

  B. An ActiveX control to store state information

  C. Settings for a control to be stored in the control's .INI file

  D. Settings for a control to be stored with the document where the control is used

20. To inspect an object library for a particular ActiveX component for use with VBA, what is the simplest approach?

  A. Examine the registry.

  B. Use the Object Browser.

  C. View the client's property sheet.

  D. View the server's property sheet.

21. Select the statement(s) which accurately describes how 16- and 32-bit ActiveX components can interoperate on a single computer.

  A. 16-bit ActiveX DLLs can be used by 32-bit ActiveX controllers.

  B. 16-bit ActiveX EXEs can be used by 32-bit ActiveX EXEs.

  C. 32-bit ActiveX DLLs can be used by 16-bit ActiveX controllers.

  D. 32-bit ActiveX EXEs can be used by 16-bit ActiveX EXEs.

22. How may an automated object be accessible?

  A. Both as a remote or local object

  B. Only as a local object

  C. Only as a remote object

  D. Only through a network connection

23. An ActiveX type library can be used to do which of the following? (Select all that apply.)

   A. Access objects

   B. Check type information for properties and methods

   C. Display object members in an Object Browser

   D. Obtain a pointer to a .CAB file

24. Using parameters in ActiveX automation requires which of the following?

   A. Careful attention to typecasting between client and server objects

   B. No special provisions

   C. Type-safe variables passed using the VARIANT data type

   D. Using the IDataType interface to inquire about parameter sizes

25. Remote (OLE) Automation is used in ActiveX controls to permit clients access to the control's features through which of the following?

   A. A client-supplied programming language

   B. A macro language

   C. The IDirect interface

   D. The VBScript programming language

26. Remote Automation supports security access rights which include which of the following? (Select two.)

   A. Allowing access to specific interfaces on a per-user basis

   B. Allowing access to specific servers for remote access

   C. Granting access to specific client applications

   D. Granting access under NT to specific users and specific groups of users

27. The ActiveX technology family includes which of the following? (Select three.)

   A. Active Scripts, Code Download and Verification, and HTML extensions

   B. ActiveX controls, ActiveX documents, and Internet ActiveX controls

   C. ActiveX server framework and Internet Data Download Services

   D. ActiveX viewer services and VB Scripts

28. What is the benefit of creating custom components?

   A. Developers can compete with large corporations.

   B. Components allow applications to be distributed over the Internet.

   C. Developers can create tools for specific tasks without creating entirely new application suites to support these tools.

   D. Developers can replace portions of existing applications without developing entirely new applications.

29. Structured storage is organized into which three object types?

   A. Discrete data objects

   B. Lock byte objects

   C. Storage objects

   D. Stream objects

30. Structured storage objects may do which of the following?

   A. Return both OLE and MAPI error messages

   B. Return custom error messages

   C. Return only MAPI error messages

   D. Return only OLE error messages

CHAPTER

10

Database Access Technologies

Microsoft Exam Objectives Covered in This Chapter:

- Given a scenario, choose the appropriate data access tool.

- Compare Data Access Objects with other potential components of a solution, such as ODBC or RDO.

- Evaluate Open Database Connectivity as a component of a given solution.

- Compare solutions that use ODBC on the basis of performance, maintainability, and interoperability.

- Explain the benefits of Remote Data Objects.

- Explain the benefits of the SQL Distributed Management Objects (SQL-DMO).

Databases are central to the role of most professional developers today. The majority of all business applications today are database applications. Databases can be as small as a client contact system on the laptop of a sales representative or as big as the huge mainframe databases maintained by governmental and educational institutions.

This chapter goes into some of the historical problems in database access and the different approaches available for accessing this data from a client application. These different approaches must be evaluated to select a model that is best suited for the specific needs of a client application and a data source. We will begin by discussing some of the general approaches for storing and accessing data, followed by a more specific look at each of the data access methods currently in use in the Windows environment. These include:

- Data Access Objects

- Open Database Connectivity

- Remote Data Objects

- OLE DB

- ActiveX Data Objects

- SQL Server 6.5 Distributed Management Objects

Finally, we will look at the various approaches to database replication, including methods provided for Microsoft Access and SQL Server 6.5.

Problems in Database Connectivity

Database connectivity has been a long-standing problem in the computer industry, presenting the challenge of accessing multiple data sources, often maintained by quite different database systems and standards, from within a single application. For example, consider an application that expects to access data stored in dBase format from a local database in a small office, but also requires access to an Oracle or SQL Server, via network, from an applications server. Such multiple access would in the past have required building separate data engines to access each of these data sources using separate protocols, record types, and data standards.

SQL (Structured Query Language) was one of the early attempts to provide a standard for database access, but SQL itself exists as a variety of different implementations and addressed only one of the problems inherent in database connectivity: how a query is phrased.

Looking at the question in its entirety, connectivity problems are found in varying programming interfaces, DBMS protocols, DBMS languages, and network protocols. Even restricting the problem to relational databases using some form of SQL, there are still a variety of problems and incompatibilities that require resolution. Four primary problems exist in connecting different databases to applications; all of these problems center around proprietary software and hardware:

- **Programming interfaces** vary as each vendor implements its own proprietary interface. Relational DBMSs may be accessed through embedded SQL or through an API.

- **DBMS protocols** also vary as each developer uses his or her own proprietary data format and proprietary methods of communication between the front-end applications and the databases proper. In the data formats alone, there are a wide variety of methods of identifying field and record extents and sizes.

- **DBMS languages** vary equally. Even though SQL has become the language of choice for relational database systems, there is no single SQL standard because each vendor offers their own extensions to SQL.

- **Networking protocols** vary as widely as any other connectivity problem with a wide selection of both LAN and WAN protocols in use. Under Windows alone, we are faced with a choice between the TCP/IP, NetBEUI, and IPX/SPX protocols (as well as AppleTalk, VINES, and DecNet Sockets), while other OSs, such as VAX, offer DecNet... to name only a few of the existing protocols.

Solutions to Database Connectivity

Over the years, a number of solutions to database connectivity have been proposed, each of which has been met with varying degrees of acceptance. The three primary approaches to solving incompatibly issues of database connectivity include:

- Using gateways
- Using a common programming interface
- Using a common protocol

Gateways

A gateway is a translation system that causes a target DBMS to appear to a calling application as a copy of the DBMS that supports a specific grammar, interface, and protocol. In operation, the gateway accepts queries from the application, translates and forwards the request to the target DBMS, and, of course, translates the returned data. The gateway approach is limited by architectural differences between varying DBMSs and the need for a separate gateway for each choice of client/server system. Figure 10.1 illustrates this translation.

FIGURE 10.1

A simplified gateway translating between two DBMS structures

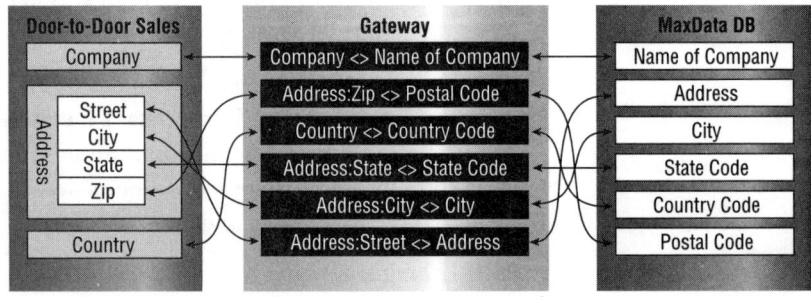

While gateways have been implemented as a valid approach to database connectivity and remain essential in some environments, they are also restricted, unwieldy, and unlikely to provide a long-term solution.

Common Programming Interfaces

A common programming interface is a feature provided by database manufacturers for the developer, providing standardization in the development environment and/or user interface across DBMSs using quite different underlying interfaces. This can be accomplished by creating a standard API, a standard macro language, or a standard set of tools for translating requests, accessing data, and returning results from each target DBMS. A common interface is typically implemented by writing a separate driver for each target DBMS.

Common Protocols

The common protocol approach is based on a single DBMS protocol, SQL grammar, and networking protocol common to all DBMSs such that all applications can use the same protocol and SQL grammar to communicate. Proposed standards are RDA (remote data access) and DRDA (distributed relational database architecture). While RDA is an emerging standard, it is not yet available. DRDA is IBM's proposed DBMS protocol.

Database Structure

Databases are often differentiated by the way that data is stored and accessed. These differences can have a significant impact on the performance of the data access method chosen. Windows desktops today usually interact with two types of databases:

- Desktop or file-server databases
- Client/server database management systems

The difference between these two general approaches focuses on how the data is accessed from the client application, and, more importantly, where the data engine resides.

File-Server Databases

File-based databases are very efficient for extracting information from large data files. Each workstation on the network has access to a central file server where the data is stored. The data file can also reside on the workstation with the client application. The PC network version of this architecture is illustrated in Figure 10.2.

FIGURE 10.2

The file-server database

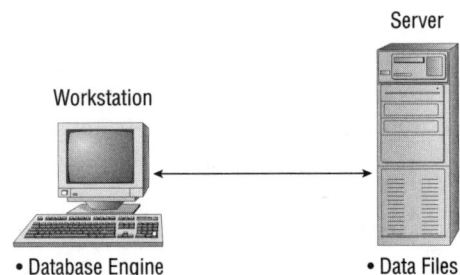

Server

Workstation

• Database Engine   • Data Files

Multiple workstations will access the same file server where the data is stored. The file server is centrally located so that it can be reached easily and efficiently by all workstations. In addition to the data, other files may be needed on the server to manage any multi-user considerations. Ensuring compliance with multi-user policy may be the responsibility of the workstation. As functionality increases on the server, it may even become a client/server system.

The user's application (including the interactive portion of the application *and* the database engine) resides on the workstation. The fact that the database engine resides on the workstation implies that ISAM database engines are essentially single-user engines. Although multi-user considerations can be a factor of the engine design or application design, the engines themselves are substantially biased toward single-user data processing.

Another fact inherent in file-server design is that the file server stores only data and support files. It is not an application server and as such does not host any server-side process. This means that the file server is a passive participant in the application process, requiring the engine residing on each individual workstation to do all of the processing in the application.

To illustrate this last point, consider the following scenario. Suppose you have a data file hosted on a file server. This data file contains 10,000 records. A user submits a request from the workstation application to extract 10 records from this data file. How many records does the file server send back to the workstation to fulfill this request?

If you answered 10,000, you are right. The file server hosts no program to process the data. The entire file requested must be sent back to the client application and processed at the workstation where the database engine resides. A few sophisticated ISAM data engines, such as Microsoft's Joint Engine Technology (JET), use a process of client-side page caching to make this process more efficient; however, even in these cases, the workstation-resident engine is still responsible for the entire process.

Client/Server (Relational) Databases

The driving concept in a client/server architecture is flexibility. A client/server architecture is often referred to as *multiple-tier* architecture because the execution of tasks is divided between applications and components in the architecture. A *tier* in client/server technology is a layer of software that accepts requests and offers services to an application. For example, the client application represents the user services layer of the application. This is a tier of the application. As a system architect, you have discretion to allocate tasks and processing to different tiers in the model. You can use a traditional two-tier model or increase application independence by moving to a multiple-tier model. Within these models, you still have full control over the technology used to implement the solution and your chosen level of systems abstraction.

Figure 10.3 illustrates a basic client/server scenario. Although this theme has many variations, you will notice some common threads running throughout all client/server implementations.

F I G U R E   10.3

Client/server
architecture

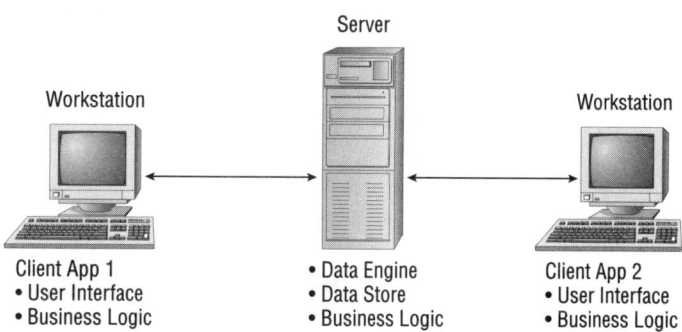

Workstation	Server	Workstation
Client App 1 • User Interface • Business Logic	• Data Engine • Data Store • Business Logic	Client App 2 • User Interface • Business Logic

With all of these choices, deciding exactly how to design your system can sometimes be difficult. However, some basic guidelines can help you choose.

Figure 10.3 illustrates some distinguishing characteristics of client/server design. You will notice immediately that the database engine has been moved from the client to the server. The server in this scenario is no longer a file server simply providing file services to the network. It is an application server hosting a process such as Microsoft SQL Server.

This transition is significant because it means that the client workstation is no longer responsible for all of the work involved in implementing the application. Tasks can be distributed between client and server, allowing each to participate in the process. In fact, you could say that the definition of client/server architecture is the intelligent distribution of tasks across tiers in the architecture.

Because the database engine now resides on the server, the behavior of the previous scenario changes. Remember that the data table held 10,000 records. Now assume that a Microsoft SQL Server is hosting this data table. When the client application submits a request for 10 records, only 10 rows will be returned across the network to the client because a process on the server can satisfy the request.

Because the server is an active participant in the process of data reduction and modification, a client/server database is not limited to small work-group applications the way file-server applications are. Because the client/ server systems usually have much larger numbers of users, an increased load might be put on the network. Managing network resources becomes paramount in a client/server design.

Since there are significant differences in the storage structure and data engines of these various databases, it has been historically true that different interfaces have been used to target these diverse database structures. A developer using Microsoft Visual Basic as a tool for creating database clients has a number of options available for accessing database resources. The next section will look at these options in more detail and evaluate the performance implications of each choice.

Microsoft JET and the Data Access Objects

Microsoft ✓ *Exam* *Objective* | **Given a scenario, choose the appropriate data access tool.**

Microsoft's Joint Engine Technologies (JET) has been one of the most popular desktop database engines of our day. Shipping with most Microsoft Office products and development tools in some form, the JET engine in many ways redefined the concept of data access from file-server and ISAM data sources.

Microsoft JET is a file-server data engine, and fits elegantly into the file-server database architecture previously described. This approach to database deployment places the data engine on each individual workstation accessing the data source. The source data file may either be a shared file located on a file server or a data file located on the workstation machine as a stand-alone application.

The native data file for JET is the Microsoft Database or MDB, known to most of us as the "Access Database." In addition to this native database structure, the JET engine can also access data in many other database file structures through a set of ISAM drivers that ship with JET. These drivers enable access to numerous other PC desktop database formats and spreadsheets including Microsoft FoxPro, Microsoft Excel, text files, and many other vendors' database and spreadsheet formats.

The programming interface for the JET engine is the Microsoft Data Access Objects (DAO). The DAOs give any development tool able to automate COM objects the ability to access data through the JET engine.

Although DAO is currently the native interface for JET and the programming model of choice for many Visual Basic and Access developers, Microsoft has shelved this object model in favor of OLE DB and the ActiveX Data Objects. You will still need to understand the structure and uses of the DAO for the exam, however, this interface should not be seriously considered for new development projects, especially those using relational data sources.

Data Access Objects

Microsoft ✔ *Exam* *Objective*	**Compare Data Access Objects with other potential components of a solution, such as ODBC or RDO.**

Data Access Objects provide a framework for applications to create and maintain databases using an object hierarchy. DAO relies on the Microsoft JET database engine to access data and database structures in the following areas:

- Microsoft JET (.MDB) databases, including databases created using Microsoft Access or Visual Basic. Includes versions 1.*x*, 2.*x*, and 3.*x* of the database engine.

- Installable ISAM databases including:

  - dBASE III, dBASE IV, and dBASE 5.0

  - Paradox (versions 3.*x*, 4.*x*, and 5.*x*)

  - FoxPro (versions 2.0, 2.5, and 2.6); can import/export to and from version 3.0 but can not create objects

  - Btrieve

  - Microsoft Excel worksheets (versions 3.0, 4.0, 5.0, and 7.0)

  - Lotus spreadsheets (WKS, WK1, WK3, and WK4)

  - Text files

- ODBC data sources (using an ODBC driver) including:

  - Microsoft SQL Server

  - SYBASE SQL Server

  - Oracle Server

WARNING   To access an ODBC database, the appropriate ODBC driver for each database is needed.

DAO functions best with databases that can be accessed using the Microsoft JET engine, including all of the preceding except for the ODBC data sources. Optimum performance is achieved with Microsoft JET (.MDB) databases. Figure 10.4 illustrates the DAO model.

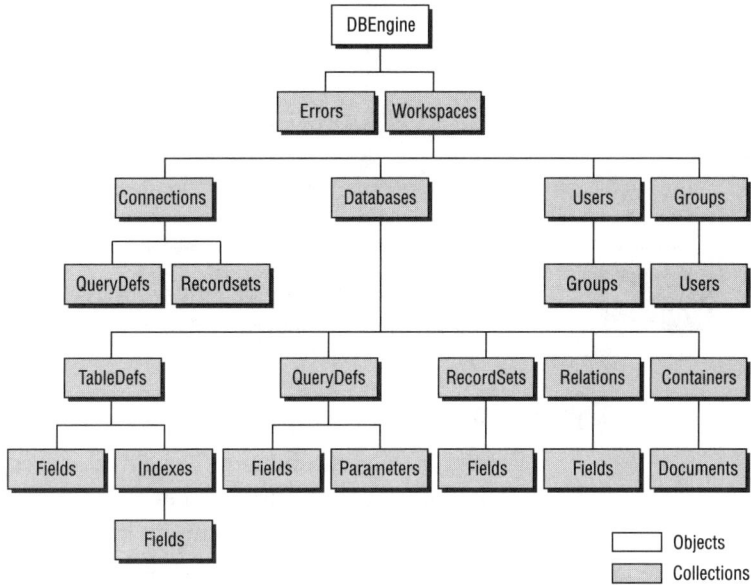

Using Recordsets in DAO

You use DAO recordset objects when you want to get access to data stored in a database through JET. There are three types of recordsets supported by DAO:

- Tables
- Dynasets
- Snapshots

These three recordset types are actually created on the client as *cursors*. A cursor is a set of pointers that reference the data stored in a database. When specific data is requested, the system follows the pointers to extract the appropriate data.

Tables

A table recordset is very similar to a dynamic cursor. It allows multiple users to see the changes that other users make in a data source. For example, assume you have two users, User A and User B. If they both built table recordset objects at the same time, each user would be able to see the results of the other user's activity in their recordset. If User A changed a record, User B would see the change. If User A added a record, User B would see the new record. If User A deleted a record, User B would see the deletion.

JET builds table recordsets with minimal resources on the client, but requires a round trip to the server whenever new data is requested from the data source. It benefits from distinct multi-user advantages, but the added network resources used may make it costly to implement.

Table recordsets can only be built from DAO based on `TableDef` objects. You cannot create a table recordset through ODBC.

Dynasets

Dynasets are keyset cursors. When a dynaset recordset type is built, a set of keys are built on the client; one key for every record in the result set at the time the keyset was built. Within this keyset, the data is somewhat dynamic, but outside the keyset, the data is static. JET caches dynaset data on the client. The same data is only downloaded again from the server if the data has been changed by another user and the cached version is obsolete.

If Users A and B from our earlier examples build dynasets at the same time, their recordsets will exhibit slightly different behavior from that previously noted. If User A modifies a record, User B will see the change because the data is in the keyset. However, if A adds a record, User B would not see the new record because there is no key for that record in his keyset. If User A deletes a record, User B would see a hole in the keyset; a key that has no data.

Dynasets are often the best possible solution. They provide much of the dynamism of tables while not requiring as many resources.

Snapshots

Snapshot recordsets are static cursors. Data cannot be updated from a snapshot and the server will never be contacted to query for data that is more current. Although this presents some obvious multi-user weaknesses, snapshots are very effective for reporting and other types of small-to-moderate data extractions.

JET caches all snapshot data on the local client and completes the snapshot as the user moves forward through the recordset. The user must therefore move to the end of the entire recordset before the snapshot is fully populated and an accurate recordcount can be obtained.

A special type of "cursorless" snapshot, called a forward-only snapshot, can be created for simple reporting. Although these recordsets lack the ability to scroll backward, they are small, efficient, and require minimal caching overhead.

Exercise 10.1 shows you how to access data in a database through the Data Access Objects. This example illustrates how to use DAO using Microsoft Excel 97 as the data client.

The exercises in this lab assume that Microsoft Office 97 Professional Edition is installed with the Northwind sample database installed in the default location. If the Northwind database is installed in an alternate location, make the necessary adjustments in the exercises.

EXERCISE 10.1

Accessing Data Using the Data Access Objects

1. Start Microsoft Excel 97.

2. Open the Visual Basic Editor by selecting Tools ➢ Macro ➢ Visual Basic Editor from the menu.

3. Add a new code module to the editor by selecting Insert ➢ Module from the menu.

4. Add a new procedure by selecting Insert ➢ Procedure from the menu. In the Add Procedure dialog box, Enter **DAOTest** in the Name text box. Make sure that Sub is selected as the Type option and Public is selected as the Scope option. Click OK.

5. Make a reference to the Microsoft DAO 3.5 object library by selecting Tools ➢ References from the menu. Scroll down the list of references to find the Microsoft DAO 3.5 object library and select the checkbox next to the listing. Click OK.

6. Between the Public Sub and the End Sub statements in the new procedure, enter the following code:

```
Dim db As database
    Dim rs As Recordset
    Dim intCounter As Integer
    Set db = Opendatabase("C:\program files\microsoft
office\office\samples\northwind.mdb")These two lines must
be on one
Set rs = db.openrecordset("products")
intCounter = 1
Do While Not rs.EOF
    Cells(intCounter, 1).Value = rs!ProductID
    Cells(intCounter, 2).Value = rs!ProductName
    Cells(intCounter, 3).Value = rs!UnitsInStock
    intCounter = intCounter + 1
    rs.movenext
Loop
```

7. Close the Visual Basic Editor by selecting File ➤ Close and Return to Microsoft Excel.

8. Select cell A1 in the spreadsheet. Select Tools ➤ Macro ➤ Macros from the menu. Select DAOTest from the list of macros and click Run to execute.

9. The spreadsheet should now display the Product ID, Product Name, and Units in Stock from the products table in the first three columns.

10. Exit Microsoft Excel. Save the file if desired.

While DAO and the JET engine are exceptional tools for accessing ISAM data sources, this model has some inherent weaknesses when accessing client/server data sources. The primary problems are:

- Engine inefficiency for client/server computing
- Object model bias

Client/Server Databases and the JET Engine

JET is a client-resident data engine. Its primary purpose is I/O exchange with local and remote data files. Since client/server databases store data in relational structures, simple file I/O is insufficient and JET is unable to access them directly. To access relational databases, JET must interface with ODBC. While this approach is workable, there are some significant performance drawbacks to this model.

When you use the DAO to access an ODBC data source, you are actually interfacing with JET. JET takes your requests issued through DAO and translates them into requests that ODBC can understand. These requests are then passed to an ODBC driver, which translates them again into the structure required by the proprietary interface of the relational database. In this scenario, you have a client-side data engine and a server-side data engine. More translation takes place than is needed.

Another problem with this scenario is the sheer weight of the JET engine. When the DAO is used, the bulky engine loads on the client, requiring more resources than necessary. Since this engine is not actually needed, this resource consumption on the client is wasteful and unnecessary.

Object Model Bias

The DAO model was designed for access to ISAM data structures. Consequently, the model is biased against relational databases. For example, since client/server data sources are managed by server-side processes, the developer must make a connection to the data engine before any requests can be made for data. These connections occupy resources on the server and proper connection management is an important part of a client/server database design.

ISAM data structures have no corresponding concept of the connection. This results in the fact that the DAO object model contains no connection object. This seemingly small omission makes the management of connection very difficult when the DAO is used to access relational data sources.

ODBC Direct

ODBC Direct acts as a partial solution to the problems described previously. This model is included in the most recent releases of DAO, and allows the developer to bypass the loading of the JET engine on the client by requesting the creation of an ODBC Direct workspace. When ODBC Direct is used, the object model changes somewhat to include elements that are more congruent with relational data sources.

ODBC Direct goes through RDO (see "Remote Data Objects" for more information on RDO) to accomplish direct connections to relational data sources without loading the JET engine. This is included in the DAO model primarily to offer a method of relational data access to developers who might not own the Enterprise editions of Microsoft's development tools, and thus would not have the option of RDO implementation.

Open Database Connectivity (ODBC)

Microsoft ✓ *Exam Objective*

Evaluate Open Database Connectivity as a component of a given solution.

Odbc is a standard programming language interface that allows an application access to a variety of data sources. Using ODBC, access is provided to any data source, either local or remote, as long as an appropriate ODBC driver is available. ODBC drivers are available as both 16-bit and 32-bit versions for a wide variety of data sources such as Microsoft SQL Server and Microsoft Access.

The ODBC Administrator applet is commonly accessed through the Control Panel (under Windows), where Data Source Names (DSNs) are created.

Where ODBC Fits

ODBC takes the common interface approach to the database connectivity problem. By providing developers with a single API to access all data sources, ODBC conforms to a CLI specification developed by a consortium of over 40 companies, including members of the SQL Access Group (SAG). Further, ODBC has broad support from both application developers and database vendors.

The ODBC interface provides a single API with full functionality to support developers, as well as an architecture suitable to provide database developers with functional interoperability.

ODBC Architecture and Function

The ODBC standard defines an API suite allowing applications access to a variety of data sources through DBMS-specific drivers. Each ODBC Driver fits between the application and the database, providing connections, query and transaction translations, and returning data in response to the queries (see Figure 10.5).

Application
Calls ODBC API functions to make connections,
transmit SQL queries, and receive data

ODBC API

Driver Manager
(ODBC.DLL)
Loads ODBC driver, passes queries to driver,
and returns results to application

DBMS Driver (.DLL)
Processes ODBC API function calls, translates SQL
requests to the DBMS, returns results of query or
instruction to the application

Networking Software
May require a DBMS-specifc network component

Data Source (DBMS)
Processes queries and returns results

The application calls on ODBC API functions that are implemented by the Driver Manager (an ODBC.DLL library) and then passed to the appropriate DBMS driver.

The DBMS driver is separate from the application and ODBC library and provides any necessary translation services, such as translating standard SQL statements into the native SQL of the data source, protocol management, or other services required by the data source. All SQL translations are the responsibility of the driver developer. Also, the front-end application is not limited to using a single DBMS driver but may make connections through several drivers to different databases or may use a single DBMS driver to connect to several similar DBMSs.

On networks, another layer of networking software may appear but is not always present. The presence or absence of this networking software layer is determined by the requirements of the data server. And, finally, the DBMS component receives the request and returns the responding data via the same route.

The Open Database Connectivity standards were designed to provide developers with a choice between utilizing a lowest common denominator of features provided by all ODBC drivers across all DBMSs, or being able to exploit extended features supported by a specific DBMS.

ODBC implements a core SQL grammar and a core set of functions both based on the SAG CLI specification. All ODBC drivers are expected to implement the core grammar and core functions. This means that any application developer who does not require functionality beyond these core provisions can use an ODBC driver without incorporating provisions to check for specific capabilities.

The core provisions consist of support for establishing a connection with a data source, the ability to execute SQL statements, and the ability to retrieve results. Core provisions also include the following standards:

- Error message reporting system

- Logon interface for the end user

- Set of data types (defined by ODBC)

- SQL grammar (defined by ODBC)

Beyond the core provisions, ODBC also defines an extended SQL grammar and extended function set, which offer developers methods of exploiting any advanced capabilities that a specific DBMS may possess. These extensions are implemented through a series of features including:

- A method for applications to query the capabilities supported by a specific driver and data source

- A SQL grammar for scalar functions, outer joins, and procedures

- Asynchronous operation

- Extended data types such as date, time, timestamp, and binary

- Scrollable cursors

Other advantages found in ODBC include the following:

- A single ODBC driver can be used by a variety of applications.

- By providing different conformance levels, developers have a choice between a minimalist approach offering access to the widest variety of DBMSs or using advanced features to fully exploit specific DBMSs.

- ODBC is an accepted industry standard and enjoys wide support.

- ODBC provides a portable API that offers a common data access language for both the Windows and Macintosh environments.

- The ODBC standards are vendor independent.

Interoperability

Microsoft ✓ *Exam* *Objective*	**Compare solutions that use ODBC on the basis of performance, maintainability, and interoperability.**

The goal of ODBC is to provide interoperability in database applications. Rather than rewrite front-end applications to a new set of native APIs whenever a new back-end data source must be supported, ODBC supplies a common API set as well as a common defined SQL grammar that allows access to databases in a generic fashion. This is not a perfect solution, however.

Occasionally, you may be interested in including some functionality in your application that is not supported by a target driver at its level of conformance. When this is the case, you will have to make some decisions concerning how to handle the desired functionality. These decisions could have a direct impact on the interoperability of the application. Your options are:

- **Provide the unsupported feature as part of the client application.** This option requires more client-side programming on your part and may not even be possible, depending on the feature that you wish to support. When you provide the feature as part of the client application without relying on the server, you maintain application interoperability.

- **Make the feature available based on the features of the driver.** If the user can choose the back-end data source from a variety of options, the feature can be restricted to only those data sources that have ODBC drivers available that support the feature. All other data sources would not be allowed to use the feature. This option does not allow full interoperability because some of the features may be disabled when using certain data sources.

- **Provide an alternative to the desired functionality.** Instead of including the desired functionality, provide an alternative that is supported by the driver. Use the alternative feature instead. This option maintains interoperability at the expense of full functionality.

- **Support the feature by calling the data source directly.** Instead of using ODBC, call the feature directly by using the native API of the server. Remember that whenever you call a native API set, you have destroyed interoperability for that feature. Future releases of your software for other data sources would require a rewrite of the feature in question.

- **Drop the feature from your application.** If you can't find a way to support the feature while remaining interoperable, the feature can be dropped from the feature set of an application. This may or may not be an acceptable solution depending on the importance of the feature for the intended application. While interoperability is maintained, the price may be very high.

The goal is to provide an application that is as functional as possible but also as interoperable as possible. Any sacrifices in interoperability must be compensated during the maintenance of the application, especially if you end up with multiple versions of the application that you must support to include all desired features.

ODBC and ISAM Performance

The architecture of ODBC is designed for access to relational data structures. Although ODBC drivers are provided for many ISAM database file types, these drivers tend to be very inefficient. This is primarily due to the amount of work offloaded to the driver by ODBC for ISAM data structures. Drivers targeting ISAM data sources are called *single-tier* drivers. Figure 10.6 compares these drivers with standard *two-tier* drivers that access relational data sources.

FIGURE 10.6

Driver processing roles

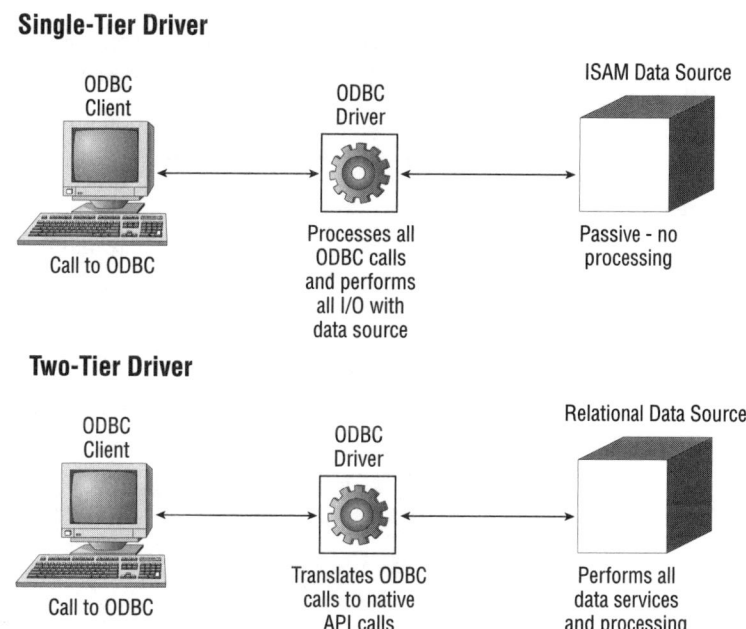

In Figure 10.6 we see that when the developer uses ODBC to access an ISAM data source, the driver must assume increased responsibility. Instead of relying on the relational database management system on the server to provide data services to the client, the driver must provide these services. This is because there is no server-side processing in a file-server database architecture.

The driver essentially becomes a client-side data engine. Because the client could have accessed the data through a client-side engine such as JET, the entire ODBC layer is unnecessary. Consequently, this approach to ISAM data access is quite inefficient.

Exercise 10.2 takes you through the process of creating an ODBC Data Source Name for the Northwind Access Database. This exercise assumes that ODBC 3.0 is installed on your computer.

EXERCISE 10.2

Creating a Data Source Name

1. From the Windows Start menu, open the Control Panel by selecting Start ➢ Settings ➢ Control Panel.

2. Locate the ODBC 32 icon in the Control Panel. Double-click this icon to open the ODBC Data Source Administrator.

3. Click the System DSN tab. This will enable your DSN to be used by any user logged on to the computer as well as any system process. Click Add.

4. From the list of drivers, select Microsoft Access Driver (*.MDB). Click Finish. This will present the Driver setup screen.

5. Enter **TestDSN** as the Data Source Name. In the Database section, click Select and navigate to the NORTHWIND.MDB file. Recall the location of this database from Exercise 10.1. The completed dialog box should look like the figure below:

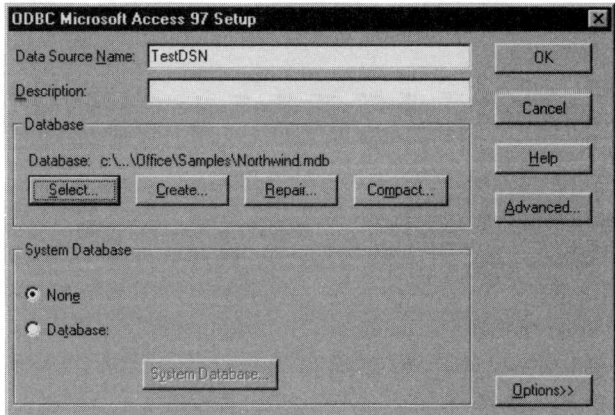

6. Click the OK button to save the DSN. Click OK again to exit the Administrator.

Remote Data Objects

Microsoft ✓ ***Exam*** ***Objective***

Explain the benefits of Remote Data Objects.

While ODBC proved to be an efficient way to access relational data sources while maintaining interoperability, there remained a few problems with using the ODBC API to access data sources. For most developers, the complexity of the ODBC API proved to be a very prohibitive factor in the development of truly interoperable applications.

The Remote Data Objects (RDO) provided a simpler approach to taking advantage of the ODBC model. By providing a thin object model over the ODBC API, RDO provided the means to harness the power of ODBC, but on a much simpler level. RDO enables programmers to open and manage a database connection, execute queries and stored procedures, manipulate query results, and to commit or roll back (cancel) changes to the database.

RDO objects and collections describe the characteristics of database components and methods used to manipulate database records. The RDO object model, illustrated in Figure 10.7, shows the objects and collections used to create relationships that represent the logical structure of the database. In many respects, this object model is very similar to the DAO model, although RDO is significantly faster in accessing relational data sources than DAO.

FIGURE 10.7

The RDO model

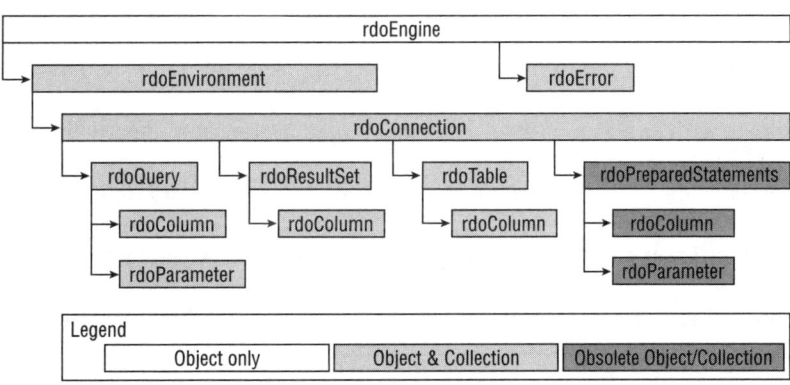

RDO is found only in the Enterprise versions of the Microsoft Developer products such as Visual Basic. If you do not own the Enterprise version, you do not have access to these objects and do not have license to use them for development.

Different types of containment relationships are provided by objects and collections. While objects and collections are similar—both represent relationships—the differentiation between objects and collections is found in the contents of each classification. Each object may contain none, one, or more collections, but each must be a different type. Collections, in contrast, contain none, one, or more objects but the objects must all be the same type.

In Table 10.1, the collection types appear in the first column, object types in the second, and a description in the third. Notice that collection names are always plural while the corresponding object names are singular.

T A B L E 10.1: RDO Collections and Objects

Collection	Object	Description
RdoConnections	rdoConnection	An open or allocated connection
n/a	rdoEngine	The remote database engine itself
RdoErrors	rdoError	ODBC error information
RdoEnvironments	rdoEnvironment	Any logical set of rdoConnection objects with a common user and password
RdoColumns	rdoColumn	A column returned as part of an rdoResultSet
RdoParameters	rdoParameter	Parameter used with rdoQuery
RdoQueries	rdoQuery	Saved query definition
RdoResultsets	rdoResultset	Rows returned by a query
RdoTables	rdoTable	Table definition statement

RDO Support for Client/Server Design Goals

RDO and the Remote Data control offer a number of remote data access advantages for client/server communications:

- **Batch management for multiple action queries.**   Using RDO, an application can issue a set of INSERT, DELETE, or UPDATE operations in a single SQL statement. This increases performance by reducing the network and remote processing overhead.

- **Continuing queries after an initial timeout period.**   If a query exhausts the interval set of the QueryTimeout property, RDO allows an override to the query cancellation, permitting the query to continue until another timeout occurs.

- **Executing asynchronous queries.**   Because a query can involve extended processing time to complete, RDO offers both an asynchronous query option and a method of canceling an asynchronous query as well as a unique event-driven asynchronous programming option that replaces the need for a polling loop. Asynchronous operation includes opening connections and the MoveLast methods.

- **High performance access to remote ODBC data sources.**   Rapid access to data in response to complex queries is a goal found in virtually every data access application. The level of performance provided by RDO is equaled only by the ODBC and DBLib API programming models. Last, by leveraging the remote data engine, RDO offers improved response times and increases user productivity.

- **Managing multiple result sets.**   Executing queries to return multiple result sets is an efficient method of database access, minimizing the demands on system resources. RDO permits filling multiple data-driven listboxes and menus in response to a single query. Further, by combining a row-count query with a SELECT query, scrollbars and progress status bars can be accurately set.

- **Managing stored procedures.**   RDO's rdoParameter object offers access to the values returned by stored procedures. Because output parameters are the only method of accessing information from an Oracle stored procedure and these are extensively used for administrative functions as well as single inquiries, the procedure's return value is commonly required to determine if the stored procedure has completed successfully.

- **Setting limits on the number of returned or processed rows.** Since queries can easily return more rows than can be handled practically, RDO includes a query limit governor which restricts the number of rows returned. Limiting excessive responses assists in predicting response times and makes it easier to manage workstation or server resources used for cursor keysets. Likewise, limits can be placed on the number of rows affected by a data-modification query statement.

- **Utilizing server-side cursors.** Some database servers, such as Microsoft SQL Server, permit cursor keysets that exist on the server rather than the workstation. Remote (server-side) cursor keysets can enhance performance while reducing both the network and client-side workloads.

- **Improved polymorphism and 'free-standing' object creation.** RDO allows the creation of free-standing rdoConnection and rdoQuery objects which can later be associated with other objects to perform specific tasks. An example would be creating an rdoQuery object without an rdoConnection object, then later associating the rdoQuery object with an open connection.

- **Supporting dissociated result sets.** RDO allows the creation of a static read-write cursor and the break of the connection with the remote server while the rdoResultset object is still available for access. Later, the rdoResultset object can be re-associated with another rdoConnection object and the BatchUpdate method used to post off-line changes to the database.

- **Creation and management of optimistic batch updates.** While ODBC supports optimistic updates, these are done on a row-by-row basis rather than a batch basis and requires both network and server bandwidth. In contrast, RDO can leverage the Client Batch cursor library to set groups of rows for insertion, updating, or deletion with a single process call, improving update performance and reducing the network load.

- **Simplifying the use of stored procedures.** RDO supports the expression of parameterized queries and stored procedures as if these were methods belonging to a parent rdoConnection object. In this fashion, parameters can be passed in the same fashion as they would be for a Visual Basic function, removing the reliance on rdoParameter objects.

- **Exposing underlying ODBC handles.** In situations where additional flexibility or control is required beyond that supplied by the object model, RDO offers access to the ODBC environment, connection, and statement handles.

- **Minimizing memory footprint.** The RDO memory footprint is minimal compared to other programming models and does not demand local memory or swapdisk space for low-level cursors. This offers advantages in client/server front-end applications where RAM may be limited as well as minimizing the demand on system resources.

The ActiveX Data Objects (ADO) also support most of the previously listed advantages. This object set should be seriously considered for new development projects as there will be no further releases or upgrades of the RDO library.

Comparing RDO and Microsoft JET/DAO

The RemoteData control can be used to create a form that contains the same bound controls as the Data control, and the result can be processed with minimal code. Remote Data Objects and their DAO/JET equivalents are shown in Table 10.2.

T A B L E 10.2 RDO and DAO/JET Equivalents	RDO Object	DAO/JET Equivalent
	Dynamic-type	n/a
	Forward-only-type	Forward-only-type
	Keyset-type	Dynaset-type
	Static-type (r/w)	Snapshot-type (r/o)
	n/a	Table-type
	rdoColumn	Field
	rdoConnection	Database
	rdoEngine	DBEngine
	rdoEnvironment	Workspace
	rdoError	Error
	rdoParameter	Parameter

	RDO Object	DAO/JET Equivalent
T A B L E 10.2 *(cont.)* RDO and DAO/JET Equivalents	rdoQuery	QueryDef
	rdoResultset	Recordset
	rdoTable	TableDef
	(cursorless)	n/a
	n/a	Index
	n/a	Relation
	n/a	Group
	n/a	User

RDO implements objects, properties, and methods used to access relational data sources through ODBC. Queries return data in the form of result sets consisting of none, one, or multiple data rows that are composed of one or more columns. Also, while DAO requires cursors to access data, RDO supports *cursorless* resultsets, which demand fewer resources than cursors.

DAO includes objects, methods, and properties designed to implement and support the ISAM structures for JET and installable ISAM databases. Examples include the Index object and Seek methods used to manage the ISAM indexes, which are used to locate data rows (records). Since RDO and relational databases take a quite different approach to managing indexes, the ISAM-support objects and methods are not required.

Referential Integrity and Security

DAO supports referential integrity, creation, and modification of the database schema, and security using DAO methods and properties; RDO does not provide any type of referential integrity, and no support for security or schema modification. Instead, these features are expected to be provided through the server's tools and utilities.

RDO does provide make-table queries and execute action queries to create, modify, or delete databases and tables using native SQL statements. Further, RDO can also execute stored procedures of any complexity to manage the database schema as well as perform maintenance operations that are not supported by DAO.

Conversions from DAO to RDO

Existing DAO and data-control applications can be converted to RDO and the RemoteData controls with minimal revisions. Those changes that are required, however, are because RDO is designed entirely for use with relational databases.

Because RDO does not implement a query processor, RDO requires the data source to process all queries and to create the returned result sets.

Conversion Exceptions

DAO/JET applications that do not use DAO ISAM objects and methods, such as the table-type Recordset object, the Seek method, or other ISAM programming methodologies, can easily be converted to ODBCDirect rather than being converted to RDO. The ODBCDirect driver routes DAO through RDO rather than through Microsoft JET, and conversion to ODBCDirect requires fewer revisions than conversion to RDO.

Although ODBCDirect can be used to easily convert applications to support relational databases, remember that Microsoft is phasing out DAO. Conversion should take place, although conversion to ADO rather than RDO may be the best move.

OLE DB and ADO

As we have seen from the previous discussion, ODBC, while a welcome technology, is not a perfect technology. Knowing that there is always room for improvement, Microsoft introduced OLE DB in an effort to improve ODBC performance and eliminate any and all biases to specific data-storage formats. Unlike ODBC, OLE DB represents a COM interface directly to the destination database. The goal of OLE DB is to provide a component solution for database access that removes the barriers presented to ODBC by allowing heterogeneous data sources to expose their full potential.

Although OLE DB and ADO are covered in detail in the next chapter, these concepts are addressed here to introduce their place in the list of options for data access.

Since OLE DB is a C++ API, it is not directly accessible to many other development environments such as Visual Basic and Internet platforms. For these environments, Microsoft has provided a set of programmable objects, the ActiveX Data Objects (ADO) that allow access to OLE DB.

ADO was introduced in March of 1997 with the release of Visual Studio 97. It was originally intended as a method through which Active Server Pages running on Internet Information Server could get access to OLE DB data sources. ADO is also usable in Visual J++- Java applications and Visual Basic 5.0, both part of the Visual Studio 97 family of products.

The most popular implementation of ADO today can be found in Active Server Pages. Active Server Pages is an IIS ISAPI extension that allows HTML and script code to be processed on the Web server rather than forcing it to run on the browser. This allows access to server-side resources. Database access can happen easily in Active Sever Pages by using ADO.

Although OLE DB is not intended to replace ODBC, many applications that at one time would have been written with ODBC and RDO may now be more appropriate for OLE DB and ADO. If your application accesses data from data sources ranging from mainframes to desktops, or if you are building a Web application designed to provide a user with an interactive experience with a data source, ADO may be exactly what you have been looking for.

SQL-Distributed Management Objects

Microsoft ✓ *Exam* *Objective* | **Explain the benefits of the SQL-Distributed Management Objects (SQL-DMO)**

The Microsoft SQL-Distributed Management Objects (SQL-DMO) stand apart from all of the other interfaces that we have discussed. While all of the other interfaces are intended to access data from heterogeneous data sources, the SQL-DMO is designed to interact only with Microsoft SQL Server. Although it is a 32-bit interface accessible from any language that can perform OLE automation, with any other database server other than SQL Server it serves no useful purpose.

The other striking difference between the other models and the SQL-DMO is that the SQL-DMO is not actually intended to be a data interface at all; rather, it is intended to access the administrative functionality of SQL Server. Those tasks that one would normally associate with the database administrator, such as adding users, assigning permissions, and allocating storage, can all be executed quite easily and efficiently from a custom administrative client application through the SQL-DMO. Figure 10.8 illustrates the SQL-DMO object model.

FIGURE 10.8

The SQL-DMO object model

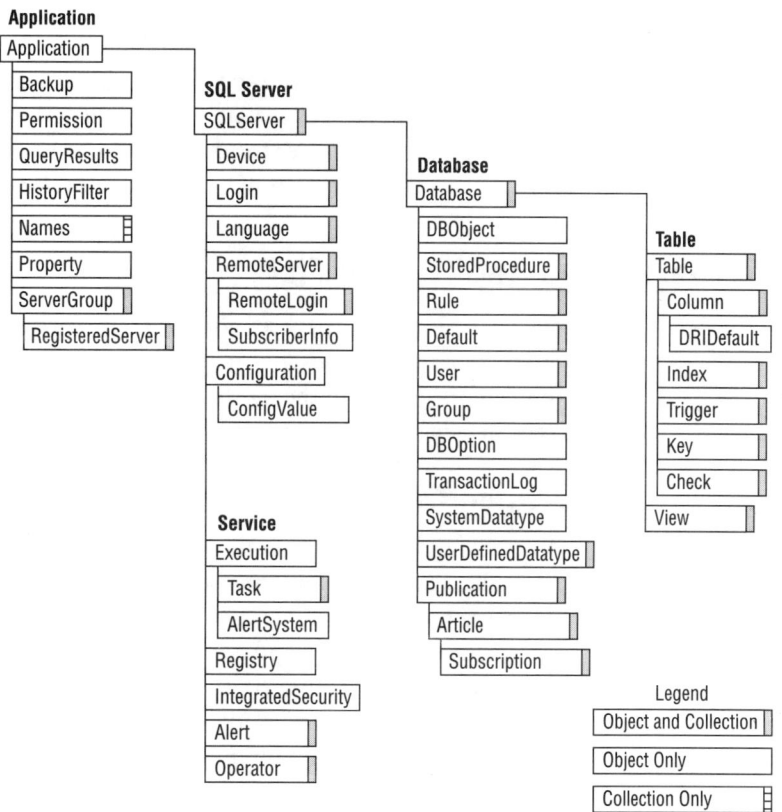

As you can see clearly from Figure 10.8, the SQL-DMO model is not a data access model at all. Although tables and stored procedures are referenced in the model, it is clearly an application model with the focus on the discovery and manipulation of database objects ranging from data storage objects to users and groups. Although the SQL-DMO can be used to access SQL Server data, this is not the intent of this model and other models should be used for data access.

Database Replication

Sometimes, one data store is not enough. Database replication has become an extremely popular approach to distributing data throughout the enterprise because it allows the people making decisions more access to actual data. When data is needed, it is available more quickly at a computer down the hall, not across the country or across the world.

This section will explore some of the general issues regarding replication strategies and their appropriate place in the enterprise. It will then look at some specific technologies for database replication including Microsoft JET replication and replication with Microsoft SQL Server.

Where Does Replication Fit?

Data can be distributed throughout the enterprise from a database source by distributed transactions and replication. Each approach is very different in terms of its goals and the mechanisms used to accomplish the distribution. Each also has its own distinct advantages and disadvantages.

Distributed Transactions

A *distributed transaction* is the process of issuing a single transaction from an application source and forcing this transaction to be atomic across servers on a network. For example, a client application might request a transaction that requires data to be updated on two different servers. If the transaction cannot commit on both servers, then the transaction will be rolled back on both servers and no data modifications will be made.

A distributed transaction may be issued in two ways:

- Through the Microsoft Transaction Server
- Directly with a distributed transaction manager

The components that actually interface with the databases may be calling different servers, yet the context of this transaction will force atomic behavior. To carry out this role, the Microsoft Transaction Server uses a service called the Microsoft Distributed Transaction Coordinator (MSDTC).

If you are using Microsoft SQL Server, you can call the Distributed Transaction Coordinator directly from your server-side application by requesting a distributed transaction in your Transact-SQL code. You can also use the DBLib API exposed by SQL Server to create a distributed transaction from the client. Either approach will have the same result.

There are distinct advantages to using distributed transactions in the effort to ensure database distribution. One advantage is that the data modified on the separate servers does not have to be identical to or a subset of the other. For example, suppose that someone placed an order for 100 widgets with a sales representative sitting in an office building. The sales representative enters the order and executes a distributed transaction. First, the order is entered into the local sales database on a server within the office building. This database is used for billing and commissions. The order is also relayed to the inventory database sitting on a server in the warehouse. Sales values are increased and inventory values are decreased, all with the same transaction. Figure 10.9 illustrates a transaction like the one just described.

FIGURE 10.9

Supporting distributed
transactions

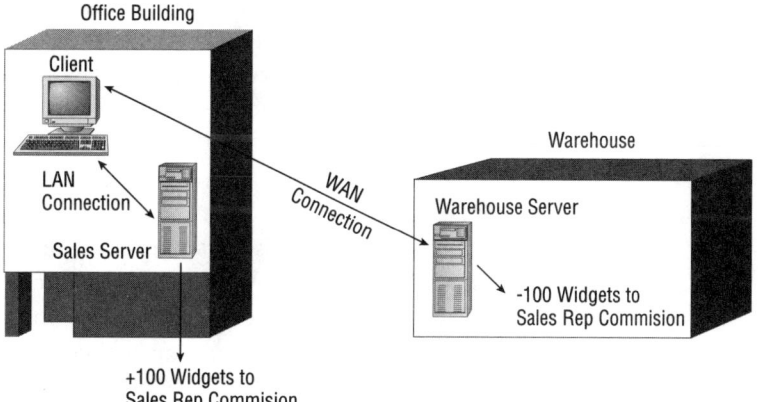

Extend this scenario and suppose that there are not 100 widgets in stock over at the warehouse. In fact, the widget model the customer ordered is actually a discontinued item. You could actually do an inventory check before you commit the transaction at the warehouse. Because the inventory is insufficient to cover the order, the transaction at the warehouse would fail, forcing the transaction at the office building to fail as well.

Using distributed transactions, you have the added advantage of *zero data latency*. Data will always be in a consistent state throughout the enterprise. It is impossible to commit any transaction that does not also update data on the other servers participating in the process.

There are some disadvantages to this approach as well. The primary problem with distributed transactions is overhead. Forcing multiple servers to participate in every transaction significantly increases the amount of network traffic produced. It also increases the likelihood that any given transaction will fail. If a single server fails, then all transactions in which that server participates will cease to function. If not resolved quickly, this can cause significant losses for a business.

Distributed transactions can be quite effective when a business has no tolerance for data latency. If the business also has the ability to handle the additional overhead and can effectively manage the risks inherent in this solution, then it may be a good choice.

Database Replication

Database replication is the process of taking existing data in a database and copying its content or portions of its content to other databases on the network. Some replication technologies even allow you to select specific fields or rows in a table for replication.

Numerous technologies provide replication services. The Microsoft JET engine supports a bidirectional replication model allowing data to be edited in any replica on the network. These edits are then replicated to other databases in the enterprise when necessary. SQL Server 6.5 supports a unidirectional replication model where data editing can take place only on a single-source database. These edits are then periodically replicated to the subscribers of the database.

Database replication also has its own advantages and disadvantages. The greatest advantage is that it does not require consistent and reliable lines of communication, as does the distributed transaction. If a server is not available for a scheduled update, the replicated changes are simply stored for the next synchronization. The advantage to this arrangement is significantly less overhead in the replication scenario. Rather than having transaction requests bouncing throughout the network on a constant basis, replication tasks and synchronizations can be delayed for relatively inactive times on the network.

If there is a substantial disadvantage to database replication, it is data latency. Although you can configure replication tasks and synchronization to take place frequently (after every data modification if needed), there is no guarantee that the data will ever be consistent across servers at any point in time.

The best implementations of replication are, therefore, those in which data latency can be tolerated. If network resources are at a premium and there can be no guarantee that communication channels will be reliable, replication is also a good choice. Finally, if you are simply unable to effectively manage the risks that come with distributed transactions, then database replication might be an acceptable alternative.

Replication Strategies

Microsoft supports two general approaches to database replication:

- A bidirectional model supported by Microsoft Access and JET
- A unidirectional model supported by Microsoft SQL Server 6.5

Each approach has different design goals. The JET replication model emphasizes application autonomy over transactional integrity, while the SQL Server model takes the opposite perspective.

Replication Using Microsoft JET

Microsoft JET uses an autonomous application approach to replication. Data modifications can be made to any replica and synchronized back to other replicas when necessary and available. This approach allows each replica in a replica set to be very independent, acting almost as a stand-alone database. However, this independence comes at the sacrifice of true transactional integrity. If two users make changes to a record at the same time on different replicas, there is a data inconsistency that must be resolved at the next synchronization.

Every JET database that supports replication is a part of a group called a *replica set*. Each replica set represents a group of databases that can replicate their data changes to other databases in the same set. Every replica set has one database called the design master. Only the design master is allowed to replicate database design modifications (such as a new table) to other databases in the replica set.

JET replication can be managed in three different ways:

- The briefcase
- The Replication Manager
- The JET DAO code

The easiest approach to set up and manage is the *briefcase*. The briefcase is a service provided by Windows 95 and Windows NT 4.0. Its purpose is to synchronize changes made to various files so that copies on disks or mobile computers can be synchronized with copies stored on a server. JET supports the briefcase through a special briefcase reconciler designed to interface JET databases with the briefcase.

JET also supports a more robust approach to replication known as the Replication Manager. The Replication Manager is a fully featured replication service that allows more flexible treatment of replicas than the briefcase does. It allows some objects inside a JET database to be replicated, while others remain local. It also allows very flexible replication topologies to be constructed to satisfy virtually any replication need.

The Replication Manager does not ship with Microsoft Office Professional Edition. If you want to use the Replication Manager, you must own the Developer Edition of Microsoft Office.

The last approach to replication is managed entirely through JET Data Access Objects (DAO) code. If you want, you can create replicas, schedule synchronizations, and work with all replication tasks through the DAO. This approach provides a great deal of flexibility, but it may be a bit cumbersome to implement.

Exercise 10.3 walks you through the process of configuring replication using the briefcase. Although this is the least flexible model, it will still give you a good idea of the functionality supported by JET replication.

EXERCISE 10.3

Configuring Briefcase Replication with an Access Database

1. On the desktop, create a new briefcase by pointing to any space not occupied by an icon and right-click. From the pop-up menu, select New ➢ Briefcase. A new briefcase object will be created on the desktop.

2. Start Microsoft Access. When prompted to open or create a database, click Blank Database and click OK. From the Save dialog box, name the database Rep and save it in the location of your choice where you will be able to access it easily later.

3. Import the categories table from the Northwind database by selecting File ➢ Get External Data ➢ Import from the Access menu. Navigate to the location of the Northwind database. If you have maintained default paths this should be \Program Files\Microsoft Office\Office\Samples\ NORTHWIND.MDB. Double-click the Northwind database file to open the import objects window.

4. From the list of tables, select categories and click OK. You should now see the categories table in your database window.

5. Exit Microsoft Access and double-click the new briefcase icon on the desktop to open the briefcase. Click Finish from the Welcome screen. Using the My Computer icon, navigate to the directory where the REP.MDB database file is stored. Close or minimize any other open windows except for the briefcase and the window containing your database.

6. Drag the REP.MDB file from inside the folder to inside the briefcase window. The first message informs you that the briefcase must make some changes to the file to make the database replicable. Click Yes to continue.

7. The next dialog box asks if you want to make a backup of the original database. Because the original database will be irrevocably changed, you will usually want to answer Yes. However, for our example, click No to continue.

8. The last dialog box asks which database you want to be the design master in your replica set. Verify that Original Copy is selected, and click the OK button.

9. You now have two copies of the database, one in the original folder and the other in the briefcase. Double-click the briefcase copy to open it inside Access. Notice the new icon next to the categories table in the database window. This icon represents a replicated object.

10. Open the categories table and change the category name "Beverages" to "Liquids." Close the Categories table and exit Access.

11. Now point to the REP.MDB icon in your original folder, which should still be open on your desktop. Double-click to open the database.

12. Open the categories table. Notice that the name of the first category is still "Beverages." Change the description in category eight from "Seaweed and Fish" to "Shrimp and other Shellfish."

13. Close the categories table and exit Access.

14. From the menu in the briefcase window, select Briefcase ➤ Update All. You will be notified that you must perform a merge because changes have been made in both databases. Click Update to perform the merge.

15. Open each of the databases and verify that your changes were replicated. When you are finished, close the briefcase and your folder window.

Replication Using Microsoft SQL Server 6.5

The SQL Server approach to replication is much different from the JET approach. JET replication favors application autonomy over transactional integrity. SQL Server takes the opposite approach. SQL Server uses a publisher/subscriber metaphor in its replication model. This is illustrated in Figure 10.10.

FIGURE 10.10

SQL Server 6.5
database replication

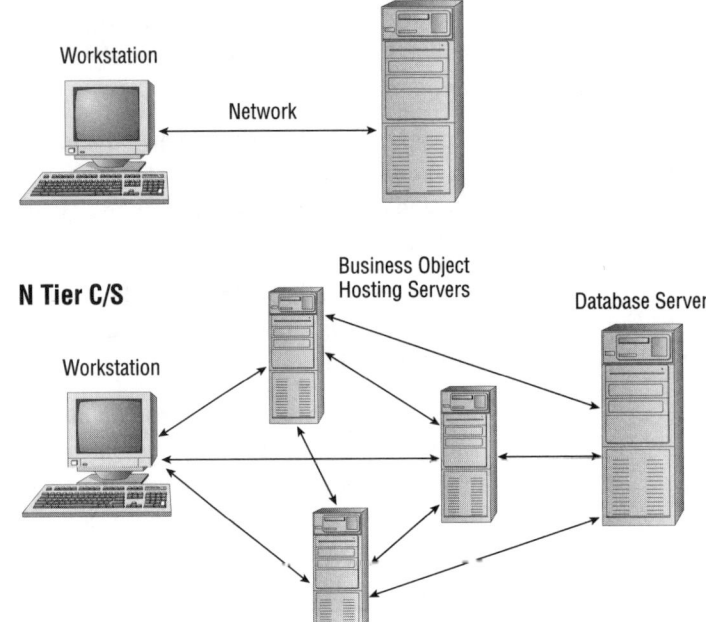

In the SQL Server replication model, data modifications can be made in only one place, on the publishing server. This ensures transactional integrity on the source database because no transactions can be issued to the subscribing databases. If a client using a subscribed database must make a change to the data, the modification must be directed to the publication server.

The distribution server hosts a special database called the *distribution database*. This database is essentially the post office. Periodically, a service on the distribution server called the Log Reader service will read the transaction log of the publishing server and pull out any transactions that affect replicated data. These transactions are then stored in the distribution database until it is time to replicate these changes to the subscribing servers. After all the transactions have replicated to all subscribing servers needing them, the stored transactions can be removed from the distribution database.

Although at first glance, it may seem that the unidirectional nature of SQL Server replication might limit its functionality, in reality the model is quite flexible. For example, assume that you have a SQL Server in New York and you wish to replicate the data to three SQL Servers in Los Angeles across a slow link. The server in New York would be the publisher, but do you really want all three L.A. servers acting as subscribers? Suppose that you set one of the L.A. servers as a subscriber, but also as a publisher, allowing it to publish the subscribed information locally to the other two servers. SQL Server can handle this task quite efficiently.

SQL Server replication is also flexible enough to handle multiple business models as well. For example, you may have a very centralized business model with a headquarters and satellite offices that report to this headquarters. Certainly, the central administration must always have the complete picture of what is going on in the field. To support this scenario, you could have a SQL Server in the headquarters office actually subscribe to the tables published by the field offices. Only the main office will have the "big picture," but then again, that is all that is needed anyway.

By contrast, what if you work with a very decentralized business model? There is no main office, but every office knows what the other is doing. In this example, you could have each office maintain their own data and replicate that data to the other offices. This would give every office the complete picture.

The key concept from this discussion is that just because SQL Server replication will only be editing on the original publishing server does not mean that this is a hobbled approach to replication in any way. In fact, it stresses the concept of data integrity above all else. In reality, that just might be the most positive element of all.

Summary

Database connectivity has been a long-standing problem in the computer industry, complicated by proprietary database protocols, language structures, and network protocols. While SQL (Structured Query Language) has attempted, in part, to address the lack of a consistent query format, SQL itself exists in a variety of forms. Other attempts to address incompatibilities have taken the form of:

- Gateways to accept queries, translate, and forward requests and translate the returned data

- Common programming interfaces using standardized APIs, macro languages, or tool sets to provide a common interface

- Common protocols to provide a consistent SQL grammar and net-working protocols common to all DBMSs

Unfortunately, none of these approaches has been universal nor has it become a de facto industry standard.

Data Access Objects (DAO) and Open Database Connectivity (ODBC) are two application programming interfaces that try to provide database-independent support for applications. ODBC drivers have gained wide support and become a popular interface for DBMSs.

DAO is optimized for .MDB database files (such as those created using Microsoft Access) but can still be used to access ODBC sources. Using ODBC, an ODBC driver acts as a translator between the front-end applica-tion and the back-end database server. Because the application can call on multiple ODBC drivers, applications may access multiple databases without having to include explicit support for each database's protocols and lan-guage requirements. This is the advantage to incorporating ODBC into an application framework.

ODBC drivers are required to implement a standard SQL grammar and a standard set of core functions based on the SAG CLI specification. Indi-vidual ODBC drivers may, however, also supply extended functionality beyond the core specifications, which consist of:

- Support for establishing a connection with a data source, the ability to execute SQL statements, and the ability to retrieve results

- A standard error message reporting system

- A standard logon interface for the end user

- A standard set of data types (defined by ODBC)

- A standard SQL grammar (defined by ODBC)

Data Access Objects (DAO) provide database support for .MDB (Microsoft JET) database engines but can also access ODBC data sources and installable ISAM databases.

Remote Data Objects (RDO) are used to access remote data sources through ODBC drivers and provide the means to open and manage database connections, execute queries and stored procedures, manipulate query results, and commit changes to the database. One advantage to RDO is that it outper-forms DAO when accessing relational databases.

The SQL Distributed Management Object (SQL-DMO) is a set of programmable COM objects used to create custom applications that control the administrative functionality of Microsoft SQL Server. The SQL DMO can be accessed by any development environment able to perform OLE automation, including Microsoft Visual Basic.

Review Questions

1. Multiple database access is hampered by differences between databases in:

   A. Protocols

   B. Record types

   C. Data standards

   D. All of the above

2. What are the three primary approaches to the database connectivity problem?

   A. Developing gateways

   B. Developing applications to handle multiple database formats

   C. Developing common programming interfaces

   D. Developing common protocols

3. The ODBC standard:

   A. Calls for the development of common interface implementations by database vendors

   B. Defines a series of object classes based on the MFC DAO classes to provide translation and protocol services

   C. Defines a series of object classes based on the MFC RDO classes to provide translation and protocol services

   D. Defines an API suite allowing a variety of applications access to a variety of data sources through DBMS-specific drivers

4. Which of the following is true of DBMS drivers under ODBC? (Select two.)

    A. They are dependent on OCX objects.

    B. They are integrated in the ODBC library.

    C. They are separate from the ODBC library.

    D. They translate standard SQL statements into native SQL for the data source.

5. Which of the following is true?

    A. Both DAO and ODBC are dependent on specific database management systems.

    B. Both DAO and ODBC are independent of specific database management systems.

    C. DAOs are dependent on specific database management systems while ODBC objects are independent.

    D. ODBC objects are dependent on specific database management systems while DAOs are independent.

6. A common programming interface provides which of the following?

    A. A copy of the DBMS that supports a specific grammar, interface, and protocol

    B. A standard API, macro language, or tool set for translating requests, accessing data, and returning results

    C. A transaction-based system of exchanging information between front-end applications and back-end servers

    D. An object-oriented interface between databases

7. ODBC is an API implemented by individual database vendors as which of the following?

    A. An extension of the Microsoft JET database engine

    B. ODBC component modules providing translation services between application standards and database native formats

    C. ODBC drivers specific to each vendor's database management system

    D. Three-tiered driver services providing multiple database format translations

8. Data Access Objects (DAO) provide data access objects consisting of a database object and which of the following? (Select three.)

    A. A querydef object

    B. A recordset object

    C. A tabledef object

    D. A SQLdef object

9. The common protocol approach to database connectivity is based on which of the following?

    A. A single protocol, SQL grammar, and networking protocol common to all DBMSs

    B. A standard API, macro language, or tool set for translating requests, accessing data, and returning results

    C. A transaction-based system of exchanging information between front-end applications and back-end servers

    D. Distributed Relational Database Architecture (DRDA)

10. Data Access Objects are optimized for:

    A. .MDB files (Microsoft Access)

    B. ISAM database files

    C. SQL database files

    D. Unstructured data files

11. Open Database Connectivity (ODBC) is best suited for access to:

A. Local data sources

B. Relational data sources

C. .MDB (Microsoft JET) databases

D. Any data source as long as an appropriate ODBC driver is available

12. To solve the database connectivity problem, what approach is used by ODBC?

A. Common interface approach

B. Common protocol approach

C. Gateway approach

D. Both B and C

13. Core provisions of the ODBC standard include which of the following? (Select three.)

A. A standard error message reporting system

B. A standard SQL grammar defined by ODBC

C. The ability to execute SQL statements

D. The ability to translate data types

14. Extensions to the ODBC core provisions include which of the following? (Select three.)

A. A SQL grammar for scalar functions, outer joins, and procedures

B. Extended data types such as date, time, timestamp, and binary

C. Scrollable cursors

D. Synchronous operations

15. Advantages of ODBC include which of the following? (Select three.)

A. A portable API offering a common data access language for both the Windows and Macintosh environments

B. Access to multiple database types through a single driver

C. Being an accepted industry standard enjoying wide support

D. Vendor-independent standards

16. Advantages of DAO over ODBC include which of the following? (Select three.)

    A. The ability to specify relations between tables

    B. Access to data validation rules

    C. ISAM database compatibility

    D. Support for the Data Definition Language (DDL) and Data Manipulation Language (DML)

17. Comparing DAO and RDO, select the false statement following:

    A. Both DAO and RDO support cursorless result sets that demand fewer resources than cursors.

    B. DAO supports ISAM structures for JET and installable ISAM databases.

    C. RDO does not require ISAM-support objects or methods.

    D. The RDO `RemoteData` control parallels the DAO `Data` control.

18. Using RDO, referential integrity and support for security are provided by which of the following?

    A. Database tables and stored procedures

    B. RDO API functions

    C. Special object classes supported by RDO

    D. The database server

19. Converting DAO and Data control applications to RDO and Remote-Data controls requires which of the following?

    A. Conversions from result sets to data sets

    B. Minimal revisions

    C. Renaming classes and objects

    D. Support for ISAM objects

20. Which of the following is true of SQL Distributed Management Objects (SQL-DMOs)? (Select three.)

    A. They are 32-bit COM objects compatible with Win98/Win95/WinNT.

    B. They are part of an integrated framework consisting of objects, properties, methods, and collections used to administer multiple SQL Servers distributed across a network.

    C. They are OLE Automation–compatible.

    D. They are dependent on the Visual Basic Script Language.

21. Remote Data Objects (RDO) consist of objects and collections. Select the false statement following:

    A. RDO collections may contain multiple objects of a single type.

    B. RDO objects may contain multiple collections of a single type.

    C. RDO permits overriding the `QueryTimeout` property.

    D. `rdoEnvironments` consist of a logical set of `rdoConnection` objects.

22. RDO provides which of the following? (Select three.)

    A. Access to values returned by stored procedures

    B. High performance access to remote ODBC data sources

    C. `rdoQuery` objects to access data sources without an associated connection object

    D. Support for server-side cursor keysets

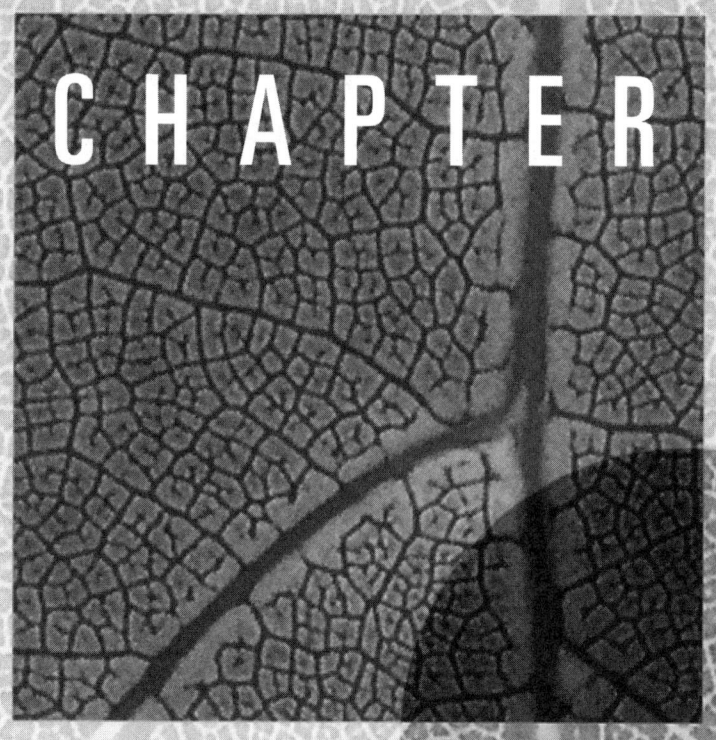

CHAPTER

11

Database Access
Using OLE DB and ADO

OLE DB supports the same basic goal as ODBC, its predecessor: to provide standard data access interfaces allowing the developer to create interoperable database client applications. In this chapter, we will explore OLE DB as a specification for standard data access. We will compare OLE DB to ODBC and discuss the relative positioning of each technology in the marketplace. Finally, we will explore the ActiveX Data Objects (ADO) as a component of an OLE DB solution.

OLE DB

There would be no reason to develop a new standard like OLE DB unless there were room for improvement. While ODBC served the industry for many years, there are some inherent problems with the ODBC approach to data access. In this section, we will first pose the problems affecting the current situation and then address some of the solutions provided by OLE DB.

Problems with Data Storage

Data can be stored in a variety of different formats. Some data structures are flat in nature, storing data in single tables with no real concern for normalization. The data engines that interact with these types of data sources seem to be primarily file I/O systems that read and write data to and from the file. Many of these systems have no sophisticated query optimization logic and tend to be very monolithic in nature. The data files might be on the same computer as the data engine or they might be located on a network server, allowing access from data engines running on a number of different clients.

Other data storage formats are more sophisticated, featuring groups of tables related in such a way that data redundancy is reduced. The most sophisticated of these database management systems will host the data engine on a network server, requiring the client application to make calls to a remote engine rather than have a local engine process remote data. These engines also have very sophisticated query processors and optimizers, ensuring that every query will be executed as efficiently as possible. This approach to data storage is called *relational* storage.

Because these types of data engines are so very different, it is impossible to create a single API set or define a single SQL grammar set that is applicable to all database formats. This is the problem posed to ODBC. While very efficient with relational data sources, ODBC was very inefficient with non-relational or non-structured data sources.

For example, although Microsoft provides an ODBC driver for the Access database file (MDB), this driver is tremendously inefficient. Don't blame the driver developers for this. They did the best that they could with the situation that they were given, however, the architecture of ODBC does not support non-relational databases with the same efficiency as with relational data sources. Figure 11.1 illustrates the current architecture when using drivers for non-relational data sources.

FIGURE 11.1

ODBC and non-relational data sources

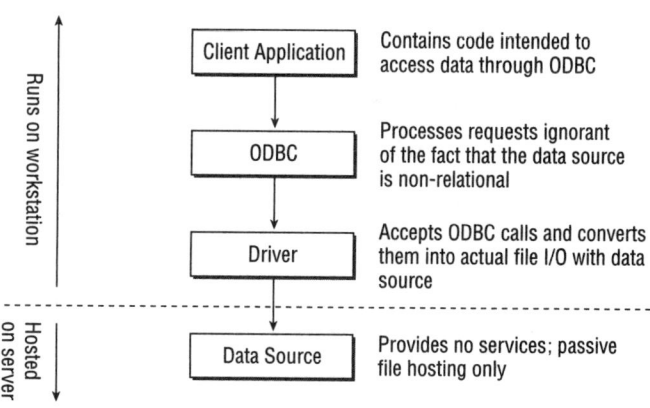

In Figure 11.1, we see that since ODBC components such as the ODBC driver manager and the ODBC driver reside on the client workstation, all data access must still take place at the client. This means that ODBC simply adds more layers to a client-side data engine that is already quite inefficient when compared to relational data engines. Since ODBC does not force the client application to call a data engine, the driver residing on the client acts as the data engine. This places an unnecessary stress on the ODBC driver, which could be avoided if a more efficient architecture were used.

The OLE DB Solution

OLE DB architecture is very flexible. By breaking the database management system into component pieces, OLE DB allows these pieces to run at both the client and the server, depending on the component and the method of implementation. The result is a solution that is less client intensive and more adaptive to the needs of the individual case.

OLE DB is a series of interfaces designed to offer data access to all data types, irrespective of format or location. OLE DB is designed to encapsulate or componentize database and related data processing functions. To achieve this aim, databases and data processing functions would be restructured as middleware components to execute on the client or server sides. The OLE DB architectural standards include provisions for components supplying such services as:

- Business rules

- Cursor engines

- Direct data access across interfaces

- Optimizers

- Query engines

- Transaction managers

In this fashion, the concept behind OLE DB is to break the database apart into basic components, making the components external to the database and, thus, making it possible for the database functionality to become a reusable component architecture. Because the components providing these services are external rather than internal to the database, they can be shared across multiple applications, systems, and data stores, and can provide a higher-level universal interface.

In keeping with the COM standards, OLE DB components can be individually upgraded without replacing the database as a whole.

OLE DB components are also known as OLE DB *Providers* or, more explicitly, as OLE DB Data Providers and OLE DB Service Providers. The OLE DB Data Providers offer direct interfaces between an application and the native data, very much like existing ODBC drivers in use today.

OLE DB Service Providers (see the "OLE DB Components" section, below) are the engines or business rule components that offer extended functionality by interacting between the Data Providers and the applications. OLE DB Service Providers include SQL engines, metadata catalogs, optimizers, and transaction managers. Applications, under OLE DB, employ one or more separate Service Providers to obtain desired functionality. This allows the application interfaces to access and manipulate data from all different types using standard mechanisms.

OLE DB Component Architecture

Because OLE DB depends on component architecture instead of creating a single monolithic application, data access and processing features can be supplied by individual components. This means that:

- A common functionality can be supplied across a variety of data sources.

- Components can be called from a variety of applications, programming languages, and tools.

- Components can be selected as needed to fulfill application requirements and changed or replaced as requirements evolve.

In addition, component architecture provides for reusability and interoperability while maintaining flexibility in client/server–based deployment. And, not least, component architecture reduces the demands for the application developer by placing many of the development demands on the service provider.

OLE DB Components

The OLE DB standard defines a series of components where each component is an OLE COM object:

- **Command objects** execute text commands such as SQL statements. When a text command specifies a rowset—as in a SQL SELECT statement—the command object serves as a factory for the rowset.

- **Data source objects** provide the mechanisms to connect to a particular data source such as a file or a DBMS. Individual data source objects can generate one or more sessions.

- **Enumerator objects** search for other enumerators, and search for and identify available data sources. Applications that are not customized for a specific data source may use enumerators to search for an alternate data source.

- **Error objects** can be generated by any interface on any OLE DB object and provide additional information about an error. Error objects may optionally include a custom error object.

- **Rowset objects** expose data in a tabbed or tabular format and include indexes.

- **Session objects** offer a context for transactions and may be explicitly or implicitly transacted. Sessions can also generate transactions, commands, and rowsets.

- **Transaction objects** are used to commit or abort nested transactions.

ODBC and OLE DB Compared

Microsoft ✓ *Exam* *Objective*	**Compare OLE Database (OLE DB) with the ODBC API and with native APIs as a means of retrieving data in a given scenario.**

As was previously mentioned, although ODBC and OLE DB share a common interoperability goal, there are differences between these two technologies in terms of both architecture and implementation. In this section we will explore those differences in more detail.

Client or Server Architecture

ODBC remains entirely a client-side implementation. All ODBC components run on the client, not on the server. Due to its component architecture, OLE DB components can be implemented at various tiers of the architecture, allowing more efficient placement and execution of each of the elements in a database application.

Allowing some server-side processing also allows the data access technology to be insulated from the client to some extent. Whenever a change or upgrade of any server-side components is deemed necessary, these components can be upgraded in one location on the server rather than requiring an entire redeployment of the application.

Call vs. COM

ODBC is a call-level interface found in standard DLLs. To use the ODBC API, these DLL references must be included in the client application and then called directly from the client code. Another popular alternative to calling the ODBC API directly is to place an object model over the ODBC API and allow the object model to make the calls for you. You simply automate the object model from your client application. In this way, the complexities of the ODBC API can be hidden from the developer. The Microsoft Remote Data Objects (RDO) provide a layer like the one just described.

OLE DB defines COM interfaces. Rather than defining a set of functions that represent certain actions taken on the data source, the COM interface exposed by OLE DB breaks the database into component objects. These object interfaces allow for a more robust and flexible environment than that found in the traditional call-level interface.

Performance Bias

Because of its architecture, ODBC is biased toward relational data sources. Non-relational data sources suffer from heavy and usually inefficient drivers, thus creating an undesirable performance scenario. This prevents ODBC from being considered a useful standard when accessing non-relational data sources.

OLE DB has no such bias. One of the driving factors behind the development of OLE DB was to create a single data access interface that would allow truly universal access to any data source without a performance bias inherent in the design. OLE DB accomplishes this feat by componentizing all data access services, allowing each data model to implement services that are relevant and efficient for their own structure.

Your exam will heavily stress this last point. OLE DB is designed to provide unencumbered and unbiased access to all data storage formats without regard to the structure or architecture of the desired data source.

When to Use Each Model

When writing client applications for databases, you have essentially three basic choices as to how to access the database functionality. It is very important to consider when these options should be used. These options are:

- Native APIs

- ODBC API

- OLE DB

The previous list does not include object models such as SQL-DMO, RDO, or ADO. This is because all of the object models are based on one of the standard technologies in the list. SQL-DMO is an object interface into the native API of Microsoft SQL Server, RDO is based on ODBC technology, and ADO is designed as a means of OLE DB implementation.

Native APIs

Even though you don't hear much about writing to the native APIs of a database management system, this does not mean that this should never be considered an option. The native APIs of a database management system will usually provide the fastest access possible to the data managed by that system. If speed is your overwhelming concern, the native APIs are still a valid choice.

You should be keenly aware, however, of the tradeoffs for using native APIs in your applications. Since they are proprietary in nature, there is usually a substantial learning curve for this type of implementation. In a world where Rapid Application Development is a driving force, the extra time to become acquainted with the native APIs may not always be available. Object models built on the native APIs such as the SQL-DMO can help the situation, but will not solve the problem entirely.

Another problem with native API implementation is that you immediately sacrifice any and all interoperability. If you ever choose to deploy this application using a database management system other than the one for which the application was written, an entire rewrite of the application will be necessary, or, at the very least, a rewrite of the business objects that encapsulate the data access logic.

ODBC

Using the ODBC API is still a valid option when an OLE DB service provider is not available for a target data source. Although OLE DB provides more flexibility overall, the ODBC API can still be used to access older systems where OLE DB is not supported.

Microsoft does ship an OLE DB service provider for ODBC that allows OLE DB to call data sources through ODBC. This enables OLE DB interfaces to be used even when the database does not directly support OLE DB. This service provider for ODBC was provided as a bridge between the two technologies and was not intended to act as a permanent solution. Because it is slow and inefficient, the service providers should be upgraded to database-specific service providers as soon as they are available from the database vendor.

OLE DB

OLE DB should be the technology of choice for data access. Because the ODBC bridge provides a temporary solution, the developer has the opportunity to implement OLE DB solutions even before OLE DB service providers are available for the target data sources.

OLE DB should especially be considered when data access to a collection of heterogeneous data sources is required, especially those that include non-relational data storage. As was previously illustrated, ODBC is extremely inefficient in handling these types of data sources. Using OLE DB in these situations now allows the best possible performance for data access in the long run.

Active Data Objects (ADO)

Microsoft
✓ *Exam*
Objective

Explain the benefits of Active Data Objects (ADO).

While OLE DB provides many advantages to the database developer, there is one problem with OLE DB that had to be overcome. OLE DB interfaces are COM interfaces, which are significantly more complex than the standard call-level interfaces of ODBC. In fact, the COM interfaces exposed by OLE DB are complex to the point that they are virtually inaccessible to some application development tools that lack support for many of the object-oriented features that these COM interfaces require. Neither Microsoft Visual Basic or VBScript in an Active Server Page are sophisticated enough to use the OLE DB interface directly. For these tools, another approach had to be developed.

Since Visual Basic–accessible object models had already been developed for the ODBC API (RDO) and even some native API (SQL-DMO), the same approach was used to create an interface for OLE DB. This interface is ADO.

Primary benefits of ADO include:

- Ease of use

- Speed

- Minimal memory overhead

- Small disk (hard drive) footprint

- Unbiased access to both relational and non-relational data sources

In ADO, a Recordset object provides the main interface to data. A Recordset object represents a single record or an entire set of records from a database table. Commonly, a Recordset contains the results returned by a query command. The current record identified by a Recordset object refers to a single record within the set.

Figure 11.2 shows three Recordset objects: The first—Recordset1—shows six consecutive records returned from a database, each record returning a name and address. The current record in Recordset1 is the index of the last record accessed.

Recordset2 holds eleven records—not consecutive—returned in response to unspecified search criteria. Each record, however, has returned a name, city, and a dollar amount. Again, the current record in Recordset2 is the index of the last record accessed.

Recordset3 holds a single record containing a name and three coded values while the current record field is the index of the record found.

F I G U R E 11.2

Three Recordset
objects holding
query results

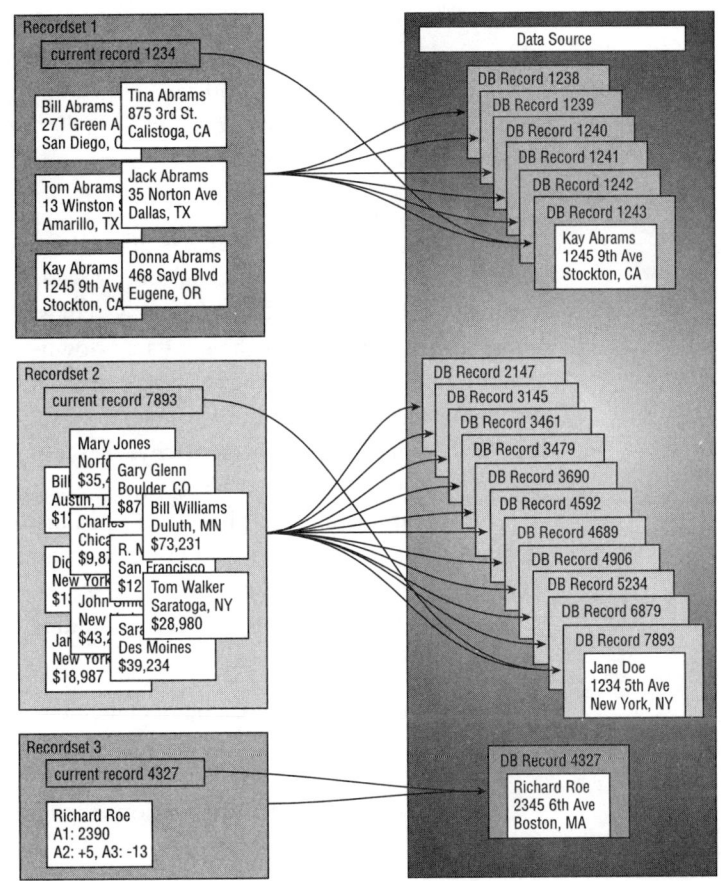

The following example uses the VBScript code and the ADODB implementation of ADO to generate a forward-only, read-only Recordset object to access an ODBC data source through OLE DB.

```
set rstMain = CreateObject("ADODB.Recordset")
rstMain.Open "SELECT * FROM authors", _
          "DATABASE=pubs;UID=sa;PWD=;DSN=Publishers"
```

A more functional, fully-scrollable and batch-updateable Recordset is generated by the following code.

```
set rstMain = CreateObject("ADODB.Recordset")
rstMain.Open "SELECT * FROM authors", _
          "DATABASE=pubs;UID=sa;PWD=;DSN=Publishers",
          adOpenKeyset, adLockBatchOptimistic
```

Because ADO objects are independently created rather than being derived from parent object classes, the object hierarchy is de-emphasized. The benefits are that you do not need to navigate through a hierarchy to create an ADO object, and, instead, you can create and track only the objects needed, resulting in fewer ADO objects and a smaller working set.

Hierarchies

A hierarchy, in computer terms, is defined as a pyramid method of organizing general groups of information, processes, and systems. For example, the file system is a hierarchy where a system is at the top of the pyramid. Systems can contain drives—the next step down—while individual drives can contain both directories (the third step in the hierarchy) and files (the fourth and final step). Directories, of course, may contain other directories or files but the bottom level of the hierarchy, files, contain data but cannot contain other files, directories, or drives.

This hierarchical de-emphasis is also in distinct contrast to both DAO (Data Access Objects) and RDO (Remote Data Objects), which do remain dependent on object hierarchies.

Key features provided by ADO for building client/server and Web-based applications include:

- Advanced recordset cache management

- Batch updating

- Efficient Web server applications through free-threaded objects

- Independently created objects

- Multiple returned recordsets from stored procedures or batch statements

- Optional limits on the number of returned rows and query responses

- Support for multiple cursor types together with support for back-end specific cursors

- Support for stored procedures including in/out parameters and return values

- Flexibility in choice of back-end data store

Exercise 11.1 demonstrates the implementation of ADO in an Active Server Page using Microsoft Visual InterDev.

WARNING   This exercise assumes that you have completed the exercises in Chapter 10. A Web server with Active Server Pages must be installed on the local machine. The Web server must be running. If you are using Microsoft Windows 95, use Personal Web Server.

EXERCISE 11.1

Implementing ADO

1. Start Microsoft Visual InterDev. Close any startup dialog boxes.

2. To create a new Web project in a new workspace, select File ➣ New from the menu. The Projects tab should be selected. If not, select this tab. Select Web Project Wizard from the bottom of the list of project options.

3. In the Project Name textbox, type **ADO_Proj** and click OK.

4. When asked to select a Web server name, type **localhost**. Click Next.

5. Click the Create New Web option. Leave the default name as ADO_ Web. Select the checkbox setting full text search for the Web. Click Finish. Your project will be created.

6. To create a new Active Server Page in the Web project, select File ➣ New from the menu. Make sure that the Files tab is selected. Click Active Server Page in the list of file types and enter **ADOTest** in the File Name textbox. Click OK. This will present the ASP code on your screen.

7. Between the open and close body tags in the Active Server Page, enter the following code:

```
<SCRIPT LANGUAGE=VBScript RUNAT=Server>
Dim intCountProd
Dim rs
Set rs=Server.CreateObject("ADODB.Recordset")
rs.Open "Select Count(*) From Products","DSN=TestDSN"
intCountProd=rs(0)
Response.write "There are " & intCountProd & _
" products in the database."
</SCRIPT>
```

8. With the cursor still active in the code window, select File ➢ Save from the menu. To view the page, right-click the ADOTEST.ASP file in the file list on the left side of the screen. Select Browse With from the pop-up menu and click Microsoft Internet Explorer in the dialog box. Click Open. The Web page should report a total of 77 products.

9. Close Internet Explorer. Exit Visual InterDev. Save if prompted.

Summary

Active Data Objects (ADO) have the advantage of de-emphasizing the object hierarchy and can be created independently without the need to navigate through a hierarchy.

Primary advantages of ADO include:

- Ease of use

- Speed

- Minimal memory overhead

- Small disk (hard drive) footprint

OLE Databases (OLE DB) is a middleware-based solution providing access to relational, non-relational, and unstructured data and incorporates ADO to provide a high-level interface for application developers with OLE DB Providers as the data access engines. OLE DB is a component-based environment with separate components providing various services. The OLE DB architectural standards include provisions for components supplying such services as:

- Business rules

- Cursor engines

- Direct data access across interfaces

- Optimizers

- Query engines

- Transaction managers

While ODBC has become the de facto standard for client/server databases, OLE DB provides comparable interoperability advantages without the performance bias towards relational data sources that is found in ODBC solutions. This makes OLE DB a more truly universal standard, providing access to resources without restrictions and encumbrances.

Review Questions

1. What are the primary benefits of Active Data Objects? (Select three.)

   A. Access to multiple database types

   B. Ease of use

   C. Minimal memory overhead

   D. Sophisticated hierarchies

2. ADO objects can do which of the following? (Select all that apply.)

   A. They can be used for batch updating.

   B. They offer efficient data access through Active Server Pages.

   C. They provide support for stored procedures including in/out parameters and return values.

   D. They return only a single recordset in response to any query.

3. OLE DB architectural standards include which of the following? (Select three.)

   A. Automation engines

   B. Business rule engines

   C. Query engines

   D. Transaction managers

4. What are the basic concepts behind the OLE DB standard? (Select all that apply.)

   A. To allow components to be shared across multiple applications

   B. To make the service component external to both the database and the application

   C. To separate database and service aspects into separate components

   D. To standardize services offered by database systems

5. The OLE DB standard is intended to do which of the following? (Select three.)

   A. Extend and leverage existing ODBC database access

   B. Offer access to unstructured as well as structured data

   C. Offer both network and Internet access to data

   D. Replace existing ODBC database access

6. How do OLE DB components differ from existing database services?

   A. They exist as independent applications functioning as a layer between client applications and the data providers.

   B. They exist either as server-side or client-side components.

   C. They provide integrated extensions to existing database services.

   D. They replace existing database services with new object-oriented services.

7. What does using OLE DB's component architecture mean? (Select three.)

   A. Common functionality can be supplied across a variety of data sources.

   B. Components can be called from a variety of applications, programming languages, and tools.

    C. Components can be selected as needed to fulfill application requirements and changed or replaced as requirements evolve.

    D. Database vendors will not need to be responsible for developing ODBC drivers.

8. OLE Databases (OLE DB) are based on which of the following?

    A. ActiveX components

    B. Metadata catalogs

    C. Structured Query Language

    D. Universal Data Access interoperability

9. Implementing Universal Data Access through ADO and OLE DB provides which of the following?

    A. Convenient access to diverse data types and sources

    B. Optimized performance for diverse data types and data storage

    C. Reusable objects and third-party components

    D. Single-source support for all database requirements

CHAPTER

12

Threads, Processes, and Scheduling

- Describe how the Windows operating systems manage threads, processes, and scheduling.

Both Windows NT and Windows 95/98 provide multitasking environments. To perform multitasking, however, the operating system itself requires the ability to execute separate tasks as processes, allowing each process a time segment for execution, then suspending a process and allowing another process its turn to execute.

About Processes and Threads

A process consists of the resources required to execute a program. Each process possesses a virtual address space, executable code, application data, object handles, environment variables, a base priority, and minimum and maximum working set sizes. Initially, a process begins with a single thread—commonly called the primary thread—but may spawn (launch) additional threads during execution. (Any thread, primary or secondary, can create a new execution thread.) Each thread within a process becomes a separate task itself.

Thread scheduling is arranged by the Windows kernel.

Windows NT supports multiprocessor systems and can simultaneously execute a separate thread on each processor, while Windows 95/98 does not support multiprocessors.

Within a process, all threads share the same virtual address space and system resources. At the same time, each thread has its own exception handlers, which schedule priority, and each has a set of structures which the system will use to save the thread context while the thread is suspended.

The system consumes memory for both thread structures and process structures.

The thread context contains the kernel stack for the thread, a series of machine registers, the thread's environment block, and a user stack in the address space of the parent process for the thread.

Multitasking creates the effect of simultaneous execution of multiple threads from multiple processes.

A thread is a unit of executable code. A process is simply the data and code associated with an application: It contains one or more threads but always starts with a single thread.

Multitasking

Multitasking operating systems function by dividing the available processor time—the available workload—across a series of processes or threads. Windows is designed for preemptive multitasking and allocates a processor time slice to each executing thread. When the time slice expires, the executing thread is suspended, allowing another thread time to execute. As a thread is suspended, the operating system saves the context of the preempted thread and restores the previously saved context for the next thread to execute.

Under Windows, each process or thread receives a time slice approximately 20 milliseconds in length, cutting each second into roughly fifty slices. Because these are small time slices, the appearance is that multiple threads are each executing at the same time.

The exact length of a time slice depends on the operating system and the CPU speed.

On multiprocessor systems, where there actually are multiple threads executing simultaneously, the appearance becomes reality.

WARNING

When using multiple threads, having too many threads executing can decrease system performance.

Symmetric versus Asymmetric Multiprocessor Systems (Windows NT Only)

On a symmetric multiprocessor system (SMP), operating system threads can execute on any processor in the system. In contrast, an asymmetric multiprocessor system assigns a processor or set of processors to handle the system threads.

Scheduling

Multitasking is controlled by the system scheduler, which uses priorities to determine which of the various competing threads should receive the next execution time slice.

Scheduling Priorities

Both processes and threads are assigned scheduling priorities and, where a process contains multiple threads, each thread may receive a different priority. Priority levels range from 0 (lowest) to 31 (highest). However, only the zero-page thread—a system thread named Idle—can receive a zero priority.

Thread priorities are determined by:

- The process's priority class
- The thread's priority level within the process
- The thread's dynamic priority boost

The priority class (belonging to the process) and the priority level (assigned to the thread) combine to create the base priority for each thread.

 Threads do not themselves have priority classes, but depend on the priority class of the process together with any dynamic priority boost assigned by the operating system.

Priority Class

Processes belong to one of four priority classes (in order, low to high):

- IDLE_PRIORITY_CLASS
- NORMAL_PRIORITY_CLASS
- HIGH_PRIORITY_CLASS
- REALTIME_PRIORITY_CLASS

When a child process is created, the CreateProcess function is used to specify the processes priority class. The SetPriorityClass and GetPriorityClass functions are used, respectively, to change or query a process's priority class.

IDLE_PRIORITY_CLASS IDLE_PRIORITY_CLASS is commonly used for background processes which monitor the system, such as a screen saver or an application that periodically updates a display. Assigning a low priority prevents threads belonging to the process (which themselves will have low priorities) from interfering with higher priority threads.

NORMAL_PRIORITY_CLASS NORMAL_PRIORITY_CLASS is the default priority class assigned to any process.

HIGH_PRIORITY_CLASS HIGH_PRIORITY_CLASS should be assigned only in special circumstances. Threads belonging to processes with this priority receive a high priority for scheduling and this class should be used only for threads which must respond to time-critical events.

If a thread executes at the highest priority level for any extended period of time, other threads do not receive a chance to execute. If several threads are set for high priority at the same time, all of them lose their effectiveness.

The appropriate use for a high priority thread is to reserve this priority for a thread that requires critical attention but to only assign a high priority—using SetPriorityClass to temporarily raise the process's priority—during the critical task. Once the task is completed, the process's priority should be reduced again to normal.

A second strategy is to create a high-priority process but to block all of the process's threads, awakening them only during the period when critical tasks are required. The key is that high-priority threads should only execute for brief periods and only while there are time-critical tasks to be executed.

REALTIME_PRIORITY_CLASS   Processes operating under REALTIME_ PRIORITY_CLASS interrupt system threads which manage mouse and keyboard inputs and handle such tasks as background disk flushing. REALTIME_PRIORITY_CLASS is used only in extremely critical cir- cumstances where applications must "talk" directly to hardware or need to perform brief tasks that have limited interruptions.

Setting REALTIME_PRIORITY_CLASS for a thread can have serious conse- quences including interfering with network operations and other system level operations.

Priority Levels

Within a priority class, individual threads are assigned one of seven thread priority levels:

- THREAD_PRIORITY_IDLE
- THREAD_PRIORITY_LOWEST
- THREAD_PRIORITY_BELOW_NORMAL
- THREAD_PRIORITY_NORMAL
- THREAD_PRIORITY_ABOVE_NORMAL
- THREAD_PRIORITY_HIGHEST
- THREAD_PRIORITY_TIME_CRITICAL

By default, all threads are created with THREAD_PRIORITY_ NORMAL, giving the thread the same priority as the process. Once a thread has been created, SetThreadPriority can be used to adjust the thread's priority relative to other threads belonging to the process.

Normally, the five priority levels available to threads within their process are: lowest (-2), below normal (-1), normal (0), above normal (+1) and highest (+2). The idle and time_critical priorities are not commonly used.

A common approach to ensure that applications are responsive is to assign THREAD_PRIORITY_ABOVE_NORMAL or THREAD_PRIORITY_HIGHEST for the process's input thread. Threads which are processor intensive—particularly background threads—are commonly assigned THREAD_PRIORITY_BELOW_NORMAL or THREAD_PRIORITY_LOWEST. This ensures that the threads can be preempted when necessary.

When one thread is waiting for another thread with a lower priority to complete a task, the process can become deadlocked with the higher process thread monopolizing the time slices and the lower priority thread prevented from being scheduled. To prevent a conflict of this type, the execution of the higher-priority thread should be blocked using a wait function, a critical section, or by calling the Sleep, SleepEx, or SwitchToThread functions.

The GetThreadPriority function is used to query the current priority level assigned to a thread.

The initial process priority, dynamic priority boost, and base priority do not necessarily give a thread higher priority than the operating system and only a thread with a priority higher than the operating system thread can preempt the operating system.

Base Priority   The base priority level of a thread is determined by combining the process priority class and the thread's priority level. The base priority is also affected by whether the process is running in the foreground or in the background. Table 12.1 shows how the process priority class and the thread's priority level combine to create a base priority.

T A B L E 12.1:   Base Priorities

Process Priority Class	Thread Priority Level	Base Priority
IDLE_PRIORITY_CLASS NORMAL_PRIORITY_CLASS or HIGH_PRIORITY_CLASS	THREAD_PRIORITY_IDLE	1
IDLE_PRIORITY_CLASS	THREAD_PRIORITY_LOWEST	2
IDLE_PRIORITY_CLASS	THREAD_PRIORITY_BELOW_NORMAL	3

T A B L E 12.1: Base Priorities *(continued)*

Process Priority Class	Thread Priority Level	Base Priority
IDLE_PRIORITY_CLASS	THREAD_PRIORITY_NORMAL	4
NORMAL_PRIORITY_CLASS (**B**) IDLE_PRIORITY_CLASS	THREAD_PRIORITY_LOWEST THREAD_PRIORITY_ABOVE_NORMAL	5
NORMAL_PRIORITY_CLASS (**B**) IDLE_PRIORITY_CLASS	THREAD_PRIORITY_BELOW_NORMAL THREAD_PRIORITY_HIGHEST	6
NORMAL_PRIORITY_CLASS (**F**) NORMAL_PRIORITY_CLASS (**B**)	THREAD_PRIORITY_LOWEST THREAD_PRIORITY_NORMAL	7
NORMAL_PRIORITY_CLASS (**F**) NORMAL_PRIORITY_CLASS	THREAD_PRIORITY_BELOW_NORMAL THREAD_PRIORITY_ABOVE_NORMAL	8
NORMAL_PRIORITY_CLASS (**F**) NORMAL_PRIORITY_CLASS	THREAD_PRIORITY_NORMAL THREAD_PRIORITY_HIGHEST	9
NORMAL_PRIORITY_CLASS (**F**)	THREAD_PRIORITY_ABOVE_NORMAL	10
HIGH_PRIORITY_CLASS NORMAL_PRIORITY_CLASS (**F**)	THREAD_PRIORITY_LOWEST THREAD_PRIORITY_HIGHEST	11
HIGH_PRIORITY_CLASS	THREAD_PRIORITY_BELOW_NORMAL	12
HIGH_PRIORITY_CLASS	THREAD_PRIORITY_NORMAL	13
HIGH_PRIORITY_CLASS	THREAD_PRIORITY_ABOVE_NORMAL	14
IDLE_PRIORITY_CLASS NORMAL_PRIORITY_CLASS or HIGH_PRIORITY_CLASS HIGH_PRIORITY_CLASS	THREAD_PRIORITY_TIME_CRITICAL THREAD_PRIORITY_HIGHEST	15
REALTIME_PRIORITY_CLASS	THREAD_PRIORITY_IDLE	16
REALTIME_PRIORITY_CLASS	THREAD_PRIORITY_LOWEST	22
REALTIME_PRIORITY_CLASS	THREAD_PRIORITY_BELOW_NORMAL	23

T A B L E 12.1: Base Priorities *(continued)*

Process Priority Class	Thread Priority Level	Base Priority
REALTIME_PRIORITY_CLASS	THREAD_PRIORITY_NORMAL	24
REALTIME_PRIORITY_CLASS	THREAD_PRIORITY_ABOVE_NORMAL	25
REALTIME_PRIORITY_CLASS	THREAD_PRIORITY_HIGHEST	26
REALTIME_PRIORITY_CLASS	THREAD_PRIORITY_TIME_CRITICAL	31

Legend: (*F*)oreground Process / (*B*)ackground Process

Notice that the Base Priorities listed are not continuous—refer to the "Priority Boosts" section, below.

 Because the actual numerical values identified by the various xxxxx_ PRIORITY_CLASS constants may vary from one operating system version to another, the constant identifiers should always be used, not the number values.

Context Switches

The scheduler maintains a queue of executable threads, known as ready threads, for each priority level. When a time slice for a processor becomes available, the system performs a context switch in four steps:

1. It saves the context for the thread which has been suspended.

2. It places the suspended thread at the end of the queue for the thread's priority.

3. It selects the highest priority queue containing ready threads.

4. It selects the thread at the head of the queue, loads the thread's context, and executes the thread.

Remember: Only ready threads are executed, and threads with the highest priority are always executed first.

Threads which are not ready threads include the following:

- Threads created with the CREATE_SUSPENDED flag

- Threads halted during execution with the SuspendThread or Switch-ToThread function

- Threads waiting for a synchronization object or input

No processor time is allocated by the scheduler for threads which are suspended or blocked—regardless of their priority—until they become ready to run.

A context switch occurs when:

- A time slice has elapsed

- A thread with a higher priority is ready to execute

- An executing thread needs to wait for some other action

When, for whatever reason, an executing thread needs to wait, the remainder of the thread's current time slice is relinquished.

Priority Boosts

Threads possess both a base priority (static) and a dynamic priority, and the dynamic priority is used by the scheduler to determine which thread should be executed next. Initially, a thread's dynamic priority is the same as its base priority, but the system will raise or lower the dynamic priority to ensure that the system remains responsive and that no ready threads become starved for processor time.

The system does not, however, boost the priority for threads with a base priority level in the range from 16 to 31. Only threads with base priorities in the 0 to 15 range receive dynamic priority boosts.

Conditions for boosting the dynamic priority of a thread are governed by three factors:

- When a process with NORMAL_PRIORITY_CLASS is brought to the foreground, the scheduler boosts the priority class of the foreground process so that it is greater than or equal to the priority class of any background processes. When the process looses the focus, i.e., is no longer in the foreground, the priority class returns to its original setting.

Windows NT only: Users can control the boosting of processes using NORMAL_PRIORITY_CLASS through the System control panel application.

- When a window receives input—such as timer messages, mouse events, or keyboard input—the scheduler boosts the priority of the thread owning the window.

- When a blocked thread's wait conditions are satisfied, the scheduler boosts the thread's priority. For example, when a wait operation is dependent on disk access or keyboard I/O and the conditions are satisfied, the thread receives a priority boost.

Windows NT only: The priority-boosting feature can be disabled by calling SetProcessPriorityBoost or SetThreadPriorityBoost. Or, to determine if this feature has been disabled, call GetProcessPriorityBoost or GetThreadPriorityBoost.

Once the scheduler has raised a thread's dynamic priority, the thread's priority is reduced one level each time the thread completes a time slice until the thread has reached its base priority. A thread's dynamic priority will never fall below the thread's base priority.

Priority Inversion

Priority inversion occurs when two or more threads with different priorities are in contention for scheduling.

For example, consider a situation with three threads: T1, T2, and T3. T1 is a high priority thread and becomes ready for scheduling but is waiting for a shared resource from T2, which is a low priority thread and is executing code in a critical section. Last, T3 is a medium priority thread. In this situation, T3 receives all of the processor time because T1 (the high priority thread) is waiting for shared resources from T2 (the low priority thread). At the same time, T2 can't leave the critical section because it does not have a high enough priority to be scheduled.

How this conflict is resolved takes two different forms under Windows NT and under Windows 95/98:

Windows NT   Under Windows NT, the scheduler resolves the conflict by randomly boosting the priority of the ready threads, i.e., the low priority thread T2 which is blocking operations. This gives the low priority thread enough time to exit the critical section, thus allowing the high priority thread (T1) the opportunity to enter the critical section.

If the low priority thread does not receive sufficient CPU time to exit the critical section immediately, it will receive another opportunity during the next round of scheduling.

Windows 95/98   Under Windows 95/98, when a high priority thread is waiting on a low priority thread that is not allowed to run because a medium priority thread (T3) is monopolizing the CPU, the system recognizes the T1 thread's dependence on T2.

In response, the low priority thread's priority (T2) is boosted to match the high priority thread's priority (T1). When this is done, the previously low priority thread becomes able to execute and, having done so, releases the high priority thread waiting on it.

Finally, T2's priority is reduced to its original priority as described previously in the "Priority Boosts" section.

Multiple Processors (NT Only)

On systems with multiple processors (CPUs), Windows NT employs a symmetric multiprocessing (SMP) model to schedule threads across two or more processors. Using the SMP model, any thread may be assigned to any processor, making scheduling on a multiprocessor system similar to scheduling on a single processor system. The difference on a multiprocessor system is that the scheduler has a pool of processors allowing two or more threads to execute concurrently while scheduling continues to be determined by thread priority (as discussed previously).

What is unique on a multiprocessor system, however, is that scheduling can also be affected by setting *thread affinity* and *thread ideal processor*.

Thread Affinity

Thread affinity forces a thread to run on a specific subset of processors. The SetProcessAffinityMask function is used to specify thread affinity for all threads of the process; the SetThreadAffinityMask function is used to set the thread affinity for a single thread.

The thread affinity must be a subset of the process affinity. The process affinity can be retrieved by calling the GetProcessAffinityMask function.

Because setting thread affinities can interfere with the scheduler's ability to assign threads effectively across multiple processors and can decrease the performance gains offered by parallel processing, such specific assignments should be avoided.

Thread Ideal Processor

Specifying a thread ideal processor—using SetThreadIdealProcessor— suggests that the scheduler should run the thread on the specified processor when possible but does not force the assignment. This type of assignment does not guarantee that the specified processor will be used, but does weigh the odds accordingly.

Multiple Threads

Initially, each process begins with a single thread. Any thread, however, can create additional threads. Also, threads can be suspended, synchronized, used to create windows, and, of course, terminated.

Creating Threads

The CreateThread function is called to create a new thread for a process. In creating a new thread, the parent thread must specify a starting address of the code which the new thread will execute, typically a function defined in the program code. Typically, an entry function for a thread accepts a single parameter and returns a DWORD value. A process may, however, have multiple threads simultaneously executing a single function.

The example following demonstrates creating a new thread to execute ThreadProc, a locally defined function.

```
DWORD WINAPI ThreadProc( LPVOID lpParam )
{
   char szMsg[80];

   wsprintf( szMsg, "ThreadProc: Parameter = %d\n", lpParam );
   MessageBox( NULL, szMsg, "Thread created.", MB_OK );
   return 0;
}

VOID main()
{
   DWORD  dwThreadId, dwThrdParam = 1;
   HANDLE hThread;

   hThread = CreateThread(
            NULL,            // no security attributes
            0,               // use default stack size
            ThreadProc,      // name of thread function
            &dwThrdParam,    // argument to thread function
            0,               // use default creation flags
            &dwThreadId );   // returns thread identifier
      // Check the return value for success.
   if( hThread == NULL )
      ErrorExit( "CreateThread failed." );
   CloseHandle( hThread );
}
```

In this example, a pointer to a DWORD value is passed as an argument to the thread function. More commonly, this might be a pointer to any type of data or structure or could be omitted entirely by passing a NULL pointer and, of course, deleting the reference to the value in ThreadProc.

One risk to be aware of is passing the address of a local variable. If the creating thread exits before the new thread, the address in the pointer becomes invalid. Alternatives are:

- Pass a pointer to dynamically allocated memory.

- Make the creating thread wait to terminate until the new thread has terminated.

Of course, data can also be passed to a new thread using a global variable (or variables). However, using global variables with multiple threads may make it necessary to synchronize access (see the "Synchronizing Threads" section, below).

Executing Multiple Threads

While multiple threads are often used to execute a single process, using a single set of global variables to control multiple threads is not a convenient approach. For example, a process used to open a file might be used as multiple threads to open several files with each thread executing the same function.

To create each thread, passing unique information to each for the filename in our example, would make using a global variable impractical. A practical alternative, however, would be to use a dynamically allocated string buffer for each argument. In other circumstances, any type of dynamically allocated structure could be used to pass a complex set of arguments.

Arguments accepted by the CreateThread function can be used to specify:

- Security attributes for the handle of the new thread including an inheritance flag to determine whether the handle can be inherited by child processes and a security descriptor for the system to perform access checks on all subsequent uses of the thread's handle before granting access.

- The initial stack size for the new thread. The thread's stack is allocated automatically in the process's memory space; the system increases the stack as needed, freeing it when the thread terminates.

- A creation flag creating the thread in a suspended state. While suspended, the thread does not run until ResumeThread is called.

Windows NT only: The CreateRemoteThread function can also be used to create a thread. This function is used by debug processes to create threads which run in the address space of the process being debugged.

Thread Handles and Identifiers

When a thread is created using CreateThread or CreateRemoteThread, a handle for the thread is returned. By default, the returned handle has all access rights and, subject to security access restrictions, can be used by all functions that accept a thread handle.

Depending on the inheritance flag specified during creation, this handle can be inherited by child processes. Alternately, the handle can be duplicated—using `DuplicateHandle`—as a thread handle with a subset of access rights. Handles remain valid until explicitly closed even when the thread the handle represents has terminated.

The `CreateThread` and `CreateRemoteThread` functions also return identifiers which uniquely identify the thread throughout the system and any thread may request its own identifier by calling `GetCurrentThreadID`. These identifiers remain valid until the thread terminates.

The Win32 API makes no provisions to obtain a thread handle from a thread identifier since providing access of this type would allow processes to access threads which they do not own and perform unexpected actions such as changing priorities, or suspending or terminating threads. Instead, access is restricted by requiring a request for a thread handle to be made to the thread creator or to the thread itself.

Threads are, however, permitted to call `GetCurrentThread` to retrieve a pseudo-handle to their own thread object. The pseudo-handle is valid only to the calling process and can not be inherited or duplicated for use by other processes.

Suspending Thread Execution

Threads are allowed to suspend or resume execution for other threads using the `SuspendThread` and `ResumeThread` functions. As long as a thread is suspended, the thread will not be scheduled for time on the CPU.

`SuspendThread` is not particularly useful for synchronization because it doesn't control the point at which a thread's execution is suspended. It can be used, however, to suspend a thread while waiting for an instruction to cancel a thread. If the thread is to be canceled, have the thread exit; otherwise, call `ResumeThread`.

If a thread was created suspended—using the CREATE_SUSPENDED flag—execution does not begin until another thread calls `ResumeThread` with a handle for the suspended thread. This practice is often used to initialize a thread's state before starting execution, or, for a one-shot synchronization, ensuring that the suspended thread will execute at its starting point when `ResumeThread` is called.

The `Sleep` or `SleepEx` functions can be called to temporarily halt a thread's execution for a specified interval. This can be useful when a thread responds to user interactions by delaying execution to allow users to observe the results of their actions. During the sleep interval, the thread is not scheduled for processing time.

The SwitchToThread function allows a thread to relinquish its time slice by changing to another thread.

Synchronizing Threads

When threads are using shared resources, to prevent race conditions and deadlocks, synchronization between threads is required. Synchronization is also used to ensure that interdependent code is executed in the appropriate sequence.

A variety of objects are supplied by the Win32 API, whose handles can be used to synchronize multiple threads. These include console input buffers, events, mutexes, processes, semaphores, threads, and timers.

Each of these objects has a state which is either signaled or unsignaled. By specifying a handle to one of these objects in a call to a wait function, the calling thread's execution is blocked until the object's state becomes signaled.

Some objects can be used to block a thread until an event occurs. A console-input buffer handle, for example, is signaled when unread input such as keyboard characters are waiting in the buffer or when a mouse event message is queued.

Process and thread handles are signaled when a process or thread terminates. This can allow, for example, a process to create a child process and then block its own execution until the child process terminates.

Mutexes

Mutex objects are useful in protecting shared resources from simultaneous access. By giving multiple threads handles to a mutex object, each thread calls one of the wait functions to wait for the mutex to be signaled. When the mutex is signaled, only one of the waiting threads is released to access the shared resource while the state of the mutex is immediately reset to unsignaled so that the threads remain blocked. When the active thread finishes using the resource, that thread sets the state of the mutex to signaled, allowing another thread access to the resource.

Single Process Threads

For threads belonging to a single process, using critical-section objects is a more efficient method of synchronization than a mutex. Like a mutex, a critical section allows one thread at a time access to a protected resource.

A thread uses the EnterCriticalSection function to request ownership of a critical section. If the section is already owned—in use—by another thread, the requesting thread is blocked. Alternately, a thread might use the

TryEnterCriticalSection function to request ownership without being blocked on failure. In either case, once a thread receives ownership of the critical block, the thread is free to use the protected resource. Execution by other threads of the process is not affected unless they also attempt to enter the same critical section.

WaitForInputIdle

The WaitForInputIdle function makes a thread wait until a specified process has been initialized and is waiting for user input, but has no input pending. WaitForInputIdle is useful for synchronizing parent and child processes because the CreateProcess function returns without waiting for the child process to complete initialization.

Multiple Threads and GDI Objects

In the interests of performance, access to graphics device interface (GDIs) objects (i.e., palettes, device contexts, regions) is not serialized. While improving performance, this also creates risks for processes which have multiple threads sharing these objects. For example, if one thread deletes a GDI object that another thread is using, the results are unpredictable.

To prevent such occurrences, two options are possible: either avoid sharing GDI objects entirely or have the application provide its own mechanisms for synchronizing access.

Thread Local Storage

When a process uses two or more threads, all of the threads share the same virtual address space and have access to global variables belonging to the process. While local variables for a thread function do remain local to each thread, all static or global variables are shared by all threads.

Thread Local Storage (TLS) allows a thread to create a unique copy of a variable. Using TLS, one thread allocates an index, then each thread—or any thread—in the process uses the index to retrieve its own unique copy of a previously global variable.

To implement TLS:

- During process or DLL initialization, use TlsAlloc to allocate a TLS index.

- Subsequently, each thread requiring the TLS index should allocate dynamic storage for the variable, then use TlsSetValue to associate the index with a pointer to the dynamic storage.

In operation:

- When a thread needs to access its own storage, the TLS index is passed in a call to TlsGetValue to retrieve the pointer.

- When a thread no longer requires the dynamic storage, it should free the index.

- When all threads are finished with the TLS index, TlsFree is called to release the index.

The minimum number of TLS indexes available for each process is specified by the constant TLS_MINIMUM_AVAILABLE and is guaranteed to be at least 64 indexes for all systems.

Creating Windows in Threads

Any thread is able to create a window and owns the window and its associated message queue. This also means that the thread must provide a message loop to process messages in the window's message queue. Further, the Msg-WaitForMultipleObjects or MsgWaitForMultipleObjectsEx functions, rather than other wait functions, must be used in the thread so that the thread does not cause a deadlock while waiting for messages.

The AttachThreadInput function allows threads to share their concept of the active window and to share the same input state. In this fashion, one thread can always activate another thread's window. Further threads can also share the focus state, keyboard state, and window Z-order state, among windows created by different threads.

Terminating a Thread

Once launched, a thread executes until one of the following events occurs:

- The thread calls ExitThread.

- Any thread in the process calls ExitProcess.

- The thread function returns.

- Any thread calls TerminateThread with a handle to the thread.

- Any thread calls TerminateProcess with a handle to the process.

The termination status of a thread is returned at any time by `GetExitCode-Thread`. While a thread is executing, the reported termination status will be STILL_ACTIVE but, on termination, changes are made to the exit code of the thread. The thread's reported exit code may be the value specified in a call to `ExitThread`, `ExitProcess`, `TerminateThread`, or `TerminateProcess`, or the exit code may be the value returned by the thread function.

Once a thread terminates, the thread object's state becomes signaled, releasing any other threads which may have been waiting on the terminating thread.

When a thread is terminated by `ExitThread`, the system calls the entry-point function for each attached DLL with a message value indicating that the thread is detaching from the library. This notification can be blocked by calling `DisableThreadLibraryCalls`.

When a thread is terminated by `ExitProcess`, the DLL entry-point function is invoked only once, indicating that the process is detaching.

When threads are terminated using `TerminateThread` or `Terminate-Process`, no notifications are sent to attached DLLs.

The `TerminateThread` and `TerminateProcess` functions do not allow threads to perform an orderly shutdown and clean up, do not notify attached DLLs, and do not free the initial stack. For this reason, these two functions should be used only in urgent circumstances.

The optimum sequence for handling threads is:

- Create an event object using the `CreateEvent` function.

- Create the threads.

- Have each thread monitor the event state by calling `WaitForSingle-Object` using a wait time-out interval of zero.

- Allow each thread to terminate its own execution when the event is set to the signaled state, i.e., when `WaitForSingleObject` returns WAIT_OBJECT_0.

Thread Times (NT Only)

The `GetThreadTimes` function reports timing information for a thread by returning the thread creation time—how long the thread has been executing in kernel mode and in user mode. These times do not include time spent executing threads or time spent waiting in a suspended or blocked state. If the thread has exited, the thread exit time is returned.

Child Processes

A child process is a process created by another (parent) process.

Creating Processes

The CreateProcess function launches a new process which executes independently of the parent process. Despite the independence, for simplicity, this relationship is referred to as a parent-child relationship.

The code fragment following shows how to create a child process.

```
void main()
{
    STARTUPINFO si;
    PROCESS_INFORMATION pi;
    BOOL                bResult;

    ZeroMemory( &si, sizeof(si) );
    si.cb = sizeof(si);
        // Start the child process.
    bResult = CreateProcess(
        NULL,             // no module name - uses command line
        "Child Process",  // command line for module name
        NULL,             // process handle not inheritable
        NULL,             // thread handle not inheritable
        FALSE,            // set handle inheritance to FALSE
        0,                // no creation flags
        NULL,             // use parent's environment block
        NULL,             // use parent's starting directory
        &si,              // pointer to STARTUPINFO structure
        &pi ) );          // pointer to PROCESS_INFORMATION
                          //    struct
    if( ! bResult )// CreateProcess returned FALSE
        ErrorExit( "CreateProcess failed." );
        // Wait until child process exits.
    WaitForSingleObject( pi.hProcess, INFINITE );
        // Close process and thread handles.
    CloseHandle( pi.hProcess );
    CloseHandle( pi.hThread );
}
```

If `CreateProcess` succeeds, the PROCESS_INFORMATION structure returns containing handles and identifiers for the new process and the primary thread. By default, the thread and process handles are created with full access rights but can be restricted if security descriptors are specified.

When the provided handles are no longer required, the `CloseHandle` function can be called to close the handles.

Processes can also be created using `CreateProcessAsUser` which allows specifying the security context of the user account where the process will execute.

Setting Window Properties with STARTUPINFO

The `CreateProcess` function accepts a pointer to a STARTUPINFO structure which allows the parent process to specify properties associated with the main window of the child process.

The `dwFlags` member contains a bit field that determines which other members of the STARTUPINFO structure are used, and allows specifications to be set for any subset of the window properties. For any properties not specified, the system uses default values. The `dwFlags` member can also force a feedback cursor to be displayed during the process initialization.

For GUI processes, the STARTUPINFO structure specifies the default values which will be used the first time the new process calls `CreateWindow` or `ShowWindow` to create and display an overlapped window. Specified values can include:

- The height and width in pixels for the window created by `CreateWindow`

- The screen location for the window created by `CreateWindow`

- The `nCmdShow` parameter for `ShowWindow`

For console processes, use the STARTUPINFO structure to specify window properties only when creating a new console, using either `CreateProcess` with CREATE_NEW_CONSOLE or with `AllocConsole`. Specified values can include:

- The console window size in character cells

- The console window location in screen coordinates

- The console window's screen buffer size (in character cells)

- The console window's text and background color attributes

- The console window's title

Process Handles and Identifiers

When CreateProcess is used to create a new process, handles are returned for the new process and the process's primary thread. The returned handles have full access rights and, subject to security access restrictions, can be used by any functions which accept thread or process handles.

The returned handles can be inherited by child processes—depending on the inheritance flag specified when the process was created—and remain valid until closed, even after the process or thread represented by the handle has been terminated.

CreateProcess also returns an identifier that uniquely identifies the process throughout the system; any process may use GetCurrentProcessID to retrieve its own process identifier. The process identifier remains valid until the process is terminated.

Given a process identifier, a process handle can be retrieved by calling OpenProcess while specifying the handle's access and inheritance rights.

Alternately, a process can call GetCurrentProcess to retrieve a pseudo-handle to the process's own process object. The pseudo-handle is valid only within the calling process, cannot be inherited, and cannot be duplicated for use by other processes.

The DuplicateHandle function can be used to retrieve a real handle to a process.

Obtaining Additional Process Information

The Win32 API offers functions to obtain information about processes. Some functions accept a process handle as a parameter and can be used to query information about any process. Others do not accept process handles and only provide information about the calling process.

Supported services include:

- Determining if a process is being debugged by using IsDebugger-Present

- Retrieving the command-line string for the current process by using GetCommandLine

- Parsing a Unicode command-line string (from the Unicode version of GetCommandLine) by using CommandLineToArgvW

- Retrieving a handle count for graphical user interface (GUI) objects in use by using `GetGuiResources`

- Retrieving the full path and filename for the executable containing the process code by using `GetModuleFileName`

- Retrieving the STARTUPINFO structure specified when the current process was created by using `GetStartupInfo`

- Retrieving version information from the executable header by using `GetProcessVersion`

Inheritance

A child process can inherit a number of properties and resources from the parent process, but can also be prevented from inheriting.

Properties which can be inherited include:

- Open handles returned by the `CreateFile` function, including handles to files, console input buffers, console screen buffers, mailslots, named pipes, and serial communication devices

- Open handles to process, thread, mutex, event, semaphore, anonymous pipe, named pipe, and file mapping objects

- Environment variables

- The current directory

- The console, except when the process is detached or when a new console is created for the process. A child console process also inherits the parent process's standard handles plus access to the input and active screen buffers.

Properties which can not be inherited include:

- Priority class

- Handles returned by `LocalAlloc`, `GlobalAlloc`, `HeapCreate`, and `HeapAlloc`

- Pseudo-handles such as the handles returned by `GetCurrentProcess` or `GetCurrentThread` which are valid only for the calling process

- Handles to DLL modules returned by the `LoadLibrary` function

- GDI or USER handles such as HBITMAP or HMENU

Inheriting Handles

Before a handle can be inherited, two conditions are required:

- The handle must be specified as inheritable when it is created, opened, or duplicated.

- The call to CreateProcess must specify that handles will be inheritable.

Specifying on creation that a child process can inherit handles from the parent process permits the child to inherit some handles but not others.

For example, the CreateProcess and CreateFile functions are called with security attributes arguments which determine whether a handle can be inherited. Similarly, the OpenMutex, OpenEvent, and DuplicateHandle functions are called with a handle inheritance flag which specifies whether the returned handle is inheritable.

When creating a child process, the fInheritHandles parameter passed to CreateProcess determines whether the parent process's inheritable handles will be inherited by the child process. An inherited handle refers to the same object in the child process as in the parent and has the same value and access privileges.

In this fashion, when one process changes the state of an object which has been inherited, the change affects all processes with handles to the object.

In order to use a handle, the child process must retrieve the handle value and must know the object to which the handle refers. Normally, the parent process passes this information to the child process through the command line, environment block, or through some type of interprocess communication.

The DuplicateHandle function is useful when a process has an inheritable open handle which should not be inherited by a child process. Before creating a child process, the DuplicateHandle function is called to open a duplicate handle—but specifying the duplicate as not-inheritable—and then calling CloseHandle to close the inheritable handle. DuplicateHandle can also be used to open an inheritable duplicate of a handle which is not inheritable.

Inheriting Environment Variables   By default, a child process inherits the parent's environment variables. However, the parent process can create a new environment block specifying a different set of environment variables and pass a pointer to the environment block as a parameter in the CreateProcess call.

Inheriting the Current Directory   By default, a child process inherits the current directory from the parent process, but the CreateProcess function permits the parent process to specify a different current directory for the child process.

GetCurrentDirectory retrieves the current directory of the calling process while SetCurrentDirectory can be used to change the current directory of the calling process.

Environment Variables

Each process has an environment block that holds a set of environment variables and values. The command processor provides the set command to display the environment block and to create new environment variables. When a program is launched by the command processor, the program (process) inherits the command processor's environment variables.

The GetEnvironmentStrings function returns a pointer to the calling process's environment block while the GetEnvironmentVariable function determines whether a specified variable is defined in the calling process's environment and, if so, what the value is.

The environment block, however, should be treated as read only and should not be modified directly. Instead, the SetEnvironmentVariable function should be used to change environment variables.

When the pointer to the environment block is no longer needed, the FreeEnvironmentStrings function should be called to free the block.

Terminating a Process

Once launched or created, a process executes until:

- Any thread in the process calls ExitProcess to terminate all threads in the process.

- The process's primary thread returns.

The primary thread, however, can avoid terminating other threads by explicitly calling ExitThread before returning. It is then the responsibility of one of the remaining threads to call ExitProcess to ensure that all threads are terminated.

- The last thread of the process terminates.

- Any thread calls TerminateProcess with a handle to the process.

This immediately terminates all threads belonging to the process without permitting clean-up or allowing data to be saved.

- The user shuts down the system and logs off.

The SetProcessShutdownParameters function is used to specify shutdown parameters including when a process should terminate relative to other system processes. GetProcessShutdownParameters retrieves the current shutdown priority and other shutdown flags for the process.

- A console process receives a Ctrl+C or Ctrl+BREAK signal causing the default handler to call ExitProcess. All console processes attached to the console receive these signals.

Detached processes and GUI processes are not affected by Ctrl+C and Ctrl+BREAK signals.

When a process terminates, all threads belonging to the process are immediately terminated and do not have any opportunity to execute additional code. In particular, this means that code in termination handler blocks will not be executed.

Termination Status   GetExitCodeProcess returns the termination status for a process. While a process is executing, the termination status is STILL_ ACTIVE. On termination, the termination status becomes the exit code of the process that is either the value supplied in the call to ExitProcess or TerminateProcess, or may be the value returned by the process's main or WinMain functions.

If a process is terminated due to a fatal exception, the exit code is the value of the exception causing the termination. Further, this value is used as the exit code for all threads which were active when the exception occurred. When a process terminates, the process object's state becomes signaled, releasing any threads which have been waiting on the process (see the "Synchronizing Threads" section, above.)

Also when a process terminates, all open handles to files or other resources are automatically closed. The objects themselves, however, continue to exist until all open handles to the object are closed. That is, if another process has a handle to an object, the object remains valid.

When a process is terminated by an ExitProcess call, the system calls the entry-point function for each attached DLL with an event notifying the DLL that the process is being detached. However, when a process is terminated by TerminateProcess, DLLs are not notified.

TerminateProcess should be called only in extreme circumstances because this function does not permit threads to perform clean-up, to save data, or to notify attached DLLs.

Optimally, for one process to terminate another process, the following steps should be used:

- Both processes should call RegisterWindowMessage to create a private message.

- One process can terminate the other process by broadcasting a private message, using BroadcastSystemMessage:

```
BroadcastSystemMessage(
    BSF_IGNORECURRENTTASK,  // do not send message to process
    BSM_APPLICATIONS,       // broadcast only to applications
    private message,        // message registered in previous
                               step
    wParam,                 // message-specific value
    lParam );               // message-specific value
```

- The process receiving the termination message should call Exit-Process to terminate execution.

When the system terminates a process, any child processes created by the process are not terminated.

Process Times (NT Only)

The GetProcessTimes function is used to report timing information for a process and returns the process creation time, the time spent by the process in kernel mode, and the time spend by the process in user mode. The time the process has spent executing system threads or waiting in a suspended or blocked state is not reported.

If the process has terminated, GetProcessTimes reports the process exit time.

Process Working Set

A program's working set is a collection of pages in the program's virtual address space which has been referenced recently. This includes both private and shared data.

The shared data includes pages containing all instructions that the application executes, including those in the application's DLLs and in the system DLLs; memory demands increase as the working set size increases.

When a DLL is loaded, the library code is not loaded directly to the process's address space but is mapped to the process's address space. In this fashion, a DLL can be loaded once and then shared by two or more processes.

Each process has an associated minimum and maximum working set size. When `CreateProcess` is called, the minimum working set size for the process is reserved. The virtual memory manager attempts to keep enough active memory to keep the minimum working set resident but does not keep more than the maximum working set size.

While the system sets the default working set sizes, the `GetProcessWorkingSetSize` will return the requested minimum and maximum sizes for the working set for the application. These sizes can be modified by calling the `SetProcessWorkingSetSize` function.

Setting minimum and maximum values is no guarantee that the memory will be reserved or resident. Also, requesting too large a minimum or maximum working set size can degrade system performance.

Fibers

Fibers, as the name may suggest, can be thought of as subsets or components of threads. The analogy, however, is not a strong one, and a better definition would be to say that a fiber is a unit of execution which is manually scheduled by an application.

Fibers run in the context of the threads that schedule them and each thread can schedule multiple fibers. Only one fiber per thread, however, will be executed at any time. As a general rule, fibers do not provide any advantages over well-designed multithreaded applications. What fibers do provide, however, is convenience in porting applications which were previously designed to schedule their own threads.

From the standpoint of the system, a fiber assumes the identity of the thread creating it. This means that for a fiber to access thread local storage (TLS), it accesses the thread local storage of the thread creating the fiber. Likewise, when a fiber calls ExitThread, the thread creating the fiber exits.

Differences between Fibers and Threads

A fiber does not possess the same state information as a thread. The fiber's only state information is its stack, a register subset, and the data provided to the fiber during its creation. The register subset consists of the registers typically preserved across a function call. Also, fibers are not preemptively scheduled. A fiber is scheduled by switching to it from another fiber.

While the system still schedules threads for execution, a fiber executes only when its thread runs and, when a thread running fibers is preempted, the currently running fiber is also preempted.

Scheduling Fibers

Before a thread can execute fibers, a call to ConvertThreadToFiber is required to create an area to save the fiber state information. Once this is done, the calling thread becomes the currently executing fiber while the stored state information for this fiber includes the fiber data passed as an argument to the ConvertThreadToFiber call.

To create a new fiber from an existing fiber, the CreateFiber function is called with the stack size, the starting address, and the fiber data. Typically, the starting address is a user-supplied function—the fiber function—which accepts one parameter, the fiber data, and which does not return a value. If the fiber function returns, the thread executing the fiber exits.

To execute a fiber created with CreateFiber, the SwitchToFiber function is called with the address of a fiber created by a different thread. This call requires the address returned when the thread called the CreateFiber function and appropriate synchronization must be used.

A fiber can retrieve the fiber data by calling GetFiberData and can retrieve the fiber address by calling GetCurrentFiber.

The DeleteFiber function is used to clean up the data associated with a fiber. When DeleteFiber is called from the currently running fiber, its thread calls ExitThread, terminating the thread. When DeleteFiber is called for a fiber created by another thread, however, the thread creating the fiber can be terminated abnormally.

Summary

Both the Windows NT and Windows 95/98 systems manage multi-tasking by managing processes and scheduling threads for execution.

A process consists of the resources necessary to execute a program containing a virtual address space, executable code, application data, object handles, environment variables, a base priority, and minimum and maximum working set sizes. Each process begins with a single thread but may spawn additional threads to perform multiple tasks.

Scheduling is a process of using priorities to determine which processes or threads should be executing. Priorities for threads are determined by the process's priority class and the thread's priority class.

A context switch is used to change between executing threads while priority boosts change the dynamic priorities of thread (but not the base priorities) to ensure that the system remains responsive, and to prevent ready threads from being starved for processor time.

Each process begins with a single thread but may spawn additional threads. Also, each process may create (launch) additional (child) processes. The rules governing both threads and processes are similar, and warrant comparison, but are not identical.

Review Questions

1. Each process possesses which of the following? (Select three.)

   A. A base priority and minimum and maximum working set sizes

   B. A virtual address space, executable code, and application data

   C. Multiple threads and thread priorities

   D. Object handles and environment variables

2. Which of the following is true?

   A. Creating multiple processes is more efficient than distributing tasks among multiple threads under a single process.

   B. Only threads execute code, while a process is the address space for the code.

   C. Processes require synchronization; threads run unsynchronized.

   D. The system reserves memory for structures required by processes but does not reserve memory for structures required by threads.

3. Which of the following is true? (Select all that apply.)

   A. A process may begin with a single thread.

   B. A process may begin with multiple threads.

   C. Any thread may create a new execution thread.

   D. Only the primary thread may create new execution threads.

4. Under Windows NT, CPU time is allocated to which of the following?

   A. A process

   B. A program

   C. A thread

   D. An application

5. Threads in a 32-bit Windows environment:

   A. Are allotted time slices in which to run

   B. Are irrelevant since the Win32 API is not designed for preemptive multitasking

   C. Cannot access the global variables or system resources belonging to the process

   D. Each have their own virtual address space which is not shared by other threads

6. Symmetric multiprocessor operating systems are characterized by which of the following?

   A. They allow the operating system to run free on any processor or on all processors simultaneously.

   B. They do not allow the operating system to be preempted by a higher priority thread requiring attention.

   C. They do not allow a single process to execute a different thread on different processors.

   D. They select one processor to run the operating system while other processors are dedicated to user jobs.

7. Which of the following is true?

   A. Windows 95/98 does not support multiple processors.

   B. Windows 95/98 supports multiple processors and can simultaneously execute a separate thread on each processor.

   C. Windows NT does not support multiple processors.

   D. Windows NT supports multiple processors and can simultaneously execute a separate thread on each processor.

8. Within a process, a thread may have how many priority levels?

   A. Two

   B. Three

   C. Five

   D. Six

9. When a thread is suspended:

   A. The context of the preempted thread is saved.

   B. The thread is saved to virtual memory.

   C. The thread is terminated.

   D. The thread must be recreated.

10. Which of the following statements is true of operating system architecture models?

    A. A multiprocessor system can execute multiple threads simultaneously but only when two separate threads are placed in the processing queue.

    B. All applications are multitasked on a multiprocessor operating system.

    C. All multitasking systems require a minimum of two processors.

    D. The multitasking model requires a 32-bit Windows operating system.

11. Scheduling priorities are:

    A. Assigned only to processes

    B. Assigned only to threads

    C. Assigned to both processes and threads

    D. Reserved for the operating system

12. Select the priority class assigned to background processes:

    A. HIGH_PRIORITY_CLASS

    B. IDLE_PRIORITY_CLASS

    C. NORMAL_PRIORITY_CLASS

    D. REALTIME_PRIORITY_CLASS

13. A thread's priority is determined by which of the following? (Select all that apply.)

    A. The priority class of the thread's process

    B. The thread's dynamic priority boost

    C. The thread's priority class

    D. The thread's task ID

14. Select the priority class used for threads which must respond to time-critical events:

A. HIGH_PRIORITY_CLASS

B. IDLE_PRIORITY_CLASS

C. NORMAL_PRIORITY_CLASS

D. REALTIME_PRIORITY_CLASS

15. Thread execution is managed and scheduled by:

A. The kernel

B. The memory manager

C. The process manager

D. USER32.EXE

16. The differences in handling for threads and processes for a symmetric multiprocessing system (SMP) and an asymmetric multiprocessing system (ASMP) are:

A. Threads can execute on any available processor on an ASMP operating system, while an SMP operating system has the system threads bound to a specific processor or set of processors.

B. Threads can execute on any available processor on an SMP operating system, while an ASMP operating system has the system threads bound to a specific processor or set of processors.

C. Threads can execute on multiple processors simultaneously on an SMP operating system, while an ASMP operating system allows threads to only execute on one processor at a time.

D. Threads can execute on multiple processors simultaneously on an ASMP operating system, while an SMP operating system allows threads to only execute on one processor at a time.

17. Thread priorities are determined by which of the following?

A. The process's priority

B. The process's priority class and the thread's priority within the process

C. The thread's base priority added to the process's priority

D. The thread's virtual priority

18. Under Windows NT, operating system code can be preempted when:

A. A thread with a dynamic priority boost requires attention.

B. A thread with a higher process priority class requires attention.

C. A thread with base priority requires attention.

D. A thread with maximum application performance priority requires attention.

19. Select the statement(s) which is true for a process.

A. A process can start with multiple threads.

B. A process consists of the code, data, and other system resources used by the process threads.

C. A process is a program which is loaded into memory.

D. More than one process can share the same virtual address space.

20. Which priority are processor-intensive threads commonly assigned?

A. THREAD_PRIORITY_HIGHEST

B. THREAD_PRIORITY_IDLE

C. THREAD_PRIORITY_LOWEST

D. THREAD_PRIORITY_TIME_CRITICAL

21. Two Windows NT applications are executing, both using the same dynamic link library. The DLL is loaded:

A. Once and is mapped to the memory space of both processes

B. Once and receives its own local heap

C. Once with global and static memory shared by the two processes

D. Twice with each process maintaining its own global and static variables

22. The base priority of a thread is determined by:

    A. The process priority class

    B. The thread's priority level

    C. Whether the process is running in the foreground or background

    D. All of the above

23. The scheduler:

    A. Maintains a queue of all threads by process priority

    B. Maintains a queue of all threads by virtual priority

    C. Maintains a queue of ready threads by base level

    D. Maintains a queue of ready threads by priority level

24. Threads which are not ready include which of the following? (Select three.)

    A. Threads created with the CREATE_SUSPENDED flag

    B. Threads halted during execution by `SuspendThread` or `SwitchToThread`

    C. Threads waiting for a synchronization object or input

    D. Threads which are currently executing

25. Priority boosts are used to do which of the following? (Select two.)

    A. They adjust priorities for threads in the 16–31 priority levels.

    B. They ensure that no ready threads become starved for processor time.

    C. They ensure that the system remains responsive.

    D. They raise threads from 0–15 priority levels to 16–31 priority levels.

26. Thread affinity is used to do which of the following?

A. Force a thread to execute on a specific processor

B. Force specific threads to execute simultaneously

C. Force threads to be shared across multiple processors

D. Force threads to cluster on certain processors

27. When creating new threads:

A. A function named `ThreadProc` must be supplied as an entry point.

B. The `CreateProcess` function is called to create a process for the thread.

C. The parent thread must specify a starting address for the code that the new thread will execute.

D. The process must request permission from the system.

28. The `CreateThread` function accepts arguments which can specify which of the following? (Select three.)

A. A creation flag placing the thread in a suspended state

B. Initial stack size for the new thread

C. Priority levels for the parent process

D. Security attributes for the handle to the new thread

29. Threads can be synchronized using which of the following? (Select three.)

A. Console input buffers

B. Events, mutexes, processes, and semaphores

C. Message queues

D. Other threads and timers

30. Critical-section objects are an efficient method of doing which of the following?

   A. Interrupting a thread's execution

   B. Synchronizing threads across processes

   C. Synchronizing threads belonging to a single process

   D. Synchronizing threads globally

31. Thread Local Storage (TLS) allows threads to do which of the following?

   A. Allocate common memory

   B. Create unique copies of global variables

   C. Exchange private messages

   D. Share common objects

32. Once a thread is launched, the thread executes until which point? (Select three.)

   A. Another process calls `TerminateThread` with a handle to the thread

   B. Any thread calls `TerminateThread` with a handle to the thread or `TerminateProcess` with a handle to the process

   C. The thread calls `ExitThread` or any thread in the process calls `ExitProcess`

   D. The thread function returns

33. The `TerminateThread` and `TerminateProcess` functions:

   A. Free the initial stack

   B. Notify all attached DLLS

   C. Provide for an orderly shutdown and clean-up

   D. None of the above

34. When `CreateProcess` is used to create a new process, which of the following occurs? (Select two.)

   A. An identifier is returned which uniquely identifies the process.

   B. Handles are returned for the new process and the process's primary thread.

   C. The process's thread immediately becomes active.

   D. The returned handles can be inherited by child processes.

35. A child process can inherit which of the following? (Select two.)

   A. Environment variables

   B. Handles to DLL modules opened using the `LoadLibrary` function

   C. Open handles to process, thread, mutex, event, semaphore, anonymous pipe, named pipe, and file mapping objects

   D. Priority class

36. A child process cannot inherit which of the following? (Select two.)

   A. Handles returned by `LocalAlloc`, `GlobalAlloc`, `HeapCreate`, and `HeapAlloc`

   B. Open handles returned by the `CreateFile` function, including handles to files, console input buffers, console screen buffers, mailslots, named pipes, and serial communication devices

   C. Pseudo-handles returned by `GetCurrentProcess` or `GetCurrentThread`

   D. The current directory

37. Comparing fibers and threads, select the true statement(s):

   A. A fiber does not possess the same state information as a thread.

   B. Fibers are executed independently of their threads.

   C. Like threads, fibers are preemptively scheduled.

   D. When a fiber calls `ExitThread`, only the fiber terminates.

CHAPTER

13

Inter-Process Communications

Microsoft Exam Objectives Covered in This Chapter:

- Given a scenario, identify the appropriate type of Inter-Process Communication to use. Types of Inter-Process Communication include:
  - DDE (Dynamic Data Exchange)
  - NetDDE (Network Dynamic Data Exchange)
  - Windows Sockets
  - Named pipes
  - Memory-mapped files
  - NetBIOS
  - RPC (Remote Procedure Calls)

Inter-Process Communications (IPC) are simply methods of exchanging information between two processes, irrespective of whether they are parent and child processes (or sibling processes) belonging to a single application, or processes belonging to separate and independent applications.

Inter-Process Communications may be either local or remote, but the primary emphasis—today and for the future—is on distributed processing involving remote communications.

In distributed computing, while not an absolute distinction, the task of inter-process computing divides applications into two categories: client and server. Originally, the intention behind IPC was to move the actual applications processing from the client side (the client workstation) to the server side (a server system) with the power to execute large applications.

The client side of a client/server application provides the user interface, runs on the client's workstation, and requires relatively light computing power. Typically, however, the client/server relationship also requires considerable bandwidth to communicate.

The server side of a client/server application, in contrast, commonly requires massive data storage, sophisticated computing power, and/or specialized hardware. This includes operations such as database lookups and updates or mainframe data access.

While contemporary systems find the distinctions in computing power blurred between the client and server sides of an operation—the desktop client system may easily have more raw power than an antiquated mainframe server or the 'mainframe' server may be simply a desktop-equivalent with multiple processors and a large array of disk storage systems—the concept behind thin-client computing remains.

More commonly, the real emphasis behind client/server systems is simply to provide distributed access to common data sources, to allow shared data, document and task processing, and to facilitate communications between distributed workstations.

In either scenario, there must be a network connection between the client and server sides of distributed applications to allow data to flow in both directions. To establish this type of data exchange, Windows supports a variety of Inter-Process Communication (IPC) mechanisms.

The earliest version of Inter-Process Communications was found in the clipboard services. However, even though the clipboard is still supported and has been enhanced from its original capabilities, the clipboard is not generally employed—except for cut and paste operations invoked by the user—for inter-process data transfers, having been supplanted by more sophisticated mechanisms.

DDE (Dynamic Data Exchange)

Dynamic Data Exchange is a form of Inter-Process Communications supported by the Win32 API. The DDE protocol consists of a set of messages and guidelines used to communicate between applications which share data and use shared memory to exchange data. DDE can be used for one-time data transfers and for ongoing exchanges, in which applications send updates as new data becomes available.

Quite commonly, DDE applications may support both client and server capabilities within a single application, though this is not required.

The Win32 API includes the Dynamic Data Exchange Management Library (DDEML) in the form of a dynamic link library (DLL) which applications running under Windows can use to share data. The DDEML provides an application programming interface (API) that simplifies the task of incorporating DDE functionality in Win32-based applications.

Rather than posting DDE transactions directly, an application using DDEML calls the provided API functions to manage the DDE conversations.

A DDE conversation is the interaction between a DDE client and a DDE server application.

DDEML also provides facilities for managing the strings and data shared between DDE applications. In lieu of using atoms and pointers to shared memory objects, DDE applications create and exchange string handles for string data, and data handles, which identify memory data objects.

Using DDEML, a DDE server can register the service names supported. The registered names are broadcast to other applications on the system and these applications can then use the service names to connect to the server. Further, DDEML provides compatibility between DDE applications by forcing them to implement DDE protocols in a consistent fashion.

Existing applications using the message-based DDE protocol are fully compatible with applications using DDEML. That is, an application using message-based DDE can establish a conversation and carry out transactions with DDEML-based applications without any special provisions or changes in protocol.

However, because the DDEML library greatly simplifies developing and implementing both DDE clients and servers, it is recommended that new applications use DDEML rather than programming for DDE messaging directly. Using the DDEML API requires including the DDEML header in the application source files, linking with the DDEML library and, of course, ensuring that the DDEML dynamic link library is in the system's search path.

DDEML.DLL will normally be found in the \Windows\System directory.

NetDDE (Network Dynamic Data Exchange)

NetDDE is a networked version of the Dynamic Data Exchange protocol which serves as a virtual hot-link by providing automatic updates to shared memory areas across a network. NetDDE provides information-exchange capabilities by opening two one-way pipes between the local and remote applications.

A NetDDE link can exchange information at any time.

The NetDDE services are not opened automatically but can be established using Control Panel services, from the command prompt or through the Server Manager utility from the Windows NT Server.

The Windows Portability Library does not support the Win32 NetDDE APIs on the Macintosh.

Windows Sockets

The Windows Sockets specification defines a network programming interface based on the *socket* paradigm popularized by Berkeley Software Distribution (BSD/UC at Berkeley).

The Windows Sockets API provides a standard API supporting application developers with services to interface to many transports with different addressing schemes such as TCP/IP and IPX/SPX, as well as XNS and DECnet. Under each version of Windows, Windows Sockets defines an application binary interface allowing an application to function with a conformant protocol implementation from any network software vendor.

Like ODBC and MAPI, the Windows Sockets API provides a standard interface for complex software, improving developer productivity and increasing the probability that network applications will be created successfully.

The basic unit for communications is the socket. A socket is a communication endpoint and a name may be bound to a socket. During use, each individual socket has a type and an associated process, and exists within a communication domain.

A communication domain is an abstraction used to bundle common properties of threads communicating through sockets.

Sockets normally exchange data only with other sockets in the same domain. While it is possible to cross domain boundaries, this requires a translation.

The Windows Sockets facilities support a single communication domain: the Internet domain, which is used by processes to communicate though the Internet Protocol Suite. Individual sockets are typed according to the communications properties which are visible to the user.

The assumption is that applications communicate only between sockets of the same type. This does not, however, prevent communications between sockets of different types as long as the underlying communication protocols support the connection.

At present, two types of sockets are available to users: stream sockets and datagram sockets. Both client-side and server-side systems use a socket call to define their endpoints and both provide bidirectional data flow, but differ in the protocol methods and reliability of the communications.

Because the sockets protocol is a standard used by FTP and HTTP applications, the Windows Sockets API should be used when writing Windows FTP and HTTP applications for the Internet. A stream socket provides a reliable, sequenced, and unduplicated flow without record boundaries.

In contrast, a datagram socket is more like a packet transmission and closely models the facilities found in packet-switched networks such as Ethernet, supporting a bidirectional data flow which is not sequenced, not reliable, and not unduplicated. A process using a datagram socket may find that messages are duplicated and may not be in the order originally transmitted. In a datagram socket, however, record boundaries in data are preserved.

It is important to realize that this distinction between reliable and not reliable, between stream and datagram sockets does not imply a failure in transmission. Packet transmission systems are predicated on an expectation of failure of individual packets and use receipt-confirmation and resend methods to ensure reliable results overall. The difference is that packets allow a higher throughput under poor communications conditions by allowing for and recovering from errors.

WinInet is an MFC interface that resolves a great deal of the complexity involved in Windows Sockets and is ideal for simple data transfers without invoking ActiveX controls. The shortcoming of WinInet is a loss of some degree of the control that is possible by writing to sockets directly.

Named Pipes

Named pipes, as well as mailslots, are actually implemented as file systems and, in the registry, entries appear for NPFS (Named Pipe File System) and MSFS (MailSlot File System).

Named pipes are not supported on Windows 95/98 but named-pipe applications—developed under Windows NT—will be treated as anonymous pipes when executed on Window 95/98. Mailslot applications, in contrast, are supported by both. (File mapping and anonymous pipes can only be used between processes on the same computer.)

As file systems, both named pipes and mailslots share a common functionality, including security, with other supported file systems. Additionally, local processes may use named pipes and mailslots with other processes locally without requiring networking components. Remote access for named pipes and mailslots, as with all file systems, is accomplished through the redirector.

Named pipes provide connection-oriented messaging permitting applications to share memory across a network and Windows NT provides a special API offering increased security for named-pipe operations.

Because named pipes and Windows Sockets are the two most important networking IPC APIs in Windows, both must provide support for Windows NT security functions.

Mailslots

Mailslots are similar to named pipes but offer the additional ability to broadcast messages to all computers in a specified domain. Windows NT's mailslot implementation is a subset of the Microsoft OS/2 LAN Manager implementation and supports only second class mailslots providing connectionless messaging for broadcast messages.

Using second class—connectionless—messaging, delivery of the message is not guaranteed even though the delivery rate for most networks is high.

Mailslots are most useful for identifying other computers or services on a network. As an example, Windows NT's Computer Browser service uses mailslots to identify available connections and services.

Impersonation

Impersonation is a feature added to named pipes which allows a server to change its security identifier to appear to be the client at the remote end of the connection. In this fashion, a database server, using named pipes to receive, read, and write client requests, can impersonate the client while attempting to perform the request. When this is done, if the client lacks the authority to perform the action, the request is denied.

Memory-Mapped Files

The Virtual Memory Manager (VMM) is designed to ensure that applications do not have access—accidentally or deliberately—to each other's memory space. In translating a virtual address to a physical address, VMM routes the memory address to safe locations, keeping the memory used by individual applications separate and secure. VMM does, however, include provisions allowing a single page frame to be visible in the virtual addresses of separate processes. At the operating system level, this block of shared memory is called a section object.

The Win32 subsystem exposes the functionality of section objects to clients in the form of memory-mapped files. While two programs cannot share memory directly, they can share the same disk file. At the same time, even when applications act as if they were accessing memory, they can actually be accessing the swap file—which is used as an extension of memory—because VMM simply masks the distinction, making translating virtual addresses to physical addresses in RAM or in the swap file with equal impartiality.

Further, any disk file can be accessed the same way, using memory addresses by creating a memory-mapped file. As an extension of this memory I/O capability, two processes may open the same block of memory as though it were a file and then read from and write to it. To share memory without creating a new disk file, the programs simply link the shared object to the system's normal page-swapping file.

Also, when the user launches multiple instances of a program, the system creates a mapped file object to enable all instances to share a single copy of the .EXE image.

NetBIOS

NetBIOS is a standard IPC programming interface in the PC environment, providing support for client/server applications. NetBIOS has been in use since its introduction in the early 1980s. NetBIOS client/server applications support various protocols including: NetBEUI (NBF), NWLink, NetBIOS (NWNBLink), and NetBIOS over TCP/IP (NetBF).

Within the Windows environment, the `Netbios` function is offered primarily for applications written for the IBM NetBIOS system. NetBIOS contains extensions to the standard IBM NetBIOS 3.0 specification which allow POST routines to be called from C and to operate efficiently in the Windows environment.

From a developer's perspective, however, any of a variety of higher level interfaces—such as named pipes and RPC—are superior to NetBIOS both in flexibility and portability.

RPC (Remote Procedure Calls)

The RPC mechanisms make use of other IPC mechanisms to establish communications between client and server processes. When both the client and server processes are physically located on the same computer, the LPC (Local Procedure Call) mechanism handles the information transfer. Between these two forms—local and remote—RPC forms the most flexible and portable IPC choice for use between applications running on different operating systems, including calls from a Windows application to an MS-DOS application running on a different computer.

For more information on the Remote Procedure Call mechanisms, see Chapter 7.

Summary

Inter-Process Communications provide a means for processes to exchange data both locally and for network (distributed) processes. IPC methods include Dynamic Data Exchange (DDE) and Network DDE, Windows sockets, named pipes and mailslots, memory-mapped files, NetBIOS, and RPC.

Review Questions

1. Inter-Process Communications are:

   A. Always local processes

   B. Always remote processes

   C. Both local and remote processes

   D. Independent of the process locations

2. Which of the following is true of the client side of a client/server application? (Select all that apply.)

    A. It commonly requires light computing power.

    B. It provides the user interface.

    C. It requires a TCP/IP connection.

    D. It requires considerable bandwidth.

3. Which of the following is true of the server side of a client/server application? (Select all that apply.)

    A. It can only function over a network.

    B. It must run on a mainframe system.

    C. It commonly provides massive data storage.

    D. It commonly provides sophisticated computing power.

4. Select the development tool(s) which would provide maximum control and efficiency for writing a new Web browser.

    A. Active Server Pages (ASPs)

    B. Java applets

    C. Windows Sockets API

    D. WinInet

5. ODBC and the Messaging API (MAPI) provide a layer of abstraction for local-area database and messaging systems. The same type of abstraction layer for WAN protocols is provided by:

    A. NetBEUI

    B. NetBIOS

    C. TCP/IP

    D. Windows Sockets

6. Which of the following is true of today's client/server systems? (Select all that apply.)

   A. They allow shared data and document and task processing.

   B. They are used to leverage legacy mainframes.

   C. They facilitate communications between distributed workstations.

   D. They provide distributed access to common data sources.

7. The Inter-Process Communications (IPC) mechanism that is used to implement a hot link over a network and automatically update a shared memory area on a client computer is:

   A. Mailslots

   B. Named pipes

   C. NetDDE

   D. Windows Sockets

8. Which of the following is true of the DDE protocol? (Select all that apply.)

   A. It consists of a set of messages and guidelines to send messages between applications.

   B. It depends on the DDEML.DLL library.

   C. It uses atoms and pointers to shared memory objects.

   D. It uses shared memory to exchange data.

9. Which of the following is true of the DDE Management Library (DDEML)? (Select all that apply.)

   A. It enforces DDE protocols in a consistent fashion.

   B. It provides compatibility between DDE applications by forcing them to implement DDE protocols in a consistent fashion.

   C. It simplifies developing and implementing DDE client applications.

   D. It simplifies developing and implementing DDE server applications.

10. What are the main components that make up a socket under the Windows Sockets API? (Select all that apply.)

   A. A port number or ID

   B. A socket type (stream or datagram)

   C. A TCP/IP network

   D. An IP address

11. How does NetDDE function?

   A. It establishes a token-ring link between local and remote applications.

   B. It opens a bidirectional pipe between local and remote applications.

   C. It opens two one-way pipes between local and remote applications.

   D. It passes messages and data using packet transmissions.

12. Select the Inter-Process Communications (IPC) mechanism that can broadcast messages to all computers across a specific network domain.

   A. Anonymous pipes

   B. File mapping

   C. Mailslots

   D. Named pipes

13. The Windows Sockets specification supports:

   A. Anonymous pipes

   B. Communications using TCP/IP and IPX/SPX only

   C. Data transfer through shared memory

   D. Services to interface with many transports with different addressing schemes

14. Select the Inter-Process Communications (IPC) or memory-sharing processes which can be used across a network.

A. Anonymous pipes

B. File mapping

C. Named pipes

D. Windows Sockets

15. Named pipes and mailslots:

A. Are immune to impersonation

B. Are implemented as file systems

C. Depend on packet data transmission

D. Support special security APIs

16. The definition of a socket is:

A. A memory address used to receive data on a TCP/IP network

B. A point-to-point connection between two processes using the TCP/IP protocols

C. A TCP or UDP connection used by a network server

D. An endpoint for bi-directional communications between processes

17. Memory-mapped files:

A. Access other process's memory directly through VMM maps

B. Use a shared disk file to exchange data

C. Use NetBEUI communications

D. Write data to reserved system files

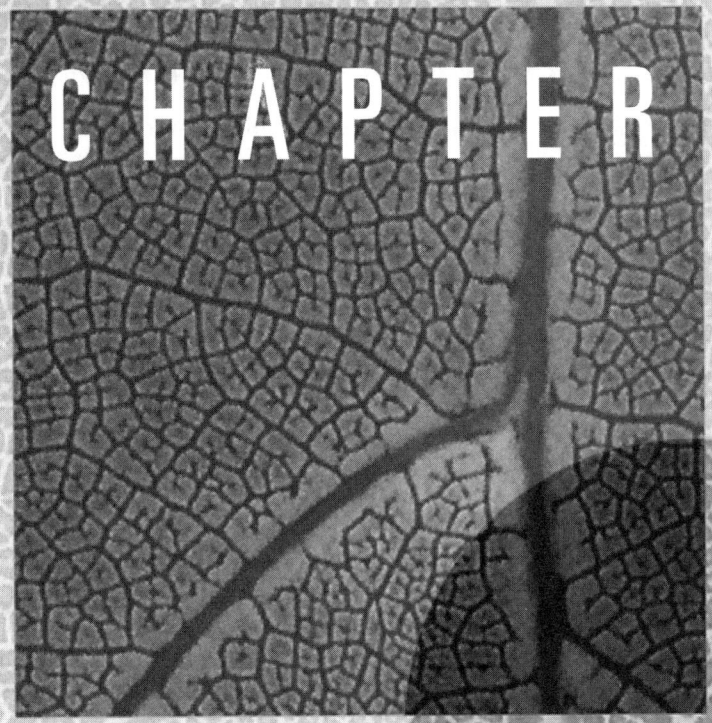

CHAPTER

14

Internet and Intranet Protocols

Microsoft Exam Objectives Covered in This Chapter:

- Choose the appropriate protocol for a given application on the Internet or on an intranet.

In many ways, the Internet is like St. Paul who, it was said, was all things to all men. It would be nice if the Internet were also, as Plutarch reports of Caesar's wife, above reproach... but that standard exists only in dreams and political rhetoric. In reality, the Internet has been better characterized by Vernor Vinge (in *A Fire Upon The Deep*) as "The Web of a Thousand Lies."

In any case, however flawed, the Internet is a massive interchange where virtually anyone (except the computer-phobic) can find something to satisfy their needs. For some, the Internet is a social venue: a place to gather and exchange ideas, philosophies, and commentary. For others, the Web forms a critical resource for collaboration and communication. For still others, it is a place to gather information, a marketplace, the ultimate library, the neighborhood post office, the morning newspaper, a stock market ticker, or a banking center where no one waits in line.

The single element shared by all of these aspects is that the Internet is a facility for communications, making it possible for many tens of millions of people—with more joining every day—to exchange and share ideas and information in new and innovative fashions.

A decade or more ago—in the heyday of Compuserve and MCI Mail when 300 baud modems were 'hot stuff'—simply being able to send electronic messages was real cutting-edge technology, even if it was limited to text and to communications with those other brave souls who were crazy enough to be out there in the wilds of cyberspace.

Today, my electronic mailbox is the regular recipient not only of mail from my son and daughter-in-law and my brothers and sisters but also from friends from Britain, Greece, India, Taiwan, Thailand, and other nations as well as the closer continental United States (and Hawaii, of course). But the point is that these messages are not from members of the techno-intelligensia but from 'just plain folks' (no offense, please) who happily avail themselves of the possibilities—often in ways which no one expected nor envisioned a very short decade ago.

And, as the world becomes increasingly connected, this trend can only continue (although it will, undoubtedly, hold further surprises) to bring more people into the 'Net'-hood.

Increasingly, just as television has become simply TV and both compact disks and compact disk players are referred to as CDs, the Internet is known simply as the Net.

Today, the Internet is a world almost in itself but also a world which simply did not exist a decade ago. The Internet today is a vast store of information, incredible volumes of content, stores of data of all types but, most of all and most important, an incredible network of people.

A decade from now, instead of writing a book like this, I may well be speaking to you over the Net, displaying graphics and applications as we talk and, of course, frantically trying to keep myself and you abreast of the newest changes in technology with feeds from a multitude of other sites.

For the present, however, the Internet is a live, growing entity and we will be looking at the structure of the Internet and at popular Internet services, including File Transfer Protocol (FTP), Gopher, search engines, and the World Wide Web in general. And, of course, we will be looking at some of the applications and services available on the Internet that relate to the Windows operating systems and at how these services are related.

Introduction to the Internet

An internetwork is, very simply, a collection of networks, while the Internet (capitalized) identifies a specific collection of networks, internationally, which are linked through the Transport Control Protocol/Internet Protocol (TCP/IP) protocol suite.

The Internet was created in the late 1960s as the ARPANET, a research project sponsored by the government through DARPA, the Defense Advanced Research Projects Agency. Originally, the Internet was envisioned as being designed to facilitate communications between research facilities.

Roughly a decade after the invention of ARPANET, when the first PCs were being invented, a group of ham operators began looking at methods for allowing personal computers to communicate over the airwaves, primarily using 40 meter and 2 meter frequencies. Because of the unreliability of transmission/reception, a scheme known as packet radio was developed where information was sent in discrete packets containing identifiers and checksum values.

These transmitted packets would be decoded on receipt, checked for validity, and their receipt acknowledged to the sending unit. If the original transmitter did not receive acknowledgment of a packet within a reasonable interval, the packet would be retransmitted. And, on the receiving end, once enough packets were received, the contents of the packets would be decoded and reassembled to recreate the original message.

Later, as traffic over the ARPANET increased, these same standards of packet transmission were incorporated in the communication protocols (as they are today) to improve the reliability of network communications.

Today, ARPANET, along with MilNet, NSI (NASA Science Internet), and the NSFNet (National Science Foundation Network) form the background of the domestic Internet while the Internet as a whole consists of more than two million hosts located in 130 countries. (The number of users connected to these two million hosts is uncertain but is estimated in the multiple tens of millions.)

While the original Internet was widely seen as a toy for computer geeks and a means for collaborative research exchanges between universities and research establishments, today the Internet reaches into businesses, schools at all levels, homes, and even coffee bars. In effect, today, the opportunity for communication is open to everyone.

And, even though the Internet is very far from being limited to computers—although it does depend on computers—the Internet is perhaps the ideal medium for disseminating information to and about computers.

Internet Standards and Protocols

The Internet, in effect, consists of a melange of different types of computer systems ranging from mainframes to minis to desktop (or tower) servers running an equally divergent assortment of operating systems, such as multiple flavors of UNIX (ZENIX, LINUX), Windows NT, OS/2, and a host of others. Perhaps this is overly obvious, but to allow such diverse systems comprising the Internet to intercommunicate simply would not be possible without a standard set of protocols.

Internet standards are proposed in documents titled Requests For Comment, or RFCs. RFCs began in 1969 and comprise the working notes of the

Internet research and development community, with each RFC consisting of a description of a protocol, procedure, or service; a status report; or a summary of research.

To date, more than two thousand RFCs have been published, but these RFCs do not become standards until they have been subjected to the review of the Internet community. However, most of the Internet standards today began as RFCs. Because, with a few exceptions, RFCs are documents in the public domain, these papers are available from a number of sources.

Requests For Comment papers are numbered sequentially and, once assigned a number, are not revised. Instead of revising an existing RFC, a new version of the RFC—with a new number—is issued. Additional information on RFCs and the Internet protocol standards process is found in RFC 1310.

Transmission Control Protocol/Internet Protocol (TCP/IP)

RFC 1310 proposed a suite of protocols including the Transmission Control Protocol/Internet Protocol (TCP/IP). The TCP/IP protocol suite actually consists of a group of protocols working across several network layers. TCP/IP is best illustrated as a four-layer system, as shown in Figure 14.1.

F I G U R E 14.1

The TCP/IP protocol stack

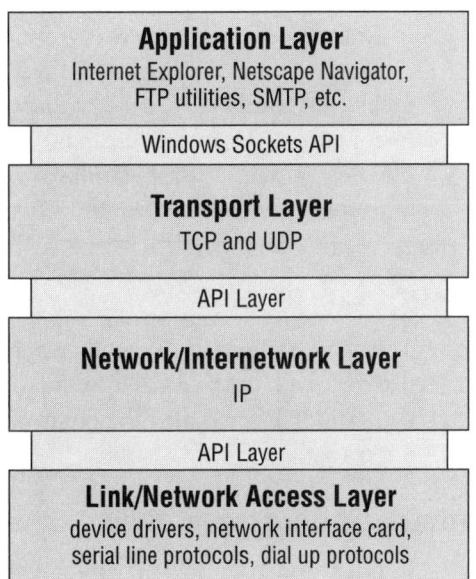

Application Layer
Internet Explorer, Netscape Navigator,
FTP utilities, SMTP, etc.

Windows Sockets API

Transport Layer
TCP and UDP

API Layer

Network/Internetwork Layer
IP

API Layer

Link/Network Access Layer
device drivers, network interface card,
serial line protocols, dial up protocols

Networks are commonly defined in layers to permit the separation of functionality. These layers can be visualized as a sequence of steps that a data packet follows while progressing from one computer in the network to the next.

Each layer in the network is joined by an Application Programming Interface (API), or convention for interpreting messages—packets—passing between layers. Under Windows, for example, the Windows Sockets API frees the developers from being concerned with the layers below, including how TCP packets are passed through the IP layer and then on to the network card in the link layer.

The Windows Sockets API is not part of the TCP/IP protocol suite itself, but does permit applications using WinSock to operate over TCP/IP implementations created by different vendors.

The Link Layer

The link layer (the bottom-most layer in Figure 14.1) is commonly associated with the network card interface or with the dial-up modem interface. The link layer's primary role is to transfer data packets to the physical network, and may include interfacing with a conventional network card, such as an Ethernet card, or may involve a serial line interface, such as a modem.

The two most common link layer protocols are Serial Line Internet Protocol (SLIP) and Point-to-Point Protocol (PPP), both of which allow systems to connect to the Internet using the TCP/IP protocols. These connections, however, are made over standard, dial-up phone lines and modems rather than conventional network links (i.e., a LAN system).

The Network Layer

The network layer is primarily responsible for moving packets across the network and, in the TCP/IP standard, is handled by the Internet Protocol (IP). The IP layer is also the point where unique Internet addresses become important.

Internet Address Schema

Internet domain and electronic mail addresses should be familiar to everyone in today's world. Domain names are ubiquitous, appearing everywhere: in print ads, on television ads, and even in the yellow pages in your local phone book.

On the very rare chance that you're not conversant with domain and e-mail addresses, a domain name consists of a name and a domain extension. Domain names take the form *sonic.net*, *ezzell.org*, or *whitehouse.gov*. The first is the domain name for Sonoma Interconnect, an Internet Service Provider (ISP). The second is your author's own registered domain name, while the third reaches the White House in Washington, D.C.

E-mail addresses consist of a personal name at a domain address. For example, to reach the author of this book, you would address your e-mail to *ben@ezzell.org*—i.e., to me at my domain. Of course, you could also reach me as *ezzell@sonic.net*, as *ezzell@wclynx.com* or as *ezzell@pcugr.org*, three aliases, in effect, which are all delivered to the same electronic mailbox.

However, while all of these names are convenient for people, computers are a little bit pickier about what kind of addresses they understand and these human-friendly mnemonic addresses just don't work for our cybernetic servants. For network traffic, where routers need to move packets efficiently over the appropriate networks, a more distinctive address scheme—or a more computer-oriented address scheme—is required. For this purpose, each host on the Internet requires a unique 32-bit address, commonly referred to as an IP address.

NOTE   Every host is required to have a globally unique IP address but is not required to have a domain name.

Are 32-bit Addresses Enough?

In the early days of the Internet, a 32-bit address surely seemed like a value which would be more than sufficient for eternity. After all, a 32-bit address is sufficient to provide unique addresses for 4,294,967,296 hosts—that is, four billion computers.

Of course, an early CEO at IBM once stated with great confidence and foresight that the world might, someday, actually need a total of nine computers... maybe. Now, in all honesty, the computer in question was a very early model with limited use... and nine of that model were never built... but the thought was there.

As for expending four billion addresses?

It's really not that difficult. First, your local IP may be using a dozen or more addresses in house—one for each computer in their local system, including routers and mail servers. And there are client accounts which reserve blocks of addresses even though they are not, at present, in actual use. Still, they are 'expended,' thus reducing the total.

But, back to our ISP who is using the 12 in-house addresses because, in addition to these in-house addresses assigned to individual machines, this same ISP also has a block of 2000 address which are assigned—on a per rota basis—to dial-in clients.

Of course, when a dial-in client logs off again, the address they were assigned on login is released and can be used again, but this is still a large block of addresses owned by a single, relatively small service provider.

Adding to the numbers are offices using networks and Internet connections. Let's assume that this company has 300 workstations as well as a half-dozen servers including their own Web server. There go another 300+ addresses.

Now, what about Web-enabled TV sets connected through their local cable systems? That's right, they need addresses as well... and they're not dialing in, they're staying connected.

Recent estimates suggest that there will be 177 million Internet/e-mail clients by the year 2000 but, remember, just five years ago, the current number of clients was orders of magnitude lower than present... and it isn't decreasing.

So, just how long will it take before our four billion addresses are exhausted? And just where are we going when they are?

How long and where are both nebulous at the moment; suffice to say that these addresses will be exhausted not too long from now. Proposals are already in the works for both a 64-bit address standard and for a variable length schema for IP addresses (refer to RFC 2050 for more details).

A 64-bit standard, of course, may actually last for a little while since this would suffice for a total of 1.84×10^{19} IP addresses. And this might—just maybe—last us for a few years.

But I'm not taking any bets on how long...

For more information on domain registration, refer to http://www
.arin.net/docs.html.

For convenience (human, not computer) the 32-bit IP addresses are
divided into four numeric fields, separated by periods, with the value for
each field in the range 0..255 (0×00..0×FF). For an example, Microsoft's
FTP server has the name ftp.microsoft.com and an IP address of
198.105.232.1.

Of course, if you prefer hex format, this address would be rendered as
C6.69.E8.01. The fact that the addresses are rendered in standard decimal
format—like the human domain names—is for human convenience, as the
computer will render this to a single 32-bit value, totally ignoring the
human conventions.

The DNS (domain name system) is used to translate between the human-
friendly domain names and the 32-bit globally unique addresses. The DNS
is a distributed static database used by the Internet to map domain names to
IP addresses specified by network administrators.

The DNS arranges host names in a hierarchical fashion, similar to a file
system, where the top names in the hierarchy are called top-level domains
and include both the familiar .COM, .NET, and .ORG classifications as well
as the two-letter international country codes.

Top-Level Domain Names

Previously, top-level organization domains have consisted of six domains
listed following:

com	Commercial organizations
edu	Educational institutions
gov	Governmental agencies (U.S.)
mil	Military departments (U.S.)
net	Network providers (ISPs)
org	Other organizations

More recently, seven new top-level domains have been added, including:

art   Sites related to cultural and artistic activities

firm   Business and commercial companies

info   Information services

nom   Domain for personal names

rec   Sites related to recreational activities

shop   Retail firms doing business on the Web

web   Web and Web related organizations

And, in addition to all of these, there is also a long list of country codes. A few representative samples are offered following:

au   Australia

ch   Switzerland

de   Germany

tm   Turkmenistan

uk   United Kingdom

The country domain for Turkmenistan, for example, has proved very popular with a variety of companies since the designation—tm—is also the abbreviation for trademark. For more on top-level domain names (and the complete list of international codes) refer to `http://registrars.net/`.

The second-level domain name—`ezzell` if you are trying to reach my site—is the portion of the domain name previously administered by the Internet Network Information Center (InterNIC) but now handled by International Domain Registrars (IDR at `registrars.net`).

The remaining elements in an Internet address, such as references to sub-network addresses, are administered by the local network. These are often broken up into additional zones to ease administration.

The local network administrator is also responsible for establishing name servers to handle requests for resolving local domain names to addresses. Further specifications for the DNS protocol can be found in RFCs 1034 and 1035.

The Transport Layer

The Transport protocol layer (see Figure 14.1) handles the data flow between networked machines running IP. The TCP/IP suite employs two different protocols in the transport layer: TCP and UDP (User Datagram Protocol).

Originally, the Internet used protocols that assumed a reliable connection between systems. However, as DARPANET grew to include remote hosts and to use a variety of link layers, the reliability of the connection could no longer be assumed and the responsibility for reliable transmissions shifted from the connection to the protocols.

UDP (User Datagram Protocol) is a simple interface used by applications to exchange user data—datagrams—through the network. UDP expects a reliable connection and does not include any provisions to ensure that the data sent will be received by the intended system. Ergo, applications using UDP must include their own checks to ensure receipt.

Conversely, TCP (Transmission Control Protocol) is a connection-oriented protocol designed to tolerate unreliable link conditions between two machines. TCP is a packet-oriented protocol accepting a message of any length before breaking the message into packets—pieces less than 64KB in length. Each packet receives a checksum value, used to validate the contents of the packet, and an identifier so that the packets can be reassembled in the correct order. Finally, the packets are passed to the network layer for routing and delivery.

When a packet is received and validated, TCP returns an acknowledgment message identifying each packet. Employing time-out delays, if a transmitted packet is not acknowledged in a reasonable period, the originating system retransmits the packet, continuing until all packets have been received (or until the protocol decides that the transmission is not possible and an error is issued).

Because all of the packaging and tracking is handled by TCP, the application layer is free to simply assume that the data will be delivered in correct fashion until and unless it is informed otherwise. Because TCP is reliable and simple—for the calling application—most applications prefer to use TCP.

The Application Layer

The application layer refers to protocols built at the application layer of the TCP/IP suite. For Windows, these will be Windows Sockets–compatible applications, and there will normally be a wide variety of implementations to select from, each with its own features and variations in the Graphical User Interface (GUI).

Table 14.1 lists a variety of the common application layer protocols that are available at or supported by the TCP/IP protocol suite. Many of the protocols or utilities listed are now superseded by modern application packages which combine what were once separate utilities or by services offered through the Web rather than as stand-alone utilities.

T A B L E 14.1:   Protocols and Utilities Using TCP/IP

Protocol/Utility	Translation	Description
Archie		Catalog of the contents of 1000+ anonymous FTP servers disseminating the location of FTP retrievable files. See search.com.
DHCP	Dynamic Host Configuration Protocol	Auto-configuration service that allows a machine to obtain an IP address without a priori knowledge at boot time
DNS	Domain Name System	Distributed database that allows applications to map between computer names and IP addresses
Eudora Lite, Eudora Pro		Probably the single most popular e-mail manager used for Internet mail
Finger		Returns information on users on a specific Internet machine. See search.com.
FTP	File Transfer Protocol	Copies files from one Internet machine to another. See HTTP, WS-FTP.
Gopher		Protocol for distributed document navigation and retrieval. The sum of Gopher resources is sometimes referred to as "gopherspace." See search.com.

T A B L E 14.1: Protocols and Utilities Using TCP/IP *(continued)*

Protocol/Utility	Translation	Description
HTTP	Hypertext Transfer Protocol	The HTTP protocol is the basis of the World Wide Web and is usually used to fetch Web pages. HTTP can be used to fetch the direct HTML of a Web page but, like FTP, can also be used to fetch binary files such as images or .zip files. See FTP, WS-FTP.
Internet Explorer		Microsoft's 'integrated' Web browser utility package that supplants many of the previous separate utilities used for the Internet. See Netscape Navigator, Opera.
IRC	Internet Relay Chat	Real-time text-based conversation system
MUD	Multi-User Dungeon	Multi-player adventure game known to consume massive network bandwidth and programmer cycles (see Quake)
Netscape Navigator		Popular Web browser utility that supplants many of the previous separate utilities used for the Internet. See Internet Explorer, Opera.
NFS	Network File System	Provides transparent file access across clients on the Internet
Opera		Web browser utility popular for its no-frills approach. See Internet Explorer, Netscape Navigator.
Outlook		Microsoft's combined contact manager, e-mail manager. See Eudora Lite, Eudora Pro.
PEM	Privacy Enhanced Mail	Protocol for electronic mail that provides for encryption and authentication using RSA and DES
PGP	Pretty Good Privacy	Widely accepted encryption technology using public key cryptography to maintain secure communications
POP 2 & 3	Post Office Protocol	Protocol for the management of electronic mail using store and forward
Quake		Multi-player game known to consume massive network bandwidth and programmer cycles. See MUD.

T A B L E 14.1: Protocols and Utilities Using TCP/IP *(continued)*

Protocol/Utility	Translation	Description
search.com, Four11 White Pages, Yahoo, Computer ESP,		The original utilities, such as Finger and Gopher, which were used to locate people and documents on the Net, are now replaced by Web-based services. CNet's search.com offers a collection of hundreds of search engines and search services. See Gopher, Archie, Veronica, Finger.
SMTP	Simple Mail Transfer Protocol	Governs the exchange of electronic mail between two message transfer agents (MTAs) on the Internet
SNMP	Simple Network Management Protocol	Protocol for remote administration and management of TCP/IP machines
Telnet	Telecommunications Network Protocol	Remote login between hosts running potentially different operating systems
USENET	Uses NNTP	Huge collection of messages and newsgroups arranged in a Network News Transport Protocol hierarchical bulletin board system
VERONICA	Very Easy Rodent-Oriented Netwide Index to Computerized Archives	Indexed search to gopherspace. See search.com.
WAIS	Wide Area Information Server	Implementation of Z39.50 content indexing and information retrieval standard
Whois	Who Is	Returns information on an Internet user voluntarily registered with InterNIC. See search.com.
WS-FTP		Windows-based FTP utility with GUI. See FTP, HTTP.
WWW (also Web or W3)	World Wide Web	Protocol for distributed hypertext document searching, navigation, and retrieval

Obviously, the protocols, services and utilities listed in Table 14.1 are only a sparse sampling of the gamut of services and utilities available on the Net overall, and the list shown is also heavily concentrated on the older, historical protocols and utilities. A few of the older utility services that are still heavily used are discussed following.

FTP

In terms of traffic, the file transfer protocol (FTP) is one of the most widely used TCP/IP application protocols. FTP is used to copy files between machines. Copying a file is not the same as remotely accessing a file, which is as service provided by the NFS (Network File Service) or CIFS (Common Internet File System) members of the application layer.

Common Internet File System (CIFS)

Whereas most Internet usage depends on simple read-only browsing or one-way file transfers, the new Common Internet File System (CIFS) protocol offers a means for collaborative applications to function over the Internet (or intranets). CIFS defines a standard remote file system access protocol allowing groups of users to share documents across the Internet or across corporate intranets. CIFS is an open, cross-platform technology based on the native file-sharing protocols found in Windows and other PC operating systems but is also supported on other platforms, including UNIX.

In some ways, the FTP protocol is analogous to the Kermit, Xmodem, or YModem applications, which were heavily used before BBS (Bulletin Board Services) were overtaken by the Internet. Unlike the earlier Kermit, XModem, and YModem services, FTP also offers some navigational functions and virtually every commercial TCP/IP version provides some form of FTP support.

RFC 959 provides the definitive reference for the FTP protocol and is available from several sources.

The FTP.EXE utility is supplied by Microsoft with most versions of Windows. FTP.EXE is a command-line utility and, under Windows, executes in a DOS window as shown in Figure 14.2.

The complete transcript of a brief FTP session appears following with our entries shown in bold italics:

ftp> *open nis.nsf.net*

Connected to nis.nsf.net.

220 nic.merit.edu FTP server (Version wu-2.4.2-academ[BETA-15](3)

 Thu Oct 30 13:16:32 EST 1997) ready.

User (nis.nsf.net:(none)): *anonymous*

331 Guest login ok, send your complete e-mail address as password

Password: *(the entry here is not echoed locally)*

230-

230-   NOTICE: This system is operated by the Merit Network, Inc.

230-   You must follow the Merit Acceptable Use Policy described in

230-   /michnet/policies/acceptable.use.policy.

230-

```
230-    The local time is Sat Mar 14 19:16:19 1998.
230-    You are user 2 out of a maximum of 100 users.
230-
230 Guest login ok, access restrictions apply.
ftp> help
Commands may be abbreviated.  Commands are:
!           delete      literal     prompt      send
?           debug       ls          put         status
append      dir         mdelete     pwd         trace
ascii       disconnect  mdir        quit        type
bell        get         mget        quote       user
binary      glob        mkdir       recv        verbose
bye         hash        mls         remotehelp
cd          help        mput        rename
close       lcd         open        rmdir
ftp> get /michnet/policies/acceptable.use.policy
200 PORT command successful.
150 Opening ASCII mode data connection for /michnet/
policies/acceptable.use.policy (4308 bytes).
226 Transfer complete.
ftp: 4404 bytes received in 1.32Seconds 3.34Kbytes/sec.
ftp: bye
221 Goodbye.
```

While our FTP session has been successful, the command-line FTP.EXE utility does, of course, give us a lot of power but it is not the most user friendly application and does not afford a great deal of flexibility in some aspects of our operation. For example, once we've opened our FTP utility, we really don't have any way to change our local directory and the file being downloaded from nis.nsf.net is going... where? Are we even sure?

Actually, in this case, the downloaded file is going to the D:\Win98 directory since this is where FTP.EXE was executed from, but the point is that the command line utility doesn't give us very much flexibility for transferring files to specific directories. Granted, we can switch to a specific drive/directory before calling FTP.EXE but we really can't change directories on the local system in midstream, so to speak.

The alternative is to use an FTP utility with a GUI interface and the ability to give us a view of both local and remote directories; see the "Graphic FTP Utilities" section, below.

FTP Operations

In order to transfer files using FTP, there are a few obvious requirements, such as a client system running TCP/IP, a client-side FTP utility, and a server-side FTP process. Of course, the one other item necessary to know is where to connect, i.e., where to find files that might be of interest.

In the example preceding, the connection was made to a known site where a library of RFC documents can be found. In other cases, we might be linking to sites which have been recommended in an e-mail message, listed in an articles or located using a search engine.

In any case, the first step is to use the Open command, using a complete host address as an argument, to connect to a server. The host address can be a string name—such as nis.nsf.net for a domain name server—or can be the dotted-decimal address: the globally unique 32-bit identifier. Simply as a courtesy, common FTP sites used to provide both their string names and address. More recently, however, most sites only list their string names.

In the example, the connection was made to an NSFNet server where the server's name is nis, the second-level domain name is nsf, and the top-level domain name is net.

Once a connection has been made to the server, the server responds by requesting a login identifier. In most cases, if the only purpose is to download software or documents, the anonymous identifier can be used. In other cases, more restricted access may require a specific identifier. In the latter case, the 'name' required for login is established by the system administration and may simply be your name, your user name, or it may be a special sequence of letters and/or numbers.

For an anonymous login, most systems request the caller's Internet e-mail address as the password. Some systems may accept a blank or may accept guest in lieu of an e-mail address, but others enforce their request by parsing the domain name from the e-mail address (everything to the right of the @-sign) and then attempt to resolve the domain name with the address the request is coming from.

However, if your e-mail address is an alias, if you are connecting through a system or network which is not the same as your mail server or if you have a firewall in place, the name can probably not be resolved and the server will probably not allow access. (In such cases, consult your system administrator for an appropriate domain name for use.)

Most servers use the password information simply to maintain a connections log and, in accord with Internet use policies, this information is not supposed to be used for any purposes other than security. For example, the information provided is not to be used for providing e-mail lists or for tracking downloads for competitive or commercial purposes. For this reason, the use of the anonymous login identifier is commonly called *anonymous FTP*.

Once a connection has been made to the server (using the command-line FTP utility), things are a little like a trip back into the past when DOS was the hottest operating system around and everything depended on simple text displays. In this archaic world, everything depends on simple text commands and long-established conventions. To navigate in this world, an understanding is required for three key elements: the FTP commands, how files and directories are structured, and standard file formats.

 The GUI-based FTP utilities introduced following offer much more convenient methods of navigation.

The FTP commands are a subset of Novell's UNIX shell commands. In the example FTP session, preceding, the `help` command was used to request a list of commands available on the server. Note that these are server-supported commands and they are not supplied by FTP.EXE and therefore may be different on different servers. What we did not receive, of course, was an explanation of what these commands mean: Table 14.2 outlines the more important commands with some explanation.

T A B L E 14.2: FTP Commands

Command	Description
help	Prints a list of available commands. In some cases, further help on a command is available by simply trying the command, but this feature varies from server to server.
open *server*	Initiates a connection with a system named *server*
ascii	Sets the current transfer mode to ASCII characters, including CR/LF translation
binary	Sets the current transfer mode to binary, i.e., all transfers occur as byte images of files
cd	Changes the directory on the server; type .. to go up one directory level
lcd	Changes the local directory. This is the same as using the cd command at a local prompt rather than an ftp> prompt.

T A B L E 14.2: FTP Commands *(continued)*

Command	Description
close	Ends the current connection but does not exit from FTP
bye	Ends the current connection and exits FTP
ls *name*	Lists a directory's contents or lists the attributes for a filename. Note that DIR works on most sites as well.
get *source* *destination*	Downloads a file named *source*. If *source* is not specified, a prompt will request a file name. The *destination* argument can sometimes be used to rename a file during the transfer.
mget *list*	Downloads the group of files in *list*, may include server-specific wildcard matching
put *file*	Uploads a file. If *file* is not specified, a prompt will request both remote and local names. (With anonymous FTP, in general, either limited or no write permissions are granted.)
mput *list*	Uploads a group of files in *list*, may include client-specific wildcard matching.

The get command, as shown in the sample session, copies a file from the host system to the local computer. Using command-line FTP, the destination is always the current directory but the lcd command can be used to change directories if desired.

While the get command does offer some feedback on the size of the file being transferred, GUI-based front-end FTP utilities are considerably more convenient and often include progress indicators during transfer. Quite commonly, FTP directories will contain an ASCII (.TXT) file which holds a list and notes describing all of the files in the directory. The directory listing file can be downloaded, opened with a text editor, and read at leisure to find out what files are available without the need to spend time downloading files at random to find out their contents.

Operating System Differences

The ASCII and binary commands are provided because text files on different operating systems may use different formats for line breaks. For example, some systems require both CR and LF characters to terminate lines while others settle for a simple CR to end a line. When the ASCII transfer format is selected, the FTP protocol includes a facility to translate the line-ending characters according to the requirement of the destination system.

Obviously, CR/LF conversions are not supported for compressed files, but you should be aware that downloading a compressed file, using the default ASCII mode transfer, is likely to corrupt the contents of the file.

Also, because the FTP specification calls for ASCII mode to be the default used by FTP utilities, it is a good idea to change to binary mode before executing a transfer of any non-text file.

GUI-based FTP utilities do not necessarily follow this format specification and may include options for automatic transfer format selection.

Another area where differences in operating systems require attention is in local and remote filenames. As you should remember, DOS and earlier versions of Windows relied on 8.3 filename formats while UNIX systems—including many public FTP sites—accept long filenames. Today, of course, Windows 95/98 and Windows NT also support long filename formats.

When files are transferred from long filename–supported systems to systems requiring 8.3 filename formats, normally the client-side software will handle the conversion automatically by truncating the long filenames to an 8.3 format, meaning that there generally will be no special problem.

What you do need to be aware of, however, is that UNIX systems, in addition to supporting long filenames, also support case-sensitive filenames. Conversely, Windows 95/98/NT systems do not differentiate between upper-case and lower-case in filenames (by default). The result is that files from UNIX hosts, which differ only in case, will overwrite each other when being downloaded.

Compressed Files

Motivated more by considerations of transmission times and bandwidth than out of concerns for storage space, FTP sites commonly store individual files or collections of files in compressed form using standard file compression formats. File compression formats (and utilities) in use are identified by their file extensions and include:

- .ZIP identifies PKZIP, which is probably the single most popular format in use. The ZIP2EXE utility can be used to convert ZIP archives to an .EXE format to provide self-extracting files (.EXE files) which, after downloading, are simply executed to decompress automatically.

- .ARC identifies an older compression format which is not common today but may still be found on some sites. The ARC.EXE utility is used to decompress files of this type.

- .SIT identifies a Macintosh compression format requiring the Stuffit utility for decompression.

- .CAB is a new compression format used primarily for Microsoft installation files. .CAB files are decompressed by the operating system and do not require decompression utilities.

Any file compression utilities required can commonly be found (uncompressed) in the \bin directory of the FTP host.

Graphic FTP Utilities

The WS-FPT utility (Windows Sockets FTP) is a GUI-based FTP utility (see Figure 14.3) which provides full FTP services without requiring the user to know the server-supported codes.

FIGURE 14.3

WS-FPT Pro

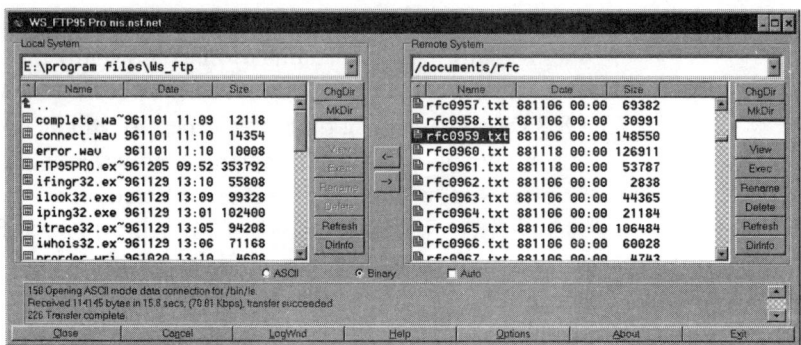

Not only does WS-FTP relieve the dependence on codes, but it offers a number of other services that simply are not supported at all by command-line FTP utilities.

To begin, WS-FTP keeps a list of FTP sites visited by the user, together with any special login names and passwords, and both local and remote working directories plus a variety of advanced and firewall options. These elements make it convenient to configure an FTP session for whatever requirement a specific server (or situation) may demand.

Second, WS-FTP provides a two-pane view showing both the local and remote (host) directories, making it easy to change directories, identify files, and see file sizes and creation dates. Perhaps almost as an afterthought, the bottom pane (showing only three lines but scrolling for review) provides a log of the actual FTP message traffic.

WS-FTP Pro is available from Ipswitch, Inc., who can be reached at www.ipswitch.com.

WS-FTP is only one of the high-level FTP services available; an excellent option is not a stand-alone utility but a integrated feature supplied by Canyon Software's Drag-and-File disk manager (see Figure 14.4).

FIGURE 14.4

Drag-and-File performing FTP services

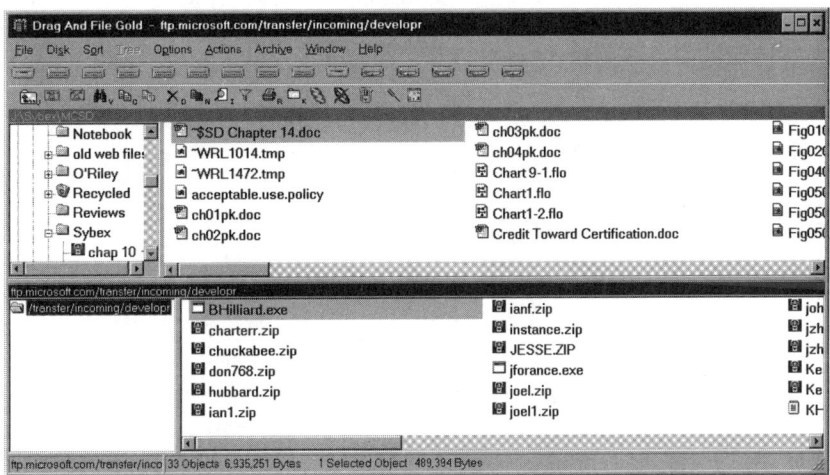

Like WS-FTP, Drag-and-File also maintains a record of FTP sites visited together with login names and passwords and provides a two-pane view to show both the local and remote directories.

Beyond this, the choice between the two is largely a matter of personal preference and convenience. And, of course, there are other graphic FTP utilities available as well.

Drag-and-File is available from Canyon Software, who can be reached at www.canyonsw.com.

As a final note on FTP operations, as you may have realized, all of the operations illustrated began with known FTP sites. The real trick, however, is to know where to find things. Sometimes, of course, references will appear in magazine articles or maybe in an e-mail message, but relying on chance to deliver the site information you need is a poor strategy.

Hypertext Transport Protocol (HTTP)

The Hypertext Transport Protocol (HTTP) is the underlying, application-level protocol using by World Wide Web clients and servers to communicate on the Internet. While HTTP browsers and servers commonly transfer Web pages in HTML format, other data formats such as Audio Video Interleaved (AVI) and Graphic Image Format (GIF) files are also handled by HTTP.

Further, HTTP is coming into use for the transfer of other types of files, functioning in a fashion similar to FTP. The primary difference between FTP and HTTP is that HTTP file transfers are programmed into Web pages and do not provide browsing or directory capabilities for the user. Instead, HTTP transfers are used to perform specific file downloads offered by the Web page creator.

Finding Your Way Around

Historically, a number of attempts have been made to provide ways to find materials on the Net. One of the earlier methods was an attempt to catalog files from an assortment of anonymous FTP sites using a TCP/IP application known as Archie, which provided a simple mechanism for locating files across more than a thousand public hosts.

The shortcomings in Archie were that it only provided indexes to filenames, not to content, so an idea of the filename was a prerequisite for finding a file.

Later, Gopher was introduced as an application layer client/server protocol for distributed document search and retrieval—in effect, an Internet card catalog. The details for the Gopher protocol specification can be found in RFC 1436.

The growth of the Internet, however, has rendered Archie, Gopher, and several other similar utilities effectively worthless simply because of the sheer mass of material. So much so, in fact, that IIS version 4 does not include a gopher service. In their place, a variety of Internet search utilities have appeared.

Some of the services are specialized, offering searches only within certain areas while others offer more generalized search engines. And some, such as Yahoo (`http://www.yahoo.com`), have not only made a splash on the Internet but also on Wall Street.

However, rather than try to offer a comprehensive list of the available search engines, since new ones appear almost every day and some are very specialized, perhaps the best place to start is a site at `www.search.com`, which offers links to hundreds of search engines, both general and specific. `Search.com` appears in Figure 14.5 and includes 14 primary categories for searches, as listed in Table 14.3.

F I G U R E   14.5

Search.Com

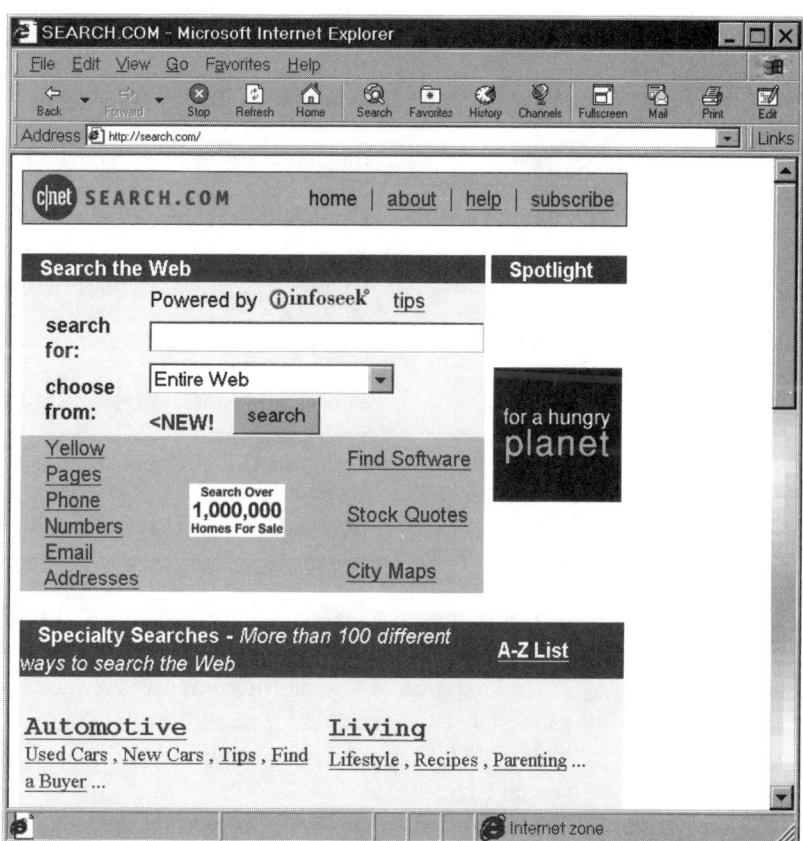

	Category	Content
TABLE 14.3 Fourteen Search Categories	Automotive	Used Cars, New Cars, Tips, Find a Buyer
	Living	Lifestyle, Recipes, Parenting
	Classifieds	Real Estate, Personals, Tickets
	Local	Businesses, Newspapers, Area Code Lookup
	Computing	Tech News, Game Downloads, Hardware
	Money	Quotes and News, Mutual Funds, Company Info
	Employment	Job Search, International Jobs, Job Postings
	News	Business News, Weather, National News
	Entertainment	Movies, Celebrities, TV, Restaurants, Music
	Shopping	Online Stores, Software, Books, CDs, Flowers
	Health	Health Tips, Medical News, Virtual Hospital
	Sports	Scores and Stats, Outdoor Sports, Golf Courses
	Learning	Colleges, Government, Sciences, Nature
	Travel	Hotels, Guides, Trip Routing, Air Fares

Under these 14 search categories, some 474 separate search engines are found. Some, such as Computer ESP, are specialized. Computer ESP provides comparative pricing for computer components and software. Others, such as 411 White Pages, are useful for locating people. Still others, such as Yahoo or Lycos, are very generalized and may themselves search other search engines.

Another area that may be of special interest to Windows developers and programmers is found at www.microsoft.com/search/.

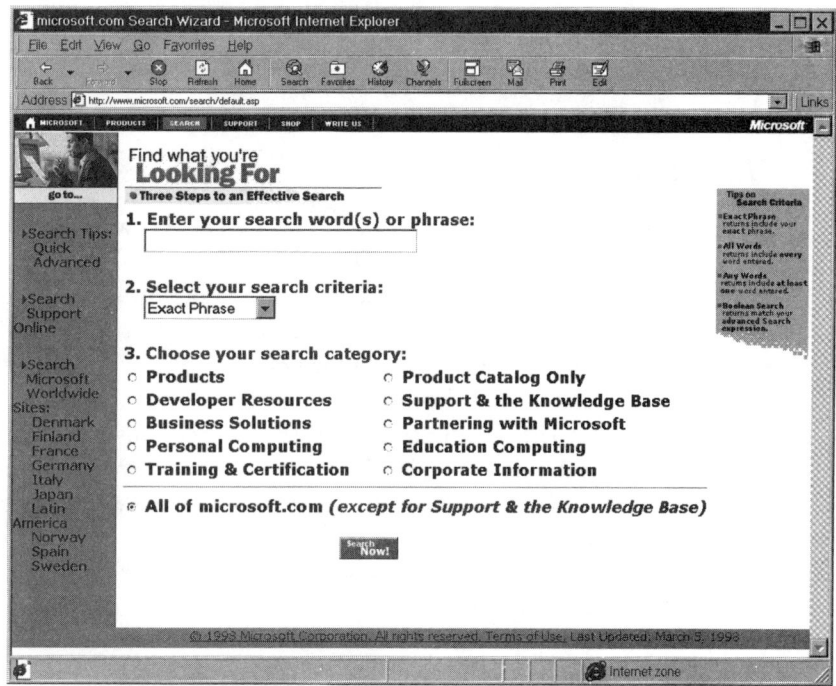

Here the Microsoft Search Wizard offers searches by category or across all categories. The ten categories for searches include:

- Business solutions
- Corporate Information
- Developer resources
- Education Computing
- Partnering with Microsoft
- Personal Computing
- Product Catalog Only
- Products
- Support and the Knowledge Base
- Training and Certification

A popular ad for the telephone Yellow Pages suggests that if something can't be found, it probably doesn't exist. But a more accurate statement might be that if it can't be found using Internet search engines... then you're probably spelling it wrong.

Web Browsers

Only a few years ago, Mosaic was the browser of choice for the Internet, if only because Mosaic was the only browser—or, at least, the only full-featured browser. But, with the Internet as a rapidly growing void waiting to be filled, it did not require long for other increasingly sophisticated browsers to appear on the market. One of the first and still the most popular was Netscape Navigator (now the Netscape Communicator suite).

The number two browser—as everyone excepting, perhaps, a few hermits—is aware, is Microsoft's Internet Explorer A third and increasingly popular contender from Norway's Opera Software is the Opera Internet browser.

While there are other contenders in the marketplace, these three—Netscape Navigator, Internet Explorer, and Opera—are the most popular browsers currently available and are discussed briefly below.

Netscape Navigator

When Netscape Navigator entered the browser scene, Navigator was the answer to the collective prayers of a growing number of Web surfers (see Figure 14.7). Providing a well-integrated browser with all of the essential features for Internet navigation—including bookmark lists and full HTML support—Navigator quickly proved itself to be the quintessential Web browser providing the standard by which all other browsers would be judged.

Like all Windows-based browsers, Navigator employs a GUI interface and graphic controls and, in current versions, includes a news group/discussion reader, e-mail support, an HTML composition editor, and, of course, support for the newest push technology (channels).

In short, Navigator is a full-featured Web browser offering as much or as little support and functionality as the user desires. Further, by offering *plug-ins*—Java applets that offer feature or service support—to extend the services supported by Navigator, adding functionality for new features is not a matter of upgrading the application as a whole but simply of downloading the desired applets, normally on a no-cost basis.

F I G U R E   14.7

Netscape Navigator

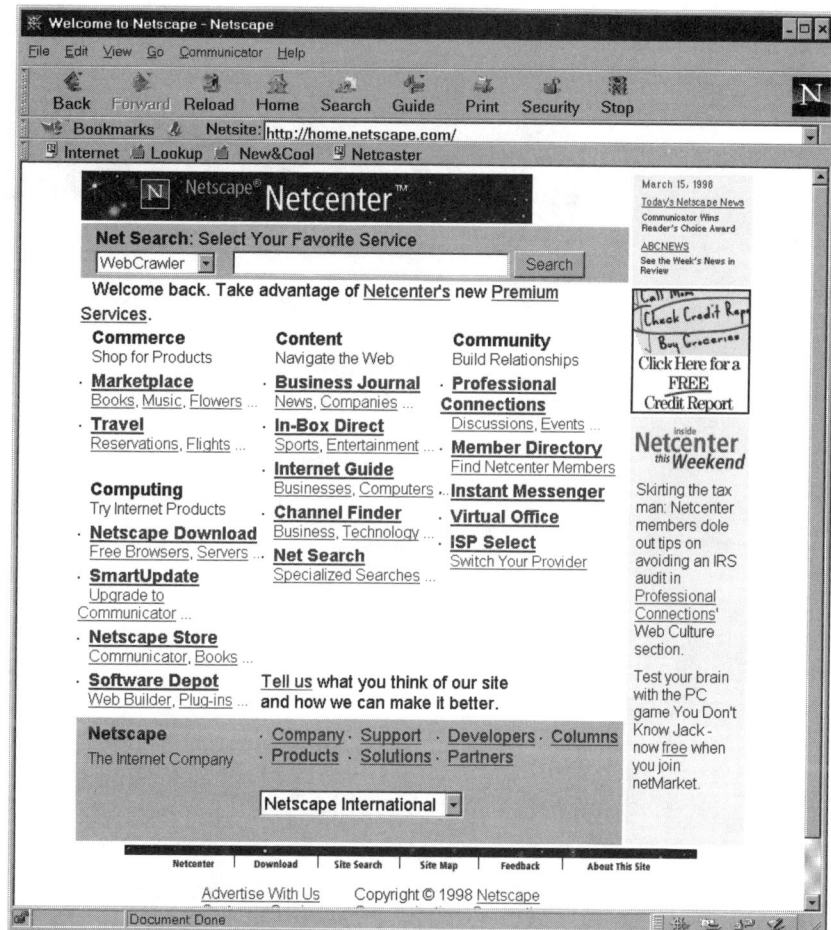

F I G U R E   14.7

Netscape Navigator

Netscape Navigator itself is available by download from www.netscape.com.

Internet Explorer

Microsoft's entry in the browser scene, Internet Explorer, offers the same functionality as Netscape Navigator (see Figure 14.8).

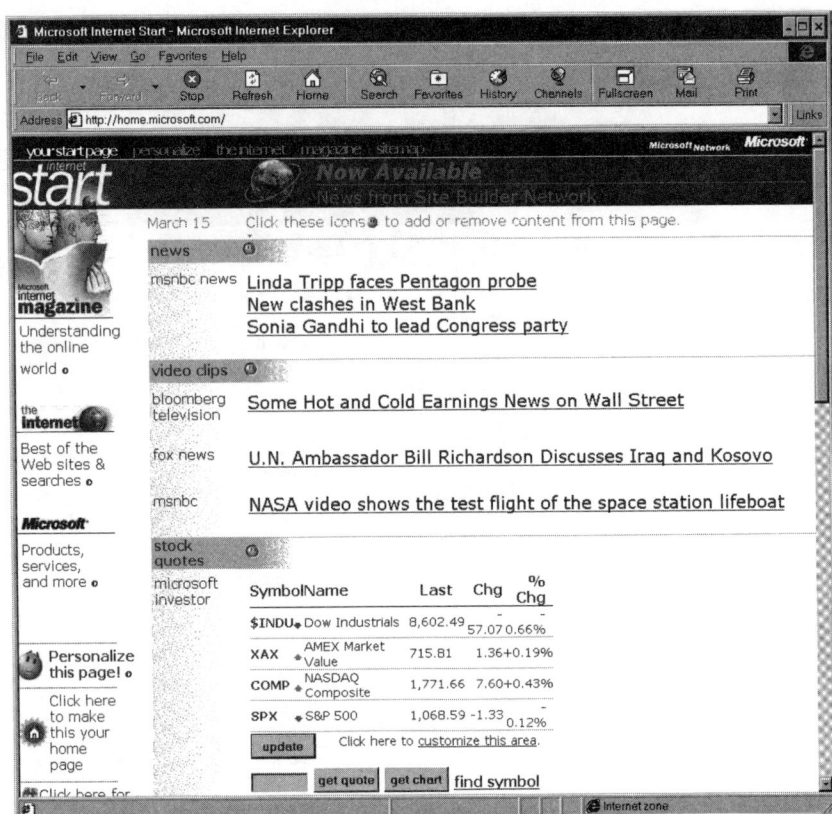

One preeminent feature of Internet Explorer that is lacking in other browsers is the OLE HTML viewer, which can be used by other applications to display HTML-format and ActiveX documents and, of course, to support rudimentary navigation and hyperlink features through established network connections. Internet Explorer also offers support for ActiveX controls that are not recognized by other browsers.

Microsoft Internet Explorer is distributed bundled with all current versions of the Windows operating system and with some developer products. Updates are available from http://www.microsoft.com/ie.

Opera

While less well known than Netscape Navigator or Internet Explorer, Opera is an increasingly strong contender with growing popularity for several reasons. While not as feature-heavy as either Netscape or Internet Explorer, Opera is also a very compact browser—on the order of one-tenth the size of either of its competitors—and capable of offering service on any platform from an archaic 80286 with 4MB of RAM up to the newest and fastest Pentium/K6/WinChip systems. The Opera browser appears in Figure 14.9.

FIGURE 14.9

Opera

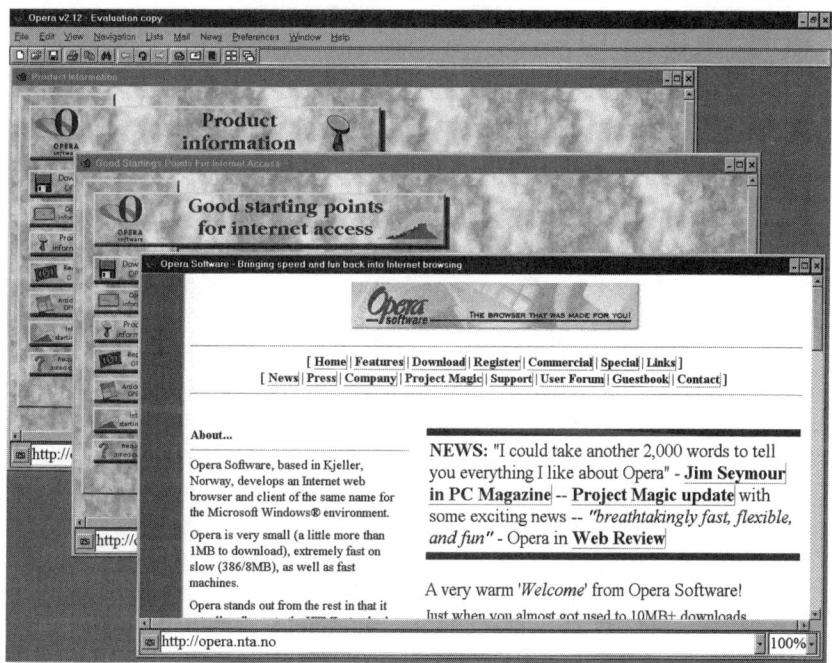

Saying that Opera is not as feature heavy as its competitors, however, is not intended to suggest that Opera is not a capable browser, because it does provide full Web access. One of the features of Opera, however, is that it has options to turn off some of the bells and whistles that Web-page designers seem so enamored of.

For example, animation on the Web may be a nice way to add flashing lights, dancing babies, and marquee banners, but not everyone appreciates these bits of flash and glitter while looking for information. Opera offers an option to simply disable animation.

Other options controlling presentations, including being able to turn off video presentations, sound clips, automatic loading for images, and documents and frames. If you're using the Web for serious research, disabling a few of these options can not only reduce clutter but speed up operations by not wasting time on downloading frills. (This can be done in IE 4.0 as well but not as conveniently.)

Also, where other browsers depend on opening multiple copies of the browser to display multiple Web pages, Opera, as shown in Figure 14.9, supports multiple windows within a single application frame.

Evaluation copies of Opera can be downloaded from `opera.nta.no` (Norway).

HTML and URLs

Even in the old days of text-based bulletin boards and commercial BBS services, a lot of effort went into primitive graphics (using graphic characters), colored text, and formatted presentations. For the World Wide Web, where information was to be presented not just on DOS ASCII platforms but across a variety of platforms, almost all of which were using graphic environments, a new approach was required—something going beyond simple text formats.

At the same time, there was also a need for a method to support navigation to make it possible for users to get from one place to another.

For text-based BBS pages, the standard method of identifying and activating links was to use hot-keys: single characters that were highlighted in labels (or placed in parentheses or underlined) and were recognized by the BBS as instructions. In effect, BBS operations were driven by a series of menu operations.

But, again for a graphic environment, something better and more flexible was needed. The solutions, eventually, were twofold: the introduction of the Hypertext Markup Language (HTML) and Uniform Resource Locators (URLs).

HTML

HTML is the lingua franca for Web-based publishing. As a non-proprietary format, HTML documents can be created using anything from simple plain-text editors to sophisticated WYSIWYG document development tools. In either form, HTML depends on tags such as <h1> and </h1> (header level 1 and end header level 1, respectively) to specify text structures to be applied to headers, paragraphs, lists, hypertext links, and anything else one may expect to find on a Web page.

The HTML standard is implemented as a Document Type Definition (DTD) in Standard Generalized Markup Language (SGML), which is a system for specifying grammars in a document.

SGML does not, in itself, define any formatting conventions but, instead, permits text to be tagged structurally. Documents are used only with a DTD that defines a style sheet or a series of allowable structure elements in a document. In general, SGML text (see the sample following) resembles an off-line formatting language such as RTF (rich text format) where the plain ASCII text contains format instructions which only appear as formatting when the document is replayed.

A sample HTML text file is shown following:

```
<HTML>
<HEAD>
    <META HTTP-EQUIV="Content-Type" CONTENT="text/html;
charset=iso-8859-1">
    <META NAME="Generator" CONTENT="Microsoft Word 97">
    <META NAME="GENERATOR" CONTENT="Mozilla/4.03 [en]
(Win95; U) [Netscape]">
    <META NAME="Author" CONTENT="Ben Ezzell">
    <TITLE>It's got a beat, you can dance to it</TITLE>
</HEAD>
```

The first line identifies the file as a hypertext source file and is followed by the file header which, among other things, identifies the ISO standard providing the basis for the HTML format, the composition engine used to create the file, the author, the file title, the platform (operating system), and the preferred browser.

All of this detail, of course, is optional and most of it was supplied automatically by Netscape Composer and by Microsoft Word (both of which were used when editing the HTML document).

Notice particularly that the header section is identified by the <HEAD> instruction and terminated by </HEAD>.

With the header out of the way, the next instruction sets the background for the page which, in this case, uses a JPEG image called whimarbbg—shorthand for "white marble backgound."

```
<BODY BACKGROUND="Whimarbbg.jpeg">
<FONT SIZE=-1> It's got a beat, you can dance to it ...</
FONT>
```

The <FONT SIZE=-1> instruction says to reduce font size by one step while the terminating </FONT> cancels the previous setting. In the following instructions, the first instruction says to center everything, use bold face (<B>), and increase font size by one.

```
<CENTER><B><FONT SIZE=+1>Computer Rhymes -- a la mode Dr.
Seuss</FONT></B></CENTER>
```

At the end of the line, the instructions are canceled and then new instructions are issued on the next line.

```
<CENTER><FONT SIZE=-1>(anonymous)</CENTER>
```

This time, the reduce font size instruction is not canceled and remains in effect for the rest of the page. The next line begins with a paragraph break <P> while subsequent lines begin with break instructions <BR>.

```
<P> Here's an easy game to play,
<BR> Here's an easy thing to say:

<P> When a packet hits a pocket on a socket on a port,
<BR> And the buss is interrupted as a very last resort,
<BR> And the address of the memory makes your floppy disk
abort,
<BR> Then the socket packet pocket has an error to report.

<P> When your cursor finds a menu item, followed by a dash,
<BR> And the double-clicking icon puts your window in the
trash,
<BR> And your data is corrupted 'cause the index doesn't hash,
<BR> Then your situation's hopeless 'cause your system's
gonna crash!
```

Blank lines in the text—even without the <BR> break instruction—still appear as breaks in the formatted text.

```
<P> You can't say this?
<BR> What a shame, sir!
<BR> We'll find you
<BR> Another game, sir.
```

The indenting in this sample—consisting of repeated   (non-breaking space) codes—has been removed for simplicity.

```
<P> If the label on the cable on the table at your house
<BR> Says the network is connected to the button on your mouse,
<BR> But your packets want to tunnel on another protocol
<BR> That's repeatedly rejected by the printer down the hall.
<BR> And your screen is all distorted by the side effects of
gauss,
<BR> So your icons in the window are as wavy as a souse,
<BR> Then you may as well reboot and exit with a bang,
<BR> 'Cause sure as I'm a poet, this sucker's gonna hang!

<P> There's no blame, sir ...
<BR> But it is a shame, sir ...
<BR> Another game, sir?

<P> When the copy of your floppy's getting sloppy on the disk,
<BR> And the microcode instructions cause unnecessary RISC,
<BR> Then you need to flash your memory,
<BR> And you'll want to RAM your ROM
<BR> So - quickly - turn off the computer,
<BR> And run and tell your mom!

<P> Did it fry, sir?
<BR> Ctrl-Abort-Retry, sir?
<BR> Please don't cry, sir ...
</FONT></BODY></HTML>
```

Last, at the end of the file, the standing reduce font instruction is canceled, the end of the body of the file is identified, and the end of the HTML text is specified.

As shown in the example preceding, HTML formatting commands always occur in pairs with the first code turning on a formatting instruction and the second ending it. A selection of common HTML formatting commands (tags) are listed in table 14.4.

T A B L E 14.4: Selected HTML Formatting Tags

HTML Tag	Meaning
A	An anchor marks the beginning of a hyperlink. Following the A tag is usually a qualifier, such as HREF, which is a reference to another document. The NAME attribute allows an anchor to itself serve as the destination of a hyperlink.
B	Boldface
BR	Line break
DT, DD	Glossary entries used to indicate a list of definitions. DT is the "term" and DD is the "definition." These are often used just to show lists.
H1, H2, H3, H4, H5, H6	HTML supports six levels of headings implying a change in font and/or emphasis, as in the sections of a document. For example, H1 is usually a large bold font, centered across a line.
I	Italic
IMG	Inline graphic displayed by the client. The standards call for GIF files (but are not limited to GIF format images) while the SRC attribute indicates the location of the graphic.
P	Marks a new paragraph
TITLE	Document title which is displayed by the client prominently
U	Underline
UL, OL, DIR	Defines a list, which is a sequence of paragraphs. There are several types of list items, each with a different suggested display. UL is generally a bulleted list. OL is generally a numbered list. DIR is a list of short elements, perhaps used to display the results of an FTP directory listing.

While it is possible to create formatted HTML text using a plain-vanilla editor, it's also a lot easier if you use a HTML editor. At the same time, finding an HTML editor usually requires looking no further than your Web browser since most contemporary browsers and many word processors incorporate HTML editor/composer features.

On the other hand, if you are doing extensive HTML editing, it may be worthwhile investing in a WYSIWYG composition package such as Microsoft FrontPage.

The same HTML file, as presented by an HTML browser, appears in Figure 14.10.

FIGURE 14.10

It's got a beat, you can dance to it!

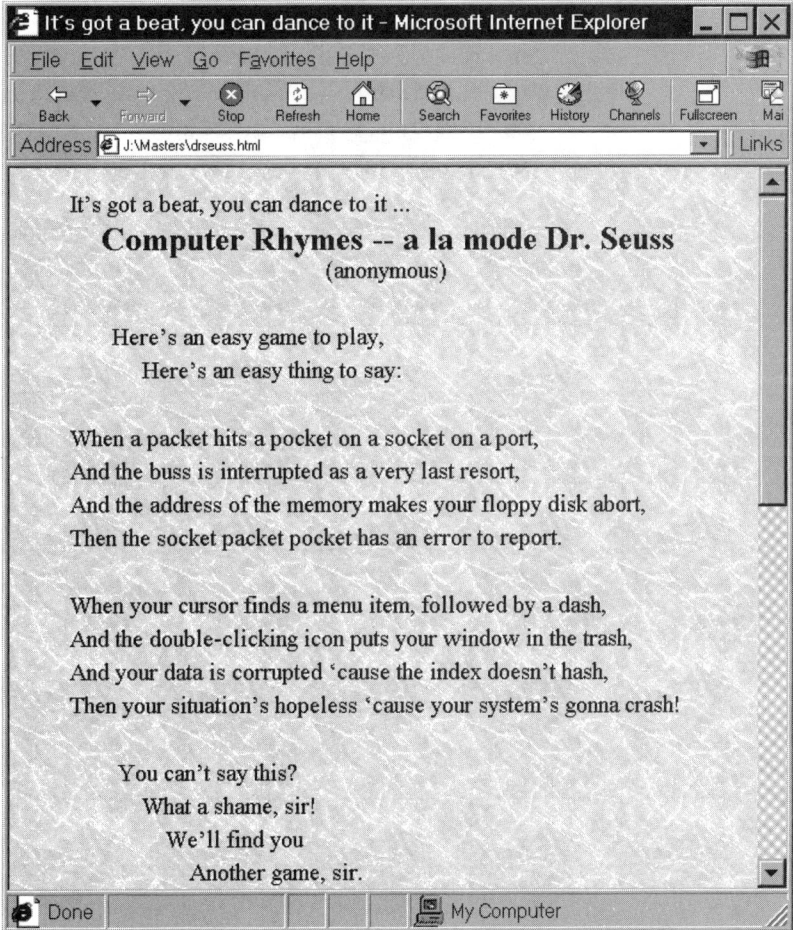

More information on HTML language standards, including HTML 3.2 and 4.0 can be found at www.w3.org. W3C is hosted by the Laboratory for Computer Science at MIT, by INRIA and Keio University with support from DARPA and the European Commission.

URLs

Where text-based BBSs depended on hotkey assignments for link operations, a graphic, hypertext environment demands a more sophisticated method both for identifying link points in the presentation and, most importantly, for identifying the places (locations) linked.

On a BBS, this was a relatively simple matter since the link locations were always local, within the confines of the BBS and its local drives. On the Internet, however, the location of any given link may be virtually anywhere in cyperspace.

To satisfy the demands of the Web, Uniform Resource Locators (URLs) were designed to refer to globally available information. In essence, URLs are simply extensions of conventional drive/path/filename specifications. After all, URLs are simply identifiers for files. There are, of course, a few differences.

Where fully qualified path/filenames customarily begin with a drive designation, URLs begin with an identifier for the retrieval method that should be used to reach the file. Following the retrieval method is a host domain name identifying the physical (cyberspace) location where the file (or other source) is located. The remainder of the URL is (usually) the pathname of the document together with any retrieval options that may be necessary (such as an account name, if required, and a password).

The URL convention does not define how the client operating system or browser should transform the URL reference into an object. The actual conversion/retrieval is left to the implementor.

The most common retrieval schemes used in URLs appear in Table 14.5.

T A B L E 14.5: URL Retrieval Schemas

Retrieval Schema	Description
FTP	The domain name is followed by a path specification giving the document or directory to be retrieved using the FTP protocol—for example: `ftp://www.`*server-name*`.net/`*filename*`.zip`
Gopher*	The domain name is followed by a valid Gopher selector to be used to retrieve a document or directory from a Gopher server—for example: `gopher://gopher.banzai.edu:1234/` where 1234 identifies the gopher port number.
FILE	The domain name is followed by any subdirectory information and the name of a file for retrieval by anonymous FTP or from the local computer—for example: `file://ftp.foobar.com/pub/files/foobar.txt`
HTTP	The domain name is followed by a full path specification to an HTML document to be retrieved using the HTTP protocol—for example: `http://www.ezzell.org/Buddy/Buddy.html`.
NEWS	For a news group link, the identifier is followed simply by the name of the UseNet news group—for example: `news:rec.fishing`
MAILTO	In place of a domain name, the string specifies a full Internet mail address. Normally, the browser will call the user's e-mail application, passing the mail address to create an e-mail message—for example: `mailto:ben@ezzell.org`
TELNET*	The domain name is followed by an optional user name and password to establish an interactive session using TELNET.
WAIS*	The domain name is followed by a path to a WAIS server along with fields used to retrieve a document from a WAIS full-text index.

* Gopher, TELNET, and WAIS retrievals are rarely used today but do still exist as URL retrieval schema.

The HTML source fragment following incorporates several URL specifications including one `mailto:` and five `http:` links. (The retrieval identifiers appear in bold for your convenience.)

```
<HTML>
<HEAD>
   <META HTTP-EQUIV="Content-Type" CONTENT="text/html;
charset=iso-8859-1">
```

```
    <META NAME="GENERATOR" CONTENT="Mozilla/4.03 [en] (Win95;
U) [Netscape]">
    <TITLE>Ben Ezzell; Author; Writer; Buddy, Can You Spare A
Crime; Handcrafted Murder; The Homeless Detective Agency; A
Warlock's Words; A Death In Memory; Mystery</TITLE>
</HEAD>
<BODY BACKGROUND="whimarbbg.jpeg">
<IMG SRC="Count.cgi" >

<P><LINK rev="owner" href="mailto:ben@ezzell.org">
<CENTER><BI>Fictional titles offered on-line.</CENTER>

<CENTER>Copyright (c) 1997 by Ben Ezzell.</BI></CENTER>

<CENTER><IMG SRC="bookendl.gif" HEIGHT=204 WIDTH=108>
<A HREF="http://www.ezzell.org/Buddy/Buddy.html">
<IMG SRC="buddy.gif" ALT="Buddy, Can You Spare A Crime"
BORDER=0 HEIGHT=220 WIDTH=41></A>
```

The link identified here is attached to a graphic image (BUDDY.GIF) and includes an alternate text label ("Buddy, Can You Spare A Crime") for systems that do not support graphics or where the graphics are turned off.

```
<A HREF="http://www.ezzell.org/Handcrafted/
Handcrafted.html">
<IMG SRC="handcrafted.gif" ALT="Handcrafted Murder" BORDER=0
HEIGHT=224 WIDTH=42></A>
<A HREF="http://www.ezzell.org/Memory/Prelude.html">
<IMG SRC="memory.gif" ALT="A Death In Memory" BORDER=0
HEIGHT=220 WIDTH =41></A>
<A HREF="http://www.ezzell.org/Warlock/Warlock_01.html">
<IMG SRC="warlock.gif" ALT="A Warlock's Words" BORDER=0
HEIGHT=220 WIDTH=41></A>
<A HREF="http://www.ezzell.org/Homeless/Homeless.html">
<IMG SRC="homeless.gif" ALT="The Homeless Detective Agency"
BORDER=0 HEIGHT=220 WIDTH=61></A>
<IMG SRC="bookendr.gif" HEIGHT=204 WIDTH=108></CENTER>
```

The graphics created by the preceding instructions are illustrated in Figure 14.11, following.

F I G U R E   14.11

Graphic images used
as URL links

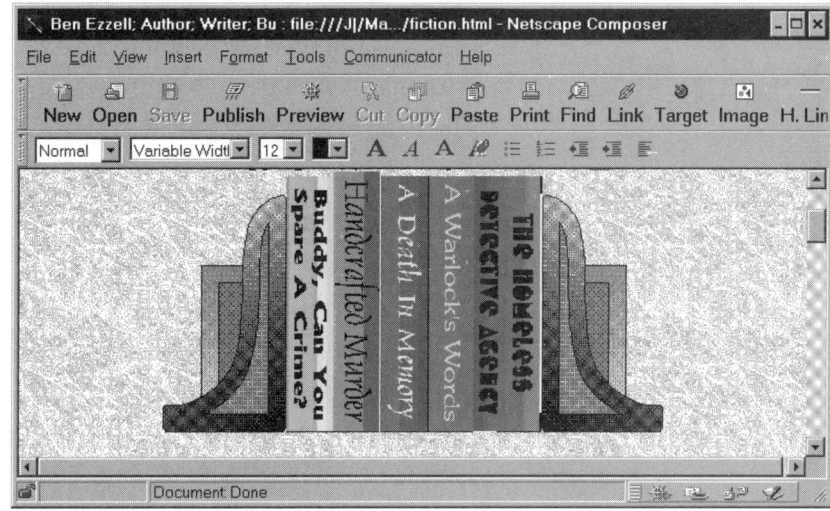

F I G U R E   14.11

Graphic images used
as URL links

Partial URLs

Partial URLs are used to point to other files which exist on the same server
and in the same directory. For example, suppose that a link in an HTML
document is intended to point to another file named EXPERIENCE.HTML.
Instead of providing a fully qualified link as:

```
<A HREF="http://www.foobar.net/experience.html">Experience</A>
```

since the document file is located in the same directory on the same server,
the simpler partial URL format can be used as:

```
<A HREF="experience.html">Experience</A>
```

In brief, as long as the documents are found in the same directory, a partial URL can be used in place of a fully qualified URL. This is particularly
convenient when developing a hypertext document on a local system which
will later be moved to a server for use.

For example, during development, the fully qualified link format might be:

```
<A HREF="http://d:\working doc\experience.html">Experience</A>
```

but this would have to be revised—along with all other links—before
moving the files to the server. Instead, using partial links, no revisions would
be required, and fewer errors would be found afterwards.

Once the HTML source is on the server system and accessed from there, the partial link is sufficient to reach any other files in the same directory. This is because the additional information (access method, hostname, port number, directory name, etc.) will simply be assumed based on the URL used to reach the first document.

More information on URLs can be found at: `www.w3.org/Addressing/Addressing.html`.

Web-Page Design Utilities

Coding HTML pages by hand can be a tedious process, so a variety of HTML editors are available, some commercial and others as shareware. For a full list of available utilities, try using any of the search engines recommended earlier.

Summary

The Internet is a collection of networks linked through the Transport Control Protocol/Interface Program (TCP/IP) protocol suite. Originating in the 1960s as ARPANet to connect research and university sites, the Internet today is as ubiquitous as the phone system, connecting millions, both domestically and internationally.

The Internet is supported by all types of computer systems but depends on a standardized set of protocols. Internet standards are proposed in documents known as RFCs.

The TCP/IP protocol suite provides layers defining functionalities to free developers from concerns with the hardware implementations required for Internet operations. The link layer in TCP/IP handles the network card and dial-up modem interfaces using Serial Line Internet Protocol (SLIP) and Point-to-Point Protocol (PPP).

For human convenience, Internet domain and e-mail addresses are based on domain names which identify top-level and second-level domains while 32-bit globally-unique IP addresses are used for the computer's purposes. The DNS (domain name system) provides the translations between the human-friendly domain names and the 32-bit IP addresses.

A variety of top-level domain names are in use today, including a series of country codes consisting of two-letter identifiers for individual countries.

The transport layer in TCP/IP is responsible for regulating data flow between networked machines and relies on two protocols: TCP and UDP.

The application layer consists of both protocols, services, and applications such as browsers which provide the means for users to access and browse (surf) the Internet.

The FTP or File Transfer Protocol is one of the application level protocols used widely for managing file transfers between computers. The FTP.EXE utility supplied with Windows systems offers command-line FTP operations but GUI-based FTP utilities such as WS-FTP offer much more popular and convenient capabilities.

While historical utilities such as Archie and Gopher were used to search the Internet for documents in the days when the Net was much smaller, today a wide variety of search engines—some generalized and other specialized—provide search services that extend far beyond the capabilities of the early Gopher and Archie utilities.

Finally, the popularity of the Internet today is produced in large part by three elements: Internet browsers such as Netscape Navigator or Internet Explorer, Hypertext Markup Language, which allows documents to be displayed across a wide variety of systems, and URLs, which provide the basis for hyperlinks between sites and documents.

Review Questions

1. The original Internet (the ARPANET) was created for what purpose?

   A. To facilitate communications between research facilities

   B. To maintain a high state of military readiness during the Cold War

   C. To share records between IRS offices

   D. All of the above

2. What is File Transfer Protocol used for?

   A. To copy files from one Internet machine to another

   B. To copy HTML files to client systems for display

   C. To provide a protocol for distributed document navigation and retrieval

   D. To provide transparent file access across Internet clients

3. What is the primary communication standard used on the Internet?

   A. Distributed Communication Procedures (DCP)

   B. Point-to-Point Protocol (PPP)

   C. Remote Computer Calls (RCC)

   D. Transmission Control Protocol / Internet Protocol (TCP/IP)

4. The link layer in TCP/IP is associated with which of the following? (Select all that apply.)

   A. Creating transmission handshaking protocols

   B. Interfacing with a network card or modem

   C. Resolving Internet address identifiers

   D. Transferring data packets to the physical network

5. An Internet domain name consists of which of the following? (Select all that apply.)

   A. A 32-bit globally unique address

   B. A primary domain name

   C. A secondary domain name

   D. A user name

6. The TCP/IP protocol stack consists of which four layers?

   A. Application, browser, e-mail, and network/internetwork layers

   B. Application, transport, network/internetwork, and link/network access layers

    C. Protocol, e-mail, FTP, and FileNet layers

    D. Transport, DNS, Windows Sockets, and serial-line/dial-up layers

7. Which of the following is true of globally unique 32-bit Internet addresses? (Select all that apply.)

    A. They are created by local network administrators.

    B. They are encoded versions of the top-level and secondary domain address names.

    C. They consist of four hex values in the range 0..0×FFFF.

    D. They consist of four numeric fields with values in the range 0..255.

8. Internet standards are proposed in what documents?

    A. Interdependent System Developments (ISD)

    B. Internet Standards Document (ISD)

    C. Request For Comment (RFC)

    D. Requirements For Communications (RFC)

9. The transport protocol layer regulates the data flow between networked machines using which protocol? (Select all that apply.)

    A. Packet Transmission Protocol (PTP)

    B. Secure Data Transmission Protocol (SDTP)

    C. Transmission Control Protocol (TCP)

    D. User Datagram Protocol (UDP)

10. Which of the following is true of the application layer? (Select all that apply.)

    A. It consists of external applications called through TCP/IP protocols.

    B. It has been superseded in part by Web-based services.

    C. It implements GUI services for the Web.

    D. It refers to protocols built at the application layer of the TCP/IP suite.

11. The Domain Name System (DNS) is:

    A. A distributed database used to map domain names to IP addresses

    B. A group of servers providing routing services for Internet connections

    C. A host system providing addressing services for Internet connections

    D. A protocol for translating IP addresses to top-level and second-level domain names

12. Universal Resource Locators (URLs) may contain which of the following? (Select all that apply.)

    A. Account names and passwords

    B. Directory and filenames

    C. File transfer retrieval schemas

    D. Host domain names

    E. Protocol to be used

13. The User Datagram Protocol (UDP) relies on which of the following?

    A. Application-supplied data validation

    B. Auto-correcting data streams

    C. Checksum data validation

    D. Reliable connections between networks

14. Post Office Protocol (POP 2 & 3) provides:

    A. A means for identifying and locating e-mail users

    B. A protocol for displaying electronic mail on a client system

    C. A protocol for managing electronic mail using store and forward

    D. A protocol to translate e-mail addresses to IP addresses

15. Transmission Control Protocol (TCP) relies on which of the following? (Select all that apply.)

   A. Application-supplied data validation protocols

   B. Automatic line condition monitoring

   C. Packet identifier and checksum values

   D. Tolerance for unreliable link conditions using packet-oriented protocol

16. Registration for second-level domain names is handled by which of the following?

   A. American Registration Internet Networks (`arin.net`)

   B. International Domain Registrars (`registrars.net`)

   C. International Registration Services (`registration.net`)

   D. Internet Network Information Center (InterNIC)

17. Network File System (NFS) is used for which of the following?

   A. To copy files from one Internet machine to another

   B. To copy HTML files to client systems for display

   C. To provide a protocol for distributed document navigation and retrieval

   D. To provide transparent file access across Internet clients

18. Simple Mail Transfer Protocol (SMTP) establishes which of the following?

   A. A means for identifying and locating e-mail users

   B. A protocol for displaying electronic mail on a client system

   C. A protocol for the exchange of electronic mail between two message transfer agents (MTAs) on the Internet

   D. A protocol to translate e-mail addresses to IP addresses

19. FTP (File Transfer Protocol) connections using the Open command can supply arguments as which of the following? (Select all that apply.)

A. 32-bit IP addresses

B. Partial URLs

C. Top-level, second-level domain names

D. All of the above

20. Anonymous FTP logins commonly request e-mail addresses as password arguments. This information may be used to do which of the following? (Select all that apply.)

A. To build e-mail name/address lists

B. To maintain a connections log

C. To parse and resolve domain names to identify the location where the request originates

D. To track downloads for commercial or competitive purposes

21. What does Simple Network Management Protocol (SNMP) offer?

A. A protocol for distributed hypertext document searching, navigation, and retrieval

B. A protocol for remote administration of TCP/IP machines

C. A protocol for transferring files between machines

D. A protocol to address remote systems

22. File Transfer Protocol (FTP) supports which transfer modes? (Select all that apply.)

A. ASCII

B. Binary

C. Compressed

D. Graphic

23. In order to find a location on the Internet for a file, service, or topic, what is the appropriate mechanism to use?

A. Any of a variety of Web-based search engines

B. Archie to catalog anonymous FTP servers

C. GOPHERSPACE for distributed document search and retrieval

D. VERONICA for an indexed search to gopherspace

24. Hypertext Markup Language (HTML) is a method providing which of the following?

A. An extension of the Standard Generalized Markup Language (SGML)

B. Format tags defining how documents should be presented

C. Hotkey links between files and file locations

D. Support for JPEG and GIF image formats

25. According to HTML standards, lists are supported as which of the following? (Select all that apply.)

A. A sequence of paragraphs

B. Automatically by indented paragraph levels

C. Bulleted list items using the UL tag

D. Numbered list items using the OL tag

26. In which of the following cases can a partial URL be used?

A. When the file referenced is located on the same server and directory as the document containing the URL

B. When the link is referring to a graphic image

C. When a fully-qualified URL is too long to fit

D. When the file or document referenced is located on the local (client) system

27. Which of the following is true of tags defined in the HTML language structure?

A. They are defined in the HTML 3.2 and 4.0 language standards.

B. They can be user defined.

C. They must always consist of begin and end codes.

D. They must always use begin and end codes for format instructions.

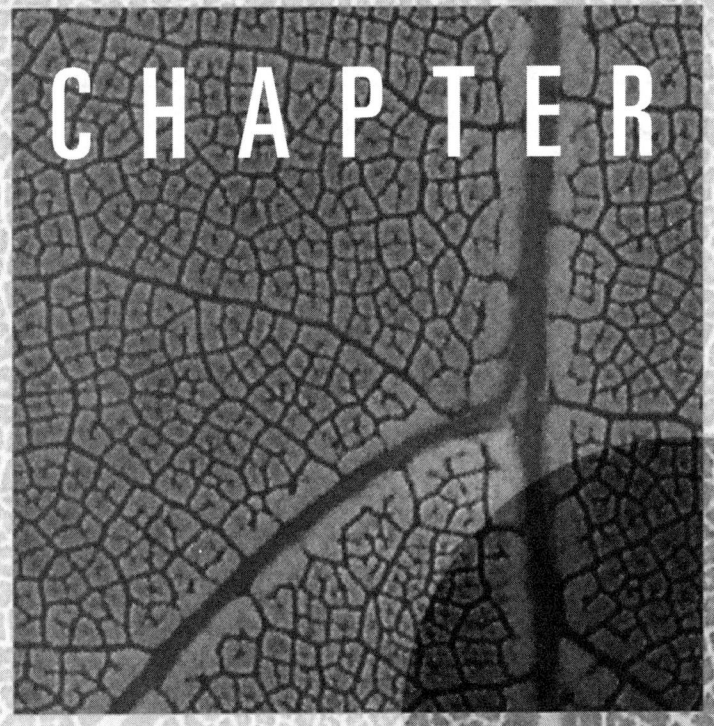

CHAPTER

15

Internet and Intranet Design Content

Microsoft Exam Objectives Covered in This Chapter:

- Choose an appropriate design for content for an intranet or for the Internet, based on bandwidth and latency considerations.

When we place a telephone call to another party, we expect a dedicated connection—that our call has a single service connection devoted to our conversation. In actual fact, of course, particularly on a long distance call, our 'dedicated' connection is being broken, frequency-shifted, switched, shared across a multi-message trunk line, and is anything but private, dedicated, or one-to-one. Still, the fact that it appears to be a dedicated connection is all that's really relevant to us.

And, for a telephone conversation, if the circuits become overloaded, then the system simply stops accepting additional connections. Existing connections, except in rare cases, do not see any degradation of service.

In the good old days of computer bulletin boards, our dial-up connections saw a similar 'steady-state' service. We would dial in to a modem over a dedicated line and, as long as there was a modem free to answer, we would receive a one-to-one connection with the system.

On the Internet and on intranets however, the situation is not quite so simple, and all network traffic is subject to limitations that are not outwardly obvious, even though their effects may be readily apparent.

Routine traffic, where two computers are exchanging information without immediately presenting any of it to a user/observer, generally conceals any delays or slowdowns in transmission simply because the protocols used allow for variations in link quality and are patient about continuing until the task is completed. This does not, of course, excuse poor connections—but it does make variations somewhat more tolerable.

When eternally impatient humans enter the equation, however, delays and poor link qualities become much more immediate.

None of this, however, excuses ignoring appropriate considerations in creating either Internet or intranet content. To understand why, however, we need to look first at how both intranet and Internet connections function.

The Nature of Internet and Intranet Connections

Basically, to reach the Internet, one of three scenarios apply: You are either dialing in to an ISP (Internet Service Provider) connected to a network with an Internet connection; or, for an intranet scenario, you are connected to a local area network with links to other local systems, or links to remote systems as well.

In each of these situations, there are limitations on the service.

In the first scenario, a dial-up link to an ISP, you might assume that the dial-up connection itself is the primary limiting factor and, in some cases, this could be correct. Very often, however, even though you may have a 56K connection to your local ISP's server, attempts to reach remote sites may be exhibiting transfer rates which are a small fraction of the theoretical baud rate supported by the immediate link. This factor is called *bandwidth*—a measure of the amount of traffic which a link can handle.

Figure 15.1 illustrates a connection with four links between the client application/system and the remote service provider.

FIGURE 15.1

How bandwidth can vary between links

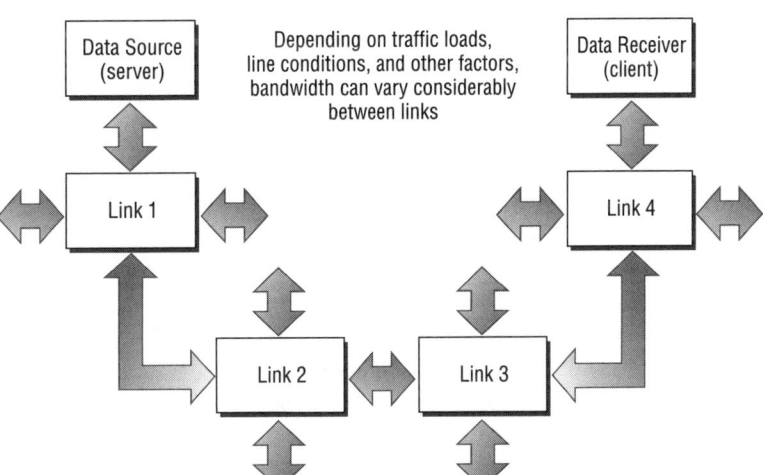

The illustration suggests a condition in which several links are providing services and connections to a variety of other links, clients, and servers even though only the immediate chain—from the remote service to the client application—is shown in full. Between these two end points, four link servers are involved in the traffic while the connections between links vary according to traffic loads, line conditions, and a variety of other factors.

In actual fact, this is a simplification since there probably won't be any single connection. Instead, traffic between the two sites could be following quite different paths at different times. But, regardless of the precise path, the point remains the same: limitations can occur anywhere along a path and may not be limited to the immediate connection to the ISP's server.

For a local network or an intranet, the paths may be simpler and more easily defined, but there still may be limits on the traffic which the connections can handle.

Bandwidth is simply the amount of data which, at any given time, can be transferred between two links. The available bandwidth can be affected by line conditions and equipment capabilities. In any case, the bandwidth of a system is a commodity that is virtually always shared among multiple clients.

On the Internet, the effective bandwidth can vary widely according to the demands of other traffic. Actually, rather than talking about bandwidth, it's more to the point to speak of the speed of the Net or about usage percentages.

Figure 15.2 shows a usage report from a local ISP (Sonoma Interconnect, a.k.a. `sonic.net`) as a graph for the past twenty-four hours.

Figure 15.3 charts speed rather than usage and shows traffic indexes internationally for a twenty-four hour and a one week period.

Naturally, both usage and overall speed are beyond our control but they are worth being aware of.

A second factor in both intranet and Internet communications is called *latency*. Latency is defined as the time that elapses between a request for data being issued and the data being received.

For a floppy drive, a hard drive, or a CD, latency is largely determined by mechanical factors. Latency also applies to intranet and Internet data connections, although in these cases, the factors are not quite so simply quantified.

FIGURE 15.2

Net server usage in a 24-hour period

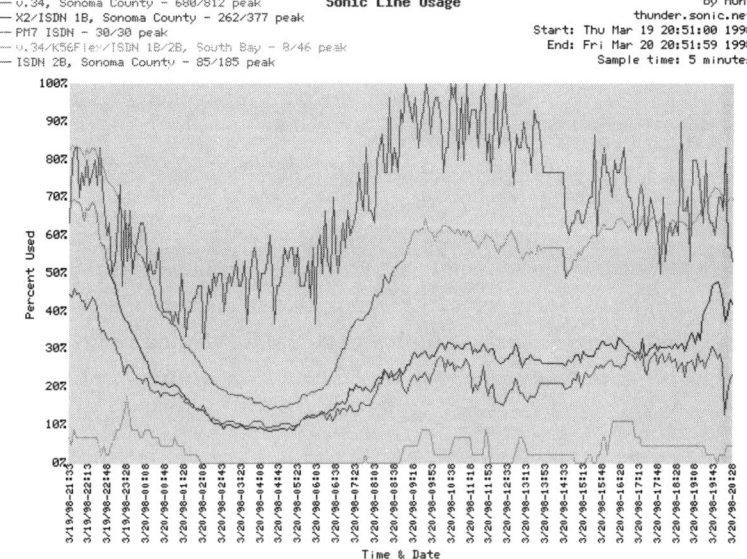

FIGURE 15.3

Internet speeds for a day and week

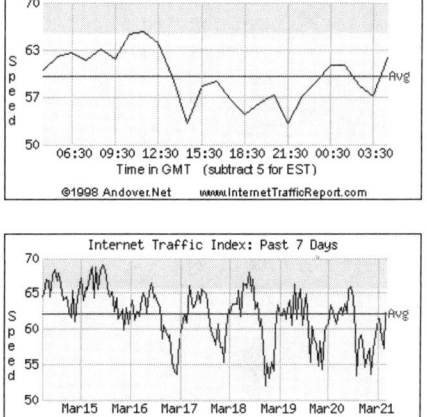

When the considerations are hardware only, latency is measured by the time required for the initial response to the request. The time taken for the requested transfer to be completed, of course, is determined by the bandwidth available and the amount of data.

In network terms, however, latency is measured as the average amount of time required for a data packet to get from the source to the destination. Latency can be affected by transmission delays, queuing delays in network systems, and delays in host protocol stacks.

A third factor which must be taken into account is *jitter*. Jitter is the irregularity in the order in which packets—originally transmitted in sequence—are received. Network data transmissions—in contrast to dedicated line connections—occur as packets of data in which each packet is essentially a separate transmission and must be acknowledged. Unacknowledged packets, presumed lost, are retransmitted with the original data reassembled at the receiving end from multiple packets.

An example of jitter is illustrated in Figure 15.4, where a sequence of nine packets are transmitted in order, but received in a different order.

FIGURE 15.4

Jitter in packet transmission

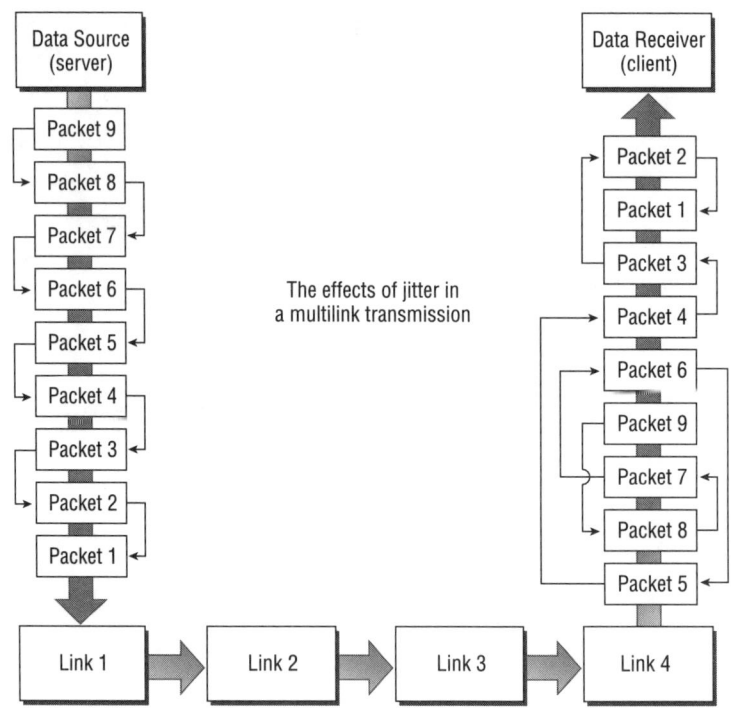

Jitter is most important when real-time multimedia data is involved and it is essential for data packets to arrive in order and on time. For multimedia purposes, jitter must be kept below a certain threshold to avoid dropped packets which produce irritating shrieks and gaps in the call. Jitter, by determining receive buffer sizes, affects latency.

These three factors—bandwidth, latency, and jitter—must all be evaluated in measuring the Quality of Service (QoS) of a network. However, because the QoS of a network is largely beyond our immediate control, when evaluating designs for intranet or Internet content, i.e., Web pages, we must take other factors into consideration.

Designing Web-Page Content

In designing network content—whether it be Web pages for Internet presentation or internal intranet use—one of the primary considerations that should be taken into account, aside from the information actually presented, is how the Web page will be seen by the users. And, most important, by all users, not just those fourteen-year-olds who like anything flashy regardless of how long it takes to load, or by those who have dedicated T1 lines and don't have to wait at all.

Esthetics aside, since we are not talking about color schemes, flash automation, scrolling banners, or garish backgrounds, the complexity of a Web page is one of the biggest factors involved in response time. Every element on a page is essentially a separate file, and the number of files that must be downloaded to complete a Web page is one of the primary factors determining the response time before a page can be viewed.

A second factor, of course, is the number of images and the size of the images on a page. Several small images can be much faster to download than a single large image.

The number of files contained in a Web page and the size of the files are the primary factors determining the time required to download and display the pages. Images, of course, on the basis of size, are one of the primary culprits.

Along with any image, a Web page should *always* supply an alternative text tag for each image. In this fashion, when a user's browser is configured for text-only display or, more often, when the user is still waiting for the images to download, the alternative text tags are displayed.

Also, in consideration of speed, page designers should also minimize the use of both ActiveX controls and Java applets, both of which require time for downloads.

Internet Graphics Formats

When images are used in Web pages, the GIF (Graphic Interchange Format) image format is the de facto standard but is not the only image standard in use. Both the JPEG (Joint Photographic Expert Group) and PNG (Portable Network Graphics) are recognized Internet image formats. These three formats—and their strengths and weaknesses—are described below.

Graphics Interchange Format (GIF)

The Compuserve GIF format was the original graphics format available on the Web and remains the de facto standard. First introduced in the mid-1980s, the GIF format was optimized for the palletized images that were the standards of the period.

Normally, GIF images are either 16 or 256 colors and use either run-length or LZW (Lempel Zev Welch) compression to minimize data size. GIF does not, however, provide support for 24-bit per pixel (i.e., true-color) images.

GIF does support an interlaced mode which offers the appearance of a 'fade-in' as an image is downloaded (see the "Interlaced versus Non-Interlaced Images" section, below).

The GIF image format allows a transparency index where one palette color is assigned to be transparent so that background images will appear through pixels using the transparent color. (Or, more accurately, the background will not be overwritten when the image is drawn.)

Support for GIF images is widely available and most graphics applications as well as Web browsers support the GIF format.

Joint Photographic Experts Group (JPEG)

In contrast to the GIF image format, the JPEG format is optimized for 24-bit photographic images and uses a DCT-based coder to achieve high compression ratios. By comparision, JPEG images can commonly be compressed by 10:1 ratios or higher without introducing visible artifacts on decompression, while GIF images rarely achieve better than 2:1 to 3:1 compression ratios.

JPEG also offers trade-offs on compression, allowing higher compression ratios to be used at the expense of restoration quality. In this fashion, lower compression can be used to preserve fine detail and higher ratios to minimize transmission time. JPEG is not the optimum choice for text or for line art where decompression will typically introduce small but visible artifacts on edge boundaries. Within these limitations, JPEG's superior performance and robust suitability for photographic images have made this the prevailing network image format since the mid-1990s.

Portable Network Graphics (PNG)

The Portable Network Graphics format has evolved as a grassroots effort created by graphics developers on the Internet. The PNG format offers a public, lossless coder with support for both palletized and photographic color images.

PNG is the contemporary replacement for the GIF format and is widely supported by many popular graphics applications. PNG has also been formally recommended by the World Wide Web Consortium (W3C).

Lastly, like GIF, PNG supports a transparency index allowing images to contain transparent areas which do not overwrite background images and also offers a choice between interlaced and non-interlaced formats.

Interlaced versus Non-Interlaced Images

Interlacing is an image format (or sub-format) that supports progressive rendering, allowing an image to be viewed gradually as it is received. The interlaced image is transmitted as alternating scan lines, which means that, when half of the image has been received, the complete image appears with half of the scan lines displayed. The remaining, alternate scan lines are added as the download progresses.

The alternatives are techniques which either display images in pieces or do not display the graphics at all until they are completely downloaded.

In general, users tend to prefer the progressive rendering simply because the image becomes visible more immediately even though the finished image does not appear any faster by interlacing than through any of the alternatives.

The interlaced format is supported by both the GIF and PNG formats.

Image Sizes

While all three of the image formats discussed support image file compression, the compression ratios do vary widely between formats, as shown in Table 15.1.

T A B L E   15.1:   Comparing Compression Ratios

Image Size	274x480 8bpp	%	672x209 8bpp	%	990x612 24bpp	%
Raw Size	131,520 bytes		140,448 bytes		1,817,640 bytes	
GIF	60,594 bytes	46	63,414 bytes	45	360,181 bytes*	59*
JPEG	20,812 bytes	16	22,758 bytes	16	211,309 bytes	12
PNG	54,144 bytes	41	54,158 bytes	38	873,482 bytes	48

* reduced to 8bpp color depth

Overall, the JPEG format provides the best compression ratio for all three image samples, with the PNG format running second. In the case of the largest image, which was also a true-color image using 24-bits per pixel color, the conversion to GIF format required a color reduction from true-color to 256 color format which, consequently, reduces the raw size from 1,817,640 bytes to 605,880 bytes. The compression percentage shown was calculated on the raw size of the reduced color image rather than the raw size of the original image.

Images should always be sized to the minimum size that can be displayed. While HTML does allow entering a size specification to reduce image sizes, downloading a larger file than is actually required simply slows connections.

Web Browsers and Optimizations

Most people today are familiar with one or more Web browsers. Depending on your individual preference, you may be using Microsoft Internet Explorer, Netscape Navigator or Communicator, Opera Software's Opera browser, or some other browser.

Given this assumption, it's also only reasonable to assume that you are familiar with how to follow links on the Net and how to enter a URL if necessary. Likewise, you should be familiar with the fact that browsers create temporary caches as files on your hard drive for the Web pages you have visited and any browser will allow you to use the forward and back arrows to step through these stored pages and graphics.

A client log file is used to store locations for previously visited sites.

When stepping through stored pages, however, you should be aware that the material being viewed is, by default, a locally stored version of the Web page and the material does not reflect changes which may have occurred to the Web site since the page was downloaded. If you would prefer, most browsers can be configured to automatically refresh pages each time they are accessed.

Configuring Web-Page Refresh Options

Internet Explorer can be configured to automatically refresh Web pages rather than using cached copy.

1. For Internet Explorer (version 4.0), begin by selecting the Internet Options selection from the View menu.

2. On the General tab, under Temporary Internet fields, click the Settings button to display the Settings dialog box.

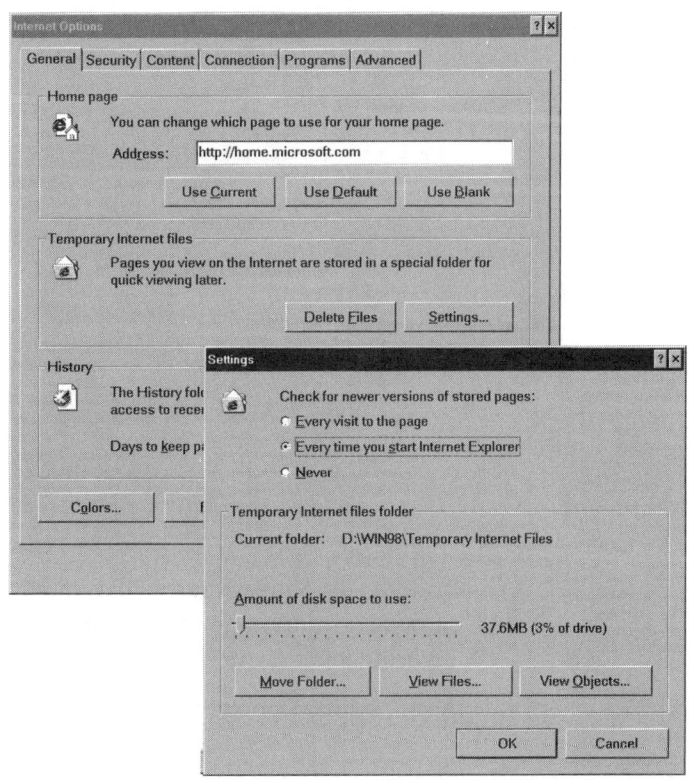

3. Select Every visit to the page to ensure that visited pages will be refreshed from the site on every visit.

Similar options, of course, are found in most Web browsers.

Speed Browsing on the Web

One of the often frustrating elements in browsing the Web is the time required for pages to load; this problem is most often caused by images, animations, and sometimes, videos. To avoid these slowdown elements:

1. Select the Internet Options selection from the View menu (for Internet Explorer 4.0).

2. Select the Advanced tab to display the options shown in Figure 15.6.

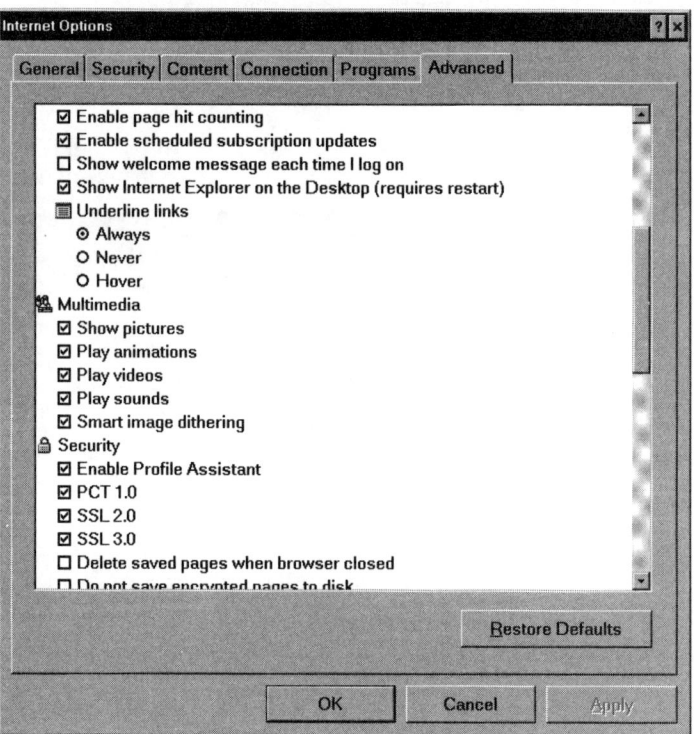

3. Clear the Show pictures, Play animations, Play videos, and Play sounds options, all of which require downloads which can slow browsing.

Again, similar options are found in most Web browsers.

When speed of navigation is a principal consideration, access can be enhanced by disabling the graphics and animation displays (i.e., selecting text only).

Internet Support Services

Windows provides a variety of controls, protocols, and services to support Internet browsing.

- The Internet Transfer control supplies implementation for the two most widely used protocols on the Internet, the Hypertext Transfer Protocol (HTTP), and the File Transfer Protocol (FTP).

  - The FTP protocol permits logging on to FTP servers to download and upload files. The FTP protocol's UserName and Password properties offer the means to log on to private servers requiring authentication, while an anonymous login can be used for other FTP servers. Common FTP commands, such as CD and GET are supported through the Execute method. (FTP is covered in more detail in Chapter 14.)

  - The HTTP protocol is used to connect to World Wide Web servers and to retrieve HTML documents. (See Chapter 14.)

Visual Basic (version 5.0) offers the Internet Transfer (ActiveX) control to support both the HTTP and FTP protocols.

- The Network News Transfer Protocol (NNTP) provides newsgroup services over the Internet. The newsgroup services can provide access to electronic bulletin boards such as UseNet, and to automatically distribute postings to subscribers using e-mail.

- The WinSock control is used to create applications which use the Internet to communicate with each other via the UDP and TCP protocols. (See Chapter 14.)

- The WebBrowser control, a.k.a. the HTML ActiveX control, is used by applications such as Visual Basic forms or Visual C++ dialog controls to display HTML pages either from local sources or through Internet connections.

- Microsoft Proxy Server provides the Web Proxy Service and WinSock Proxy Service.

  - The Web Proxy Service offers caching, client authentication, and domain filtering through the WinSock Proxy Service. The caching service is always active and automatically retrieves new Web page versions—when enabled—prior to client requests.

  - The WinSock Proxy Service works with the WinSock API to monitor and control network traffic across the Proxy Server gateway.

Summary

Internet and intranet operations are governed by a different set of considerations than those applied in the old days of bulletin board services. Where BBSs used dedicated connections, the Internet and intranets function on the basis of shared connections between network links. This change makes bandwidth a variable subject to fluctuating load conditions and introduces concerns for latency and for jitter in data transmissions.

At the same time, by moving from text-based displays to graphics displays, the transmission requirements for Web presentations have risen sharply with images, ActiveX controls, and Java applets all contributing to download time requirements.

Also, since graphics are a primary consideration in Web pages—download times not withstanding—three popular image formats are in common use: GIF, JPEG, and PNG.

Of these, GIF images are limited to low-color resolution (16- or 256-color palettes) and offer relatively poor compression ratios. JPEG images provide both high compression ratios and true-color images but are not the optimum choice for line drawings. The newest format, PNG, provides true-color support as well as lower color resolutions but does not provide compression ratios equal to JPEG image formats.

Both GIF and PNG images—in interlaced format—offer the advantage of displaying an image before the image download is completed.

By default, Web browsers download Web pages only once during a session and refer to stored copies for subsequent access. There are options, however, which can enabled browsers to update pages automatically each time a page is accessed. To speed browsing operations, options are also provided in most browsers to disable images, videos, animation, and sounds.

Finally, Internet operations under Windows are supported by a variety of controls, protocols, and services.

Review Questions

1. The Network News Transfer Protocol is used to:

   A. Display HTML pages from either local sources or through Internet connections

   B. Connect to newsgroup services over the Internet

   C. Create applications that use the Internet for intercommunications

   D. Locate headlines and sports scores over the Internet

2. The time required for downloading Web pages can be reduced by:

   A. Employing a Web browser supporting ActiveX controls

   B. Employing a Web browser supporting Java applets

   C. Turning off graphics display by the browser

   D. Turning off security checks by the browser

3. The Internet Transfer control supplies implementation for which of the following? (Select all that apply.)

   A. The WinSock Proxy Service

   B. The File Transfer Protocol (FTP)

   C. The Hypertext Transfer Protocol (HTTP)

   D. The Network News Transfer Protocol (NNTP)

4. Select the file format supported by Web browsers that provides progressive rendering for graphic images.

A. ActiveX compound documents

B. Auto-download files

C. Interlaced files

D. Java files

5. The WebBrowser ActiveX control is used to:

A. Display HTML pages from either local sources or through Internet connections

B. Connect to newsgroup services over the Internet

C. Create applications that use the Internet for intercommunications

D. Locate headlines and sports scores over the Internet

6. When using the Network News Transport Protocol (NNTP) over the Internet, the service most likely to be accessed is:

A. A BBS (bulletin board) service or newsgroup

B. A file download service

C. A Gopher or document location service

D. A World Wide Web service

7. Browsers cache visited Web locations by:

A. Using read-ahead functions to predict which pages will be required next

B. Keeping a list of previously visited URLs

C. Writing temporary files to the local drive

D. Writing temporary files to your IP server

8. Visual Basic (version 5.0) provides a number of Internet-specific ActiveX controls including one which supports both the HTTP and FTP protocols. The control supporting both services is:

A. Internet Protocol control

B. Internet Transfer control

C. WebBrowser control

D. WinSock control

9. Optimum compression ratios for images used in Web pages are provided using:

A. The GIF format

B. The JPEG format

C. The PNG format

D. All of the above

10. While using Internet Explorer, you are alternating between a page listing parts and price information and pages offering detailed descriptions of equipment. How does Internet Explorer determine which pages should be updated when stepping back and forth between cached material?

A. The HTTP protocol checks the date and time stamps for each page accessed, downloading the .HTML file if it is newer than the cached version.

B. The HTTP protocol refers to the CLASS ID for every page and refreshes both text and graphics if the .HTML file is newer than the cached version.

C. Internet Explorer does not update any cached pages unless the Refresh button is clicked.

D. Internet Explorer may be configured to refresh pages when they are accessed a second time during a session.

11. True-color (24-bit-per-pixel) images can be displayed from Web pages using which format(s)? (Select all that apply.)

    A. GIF

    B. JPEG

    C. PNG

    D. All of the above

12. Active caching of frequently visited Web pages is provided by which Microsoft Proxy Server service?

    A. Domain Filtering

    B. Web Proxy Service

    C. Windows NT Challenge/Response Authentication

    D. WinSock Proxy Service

CHAPTER

16

Internet and Intranet Database Connectivity

Microsoft Exam Objectives Covered in This Chapter:

- Use Internet Data Connector (IDC), Active Server Pages (ASP), or Microsoft FrontPage to provide Internet or intranet database connectivity.

Originally, Web pages contained only static content, i.e., content that was prepared in advance by a developer. It is still quite common today for many sites to remain static.

In the static model, a browser uses the Hypertext Transport Protocol (HTTP) to request an HTML file from a Web server. In return, the server sends the requested HTML page to the browser, which handles the formatting and display for the contents. This model does provide ready access to formatted data but is deficient in that it offers only limited interactions—in the form of links to other pages—between the user and the Web server. And, of course, to change the content of a Web page, the page must be manually edited.

Dynamic HTML content, in contrast to the static model, provides varying degrees of interaction between the user and the Web server. Dynamic HTML content is supported by such gateway interfaces as CGI (Common Gateway Interface), ISAPI (Internet Server Application Programming Interface), and others.

Using these various interfaces, browsers (i.e., users) can send HTTP requests to executable applications rather than static HTML files, with the Web server executing the requested application.

On the server side, the called application can read information associated with the request, such as values submitted by filling out an HTML form, parse the information for relevant data, and then generate an HTML page to return to the browser.

The shortcoming of gateway programs is that they are difficult to create and to maintain.

Functionally, gateway programs require a design process that is quite different from HTML files, and gateway programs cannot be integrated into HTML files.

Internet Data Connector (IDC)

IDC (Internet Data Connector) is an interface supplied with IIS (Internet Information Server) that provides a means to support complex data retrieval from ODBC data sources. Together with HTML extension (HTX) services, the IDC/HTX combination is used by Microsoft Internet Information Server to query information from a database and to display the information in a Web page.

For example, using Microsoft Access, assume that a table, form, or query datasheet is saved as Internet Connector files. Microsoft Access creates two files: an Internet Database Connector (.IDC) file and an HTML extension (.HTX) file which, together, are used to generate a Web page displaying current data from the database.

The IDC file contains all necessary information to connect to a specific ODBC (Open Database Connectivity) database source and to execute an SQL statement querying the database. This information includes the data source name and—if required by user-level security on the database—the user name and password necessary for access.

The generated Internet Database Connector file (.IDC) includes a query datasheet, form, or table together with information identifying an ODBC data source name (DSN). The companion HTML extension file (.HTX) provides the information necessary to format and display the query results through a Web browser. The .IDC and .HTX files must have the same filename (but, obviously, different extensions) and must be located in the same directory on the Web server.

To continue the example, using the Northwind sample application provided with Access, saving the Current Product List query datasheet will generate an IDC file—named Current Product List.IDC—as:

```
Datasource:Northwind
Template:Current Product List.htx
SQLStatement:SELECT ⌟
    [Product List].ProductID, [Product List].ProductName
+FROM Products AS [Product List]
+WHERE ((([Product List].Discontinued)=No))
+ORDER BY [Product List].ProductName;
Password:
Username:
```

In the example, the data source and SQL statement appear in bold but neither user name nor password are required for access. However, notice that the .IDC file does contain—as the Template entry—the name of an HTML extension (.HTX) file.

The .HTX file is a template for creating an HTML document and contains field merge codes, which are replaced by values returned when the SQL statement is executed.

Again, using the Northwind sample application, Access generates a .HTX file that looks something like this:

```
<HTML>
<TITLE>Current Product List</TITLE>
<BODY>
<TABLE BORDER=1 BGCOLOR=#ffffff><FONT FACE="Arial"
COLOR=#000000>
<CAPTION><B>Current Product List</B></CAPTION>
<THEAD>
<TR><FONT SIZE=2 FACE="Arial" COLOR=#000000>
<TD>Product ID</TD>
<TD>Product Name</TD>
</TR>
</THEAD>
<TBODY>
<%BeginDetail%>
<TR VALIGN=TOP><TD><%ProductID%><BR></TD>
<TD><%ProductName%></TD><BR>
</FONT></TR>
<%EndDetail%>
</TBODY>
<TFOOT></TFOOT>
</BODY>
</HTML>
```

The heart of the .HTX file is the result set which appears embedded within a <%BeginDetail%>/<%EndDetail%> tag set. Within the Begin/End tags, field names corresponding to the SQL query in the associated .IDC file appear in the form <%fieldname%>. These key elements are shown in bold in the example code shown above.

Once the information returned by the SQL query is merged into the .HTX template to generate a finished .HTML file, the HTML file is passed to the Web browser for display.

An HTML template can also be referenced when creating .IDC and .HTX files and is merged with the .HTX template file. The optional template can provide additional HTML code to be included in the generated .HTML Web page file, offering the opportunity to embellish the appearance of the displayed page.

Converting from IDC to ASP

An existing Web site or corporate intranet displaying data via the Internet Data Connector (IDC) can be converted to ASP (Active Server Pages) using the IDC2ASP tool. While IDC is a functioning technology, ASP holds several advantages, including being more powerful, more efficient, and easier to work with.

The IDC2ASP tool is available as a free download from Microsoft and is supplied in two versions. IDC2ASP.EXE is a command-line utility that automatically converts IDC files into ASP format. A series of command line switches are provided that control all aspects of the conversion. Further, since the original files remain intact, the conversion results can be tested without demanding a complete commitment to the ASP.

Second is an active server component version of IDC2ASP that can be instantiated within an ASP page—in the same fashion as any other component. Once the component properties are set, all that is required is to call the Convert method.

The IDC2ASP utilities appear under the name IntraActive and are not supported by Microsoft. The potential usefulness of the product, however, can make this well worth investigation when there are a number of IDC files requiring conversion.

Active Server Pages (ASP)

Active Server Pages are the latest extension in providing database connectivity for the Internet and intranets. ASP is a server-side scripting technology which can dynamically build .HTML files in response to URL requests. Like .IDC files, .ASP files can access ODBC data sources through a data source name (DSN).

Once references to a specific DSN have been made in an ASP or IDC file, the database indicated can be changed by deleting the existing DSN in the ODBC Administrator, then creating a new data source using the same name.

Active Server Pages provide a means for incorporating executable scripts directly in HTML files. This integration allows HTML development and scripting development to become a single process, permitting developers to focus on the look and feel issues during creation, adding dynamic elements directly rather than as an after-thought or add-in.

ASP applications provide the following advantages:

- Complete integration with HTML files

- Convenient design without requiring manual compiling or linking of programs

- Object-oriented design

- Extensibility using ActiveX server components

These advantages translate directly into tangible benefits, making it possible for Web developers to create interactive business applications rather than simply publishing static content. Examples of ASP Web pages can be found in online bookstores, airline sites, Web computer stores and many others where interactive content allows browsing customers not only to check available items and prices but to place both simple and complex orders.

ASP applications can be developed using any scripting language with an appropriate scripting engine, including Visual Basic Scripting Edition (VBScript) and JScript. Visual InterDev can also be used for creating applications using Active Server Pages.

Regardless of the scripting language or development tools, additional functionality can be provide by incorporating ActiveX server components (previously Automation servers) to process data and generate response information.

Download on Demand

Because data transmission expends system resources and network bandwidth, data should remain in the server-side databases until required, using Active Server Pages to perform downloads on a demand basis. Further, while there are a number of tools and techniques addressing the download-on-demand question for client/server LAN/WAN environments, ASPs are one of the few tools appropriate for Web-based applications.

Download on demand using ASPs is particularly useful when accessing large databases as, for example, online ordering systems.

 ASP-generated content is compatible with standard Web browsers.

Microsoft FrontPage

Microsoft FrontPage is probably best known as an editor for preparing HTML Web pages, but it is also an editor for Visual InterDev, an integrated version of the FrontPage WYSIWYG HTML editor. FrontPage can be used to edit and create advanced Web page designs within a Visual InterDev project.

Scripts in FrontPage

Among the features provided by FrontPage are the ability to add VBScript or JScript to pages using the point-and-click Script Wizard.

The Script Wizard allows the developer to select events and objects associated with events and to selection actions to be taken in response to these events. Once trigger events and responses have been determined, the Script Wizard generates either a VBScript or JScript.

The FrontPage Editor for Visual InterDev should be used to open existing .HTM/.HTML files only. Opening .ALX, .ASA, or .ASP files may produce unpredictable results.

Forms and Form Fields

A popular method of making interactive Web pages using FrontPage is to use forms as collections of fields that accept user entries. Forms, of course, are not limited to collections of fields but can also contain styled text, tables, images, and most other objects that can be inserted in a page.

In operation, each form has an assigned form handler, which consists of a program on the Web server that reads data from the form's fields and subsequently processes the submitted data in some fashion.

When a form is submitted, form data—consisting of the name of each field in the form and the data in the field—is returned to the form handler as a series of name-value pairs.

The form handler is responsible for processing the data submitted, but how the data is handled and the response are dependent on the form handler's design. In some cases, form handlers may simply pass the processed data to a database; in others, the form handler may return an HTML page to the browser to reflect the data processing results.

Quite commonly, form handlers may include checks to ensure that all requested data—or all required data—has been correctly supplied and, if not, may post a message requesting additional data be submitted before the form will be accepted. Normally, this involves returning the user to the previous HTML page for completion of the form.

Form handlers may also perform various types of calculations or look up additional data from databases before generating an HTML page to report the results.

For example, a form handler might be designed to estimate fabric required to reupholster furniture by displaying common types of chairs or couches, and offering sample fabric patterns. Then, after the user had made their selections, the form handler could 'look up' the amount of fabric required and the current price for the fabric and report back with costs, including shipping and any applicable taxes, by generating a HTML page for the browser to display.

FrontPage includes a variety of built-in form handlers for common purposes, such as collecting data from a form and storing the data in a variety of formats, registering visitors to a Web page, or supporting a discussion group.

Forms can also be designed to interact with the Internet Database Connection (IDC), and experienced developers can create their own form handlers and assign these to forms created in FrontPage.

When new files are created using the FrontPage Editor, they are not automatically added to a Web project; instead, they must be inserted into the project manually.

Customizing Links

Normally when a link is created in a Web document, the followed link is displayed in the same frame or window where the source document was displayed. For example, the following code illustrates an anchor which displays an image—SAMPLE.GIF—as a hypertext link to a page—SAMPLE.HTML.

```
<A HREF="http://www.nowhere.net/sample.html"><IMG
SRC="sample.gif" ALT="Sample" BORDER=0 HEIGHT=220
WIDTH=41></A>
```

Several things have been done in this statement. For one, an alternate (ALT) text label has been supplied for browsers that are not displaying graphics. Also, for browsers that are displaying graphics, the graphic image has been specified with no border and a fixed height and width.

The <A...> statement is an anchor, while the </A> statement identifies the end of the anchor. The <IMG SRC...> statement is associated with the anchor.

The anchor statement is the important element here because the bare anchor statement, as shown above, is only one form this statement can take. The anchor statement is defined as:

```
<A HREF=reference
   NAME=name
   TARGET=window
   TITLE=title >
```

In the example—and most commonly—the HREF=*reference* attribute is used to specify a link to another document. The second most common anchor is the NAME=*name* attribute, which links to a named reference, normally within the same document. The use of an anchor, however, is more flexible than the common usage, and the four parameters with their special variations appear below.

HREF   The HREF parameter takes the form HREF=*reference*, where the reference is either a destination address or a destination file, in URL format. For a file reference, this must be the name of a file and must appear in the format of the file system (i.e., the name case must match if the system—UNIX, for example—is case sensitive). When no path or domain name are specified, the file must be located in the same directory or location as the referring document.

NAME   The NAME parameter takes the form NAME=*name*, where the name identifies a reference within the current HTML document or may be a reference within an external document. To link to a reference location in an external document, the HREF parameter would supply the document, as a URL, and the NAME parameter would be prefaced by the pound sign (#).

```
<A NAME="my_reference_location"></A>
```

```
<A HREF="http://www.nowhere.net/sample2.html" #NAME="my_
reference_location"></A>
```

TARGET   The TARGET parameter takes the form TARGET=*window*, where window identifies a named window where the linked document is loaded. This is normally used with a frameset where a frame has been named in the FRAME element, i.e., an SRC parameter is placed within the <FRAMESET> tag to show which document is being displayed within the frame.

This parameter can, however, also be used with four predefined window names, as well as the variable:

window   The linked page (document) is loaded to the named window. With the exception of the four predefined window names, the window names must begin with an alphanumeric character.

_blank   The linked page (document) is loaded to a new blank window. This window is not named.

_parent   The linked page (document) is loaded to the immediate parent of the document where the link appears.

_self   The linked page (document) is loaded to the same window where the link appears. (This is the default when nothing else is specified.)

_top   The linked page (document) is loaded to the full body of the window. (Frames are overwritten.)

```
<A HREF="http://www.nowhere.net/sample2.html" TARGET=
"_blank"></A>
```

Rather than opening a new browser, the Opera browser simply opens a new window within the browser.

TITLE   The TITLE parameter takes the form TITLE=*title*, where title is the title appearing when the hyperlink is selected. The TITLE parameter can be combined with any of the other parameters to produce a pop-up caption window.

```
<A HREF="http://www.nowhere.net/sample2.html" TARGET=
"_blank" TITLE="Opens a new browser"></A>
```

> ### Why New Browser Windows?
>
> For reasons which are often obscure (or even downright cryptic), a number of Web sites like to open new browser windows in response to certain links. In some cases, this may come from a frame with the intention of opening a full window for the linked page, but many other examples on the Web today seem to have less excuse for their action.
>
> Opening a new browser window to display a page does disrupt the chain of pages, i.e., the Back button in the new page does not return to the URL where the original link appears.

Summary

While Web pages began as displays with static content where browsers would used the Hypertext Transport Protocol to request HTML pages from a Web server, today's Web pages can be—and often are—much more sophisticated. Quite commonly, Web pages are used to display information derived from database sources or to present forms to request user information and to then prepare HTML pages to display information in response.

One method of linking database information to a Web page is to use the Internet Data Connector, an interface provided by the IIS (Internet Information Service), to retrieve complex data from ODBC data sources. Together with the HTML extension (HTX) services, information from database sources can be formatted and displayed by Web pages.

Another method of displaying database information on a Web site is to use Active Server Pages (ASP) to incorporate executable scripts directly in HTML files. Active Server Pages are used for a variety of interactive Web sites, such as online book stores, airline booking pages, or other sales sites.

Microsoft FrontPage and the Script Wizard provide a means of creating interactive forms that use server-side form handler engines to process and respond to submitted data. FrontPage includes a variety of built-in form handlers for varying purposes while custom form handlers can be created to meet special requirements.

Review Questions

1. Often ODBC databases require a user name and password for access. Where does an Internet application commonly store this information?

   A. In an .ASP file

   B. In an .HTX file

   C. In an .IDC file

   D. Either A or C

2. What is the appropriate visual tool to create Active Server Pages (ASP)?

   A. Microsoft FrontPage

   B. Microsoft Internet Information Server

   C. Microsoft Visual Basic

   D. Microsoft Visual InterDev

3. When using the Internet Database Connector to publish an Access database on the Internet, where is the ODBC data source name stored?

   A. In the .HTM file

   B. In the .HTX file

   C. In the .IDC file

   D. In the .ISP file

4. Which of following is true of the design process used by gateway programs?

   A. It is dependent on the TCP/IP protocols and must be integrated into HTML pages.

   B. It is dependent on the HTML protocol and must be integrated into HTML pages.

   C. It is dependent on the TCP/IP protocols and cannot be integrated into HTML pages.

   D. It is quite different from HTML files and cannot be integrated into HTML pages.

5. An .IDC file is used to retrieve the `Itemprice` field from a catalog database. In the resulting HTML file, which tag displays the `Item-price` field?

    A. `<%itemprice%>`

    B. `<htx.itemprice>`

    C. `<idc.itemprice>`

    D. `<itemprice>`

6. Which of the following is true of the Internet Data Connector? (Select all that apply.)

    A. It is a gateway-based service.

    B. It is a protocol supplied by an ActiveX component.

    C. It is an interface supplied by the Internet Information Server.

    D. It is used together with the HTML extension services.

7. In designing a Web page using Microsoft FrontPage, a hyperlink leaves the existing page displayed in the current browser window and opens a second browser to display the linked page. To fill this requirement, the TARGET parameter in the <FRAMESET> tag is assigned which value?

    A. _blank

    B. _new

    C. _top

    D. _window

8. In creating an Internet shopping application, the Active Server Pages (ASPs) permit which of the following?

    A. Product data can be accessed from the Web browser's data cache.

    B. Product data can be accessed on demand using a database server.

    C. Product data can be stored on a single ASP.

    D. Product data can be stored on the client computer using HTML pages.

9. Once an ASP (Active Server Page) or IDC (Internet Data Connector) file has incorporated references to an existing DSN (Data Source Name), how can the reference be changed?

   A. By linking the DSN through a database reference to a new data source

   B. By deleting the existing DSN and creating a new source using the same name

   C. By using an alias to redirect the DSN to a new data source

   D. Only by recreating the ASP or IDC source

10. The Microsoft Internet Information Server uses .IDC and .HTX files together. What are the functions filled by these two files are?

   A. .IDC files contain database queries while .HTX files contain templates to display the results of a database query in an HTML format.

   B. .IDC files contain templates to display the results of a database query in an HTML format while .HTX files contain the login ID and password for database access.

   C. .IDC files contain the login ID and password for database access while .HTX files contain the data to be displayed.

   D. .IDC files contain the names of data sources while .HTX files provide the data to be displayed.

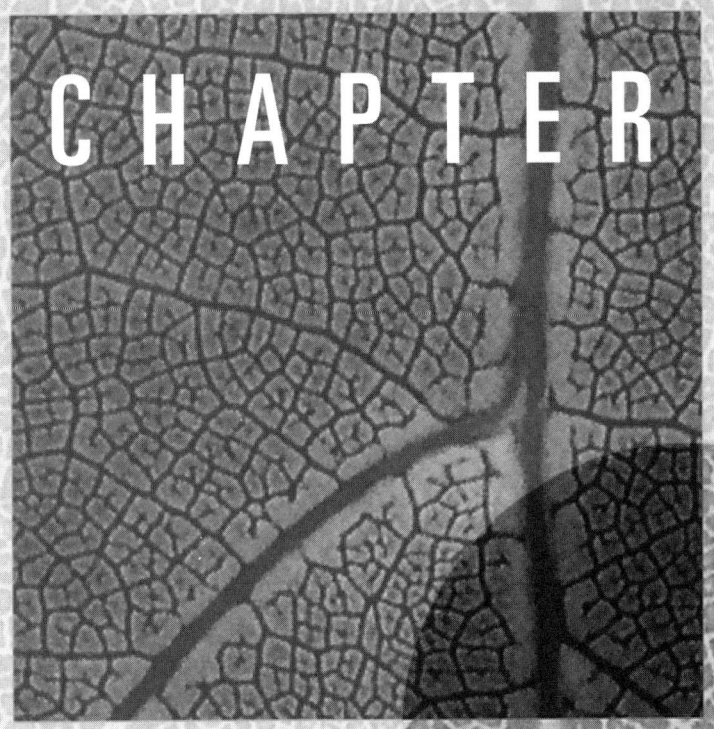

CHAPTER

17

ActiveX Technologies for
Web-Based Applications

ActiveX components, including ActiveX documents, form an important base for creating Web-based applications. Both ActiveX components and documents can be downloaded on demand and provide data persistence. An important facility supporting the distribution of ActiveX technologies is found in the use of .CAB (cabinet) files.

ActiveX Documents in Internet Applications

Active X documents, developed using Visual Basic or Visual C++, are simply applications which integrate with other elements of an Internet or intranet site. ActiveX documents can be deployed in such a fashion that users can navigate transparently between HTML pages and ActiveX documents.

Essentially, ActiveX documents can be thought of as applications for the Internet and virtually anything done with a standard application can be handled using an ActiveX document. For example, a user interface component could be part of a three-tiered client/server application, calling business services provided by other components, submitting queries to a remote database, or presenting returned results in a table or grid format. Among the advantages in using an ActiveX document are a more complex client-side process and a more sophisticated presentation than is possible using HTML pages. ActiveX documents can also provide a more sophisticated environment for the design and debugging of forms.

ActiveX documents are hosted by an ActiveX document container, such as Microsoft's Intenet Explorer or the Microsoft Office Binder, where the document container supplies support services for the document, including menu integration and persistent data storage through a `PropertyBag` object on the client side.

The scripting tools used on HTML pages are not valid for ActiveX document pages. Instead, jumps between links (URLs) on the Internet are accomplished using the Visual Basic Hyperlink object.

Just as components that are not installed on the user's system can be automatically downloaded when required, ActiveX documents can be retrieved on demand or can be upgraded automatically when more recent versions become available. ActiveX document features include the following:

Download   Links can be created to ActiveX documents that cause the browser to automatically find and download all components that are required to execute the document. (See the "Deploying ActiveX Components" section, below.)

Menu negotiation   ActiveX documents have the ability to merge their menus with those of the browser. Documents loaded in Internet Explorer, for example, can merge their menu items with the browser's menu.

Navigation   Hyperlink-aware containers can use the Visual Basic Hyperlink object properties and methods to jump to a given URL or to navigate through a history list.

Persistence   ActiveX documents deployed in Internet Explorer can persist data through the `PropertyBag` object.

Other examples of ActiveX documents are Microsoft Word document files or Excel spreadsheets. To function as components, these require an ActiveX server, such as WINWORD.EXE or EXCEL.EXE, and an ActiveX container, a browser such as Internet Explorer or Office Binder.

Internet Explorer, for example, can display an ActiveX document without requiring an HTML page. This can be exhibited by opening a Word document or an Excel spreadsheet from inside Internet Explorer.

Type libraries for ActiveX components provide descriptions of objects and provide data type information for object properties and methods. Type libraries also provide help information for objects or provide pointers to help files.

Deploying ActiveX Components

Any ActiveX-enabled Web browser downloading a page that contains an ActiveX component—identified by information contained in an <OBJECT...> tag—will download the component (unless, of course, the component already exists on the local system). The download process involves seven steps:

1. The browser begins by checking the class ID parameter— in the <OBJECT...> tag—to determine if the component exists locally. If the component exists, obviously, no further action is required. If the component does not exist locally, the browser initiates steps to download the .CAB file identified by the CODEBASE parameter.

2. The OBJECT tag is parsed to extract the CODEBASE= attribute. If the CODEBASE= attribute is absent or if it is preceded by a URL-to-object index server (found in the CodeBaseSearchPath), the index is used to retrieve the .CAB (cabinet) file (see the ".CAB (Cabinet) Files" section, below).

3. The CODEBASE= attribute is used to identify the .CAB file.

4. The browser expands the files from the .CAB file, copying the expanded files to the user's computer (by default, the files are placed in the \WINDOWS\OCCACHE directory). The .CAB file contains a compressed (archive) version of the component together with an .INF file, which identifies any required support files and the locations for these files.

5. The browser downloads any files listed in the .INF file which are not already present on the system.

6. The browser registers any object(s) and/or file(s) requiring registration.

7. The browser calls the COM `CoCreateInstance` function to create an instance of the specified object.

The OBJECT Tag Structure

The `<OBJECT>` tag is used to insert an object, i.e., an image, document, applet, or control, into an HTML document. Any object may contain any elements ordinarily used within the body of an HTML document, including section headings, paragraphs, lists, forms, and nested objects, or, of course, ActiveX components.

The `<OBJECT>` tag is defined as follows:

```
<OBJECT
    ALIGN=LEFT|TEXTTOP|MIDDLE|TEXTMIDDLE|
          BASELINE|TEXTBOTTOM|CENTER|RIGHT
    BORDER=n
    CLASSID=url
    CODEBASE=url
    CODETYPE=codetype
    DATA=url
    DECLARE
    HEIGHT=n
    HSPACE=n
    ID=name
    NAME=url
    NOTAB
    SHAPES
    STANDBY=message
    TABINDEX=n
    TITLE=text
    TYPE=type
    USEMAP=url
    VSPACE=n
    WIDTH=n >
```

The <OBJECT...> tag statement must always be terminated by the end tag:

</OBJECT>

The <OBJECT...> parameters are listed below, beginning with the parameters used for an ActiveX control (in bold):

ID=*name* identifies the object.

CLASSID=*url* identifies the object implementation. The *url* syntax depends on the object type. For example, for a registered ActiveX control, the syntax is: CLSID:*class-identifier*.

CODEBASE= *url* identifies the object code base. The *url* syntax depends on the object type.

ALIGN=*alignment* sets the alignment for text surrounding the object (default: LEFT). Possible alignments are as follows:

BASELINE	Object is drawn bottom aligned with the baseline of the continuous text.
LEFT	Object is drawn as a left-flush "floating object" with text flowing around the object. (This is the default setting.)
MIDDLE	Object is drawn as a middle-centered "floating object" with text flowing around the object.
RIGHT	Object is drawn as a right-flush "floating object" with text flowing around the object.
CENTER	Any surrounding text is aligned with the center of the object.
TEXTBOTTOM	Any surrounding text is aligned with the bottom of the object.
TEXTMIDDLE	Any surrounding text is aligned with the middle of the object.
TEXTTOP	Any surrounding text is aligned with the top of the object.

BORDER= *n* sets the border width for objects defined as hyperlinks.

CODETYPE= *codetype* sets the Internet media type for code.

DATA= *url* identifies object data. The *url* syntax varies depending on the object type.

DECLARE declares an object but does not instantiate the object. This is used to create a cross-reference to any object later in the document or when the object is used as a parameter in another object.

HEIGHT= *n* sets the suggested height for the object.

HSPACE= *n* sets the horizontal gutter, i.e., the empty space between the object and any surrounding text or images to the right or left of the object.

NAME= *url* specifies an object name when submitted as a part of a form.

NOTAB specifies the object is not included in tab order (i.e., can not be selected by tabbing).

SHAPES specifies the object uses shaped hyperlinks.

STANDBY= *message* specifies a message to show while the object is being loaded.

TABINDEX= *n* sets the tab order for the object.

TITLE= *text* sets an advisory title.

TYPE= *type* sets the Internet media type for object data.

USEMAP= *url* identifies the image map to be used with the object.

VSPACE= *n* sets the vertical gutter, i.e., the empty space between the object and any surrounding text or images above or below the object.

WIDTH= *n* sets the suggested width for the object.

ActiveX components used in Web pages can be stored in .CAB (cabinet) files and downloaded by specifying the location of the cabinet file in the CODEBASE attribute of the OBJECT tag.

While the .CAB file can be located anywhere on the Internet, common practice is to have the .CAB file located in the same directory as the Web page.

The <OBJECT...> tag for an ActiveX control contains three major attributes: the ID attribute, the CLASSID attribute, and the CODEBASE attribute containing the path of the .CAB file.

Using the Spindial ActiveX object (an MFC-supplied sample control) as an example, the following code shows how the <OBJECT...> tag packages the control.

```
<OBJECT
    ID="Spindial1"
    WIDTH=100
    HEIGHT=51
    CLASSID="CLSID:06889605-B8D0-101A-91F1-00608CEAD5B3"
    CODEBASE="http://sample_site/spindial
    .cab#Version=1,0,0,001">
```

The <OBJECT...> tag, in addition to the ID, CLASSID, and CODEBASE, also includes WIDTH and HEIGHT parameters. The <OBJECT...> tag is followed by a list of control-specific parameters:

```
<PARAM NAME="_Version" VALUE="65536">
<PARAM NAME="_ExtentX" VALUE="2646">
<PARAM NAME="_ExtentY" VALUE="1323">
<PARAM NAME="_StockProps" VALUE="0">
<PARAM NAME="NeedlePosition" VALUE="2">
```

And, last, the end tag, </OBJECT>, terminates the statement.

```
</OBJECT>
```

.CAB (Cabinet) Files

The Cabinet (.CAB) files format has been used for some years by Microsoft to compress software for distribution on disks or CDs. Today, in addition to using .CAB files to minimize media requirements for shipment, .CAB files are also used to reduce file size and the associated download times for components used with Web pages.

The .CAB file format is a non-proprietary compression format, also known as MSZIP, which is based on the Lempel-Ziv data compression algorithms.

A newer format, LZX (also known as Lempel-Ziv), is available but is only supported by Internet Explorer 4.0 or later.

Cabinet files are organized around the concept of a folder, where a folder is a collection of one or more files which are compressed together as a single entity. The strength of this approach is to improve compression ratios. Conversely, however, random access to compressed files suffers because decompressing any single file in a folder means that all preceding files in the folder must be decompressed as well.

Cabinet files focus on maximum compression rather than speed of decompression and are designed to deliver file content as opposed to stream media.

Creating a .CAB File

To create a .CAB archive for the SpinDial control used in the preceding example, the SPINDIAL.CAB archive requires two files: SPINDIAL.OCX and SPINDIAL.INF. Using the command line CABARC.EXE utility, the cabinet file would be created as follows:

```
C:\CabDevKit\cabarc.exe -s 6144 N spindial.cab spindial.ocx
spindial.inf
```

The –s 6144 parameter reserves space in the cabinet file for a digital signature; see the "Digital Signatures" section, below.

Cabinet Tools

Microsoft supplies a CABinet resource kit (CABSDK.EXE) containing the tools required by developers to build .CAB files.

Also, extensive documentation on how to create .CAB files for different purposes is available online, and is supplied with the CabSdk resource kit.

Archiving Library Files

When a cabinet file is use to supply library files, the library files are compressed first in a .CAB file called the inner cabinet. The inner cabinet is then archived in a second .CAB file—the outer cabinet—with an .INF file containing the names of the libraries, the locations where the libraries should be installed, the class identifier used in the <OBJECT...> tag, etc.

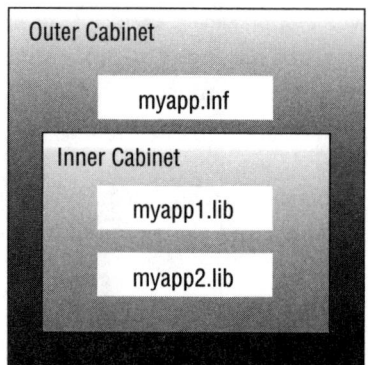

This use of the .INF file applies only to libraries which are referenced by an HTML <OBJECT...> tag and does not apply to applets.

The .INF file can be based on the MASTER.INF template supplied with the software development kit (SDK).

Internet Component Download

The Internet Download Service uses two types of .CAB files. A primary .CAB file always contains an .INF file which serves as a script pointing to additional files required by a component.

The browser will use the .INF file information to determine if the required support files already exist on the client (local) system or if these need to be downloaded as a secondary .CAB file.

To minimize Internet download times, the primary .CAB file should contain as few files as necessary, while the .INF file should contain pointers (URL addresses) to secondary .CAB files. Optionally, the primary .CAB file may only contain an .INF file with all additional components, libraries, etc., located in secondary .CAB files.

FIGURE 17.2

Primary and secondary .CAB files

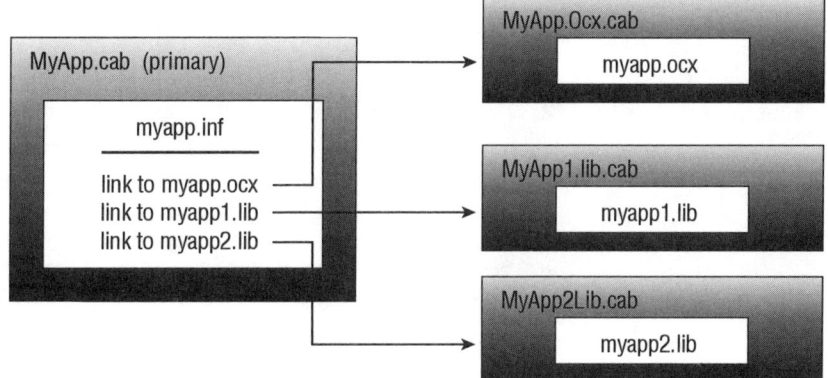

Alternately, for corporate intranet applications, where bandwidth is less of a consideration, it may simply be more convenient to keep all files in a single .CAB file.

Digital Signatures

When an application is purchased in a store—whether in person, by mail, or over the Internet—the physical package enclosing the application identifies the developer and provides some assurance of reliability. However, applications received by download, i.e., directly over the Internet, lack the packaging, shrink-wrap, and holographic logos. In lieu of these, a digital signature offers source verification by providing a link through the certificate authority issuing the signature to the source company or developer.

While a digital signature does offer confirmation of identity, it is not an assurance that the product is free from problems, only that the developer is known.

Certificate authorities provide and renew digital signature certificates, authenticate the identity of the certificate holder, and take responsibility for legal and liability issues if security is broken. In turn, the developer should use the digital certificate with all the code and components that are distributed over the Internet.

Digital signing for Internet distribution works something like this:

1. A function, supplied by the certificate authority, is applied to create a separate file (a digest) which represents a unique abstract of the application code.

2. The digest file is encrypted together with the name of the function's hash algorithm, the developer's digital certificate, the Certificate Authority's certificate, and the means for decrypting the digest. The encrypted file is called a signature block.

3. When a component is packaged for Internet distribution, using, for example, the Visual Basic Setup Wizard, space is left within the created .CAB package to hold the signature block.

4. When the .CAB file is downloaded from the Internet, the Web browser extracts the signature file, identifies the CA authenticating the signature, and decrypts the digest file.

5. The hash algorithm from the digest file is used on the component code to create a new digest which is compared with the extracted digest.

6. Any modifications to the code since the signature was originally created will prevent the two digest versions from matching. If a mismatch is found, the component is suspect and a warning is issued to the user.

Just as ActiveX controls can be digitally signed, a .CAB file can also include a digital signature—using the Authenticode technology—offering accountability by identifying the software developer.

Under Internet Explorer 3.0, for example, an ActiveX component will not be automatically downloaded unless it contains a digital signature.

While digital signatures are optional rather than required, including a code signature is important to users who will make the decision whether to allow a component into their systems or not.

Component Safety

When components are downloaded from the Internet—or, for that matter, from an intranet—component security is based on knowing that the component has been certified both as *safe for scripting* and *safe for initialization*.

WARNING The certification for component safety is set by the component developer and is not validation from a third-party certification authority. Because a malicious script or data or even a malicious component design could have serious consequences, the digital signature certifying the origin of a component becomes doubly important.

This certification of component safety is the developer's assurance that the component has been designed to interact safely with script and data passed to the component during initialization. By default, Internet Explorer will not download components that are not identified as safe for scripting and initialization but, instead, will display a warning when such a component is located.

The safe for scripting and initialization designation for a component is set when the component is packaged—using the Visual Basic Setup Wizard, for example—for Internet distribution.

Safe for Scripting

Components on HTML pages rely on scripting—such as events handled through VBScript—to access component functionality. Likewise, for ActiveX controls, scripting is the only method of enabling a control's features within a browser.

A component should be marked safe for scripting only when the control will remain secure regardless of the script, i.e., the component will not function in an unsafe or unreasonable manner even if a malicious script is executed. In essence, the certification is the developer's assurance that the component is immune to subversion by a malicious or malignant script.

Commonly, ActiveX components depend on client- or server-side scripts to read and write properties and to invoke component methods. While it is acceptable for an ActiveX component to read or write to a file, a script should never be permitted to read or write to any system file except with the express permission of the user.

Likewise, ActiveX components (and scripts) should not be able to collect information about the user or the user's system, including e-mail addresses, except and unless the user gives explicit permission for such information to be collected.

Neither should scripts be able to use controls marked as safe to create, change, or delete files, or change any system settings without the user's explicit permission and knowledge.

NOTE While the Component Object Model is used by ActiveX components, COM is not required for safe scripting and initialization.

Safe for Initialization

A second potential security hazard occurs when an ActiveX control's state is initialized using untrusted data. When an ActiveX control or component is embedded in an HTML page, the object's initial state is set by the PARAM NAME attributes accompanying the OBJECT tag (see the SpinDial example in the "The OBJECT Tag Structure" section, above).

A component can be certified as safe for initialization when the component's properties can not be passed data in such a fashion that the component can cause damage to the user's system.

This is normally assured by using code with validated changes in property values including, particularly, the `InitProperties` and `ReadProperties` events.

Again, safe initialization should ensure that the component cannot corrupt the user's system by creating, changing, or deleting files or changing system settings without the user's explicit permission and knowledge.

A component should be marked safe for initialization only when the control will remain secure regardless of the data used to initialize the component, i.e., the component will not function in an unsafe or unreasonable manner even if malicious data is supplied. In essence, the certification is the developer's assurance that the component is immune to subversion by malicious or malignant data.

Summary

ActiveX documents can be used as applications for the Internet or intranet deployment and can be linked with HTML pages and other ActiveX documents. Like other components, ActiveX elements can be downloaded on demand, and support installation, menu negotiation, navigation, and persistence. In an HTML page, the <OBJECT…> tag provides a link to an .INF file which provides information on the object implementation and code base, i.e., the location where the object is found on the Web or intranet.

Cabinet (.CAB) files are used to compress software for both media and Internet distribution using a non-proprietary compression format based on the Lempel-Ziv data compression algorithms and optimized for maximum compression. Cabinet files may be nested but are often used as primary and secondary cab files, where the primary .CAB file contains an .INF file with links to one or more secondary files.

Both components and archives may use digital signatures—issued by Certificate Authorities—to authenticate the identity of a developer and the validity of a package downloaded over the Internet. Conversely, the developer alone is responsible for certifying components as safe for scripting and initialization.

Review Questions

1. Before an ActiveX component can be marked as safe for scripting and initializing, what must the developer certify?

A. That the component script cannot be used to read or write to any file

B. That the component script cannot be used to set component properties

C. That the component script cannot read users' names or e-mail addresses without their permission

D. That the component script uses the COM (Component Object Model) library for execution

2. When an ActiveX component is identified as Safe for Initialization, this indicates that:

A. A test agency certifies that a user's data cannot be harmed by data accepted by the control's properties.

B. A test agency certifies that a user's data cannot be harmed by data accepted by the control's methods.

C. The developer certifies that a user's data cannot be harmed by data accepted by the control's methods.

D. The developer certifies that a user's data cannot be harmed by data accepted by the control's properties.

3. Select the HTML code which will instruct Internet Explorer to download and register an ActiveX component:

A. ```
<COMDOC
    CLASSID="clsid:2A356098-2AF4-33C4-7567-2345BDEF8745"
    CODEBASE="Example.cab#version=1,0,0,0">
</COMDOC>
```

**B.** ```
<COMDOC
    CLASSID="clsid:2A356098-2AF4-33C4-7567-2345BDEF8745"
    docfile="Example.doc#version=1,0,0,0">
</COMDOC>
```

C. ```
<OBJECT
    CLASSID="clsid:2A356098-2AF4-33C4-7567-2345BDEF8745"
    CODEBASE="Example.cab#version=1,0,0,0">
</OBJECT>
```

**D.** ```
<OBJECT
    CLASSID="clsid:2A356098-2AF4-33C4-7567-2345BDEF8745"
    docfile="Example.doc#version=1,0,0,0">
</OBJECT>
```

4. When an ActiveX-enabled Web browser downloads a page containing an ActiveX component, what does the browser do first?

A. It automatically downloads any files listed in the .INF file.

B. It automatically downloads the component .CAB file.

C. It checks the class ID parameter to determine if the component presently exists on the local system.

D. It extracts the CODEBASE= attribute to identify the .CAB file.

5. Select the element from the `<OBJECT>` tag on an HTML page which indicates the location of the .CAB file used to download an ActiveX component.

A. CLASSID

B. CODEBASE

C. ID

D. OBJECTID

6. Assuming that Internet Explorer (version 3.0) is configured with all default settings, what must be true for an ActiveX component to be automatically downloaded by the browser from the Internet?

 A. It must be digitally signed.

 B. It must be packaged in a .CAB file.

 C. It must be packaged in a .ZIP file.

 D. It must have a security rating less than four.

7. Which of the following is true of the HTML <OBJECT...> tag?

 A. It can only be used for ActiveX components.

 B. It can only be used for ActiveX controls.

 C. It must always be terminated by a </END> tag.

 D. It must always be terminated by a </OBJECT> tag.

8. An HTML page uses an <OBJECT...> tag identifying a .CAB file as the source of an object to be included in the page. The .CAB file may contain which of the following?

 A. Any number of files and may contain one .INF file

 B. Any number of files but must contain one .INF file

 C. Exactly one file

 D. One .INF file and one other file

9. The <OBJECT...> tag for an ActiveX control contains what three major attributes? (Select all that apply.)

 A. the CLASSID attribute

 B. the CODEBASE attribute

 C. the ID attribute

 D. the USEMAP attribute

10. An ActiveX document created using Visual Basic supplies which of the following features?

   A. A property page for saving persistent data to the server

   B. Menu placement services for visual editing

   C. The ability to write client-side scripts using the Visual Basic scripting tool

   D. The Visual Basic HTTP component object allowing Internet navigation.

11. Where are cabinet (.CAB) files for ActiveX components customarily stored?

   A. On the client system in the \WINDOWS directory

   B. On the client system in the \WINDOWS\OCCACHE directory

   C. On the server in the \WINDOWS\OCCACHE directory

   D. On the server in the same directory as the HTML page using the component

12. Object information contained in an ActiveX component type library consists of which of the following?

   A. Methods

   B. Properties and methods

   C. Properties, methods, and help information

   D. Properties, methods, and linking information

13. While the cabinet (.CAB) file format supports more than one compression format, for widest access by browsers, which format should be selected?

   A. ARC

   B. LZX

   C. MSZIP

   D. PKZIP

14. Certification for component safety is established by:

 A. A consortium of Internet Service providers

 B. A Microsoft certification service

 C. An independent Certificate Authority

 D. The component developer

15. A digital signature in an ActiveX component offers users of the component the assurance that:

 A. The component has been licensed for distribution in the developer's name or the company's name.

 B. The developer's name or company's name is attached to the code.

 C. The developer's or company's identity has been verified by Microsoft.

 D. The developer's or company's identity has been verified by the InterNIC Corporation.

16. Cabinet files are organized around folders to:

 A. Maximize compression

 B. Minimize decompression

 C. Preserve directory structures

 D. All of the above

17. To optimize performance over the Internet, a component object should be packaged by:

 A. Placing all required files in a single .CAB file

 B. Placing each library and component object in separate .CAB files

 C. Placing the .INF and component object in a primary .CAB file and the library files in a secondary .CAB file

 D. Placing the .INF file in a primary .CAB file and placing all other files in secondary .CAB files

18. When using .CAB files to distribute ActiveX components over the Internet, if the component requires supporting files, how are these identified?

   A. By an .ASP file

   B. By an .HTM file

   C. By an .IDC file

   D. By an .INF file

19. What is a digital signature?

   A. A certificate issued by a Certificate Authority

   B. A graphic reproduction of a handwritten signature

   C. An encrypted fingerprint image

   D. An encrypted key supplied by the Internet Security Agency

20. Which one of the following best describes how ActiveX documents and ActiveX controls can be used?

   A. ActiveX controls can be used to replace ActiveX documents.

   B. ActiveX controls can be used to replace HTML pages.

   C. ActiveX documents can be used to replace ActiveX controls.

   D. ActiveX documents can be used to replace HTML pages.

APPENDIX

A

Review Question Answers

Chapter 1

1. Registry entries contained in the HKEY_LOCAL_MACHINE hive will be overridden by data contained in which of the following?

   A. The CONFIG.SYS file

   B. The HKEY_CURRENT_CONFIG hive

   C. The HKEY_CURRENT_USER hive

   D. The WIN.INI file

   Answer: C

2. The functional scope supported by the registry services includes which of the following? (Select all that apply.)

   A. Enumerating and tracking a system's hardware configuration

   B. Providing keys to enumerate, track, and configure applications, device drivers, and operating system control parameters

   C. Providing multi-user configuration support

   D. Providing system global storage for information exchanged between applications

   Answer: A, B, C

3. In which two disk files is the Windows NT/95/98 registry stored?

   A. SYSTEM.DAT and USER.DAT

   B. SYSTEM.DAT and WIN.DAT

   C. SYSTEM.INI and USER.INI

   D. SYSTEM.INI and WIN.INI

   Answer: A

4. The registry is organized into sections called:

   A. Hives

   B. Keys

   C. Nests

   D. Swarms

   Answer: A

5. Information in the registry is accessed through keys and subkeys that serve which of the following functions?

   A. They are required to unlock successive layers of security for access.

   B. They are used like directories and subdirectories to identify where the information is stored.

   C. They are used to decode the encrypted information.

   D. Both A and C

   Answer: B

6. A registry key under Windows 95/98 or Windows NT may contain how many individual values?

   A. One

   B. Two

   C. Four

   D. Eight

   E. Any number

   Answer: E

7. Individual key data entries may take which of the following forms? (Select all that apply.)

   A. Names and object class names

   B. Pointers to memory

   C. Security descriptors and time stamps

   D. Values

   Answer: A, C, D

8. All registry data entries:

   A. May be of any data type, including custom and binary data

   B. Must be ASCIIZ string values

   C. Must conform to either a predefined or a registered custom data format

   D. Must match a predefined data format

   Answer: B

9. What does the registry enforce?

   A. Consistency across registry data values

   B. Security for read and read/write access

   C. Strict granularity (atomicity) to ensure that changes are committed entirely

   D. Unicode string formats for string entries

   Answer: C

10. Before an application can open a registry key, the application must first do which of the following?

   A. Create a new registry entry

   B. Have security rights for access

   C. Use any existing handle to find a registry entry point

   D. Use one of the predefined handles as an entry point

   Answer: D

11. A registry key value consists of which of the following segments? (Select three.)

A. Data

B. Name

C. Security access

D. Type

Answer: C

12. A key entry for an OLE class would be found under which root key?

A. HKEY_CLASSES_ROOT

B. HKEY_CURRENT_CONFIG

C. HKEY_DYN_DATA

D. HKEY_LOCAL_MACHINE

Answer: A

13. HKEY_CLASSES_ROOT is an alias to a subkey under which of the following?

A. HKEY_CURRENT_CONFIG\Software\Classes

B. HKEY_CURRENT_USER\Software\Classes

C. HKEY_DYN_DATA\Software\Classes

D. HKEY_LOCAL_MACHINE\Software\Classes

Answer: D

14. User preferences, including color settings, environment variables, program groups, and network connections would be found under which key?

A. HKEY_CURRENT_CONFIG

B. HKEY_CURRENT_USER

C. HKEY_DYN_DATA

D. HKEY_LOCAL_MACHINE

Answer: B

15. System configuration identifying the bus type, system memory, and installed software and hardware would be found under which key?

A. HKEY_CLASSES_ROOT

B. HKEY_CURRENT_CONFIG

C. HKEY_DYN_DATA

D. HKEY_LOCAL_MACHINE

Answer: D

16. Where should application-specific information be stored?

   A. In .INI files outside the registry

   B. Under HKEY_CURRENT_CONFIG\Software\Vendor\ AppName\Version key entries for all application data

   C. Under HKEY_CURRENT_USER\Software\Vendor\AppName\ Version key entries for user-specific preferences

   D. Under HKEY_LOCAL_MACHINE\Software\Vendor\AppName\ Version key entries for initialization and run-time data which applies to all users

Answer: C, D

17. Windows Open Services Architecture (WOSA) proposes:

   A. A cooperative development effort toward a single unified operating system

   B. A single integrated API providing functional database access across multiple types of operating systems

   C. Standards for seamless access in information resource services

   D. Standards for transporting the Windows operating system to Macintosh, Unix, and Sun workstation platforms

Answer: C

18. In a 32-bit Windows environment, when two processes use the same DLL:

   A. The DLL is loaded once and mapped to the virtual address space of the first process calling the DLL.

   B. The DLL is loaded only once but mapped to the virtual address space of both processes.

   C. The DLL is loaded twice but each process shares one set of global and static variables.

   D. The DLL is loaded twice, giving each process its own copy.

Answer: B

19. The WOSA Common Application Services include which of the following? (Select three.)

   A. Financial Services API (FSAPI)

   B. Messaging API (MAPI)

   C. Open Database Connectivity (ODBC)

   D. Windows Telephony API (TAPI)

Answer: B, C, D

20. The Windows Telephony API offers applications access to interact with which of the following?

   A. Broadcast video transmissions

   B. Desktop audio and video conferencing

   C. Electronic mail

   D. The telephone network

Answer: B, D

21. What is the advantage of dynamic linking over static linking?

A. It allows global and static variables to be shared between processes for Dynamic Link Libraries.

B. It gives 32-bit DLLs their own local heaps.

C. It allows multiple copies of a DLL to be created in memory.

D. It requires that only one copy of a DLL be created in memory.

Answer: D

Chapter 2

1. Both Windows 95 and Windows NT fully support which of the following? (Select all that apply.)

A. MAPI

B. ODBC

C. Unicode

D. User-level security functions

Answer: A, B

2. Which of the following is true?

A. Both Windows NT and Windows 95/98 enforce protected memory for all applications.

B. Protected memory is enforced by application design only.

C. Windows NT and Windows 98 enforce protected memory but Windows 95 does not.

D. Windows NT enforces protected memory but Windows 95/98 does not.

Answer: D

3. The virtual address space shared by 16-bit applications and 32-bit DLLs in Windows 95 is:

A. 1GB to 2GB

B. 1MB to 4MB

C. 2GB to 3GB

D. 3GB to 4GB

Answer: C

4. The only file system recognized by DOS, Windows 95, Windows 98, and Windows NT is:

A. FAT16

B. FAT32

C. HPFS

D. NTFS

Answer: A

5. Virtual memory address space in the 32-bit Windows environment is arranged with:

A. The lower 2GB allocated to the application and the upper 2GB allocated to the system.

B. The lower 2GB allocated to the system and the upper 2GB allocated to the application.

    C. The lower 2MB allocated to the application and the upper 2MB allocated to the system.

    D. The lower 2MB allocated to the system and the upper 2MB allocated to the application.

Answer: A

6. Which of the following are true? (Select all that apply.)

    A. FAT file systems provide efficient support for larger hard drives.

    B. FAT32 file systems provide efficient support for larger hard drives.

    C. FAT32 file systems support file access security.

    D. NTFS file systems provide efficient support for larger hard drives.

Answer: B, D

7. In a 32-bit Windows process, the termination of which thread causes the process to terminate?

    A. The initial thread

    B. The last thread executing

    C. The primary thread

    D. The semaphore thread

Answer: B

8. Multiple processors are supported by which of the following?

    A. Both Windows 95/98 and Windows NT

    B. Windows 95/98 only

    C. Windows NT only

    D. None of the above

Answer: C

9. Which of the following elements are features of Windows 95? (Select all that apply.)

    A. Portability to non-Intel platforms

    B. Preemptive multitasking

    C. Support for symmetric multi-processors

    D. Virtual memory management

Answer: B, D

10. Which of the following are true? (Select all that apply.)

    A. 16-bit Windows operating systems offer a method of leveraging older, legacy systems.

    B. Windows 3.1 supports 32-bit addressing.

    C. Windows 95 operates independently of the DOS operating system.

    D. Windows for Workgroups adds networking support to Windows 3.1.

Answer: A, C, D

11. In a 32-bit Windows environment, what is the maximum amount of virtual address space each process can use?

   A. 4MB

   B. 2GB

   C. 4GB

   D. 8GB

Answer: C

12. Which of the following are true of the Windows 95/98 operating system? (Select all that apply.)

   A. It's aimed at top-end, leading-edge power users with high performance workstations.

   B. It's an independent 32-bit operating system.

   C. It's designed to deliver responsive performance for a broad range of applications while still conserving system resources.

   D. It's designed to support multiple-processor RISC systems.

Answer: B, C

13. Which of the following is true of the Windows NT operating system? (Select all that apply.)

   A. It's aimed at the mainstream market.

   B. It's designed to exploit the full capabilities of top-end hardware systems.

   C. It's designed to provide the most advanced services for the most demanding applications.

   D. It's optimized for 16-bit applications.

Answer: B, C

14. C2-level file security is supplied by which of the following?

   A. Windows 3.11

   B. Windows 95/98

   C. Windows NT

   D. All of the above

Answer: C

15. What are units of virtual memory called?

   A. Allocation units

   B. Extents

   C. Pages

   D. RAM

Answer: C

16. For which of the following situations is the Windows 95/98 operating system a valid selection? (Select all that apply.)

   A. Engineering and scientific applications requiring intensive data analysis

   B. General office environments

C. Manufacturing systems using multiple 16-bit applications to manage production lines

D. Sales and field representatives who use portable computers

Answer: B, C, D

17. How is multitasking handled?

A. On a cooperative basis by Windows NT, but on a preemptive basis by Windows 3.*x* and Windows 95/98

B. On a preemptive basis by all versions of Windows, including Windows 3.*x*, Windows NT, and Windows 95/98

C. On a preemptive basis by Windows NT, both a preemptive and cooperative basis by Windows 95/98, and on a cooperative basis by Windows 3.*x*

D. On a preemptive basis by Windows NT, but on a cooperative basis by Windows 3.*x* and Windows 95/98

Answer: C

Chapter 3

1. The sales department is interested in creating a slide presentation that will include audio/visual clips and that will be used for live presentations as well as being distributed both on CD and over the Internet. What would your recommendation for this project be?

A. Microsoft FrontPage

B. Microsoft Outlook

C. Microsoft PowerPoint

D. Microsoft Publisher

Answer: C

2. Your office manager asks for a recommendation for a package which can be used to create the company newsletter and prepare brochures and documents for internal distribution. What would your recommendation(s) be?

A. Microsoft FrontPage

B. Microsoft InterDev

C. Microsoft Publisher

D. Microsoft Word

Answer: C, D

3. Microsoft Outlook supplies support for which of the following? (Select all that apply.)

A. Creating and printing formatted text

B. Performing calculations on data

C. Sending e-mail

D. Tracking schedules

Answer: C, D

4. The Microsoft Internet Information Server supports Internet publishing, providing all of the basic services required including:

   A. Dynamic Host Configuration Protocol (DHCP) services

   B. Internet Database Connector gateway supporting publication of database information on the Internet

   C. Internet Service Manager supporting encrypted communications between client and server

   D. Windows Internet Naming Services (WINS) for automatic IP address configuration

Answer: B

5. Microsoft Project supplies support for which of the following? (Select all that apply.)

   A. Creating and printing formatted text

   B. Performing calculations on data

   C. Sending e-mail

   D. Tracking schedules and budgets

Answer: D

6. The corporate sales force needs e-mail, contact, task and schedule management both in the office and in the field. Select the optimum package(s) for in-house support for these functions.

   A. Internet Explorer with Microsoft Team Manager

   B. Lotus cc:Mail, Lotus Notes, and Novell Groupwise XTD

   C. Microsoft Outlook and Exchange Server

   D. Microsoft Word and MS Mail

Answer: C

7. Microsoft FrontPage supplies support for which of the following? (Select all that apply.)

   A. Creating formatted text

   B. Managing Web sites

   C. Sending e-mail

   D. Tracking schedules and budgets

Answer: A, B

8. Internet Information Server supports a number of standards, including:

   A. APPC

   B. HTML and HTTP

   C. ISDN services

   D. SNMP and SNMP MIB

Answer: B

9. To setup an Excel spreadsheet for calculating point spreads for NFL teams without needing to enter the data manually, the optimum solution would be to:

   A. Ask the receptionist to maintain the spreadsheet as a shared intranet link.

   B. Link the spreadsheet to an Access database containing updated scores.

   C. Subscribe to a data service to have scores sent by e-mail in an import-compatible format.

   D. Use Web Queries to directly import dynamic, real-time data.

   Answer: D

10. To share an Excel spreadsheet across a workgroup or enterprise, what would be the optimum solution?

    A. Distribute printed copies via company mail.

    B. E-mail exported copies of the spreadsheet to all interested parties.

    C. Import the spreadsheet into PowerPoint and use the viewer to create a distributable package.

    D. Save the spreadsheet directly to a URL, allowing the spreadsheet to be viewed via the corporate intranet.

    Answer: D

11. The Microsoft SNA Server supports a number of APIs including:

    A. APPC

    B. HTML and HTTP

    C. ISDN services

    D. SNMP and SNMP MIB

    Answer: A

12. Microsoft Word supplies support for which of the following? (Select all that apply.)

    A. Creating and printing formatted text

    B. Performing calculations on data

    C. Sending e-mail

    D. Tracking schedules and budgets

    Answer: A, C

13. Using Microsoft SQL Server Web Assistant, which of the following database operations can be accomplished? (Select all that apply.)

    A. A GROUP BY operation within a SELECT statement

    B. A sub-query operation within a DELETE statement

    C. A sub-query operation within an INSERT statement

    D. An ORDER BY operation within a SELECT statement

    Answer: A, D

14. The sales and engineering departments are collaborating on the creation of a company Web site. To maintain compatibility between the departments while offering both the optimum development package for the joint project, you select:

A. Microsoft Explorer

B. Microsoft FrontPage

C. Microsoft InterDev

D. Microsoft Word

Answer: B, C

15. PowerPoint presentations can be which of the following? (Select all that apply.)

A. Converted to HTML Web pages

B. Printed in book or brochure format

C. Run without having PowerPoint installed

D. Sent as e-mail messages

Answer: A, C

16. In a company with an increasing number of computers, the need is for software which will make it possible to troubleshoot problems remotely. Objectives include being able to examine the registry on a remote computer and being able to consult an inventory database to determine what software is installed on a specific computer. Select the BackOffice component which would provide these features from a server computer.

A. Microsoft Internet Information Server

B. Microsoft SNA Server

C. Microsoft SQL Server

D. Microsoft Systems Management Server

Answer: D

17. HTML pages can be automatically created and updated:

A. From the SQL Server using SQL Server Web Assistant

B. Through Excel pages and Shared Workbooks

C. Using ActiveX components to search for changed data

D. Using Stored Procedures on UNIX database servers

Answer: A

18. Which of the following is true of BackOffice applications? (Select all that apply.)

A. They are hardware dependent.

B. They operate only on RISC systems.

C. They operate only on multiple-CPU systems.

D. They support the Open Systems standard.

Answer: D

19. A company desires to create an Internet server with support for interactive Web pages allowing clients to access company database records for product pricing and availability and to place orders. This application design would be best satisfied by:

    A. Using a UNIX/XENIX Server with a FoxPro database using the Publish To The Web Wizard

    B. Using a UNIX/XENIX Server with an Access database for calculations and ActiveX objects to render data in HTML format

    C. Using a Windows NT Server with an Access database using the Publish To The Web Wizard

    D. Using a Windows NT Server with an Excel spreadsheet for calculations and ActiveX objects to render data in HTML format

Answer: C

20. How is it that BackOffice applications work on an integrated basis?

    A. They are fully designed for the Windows NT Server and cross-application compatibility.

    B. They rely on SQL transaction commands and the Windows SQL Server.

    C. They use ActiveX components to promote transaction compatibility between applications.

    D. They use the Performance Analyzer Wizard to recommend changes to improve performance.

Answer: A

21. Which standards does BackOffice support? (Select all that apply.)

    A. AppleTalk, DECnet, IPX/SPX, NETBEUI, OSI, SMB, and TPC/IP network protocols

    B. ASCII and FTP file transfer protocols

    C. DMFT and SNMP management standards

    D. SSL and WWW encrypted communications

Answer: C

22. What does Outlook use to add a new Appointment object to the Appointments folder?

    A. The `AddAppointment` method

    B. The `AddFolder` method

    C. The `CreateFolder` method

    D. The `CreateItem` method

Answer: D

23. IT managers and administrators using Microsoft BackOffice:

    A. Are able to deploy and administer desktop and server system using a single tool set

    B. Are able to deploy and administer server systems using Back-Office tools while desktop systems require the Windows NT or Windows 95/98 tool sets

    C. Are expected to choose from third-party tools for deploying and administering desktop and server systems

    D. Are provided with separate tools for deploying and administering desktop and server systems but each with a common look and feel

Answer: A

24. Select the product(s) included with Windows NT Server 4.0:

   A. FrontPage

   B. Internet Information Server (IIS)

   C. SQL Server

   D. Systems Management Server (SMS)

Answer: B

25. BackOffice is designed to run on which of the following? (Select all that apply.)

   A. Windows 95/98

   B. Windows for Workgroups

   C. Windows NT Server

   D. All of the above

Answer: C

26. Select the items that are designed to operate as integrated components under Outlook.

   A. Excel PivotTables

   B. Exchange Server Public Folders

   C. Team Manager

   D. Word spell checker

Answer: B, C

27. Windows NT supplies which of the following? (Select all that apply.)

   A. Built-in support for Internet standards: CGI, HTTP, ISAPI, ODBC, and Perl

   B. Built-in support for fault-tolerant features including disk-striping, mirroring, duplexing, and UPS-support

   C. C-2 level security for protection against unauthorized access to data

   D. Memory protection permitting securing execution for multiple applications on a single computer

Answer: B, C, D

28. While using the Microsoft SQL Server 6.5 Web Assistant to develop a Web page, the results set to be displayed can be specified by:

   A. Selecting a rule

   B. Selecting a stored procedure

   C. Selecting a view

   D. Writing a SELECT statement

Answer: B, C, D

29. Microsoft BackOffice offers which of the following advantages? (Select three.)

A. A common user environment

B. A single, integrated server supplying complete server-side functionality

C. Common development tools

D. Common system management tools

Answer: A, C, D

30. The Microsoft BackOffice suite includes which of the following?

A. Microsoft Exchange Server

B. Microsoft SQL Server

C. Microsoft Systems Management Server

D. Microsoft Transaction Server

E. All of the above

Answer: E

31. To send a document to several developers for review, while working in Microsoft Word 97, which of the following should you select?

A. The Exchange item from the Tools menu

B. The Exchange item from the Windows menu

C. The Send To item from the File menu

D. The Send To item from the Windows menu

Answer: C

32. BackOffice offers a complete server solution, including:

A. A single management model using the Window for Workgroups administration tools

B. A single management model using Windows-based administration tools

C. Two management models for Professional and Enterprise platforms

D. Two management models for the client and server sides of the database enterprise

Answer: B

33. Your objective is to design a Web site where customers can (a) query the company database for price and availability information, (b) place order requests, and (c) provide contact information. To handle pricing and stock availability, you would choose:

A. Microsoft Access

B. Microsoft FrontPage

C. Microsoft Visual Basic

D. Microsoft Visual J++

Answer: A

34. Microsoft Access offers developers a variety of tools used in form design, including which of the following? (Select all that apply.)

 A. Auto-conversion tools to convert ODBC and SQL data sources

 B. Edit boxes with built-in spell checking

 C. Image Controls providing a means of displaying graphical information in forms or reports

 D. Multi-select list boxes permitting either single or multiple selections

 Answer: B, C, D

35. Static database information can be presented on a Web site by saving the output from a Microsoft Access query, table, or report as an HTML file. To present dynamic data on the Web, Access objects would be created by saving:

 A. Access forms as .ASP files

 B. Access forms as .HTML files

 C. Access macros as .ASP files

 D. Access macros as .HTML files

 Answer: A

36. A development application requires maintaining an index to a large number of Web sites as hyperlinks. To satisfy this requirement, what is the optimum development tool?

 A. Microsoft Access

 B. Microsoft InterDev

 C. Microsoft Visual C++

 D. Microsoft Visual J++

 Answer: A

37. Using Visual Basic for Applications in Microsoft Excel, what should the instruction to reference the value in cell A1 be?

 A. `Excel("Book1").Range("A1:A1")`

 B. `Excel("Sheet1").Cell "A1"`

 C. `Worksheet("Book1").Cells("A1:A1")`

 D. `Worksheet("Sheet1").Range("A1")`

 Answer: D

38. In order to use Visual Basic for Applications (VBA) to create e-mail macros within Word, what is the first requirement?

 A. Add the OLE Messaging control to the Word document

 B. Register the MAPI control in a Word macro

 C. Set a reference to the OLE Messaging library

 D. Set a reference to the TAPI custom controls

 Answer: C

39. A replica and a design master would be used to synchronize a local database with a Web-based database by:

    A. Access

    B. Internet Explorer

    C. Internet Information Server

    D. SQL Server

Answer: A

40. Microsoft Access supports which of the following? (Select all that apply.)

    A. Distributed n-tier applications including middle-tier business rule servers

    B. Parameterized Queries allowing Internet users to create a data source which is both dynamic and interactive

    C. Partial Table Replication to replicate database objects across corporate networks

    D. Reverse engineering using the Microsoft Visual Modeler

Answer: B, C

41. What is the appropriate tool to visually display an Entity-Relationship diagram for a database?

    A. Access

    B. SQL Server

    C. Visual Basic

    D. Visual C++

Answer: A

42. Using Visual Basic for Applications (VBA), a generic object named x1 has been dimensioned (declared). Before methods can be invoked and properties set using x1 as a Microsoft Excel object, x1 must be assigned as an Excel object as:

    A. `Set x1 = CreateObject("Excel.Application")`

    B. `Set x1 = GetObject("Excel.Application")`

    C. `Set x1 As Excel.Application`

    D. `Set x1 As New Excel.Application`

Answer: A

43. An existing mainframe database application is designed to track interest rates and calculate closing costs, payments, and total interest paid for loans, presenting the information on screen. The existing mainframe application is to be replaced with Microsoft Windows applications. To convert the load amortization program to a Microsoft Office application, what would be the optimum tool?

    A. Access

    B. Excel

    C. Outlook

    D. Project

Answer: A

44. Microsoft Access objects include forms, macros, modules, reports, and tables, each of which constitute a document. Which Access object is used to group these documents into collections?

  A. Container

  B. Database

  C. DBEngine

  D. Workspace

  Answer: A

45. A decision-support application is designed to show cross-tab reports by customer, product, sales, and salesperson. Reports should cover all combinations of sales according to customer, customer region, product, and salesperson as well as sales by date by week, month, and year. Having developed a stored procedure within the database to extract the raw data, the next step is to create a configurable drag-and-drop crosstab report with a minimum of programming. What is the ideal tool for this purpose?

  A. A Visual Basic ActiveX control

  B. An Access AutoTable

  C. An Access dynaset

  D. An Excel PivotTable

  Answer: D

46. The objective is to create a Gantt chart showing task start and end times together with critical paths. The chart data will be stored in ODBC database and the application created using Visual Basic for Applications. Which VBA and ODBC-enabled application is best suited for this task?

  A. Microsoft Excel

  B. Microsoft Outlook

  C. Microsoft Project

  D. Microsoft Word

  Answer: C

47. After creating a slideshow in PowerPoint, the finished .PPT file will be distributed over the Internet. In order for people who do not have PowerPoint installed to be able to view the presentation, which tool is available on the Internet to show the presentation in the original format and backgrounds?

  A. Microsoft FrontPage

  B. Microsoft Internet Explorer

  C. Microsoft Office document viewer

  D. PowerPoint document viewer

  Answer: D

Chapter 4

1. An ActiveX control created with Visual Basic can be embedded in an Active Server Page (ASP) or in:

A. A macro for an Access .MDB file

B. A Visual Basic .CLS file

C. A Visual Basic .FRM file

D. The code for a Visual FoxPro .PRG file

Answer: C

2. Visual FoxPro uses the Internet Search Wizard to:

A. Access data tables through the Microsoft Internet Server

B. Create search pages where users can formulate queries which are passed to a Visual FoxPro database.

C. Execute topic searches across the Internet to locate requested Web pages

D. Locate Internet URLs where data tables are stored

Answer: B

3. In creating a Visual Basic ActiveX controller application to send e-mail messages, which Outlook collection would be used to add a new message to the Outbox?

A. Items

B. Messages

C. Outbox

D. Profiles

Answer: A

4. Visual FoxPro supports which of the following? (Select all that apply.)

A. Distributed n-tier applications including middle-tier business rule servers

B. Removable source code to reduce size, make applications run faster, and provide protection for intellectual property

C. Auto-conversion to migrate Access databases to FoxPro databases

D. Reverse engineering using the Microsoft Visual Modeler

Answer: A

5. For database development, why would Visual FoxPro be selected over Access 97?

A. FoxPro can be used to create ActiveX controls.

B. FoxPro is more compatible with other Microsoft tools than Access Visual Basic for Applications.

C. FoxPro is more efficient than the Jet Database Engine.

D. FoxPro provides more object-oriented programming capabilities.

Answer: D

6. Byte codes—Java executables which are not compiled into machine code until run time—offer which of the following advantages? (Select all that apply.)

   A. Direct hardware access at run time

   B. DirectX technology

   C. Faster performance at run time

   D. Platform independence

   Answer: D

7. Visual FoxPro provides support for outer joins using:

   A. ActiveX controls

   B. Custom classes representing fields

   C. Multiple SQL statements

   D. Native ANSI-standard SQL

   Answer: D

8. The Microsoft Visual Modeler is provided in which of the following tools:

   A. Microsoft Visual Basic Enterprise Edition

   B. Microsoft Visual Basic Professional Edition

   C. Microsoft Visual C++ Enterprise Edition

   D. Microsoft Visual J++ Professional Edition

   Answer: A

9. To what kind of user-defined function do a number of Windows API functions accept a pointer, as an argument?

   A. Aggregate

   B. Allocation

   C. Callback

   D. Thunking

   Answer: C

10. The results of queries submitted to a Visual FoxPro database through the Internet Search Wizard are:

   A. Automatically converted to HTML pages for presentation

   B. Passed to an ActiveX control for presentation

   C. Returned in raw format to be displayed by the client's own FoxPro forms

   D. Viewed using a Visual Basic supplied display control

   Answer: A

11. The Visual Basic Enterprise Edition includes which of the following? (Select all that apply.)

   A. Internet Search Wizard

   B. SQL Server, Developer Edition

   C. Visual Database Tools

   D. Visual SourceSafe

   Answer: B, C, D

12. Which Microsoft Visual Basic module is used to create an ActiveX control?

   A. A Control (.CTX file) module

   B. A Custom Control (.OCX file) module

   C. A UserControl (.CTL file) module

   D. A UserDocument (.OCA file) module

   Answer: C

13. Visual Basic supports creating documents with which of the following? (Select all that apply.)

   A. Explorer-style document interface applications

   B. HTML document interface applications

   C. Multiple-document interface applications

   D. Single-document interface applications

   E. All of the above

   Answer: E

14. The Microsoft Visual Modeler is a tool for which of the following? (Select all that apply.)

   A. Creating graphic models of database structures

   B. Creating models of application prior to development

   C. Reverse engineering Visual Basic applications

   D. Reverse engineering Visual C++ applications

   Answer: B, C

15. Using Microsoft Visual J++ as a Java development tool, how do Visual J++ components interact with ActiveX components?

   A. Visual J++ applications may act as ActiveX components.

   B. Visual J++ applications may use ActiveX components.

   C. Both A and B

   D. Neither A nor B

   Answer: C

16. As the IS manager for a company with mainframe, Macintosh, and PC systems running Windows, you are considering using Visual J++ as one of the development tools because applications written in Visual J++:

    A. Are easily integrated with other Microsoft applications

    B. Are specifically designed for the Internet

    C. Offer a single compiled application which can execute on any platform including Windows, Macintosh, and UNIX

    D. Operate faster than applications developed in Visual C++ or Visual Basic

    Answer: C

17. For an application requiring computation-intensive data processing, what is the optimum development tool?

    A. Visual Basic

    B. Visual C++

    C. Visual FoxPro

    D. Visual J++

    Answer: B

18. A series of applications are needed for in-house use to perform specialized calculations. These applications will require a user interface for data entry and responses but are not computation-intensive. Because the coding staff is heavily invested in other critical development tasks, you decide that these modules can best be developed by:

    A. Assigning a relatively inexperienced programmer to create the modules using Visual Basic

    B. Creating ActiveX components using Visual J++

    C. Reassigning your top Visual C++ engineer to the development project

    D. Hiring additional engineering staff on a contract basis for the development

    Answer: A

19. After developing a Visual Basic application, you discover that the application as a whole is running too slow. After further profile testing, three computation-intensive functions in the application account for better than 90 percent of the execution time. In order to speed up the application to suitable performance standards, the optimum choice is to:

    A. Create a dynamic link library, using Visual C++, to support the three computation-intensive operations.

    B. Create ActiveX components, using Visual J++, to handle the three computation-intensive operations.

    C. Rewrite the entire application in Visual C++ to speed up all operations in the application.

    D. Rewrite the Visual Basic application to speed up the three computation-intensive operations.

    Answer: A

20. Microsoft Visual J++ offers which of the following? (Select all that apply.)

    A. A Just-In-Time (JIT) compiler

    B. ActiveX technology

    C. Pointer addressing

    D. The Component Object Model (COM)

    Answer: A, B, D

21. Functionality can be added to Java applets using which of the following? (Select all that apply.)

    A. COM objects such as Data Access Objects and Remote Data Objects

    B. Dynamic link libraries

    C. Prebuilt ActiveX controls

    D. Visual InterDev

    Answer: A, C

22. What is required in order to run a Visual J++ application in the Windows environment?

    A. Web browser

    B. Web server

    C. Win32 virtual machine

    D. Windows virtual machine

    Answer: C

Chapter 5

1. The Total Cost of Ownership model weighs costs based on which of the following? (Select all that apply.)

    A. Cost versus value

    B. Current interest rates

    C. International exchange rates

    D. Return on investment (ROI) rates

    Answer: A

2. The Vericard Corporation provides credit card validation for Internet sales orders, employing Microsoft Transaction Server to provide credit card validation objects. The credit card validation object belongs to which component of the Microsoft Solutions Framework (MSF) Application Model?

    A. Active Servers

    B. Business Services

    C. Interface Services

    D. ODBC Services

    Answer: B

3. Cost baselines in the TCO model account for which of the following? (Select all that apply.)

    A. Costs as reported in industry averages

    B. Costs of acquiring technological assets

    C. Costs of managing and maintaining technological assets

    D. Costs of retiring technological assets

    Answer: B, C, D

4. The Team model aims to ensure that an effective team consists of members who:

    A. Are accountable for results in the areas each own

    B. Are empowered to use their expertise

    C. Are exam-certified professionals

    D. Possess the appropriate expertise for the project

    Answer: A, B, D

5. The managing phase in the TCO model is used to:

    A. Control expenses during implementation of the model processes

    B. Develop alternative strategies for maximizing return on investment (ROI)

    C. Treat costs as primary acquisition expenses

    D. Validate the optimization strategy by measuring actual results against projections

    Answer: D

6. The Solutions Framework Infrastructure model is used to:

    A. Anticipate user requirements

    B. Assess development tradeoffs

    C. Guide systems deployment

    D. Support infrastructures according to business growth requirements

    Answer: C

7. Major milestones defined by the Microsoft Solutions Framework (MSF) include which of the following? (Select all that apply.)

    A. Application Design

    B. Code Complete

    C. Project Analysis

    D. Project Definition

    Answer: B

8. The Solutions Framework defines an infrastructure as:

    A. Personnel and services performed.

    B. The physical elements forming a network.

C. The software elements appropriate to a computing environment

D. The total set of resources necessary to support the enterprise computing environment

Answer: D

9. The Infrastructure model applies the roles, functions, and expectations of which model or models to the requirements of rolling out a successful infrastructure?

   A. The Enterprise Architecture model

   B. The Process and Development/Application models

   C. The Process and Team models

   D. The Solution Design and Development/Application models

   Answer: C

10. The Microsoft Solutions Framework (MSF) consists of which three major models?

    A. The Process model, System Development Life Cycle (SDLC) model, and Team model

    B. The Team model, Client/Server model, and Application model

    C. The Team model, Process model, and Development/Application model

    D. The Team model, System Development Life Cycle (SDLC) model, and Application model

    Answer: C

11. The Microsoft Solutions Framework assigns responsibility for ensuring that the functional specifications for a project fit the requirements of the business to the:

    A. Development Manager

    B. Product Manager

    C. Program Manager

    D. Project Manager

    Answer: B

12. The Enterprise Architecture model is based on managing a technology infrastructure by encompassing which four perspectives?

    A. Application and Business

    B. Component and Services

    C. Information and Technology

    D. Infrastructure and Networking

    Answer: A, C

13. The planning phase in the TCO model is used to calculate which of the following? (Select all that apply.)

    A. Cost baselines

    B. Cost benchmarks

    C. Return on investment (ROI) estimates

    D. The impact of improvement costs on return on investment (ROI)

    Answer: A, B, C

14. What are the major milestones in the software development process (according to the Microsoft Solutions Framework)? (Select all that apply.)

    A. Code Complete

    B. Envisioning

    C. Planning

    D. Release of Product

    Answer: A, D

15. Problems that occur between businesses and old and new technologies in the absence of regular improvements to the infrastructure include which of the following? (Select all that apply.)

    A. Companies are unable to compete against rivals who are investing in newer systems and applications.

    B. Continuing support for legacy systems makes it impossible to define new technical guidelines.

    C. IT professionals loose touch with industry vendors and lack familiarity with state-of-the-art developments.

    D. Technology changes faster than new corporate standards can be defined.

    Answer: B, D

16. What are the perspectives used by the Solutions Design model? (Select all that apply.)

    A. Conceptual Design

    B. Industrial Design

    C. Logical Design

    D. Physical Design

    Answer: A, C, D

17. The Solutions Design model involves users:

    A. In both the initial planning and final testing stages

    B. In study groups to determine user needs and expectations

    C. Only in the initial planning stages

    D. Throughout the design process

    Answer: D

18. The Solutions Framework Process model is aimed at:

    A. Anticipating user needs

    B. Designing for flexibility

    C. Identifying and weighing development tradeoffs

    D. Producing customer-focused products or services

    Answer: C

19. Information Architecture (in the Enterprise Architecture model) is concerned with which key questions? (Select all that apply.)

    A. Is the present market expanding or contracting?

    B. What functional data requirements exist?

    C. What industry requirements and standards exist?

    D. What integration issues exist with current application systems?

Answer: B, C

20. What are the reasons cited by development professionals for keeping users from being involved in the design process? (Select all that apply.)

    A. Users are frivolous and tend to make impractical suggestions.

    B. Users are reluctant to consider innovation and are not interested in being involved in the design process.

    C. Users become overly demanding and expect all requests to be immediately implemented.

    D. Users have divergent opinions about what features new applications should and shouldn't include.

Answer: B, D

21. Benefits offered by the Solutions Framework Team model include which of the following? (Select all that apply.)

    A. A team culture encouraging clarity, efficiency, participation, commitment, and mutual cooperation

    B. Centralized maintenance of application logic

    C. Producing customer-focused products or services

    D. Tight, compact application code with well developed features

Answer: B, D

22. What are the three categories of services which compose an application, as defined by the Solutions Framework Development/Application model?

    A. Business services, including business rules, sequencing, and transaction integrity

    B. Data services, including data manipulation abstractions

    C. Internet services, including posting and HTML support

    D. User services, including the user interface and supporting logic

Answer: A, C, D

23. The Solutions Framework Process model is aimed at:

    A. Creating a higher quality product

    B. Directing development along profitable lines

    C. Improving developer morale

    D. Producing better design decisions

Answer: A, C, D

24. The Solutions Framework Process model departs from traditional development models in several fashions, including which of the following? (Select all that apply.)

   A. Directing development toward versioned releases

   B. Placing the emphasis on product Vision and Scope rather than requirements

   C. Placing the emphasis on realizable milestones

   D. Using customer-oriented rather than development-oriented milestones

   Answer: A, B, D

25. The Team model is structured around clearly defined roles which include which of the following? (Select all that apply.)

   A. Design and Cost Containment

   B. Development and Logistics

   C. Product Management and Testing

   D. Program Management and User Education

   Answer: B, C, D

26. Select the Microsoft Solutions Framework (MSF) Application Model component which resides between User Services and Data Services.

   A. Active Servers

   B. Business Services

   C. Interface Services

   D. ODBC Services

   Answer: B

Chapter 6

1. Source control applications commonly provide which of the following? (Select all that apply.)

   A. A means of tracking successive versions of a file

   B. A method of debugging source files

   C. A repository for maintaining application source files

   D. Facilities for viewing all types of file formats

   Answer: A, C

2. Source control software organizes files using which of the following?

   A. Directory trees

   B. Linked lists

   C. Projects

   D. Virtual drives

   Answer: C

3. A successful team development project depends on which of the following? (Select all that apply.)

   A. Balancing the skill levels of the project developers

   B. Coordinating and synchronizing changes to project files

   C. Developers being able to enhance application elements without interfering with efforts by other developers

   D. Multiple developers being able to access project, database, and source files

   Answer: B, C, D

4. Version 1.0 of an application is presently being shipped while two new projects are under development. One is a service pack for version 1.0 while the second project is version 2.0 of the application. Using Visual SourceSafe, changes to the service pack code modules made to correct bugs can be incorporated in the version 2.0 project source code using which SourceSafe feature?

   A. Encapsulating

   B. Linking

   C. Merging

   D. Sharing

   Answer: C

5. Services offered by source control applications include which of the following? (Select all that apply.)

   A. Automatic check-in of source files when the developer applications close

   B. Automatic check-out of source files when opened by developer applications

   C. Automatic tracking for different versions of each file

   D. Automatic version numbers to identify file versions

   Answer: C, D

6. Files removed from Visual SourceSafe: (Select all that apply.)

   A. Are always permanently lost

   B. Are removed permanently if the Destroy Permanently option is selected

   C. Can be permanently removed later using the Purge option

   D. Can be recovered if not destroyed permanently or purged

   Answer: B, C, D

7. Files under source control can:

   A. Be duplicated across projects

   B. Be shared between projects

   C. Belong to only one project

   D. Only be unique

   Answer: B

8. Visual SourceSafe allows users to recover which of the following? (Select all that apply.)

    A. All file versions at once

    B. Any file version selected

    C. Any pinned file version

    D. Only the most recent file version

Answer: B

9. Version-control change tracking: (Select all that apply.)

    A. Can only be used with text-based files

    B. Compares separate copies of file versions to identify changes

    C. Preserves a record of incremental changes made to individual files each time a file is checked in

    D. Shows binary files in hexadecimal format

Answer: C

10. A shared file exists as which of the following? (Select all that apply.)

    A. A separate file for each project

    B. A single file belonging to more than one project

    C. A specific version copied to each project

    D. None of the above

Answer: B

11. In addition to using Visual SourceSafe to maintain archival and current copies of project files, SourceSafe can also be used maintain a central up-to-date copy of these files that is not in the archives but is accessible to users who do not have access to the archives (and who are not intended to change or revise the contents of these files). What is this central storage called?

    A. Mirror image

    B. Mirror project

    C. Project replica

    D. Shadow folder

Answer: D

12. Visual SourceSafe identifies file versions by which of the following? (Select all that apply.)

    A. Both decimal and letter increments

    B. Decimal increments only

    C. Integer version numbers only

    D. Letter increments only

Answer: C

13. Custom version labels in Visual SourceSafe are commonly applied to which of the following?

    A. Both project and file versions

    B. Individual files

    C. Project level versions

    D. None of the above

    Answer: C

14. In Visual SourceSafe, which of the following is true? (Select all that apply.)

    A. Labels can be up to 128 characters in length.

    B. More than one user-defined label can be applied to a project version.

    C. Only one user-defined label can be applied to a project version.

    D. When applying multiple labels to a project, only the most recent label is retained.

    Answer: B

15. Differencing files in Visual SourceSafe shows which of the following? (Select all that apply.)

    A. Added lines in the newer version

    B. Changed lines in each version

    C. Deleted lines in the older version

    D. Whether binary files are the same or different

    Answer: A, B, C, D

16. Source control applications commonly support merging for which of the following file types? (Select all that apply.)

    A. Binary files

    B. Database files

    C. Text-based files

    D. Word-processing document files

    Answer: C

17. Using Visual SourceSafe with a Web server requires which of the following? (Select all that apply.)

    A. Installing the client version of Visual SourceSafe on all workstations

    B. Installing the client version of Visual SourceSafe on the network server

    C. Installing Visual SourceSafe on the network server

    D. Installing Visual SourceSafe on the Web server

    Answer: D

Chapter 7

1. The Component Object Model depends on which of the following?

    A. The use of object-oriented programming languages such as C++, Smalltalk, or Delphi

    B. Developing ActiveX and OLE components as COM implementations

    C. Making use of the Windows common dialog boxes in application interfaces

    D. Employing third-party libraries in application development

    Answer: B

2. Benefits of the Component Object Model include:

    A. Offering users a greater range of software choices

    B. Offering users a wider variety of specialized components

    C. Reducing the cost of redeveloping legacy applications

    D. All of the above

    Answer: D

3. In COM objects, a GUID (Globally Unique IDentifier) is created for each:

    A. Object

    B. Interface

    C. Method

    D. All of the above

    Answer: B

4. Local servers:

    A. Are commonly DLLs

    B. Are commonly EXEs

    C. Execute in a separate process space

    D. Execute in the same process space as the client

    Answer: B, C

5. Three types of Component Object Model servers are:

    A. In-process

    B. Local

    C. Remote

    D. Internal

    Answer: A, B, C

6. An individual COM object may act as:

    A. A server object

    B. A client object

C. Both a client and a server object at the same time

D. Either a client or a server object but not both at once.

Answer: C

7. The Component Object Model is supported by which of the following?

   A. Windows NT and Windows 98

   B. Windows NT, Windows 95, Windows 98, Windows 3.x

   C. Apple Macintosh

   D. Both B and C

   E. Any operating system providing COM services

   Answer: E

8. Which of the following is applicable to the COM IUnknown interface? (Select two.)

   A. It must be supported by all COM objects.

   B. It provides a binary standard for function calls between components.

   C. It provides methods to query which interfaces an object supports.

   D. It reports the GUID identifier for a component object.

   Answer: A, C

9. When a component calls an executable server object, what does COM do? (Select two.)

   A. It launches the .EXE file.

   B. It calls the CoRegisterClassFactory to instantiate the component object.

   C. It calls DllGetClassFactory to create an instance of the component object.

   D. It returns a pointer to the component object.

   Answer: A, D

10. The Component Object Library supplies which of the following? (Select three.)

    A. Connections between components

    B. Mechanisms to make IUnknown calls across processes

    C. Mechanisms to launch components

    D. Mechanisms to create UUID values for component objects

    Answer: A, B, C

11. Where is the CLSID value for a component stored for public reference?

    A. Only in the .DLL or .EXE binary file

    B. In the system registry

    C. In the SYSTEM.INI initialization file

    D. In the WIN.INI initialization file

    Answer: B

12. After calling the `QueryInterface` method for a component, which of the following is true?

    A. If the result returned is failure, the `IUnknown` method should be called to report that the object is not valid.

    B. If the result returned is failure, the `Release` method should be called to close the component object.

    C. If the result returned is success, the `AddRef` method should be called to increment the reference count for the component object.

    D. If the result returned is success, the object's reference count is automatically incremented.

Answer: D

13. Developing component objects requires a language/development platform which supports which of the following?

    A. Passing pointers to data elements

    B. Passing pointers to functions

    C. Passing data elements by value

    D. Exposing internal data elements by address

Answer: B

14. How does the COM standard manage connections between components?

    A. By using a vtable (virtual function table) to supply addresses for object functions

    B. By using a vtable (virtual function table) to supply addresses for object interfaces

    C. By querying an object's `IUnknown` function to retrieve the address of a function

    D. By querying an object's `IUnknown` function to retrieve the address of an interface

Answer: B

15. Dynamic Link Libraries are:

    A. Fully cross-compatible on a binary level and can be used on a cross-platform basis

    B. Provide the same version independence as component objects

    C. May be used for local component objects

    D. May be used for remote component objects

Answer: C

16. The Component Object Model:

    A. Provides compatibility between objects by translating parameter syntaxes between languages

    B. Provides encapsulation to ensure language independence between objects

    C. Requires compatible objects to be created using the same language

    D. Requires compatible objects to be created using the same operating system

Answer: B

17. The Component Object Model relies on which of the following?

    A. ODBC handling for transparent communications between component objects

    B. RPC handling for transparent communications between component objects

C. Static data structures for transparent communications between component objects

D. Strict typecasting for transparent communications between component objects

Answer: B

18. Which of the following statements are valid? (Select two.)

A. Existing COM interfaces always remain immutable.

B. Existing COM interfaces may be modified to handle new provisions.

C. New COM interfaces are identified by universally unique IDs.

D. New COM interfaces are identified by version numbers.

Answer: A, C

19. Universally Unique ID values can be created by which of the following? (Select two.)

A. The COM API `CoCreateGuid` function

B. The Microsoft-supplied `uuidgen` tool

C. The Universal ID Formula algorithm

D. Tossing dice

Answer: A, B

20. Universally Unique ID values include which of the following? (Select two.)

A. CLSIDs to identify component classes

B. DIDs to identify component data elements

C. FIDs to identify component files

D. IIDs to identify component interfaces

Answer: A, D

21. Each component object interface:

A. Receives a sequentially numbered GUID

B. Receives a unique IID value

C. Receives a GUID value supplied by the Open Software Foundation

D. Shares the component object class's GUID

Answer: B

22. Component objects (COM objects) may contain:

A. Both functions and data objects which are publicly exposed

B. Neither publicly exposed functions nor data elements

C. Publicly exposed functions and data elements that are never exposed

D. Publicly exposed interfaces which provide access to functions and data elements that are never exposed

Answer: D

23. Which of the following are true about pointers to component objects? (Select two.)

    A. They are actually pointers to component object interfaces.

    B. They can be used to modify object data.

    C. They can only access object methods.

    D. They provide access to all methods belonging to an object.

Answer: A, C

24. Before a COM object can be used, which of the following must happen?

    A. The object interface must be instantiated.

    B. The object itself must be instantiated.

    C. The object methods must be instantiated.

Answer: B

Chapter 8

1. The ACTXPRXY.DLL library supporting out-of-process marshalling for Active Document interfaces requires which of the following?

    A. A single version for Windows 95, Windows 98, and Windows NT 4.0

    B. Either Office 97 or Internet Explorer (3.0 or later) to be installed

    C. One version for Windows 95 and Windows 98 and a separate version for Windows 4.0

    D. Separate versions for Windows 95, Windows 98, and Windows NT 4.0

Answer: A

2. What is the advantage of OLE embedding over OLE linking?

    A. OLE embedding allows concurrent data access to multiple users.

    B. OLE embedding offers improved data security.

    C. OLE embedding prevents file sizes from expanding.

    D. OLE embedding supports in-place editing.

Answer: D

3. When an Active Document is being deactivated, what is the Active Document server responsible for?

    A. Adding its menus to the container object's menu bar

    B. Displaying all UI objects such as toolbars and status bars

    C. Hiding all UI objects such as toolbars and status bars

    D. Removing its menus from the container object's menu bar

Answer: C

4. When memory resources are limited, what is the best type of OLE object for drag-and-drop operations?

   A. An Internet object

   B. An OLE Java object

   C. An OLE-embedded object

   D. An OLE-linked object

Answer: D

5. When an Active Document is being activated, what is the Active Document server responsible for? (Select two.)

   A. Calling the server's `IOleDocumentView::SetInPlaceSite` method

   B. Calling the server's `IOleDocumentView::UIActivate` method with a non-zero (TRUE) `fActivate` parameter

   C. Displaying all UI objects such as toolbars and status bars

   D. Merging the server's menus to the container object's menu bar

Answer: C, D

6. To respond to an `IDataObject` request, how does the server store the document's data in the `IStorage` interface?

   A. Through the `IDataObject::GetDataHere` method

   B. Through the `IOleDocument` interface

   C. Through the `OleSave` API function

   D. Through the `STGMEDIUM` structure

Answer: D

7. Assume a Word document contains a linked Exel spreadsheet. If the Word document is opened after all references to Microsoft Excel are deleted from the registry:

   A. The linked spreadsheet will be visible but cannot be edited until Excel is reinstalled.

   B. The linked spreadsheet will be visible but must be relinked before it can be edited.

   C. The linked spreadsheet will be visible but the Excel type library must be reinstalled before editing.

   D. The linked spreadsheet will not be visible.

Answer: A

8. What is the advantage of OLE linking over OLE embedding?

   A. Linking does not inflate file sizes.

   B. Linking ensures that data is encapsulated within an application.

   C. Linking supports frame adornment.

   D. Linking supports in-place editing.

Answer: A

9. When registering an Active Document server, the \Insertable and \DocObject registry keys:

   A. Are always required

   B. Are required only if the CATID_Insertable and CATID_DocObject component categories have already been registered

   C. Are not required if the CATID_Insertable and CATID_DocObject component categories have already been registered

   D. Are never required

   Answer: C

10. The Active Document IOleDocument interface is *not* used to:

   A. Activate and deactivate a document's view object

   B. Create views of an Active Document

   C. Enumerate the views the object supports

   D. Provide miscellaneous information about the object's capabilities

   Answer: A

11. An iAdviseSink interface would offer the greatest benefit to:

   A. A budget application using linked Excel spreadsheets

   B. A DCOM application relying on synchronous event notification

   C. A document control application managing large print jobs

   D. A remote automation application using standard marshalling

   Answer: A

12. The Active Document IDataObject interface is used to:

   A. Activate and deactivate the view object

   B. Get and set data in the object

   C. Initialize the document object and place it in the loaded or running state

   D. Perform various save operations or to release storage

   Answer: B

13. Assume that a new hard drive has been added to a desktop system and that Microsoft Excel has been moved to the new drive without re-installation. After this is done, a Word document is opened which contains an embedded Excel spreadsheet. What is the effect of moving the EXCEL.EXE application on the document?

   A. The Adaptable Links feature of ActiveX will allow the embedded spreadsheet to be edited.

   B. The embedded spreadsheet can only be updated from within Excel.

   C. The embedded spreadsheet will appear but the system registry must be updated before the spreadsheet can be edited.

   D. The embedded spreadsheet will not appear but will be replaced by an icon.

   Answer: C

14. An Active Document:

    A. Assumes full control of the container application's client window

    B. Assumes full control of the container application's frame window

    C. Acts as an embedded object

    D. Acts as a linked object

Answer: A

15. When an OLE-embedded or linked object is selected in an OLE document, the container application may perform object-specific operations which are identified by data entries stored in:

    A. An .INI file

    B. The container

    C. The OLE object

    D. The registry

Answer: D

16. When an Active Document is displayed by a container:

    A. The Active Document's menu replaces the container application's menu.

    B. The Active Document's menu is merged with the container application's menu.

    C. The Active Document's menu appears below the container application's menu.

    D. The Active Document supplies a composite menu for both the server and client applications.

Answer: B

17. Assume that a Word document has a link to a Paintbrush bitmap image file which is stored on the same drive as the document file. When the document file is copied to a floppy disk, without copying the bitmap file, and then opened from the floppy disk on another computer, what will occur:

    A. An icon will appear in place of the bitmap image.

    B. The bitmap image will appear but an error will occur if the image is deleted.

    C. The bitmap image will appear in the document but the original image file can not be updated.

    D. The bitmap image will not appear in the document.

Answer: C

18. In Visual C++, Active Documents are supported by what two classes? (Select two.)

    A. `CDocObject` class

    B. `CDocObjectServer` class

    C. `CDocObjectServerItem` class

    D. `CDocObjectClientItem` class

Answer: B, C

19. The COM Structured Storage System provides two types of objects:

   A. A binary object and a file object

   B. A binary object and a stream object

   C. A storage object and a file object

   D. A stream object and a storage object

   Answer: D

20. Which statement is false?

   A. Active Documents have the advantage of owning their pages and exercise complete control over their presentation.

   B. Active Documents have the freedom to exploit the full native functionality of their servers.

   C. Objects embedded in documents are at least partially at the mercy of the container document.

   D. Objects embedded in documents have the freedom to exploit the full native functionality of their servers.

   Answer: D

21. Interfaces provided by the COM Structured Storage SDK can be implemented using inheritance in Visual C++. Select the interface(s) which allow separate applications to share data in a storage object without relying on global memory.

   A. `iCreateFileMoniker`

   B. `iMemAlloc`

   C. `iPersist`

   D. `iVirtualAlloc`

   Answer: C

22. What can Active Documents be presented by?

   A. ActiveX containers

   B. OLE client applications

   C. OLE servers applications

   D. Web browsers

   Answer: A

23. Which of the following do compound files offer?

   A. Direct access mode which makes differed changes to a document

   B. Direct access mode which makes immediate changes to a document

   C. Transacted access mode which makes differed changes to a document

   D. Transacted access mode which makes immediate changes to a document

   Answer: B, C

24. Which of the following are structured storage features? (Select all that apply.)

   A. Compound files

   B. Directory objects

   C. Folder objects

   D. Two-phase commits

   Answer: A, D

25. In comparing embedded and linked data using OLE, which of the following is correct? (Select two.)

   A. Embedded data is static.

   B. Embedded data occupies less space in a document file.

   C. Linked data is static.

   D. Linked data occupies less space in a document file.

   Answer: A, D

26. Which of the following are true of the Component Object Model (COM) Structured Storage System?

   A. Storage objects are analogous to files within directories.

   B. Storage objects can contain both streams and other storage objects.

   C. Storage objects can contain streams but cannot contain other storage objects.

   D. Storage objects form the highest level object in the ActiveX storage system.

   Answer: B

27. The Component Object Model (COM) reduces the use of global system resource through dependence on:

   A. ActiveX components

   B. ActiveX controls

   C. ActiveX documents

   D. Uniform Data Transfer

   Answer: D

28. An ActiveX object created using Visual Basic has control of a Microsoft Excel object. When a new hard drive is installed on a system and the user moves Microsoft Excel to the new drive (including all associated files) without reinstalling Excel, what is required for the ActiveX object to retain control of the Excel object?

   A. The ActiveX object must be rewritten.

   B. The adaptable links in ActiveX will allow everything to function unchanged.

   C. The registry entries for Excel must be updated.

   D. The user must reinstall the VBRun Dynamic Link Library.

   Answer: B

Chapter 9

1. How may a remote automation service be used?

    A. By many different client applications for different purposes

    B. By more than one instance of the same client application

    C. By multiple clients if they are using different interfaces

    D. By one client application at a time

Answer: A

2. Both Remote Automation and the Distributed Component Object Model (DCOM) enable remote communications between processes. On what do Remote Automation components execute?

    A. On a client system only

    B. On a server system only

    C. On either a client or server system with modifications to match the system

    D. On either a client or server system without modification

Answer: D

3. ActiveX controls are *not* based on:

    A. Local client objects and clipboard data transfers

    B. OLE automation and persistent storage

    C. Property pages and Uniform Data Transfer

    D. The COM model, compound documents, and connectable objects

Answer: A

4. Where are the proxies and stubs used for Remote Automation located?

    A. A proxy is located in the client's process space while the stub is located in the server's process space.

    B. A proxy is located in the client's process space while the stub may be located in either the client or server's process space.

    C. A stub is located in the client's process space while the proxy is located in the server's process space.

    D. A stub is located in the client's process space while the proxy may be located in either the client or server's process space.

Answer: A

5. In order to write an ActiveX control which will function in both the 16- and 32-bit environments, which of the following must be true?

    A. Only one version of the control is required, but it must be a 16-bit version with only one type library.

    B. Only one version of the control is required, but it must be a 32-bit version with only one type library.

C. Two versions of the control (16- and 32-bit) are required but with only one type library.

D. Two versions of the control (16- and 32-bit) are required, each with its own type library.

Answer: A

6. What is a compound document?

A. A control activated to initiate an action in a container application

B. Any ActiveX control containing data

C. Any document containing an embedded Active Document

D. Any document containing both its own native data and any linked or embedded object.

Answer: D

7. Given an application which uses object interfaces provided by two external ActiveX server applications—one local and one remote—how many proxy and stub objects are used?

A. One stub and one proxy

B. One stub and two proxies

C. Two stubs and one proxy

D. Two stubs and two proxies

Answer: D

8. ActiveX controls may support which of the following?

A. Both incoming and outgoing interfaces

B. Either incoming or outgoing interfaces

C. Only incoming interfaces

D. Only outgoing interfaces

Answer: A

9. Which of the following is the ActiveX-server remoting mechanism to use with a client application executing under a 16-bit operating system?

A. ActiveX documents

B. DCOM

C. RCOM

D. Remote Automation

Answer: D

10. An ActiveX control: (Select two.)

A. Can implement one or more persistence interfaces

B. Cannot implement more than one persistence interface

C. Must implement at least one `IPersist` interface

D. Must implement at least one `IPersist` interface if it has a persistent state

Answer: A, D

11. Select the appropriate (fastest) ActiveX component type for a processor-intensive application:

   A. A Java server

   B. An .EXE file

   C. An ActiveX library

   D. An in-process server

   Answer: D

12. Which of the following is true about ActiveX controls property pages?

   A. A component object can display its property page independent of the client.

   B. Property pages from multiple contained objects may be displayed in a single property sheet.

   C. The property sheet permits users to view and change a control's properties.

   D. All of the above

   Answer: D

13. In developing a multi-tier client-server application, which components would be good candidates for development as ActiveX controls?

   A. Business-rule processing components

   B. Custom remote automation objects

   C. Database access components

   D. Local user interface components

   Answer: D

14. When do ActiveX controls check for license (.LIC) files?

   A. In both design and run modes

   B. In design mode

   C. In run mode

   D. When the control appears on a Web page

   Answer: B

15. What is the greatest benefit to the user employing ActiveX technology?

   A. The user knows how the registry works.

   B. The user can manage and maintain information.

   C. The user can manage applications and versions.

   D. The user can use the events incorporated in ActiveX components.

   Answer: B

16. For an ActiveX control to interact efficiently with a control container, which of the following programmatic elements are employed? (Select three.)

   A. A dispatch map

   B. A series of event-firing functions

   C. The `COleControl` class

   D. The `IPersist` interface

Answer: A, B, C

17. Given the objective of changing the interface to an existing ActiveX server in order to add additional features and to reduce memory overhead when multiple instances of the objects are created, what should be created?

   A. A new interface should be created to include both the new and existing features but without supporting the previously existing interfaces.

   B. A new interface should be created to include both the new and existing features while keeping the previously existing interfaces in the new server as well.

   C. A new interface should be created which supports only the new features while previously existing features would be accessible through the previously existing interfaces.

   D. The new features should be added to the existing interface.

Answer: B

18. Information about properties and methods can be provided to the controller of an ActiveX component by using which of the following?

   A. A .CAB file

   B. A type library

   C. An .INI file

   D. Dynamic Data Exchange (DDE)

Answer: B

19. Serialization is used to permit which of the following? (Select two.)

   A. An ActiveX control container to store state information for the control

   B. An ActiveX control to store state information

   C. Settings for a control to be stored in the control's .INI file

   D. Settings for a control to be stored with the document where the control is used

Answer: A, D

20. To inspect an object library for a particular ActiveX component for use with VBA, what is the simplest approach?

   A. Examine the registry.

   B. Use the Object Browser.

   C. View the client's property sheet.

   D. View the server's property sheet.

Answer: B

21. Select the statement(s) which accurately describes how 16- and 32-bit ActiveX components can interoperate on a single computer.

   A. 16-bit ActiveX DLLs can be used by 32-bit ActiveX controllers.

   B. 16-bit ActiveX EXEs can be used by 32-bit ActiveX EXEs.

   C. 32-bit ActiveX DLLs can be used by 16-bit ActiveX controllers.

   D. 32-bit ActiveX EXEs can be used by 16-bit ActiveX EXEs.

   Answer: B, D

22. How may an automated object be accessible?

   A. Both as a remote or local object

   B. Only as a local object

   C. Only as a remote object

   D. Only through a network connection

   Answer: A

23. An ActiveX type library can be used to do which of the following? (Select all that apply.)

   A. Access objects

   B. Check type information for properties and methods

   C. Display object members in an Object Browser

   D. Obtain a pointer to a .CAB file

   Answer: A, B, C

24. Using parameters in ActiveX automation requires which of the following?

   A. Careful attention to typecasting between client and server objects

   B. No special provisions

   C. Type-safe variables passed using the VARIANT data type

   D. Using the `IDataType` interface to inquire about parameter sizes

   Answer: C

25. Remote (OLE) Automation is used in ActiveX controls to permit clients access to the control's features through which of the following?

   A. A client-supplied programming language

   B. A macro language

   C. The `IDirect` interface

   D. The VBScript programming language

   Answer: A

26. Remote Automation supports security access rights which include which of the following? (Select two.)

   A. Allowing access to specific interfaces on a per-user basis

   B. Allowing access to specific servers for remote access

   C. Granting access to specific client applications

   D. Granting access under NT to specific users and specific groups of users

   Answer: B, D

27. The ActiveX technology family includes which of the following? (Select three.)

   A. Active Scripts, Code Download and Verification, and HTML extensions

   B. ActiveX controls, ActiveX documents, and Internet ActiveX controls

   C. ActiveX server framework and Internet Data Download Services

   D. ActiveX viewer services and VB Scripts

   Answer: A, B, C

28. What is the benefit of creating custom components?

   A. Developers can compete with large corporations.

   B. Components allow applications to be distributed over the Internet.

   C. Developers can create tools for specific tasks without creating entirely new application suites to support these tools.

   D. Developers can replace portions of existing applications without developing entirely new applications.

   Answer: C

29. Structured storage is organized into which three object types?

   A. Discrete data objects

   B. Lock byte objects

   C. Storage objects

   D. Stream objects

   Answer: B, C, D

30. Structured storage objects may do which of the following?

   A. Return both OLE and MAPI error messages

   B. Return custom error messages

   C. Return only MAPI error messages

   D. Return only OLE error messages

   Answer: D

Chapter 10

1. Multiple database access is hampered by differences between databases in:

   A. Protocols

   B. Record types

   C. Data standards

   D. All of the above

   Answer: D

2. What are the three primary approaches to the database connectivity problem?

   A. Developing gateways

   B. Developing applications to handle multiple database formats

   C. Developing common programming interfaces

   D. Developing common protocols

   Answer: A, C, D

3. The ODBC standard:

   A. Calls for the development of common interface implementations by database vendors

   B. Defines a series of object classes based on the MFC DAO classes to provide translation and protocol services

   C. Defines a series of object classes based on the MFC RDO classes to provide translation and protocol services

   D. Defines an API suite allowing a variety of applications access to a variety of data sources through DBMS-specific drivers

   Answer: D

4. Which of the following is true of DBMS drivers under ODBC? (Select two.)

   A. They are dependent on OCX objects.

   B. They are integrated in the ODBC library.

   C. They are separate from the ODBC library.

   D. They translate standard SQL statements into native SQL for the data source.

   Answer: B, D

5. Which of the following is true?

   A. Both DAO and ODBC are dependent on specific database management systems.

   B. Both DAO and ODBC are independent of specific database management systems.

   C. DAOs are dependent on specific database management systems while ODBC objects are independent.

   D. ODBC objects are dependent on specific database management systems while DAOs are independent.

   Answer: B

6. A common programming interface provides which of the following?

A. A copy of the DBMS that supports a specific grammar, interface, and protocol

B. A standard API, macro language, or tool set for translating requests, accessing data, and returning results

C. A transaction-based system of exchanging information between front-end applications and back-end servers

D. An object-oriented interface between databases

Answer: B

7. ODBC is an API implemented by individual database vendors as which of the following?

A. An extension of the Microsoft JET database engine

B. ODBC component modules providing translation services between application standards and database native formats

C. ODBC drivers specific to each vendor's database management system

D. Three-tiered driver services providing multiple database format translations

Answer: C

8. Data Access Objects (DAO) provide data access objects consisting of a database object and which of the following? (Select three.)

A. A `querydef` object

B. A `recordset` object

C. A `tabledef` object

D. A `SQLdef` object

Answer: A, B, C

9. The common protocol approach to database connectivity is based on which of the following?

A. A single protocol, SQL grammar, and networking protocol common to all DBMSs

B. A standard API, macro language, or tool set for translating requests, accessing data, and returning results

C. A transaction-based system of exchanging information between front-end applications and back-end servers

D. Distributed Relational Database Architecture (DRDA)

Answer: A

10. Data Access Objects are optimized for:

A. .MDB files (Microsoft Access)

B. ISAM database files

C. SQL database files

D. Unstructured data files

Answer: A

11. Open Database Connectivity (ODBC) is best suited for access to:

    A. Local data sources

    B. Relational data sources

    C. .MDB (Microsoft JET) databases

    D. Any data source as long as an appropriate ODBC driver is available

    Answer: B

12. To solve the database connectivity problem, what approach is used by ODBC?

    A. Common interface approach

    B. Common protocol approach

    C. Gateway approach

    D. Both B and C

    Answer: A

13. Core provisions of the ODBC standard include which of the following? (Select three.)

    A. A standard error message reporting system

    B. A standard SQL grammar defined by ODBC

    C. The ability to execute SQL statements

    D. The ability to translate data types

    Answer: A, B, C

14. Extensions to the ODBC core provisions include which of the following? (Select three.)

    A. A SQL grammar for scalar functions, outer joins, and procedures

    B. Extended data types such as date, time, timestamp, and binary

    C. Scrollable cursors

    D. Synchronous operations

    Answer: A, B, C

15. Advantages of ODBC include which of the following? (Select three.)

    A. A portable API offering a common data access language for both the Windows and Macintosh environments

    B. Access to multiple database types through a single driver

    C. Being an accepted industry standard enjoying wide support

    D. Vendor-independent standards

    Answer: A, C, D

16. Advantages of DAO over ODBC include which of the following? (Select three.)

    A. The ability to specify relations between tables

    B. Access to data validation rules

    C. ISAM database compatibility

    D. Support for the Data Definition Language (DDL) and Data Manipulation Language (DML)

    Answer: A, B, D

17. Comparing DAO and RDO, select the false statement following:

    A. Both DAO and RDO support cursorless result sets that demand fewer resources than cursors.

    B. DAO supports ISAM structures for JET and installable ISAM databases.

    C. RDO does not require ISAM-support objects or methods.

    D. The RDO `RemoteData` control parallels the DAO `Data` control.

    Answer: A

18. Using RDO, referential integrity and support for security are provided by which of the following?

    A. Database tables and stored procedures

    B. RDO API functions

    C. Special object classes supported by RDO

    D. The database server

    Answer: D

19. Converting DAO and Data control applications to RDO and RemoteData controls requires which of the following?

    A. Conversions from result sets to data sets

    B. Minimal revisions

    C. Renaming classes and objects

    D. Support for ISAM objects

    Answer: B

20. Which of the following is true of SQL Distributed Management Objects (SQL-DMOs)? (Select three.)

    A. They are 32-bit COM objects compatible with Win98/Win95/WinNT.

    B. They are part of an integrated framework consisting of objects, properties, methods, and collections used to administer multiple SQL Servers distributed across a network.

    C. They are OLE Automation–compatible.

    D. They are dependent on the Visual Basic Script Language.

    Answer: A, B, C

21. Remote Data Objects (RDO) consist of objects and collections. Select the false statement following:

    A. RDO collections may contain multiple objects of a single type.

    B. RDO objects may contain multiple collections of a single type.

    C. RDO permits overriding the `QueryTimeout` property.

    D. `rdoEnvironments` consist of a logical set of `rdoConnection` objects.

    Answer: B

22. RDO provides which of the following? (Select three.)

    A. Access to values returned by stored procedures

    B. High performance access to remote ODBC data sources

    C. `rdoQuery` objects to access data sources without an associated connection object

    D. Support for server-side cursor keysets

    Answer: A, B, D

Chapter 11

1. What are the primary benefits of Active Data Objects? (Select three.)

    A. Access to multiple database types

    B. Ease of use

    C. Minimal memory overhead

    D. Sophisticated hierarchies

    Answer: A, B, C

2. ADO objects can do which of the following? (Select all that apply.)

    A. They can be used for batch updating.

    B. They offer efficient data access through Active Server Pages.

    C. They provide support for stored procedures including in/out parameters and return values.

    D. They return only a single recordset in response to any query.

    Answer: A, B, C

3. OLE DB architectural standards include which of the following? (Select three.)

    A. Automation engines

    B. Business rule engines

    C. Query engines

    D. Transaction managers

    Answer: B, C, D

4. What are the basic concepts behind the OLE DB standard? (Select all that apply.)

   A. To allow components to be shared across multiple applications

   B. To make the service component external to both the database and the application

   C. To separate database and service aspects into separate components

   D. To standardize services offered by database systems

   Answer: A, B, C

5. The OLE DB standard is intended to do which of the following? (Select three.)

   A. Extend and leverage existing ODBC database access

   B. Offer access to unstructured as well as structured data

   C. Offer both network and Internet access to data

   D. Replace existing ODBC database access

   Answer: A, B, C

6. How do OLE DB components differ from existing database services?

   A. They exist as independent applications functioning as a layer between client applications and the data providers.

   B. They exist either as server-side or client-side components.

   C. They provide integrated extensions to existing database services.

   D. They replace existing database services with new object-oriented services.

   Answer: A

7. What does using OLE DB's component architecture mean? (Select three.)

   A. Common functionality can be supplied across a variety of data sources.

   B. Components can be called from a variety of applications, programming languages, and tools.

   C. Components can be selected as needed to fulfill application requirements and changed or replaced as requirements evolve.

   D. Database vendors will not need to be responsible for developing ODBC drivers.

   Answer: A, B, C

8. OLE Databases (OLE DB) are based on which of the following?

   A. ActiveX components

   B. Metadata catalogs

   C. Structured Query Language

   D. Universal Data Access interoperability

   Answer: D

9. Implementing Universal Data Access through ADO and OLE DB provides which of the following?

   A. Convenient access to diverse data types and sources

   B. Optimized performance for diverse data types and data storage

   C. Reusable objects and third-party components

   D. Single-source support for all database requirements

   Answer: A, B, C

Chapter 12

1. Each process possesses which of the following? (Select three.)

   A. A base priority and minimum and maximum working set sizes

   B. A virtual address space, executable code, and application data

   C. Multiple threads and thread priorities

   D. Object handles and environment variables

   Answer: A, B, D

2. Which of the following is true?

   A. Creating multiple processes is more efficient than distributing tasks among multiple threads under a single process.

   B. Only threads execute code, while a process is the address space for the code.

   C. Processes require synchronization; threads run unsynchronized.

   D. The system reserves memory for structures required by processes but does not reserve memory for structures required by threads.

   Answer: B

3. Which of the following is true? (Select all that apply.)

   A. A process may begin with a single thread.

   B. A process may begin with multiple threads.

   C. Any thread may create a new execution thread.

   D. Only the primary thread may create new execution threads.

   Answer: A, B

4. Under Windows NT, CPU time is allocated to which of the following?

   A. A process

   B. A program

   C. A thread

   D. An application

   Answer: C

5. Threads in a 32-bit Windows environment:

   A. Are allotted time slices in which to run

   B. Are irrelevant since the Win32 API is not designed for preemptive multitasking

   C. Cannot access the global variables or system resources belonging to the process

   D. Each have their own virtual address space which is not shared by other threads

   Answer: A

6. Symmetric multiprocessor operating systems are characterized by which of the following?

   A. They allow the operating system to run free on any processor or on all processors simultaneously.

   B. They do not allow the operating system to be preempted by a higher priority thread requiring attention.

   C. They do not allow a single process to execute a different thread on different processors.

   D. They select one processor to run the operating system while other processors are dedicated to user jobs.

   Answer: A

7. Which of the following is true?

   A. Windows 95/98 does not support multiple processors.

   B. Windows 95/98 supports multiple processors and can simultaneously execute a separate thread on each processor.

   C. Windows NT does not support multiple processors.

   D. Windows NT supports multiple processors and can simultaneously execute a separate thread on each processor.

   Answer: A, D

8. Within a process, a thread may have how many priority levels?

   A. Two

   B. Three

   C. Five

   D. Six

   Answer: C

9. When a thread is suspended:

   A. The context of the preempted thread is saved.

   B. The thread is saved to virtual memory.

   C. The thread is terminated.

   D. The thread must be recreated.

   Answer: A

10. Which of the following statements is true of operating system architecture models?

    A. A multiprocessor system can execute multiple threads simultaneously but only when two separate threads are placed in the processing queue.

    B. All applications are multitasked on a multiprocessor operating system.

    C. All multitasking systems require a minimum of two processors.

    D. The multitasking model requires a 32-bit Windows operating system.

    Answer: A

11. Scheduling priorities are:

    A. Assigned only to processes

    B. Assigned only to threads

    C. Assigned to both processes and threads

    D. Reserved for the operating system

    Answer: C

12. Select the priority class assigned to background processes:

    A. HIGH_PRIORITY_CLASS

    B. IDLE_PRIORITY_CLASS

    C. NORMAL_PRIORITY_CLASS

    D. REALTIME_PRIORITY_CLASS

    Answer: B

13. A thread's priority is determined by which of the following? (Select all that apply.)

    A. The priority class of the thread's process

    B. The thread's dynamic priority boost

    C. The thread's priority class

    D. The thread's task ID

    Answer: A, B

14. Select the priority class used for threads which must respond to time-critical events:

    A. HIGH_PRIORITY_CLASS

    B. IDLE_PRIORITY_CLASS

    C. NORMAL_PRIORITY_CLASS

    D. REALTIME_PRIORITY_CLASS

    Answer: A

15. Thread execution is managed and scheduled by:

   A. The kernel

   B. The memory manager

   C. The process manager

   D. USER32.EXE

Answer: A

16. The differences in handling for threads and processes for a symmetric multiprocessing system (SMP) and an asymmetric multiprocessing system (ASMP) are:

   A. Threads can execute on any available processor on an ASMP operating system, while an SMP operating system has the system threads bound to a specific processor or set of processors.

   B. Threads can execute on any available processor on an SMP operating system, while an ASMP operating system has the system threads bound to a specific processor or set of processors.

   C. Threads can execute on multiple processors simultaneously on an SMP operating system, while an ASMP operating system allows threads to only execute on one processor at a time.

   D. Threads can execute on multiple processors simultaneously on an ASMP operating system, while an SMP operating system allows threads to only execute on one processor at a time.

Answer: B

17. Thread priorities are determined by which of the following?

   A. The process's priority

   B. The process's priority class and the thread's priority within the process

   C. The thread's base priority added to the process's priority

   D. The thread's virtual priority

Answer: B

18. Under Windows NT, operating system code can be preempted when:

   A. A thread with a dynamic priority boost requires attention.

   B. A thread with a higher process priority class requires attention.

   C. A thread with base priority requires attention.

   D. A thread with maximum application performance priority requires attention.

Answer: A

19. Select the statement(s) which is true for a process.

   A. A process can start with multiple threads.

   B. A process consists of the code, data, and other system resources used by the process threads.

   C. A process is a program which is loaded into memory.

   D. More than one process can share the same virtual address space.

Answer: B, C

20. Which priority are processor-intensive threads commonly assigned?

  A. THREAD_PRIORITY_HIGHEST

  B. THREAD_PRIORITY_IDLE

  C. THREAD_PRIORITY_LOWEST

  D. THREAD_PRIORITY_TIME_CRITICAL

Answer: A

21. Two Windows NT applications are executing, both using the same dynamic link library. The DLL is loaded:

  A. Once and is mapped to the memory space of both processes

  B. Once and receives its own local heap

  C. Once with global and static memory shared by the two processes

  D. Twice with each process maintaining its own global and static variables

Answer: A

22. The base priority of a thread is determined by:

  A. The process priority class

  B. The thread's priority level

  C. Whether the process is running in the foreground or background

  D. All of the above

Answer: D

23. The scheduler:

  A. Maintains a queue of all threads by process priority

  B. Maintains a queue of all threads by virtual priority

  C. Maintains a queue of ready threads by base level

  D. Maintains a queue of ready threads by priority level

Answer: D

24. Threads which are not ready include which of the following? (Select three.)

  A. Threads created with the CREATE_SUSPENDED flag

  B. Threads halted during execution by SuspendThread or SwitchToThread

  C. Threads waiting for a synchronization object or input

  D. Threads which are currently executing

Answer: A, B, C

25. Priority boosts are used to do which of the following? (Select two.)

  A. They adjust priorities for threads in the 16–31 priority levels.

  B. They ensure that no ready threads become starved for processor time.

C. They ensure that the system remains responsive.

D. They raise threads from 0–15 priority levels to 16–31 priority levels.

Answer: B, C

26. Thread affinity is used to do which of the following?

A. Force a thread to execute on a specific processor

B. Force specific threads to execute simultaneously

C. Force threads to be shared across multiple processors

D. Force threads to cluster on certain processors

Answer: A

27. When creating new threads:

A. A function named `ThreadProc` must be supplied as an entry point.

B. The `CreateProcess` function is called to create a process for the thread.

C. The parent thread must specify a starting address for the code that the new thread will execute.

D. The process must request permission from the system.

Answer: C

28. The `CreateThread` function accepts arguments which can specify which of the following? (Select three.)

A. A creation flag placing the thread in a suspended state

B. Initial stack size for the new thread

C. Priority levels for the parent process

D. Security attributes for the handle to the new thread

Answer: A, B, D

29. Threads can be synchronized using which of the following? (Select three.)

A. Console input buffers

B. Events, mutexes, processes, and semaphores

C. Message queues

D. Other threads and timers

Answer: A, C, D

30. Critical-section objects are an efficient method of doing which of the following?

A. Interrupting a thread's execution

B. Synchronizing threads across processes

C. Synchronizing threads belonging to a single process

D. Synchronizing threads globally

Answer: C

31. Thread Local Storage (TLS) allows threads to do which of the following?

    A. Allocate common memory

    B. Create unique copies of global variables

    C. Exchange private messages

    D. Share common objects

    Answer: B

32. Once a thread is launched, the thread executes until which point? (Select three.)

    A. Another process calls `TerminateThread` with a handle to the thread

    B. Any thread calls `TerminateThread` with a handle to the thread or `TerminateProcess` with a handle to the process

    C. The thread calls `ExitThread` or any thread in the process calls `ExitProcess`

    D. The thread function returns

    Answer: B, C, D

33. The `TerminateThread` and `TerminateProcess` functions:

    A. Free the initial stack

    B. Notify all attached DLLS

    C. Provide for an orderly shutdown and clean-up

    D. None of the above

    Answer: D

34. When `CreateProcess` is used to create a new process, which of the following occurs? (Select two.)

    A. An identifier is returned which uniquely identifies the process.

    B. Handles are returned for the new process and the process's primary thread.

    C. The process's thread immediately becomes active.

    D. The returned handles can be inherited by child processes.

    Answer: A, B

35. A child process can inherit which of the following? (Select two.)

    A. Environment variables

    B. Handles to DLL modules opened using the `LoadLibrary` function

    C. Open handles to process, thread, mutex, event, semaphore, anonymous pipe, named pipe, and file mapping objects

    D. Priority class

    Answer: A, C

36. A child process cannot inherit which of the following? (Select two.)

    A. Handles returned by `LocalAlloc`, `GlobalAlloc`, `HeapCreate`, and `HeapAlloc`

    B. Open handles returned by the `CreateFile` function, including handles to files, console input buffers, console screen buffers, mailslots, named pipes, and serial communication devices

C. Pseudo-handles returned by `GetCurrentProcess` or `GetCurrentThread`

D. The current directory

Answer: A, C

37. Comparing fibers and threads, select the true statement(s):

A. A fiber does not possess the same state information as a thread.

B. Fibers are executed independently of their threads.

C. Like threads, fibers are preemptively scheduled.

D. When a fiber calls `ExitThread`, only the fiber terminates.

Answer: B

Chapter 13

1. Inter-Process Communications are:

A. Always local processes

B. Always remote processes

C. Both local and remote processes

D. Independent of the process locations

Answer: C

2. Which of the following is true of the client side of a client/server application? (Select all that apply.)

A. It commonly requires light computing power.

B. It provides the user interface.

C. It requires a TCP/IP connection.

D. It requires considerable bandwidth.

Answer: A, B, D

3. Which of the following is true of the server side of a client/server application? (Select all that apply.)

A. It can only function over a network.

B. It must run on a mainframe system.

C. It commonly provides massive data storage.

D. It commonly provides sophisticated computing power.

Answer: C, D

4. Select the development tool(s) which would provide maximum control and efficiency for writing a new Web browser.

A. Active Server Pages (ASPs)

B. Java applets

C. Windows Sockets API

D. WinInet

Answer: C

5. ODBC and the Messaging API (MAPI) provide a layer of abstraction for local-area database and messaging systems. The same type of abstraction layer for WAN protocols is provided by:

A. NetBEUI

B. NetBIOS

C. TCP/IP

D. Windows Sockets

Answer: D

6. Which of the following is true of today's client/server systems? (Select all that apply.)

A. They allow shared data and document and task processing.

B. They are used to leverage legacy mainframes.

C. They facilitate communications between distributed workstations.

D. They provide distributed access to common data sources.

Answer: A, C, D

7. The Inter-Process Communications (IPC) mechanism that is used to implement a hot link over a network and automatically update a shared memory area on a client computer is:

A. Mailslots

B. Named pipes

C. NetDDE

D. Windows Sockets

Answer: C

8. Which of the following is true of the DDE protocol? (Select all that apply.)

A. It consists of a set of messages and guidelines to send messages between applications.

B. It depends on the DDEML.DLL library.

C. It uses atoms and pointers to shared memory objects.

D. It uses shared memory to exchange data.

Answer: A, D

9. Which of the following is true of the DDE Management Library (DDEML)? (Select all that apply.)

A. It enforces DDE protocols in a consistent fashion.

B. It provides compatibility between DDE applications by forcing them to implement DDE protocols in a consistent fashion.

C. It simplifies developing and implementing DDE client applications.

D. It simplifies developing and implementing DDE server applications.

Answer: A, B, C, D

10. What are the main components that make up a socket under the Windows Sockets API? (Select all that apply.)

  A. A port number or ID

  B. A socket type (stream or datagram)

  C. A TCP/IP network

  D. An IP address

  Answer: A, B, D

11. How does NetDDE function?

  A. It establishes a token-ring link between local and remote applications.

  B. It opens a bidirectional pipe between local and remote applications.

  C. It opens two one-way pipes between local and remote applications.

  D. It passes messages and data using packet transmissions.

  Answer: C

12. Select the Inter-Process Communications (IPC) mechanism which can broadcast messages to all computers across a specific network domain.

  A. Anonymous pipes

  B. File mapping

  C. Mailslots

  D. Named pipes

  Answer: C

13. The Windows Sockets Specification supports:

  A. Anonymous pipes

  B. Communications using TCP/IP and IPX/SPX only

  C. Data transfer through shared memory

  D. Services to interface with many transports with different addressing schemes

  Answer: D

14. Select the Inter-Process Communications (IPC) or memory-sharing processes which can be used across a network.

  A. Anonymous pipes

  B. File mapping

  C. Named pipes

  D. Windows sockets

  Answer: C, D

15. Named pipes and mailslots:

A. Are immune to impersonation

B. Are implemented as file systems

C. Depend on packet data transmission

D. Support special security APIs

Answer: B

16. The definition of a socket is:

A. A memory address used to receive data on a TCP/IP network

B. A point-to-point connection between two processes using the TCP/IP protocols

C. A TCP or UDP connection used by a network server

D. An endpoint for bi-directional communications between processes

Answer: D

17. Memory-mapped files:

A. Access other process's memory directly through VMM maps

B. Use a shared disk file to exchange data

C. Use NetBEUI communications

D. Write data to reserved system files

Answer: B

Chapter 14

1. The original Internet (the ARPANET) was created for what purpose?

A. To facilitate communications between research facilities

B. To maintain a high state of military readiness during the Cold War

C. To share records between IRS offices

D. All of the above

Answer: A

2. What is File Transfer Protocol used for?

A. To copy files from one Internet machine to another

B. To copy HTML files to client systems for display

C. To provide a protocol for distributed document navigation and retrieval

D. To provide transparent file access across Internet clients

Answer: A

3. What is the primary communication standard used on the Internet?

A. Distributed Communication Procedures (DCP)

B. Point-to-Point Protocol (PPP)

    C. Remote Computer Calls (RCC)

    D. Transmission Control Protocol / Internet Protocol (TCP/IP)

Answer: D

4. The link layer in TCP/IP is associated with which of the following? (Select all that apply.)

    A. Creating transmission handshaking protocols

    B. Interfacing with a network card or modem

    C. Resolving Internet address identifiers

    D. Transferring data packets to the physical network

Answer: B, D

5. An Internet domain name consists of which of the following? (Select all that apply.)

    A. A 32-bit globally unique address

    B. A primary domain name

    C. A secondary domain name

    D. A user name

Answer: B, C

6. The TCP/IP protocol stack consists of which four layers?

    A. Application, browser, e-mail, and network/internetwork layers

    B. Application, transport, network/internetwork, and link/network access layers

    C. Protocol, e-mail, FTP, and FileNet layers

    D. Transport, DNS, Windows Sockets, and serial-line/dial-up layers

Answer: B

7. Which of the following is true of globally unique 32-bit Internet addresses? (Select all that apply.)

    A. They are created by local network administrators.

    B. They are encoded versions of the top-level and secondary domain address names.

    C. They consist of four hex values in the range 0..0×FFFF.

    D. They consist of four numeric fields with values in the range 0..255.

Answer: D

8. Internet standards are proposed in what documents?

    A. Interdependent System Developments (ISD)

    B. Internet Standards Document (ISD)

    C. Request For Comment (RFC)

    D. Requirements For Communications (RFC)

Answer: C

9. The transport protocol layer regulates the data flow between networked machines using which protocol? (Select all that apply.)

    A. Packet Transmission Protocol (PTP)

    B. Secure Data Transmission Protocol (SDTP)

    C. Transmission Control Protocol (TCP)

    D. User Datagram Protocol (UDP)

    Answer: C, D

10. Which of the following is true of the application layer? (Select all that apply.)

    A. It consists of external applications called through TCP/IP protocols.

    B. It has been superseded in part by Web-based services.

    C. It implements GUI services for the Web.

    D. It refers to protocols built at the application layer of the TCP/IP suite.

    Answer: B, D

11. The Domain Name System (DNS) is:

    A. A distributed database used to map domain names to IP addresses

    B. A group of servers providing routing services for Internet connections

    C. A host system providing addressing services for Internet connections

    D. A protocol for translating IP addresses to top-level and second-level domain names

    Answer: A

12. Universal Resource Locators (URLs) may contain which of the following? (Select all that apply.)

    A. Account names and passwords

    B. Directory and filenames

    C. File transfer retrieval schemas

    D. Host domain names

    E. Protocol to be used

    Answer: A, B, C, D, E

13. The User Datagram Protocol (UDP) relies on which of the following?

    A. Application-supplied data validation

    B. Auto-correcting data streams

    C. Checksum data validation

    D. Reliable connections between networks

    Answer: A, D

14. Post Office Protocol (POP 2 & 3) provides:

    A. A means for identifying and locating e-mail users

    B. A protocol for displaying electronic mail on a client system

C. A protocol for managing electronic mail using store and forward

D. A protocol to translate e-mail addresses to IP addresses

Answer: C

15. Transmission Control Protocol (TCP) relies on which of the following? (Select all that apply.)

A. Application-supplied data validation protocols

B. Automatic line condition monitoring

C. Packet identifier and checksum values

D. Tolerance for unreliable link conditions using packet-oriented protocol

Answer: C, D

16. Registration for second-level domain names is handled by which of the following?

A. American Registration Internet Networks (`arin.net`)

B. International Domain Registrars (`registrars.net`)

C. International Registration Services (`registration.net`)

D. Internet Network Information Center (InterNIC)

Answer: B

17. Network File System (NFS) is used for which of the following?

A. To copy files from one Internet machine to another

B. To copy HTML files to client systems for display

C. To provide a protocol for distributed document navigation and retrieval

D. To provide transparent file access across Internet clients

Answer: D

18. Simple Mail Transfer Protocol (SMTP) establishes which of the following?

A. A means for identifying and locating e-mail users

B. A protocol for displaying electronic mail on a client system

C. A protocol for the exchange of electronic mail between two message transfer agents (MTAs) on the Internet

D. A protocol to translate e-mail addresses to IP addresses

Answer: C

19. FTP (File Transfer Protocol) connections using the Open command can supply arguments as which of the following? (Select all that apply.)

A. 32-bit IP addresses

B. Partial URLs

C. Top-level, second-level domain names

D. All of the above

Answer: A, C

20. Anonymous FTP logins commonly request e-mail addresses as password arguments. This information may be used to do which of the following? (Select all that apply.)

    A. To build e-mail name/address lists

    B. To maintain a connections log

    C. To parse and resolve domain names to identify the location where the request originates

    D. To track downloads for commercial or competitive purposes

Answer: B, C

21. What does Simple Network Management Protocol (SNMP) offer?

    A. A protocol for distributed hypertext document searching, navigation, and retrieval

    B. A protocol for remote administration of TCP/IP machines

    C. A protocol for transferring files between machines

    D. A protocol to address remote systems

Answer: B

22. File Transfer Protocol (FTP) supports which transfer modes? (Select all that apply.)

    A. ASCII

    B. Binary

    C. Compressed

    D. Graphic

Answer: A, B

23. In order to find a location on the Internet for a file, service, or topic, what is the appropriate mechanism to use?

    A. Any of a variety of Web-based search engines

    B. Archie to catalog anonymous FTP servers

    C. GOPHERSPACE for distributed document search and retrieval

    D. VERONICA for an indexed search to gopherspace

Answer: A

24. Hypertext Markup Language (HTML) is a method providing which of the following?

    A. An extension of the Standard Generalized Markup Language (SGML)

    B. Format tags defining how documents should be presented

    C. Hotkey links between files and file locations

    D. Support for JPEG and GIF image formats

Answer: A, B

25. According to HTML standards, lists are supported as which of the following? (Select all that apply.)

   A. A sequence of paragraphs

   B. Automatically by indented paragraph levels

   C. Bulleted list items using the UL tag

   D. Numbered list items using the OL tag

   Answer: A, C, D

26. In which of the following cases can a partial URL be used?

   A. When the file referenced is located on the same server and directory as the document containing the URL

   B. When the link is referring to a graphic image

   C. When a fully-qualified URL is too long to fit

   D. When the file or document referenced is located on the local (client) system

   Answer: A

27. Which of the following is true of tags defined in the HTML language structure?

   A. They are defined in the HTML 3.2 and 4.0 language standards.

   B. They can be user defined.

   C. They must always consist of begin and end codes.

   D. They must always use begin and end codes for format instructions.

   Answer: A

Chapter 15

1. The Network News Transfer Protocol is used to:

   A. Display HTML pages from either local sources or through Internet connections

   B. Connect to newsgroup services over the Internet

   C. Create applications that use the Internet for intercommunications

   D. Locate headlines and sports scores over the Internet

   Answer: B

2. The time required for downloading Web pages can be reduced by:

   A. Employing a Web browser supporting ActiveX controls

   B. Employing a Web browser supporting Java applets

   C. Turning off graphics display by the browser

   D. Turning off security checks by the browser

   Answer: C

3. The Internet Transfer control supplies implementation for which of the following? (Select all that apply.)

A. The WinSock Proxy Service

B. The File Transfer Protocol (FTP)

C. The HyperText Transfer Protocol (HTTP)

D. The Network News Transfer Protocol (NNTP)

Answer: B, C

4. Select the file format supported by Web browsers that provides progressive rendering for graphic images.

A. ActiveX compound documents

B. Auto-download files

C. Interlaced files

D. Java files

Answer: C

5. The WebBrowser ActiveX control is used to:

A. Display HTML pages from either local sources or through Internet connections

B. Connect to newsgroup services over the Internet

C. Create applications that use the Internet for intercommunications

D. Locate headlines and sports scores over the Internet

Answer: A

6. When using the Network News Transport Protocol (NNTP) over the Internet, the service most likely to be accessed is:

A. A BBS (bulletin board) service or newsgroup

B. A file download service

C. A Gopher or document location service

D. A World Wide Web service

Answer: A

7. Browsers cache visited Web locations by:

A. Using read-ahead functions to predict which pages will be required next

B. Keeping a list of previously visited URLs

C. Writing temporary files to the local drive

D. Writing temporary files to your IP server

Answer: C

8. Visual Basic (version 5.0) provides a number of Internet-specific ActiveX controls including one which supports both the HTTP and FTP protocols. The control supporting both services is:

   A. Internet Protocol control

   B. Internet Transfer control

   C. WebBrowser control

   D. WinSock control

   Answer: B

9. Optimum compression ratios for images used in Web pages are provided using:

   A. The GIF format

   B. The JPEG format

   C. The PNG format

   D. All of the above

   Answer: B

10. While using Internet Explorer, you are alternating between a page listing parts and price information and pages offering detailed descriptions of equipment. How does Internet Explorer determine which pages should be updated when stepping back and forth between cached material?

    A. The HTTP protocol checks the date and time stamps for each page accessed, downloading the .HTML file if it is newer than the cached version.

    B. The HTTP protocol refers to the CLASS ID for every page and refreshes both text and graphics if the .HTML file is newer than the cached version.

    C. Internet Explorer does not update any cached pages unless the Refresh button is clicked.

    D. Internet Explorer may be configured to refresh pages when they are accessed a second time during a session.

    Answer: D

11. True-color (24-bit-per-pixel) images can be displayed from Web pages using which format(s)? (Select all that apply.)

    A. GIF

    B. JPEG

    C. PNG

    D. All of the above

    Answer: B, C

12. Active caching of frequently visited Web pages is provided by which Microsoft Proxy Server service?

    A. Domain Filtering

    B. Web Proxy Service

    C. Windows NT Challenge/Response authentication

    D. WinSock Proxy Service

    Answer: B

Chapter 16

1. Often ODBC databases require a user name and password for access. Where does an Internet application commonly store this information?

   A. In an .ASP file

   B. In an .HTX file

   C. In an .IDC file

   D. Either A or C

   Answer: D

2. What is the appropriate visual tool to create an Active Service Page (ASP)?

   A. Microsoft FrontPage

   B. Microsoft Internet Information Server

   C. Microsoft Visual Basic

   D. Microsoft Visual InterDev

   Answer: D

3. When using the Internet Database Connector to publish an Access database on the Internet, where is the ODBC data source name stored?

   A. In the .HTM file

   B. In the .HTX file

   C. In the .IDC file

   D. In the .ISP file

   Answer: C

4. Which of following is true of the design process used by Gateway programs?

   A. It is dependent on the TCP/IP protocols and must be integrated into HTML pages.

   B. It is dependent on the HTML protocol and must be integrated into HTML pages.

   C. It is dependent on the TCP/IP protocols and cannot be integrated into HTML pages.

   D. It is quite different from HTML files and can not be integrated into HTML pages.

   Answer: D

5. An .IDC file is used to retrieve the `Itemprice` field from a catalog database. In the resulting HTML file, which tag displays the `Itemprice` field?

   A. `<%itemprice%>`

   B. `<htx.itemprice>`

C. `<idc.itemprice>`

D. `<itemprice>`

Answer: A

6. Which of the following is true of the Internet Data Connector? (Select all that apply.)

A. It is a gateway-based service.

B. It is a protocol supplied by an ActiveX component.

C. It is an interface supplied by the Internet Information Server.

D. It is used together with the HTML extension services.

Answer: C, D

7. In designing a Web page using Microsoft FrontPage, a hyperlink leaves the existing page displayed in the current browser window and opens a second browser to display the linked page. To fill this requirement, the TARGET parameter in the <FRAMESET> tag is assigned which value?

A. _blank

B. _new

C. _top

D. _window

Answer: A

8. In creating an Internet shopping application, the Active Server Pages (ASPs) permit which of the following?

A. Product data can be accessed from the Web browser's data cache.

B. Product data can be accessed on demand using a database server.

C. Product data can be stored on a single ASP.

D. Product data can be stored on the client computer using HTML pages.

Answer: B

9. Once an ASP (Active Server Page) or IDC (Internet Data Connector) file has incorporated references to an existing DSN (Data Source Name), how can the reference be changed?

A. By linking the DSN through a database reference to a new data source

B. By deleting the existing DSN and creating a new source using the same name

C. By using an alias to redirect the DSN to a new data source

D. Only by recreating the ASP or IDC source

Answer: B

10. The Microsoft Internet Information Server uses .IDC and .HTX files together. The functions filled by these two files are:

A. .IDC files contain database queries while .HTX files contain templates to display the results of a database query in an HTML format.

B. .IDC files contain templates to display the results of a database query in an HTML format while .HTX files contain the login ID and password for database access.

C. .IDC files contain the login ID and password for database access while .HTX files contain the data to be displayed.

D. .IDC files contain the names of data sources while .HTX files provide the data to be displayed.

Answer: A

Chapter 17

1. Before an ActiveX component can be marked as safe for scripting and initializing, what must the developer certify?

A. That the component script cannot be used to read or write to any file

B. That the component script cannot be used to set component properties

C. That the component script cannot read users' names or e-mail addresses without their permission

D. That the component script uses the COM (Component Object Model) library for execution

Answer: B

2. When an ActiveX component is identified as Safe for Initialization, this indicates that:

A. A test agency certifies that a user's data cannot be harmed by data accepted by the control's properties.

B. A test agency certifies that a user's data cannot be harmed by data accepted by the control's methods.

C. The developer certifies that a user's data cannot be harmed by data accepted by the control's methods.

D. The developer certifies that a user's data cannot be harmed by data accepted by the control's properties.

Answer: D

3. Select the HTML code which will instruct Internet Explorer to download and register an ActiveX component:

A.
```
<COMDOC
    CLASSID="clsid:2A356098-2AF4-33C4-7567-2345BDEF8745"
    CODEBASE="Example.cab#version=1,0,0,0">
</COMDOC>
```

B.
```
<COMDOC
    CLASSID="clsid:2A356098-2AF4-33C4-7567-2345BDEF8745"
```

```
    docfile="Example.doc#version=1,0,0,0">
</COMDOC>
```

C.
```
<OBJECT
    CLASSID="clsid:2A356098-2AF4-33C4-7567-2345BDEF8745"
    CODEBASE="Example.cab#version=1,0,0,0">
</OBJECT>
```

D.
```
<OBJECT
    CLASSID="clsid:2A356098-2AF4-33C4-7567-2345BDEF8745"
    docfile="Example.doc#version=1,0,0,0">
</OBJECT>
```

Answer: C

4. When an ActiveX-enabled Web browser downloads a page containing an ActiveX component, what does the browser do first?

  A. It automatically downloads any files listed in the .INF file.

  B. It automatically downloads the component .CAB file.

  C. It checks the class ID parameter to determine if the component presently exists on the local system.

  D. It extracts the CODEBASE= attribute to identify the .CAB file.

Answer: C

5. Select the element from the <OBJECT> tag on an HTML page which indicates the location of the .CAB file used to download an ActiveX component.

  A. CLASSID

  B. CODEBASE

  C. ID

  D. OBJECTID

Answer: B

6. Assuming that Internet Explorer (version 3.0) is configured with all default settings, what must be true for an ActiveX component to be automatically downloaded by the browser from the Internet?

  A. It must be digitally signed.

  B. It must be packaged in a .CAB file.

  C. It must be packaged in a .ZIP file.

  D. It must have a security rating less than four.

Answer: A

7. Which of the following is true of the HTML <OBJECT...> tag?

  A. It can only be used for ActiveX components.

  B. It can only be used for ActiveX controls.

  C. It must always be terminated by a </END> tag.

  D. It must always be terminated by a </OBJECT> tag.

Answer: D

8. An HTML page uses an <OBJECT...> tag identifying a .CAB file as the source of an object to be included in the page. The .CAB file may contain:

   A. Any number of files and may contain one .INF file

   B. Any number of files but must contain one .INF file

   C. Exactly one file

   D. One .INF file and one other file.

   Answer: A

9. The <OBJECT...> tag for an ActiveX control contains what three major attributes? (Select all that apply.)

   A. the CLASSID attribute

   B. the CODEBASE attribute

   C. the ID attribute

   D. the USEMAP attribute

   Answer: A, B, C

10. An ActiveX document created using Visual Basic supplies which of the following features?

    A. A property page for saving persistent data to the server

    B. Menu placement services for visual editing

    C. The ability to write client-side scripts using the Visual Basic scripting tool

    D. The Visual Basic HTTP component object allowing Internet navigation.

    Answer: B

11. Where are cabinet (.CAB) files for ActiveX components customarily stored?

    A. On the client system in the \WINDOWS directory

    B. On the client system in the \WINDOWS\OCCACHE directory

    C. On the server in the \WINDOWS\OCCACHE directory

    D. On the server in the same directory as the HTML page using the component

    Answer: D

12. Object information contained in an ActiveX component type library consists of:

    A. Methods

    B. Properties and methods

    C. Properties, methods, and help information

    D. Properties, methods, and linking information

    Answer: C

13. While the cabinet (.CAB) file format supports more than one compression format, for widest access by browsers, which format should be selected?

   A. ARC

   B. LZX

   C. MSZIP

   D. PKZIP

   Answer: C

14. Certification for component safety is established by:

   A. A consortium of Internet Service providers

   B. A Microsoft certification service

   C. An independent Certificate Authority

   D. The component developer

   Answer: D

15. A digital signature in an ActiveX component offers users of the component the assurance that:

   A. The component has been licensed for distribution in the developer's name or the company's name.

   B. The developer's name or company's name is attached to the code.

   C. The developer's or company's identity has been verified by Microsoft.

   D. The developer's or company's identity has been verified by the InterNIC Corporation.

   Answer: B

16. Cabinet files are organized around folders to:

   A. Maximize compression

   B. Minimize decompression

   C. Preserve directory structures

   D. All of the above

   Answer: A

17. To optimize performance over the Internet, a component object should be packaged by:

   A. Placing all required files in a single .CAB file

   B. Placing each library and component object in separate .CAB files.

   C. Placing the .INF and component object in a primary .CAB file and the library files in a secondary .CAB file.

   D. Placing the .INF file in a primary .CAB file and placing all other files in secondary .CAB files.

   Answer: D

18. When using .CAB files to distribute ActiveX components over the Internet, if the component requires supporting files, how are these identified?

A. By an .ASP file

B. By an .HTM file

C. By an .IDC file

D. By an .INF file

Answer: D

19. What is a digital signature?

A. A certificate issued by a Certificate Authority

B. A graphic reproduction of a handwritten signature

C. An encrypted fingerprint image

D. An encrypted key supplied by the Internet Security Agency

Answer: A

20. Which one of the following best describes how ActiveX documents and ActiveX controls can be used?

A. ActiveX controls can be used to replace ActiveX documents.

B. ActiveX controls can be used to replace HTML pages.

C. ActiveX documents can be used to replace ActiveX controls.

D. ActiveX documents can be used to replace HTML pages.

Answer: D

APPENDIX

B

Glossary

Access See *Microsoft Access.*

Active Data Object (ADO) An interface for OLE DB that shields Visual Basic programmers from the COM interfaces necessary to implement database connectivity.

Active Document Server An application functioning as a container application.

Active Documents Also known as Doc Objects or Document Objects. Objects which are embedded in a container application such as a Web browser or an ActiveX container.

Active Scripts Scripting languages, including VBScript, JavaScript, and others, used to connect controls and add interactive functionality to Web pages.

Active Server Pages An IIS ISAPI extension that allows script code to be processed on the Web server rather than forcing it to run on the browser. ASP can dynamically build .HTML files in response to URL requests. Like .IDC files, .ASP files can access ODBC data sources through a data source name (DSN).

ActiveX Collectively applied to the Component Object Model and to COM-based objects such as ActiveX controls; also Microsoft's name for interoperable technologies based on the Component Object Model (COM). Microsoft's ActiveX technology includes, but is not limited to, OLE.

ActiveX automation controls Objects which expose programmable objects to client applications (automation clients).

ActiveX control Previously an OLE control; a reusable component supporting a variety of OLE functionality. ActiveX control objects can be incorporated in Web pages and other ActiveX containers.

ActiveX Data Objects (ADO) Similar to *RDO.* This object set should be seriously considered for new development projects as there will be no further releases or upgrades of the RDO library.

ActiveX documents Applications developed using Visual Basic or Visual C++ which integrate with other elements of an Internet or intranet site. ActiveX documents can be deployed in such a fashion that users can navigate transparently between HTML pages and ActiveX documents.

ActiveX server framework Provides support for customized Web pages using database content and other customizations.

ActiveX technology family   A group of technologies with one primary function: to allow the developer to create Internet applications using familiar tools and technologies.

ADA   Another D***ed Acronym. See also *TLA*.

ADO   See *Active Data Object*.

AFTP   See *APPC File Transfer Protocol*.

ANSI   American National Standards Institute.

API   Application Program Interface.

APPC   Advanced Program to Program Communications.

APPC File Transfer Protocol (AFTP)   Performs high-speed file transfers between IBM hosts and Windows NT–based systems.

AppleTalk   Macintosh network protocol.

Application layer   Protocols built at the application layer of the TCP/IP suite. For Windows, these will be Windows Sockets–compatible applications.

.ARC   Identifies an older compression format which is not common today but may still be found on some sites.

Archie   A TCP/IP application that served as one of the earlier methods for cataloging files from an assortment of anonymous FTP sites. Archie provided a simple mechanism for locating files across more than a thousand public hosts.

ASP   See *Active Server Pages*.

Asymmetric multiprocessor   A system that assigns a processor or set of processors to handle the system threads.

ATL   Active Template Library.

Automation   (1) A means of manipulating an application's objects from outside the application. (2) A process used to create applications which expose object methods to programming tools and macro languages. (3) A process used to create and manipulate one application's objects from another applications. (4) A process used to create tools for accessing and manipulating objects.

Automation client Also known as automation controller; any application which manipulates exposed objects belonging to another application.

Automation server Also known as automation component; any application which exposes programmable objects to other interfaces.

BackOffice See *Microsoft BackOffice*.

Banyan VINES/IP Internet protocol from Banyan Systems.

Basic See *Microsoft Visual Basic*.

Basic interoperability Standards allowing developers to be free to create their own custom designs while still being able to determine that their applications will be interoperable with applications and components created by other developers.

Briefcase A service provided by the Windows 95 or Windows NT 4.0 operating systems that synchronizes changes made to various files so that copies on disks or mobile computers can be synchronized with copies stored on a server or desktop system.

Byte codes Uncompiled Java application code, requires *Just-In-Time compiler* for execution.

C++ See *Microsoft Visual C++*.

CAB A new compression format used primarily for Microsoft installation files. .CAB files are decompressed by the operating system and do not require decompression utilities.

Callback functions User-defined functions within applications which are called directly by the operating system message handler.

CD-ROM Compact disk, read-only memory.

CGI Common Gateway Interface.

Child process A process created by another (parent) process.

CISC (Complex instruction set computing) Refers to the architecture of a CPU design.

Class   An abstraction of an object-oriented component. In C++, object classes are defined as data types but may be defined differently in other languages. Since OLE can be coded in any language, the term class is used to refer to the general object definition.

CLSID   CLaSsID, a GUID identifying a component object class. See also *Globally Unique ID*.

CMC (Common Mail Calls)   Support for cross-platform API.

COM   See *Component Object Model*.

COM Object   See Component object.

Component   See Component object.

Component object   In the COM model, an object is a body of compiled code which provides some service or services to other system components. Also known as object or component.

Component Object Interfaces   Component objects expose groups of internal methods through interfaces, enforcing strict encapsulation of both data and processing.

Component Object Library   A library provided by the Windows system to supply the basic mechanisms supporting the COM model.

Component Object Model   The concept of reusability applied on a component level where different software components—services—can work together to provide features used by applications. An underlying architecture and standard defining components as resuable objects, software services, which can be 'plugged in' to work with other components. A.k.a. COM.

Component Object Servers   A body of code implementing a *component object* such that the *Component Object Library* can use that code to create component object instances to provide services to component object clients.

Compound documents   Any documents which contain linked or embedded objects in addition to the documents' own native data.

Compound files   A standard file format allowing compound documents to be stored as structures, providing internal support for the formats required by different components. See also *OLE Structured Storage*.

Conditional Compilation Compilation flags within the code allow developers to control application behavior, making it easy to create both debug and release compilations simply by setting or clearing flags.

Connectable objects ActiveX controls may support both incoming and outgoing interfaces, using outgoing interfaces through connectable objects, allowing the control to communicate with the client object.

Controls See *ActiveX control.*

Cooperative multitasking Applications and threads must relinquish control of the CPU so that the operating system can handle its own tasks and manage the rotation of tasks to allow other applications or threads an opportunity to perform their tasks. A.k.a. Permissive multitasking.

Cross-network call Call made between COM components located on different computers.

Cross-process call Call made between COM components in different processes on the same computer.

Cross-process functionality The development model must provide the flexibility for developers to create components which will function not only in-process but also cross-process, and eventually, cross-network, all within a single programming model.

CSS (Cascading Style Sheets) Provides a simple means to style HTML pages, offering control for visual and aural characteristics, fonts, margins, line spacing, borders, colors, layers, and more.

CSV Common Service Verb.

Cursors Used in reference to Recordsets for databases. A cursor is a set of pointers that reference the data stored in a database.

Data Access Objects (DAO) A programming interface for the Jet engine. Data Access Objects (DAO) provide a framework for applications to create and maintain databases using an object hierarchy. DAO should not be seriously considered for new development projects, especially those using relational data sources. It is superceded by *OLE DB.*

Data transfer Any process for transferring data between objects.

Database replication   The process of taking existing data in a database and copying its content or portions of its content to other databases on the network.

Database Tools   See *Microsoft Visual Database Tools*.

Database Wizard   Provides connections from Java applications to popular ODBC and SQL databases through DAO and RDO interfaces (part of Microsoft Visual Foxpro).

Datagram socket   Closely models the facilities found in packet-switched networks such as Ethernet, supporting a bidirectional data flow which is not sequenced, not reliable, and not unduplicated.

DBMS   Database Management System.

DCE   Distributed Computing Environment.

DCOM   Distributed COM; functions across networks.

DDE (Dynamic Data Exchange)   A form of inter-process communications supported by the Win32 API. The DDE protocol consists of a set of messages and guidelines used to send messages between applications which share data and use shared memory to exchange data.

DDEML (Dynamic Data Exchange Management Library)   A Dynamic-Link Library (DLL) which applications running under Windows can use to share data.

DDK   Device driver development kit.

Design master   Under Microsoft Access Jet Database Engine Replication, one copy of an .MDB file is designated as a design master. See also *Replica*.

DHCP (Dynamic Host Configuration Protocol)   Auto-configuration service that allows a machine to obtain an address without a priori knowledge at boot time.

Disk striping   A fault-tolerant system of storing information across multiple physical disk drives.

Distributed transaction   The process of issuing a single transaction from an application source and forcing this transaction to be atomic across servers on a network.

Distributed Transaction Coordinator (MSDTC)   Microsoft SQL Server 6.5 support for distributed RDO transactions.

Distribution database   In SQL Server, a special database in the distribution server host that is essentially the "post office."

DLL   See *Dynamic Link Library*.

DMI   DMTF Desktop Management Interface.

DMO (SQL-DMO)   Distributed Management Objects.

DNS (Domain Name Service)   Used to translate between the human-friendly domain names and the 32-bit globally unique addresses. The DNS is a distributed static database used by the Internet to map domain names to IP addresses specified by network administrators.

DOM (Document Object Model)   Provides methods for scripts to manipulate HTML documents using methods and data types that are independent of specific programming languages or computer platforms.

DOS   Disk Operating System, a.k.a. MS DOS or Microsoft DOS; an operating system.

Drag-and-Drop   Any operation using the mouse or another pointing device to select an element or block of data and to transfer the element or block to another location within the same window, to another window within the application, or to a window belonging to another application.

DRDA   Distributed Relational Database Architecture.

DSMN   Directory Services Manager for NetWare.

Duplexing   A method of simultaneous bidirectional transmission.

Dynamic binding   Binding at run time (i.e., on execution) as opposed to static binding.

Dynamic Link Library   A program module that contains executable code and data that can be used by applications or by other DLLs.

Dynasets Keyset cursors used in reference to Recordsets. When a dynaset recordset type is built, a set of keys are built on the client, one key for every record in the result set at the time the keyset was built.

Embedded item An item which can be edited (activated) in-place by invoking the OLE server application.

Embedding One of two methods for storing items created by external server applications within an OLE document.

Excel See *Microsoft Excel*.

Exchange Server See *Microsoft Exchange Server*.

FAT (File Allocation Table) Commonly refers to the 16-bit file system used by DOS and all versions of Windows.

FAT32 32-bit File Allocation Table system introduced in Windows 95 (OSR2) and subsequently used by Windows 98 and Windows NT version 5.0 and later.

Fiber In reference to threads, a unit of execution which is manually scheduled by an application.

FoxPro See *Microsoft Visual FoxPro*.

FPNW File and Print Services for NetWare.

FrontPage See *Microsoft FrontPage*.

FTP (File Transfer Protocol) One of the most widely used TCP/IP application protocols. FTP is used to copy files between machines. Copying a file is not the same as remotely accessing a file, which is as service provided by the NFS (Network File Service) member of the application layer.

Gateway A shared connection between a Local Area Network and a larger system such as the Internet. The gateway causes a target DBMS to appear to a calling application as a copy of the DBMS which supports a specific grammar, interface, and protocol.

get FTP command-line command that copies a file from the host system to the local computer.

GIF (Graphic Image Format) The original graphics format available on the Web, first used by Compuserve, and remains the de facto standard. Normally, GIF images are either 16 or 256 colors and use either run-length or LZW compression to minimize data size. GIF does not provide support for 24-bit per pixel (i.e., true-color) images.

Globally Unique ID (GUID) Unique 128-bit integer values, ostensibly guaranteed to be unique, both throughout the world and throughout time, which are used to identify each interface and each component object class. GUIDs are generated to prevent collisions between similar names used by different component objects. GUID or UUID (Universally Unique IDs) values are defined by the Open Software Foundation's Distributed Computing Environment and—for all practical purposes—will not be duplicated accidentally. Also known as UUID.

Gopher Introduced as an application layer client/server protocol for distributed document search and retrieval—in effect, an Internet card catalog. The details for the Gopher protocol specification can be found in RFC 1436.

GSNW Gateway Service for NetWare.

GUID See *Globally Unique ID*.

Hierarchical Object Browser Allows developers to explore an object hierarchy to locate development information by differentiating between built-in properties, custom properties, methods, event handlers, and user-defined procedures.

Hierarchy In computer terms, a hierarchy is defined as a pyramid method of organizing general groups of information, processes, and systems.

Hive Root or primary registry key.

HREF The HREF parameter takes the form HREF=reference where the reference is either a destination address or a destination file, in URL format.

HTML (Hypertext Markup Language) The HTML standard is implemented as a Document Type Definition (DTD) in Standard Generalized Markup Language (SGML), which is a system for specifying grammars in a document.

HTML extensions Provide support for controls and scripting.

HTTP (Hypertext Transport Protocol) Used to connect to World Wide Web servers and to retrieve HTML documents.

HTX file format   HTML extension (.HTX) file which is used with an .IDC in IIS 4 to generate a Web page displaying current data from the database.

Hyperlink   Provides links between documents either locally, or over the intranet or Internet.

IDC (Internet Data Connector)   An interface supplied with IIS (Internet Information Server) which provides a means to support complex data retrieval from ODBC data sources.

IDC/HTX   See *HTX file format.*

IDC2ASP   A tool available free from Microsoft that converts an existing Web site or corporate intranet displaying data via the Internet Data Connector (IDC) to ASP (Active Server Pages).

IDL   Interface Definition Language (used with the COM model).

IDR   International Domain Registrars at `registrars.net`.

IID (Interface ID)   A GUID identifying a COM interface. See also *Globally Unique ID.*

IIS   See *Microsoft Internet Information Server.*

IMAP4   See *Internet Mail Access Protocol 4.*

Impersonation   A feature added to named pipes that allows a server to change its security identifier to appear to be the client at the remote end of the connection.

Incremental File Access   Allows individual objects within the compound file—such as stream or storage objects—to be accessed without loading the entire file.

Initialization (.INI) files   Files used to store information to initialize software and hardware configurations, user preferences, and status information.

In-Place Activation   The process of invoking an OLE server to edit an embedded OLE object. Also known as visual editing.

In-process call   Call made between COM components in the same process.

Instantiation   The process of creating an actual instance of an object class, i.e., creating the concrete instance (object) from an abstraction (class).

InterDev   See *Microsoft Visual InterDev.*

Interface Definition Language   A language standard tool provided for the convenience of the programmers and not defined by the Component Object Model standards.

Interface Pointers   Address pointers to methods (functions) exposed by component objects.

Interlacing   An image format (or sub-format) that supports progressive rendering.

Internet   An international computer network.

Internet ActiveX controls   ActiveX controls for including browser and Internet communications capabilities in applications.

Internet Data Download Services   APIs providing Internet access to data.

Internet Database Connector gateway   ODBC database gateway for the WWW service, supporting publication of database information on the Internet.

Internet Information Server   See *Microsoft Internet Information Server.*

Internet Mail Access Protocol 4 (IMAP4)   An Internet standard for e-mail and server-based mail storage providing a superset of POP/SMTP features, including the ability to store e-mail messages in multiple folders. Outlook 98 supports IMAP4, including full support for multiple IMAP4 e-mail accounts. See also *Post Office Protocol 3 (POP3)*, *Simple Mail Transport Protocol (SMTP).*

Internet Service Manager   Provides remote, secure administration of all Internet Information Servers and services.

Internetwork   A collection of networks, as opposed to the Internet, which identifies a specific collection of networks.

InterNIC   Internet Network Information Center.

Intranet   A local or corporate network.

IPX (Internetwork Packet eXchange)   A Novell NetWare protocol used to route messages from one network node to another; see also *SPX.*

ISAM   Indexed Sequential Access Method file structure used for distributed transaction processing.

ISAPI   Internet Server API.

ISP   Internet Service Provider.

ISV   Independent Software Vendor.

IT   Information Technology.

J++   See *Microsoft Visual J++*.

Java   An object-oriented cross-platform programming language for building Web applets and components that can run on either the Web client (inside the browser) or on the Web server. See also *Microsoft Visual J++*.

Java Type Library Wizard   Provides the means to integrate COM-based applications, written in other programming languages, into Java applications without needing to rewrite the applications from scratch.

Java Virtual Machine   A platform-specific component supporting Java applications.

JET (Joint Engine Technologies)   A file-server data engine that fits into the file-server database architecture. This approach to database deployment places the data engine on each individual workstation accessing the data source.

Jitter   The irregularity in the order in which packets—originally transmitted in sequence—are received.

JPEG (Joint Photographic Experts Group)   A graphics format that is optimized for 24-bit photographic images and uses a DCT-based coder to achieve high-compression ratios.

Just-In-Time Compiler   Platform-specific compiler to prepare Java byte code for execution. See also *Java Virtual Machine*.

JV Machine   See *Java Virtual Machine*.

Kernel   The core portion of an operating system.

LAN   See *Local Area Network*.

Language independence   A standard requiring applications to be capable of interoperation regardless of the development tools and/or languages used in their creation.

lcd   FTP command used to change the local directory directories.

LDAP   Lightweight Directory Access Protocol.

License Service API (LSAPI)   Services designed to automate software licensing and to reduce the overhead involved in implementing custom licensing systems.

Linked item   Item displayed within an application's document but stored as a separate file; cannot be edited in-place.

Linking   One of two methods for storing items created by external server applications within an OLE document.

Local Area Network (LAN)   Any group of computers and associated peripherals connected to form a network.

LPR/LPD   Protocols for printing from a PC to a print server (LPR), and for turning a PC into a print server (LPD).

LSAPI   See *License Service API.*

LUA   Logical Unit Application.

Mailslots   Similar to *named pipes* but offer the additional ability to broadcast messages to all computers in a specified domain.

MAPI   See *Messaging API.*

Marshalling   The process of packaging and sending interface method calls across thread or process boundaries.

Memory-mapped files   A memory object shared between processes.

Messaging API (MAPI)   An open standard to offer a common method for Windows-based applications to gain access to a wide variety of electronic messaging services in enterprise environments; a medium-independent messaging architecture enabling a variety of applications to interact with different systems on different hardware platforms.

MFC   See *Microsoft Foundation Classes.*

Microkernel architecture   Alternative kernel design developed by researchers at Carnegie Mellon University and dedicated to only loading, running, and scheduling tasks.

Microsoft Access   ISAM-based relational database.

Microsoft BackOffice   An application that provides a group of server-side components for Internet and intranet support.

Microsoft Database (MDB)   Known universally as the Access database.

Microsoft Developer Network Library   CD-ROM offering a comprehensive source for technical information about Microsoft tools, platforms, and technologies.

Microsoft Excel   Supports spreadsheets and Shared Workbooks; enables groups to work together more effectively.

Microsoft Exchange Server   Provides the e-mail server with integrated groupware supporting communications and the distribution of information.

Microsoft Foundation Classes (MFC)   Object-oriented class library of functions for Windows application development.

Microsoft FrontPage   A tool for creating and managing Web sites with no programming required. Also used to edit and create advanced Web page designs within a Visual InterDev project.

Microsoft Internet Information Server   Provides both HTTP and FTP services as well as software for Internet security and database access, offering a platform for publishing on both the Internet and intranets.

Microsoft Office   Offers applications to satisfy a variety of the most common office requirements including document processing (Microsoft Word), spreadsheets and financial tools (Microsoft Excel), and database creation (Microsoft Access).

Microsoft Outlook   Provides e-mail and contact and schedule management.

Microsoft PowerPoint   Tool suite for presentations both in person and via the Web.

Microsoft Project   Project management tools for tracking schedules and budgets.

Microsoft Publisher   A tool for creating both hardcopy publications and Web pages.

Microsoft Repository   Database used with *Microsoft Visual Basic* to store and share components, models, objects, and relationships together with descriptive information.

Microsoft Schedule+   Provides time management, task organizing, and schedule sharing.

Microsoft SNA Server   Connects personal computers and servers with IBM mainframe and AS/400 systems.

Microsoft Solutions Framework   A collection of business practices integrated into reusable models which incorporate measurable milestones to guide technological decisions in a business context.

Microsoft SQL Server   Provides a scalable, high-performance database management system for managing and storing data. Designed specifically for distributed, client/server environments.

Microsoft Systems Management Server (SMS)   Provides a comprehensive solution for managing networked PCs, including software and hardware inventory management, automated software distribution and installation, management for shared applications, remote help desk functions, and remote diagnostics, as well as network and computer performance monitoring and troubleshooting.

Microsoft Team Manager   A product that consolidates, coordinates, and tracks team activities.

Microsoft Transaction Server   A component-based transaction processing system for developing, deploying, and managing high performance, scalable, and robust enterprise, Internet, and intranet server applications.

Microsoft Visual Basic   A language for application development demanding only minimal knowledge of Windows APIs, messaging protocols, and information structures.

Microsoft Visual C++   Object-oriented development tool for Windows-based applications, offering fast, efficient execution, full access to system functionality, and flexibility in application design.

Microsoft Visual Database Tools   Allows developers to visualize and edit key database objects used in applications.

Microsoft Visual FoxPro   An object-oriented database development system featuring ActiveX extensibility.

Microsoft Visual InterDev   An integrated Web application development system offering tools to develop, publish, and manage database-driven Web applications, creating applications which are accessible from any Web browser.

Microsoft Visual J++   An object-oriented cross-platform programming language for building Web applets and components that can run on either the Web client or on the Web server.

Microsoft Visual Modeler   A tool for reverse engineering existing Visual Basic applications and creating models of applications prior to development.

Microsoft Visual SourceSafe   A file repository that stores project source files, tracks differences between file versions, and allows developers access to either current or previous version of the source files.

Microsoft Visual Studio   Supplies application development tools, including Visual Basic, Visual C++, and Visual FoxPro, for creating complete, custom applications.

Microsoft Word   Word-processing program with capabilities for efficient online communication and collaboration.

MIDL (Microsoft IDL compiler)   See *Interface Definition Language*.

MIME (Multipurpose Internet Mail Extensions)   Provide full-fidelity exchange of file attachments and multimedia objects.

Mirroring   A fault-tolerant disk storage system using two identical drives to maintain mirrored data on both.

MSDN   Microsoft Developer Network.

MTA   Message Transfer Agent (Exchange Server).

Multiple CPU support   See *Symmetric multiprocessing.*

Multiple Document Container   A container object (application) which can hold (display) more than one Active Document.

Multitasking   A process by which one application is suspended, preserving its registers, memory, and execution status, in order to permit another application an opportunity to execute.

Multithreading   Similar to multitasking except that a single application or process is executing two or more tasks as independent or semi-independent threads.

Multi-tiered architecture   The execution of tasks is divided between applications and components in the architecture where separate components provide different portions of the application services. Another name for client/server architecture.

NAME   The NAME parameter in HTML takes the form NAME=name where the name identifies a reference within the current HTML document or may be a reference within an external document.

Named pipes   A communications API used in network applications to transfer information.

NetBEUI   NetBIOS Extended User Interface.

NetBIOS   A standard IPC programming interface in the PC environment, providing support for client/server applications. NetBIOS has been in use since its introduction in the early 1980s.

NetDDE   A networked version of the Dynamic Data Exchange protocol which serves as a virtual hot link by providing automatic updates to shared memory areas across a network.

NetWare   Novell network system.

NFS   Network File System.

NIST   National Institute of Standards and Technology.

NNTP (Network News Transport Protocol)   Provides newsgroup services over the Internet.

NTFS   Windows NT File System; a 32-bit file allocation system providing support for larger hard drives as well as system (file) access security. NTFS conforms to C2-level certification requirements.

NVAlert   NetView Alerter; used with an SNA Server to send predefined Windows NT events to Novell NetView.

NVRunCMD   NetView Run Command; allows a Novell NetView host to send commands to an SNA Server run under Windows NT.

NWLink   Component of Novell network.

<OBJECT> tag   A tag used to insert an object, i.e., an image, document, applet, or control, into an HTML document. An object may contain any elements ordinarily used within the body of an HTML document, including section headings, paragraphs, lists, forms, and nested objects or, of course, ActiveX components.

Object   A body of compiled code that provides some service—or multiple services—to other system components. See also *Component Object*.

Object Linking and Embedding (OLE)   An early standard in the creation of component software allowing separate applications to share services or permitting one application to supply services used within the framework of another application. All OLE services are simply COM interfaces. A mechanism allowing users to create and edit compound documents.

OCX   Optical character recognition, or a compiled, shared object in Visual Basic 4.

ODBC   See *Open Database Connectivity*.

ODS   Open Data Services gateway.

Office   See *Microsoft Office*.

OLAP   Online analytical query processing.

OLE   See *Object Linking and Embedding*.

OLE automation   OLE automation can be used in ActiveX controls to permit clients access to the control's features through a client-supplied programming language. See also *Automation*.

OLE controls   See *ActiveX controls*.

OLE DB   OLE Database is a series of interfaces designed to offer data access to all data types, irrespective of format or location. OLE DB is designed to encapsulate or componentize database and related data processing functions.

OLE DB Providers   Also known as OLE DB components or, more explicitly, as OLE DB Data Providers and OLE DB Service Providers. Offer direct interfaces between an application and the native data, very much like existing ODBC Drivers in use today.

OLE documents   Documents that contain objects created and maintained by multiple applications. Also known as compound documents.

OLE Structured Storage   An OLE-supported technology for storing and maintaining compound files in native file systems, i.e., for storing a file composed of two or more OLE elements from different sources in a single document file. See also *Compound Files*.

OOP   Object-Oriented Programming.

Open Database Connectivity (ODBC)   A standard programming language interface that allows an application access to a variety of data sources. Using ODBC, access is provided to any data source—either local or remote—as long as an appropriate ODBC driver is available. ODBC drivers are available as both 16-bit and 32-bit versions, for a wide variety of data sources such as Microsoft SQL Server and Microsoft Access.

Open Systems Environment (OSE)   A standard intended to increase the number and variety of products for business solutions available to users, assuming functionality and price, by encouraging third-party add-on product developers.

Outlook   See *Microsoft Outlook*.

PAN   See *Personal Area Network*.

Partial Table Replication   Used to replicate database object subsets across corporate networks.

Perl   Common language for developing simple Web applications.

Permissive multitasking   See *Cooperative multitasking*.

Persisted data   Data or information that is written to persistent storage (i.e., a file on a hard or floppy drive).

Persistence storage   An ActiveX control can implement one (or more) of several persistence interfaces to support a means of saving a control's state.

Personal Area Network (PAN)   Wireless network used for communications with peripherals over very localized distances.

PIM   Personal Information Manager.

PNG   See *Portable Network Graphics*.

Pointer   An address of a function or variable.

Post Office Protocol 3 (POP3)   One of the most commonly used protocols for sending and receiving e-mail over the Internet. Outlook 98 provides industry-leading support for POP3/SMTP, including full support for multiple Internet e-mail accounts, authenticated SMTP, Distributed Password Authentication, and the ability to store messages on the server. See also *Internet Mail Access Protocol 4 (IMAP4)*, *Simple Mail Transport Protocol (SMTP)*.

POP3   See *Post Office Protocol 3*.

Portable Network Graphics (PNG)   The possible replacement for the GIF format that has evolved as a grassroots effort created by graphics developers on the Internet. The PNG format offers a public, lossless coder with support for both palletized and photographic color images.

POTS   Plain old telephone service.

PowerPoint   See *Microsoft PowerPoint*.

PPP (Point-to-Point Protocol)   Allows systems to connect to the Internet using the TCP/IP protocols.

PPT (.PPT)   PowerPoint document extension.

Preemptive multitasking   The operating system itself is able to suspend an application or thread without waiting for the executing process to relinquish control.

Process With regard to threading and the Win32 kernel, a process consists of the resources required to execute a program. Each process possesses a virtual address space, executable code, application data, object handles, environment variables, a base priority, and minimum and maximum working set sizes.

POST Power-On Self Test.

Programmable Command Bars Customizable toolbars which can be modified by dragging and dropping menus, commands, and buttons, and by setting properties.

Project See *Microsoft Project*.

Property pages Allow ActiveX controls to display its internal properties in a tabbed dialog box called a property sheet.

Protected Memory A block of memory address space allocated to an executing process and protected from access by other threads or processes.

Proxy Source object in a cross-process or cross-network remote procedure call. See also *Stub*.

PSTN Public switched telephone network.

Publisher See *Microsoft Publisher*.

QuickTime Apple Computer's standard for video and sound playback on both PCs and Macintoshes.

RAC Manager (Remote Automation Connection manager) Used to set security options for server objects.

RAD Rapid Application Development.

RAM (Random Access Memory) The physical memory used in a computer.

RAS Remote Access Service.

RDA Remote Data Access.

RDO See *Remote Data Objects*.

.REG Extension used by default to identify an exported registry file.

REGEDIT.EXE Windows-supplied utilities providing access to the system registry.

Registry See *Windows Registry*.

Registry key Identifier used to label and delineate registry data.

Remote Data Objects (RDO) A simpler implementation of ODBC. Enables programmers to open and manage a database connection, execute queries and stored procedures, manipulate query results, and to commit or roll back (cancel) changes to the database.

Remote Procedure Call (RPC) A call to a remote procedure, i.e., a function or method supplied by a process on a remote computer via a network connection.

Removable Source Code Permits developers to remove the source code from Access applications, reducing size, improving speed, and offering protection for intellectual property.

Replica Under Microsoft Access Jet Database Engine Replication, copies (replicas) of an .MDB file are derived from a design master. See *Design master*.

Replica set In the Jet engine, a group of databases that can replicate their data changes to other databases in the same set.

Replication Manager In the Jet engine, a full-featured replication service that allows more flexible treatment of replicas than the briefcase does.

Repository See *Microsoft Repository*.

RFC (Request For Comment) RFCs began in 1969 and comprise the working notes of the Internet research and development community, with each RFC consisting of a description of a protocol, procedure, service, status report, or a summary of research. RFCs are identified by a number, such as RFC 1310 (contains proposals for TCP/IP protocols) or RFC 959 (FTP protocol).

RISC (Reduced instruction set computing) Refers to the architecture of a CPU design.

ROM Read-Only Memory.

RPC   See *Remote Procedure Call.*

S/MIME   Secure Multipurpose Internet Mail Extension.

Schedule+   See *Microsoft Schedule+.*

SCSI   Small Computer System Interface.

SDK   Software Development Kit.

Secure Sockets Layer (SSL)   Supports encrypted communications between client and server.

SGML (Standard Graphics Markup Language)   Precursor of and basis for HTML.

Shadow Folders   A directory where a separate copy of all up-to-date project files are stored outside of the *SourceSafe* repository.

.SIT   Identifies a Macintosh compression format requiring the Stuffit utility for decompression.

SLIP (Serial Line Internet Protocol)   Allow systems to connect to the Internet using the TCP/IP protocols.

SMB   Service Message Block protocol.

SMP (Symmetric Multiprocessor System)   With NT, threads can execute on any processor in the system.

Simple Mail Transport Protocol (SMTP)   One of the most commonly used protocols for sending and receiving e-mail over the Internet. Outlook 98 provides industry-leading support for POP3/SMTP, including full support for multiple Internet e-mail accounts, authenticated SMTP, Distributed Password Authentication, and the ability to store messages on the server. See also *Internet Mail Access Protocol 4 (IMAP4)*, *Post Office Protocol 3 (POP3)*.

SMTP/MIME   Simple Mail Transfer Protocol/Multipurpose Internet Mail Extensions.

SNA   Systems Network Architecture.

SNA API   Standard for corporate host connectivity providing open access to the existing IBM SNA API categories.

SNA Server See *Microsoft SNA Server*.

Snapshot Recordsets are static cursors. Data cannot be updated from a snapshot and the server will never be contacted to query for data that are more current.

SNMP Simple Network Management Protocol.

SNMP MIB SNMP Management Information Base.

Socket The basic unit for communications. A socket is a communication endpoint; a name may be bound to a socket.

Sockets API A single Windows-based application interface supporting communications with Sockets-based applications through a variety of transport protocols including TCP/IP, AppleTalk, and IPX/SPX.

SOHO Small office, home office.

Solutions Framework See *Microsoft Solutions Framework*.

SourceSafe See *Microsoft Visual SourceSafe*.

SPX A series of commands implemented on top of Novell's IPX protocol to form a transport layer interface.

SQL Distributed Management Objects (SQL-DMO) Designed to interact only with Microsoft SQL Server.

SQL Server See *Microsoft SQL Server*.

SQL/DS Structured Query Language/Data System.

SSL See *Secure Sockets Layer*.

Static binding Binding between application code and function libraries performed at link time. See also *Dynamic Binding*.

Storage object A COM object implementing the IStorage interface; may contain nested storage objects or *stream objects*, resulting in the equivalent of a directory/file structure within a single file.

Stream object A COM object implementing the IStream interface. Analogous to a file in a directory/file system.

Stream socket   Provides a reliable, sequenced, and unduplicated flow without record boundaries.

Structured exception handling   A mechanism for handling hardware- and software-generated exceptions during application execution.

Stub   Receiver object in a cross-process or cross-network remote procedure call. See also *Proxy*.

Symmetric multiprocessors   Supported by Windows NT, allows multiple CPUs to support multitasking and multithreading.

SYSTEM.DAT   Registry file containing system-specific information.

Systems Management Server   See *Microsoft Systems Management Server*.

TAPI   Telephony API. See *Windows Telephony*.

TARGET   The TARGET parameter in HTML takes the form TARGET=window where window identifies a named window where the linked document is loaded.

TCP (Transmission Control Protocol)   A connection-oriented protocol designed to tolerate unreliable link conditions between two machines. TCP is a packet-oriented protocol accepting a message of any length before breaking the message into packets—pieces smaller than 64KB.

TCP/IP   Transmission Control Protocol/Internet Protocol.

Team Manager   See *Microsoft Team Manager*.

Telnet   Part of the TCP/IP protocol suite used for remote login and terminal emulation.

Thread   The executing part of a process; a process may execute more than one thread for different tasks.

Thread affinity   Forces a thread to run on a specific subset of processors.

Tier   In client/server technology, a layer of software that accepts requests and offers services to an application.

TLA Three-Letter Acronym, computer shorthand format used to simplify otherwise awkward terminology. See also *ADA*.

Transaction Server See *Microsoft Transaction Server.*

Transparency Characteristic of the COM model which makes local and remote interface calls indistinguishable to the COM object.

UDP (User Datagram Protocol) A simple interface used by applications to exchange user data (datagrams) through the network.

Unicode 16-bit character code supporting international alphabets and character sets.

Uniform Data Transfer (UDT) A set of interfaces allowing data to be exchanged between OLE client and server applications in a standard fashion, independent of the method used to effect the transfer; provides the basis for drag-and-drop transfers was well as clipboard and Dynamic Data Exchange (DDE) operations.

UNIX 32-bit, multiuser, multitasking, portable operating system originally developed by AT&T.

UPS Uninterruptable Power Supply.

USER.DAT Registry file containing user-specific information.

UUDECODE Used to decode non-text attachments accompanying messages.

UUENCODE Used to encode non-text attachments accompanying messages.

UUID Universally Unique ID. See *Globally Unique ID.*

uuidgen Tool supplied by Microsoft to generate GUID values.

VAR Value added resellers.

VAX Digital Equipment's (DEC's) line of minicomputers and workstations.

VB UserControl module   A container holding the source code for an ActiveX control; unless the project itself is an ActiveX Control project, the control defined in the UserControl module will only be available within the project application.

VBA   Visual Basic for Applications.

Version compatibility   A requirement for applications to be capable of upgrading without requiring all other components to be upgraded correspondingly.

Vertical Market Extensions   Extensions that provide specialized services to support or extend tasks required by particular market segments.

VIM-compliant   Vendor-Independent Messaging (for e-mail).

Virtual Function Table (vtable)   A table of address pointers to functions within a COM object. Indirect addressing through vtables allows object instances to be shared while reducing memory requirement.

Virtual memory   A physical swap file on the hard drive used as an extension of RAM.

Virtual Memory Manager (VMM)   The Virtual Memory Manager (VMM) is designed to ensure that applications do not have access—accidentally or deliberately—to each other's memory space.

Visual Basic   See *Microsoft Visual Basic*.

Visual C++   See *Microsoft Visual C++*.

Visual Database Tools   See *Microsoft Visual Database Tools*.

Visual FoxPro   See *Microsoft Visual FoxPro*.

Visual InterDev   See *Microsoft Visual InterDev*.

Visual J++   See *Microsoft Visual J++*.

Visual Modeler   See *Microsoft Visual Modeler*.

Visual Schema Designer   A Visual C++ tool that provides the means to remotely analyze the schema for a Microsoft SQL Server database and to enhance database application development.

Visual SourceSafe   See *Microsoft Visual SourceSafe.*

Visual Studio   See *Microsoft Visual Studio.*

VLDB   Very large database.

vtable   See *Virtual Function Table.*

WAN   See *Wide Area Network.*

Web Proxy Service   Offers caching, client authentication, and domain filtering through the WinSock Proxy Service.

Wide Area Network (WAN)   A network connected across a large area; often connecting between cities, states, or countries.

Win32   The 32-bit Windows application programming interface.

Windows 3.*x*   16-bit versions of Windows executing as shells on top of the DOS operating system, includes Windows 3.0, 3.1, and 3.11 (Windows for Workgroups).

Windows 9*x*   32-bit versions of Windows consisting of Windows 95 and Windows 98.

Windows NT 3.*x*   32-bit versions of Windows offering a true operating system rather than working on top of DOS, includes Windows NT 3.1, 3.5, and 3.51.

Windows NT 4.0   Consists of Windows NT Workstation and *Windows NT Server* versions, collectively referred to simply as Windows NT.

Windows NT Server   Provides the network foundation for BackOffice, providing fast file-and-print services together with application and communication services.

Windows Open Services Architecture (WOSA)   Microsoft's standard to provide an open environment for Windows-based applications.

Windows Registry   A database where system and application configuration information is registered. Replaces the WIN.INI, SYSTEM.INI, PROTOCOL.INI, AUTOEXEC.BAT, and CONFIG.SYS files.

Windows Sockets   Named after the *socket* paradigm popularized by Berkeley Software Distribution.

Windows Telephony API (TAPI)   Provides easy access for applications to interact with the telephone network, to facilitate visual call control, integrate electronic mail, voice mail and fax; and to support desktop audio and video conferencing.

WININET.DLL   The DLL that supplies Internet API functionality.

WINS   Windows Internet Naming Service.

WinSock   Windows Sockets protocol.

WinSock control   Used to create applications that use the Internet to communicate with each other via the UDP and TCP protocols.

WinSock Proxy Service   Works with the WinSock API to monitor and control network traffic across the Proxy Server gateway.

Word   See *Microsoft Word*.

WOSA   See Windows Open Services Architecture.

WWW   World Wide Web.

WYSIWYG   What you see is what you get.

XWindows   Standard allowing applications to work across a variety of graphics terminals.

Yahoo!   A popular entry point for the Web; contains site recommendations submitted by users.

Zero data latency   Data will always be in a consistent state throughout the enterprise. It is impossible to commit any transaction that does not also update data on the other servers participating in the process.

ZIP   Identifies PKZIP format compressed files.

Index

Note to the Reader: Throughout this index **boldface** page numbers indicate primary discussions of a topic. *Italicized* page numbers indicate illustrations.

MCSE CORE REQUIREMENT STUDY GUIDES FROM NETWORK PRESS

Sybex's Network Press presents updated and expanded second editions of the definitive study guides for MCSE candidates.

MCSE: NETWORKING ESSENTIALS Study Guide SECOND EDITION
EXAM 70-058
JAMES CHELLIS
CHARLES PERKINS
MATTHEW STREBE

ISBN: 0-7821-2220-5
704pp; 7$\frac{1}{2}$" x 9"; Hardcover
$49.99

MCSE: NT WORKSTATION 4 Study Guide SECOND EDITION
EXAM 70-073
CHARLES PERKINS
MATTHEW STREBE
AND JAMES CHELLIS

ISBN: 0-7821-2223-X
784pp; 7$\frac{1}{2}$" x 9"; Hardcover
$49.99

MCSE: NT SERVER 4 Study Guide SECOND EDITION
EXAM 70-067
MATTHEW STREBE
CHARLES PERKINS
WITH JAMES CHELLIS

ISBN: 0-7821-2222-1
832pp; 7$\frac{1}{2}$" x 9"; Hardcover
$49.99

MCSE: NT SERVER 4 IN THE ENTERPRISE Study Guide SECOND EDITION
EXAM 70-068
LISA DONALD
WITH JAMES CHELLIS

ISBN: 0-7821-2221-3
704pp; 7$\frac{1}{2}$" x 9"; Hardcover
$49.99

MCSE: WINDOWS 95 STUDY GUIDE
EXAM 70-064
LANCE MORTENSEN
RICK SAWTELL

ISBN: 0-7821-2256-6
800pp; 7$\frac{1}{2}$" x 9"; Hardcover
$49.99

A $50.00 SAVINGS!

MCSE Core Requirements
Box Set
ISBN: 0-7821-2245-0
4 hardcover books;
3,024pp total; $149.96

Microsoft® Certified
Professional
Approved Study Guide

NETWORK PRESS®
SYBEX

STUDY GUIDES FOR THE MICROSOFT CERTIFIED SYSTEMS ENGINEER EXAMS

MCSD: Windows® Architecture I Study Guide

Exam 70-160

OBJECTIVE	PAGE
Component Technologies	
Explain the benefits of the Component Object Model (COM) as a model for the developing of software.	220
Discuss the use of the ActiveX™ and the OLE technologies as implementations of the COM.	286
Explain the implementation of Automation in the Microsoft Windows operating systems.	296
Identify situations in which Remote Automation is an appropriate technology to use in order to provide a desirable solution.	301
Compare component architectures on the basis of performance, maintainability, and extensibility.	220
Identify which ActiveX technologies are appropriate for use in implementing a given business solution.	289
Assess structured storage as a component of a given solution.	307
Discuss the use of Uniform Data Transfer (UDT) as part of a component solution.	304
Evaluate the use of one or more of the following in a given component solution: compound documents, OLE embedding and linking, and OLE drag and drop.	257
Evaluate the use of Active Documents as a component of a solution for a given business problem.	265
Identify the appropriate use of ActiveX controls within component solutions.	285
Database Access Technologies	
Given a scenario, choose the appropriate data access tool.	326
Evaluate Open Database Connectivity (ODBC) as a component of a given business solution.	334
Compare solutions that use ODBC, on the basis of performance, maintainability, and interoperability.	337
Explain the benefits of Active Data Objects (ADO).	366, 373
Explain the benefits of Remote Data Objects (RDO).	341
Compare Data Access Objects (DAO) with other potential components of a solution, such as ODBC or RDO.	327
Explain the benefits of SQL Distributed Management Objects (SQL-DMO).	348
Compare OLE Database (OLE DB) with the ODBC API and with native APIs as a means of retrieving data in a given scenario.	366, 370

 Exam objectives are subject to change at any time without prior notice and at Microsoft's sole discretion. Please visit Microsoft's Training & Certification Web site (www.microsoft.com/Train_Cert) for the most current listing of exam objectives.